From Concept to Monument:
Time and Costs of Construction in the Ancient World

From Concept to Monument:

Time and Costs of Construction in the Ancient World

Papers in Honour of Janet DeLaine

Edited by

Simon J. Barker, Christopher Courault,

Javier Á. Domingo, Dominik Maschek

ARCHAEOPRESS ARCHAEOLOGY

ARCHAEOPRESS PUBLISHING LTD
Summertown Pavilion
18-24 Middle Way
Summertown
Oxford OX2 7LG
www.archaeopress.com

ISBN 978-1-78969-422-2
ISBN 978-1-78969-423-9 (e-Pdf)

Cover: Rilievo con scena di costruzione; foto n. 551155, Servizio Fotografico MNR. Su concessione del Ministero della cultura – Museo Nazionale Romano.

This volume is the result of generous support from The Ancient World Research Cluster, Wolfson College (Oxford), who provided funding for the conference from which this volume arose, and the Universität Trier, who provided funding towards printing.

Contents

Contributors

Dr. Jeanine Abdul Massih is Professor of Classical Archaeology at the Lebanese University. She holds a PhD in the architecture and town planning of Hellenistic cities with special focus on Dura Europos (Syria). She directed the excavations in Cyrrhus (Syria) and has carried out research since 2004 on the quarries in Baalbek in collaboration with the German Archaeological Project (DAI). Since 2011, she has conducted a research programme on the maritime quarries of Lebanon: Byblos, Batroun, and Enfeh, and she has co-directed the Batroun Archaeological Project and the Southern Beqaa Archaeological Project in Lebanon with Chubu University, Japan.

Simon J. Barker is a posdoctoral research fellow at the Department of Architecture and Urban Planning, Ghent University. His research focuses on many aspects of the ancient world, including Roman architecture and the building industry, late-antique urbanism, and recycling practices. In addition, the application of architectural energetics to questions of construction and the economy, with emphasis on the labour of stoneworking and the cost of stone architectural decoration, has been a long-standing aspect of his research in Roman architecture.

Paolo Barresi is Associate Professor of Classical Archaeology at the Università Kore, Enna. He specialises in Roman architecture and archaeology, particularly in Asia Minor, Crete, and Sicily. He took his first degree in Classical Archaeology at Rome, La Sapienza, before specialising at the Italian School of Archaeology at Athens. His PhD focused on the costs of marble architecture in imperial Asia Minor. From 2004 to 2014 he took part in the excavations at the Villa del Casale (Piazza Armerina, Sicily), directed by Patrizio Pensabene. His ongoing research focuses on the Villa del Casale and in general on architectural and decorative aspects of late Roman villa architecture, including its continuity into the medieval period. He is also working on Roman art and architecture in Sicily (Erice, Catania), Greece, and Asia Minor, and on wall paintings from Roman Sicily, particularly Agrigento.

Chris Beckett joined the University of Edinburgh as Lecturer in Geotechnical Engineering in 2017. His research specialises in earthen construction materials from a geotechnical, structural, and thermal perspective. Chris chairs the technical committee of the Australian Earth Building Handbook and is currently the Co-Investigator of the Leverhulme Trust funded research *Earthen Empire* project.

Grzegorz Jan Blicharz completed post-graduate studies in Roman law at the University of Rome La Sapienza and the Program for the Development of Soft Skills and Entrepreneurship at Alberta School of Business in Edmonton. He is Executive Manager of the Utriusque Iuris Foundation and co-editor of Forum Prawnicze (Legal Forum journal). He also received the NCN PhD Grant Sonata 14 and the Scholarship of the Polish Ministry of Science and Higher Education for outstanding young scholars 2018–2021. In 2020 he was an academic visitor at the University of Oxford. His research focuses on Roman law, comparative private law, the European legal tradition, governing the commons, smart city development, and comparative public law (freedom, religion, and public policy).

Francesca Bologna completed her PhD at King's College London in 2018, with a thesis focusing on Roman wall painters and their working practices in the city of Pompeii. Between 2019 and 2021 she worked as project curator for the exhibition 'Nero: the man behind the myth' organised by the British Museum. Her research interests include ancient craft production, its economics, workforce organisation, and the social status and mobility of craftspeople in Antiquity.

Ann Brysbaert is Professor of Ancient Technologies, Materials, and Crafts at Leiden University and is also a trained conservator. She is PI of the SETinSTONE project funded by an ERC CoG grant. Prior to her position at Leiden University, she held academic posts at the University of Leicester, the University of Glasgow, and DIKEMES (Athens), and several senior research fellowships (A. von Humboldt and Marie Curie-Gerda Henkel at Heidelberg University and Leiden University, respectively). She has published extensively on workshop studies, pyrotechnologies, and on the socio-technological interactions between architectural production and landscape modifications

Francesca Caprioli's research looks at Roman architecture, with a special focus on the stylistic and typological characteristics of architectural decoration. Her work on Roman architecture began with the analysis of the architectural decoration of the *Aedes Vestae* in Rome, which was published as a monograph in 2007. Her PhD thesis in Classical Archeology, completed in 2009, focused on the history of Temple B of Largo Argentina in Rome and will be published in 2023. Her work has included a number of collaborations, such as the international conference *DECOR Il Linguaggio architettonico romano*, which she co-organised with Marina Milella, Javier Á. Domingo, and Patrizio Pensabene. She also started an educational program with Patrizio Pensabene at Università degli Studi di Roma 'La Sapienza' that focuses on Roman architectural decoration. Over the last 10 years, her work has mainly been dedicated to the architectural decoration of the imperial palaces on the Palatine Hill in Rome.

Christopher Courault is a Research Associate at the University of Geneva and member of the research group *Ciudades de Andalucía* (PAI-HUM 882) at the University of Cordoba. His research is focused on city walls during the Roman and late-antique periods. Based on quantitative studies, his research uses estimates of labour costs and the concept of *chaîne opératoire* in order to understand the impact of institutional organisation on the process of construction and to arrive at new interpretations in regard to historical events. In this respect, his research is based on developing a new methodology for calculating the cost of building stone in Antiquity.

Javier Á. Domingo is Professor of Christian Archaeology at the Pontifical University of the Holy Cross. Through several post-doctoral fellowships, he has undertaken various research activities at the University of Rome 'La Sapienza' and the Escuela Española de Historia y Arqueología in Rome. His studies are focused on Roman and late Roman architectural decoration, a subject to which he has dedicated a wide range of research in collaboration with Patrizio Pensabene, in addition to developing a methodology for calculating the economic costs of construction in the ancient world.

Michael Gervers is Professor of History at the University of Toronto. His interest in rock-hewn churches began as a graduate student at the Université de Poitiers, when he excavated the church of St. Georges (1965–74), which is carved out of the limestone cliff below the village of Gurat (Charente, France). Searching for comparative material, he studied the rock-cut monastic complexes in and around Göreme (Cappadocia, Turkey) and at Matera (Basilicata) in southern Italy. He extended his research to Ethiopia in 1982 and since 2000 has made annual field trips to Ethiopia's highland regions to document Christian antiquities. From 2015 to 2020, with the support of the Arcadia Foundation, he recorded video interviews with contemporary master craftsmen responsible for hewing out churches from the rock, in order to preserve oral accounts of this ancient activity, now endangered by modernisation. He has published widely on medieval history, architectural history, ancient textiles, and archaeology.

Anna Gutiérrez Garcia-M. holds an MA in Lithic and Ceramic Analysis for Archaeologists (University of Southampton) and a PhD in Archaeology (Autonomous University of Barcelona). She has developed her research at the Laboratory for the Study of Stones in Antiquity (LEMLA) of the Autonomous University of Barcelona, the Catalan Institute of Classical Archaeology (Tarragona, Spain), and at IRAMAT-CRP2A (UMR 5060 CNRS-UBM, Bordeaux, France) as Chaire Junior of the Laboratoire d'Excellence LaScArBx. Currently she is a Ramón y Cajal researcher at ICAC, director of the Archaeometric Studies Unit (UEA), and coordinator of the Archaeometry and Artistic Productions (ArPA) research group. She focuses on the interdisciplinary study of the stone industry in Antiquity, with a long publishing record in both archaeometry and archaeology. She has also taught in several MA degrees and acts as MA, PhD, and MSCA-IF supervisor.

Alfred Hirt is Lecturer in Roman History at the University of Liverpool. He studied Ancient History, Modern History, and Near Eastern Archaeology at the University of Bern, Switzerland, and wrote his doctoral thesis at the University of Oxford on imperial mines and quarries. His research interests are the study of extractive industries and their economic and social impact on provincial communities of the Roman Empire.

Anaïs Lamesa holds a PhD (Paris-Sorbonne University) in Ancient History. She is currently an associated member of the French Centre for Ethiopian Studies. As PI, she conducted postdoctoral research in Ethiopia (2019–2021), funded by the DIM-Matériaux anciens et patrimoniaux/ Île de France and hosted at the Orient et Méditerranée/CNRS laboratory. She has recently authored a publication on ancient Anatolia in the *Supplements – Dialogues d'histoire ancienne*.

Eneko López-Marigorta is Assistant Professor at the University of the Basque Country. He has been trained as a historian, archaeologist, and Arabic philologist. His research focuses on the Umayyad socio-economic history in al-Andalus (8th-11th centuries) and in particular on two strands: urban and commercial development; and economic production and political use of material culture. He is the author of the monograph *Mercaderes, artesanos y ulemas. Las ciudades de las coras de Ilbīra y Pechina en época omeya* (UJA, 2020), co-author of the book *Medina Azahara* (National Geographic, 2018), and editor of the collective volume *Una nueva mirada a al-Andalus. Retos de la investigación arqueológica y textual del periodo omeya* (UPV/EHU, forthcoming).

Daniela Matetić Poljak is Senior Lecturer at the Arts Academy of the University of Split. She holds a PhD in Archaeology from Aix-Marseille Université. Over the course of a decade, she taught at the Department of Art History at the Faculty of Humanities and Social Sciences in Split. Since 2009, she has been an associate member of the Institut de Recherche sur l'Architecture Antique in Aix-en-Provence. Her research interests focus on the architectural decoration of ancient and medieval Dalmatia. She has participated in several research projects dedicated to Diocletian's Palace and the medieval heritage of Croatia.

Dominik Maschek is Professor of Roman Archaeology at the University of Trier and Head of the Department of Roman Archaeology at the Leibniz-Zentrum für Archäologie in Mainz. A trained Classical archaeologist, his research covers a wide array of topics from Archaic Greece to the Roman Empire, with a special focus on late Republican architecture and material culture in Rome and central Italy. He has been a Rome Fellow of the Austrian Academy of Sciences and currently conducts archaeological fieldwork at Fregellae (Lazio) and Carnuntum (Austria).

Alessandro Mortera is part of the research team working on the architecture and architectural decoration of the Imperial Palace on the Palatine Hill (led by Patrizio Pensabene and Francesca Caprioli). Since 2015, he has been collaborating with Domenico Palombi (University of Rome 'La Sapienza') and Francesca Caprioli in the Seminar *Decor. Il linguaggio architettonico romano*. He graduated from Roma Tre University in 2014 and took his Masters from the University of Rome 'La Sapienza' in 2016.

Here he also attended the 'Scuola di Specializzazione in Beni Archeologici', graduating in 2018. He has taken part in several archaeological excavations in Rome (*Templum Pacis*, Circus Maximus, Colosseum, *Horrea Piperataria*) and Ostia.

Jari Pakkanen is Professor of Greek Archaeology at Royal Holloway, University of London. He has directed and co-directed several fieldwork projects in Greece and Italy that concentrate on the built environment, most recently at the harbour of Kyllene and the urban landscapes of Naxos in Sicily and Salamis in Attica. Developing three-dimensional digital documentation techniques is an important aspect of his archaeological projects. Statistical analyses of archaeological data are also at the core of his research. His labour cost studies of Greek architecture combine the study of archaeological remains with ancient building accounts.

Patrizio Pensabene is Emeritus Professor of Classical Archeology at the University of Rome 'La Sapienza' where, from 1991 to 2012, he coordinated the PhD in Classical Archaeology. He directed the excavations of the Sanctuary of Magna Mater from 1977 to 2003 and of the late Roman and medieval settlement on the Villa del Casale in Piazza Armerina from 2004 to 2014. He has worked mainly on architecture, marble, and architectural decoration of the Roman period and the use of architectural remains in Late Antiquity and the Middle Ages. He has published widely and on key monuments, such as the Temple of Saturn, the Arch of Constantine, the Arch of Janus, and the theatres of Ferento, Cassimo, Taormina, and Catania. In other publications, he has dealt with the use of *spolia* in late-antique and medieval churches in Rome, the Norman architecture of southern Italy and Sicily, the basilica of S. Salvatore at Spoleto, and the cathedral of Aquileia. His more recent publications are dedicated to his excavations in Rome (Palatine) and Piazza Armerina, to the phenomenon of reuse in Lombard architecture, and to architectural decoration in local stones in *Gallia* and *Hispania*. Currently he works with a Polish-Cypriot archaeological mission on the architecture of the house of Orpheus at Paphos (Cyprus).

Caterina Previato is Associate Professor of Classical Archaeology at the University of Padua where she also gained her PhD in 2012. Her research focuses on Classical archaeology and Roman architecture, with particular attention to topics such as the history of ancient settlements and monumental complexes, building materials, the relationships between ancient cities and environmental resources, construction processes, and building techniques, considered from historical and economic points of view. She has taken part in several archaeological excavations and survey activities in Italy and abroad (Aquileia, Altinum, Padova, Nora, Pompeii, Kos, Virunum, Tautavel). At present, she is involved in research on northern Italy (Aquileia, Padova), Sardinia (Nora), and Pompeii. She has published two monographs and several papers on Roman architecture, building materials and techniques, and ancient quarries, as well as on the archaeological excavations and research projects at Aquileia, Nora, Pompeii, and Padova.

Cathalin Recko finished her PhD thesis, which examined the building materials, building processes, and labour estimates for the Forum of Pompeii, within the DFG Research Training Group 1878 'Archaeology of pre-modern economies' at the University of Cologne. She is currently a member of the Archaeological Institute of the University of Cologne. Her research interests lie in the ancient building economy and quantification methods for the material and labour requirements of Roman construction.

Tanja Romankiewicz is a Research Fellow in Later Prehistoric and Roman Archaeology at the University of Edinburgh and part of the Leverhulme Trust funded *Earthen Empire* project team. From her background in architecture and archaeology, she investigates Roman, Iron Age, and Bronze Age building and dwelling practices across Europe. Her research interests lie in the ancient building economy and quantification methods for the material and labour requirements of Roman construction.

Marguerite Ronin is a permanent research fellow at the CNRS (Paris), specialising in the environmental history of the Roman Empire and in Roman legal texts. Since 2012, her publications have focused on water management and hydraulic risks, specifically from legal, institutional, and economic points of view. More recently she has been investigating other kinds of natural resources and commodities, the solutions developed for their control and exploitation, and the role this exploitation played within the larger framework of the ancient economy.

Ben Russell is Senior Lecturer in Classical Archaeology at the University of Edinburgh. His research focuses on Roman building materials, urbanism, trade, and craft production. He is the Principal Investigator of the *Earthen Empire* project, funded by the Leverhulme Trust, which investigates earth and turf building in the Roman North-West.

Santiago Sánchez de la Parra Pérez is a pre-doctoral fellow funded by the Junta de Castilla y León and the European Social Fund (Order EDU/556/2019). Currently associated with the Department of Prehistory, Ancient History, and Archaeology at the University of Salamanca, he is working on his doctoral thesis on public buildings in the western provinces of the Roman Empire, construction processes, and the costs of public buildings based on epigraphy, archaeological remains, and classical sources.

J. Riley Snyder is currently based at the University of Edinburgh's School of Engineering as a Research Fellow on the Leverhulme Trust funded *Earthen Empire* project. His research focuses on the energetics of building in earthen materials, which stems from his previous work on late-antique Ravenna and Constantinople where he specialised in the technological change, environmental reliance, and economic impact of lime mortar within large-scale masonry construction projects.

Natalia Toma is a postdoctoral fellow at the Department of Natural Sciences of the German Archaeological Institute (PhD Kiel, Germany, 2015). Her primary research interests are the urbanism and architecture of the Roman Mediterranean, architectural decoration with a focus on stoneworking techniques, archaeometry, in particular the provenance of white marble, and the archaeology of the Pontic region. She is currently engaged in archaeological field work at Miletus, Turkey, thanks to a research grant (2016–2021) from the German Research Foundation. She received the Wülfing-Scholarship from the German Archaeological Institute (2016/2017) and the Philippika-Prize of the Harrassowitz publishing house (2016) for her doctoral thesis. She has published widely on aspects of Roman marble architecture, stone carving, building costs, and aspects of 'standardisation' in ancient construction.

Maria Serena Vinci is a postdoctoral researcher at UNED (Madrid). She conducted a postdoctoral research project at the AUSONIUS Institute (CNRS-Université Bordeaux Montaigne) from 2017 to 2020. Her research deals mainly with the management of building sites for the construction of public monuments, first and foremost in Roman Spain. She has analysed and published the archaeological evidence for construction techniques and processes at the Provincial Forum of Tarraco. Recently her research has focused on the relationship between quarry and monument, with special attention to the use and meaning of quarry and mason's marks. She also studies carving instructions and markings on building stones in order to reconstruct ancient work processes and the transfer of knowledge between workshops.

Participants of the international conference 'From Concept to Monument: Time and Cost of Construction in the Ancient World' at Wolfson College, 16-18 January 2020; photo: Alice Poletto.

Preface

Visionary and Pragmatic: Studying the Nuts and Bolts of Roman Architecture

Simon J. Barker and Dominik Maschek

Writing the preface to this edited volume gives us special pleasure. The book originates from an Oxford conference, held at Wolfson College in January 2020, right before the Covid-pandemic forcefully interrupted what used to be called 'normality'. In hindsight it thus feels even more gratifying that, in the very last moments before international travel came to a standstill, we were able to convene in person in order to celebrate one of the most distinguished scholars of Roman architecture, Janet DeLaine.

Through her work on Rome and Ostia, Janet is widely recognised as an expert on ancient building technologies, materials, and principles of design. Now an Emeritus Fellow at Wolfson College, Oxford, and a Fellow of the Society of Antiquaries of London (from 1999 onwards), Janet's career began studying Civil Engineering followed by Classical Studies. She received her BA and PhD from the University of Adelaide, where she worked under the supervision of Frank Sear. During her MA and the first years of her doctorate, she worked in the field as part of the Australian Expedition to Pompeii. From 1981 to 1986, Janet continued at the Classics Department of the University of Adelaide, both as a postgraduate student and as a Tutor in Classics. Between 1980 and 1988, Janet was also a frequent visitor to the British School at Rome (BSR), where she was a Rome Scholar in Ancient, Medieval and Later Italian Studies in 1986–1987. Her association with the University of Oxford began in 1988 when she was awarded a Junior Research Fellowship at St John's College Oxford. It was during this time that Janet completed her PhD, *Design and construction in Roman imperial architecture: the Baths of Caracalla in Rome* (1992), which she later revised while at the University of Reading and which found a home in the Supplements volume of the *Journal of Roman Archaeology*. The volume would go on to win the Archaeological Institute of America's James R. Wiseman Award for the most important work in archaeology in 1998.

Janet's time at St John's College also marked an event that would have far reaching consequence for those following in her footsteps, studying the quantification of manpower and the cost of construction: the discovery of Giovanni Pegoretti's *Manuale pratico per l'estimazione dei lavori architettonici, stradali, idraulici e di fortificazione*, which has become the most cited of the numerous nineteenth-century building manuals detailing pre-industrial construction and labour times. Janet's seminal work, which revised her thesis using this manual, provided a radical new foundation for studies of the 'real' costs of Roman building in a wider, socio-economic context.

Janet was the AIA's Samuel Kress Lecturer in Ancient Art in 1994, and she went on to hold the positions of Lecturer and Senior Lecturer in Archaeology at the University of Reading, during which time she helped to create the MA in the City of Rome. While Janet quickly established herself as a notable expert on Roman baths and the building industry of ancient Rome, her interests in Roman urbanism led her to Roman Ostia, where she undertook the survey of I.IV.2-4. This was later extended to the study (with some excavations) of the whole Insula of the Paintings (I.IV.1–5) with David Wilkinson. Her work on Ostia maintained her long (and continuing) association with the BSR, where she returned as a Hugh Last Fellow 1999–2000, working on the re-examination of the urban development of Roman Ostia.

In 2005, Janet moved to the University of Oxford as lecturer at the Institute of Archaeology, later becoming an Associate Professor in Roman Archaeology and faculty member of the Ioannou Centre for Classical and Byzantine Studies. During her time at Oxford, Janet's profound contribution to the field was recognised in numerous ways: for example, she was elected as Corresponding Member of the Archaeological Institute of America (2010), and she held the Japan Society for the Promotion of Science Senior Research Fellowship at Kyushu University in the Department of Architecture and Urban Design (2014). She has also lectured widely in a number of countries, acted as reviewer for articles and grant applications, and sat on editorial boards for numerous journals. In more recent years, Janet was appointed an architectural specialist on the British School at Rome's major project at Portus. After retiring from the University of Oxford in 2018, Janet became the Director of the Ancient World Research Cluster at Wolfson College.

This brief overview outlines only the bare bones of Janet's impressive career. Anyone working on Roman architecture during the last few decades is greatly indebted to her work. Her landmark study on the Baths of Caracalla is complemented by a number of incisive contributions which deal with all aspects of Roman construction, from the extraction and transport of raw materials to the organisation of the building site and the nature of the workforce. From the perspective of a civil engineer, Janet's take on the subject shuns mere aestheticism and abstract reflections; rather, she studies the nuts and bolts of Roman architecture. She always aims to ground her ideas in practice, asking the questions that really matter but are rarely asked: How was this done? Who were the people who did it? What obstacles did they have to overcome, how demanding and exhausting was their work, and how did they make a living from it? In doing so, she accomplishes a rare feat, producing scholarship that is both visionary and extremely pragmatic.

Janet's impressive list of publications, however, does not convey the full story. Her leading role as a teacher and mentor, in particular during her time at Oxford, is at least as important for the field as her published work. She has taught countless undergraduates in lectures and tutorials on Roman archaeology, architecture, and art, and she has fostered a most lively community of postgraduate students who took her papers on Pompeii and Ostia, the City of Rome, and Roman architecture. Pursuing a doctorate with Janet was always set to be an exciting academic journey, both demanding and extremely rewarding (as Simon Barker knows from first-hand experience!). As many of her current and former students and colleagues will confirm, Janet is astute and probing in her criticism but always most generous with advice and comments. Janet's name is to be found in many a preface to some of the most important volumes on Roman architecture of the recent decades, with many a distinguished author offering their thanks for clarifying aspects of the subject.

Through her energy and enthusiasm in teaching and research, Janet established Oxford as an Anglophone powerhouse of Roman architectural history. Those who know her will not be surprised to hear that, as co-organiser of the fifth international workshop on 'The Archaeology of Roman Construction', held in Oxford in April 2015, Janet hugely impressed the attendants by her meticulous planning and organisation and her strict punctuality. She paired these virtues with an unfailingly English sense of courtesy by which she made her speakers feel welcome and valued, in particular during the magnificent conference dinner at Wolfson. Organised along similar lines of enthusiasm and congeniality, the Roman Architecture Discussion Group, even in times of Covid, brings together students and distinguished speakers from across the globe, not least because they can be sure to get Janet's unerring advice in all matters related to the construction and design of Roman buildings.

Overall, our knowledge of Roman architecture owes a great deal to Janet's work and commitment. She constantly reminds us that the most important questions quite often fly under the radar of academic intellectualism and fashionable theory. They might even lurk behind statements which are so obvious that most people have not yet thought about their implications. Everyone knows that Rome wasn't built in a day – but how long did it actually take to build it?

Such questions are at the core of many of the papers packaged into the present volume in honour of Janet DeLaine. The papers not only cover a wide chronological and geographical area of the ancient world but also take up many of the themes explored by Janet throughout her career on Roman architecture, urbanism, building technologies, materials, and principles of design. The wide range of papers reflects the scope and vibrancy of Janet's scholarship on Roman architecture and her enormous contribution to the discipline. Many of the contributions are provided by scholars for which Janet's work has served as a direct catalyst, both in their own research more generally and in the work presented here. Likewise, papers from former students as well as distinguished colleagues correspondingly reflect the impact of Janet's mentorship and scholarship. The common factor throughout is of course the undeniable influence of Janet's pioneering work in the field.

Dominik Maschek's opening paper sets the scene by highlighting many of the themes explored throughout the volume. Most importantly, it sketches out the great value and merit of Janet's work, discussing it within a wider context by considering its importance for our understanding not only of ancient Greek and Roman architecture but also of economic history more widely. The remaining papers collected in the present volume touch on many themes which have been at the core of Janet's work. While most papers concern Roman architecture, several (those by Jari Pakkanen and Ann Brysbaert) pose questions similar to those asked by Janet but for the Greek world during the Aegean Late Bronze Age, Classical, and Hellenistic periods.

Several contributions tackle questions related to building materials and the problems associated with their supply and organisation, a theme very much explored in Janet's own work on Rome and Ostia. Fred Hirt's paper reviews ostraca discovered at Mons Claudianus to outline some of the administrative concerns that the quarrying organisation faced as a whole, while Anna Gutiérrez Garcia-M.'s contribution mirrors Janet's interest in the procurement and supply of ordinary, less expensive and everyday building material (the bulk of material from

Roman building projects). Gutiérrez Garcia-M.'s paper explores the different types of stone in the territory around Tarraco and its employment in the town's monumental building programmes, considering the possible factors behind their selection, exploitation, and procurement.

Other key themes of Janet's work—building technology and the organisation of the building industry, including the social and economic status of builders and their place in society—are touched upon in numerous papers. For example, building technology is explored in-depth by Jeanine Abdul Massih in her paper on quarrying megaliths in Heliopolis (Baalbek). Massih's paper establishes the sequence of quarrying operations in relation to the monument, and her close examination of the organisation of the quarrying area, the extraction and transportation techniques, and daily life in the quarry made it possible to propose a reconstruction of the *chaîne opératoire* from the quarry to the temple. The paper by Anaïs Lamesa and Michael Gervers explores the status of medieval stonemasons employed on rock-hewn projects, asking questions about the organisation and skill-levels of the labour force for such projects. In Maria Serena Vinci's paper, the so-called Provincial Forum of Tarraco is used to identify the main stages in the construction of the Tarraco monumental complex and to reflect on some aspects of the building site that influenced its management, organisation, and construction times. Similarly, Santiago Sánchez de la Parra Pérez's paper addresses another avenue of research relating to building processes in Roman *Hispania*. Using epigraphic evidence, his paper examines the individuals or bodies responsible for initiating building projects, those responsible for its financing, and those responsible for aspects of the actual construction process.

The quantification of manpower and the 'cost' of construction in Roman building projects has been at the heart of Janet's work from the very beginning with her ground-breaking study of the Baths of Caracalla through to more recent forays into the economic factors involved in the choice of material and building techniques in Roman construction at Ostia. Janet's many papers on the subject have highlighted the fundamental importance of studying the labour involved in the construction processes of Roman buildings in order to understand these structures in their proper social and economic contexts. She expertly demonstrates the powerful tool architectural energetics can be when examining the role of architecture in the wider Roman economy. This methodology forms the basis of many of the papers in this volume. Contributions by Christopher Courault, Caterina Previato, Cathalin Recko, Francesca Bologna, Paolo Barresi, Javier Domingo, Daniela Matetić Poljak, and Natalia Toma apply the principles of reverse quantity surveying, which Janet pioneered, to quantify

the manpower required for a range of buildings (amphitheatres, temples, mausolea, and houses).

Applying this methodology to ancient buildings is not without difficulty; first and foremost is the problem of assigning values to tasks in terms of the time and level of skill required. The use of pre-industrial labour handbooks to reconstruct estimates for tasks in ancient construction, estimating labour rates, of course requires a meticulous methodology, and Janet's work provided significant methodological contributions to the field, setting benchmarks in terms of method and interpretation. The rigorous way in which Janet approaches the study of Roman architecture has been a common thread across all her work. In an effort to mirror her important methodological contributions, a number of papers in this volume offer reflections and new approaches to architectural energetics in order to better define the parameters for energetic studies concerning ancient construction. Simon Barker and Ben Russell's work on stone carving highlights alternative comparative data, such as price–books, building and other accounts, and modern restoration projects, to explore a range of 'hidden' costs beyond labour and materials. Riley Synder *et al.* take architectural energetics beyond its traditional application to construction projects in stone, brick, and concrete to examine neglected earth and turf construction. Their paper demonstrates the range of other sources, including the data generated by experimental archaeology, that can be used to explore the labour requirements of ancient construction. At the same time, it also offers new methodological horizons with a compilation of collected rates for each task rather than choosing one rate or group of rates from a single source.

No volume in honour of Janet DeLaine would be complete without papers focusing on the eternal city, as her work has done so much to illuminate its architecture and building industry. The paper by Francesca Caprioli *et al.* takes up the theme of imperial building projects through the case-study of the so-called Lower Peristyle of the Domus Augustana on the Palatine Hill. Roman literary sources and Roman legal texts provide the data for Marguerite Ronin's paper, which examines issues related to the development of the housing market in late Republican and imperial Rome.

As Vitruvius remarked in his opening of Book 1 of *De Architectura*, 'Architecture is a science arising out of many other sciences, and adorned with much and varied learning'. This is something paralleled in Janet's own approach to the discipline. Her work has encompassed many facets from expertise in civil engineering to the fundamentals of Roman architecture, in order to illuminate aspects such as processes of design and construction technologies, which lie at the heart of Roman architectural innovation.

While this volume celebrates Janet's career and her contribution to the field of Roman architecture, Janet will undoubtedly continue to have a significant impact on scholarship, not least with her own volume on Roman architecture for the Oxford History of Art series. All the editors of the current volume offer thanks to Janet for her work and hope this volume stands in some small way as a fitting tribute to her accomplishments and inspiration.

Simon J. Barker and Dominik Maschek

München and Mainz

List of published works

J. DeLaine, *Roman Architecture* (Oxford: OUP 2023).

J. DeLaine, Production, transport and on-site organisation of Roman mortars and plasters, *Archaeological and Anthropological Sciences* 13 (2021), https://doi.org/10.1007/s12520-021-01401-5.

J. DeLaine, Concluding remarks, in G. Mainet and S.M. Graziano (eds), *Ad Ostium Tiberis. Proceedings of the Conference Ricerche Archeologiche alla Foce del Tevere (Rome-Ostia, December 2018, 18-20th)* (Leuven: Peeters 2021), 353–358.

J. DeLaine and Y. Hori, Embellishing the Streets of Ostia, in H. Kamermans and L. Bouke van der Meer (eds), *Designating place: archaeological perspectives on built environments in Ostia and Pompeii*, (Leiden: Leiden University Press 2020), 65–81.

J. DeLaine, Strategies and technologies of environmental manipulation in the Roman world: the thermal economy of baths, in C. Schliephake, N. Sojc, and G. Weber (eds), *Nachhaltigkeit in der Antike: Diskurse, Praktiken, Perspektiven* (Stuttgart: Franz Steiner 2020), 75–93.

J. DeLaine, Conclusions, in M. Medri and A. Pizzo (eds), *Le terme pubbliche nell'Italia romana (II secolo a.C. - fine IV d.C.): architettura, tecnologia e società* (Rome: RomaTre Press 2019), 549–554.

J. DeLaine, Imperial Rome and the Roman Empire, c. 31 BCE– 284 CE, in M. Fraser (ed.), *Sir Banister Fletcher's Global History of Architecture* (London: Bloomsbury 2018 on-line, 2020 print), 368–416.

J. DeLaine, Street plaques (and other signs) at Ostia, in C.M. Draycott, R. Raj, K. Welch, and W. Wootton (eds), *Visual Histories: Essays in Honour of R.R.R. Smith*, (Turnhout: Brepols 2018), 331–343.

J. DeLaine, Economic choice in Roman construction: case studies from Ostia, in A. Brysbaert, V. Klinkenberg, A. Gutiérrez Garcia-M., and I. Vikatou (eds), *Constructing Monuments, Perceiving Monumentality and the Economics of Building* (Leiden: Sidestone Press 2018), 243–269.

J. DeLaine, Insulae; The imperial *thermae*; The construction industry, in C. Holleran and A. Claridge (eds), *A Companion to the City of Rome* (Chichester: Wiley Blackwell 2018), 317–323; 325–342; 473–490.

J. DeLaine, Quantifying manpower and the cost of construction in Roman building projects: research perspectives, *Archeologia dell'Architettura* 22 (2017), 13–19.

J. DeLaine, Gardens in Baths and Palaestras, in W.F. Jashemski, K.L. Gleason, K.J. Hartswick, and A. Malek (eds), *Gardens of the Roman Empire*, (Cambridge: CUP 2017), 165–184.

J. DeLaine, S. Camporeale, and A. Pizzo (eds), *5th International Workshop on the Archaeology of Roman Construction: Arqueología de la Construcción. V, Man-made materials, engineering and infrastructure (University of Oxford, 11-12 April 2015)*, Anejos de AEspA LXXVII (Madrid: Consejo Superior de Investigaciones Científicas 2016).

J. DeLaine, S. Camporeale, and A. Pizzo (eds), *Materials, transport and production. Posters presented at the 5th International Workshop on the Archaeology of Roman Construction: Arqueología de la Construcción V. Man-made materials, engineering and infrastructure (University of Oxford, 11-12 April 2015)*, Arqueología de la Arquitectura (2016)

J. DeLaine, Ostia, in A. Cooley (ed.), *A Companion to Roman Italy* (Chichester: Wiley Blackwell 2016), 417–438.

J. DeLaine, The production, supply and distribution of brick, in E. Bukowiecki, R. Volpe, and U. Wulf-Rheidt, *Il laterizio nei cantieri imperiali. Roma e il Mediterraneo. Atti del I workshop Laterizio (Roma, 27-28 novembre 2014)*, Archeologia dell'Architettura 20, 2015 [2016], 226–230.

J. DeLaine, The Pantheon builders - a preliminary estimate of manpower for construction, in T. Marder and M. Wilson Jones (eds), *The Pantheon: From Antiquity to the Present* (CUP 2015), 160–192.

J. DeLaine, Housing Roman Ostia, in D. L. Balch and A. Weissenrieder (eds), *Contested Spaces: Houses and Temples in Roman Antiquity and the New Testament* (Tübingen: Mohr Siebeck 2012), 327–351.

J. DeLaine, Roman architecture, *Oxford Bibliographies On-Line* (Oxford: OUP, 2011).

J. DeLaine, Baths, in A. Grafton, G.W. Most, and S. Settis (eds), *The Classical Tradition* (Harvard UP, 2010), 121–122.

J. DeLaine, On the (marble) road to a new Ostia – Patrizio Pensabene, con il contributo archeometrico di L. Lazzarini, M. Preite Martines, B. Turi, Ostiensium Marmorum Decus et Décor. Studi Architettonici Decorativi e Archeometrici (Studi Miscellanei 33, Dipt. Di Scienze storiche archeologiche e anthropologiche dell'Antichità, Università di Roma

"La Sapienza"; L'Erma di Bretschneider, Rome 2007). Pp. Xxi 715, tav. 179, figg. 265, 16 colour pls. ISBN 88-8265-345-5. – Carlo Pavolini, Ostia. Guide Archeologiche Laterza (Editori Laterza, Bari, new revised and enlarged edition 2006). Pp. Xii 339, figs. 124. ISBN 88-420-7784-4. *Journal of Roman Archaeology* 23 (2010), 548–60.

J. DeLaine, Terme imperiali, in H. von Hesberg, and P. Zanker (eds), *Storia dell'architettura italiana. Dagli Etruschi a Costantino. 1. Architettura romana. I grandi monumenti di Roma* (Mondadori Electa 2009), 250–67.

J. DeLaine, Between Concept and Reality: Case Studies in the Development of Roman Cities in the Mediterranean, in J. Marcus and J. Sabloff (eds), *Early Cities: New perspectives on pre-industrial urbanism* (Washington: National Academy of Sciences 2008), 95–118.

J. DeLaine, Conclusions, in S. Camporeale, H. Dessales, and A. Pizzo (eds), *Arqueología de la Construcción I. Los procesos constructivos en el mundo romano. Italia y provincias Occidentales*, Anejos de *AEspA* L (Madrid-Mérida: Consejo Superior de Investigaciones Científicas 2008), 319–326.

J. DeLaine, Historiography - origins, evolution and convergence. In M. Guérin-Beauvois and J.-M. Martin *Bains curatifs et bains hygiéniques en Italie de l'Antiquité au Moyen Âge*. Collection de l'École Française de Rome 383 (Rome: École Française, 2007), 21–35.

J. DeLaine, The cost of creation: technology at the service of construction. In E. Lo Cascio (ed.), *Innovazione tecnica e progresso economico nel mondo romano: Atti degli incontri capresi antica. Capri, 13-16 aprile 2003* (Edipuglia: 2007), 237–252.

J. DeLaine, Baths and bathing in late antique Ostia. In C. Mattusch and A. Donohue (eds), *Proceedings of the XVIth International Congress of Classical Archaeology, Boston 2003* (Oxford: Oxbow, 2007), 338–343.

J. DeLaine, The commercial landscape of Ostia, in A. MacMahon and J. Price (eds), *Roman Working Lives and Urban Living* (Oxford: Oxbow 2005), 29–47.

J. DeLaine, Designing for a market: *medianum* apartments at Ostia. *Journal of Roman Archaeology* 17 (2004), 146–175.

J. DeLaine, The builders of Roman Ostia: organisation, status and society, in S. Huerta (ed.), *Proceedings of the First International Congress on Construction History, Madrid 20-24 January 2003, Vol. II* (Madrid: Instituto Juan de Herrera 2003), 723–732.

R. Early, with C. Crowther, J. DeLaine, M. Önal, Y. Yavas, The rescue mission carried out at Zeugma, south-eastern Anatolia in 2000, in *Recent work at Zeugma*, Journal of Roman Archaeology Supplement 51 (2003), 9–56.

J. DeLaine, The building of the Baths of Caracalla. *Construction History Society Newsletter* 65 (2003), 43–46.

J. DeLaine, Building activity in Ostia in the second century AD, in C. Bruun, and A. Gallina Zevi (eds),

Ostia e Portus nelle loro relazioni con Roma (Rome: *Acta Instituti Romani Finlandiae* 27 2002), 41–101.

J. DeLaine, The Temple of Hadrian at Cyzicus and Roman attitudes to exceptional construction. *Papers of the British School at Rome* 70 (2002), 205–230.

J. DeLaine, Building for eternity: the concrete architecture of ancient Rome, in H. Louw (ed.) *The Place of Technology in Architectural History. Papers from the Joint Symposium of the Society of Architectural Historians of Great Britain and the Construction History Society, 2001* (London: The Society of Architectural Historians of Great Britain 2002), 9–14.

J. DeLaine, Techniques et industrie de la construction à Ostie. In J.-P. Descoeudres, *Ostia. Port et porte de la Rome antique* (Geneva: Musées d'Art et d'Histoire 2001), 91–99.

J. DeLaine, Building the Eternal City: the building industry of imperial Rome, in J. Coulston and H. Dodge (eds), *Ancient Rome: the Archaeology of the Eternal City* (Oxford: Oxbow 2000), 119–141.

J. DeLaine, The East baths at Leptiminus: an overview and suggested reconstruction, in L. Stirling, D. Mattingly, and N. Ben Lazreg (eds), *Leptiminus 2, Journal of Roman Archaeology*, Supplement 41 (Portsmouth RI 2000), 9–24.

J. DeLaine, Bricks and mortar: exploring the economics of building techniques at Rome and Ostia, in D. Mattingly and J. Salmon (eds), *Economies beyond agriculture in the Classical World*, Leicester-Nottingham Studies in Ancient History 9 (London: Routledge 2000), 230–268.

J. DeLaine and D.E. Johnston (eds). *Roman Baths and Bathing. Proceedings of the First International Conference on Roman Baths, Part 1: Bathing and Society, Journal of Roman Archaeology* Supplement 37.1 (Portsmouth RI 1999). Includes:

J. DeLaine, Foreword: Bathing and society, in *Part 1, Bathing and Society* 7–16.

J. DeLaine, Benefaction and urban renewal: baths in Roman Italy, in *Part 1, Bathing and Society*, 63–70.

J. DeLaine and D.E. Johnston (eds). *Roman Baths and Bathing. Proceedings of the First International Conference on Roman Baths, Part 2: Design and Construction, Journal of Roman Archaeology* Supplement 37.2 (Portsmouth RI 2000). Includes:

J. DeLaine, Foreword: Baths - the urban phenomenon, in *Part 2, Design and Construction* 157–163.

J. DeLaine, High status *insula* apartments in early imperial Ostia – a reading, *Mededelingen van het Nederlands Instituut te Rome, Antiquity* 58 (1999), 175–187.

J. DeLaine and D. Wilkinson, The House of Jove and Ganymede, *Mededelingen van het Nederlands Instituut te Rome, Antiquity* 58 (1999), 77–79.

J. DeLaine, The *romanitas* of the railway station, in M. Wyke and M. Biddiss (eds), *Uses and Abuses of Antiquity* (Bern), 145–160.

J. DeLaine, The Pantheon at Rome; The Colosseum at Rome; Hadrian's Villa at Tivoli; The Baths of

Caracalla, Rome; Roman Aqueducts; Roman Roads; The harbour at Caesarea; La Turbie: the Trophy of the Alps, in C. Scarre (ed.), *The Seventy Wonders of the Ancient World* (London: Thames and Hudson, 1999), 127–131, 167–181, 234–245, 278–280.

J. DeLaine and D. Wilkinson *Survey and Excavation at Regio I, Insula IV.2-4, Ostia. Interim Report on the 1998 Season* (Reading 1998).

J. DeLaine, *The Baths of Caracalla in Rome: a study in the design, construction and economics of large-scale building projects in imperial Rome, Journal of Roman Archaeology*, Supplement 25 (Portsmouth RI 1997).

J. DeLaine, Bath house; Temple-tomb or mausoleum; Architectural elements. In T. Potter, and A. King (eds), *Excavations at the Mola di Monte Gelato*, (London: British School at Rome 1997), 35–45, 228–230.

J. DeLaine, '*De aquis suis*'? The '*commentarius*' of Frontinus, in C. Nicolet (ed.), *Les Littératures Techniques dans l'Antiquité Romaine, Statut, public et destination, tradition* 42 (Vandoeuvres-Genève: Fondation Hardt 1996), 117–145.

J. DeLaine, The Insula of the Paintings. A model for the economics of construction in Hadrianic Ostia, in A. Zevi and A. Claridge (eds), *Roman Ostia Revisited: archaeological and historical papers in memory of Russell Meiggs* (London: British School at Rome 1996) 165–184.

J. DeLaine, Ancient Roman architectural theory and concepts; Basilica of Maxentius; Baths of Caracalla; Colosseum; Rabirius; Roman palaces, in *Macmillan Dictionary of Art* (London: Macmillan 1996).

J. DeLaine, Amphitheatres; Ara Pacis; Atrium Vestae; Wall of Aurelian; Baths; Circus; Cloaca Maxima; Colosseum; Columbarium; Comitium; Curia; Domus Aurea; Forum Augustum; Forma Urbis; Forum Nervae; Templum Pacis; Forum Traiani; Forum; Heating; Hypocaust; Monte Testaccio; Pantheon; Roman architecture; Rostra; Saepta Iulia; Septizodium; Horologium Augusti; Tabularium; Triumphal Arch; Tullianum, in S. Hornblower and A. Spawforth (eds), *The Oxford Classical Dictionary* (3rd revised edition, Oxford: OUP 1996).

J. DeLaine and D. Wilkinson *Survey and Excavation at Regio I, Insula IV.2-4, Ostia. Interim Report on the 1996 Season* (Reading 1996).

J. DeLaine, The Insula of the Paintings at Ostia (I.iv.2-4): Paradigm for a city in flux, in T. Cornell and K. Lomas (eds), *Urban Society in Roman Italy* (London: UCL Press 1995), 79–106.

J. DeLaine, Designing the Baths of Caracalla in Rome, in D. Ahrens and W. Rottlander, *Ordo et Mensura III. III Internationaler interdisziplinärer Kongress für Historische Metrologie, vom 17. Bis 21. November 1993 Städtischen Museum Simeonstift Trier* (St Katherinen 1995), 151–154.

J. DeLaine, The supply of building materials to the city of Rome. In N. Christie (ed.), *Settlement and Economy in Italy 1500 BC to AD 1500, Papers of the Fifth Conference of Italian Archaeology* (Oxford 1995), 555–562.

J. DeLaine and D. Wilkinson *Survey and Excavation at Regio I, Insula IV.2-4, Ostia. Interim Report on the 1995 Season* (Reading 1995).

J. DeLaine, M.G. Fulford and A. Wallace-Hadrill *Urban Development at Pompeii. Regio I, Insula 9. Excavations and Survey in 1995. Interim Report* (Reading 1995).

J. DeLaine, Descrizione e funzionamento del complesso monumentale, in P. Arthur (ed.), *Il complesso archeologico di Carminiello ai Mannesi, Napoli (Scavi 1983-1984)* (Galatina 1994), 13–46.

S. Gibson, J. DeLaine, and A. Claridge, The Triclinium of the Domus Flavia: a new reconstruction, *Papers of the British School at Rome* 62 (1994), 67–97.

S. Corcoran and J. DeLaine. The unit measurement of marble in Diocletian's Prices Edict, *Journal of Roman Archaeology* 7 (1994), 263–273.

J. DeLaine, The economics of public building in Rome: the Baths of Caracalla, in X. Dupré I Raventós (ed.), *La ciudad en el mundo romano. Actas XIV Congreso Internacional de Arqueología Clásica* (Tarragona 1994), 121–123.

J. DeLaine, New models, old modes: continuity and change in the design of public baths, in H. von Hesberg, H.J. Schalles, and P. Zanker (eds), *Die römische Stadt im 2. Jahrhundert n. Chr.: Der Funktionswandel des öffentlichen Raumes. Kolloquium in Xanten vom 2. bis 4. Mai 1990* (Köln 1992), 257–275.

J. DeLaine, The Roman and medieval architectural material and Roman sculptural fragments, in N. Christie and C.N. Daniels, Santa Cornelia: the excavation of an early medieval Papal estate and a medieval monastery, in N. Christie (ed.), *Three South Etrurian Churches*, Archaeological Monographs of the British School at Rome 4 (London 1991), 83–105.

J. DeLaine, Structural experimentation: the lintel arch, corbel and tie in western Roman architecture, *World Archaeology* 21.3 (1990), 407–424.

J. DeLaine, Some observations on the transition from Greek to Roman baths in Hellenistic Italy, *Mediterranean Archaeology* 2 (1989), 111–125.

J. DeLaine, Recent Research on Roman Baths, *Journal of Roman Archaeology* 1 (1988), 11–32.

J. DeLaine, Fase IB: the Roman bath, 263–266, and I reperti: 4. Amporiskos vitreo, 280–282, in T.W. Potter and A.C. King, Scavi a Mola di Monte Gelato presso Mazzano Romano, Etrurio meridionale. Primo rapporto preliminare, *Archeologia Medioevale* 20 (1988), 253–311.

J. DeLaine, The 'Cella Solearis' of the Baths of Caracalla in Rome: a Reappraisal, *Papers of the British School in Rome* 55 (1987), 147–156.

J. DeLaine, An engineering approach to Roman building techniques: the Baths of Caracalla in Rome, in C. Malone and S. Stoddart (eds), *Papers in Italian Archaeology IV, Part iv: Classical and Medieval*, BAR IS 246 (Oxford 1985), 195–206.

Reviews:

Two conferences on Ostia. Review of C. De Ruyt, T. Morard, and F. Van Haeperen, eds. 2018. *Ostia Antica. Nouvelles études et recherches sur les quartiers occidentaux de la cité. Actes du colloque international Rome-Ostia Antica, 22-24 septembre 2014.* Institut Historique Belge de Rome Artes / Belgisch Historisch Instituut te Rome Artes 8. Brussells; Rome: Belgisch Historisch Instituut te Rome / Institut Historique Belge de Rome; Instituto Storico Belga di Roma. Pp. 311, tables 4, pls 199 many in color. ISBN 978-90-74461-89-4. *Journal of Roman Archaeology* 35(1) (2022), 413-422.

Review of J.P. Oleson (ed.) *Building for eternity. The history and technology of Roman concrete engineering in the sea, International Journal of Nautical Archaeology* 45 (2016), 212–213.

Review of R. Ulrich and C. Quenemoen, *A companion to Roman architecture, American Journal of Archaeology* 119 (2015) (on-line).

Review of J. Anderson, Jnr, *Roman architecture in Provence, Journal of Roman Studies* 104 (2014), 257–259.

Review of J.R. Senseney, *The Art of Building in the Classical World, JSAH* 73.1 (2014), 171–173.

Review of D. Boin, *Ostia in Late Antiquity, Medieval Archaeology* 58.1 (2014) (on-line).

Review of Richard Neudecker and Paul Zanker (eds), *Lebenswelten. Bilder und Räume in der römischen Stadt der Kaiserzeit, DAI Rom, Palilia* 16 (Wiesbaden, 2005), *Bonner Jahrbücher* 208 (2008) [2010], 349–352.

Review of A. Bouet, *Les thermes privés et publics en Gaule Narbonnaise* (Rome: Ecole française, 2003), *Britannia* (2007), 376–377.

Review of P. Gros, *L'architecture romaine 2* (Paris: Picard 2001). *JRA* 18 (2005), 577–582.

Review of X. Lafon and G. Sauron (eds), *Théorie et pratique de l'architecture romaine: etudes offertes à Pierre Gros* (2005), *Antiquity* 80.310 December (2006), 1020–1021.

Review of L. Ball, *The Domus Aurea and the Roman Architectural Revolution* (Cambridge: CUP 2003), *Construction History Society Newsletter* 67 (2004), 36–37.

Review of J. Anderson Jnr, *Architecture and Roman Society* (Baltimore 1997), *Journal of Roman Archaeology* 13 (2000), 486–492.

Roman baths and bathing. Review of Inge Nielsen, *Thermae et Balnea. The Architectural and Cutural History of Roman Public Baths* (Aarhus: Aarhus University Press 1990). 2 vols, pp. 194 (text) 212 (catalogue and 260 figs). ISBN 87-7288-212-3. - Hubertus *Manderscheid, Bibliographie zum Römischen Badewesen unter besonderer Berücksichtigung der Öffentlichen Thermen* (München: Wasmuth 1988). Pp. 244 431 figs. - Fikret Yegul, *Baths and Bathing in Classical Antiquity* (Cambridge MA: Architectural History Foundation, New York, and Massachusetts Institute of Technology Press 1992). Pp. ix 501, including 506 figs. ISBN 0-262-24035-1. - *Les Thermes Romains* (Actes de la table ronde organisée par l'École Française de Rome, Rome 11-12 Novembre1988) (Collection de l'École française de Rome 142, Roma 1991) (Paris: De Boccard). Pp. viii 219 and ills. ISSN 0223-5099, ISBN 02-7283-0212-6. *Journal of Roman Archaeology* 6 (1993), 348-358. doi:10.1017/S1047759400011685

Review of J.R. Clarke, *The Houses of Roman Italy, 100 B.C. - A.D. 250: Ritual, Space and Decoration, Classical Review,* 43.2 (1993), 397–398.

Review of Ch. Bruun, *The Water Supply of Ancient Rome. A Study of Roman Imperial Administration, Antiquaries Journal* 71 (1993), 286.

Review of F.K. Yegül, *Sardis 3: The Bath-Gymnasium Complex at Sardis, Journal of the Society of Architectural Historians* 50 (1991), 72–73.

Review of H. Broise and J. Scheid, *Le Balneum des Frères Arvales, Journal of Roman Archaeology* 3 (1990), 321–324.

Review of I.M. Barton, *Roman Public Buildings, JACT Ancient History Broadsheet* December 1989.

Review of M.T. Boatwright, *Hadrian and the City of Rome, Journal of Roman Studies* 79 (1989), 218–220.

often than not they might have been specifically about skilled workers and contractors, not covering the *actual* number of participants in such projects; and, last but not least, the origin and social status of the skilled workers is clearly no valid argument against their important role for the local economy: they obviously received wages, from which, in return, they must have paid for their living expenses in the city, hence, in economic terms, their ethnic or social background is far less relevant than their firmly attested pay and impact on the urban economy.

As with the notion of 'occasional' building, this view of the workforce involved in construction projects is founded upon yet another powerful undercurrent of long-lived and deeply enshrined misconceptions: apart from sustaining only a few skilled workers, construction work in ancient Greece and Rome was often seen to have been unprofitable as it allegedly depended for the most part on large masses of slaves and convicts.[35] This idea is reminiscent of similar preconceptions about the slave mode of production ('*produzione schiavistica*') in the study of Roman agriculture, as encapsulated in Andrea Carandini's proposition of the '*villa perfecta*', which he derived from late Republican and early imperial authors and then projected onto the archaeological evidence he uncovered at Settefinestre.[36] But when we actually search for examples of the mass employment of slaves in Graeco-Roman construction, the situation becomes very unclear, as indeed in the case of the Roman villa economy where the recent reassessments by Annalisa Marzano, Alessandro Launaro, Rita Volpe, and others have shown that the situation, due to the topography of Italy with its diverse opportunities for crop production and landscape exploitation, was actually much more varied than the uniform model of '*produzione schiavistica*' would suggest.[37] The same is true for the construction industry and its dependence on highly *local* and *regional* conditions such as access to labour, transport routes, and specific resources and raw materials.[38] Therefore, the ancient construction industry, rather than being just represented by the allegedly 'sporadic' erection of Greek temples and Roman public buildings, can only be

properly understood as a continuous undertaking in a variety of local, regional, and interregional contexts.

Quantifying scale and impact: 'rationalisation' and the production of building materials

When asking questions about how these various contexts can be quantified in terms of scale and impact, the procurement and transport of building materials play a key role. The crucial importance of transport costs is already pertinent in the books of Vitruvius: he advised commissioners to make the best use of local materials to avoid higher costs (*De Arch.* 1.2.8), and at a later point in his treatise he states that if the quarries of Tarquinian stone (so-called *peperino*) were closer to Rome, the *urbs* would be built with it (*De Arch.* 2.7.4).

In very much the same vein, comparative studies of the Roman and post-Roman economy have rightly emphasised that the evidence for the transport of bulk goods is more important than the archaeology of luxury goods which are 'only for the few, not the many'; or, in the words of Chris Wickham, 'bulk exchange is the main marker of the scale of economic systems'.[39] In general, the existence of administrative systems or socio-political elites with a high efficiency in extracting resources will increase the potential for long-distance bulk-commerce and transport; this, in turn, can also become economically beneficial for larger parts of sub-elite society. As frequently emphasised by Janet throughout her work, the procurement and transport of building materials, arguably the 'bulkiest' cargoes possible, are therefore particularly relevant for a deeper understanding of the structure and scale of the Roman economy.[40] This is further corroborated by recent advances in provenance studies for local and regional building materials that fruitfully complement the conventional focus on the long-range transport of marble.[41] This prepares the ground for future inquiries into the decision-making of Roman builders which can be closely tied to the institutional and legal constraints under which they were operating, thereby supplementing traditional labour-cost analysis with the crucial, but often neglected, factor of transaction costs.[42]

Closely associated with procurement and transport of materials is the idea of 'rationalisation' in Roman architecture, which was first brought up, with respect to buildings in *opus caementicium*, by Richard

---

[35] Cf. the sweeping statement in Goldthwaite 1980: 118: 'The immense labor forces that were required, including all kinds and degrees of skills, consisted largely of dependent and involuntary workers who did not work for wages contracted freely in the market. They were pressed into service by the force of arms or compelled by customary and legal authority working through social institutions like slavery and clientage, that are peculiar to the ancient world'. For important recent reassessments of the Roman labour force working in construction, see Bernard 2016, Gerding 2019, and the paper of Alfred Hirt in this volume.

[36] Wickham 1988: 185–190; Marzano 2007: 125–153; Roth 2007: 25–26, 55–57; Capogrossi Colognesi 2009: 36–49.

[37] Marzano 2007; Launaro 2011, 2015; Volpe 2012.

[38] Cf. DeLaine 1995, 1997: 85–91, 219–220, 2015b; Erdkamp 2001, 2016; Lancaster 2005: 12–18, 2015: 21–38; Jackson and Marra 2006; Lancaster and Ulrich 2014; Peveler 2018.

[39] Wickham 2004: 163. Cf. Wickham 2005: 699–702.

[40] DeLaine 1995: 85–101, 109–122, 195–205, 2000a, 2001, 2015b. Cf. Russell 2013; Pensabene 2015.

[41] E.g. Jackson and Marra 2006; Jackson *et al.* 2011; Lancaster *et al.* 2011; Marra *et al.* 2013; D'Ambrosio *et al.* 2015; Farr *et al.* 2015; Marra *et al.* 2018; Diffendale *et al.* 2019.

[42] For propositions of such an approach on the macro-scale of Mediterranean exchange patterns across the centuries, see recently Terpstra 2019.

Delbrueck and later in the works of Filippo Coarelli and Mario Torelli who explicitly linked it to the Marxist model of 'produzione schiavistica'.[43] The very notion of 'rationalisation' implies a particular way of thinking which consciously aims at maximising output or profit in production by introducing new technology or ways of organising the workforce. Indeed, we can see that the facing styles of Roman concrete, and in particular reticulate masonry of the later 1st century BC, relied on the use of an immense number of pre-fabricated small stones of a more or less uniform shape which, in principle, could have been produced off-site by specialised workers. This means that masons building the concrete walls would only have had to put the facing stones in place, saving time and, as this view implies, money. The underlying proposition is that, at all times in human history, it is a constant trait of human behaviour to rationalise production: either because people act in line with a *natural* economic drive to save labour and gain profit, or because it is an outcome of *proto-capitalist or full-blown* capitalist structures of exploitation which rely on a docile workforce.[44]

Recently, this problem, including the closely related concepts of 'standardisation' and 'mass production', has been revisited by Natalia Toma. Looking specifically at the trade of architectural elements in marble in the imperial period, she rightly states that we should not be misled by modern concepts and terminology, as 'indeed, mass production depends on standardization, but not vice versa. The proof of standard dimensions is by no means a sufficient argument for production to stock'.[45] Ben Russell, in his book on the Roman stone trade, discusses similar issues, basically arguing against mass production in Roman architecture.[46] It is important to emphasise that this debate goes far beyond the particular question of whether 'rationalisation' actually *happened* in the ancient world (as, under very limited and specific conditions, it possibly did). More importantly, it is also closely related to the much bigger field of trade, demand, and supply in ancient architecture, where so-called 'primitivist' propositions still dominate the literature. This is well-reflected in Richard Goldthwaite's statement that the pre-modern construction industry in general 'was labor intensive, with even cost of materials representing primarily *labor charges*, and all the labor was concentrated in an area

extending no farther beyond the city walls than the quarries and kilns that supplied materials'.[47]

This model is plainly contradicted by the archaeological evidence, as it does not account for phenomena like the Roman marble trade which involved much longer distances of transport. More importantly, it also runs counter to the complex supply chains of low-value materials needed for structures in *opus caementicium*, and it is equally invalid for architectural terracottas and other types of ceramic building material which were often shipped to faraway places.[48] Likewise, the assumption that the value of basic building materials had only one major component – the cost of labour – is put into serious doubt when we look at the abundance of manufactured or significantly processed materials in Graeco-Roman architecture, such as brick, tile, lime, timber, metal elements, or quarried stone, all of which, if not the property of the building managers, had to be acquired from a wide range of different sources, and arguably for a price that must not only have covered their production, from the extraction of the raw materials to the finished end product, but also the relative scarcity of the prime resources. In principle, this would to some degree still reflect the cost of labour involved in the manufacture of these goods, but in fact the market for such manufactured building materials would have been subject to supply and demand, and therefore to inflationary or deflationary processes which surely would have impacted upon the value of the end product.

This is corroborated by Diocletian's Price Edict in which bricks used for building come at a higher price than simple ceramic vessels, demonstrating that, by the late 3rd and early 4th centuries AD, brick making could in principle have been more profitable than producing some types of pottery, in particular when considering economies of scale. Brick and tile used for building could fetch double the price of a small ceramic jar, and the maximum price for a specialised flue tile (*tubulus*) was even set at three times the sum for the jar.[49] In the time of the Price Edict, an order of 50 bricks of the ordinary type would therefore have represented a marketable value of 200 *denarii*, whilst 50 small ceramic jars would have been priced at 100 *denarii*. It is evident that these prices must stand for more than just 'labour charges', as it needs more skill to produce even the smallest and coarsest wheel-thrown vessel than to form bricks in a mould. Far from reflecting just the underlying effort of

[43] Delbrueck 1912: 179–180; Lugli 1957: 363–444; Coarelli 1977: 9–19; Torelli 1980, 1983: 247–250; Rakob 1983; Adam 1984: 79–90; Pfanner 1989: 172–176; Anderson 1997: 145–151; Wilson 2006: 226–227; D'Alessio 2010: 52, 54–55; Davies 2017a: 161–165; 2017b: 83–99; Van Oyen 2017: 136–150; *contra* Maschek 2016b; Mogetta 2019.
[44] Depending on the intended outcomes, the specific organisation of the workforce was actually much more varied than the simplistic and ultimately teleological idea of 'rationalisation' suggests: cf. the various ways of organising the workforce in Roman quarries outlined by Hirt 2010: 291–331 and the paper by Alfred Hirt in this volume.
[45] Toma 2018: 162 n. 7. Cf. Toma 2020.
[46] Russell 2013: 237–247, 250–254.

[47] Goldthwaite 1980: 399.
[48] For the transport of ceramic building materials on ships, see Rice 2016: 172–174, 192.
[49] Ceramic vessels: *lagoena* (jar): 12 *denarii*; terracotta lamp: 4 *denarii*; small jar of 2 *sextarii*: 2 *denarii*. Bricks: *later pudalis* (read: *pedalis*) and *later rutundus*: 4 *denarii*; *tubulus* (flue tile): 6 *denarii*; various water pipes: 4, 6, and 12 *denarii*; Frank 1940: 339; Erim and Reynolds 1973: 103, 108.

production, the striking difference in the Edict's pricing could thus be seen as an attempt to compensate brick producers for higher transport costs: indeed, the limited geographical distribution of regionally produced bricks and tiles beyond the obvious connective corridors of major waterways shows the constraints on export.[50] This does not mean that long-distance transport was inconceivable, in particular with respect to very large shipments which would have generated considerable profit. But even for less venturing or financially potent producers, providing modest quantities of brick and tile on a local and regional level would always have been a lucrative business when compared to other types of pottery.[51]

Concluding remarks

Last but not least, this deeply integrated nature of supply and demand in ancient construction would have sustained a substantial workforce, especially in peak periods of building and contrary to the orthodox views discussed before. For the high Middle Ages and for the construction industry in Renaissance Florence, it has been estimated that up to 10% of the total labour force, in boom times even more, would have worked on urban building projects.[52] The same may well have been true for Rome and central Italy in the late Republican and early imperial periods, especially when we consider the significant contribution of unskilled workers and day-labourers who would have boosted the number of people employed in specific moments of high demand.[53] This raises the crucial question of *how much* work of different kinds it would have taken to satisfy a construction worker's needs in an urban environment in the Graeco-Roman world? In an excellent study on wall painting in Pompeii, Francesca Bologna has addressed exactly this issue by comparing her estimates of labour costs and working hours with estimated living costs for 1st-century Roman Italy, in order to get a better understanding of how many artisans of that kind a town like pre-79 AD Pompeii could have sustained on a permanent basis and what their status in society, based upon their income, would have been.[54]

Although more studies of this kind are needed to arrive at a better understanding of chronological and geographical variation within the Roman Empire, it is beyond any reasonable doubt that people's livelihoods depended on large-scale and extended construction projects, and we should constantly remind ourselves that this actually stands behind exciting evidence, such as the famous *dipinti* of daily and monthly progress in brick construction from the Baths of Trajan on the Esquiline Hill.[55] These seemingly small and ephemeral signs reveal much more in terms of people's lives than we usually tend to think: they stand for a type of work which was organised to a firmly set timetable. They also show that there would have been pressure at different levels, from the contractor to the overseers to the individual bricklayer or even their most humble, unskilled assistants. Time as defined in the Roman calendar was used to closely monitor the building progress and, thus, the fulfilment of contractual obligations under the rules of Roman law.[56] Moreover, the *dipinti* also encapsulate the complex supply chains which had to function and a huge number of workers which had to perform more or less specialised tasks and must mostly have led very monotonous lives, presumably from a very young age onwards, in order to keep the project going.[57]

Thus, from the macro-level of frequency and impact of building projects down to the micro-level of the individual worker's life, archaeology has an invaluable and massive dataset at its disposal which enables us to ask, and potentially answer, a whole range of fundamental questions about how we imagine the nature and impact of ancient building projects. Were they deeply embedded into economic practices or were they, as Finley and others tended to argue, essentially exceptional? Were they only driven by the deficit spending and the conspicuous consumption of the urban social elites who invested in their prestige and public status? Were they driving forces for innovation and change, or were they firmly conservative in nature? Were such building projects essentially *urban* undertakings, or were they intrinsically linked with the sector of agricultural production? Were they an expression of what has been called the 'slave mode of production' and therefore virtually impossible without a large number of unfree workers? Were ancient construction sites more wasteful than productive? And, ultimately, what about the institutions which underpinned building projects in the ancient world: were they stable over longer periods of time or did they themselves become subject to change?

---

50 Cf. Darvill and McWhirr 1984; Graham 2006.
51 See Millett 1990: 177–178: 'tiles can potentially provide a market for local distributions from minor market centres, as it seems valid to assume that they were low-value products of high bulk which generally achieved only a local distribution'. In the light of the Price Edict, this notional 'low-value' status of brick and tile seems at least questionable. On brick production cf. Bukowiecki *et al.* 2015; Bukowiecki and Wulf-Rheidt 2015; DeLaine 2015b; Gerding and Östborn 2015, 2016; Schmidts 2018; Bonetto *et al.* 2019.
52 Goldthwaite 1980: 399.
53 Cf. Brunt 1980; Bernard 2016; Erdkamp 2016; Maschek 2016b, 2018; Gerding 2019.
54 Bologna 2019. Cf. Flohr 2019 and the paper of Francesca Bologna in this volume.

55 Volpe 2002, 2008, 2010; Volpe and Rossi 2012.
56 On the legal framework and contractual obligations in Roman construction, see Martin 1989.
57 The social and demographic makeup of the Roman workforce engaged in construction, including vital tasks like brickmaking, is still in need of much more incisive discussion which should ideally be complemented by the use of comparative material from anthropology and ethnography: cf. Anderson 1997: 151–166; Bernard 2016, 2019.

The papers collected in this volume go right to the core of many of these questions, presenting an impressive selection of case studies from all across the Graeco-Roman world, from Rome and Italy to Greece, Lebanon, North Africa, and Britain, whilst also setting benchmarks in terms of method and interpretation. But, most importantly, they all owe a great deal to the inspiring and rigorous way in which Janet, almost single-handedly, established this field of research 35 years ago. As we all know, there are two types of *Festschrift* in the academic world: the first type is mostly a collection of interesting and widely diverse papers, presented by a large number of former students and colleagues to celebrate a distinguished scholar; the second type, however, is the much rarer collection of thematic papers which celebrate both the individual scholar and their particular contribution to the field: such is the case with this volume. The papers collected here serve as a scholarly tribute to Janet's groundbreaking studies which have unlocked an entirely new dimension of research on ancient architecture, and thus they shall form a lasting monument and a true *Festschrift* to both Janet as a person and her impact on the field of ancient architecture.

Bibliography

Abrams, E.M. 1987. Economic Specialization and Construction Personnel in Classic Period Copan, Honduras. *AmerAnt* 52 (3): 485–499.

Abrams, E.M. 1989. Architecture and Energy: An Evolutionary Perspective, in M. Schiffer (ed.) *Archaeological Method and Theory*: 47–88. Tucson: University of Arizona Press.

Abrams, E.M. 1994. *How the Maya Built their World: Energetics and Ancient Architecture*. Austin, TX: University of Texas Press.

Abrams, E.M. and T.W. Bolland 1999. Architectural Energetics, Ancient Monuments, and Operations Management. *Journal of Archaeological Method and Theory* 6: 263–291.

Adam, J.-P. 1984. *La construction romaine: matériaux et techniques*. Paris: Picard.

Anderson, J.C. 1997. *Roman Architecture and Society*. Baltimore: Johns Hopkins University Press.

Anderson, J.C. 2014. Architect and Patron, in R.B. Ulrich and C.K. Quenemoen (eds) *A Companion to Roman Architecture*: 127–139. Malden, MA: Blackwell.

Barker, S. and B. Russell 2012. Labour Figures for Roman Stone-Working: Pitfalls and Potential, in S. Camporeale, H. Dessales and A. Pizzo (eds) *Arqueología de la construcción III: los procesos constructivos en el mundo romano: la economía de las obras, Ecole normale supérieure, Paris, 10-11 de diciembre de 2009* (Anejos de Archivo Español de Arqueología 64): 83–94. Madrid: Consejo Superior de Investigaciones Científicas.

Barresi, P. 2003. *Province dell'Asia minore: costo dei marmi, architettura pubblica e committenza* (StArch, 125). Rome: 'L'Erma' di Bretschneider.

Barresi, P. 2004. Anfiteatro flavio di Pozzuoli, portico *in summa cavea*: una stima dei costi, in E.C. De Sena and H. Dessales (eds) *Metodi e approcci archeologici: l'industria e il commercio nell'Italia antica: Archaeological Methods and Approaches: Industry and Commerce in Ancient Italy* (BAR Int. Ser. 1262): 262–267. Oxford: Archaeopress.

Bernard, S.G. 2016. Workers in the Roman Imperial Building Industry, in K. Verboven and C. Laes (eds) *Work, Labour, and Professions in the Roman World* (Impact of Empire: Roman Empire, *c.* 200 B.C.-A.D. 476 23): 62–86. Leiden and Boston: Brill.

Bernard, S.G. 2018. *Building Mid-republican Rome: Labor, Architecture, and the Urban Economy*. Oxford: Oxford University Press.

Bernard, S.G. 2019. The Economy of Work, in E. Lytle (ed.) *A Cultural History of Work in Antiquity*: 19–32. London: Bloomsbury Academic.

Blake, M.E. 1947. *Ancient Roman Construction in Italy from the Prehistoric Period to Augustus: a Chronological Study Based in Part upon the Material Accumulated by the Late Dr. Esther Boise van Deman* (Carnegie Institution of Washington Publication 570). Washington, D.C.: Carnegie Institution of Washington.

Bologna, F. 2019. Water and Stone: the Economics of Wall-painting in Pompeii (A.D. 62–79). *JRA* 32 (1): 97–128.

Bonetto, J., E. Bukowiecki and R. Volpe (eds) 2019. *Alle origini del laterizio romano: nascita e diffusione del mattone cotto nel Mediterraneo tra IV e I secolo a.C.: atti del II Convegno internazionale 'Laterizio', Padova, 26-28 aprile 2016*. Rome: Edizioni Quasar.

Bonetto, J., S. Camporeale and A. Pizzo (eds) 2014. *Arqueología de la construcción IV: las canteras en el mundo antiguo: sistemas de explotación y procesos productivos, Padova, 22-24 de noviembre de 2012* (Anejos de Archivo Español de Arqueología 69). Madrid: Consejo Superior de Investigaciones Científicas.

Brunt, P.A. 1980. Free Labour and Public Works at Rome. *JRS* 70: 81–100.

Brysbaert, A., V. Klinkenberg, A. Gutiérrez Garcia-M. and I. Vikatou (eds) 2018. *Constructing Monuments, Perceiving Monumentality and the Economics of Building: Theoretical and Methodological Approaches to the Built Environment*. Leiden: Sidestone Press.

Bukowiecki, E., R. Volpe and U. Wulf-Rheidt (eds) 2015. *Il laterizio nei cantieri imperiali: Roma e il Mediterraneo: atti del I workshop 'Laterizio', Roma, 27-28 novembre 2014* (Archeologia dell'Architettura 20). Florence: All'Insegna del Giglio.

Bukowiecki, E. and U. Wulf-Rheidt 2015. I bolli laterizi delle residenze imperiali sul Palatino a Roma. *RM* 121: 311–482.

Burford, A. 1965. The Economics of Greek Temple Building. *PCPS* 11: 21–34.

Burford, A. 1966. Notes on the Epidaurian Building Inscriptions. *BSA* 61: 254–399.

Burford, A. 1969. *The Greek Temple Builders at Epidauros: a Social and Economic Study of Building in the Asklepian Sanctuary, During the Fourth and Early Third Centuries B.C.* Liverpool: Liverpool University Press.

Camporeale, S., H. Dessales and A. Pizzo (eds) 2008. *Arqueología de la construcción I: los procesos constructivos en el mundo romano: Italia y provincias occidentales, Mérida, Instituto de Arqueología, 25-26 de Octubre de 2007* (Anejos de Archivo Español de Arqueología 50). Mérida: Consejo Superior de Investigaciones Científicas.

Camporeale, S., H. Dessales and A. Pizzo (eds) 2010. *Arqueología de la construcción II: los procesos constructivos en el mundo romano: Italia y provincias orientales, Certosa di Pontignano, Siena, 13-15 de noviembre de 2008* (Anejos de Archivo Español de Arqueología 57). Madrid: Consejo Superior de Investigaciones Científicas.

Camporeale, S., H. Dessales and A. Pizzo (eds) 2012. *Arqueología de la construcción III: los procesos constructivos en el mundo romano: la economía de las obras, Ecole normale supérieure, Paris, 10-11 de diciembre de 2009* (Anejos de Archivo Español de Arqueología 64). Madrid: Consejo Superior de Investigaciones Científicas.

Capogrossi Colognesi, L. 2009. Una lunga storia, in J. Carlsen and E. Lo Cascio (eds) *Agricoltura e scambi nell'Italia tardo-repubblicana*: 15–61. Bari: Edipuglia.

Carmean, K. 1991. Architectural Labor Investment and Social Stratification at Sayil, Yucatan, Mexico. *Latin American Antiquity* 2: 151–165.

Carter, J.C. 2006. *Discovering the Greek Countryside at Metaponto*. Ann Arbor, Mich.: University of Michigan.

Clarke, J.R. 1991. *The Houses of Roman Italy, 100 B.C. - A.D. 250: Ritual, Space and Decoration*. Berkeley, CA: University of California Press.

Coarelli, F. 1977. Public Building in Rome Between the Second Punic War and Sulla. *PBSR* 45: 1–23.

Coulton, J.J. 1977. *Greek Architects at Work: Problems of Structure and Design*. London: P. Elek.

D'Alessio, A. 2010. Fascino greco e 'attualità' romana: la conquista di una nuova architettura, in E. La Rocca and C. Parisi Presicce (eds) *I giorni di Roma: L'età della conquista: Mostra Roma, Musei Capitolini, marzo 2010 - settembre 2010*: 49–64. Milan: Skira.

D'Ambrosio, E., F. Marra, A. Cavallo, M. Gaeta and G. Ventura 2015. Provenance Materials for Vitruvius' *harenae fossiciae* and *pulvis puteolanis*: Geochemical Signature and Historical–archaeological Implications. *Journal of Archaeological Science: Reports* 2: 186–203.

Darvill, T. and A. McWhirr 1984. Brick and Tile Production in Roman Britain: Models of Economic Organisation. *WorldArch* 15 (3): 239–261.

Davies, P.J.E. 2017a. *Architecture and Politics in Republican Rome*. Cambridge: Cambridge University Press.

Davies, P.J.E. 2017b. A Republican Dilemma: City or State? Or, the Concrete Revolution Revisited. *PBSR* 85: 71–107.

Davis, P.H. 1937. The Delian Building Contracts. *BCH* 61: 109–135.

DeLaine, J. 1995. The Supply of Building Materials to the City of Rome, in N. Christie (ed.) *Settlement and Economy in Italy, 1500 BC-AD 1500: Papers of the 5th Conference of Italian Archaeology*: 555–562. Oxford: Oxbow.

DeLaine, J. 1997. *The Baths of Caracalla: A Study in the Design, Construction, and Economics of Large-scale Building Projects in Imperial Rome* (JRA Suppl. 25). Portsmouth, RI: Journal of Roman Archaeology.

DeLaine, J. 2000a. Building the Eternal City: the Construction Industry of Imperial Rome, in J. Coulston and H. Dodge (eds) *Ancient Rome: the Archaeology of the Eternal City*: 119–141. Oxford: Oxbow.

DeLaine, J. 2000b. Organising Roman Building and Space. *JRA* 13 (2): 486–492.

DeLaine, J. 2001. Bricks and Mortar: Exploring the Economics of Building Techniques at Rome and Ostia, in D.J. Mattingly and J. Salmon (eds) *Economies Beyond Agriculture in the Classical World* (Leicester-Nottingham Studies in Ancient Society 9): 230–268. London and New York: Routledge.

DeLaine, J. 2006. The Cost of Creation: Technology at the Service of Construction, in E. Lo Cascio (ed.) *Innovazione tecnica e progresso economico nel mondo romano: Atti degli incontri capresi di storia dell'economia antica, Capri, 13-16 aprile 2003* (Pragmateiai 10): 237–252. Bari: Edipuglia.

DeLaine, J. 2015a. The Pantheon Builders: Estimating Manpower for Construction, in T.A. Marder and M. Wilson Jones (eds) *The Pantheon: from Antiquity to the Present*: 160–192. New York: Cambridge University Press.

DeLaine, J. 2015b. The Production, Supply and Distribution of Brick, in E. Bukowiecki, R. Volpe and U. Wulf-Rheidt (eds) *Il laterizio nei cantieri imperiali: Roma e il Mediterraneo: atti del I workshop 'Laterizio', Roma, 27-28 novembre 2014* (Archeologia dell'Architettura 20): 226–230. Florence: All'Insegna del Giglio.

DeLaine, J. 2017. Quantifying Manpower and the Cost of Construction in Roman Building Projects: Research Perspectives. *Archeologia dell'Architettura* 22: 13–19.

DeLaine, J. 2018. Economic Choice in Roman Construction: Case Studies from Ostia, in A. Brysbaert, V. Klinkenberg, A. Gutiérrez García-M. and I. Vikatou (eds) *Constructing Monuments, Perceiving Monumentality and the Economics of Building: Theoretical and Methodological Approaches to the Built Environment*: 243–270. Leiden: Sidestone Press.

DeLaine, J., S. Camporeale and A. Pizzo (eds) 2016. *Arqueología de la construcción V: Man-made Materials, Engineering and Infrastructure: Proceedings of the 5th International Workshop on the Archaeology of Roman Construction, Oxford, April 11-12, 2015* (Anejos de Archivo Español de Arqueología 77). Madrid: Consejo Superior de Investigaciones Científicas.

Delbrueck, R. 1912. *Hellenistische Bauten in Latium II.* Strassburg: Karl J. Trübner.

Dickmann, J.-A. 1999. *Domus frequentata: Anspruchsvolles Wohnen im pompejanischen Stadthaus* (Studien zur antiken Stadt 4). München: F. Pfeil.

Diffendale, D.P., F. Marra, M. Gaeta and N. Terrenato 2019. Combining Geochemistry and Petrography to Provenance Lionato and Lapis Albanus Tuffs Used in Roman Temples at Sant'Omobono, Rome, Italy. *Geoarchaeology* 34: 187–199.

Dinsmoor, W.B. 1913a. Attic Building Accounts I: The Parthenon. *AJA* 17: 53–80.

Dinsmoor, W.B. 1913b. Attic Building Accounts II: The Erechtheum. *AJA* 17: 242–265.

Dinsmoor, W.B. 1913c. Building Accounts III: The Propylaea. *AJA* 17: 371–398.

Dinsmoor, W.B. 1921a. Attic Building Accounts V: Supplementary Notes. *AJA* 25: 233–247.

Dinsmoor, W.B. 1921b. Building Accounts IV: The Statue of Athena Promachos. *AJA* 25: 118–129.

Domingo, J.Á. 2012. Los costes de la arquitectura romana: el capitolio de Volúbilis (Mauretania Tingitana). *ArchCl* 63: 381–418.

Domingo, J.Á. 2013. The Differences in Roman Construction Costs: The Workers' Salary. *Boreas* 36: 119–143.

Domingo, J.Á. and J.R. Domingo 2017. El coste del Arco de Caracalla en Theveste (Tébessa, Argelia): verificación empírica de una metodologia de cálculo. *Archeologia dell'Architettura* 22: 35–53.

Drerup, H. 1966. Architektur als Symbol: Zur zeitgenössischen Bewertung der römischen Architektur. *Gymnasium* 73: 181–196.

Duncan-Jones, R. 1965. An Epigraphic Survey of Costs in Roman Italy. *PBSR* 33: 189–306.

Duncan-Jones, R. 1990. *Structure and Scale in the Roman Economy.* Cambridge: Cambridge University Press.

Erdkamp, P. 2001. Beyond the Limits of the 'Consumer City': A Model of the Urban and Rural Economy in the Roman World. *Historia* 50: 332–356.

Erdkamp, P. 2012. Urbanism, in W. Scheidel (ed.) *The Cambridge Companion to the Roman Economy*: 241–265. Cambridge: Cambridge University Press.

Erdkamp, P. 2016. Seasonal Labour and Rural-Urban Migration in Roman Italy, in L. de Ligt and L.E. Tacoma (eds) *Migration and Mobility in the Early Roman Empire* (Studies in Global Migration History 7): 33–49. Leiden: Brill.

Erim, K.T. and J. Reynolds 1973. The Aphrodisias Copy of Diocletian's Edict on Maximum Prices. *JRS* 63: 99–110.

Farr, J.M., F. Marra and N. Terrenato 2015. Geochemical Identification Criteria for 'Peperino' Stones Employed in Ancient Roman Cuildings: A Lapis Gabinus Case Study. *Journal of Archaeological Science: Reports* 3: 41–51.

Favro, D.G., F.K. Yegül, J.A. Pinto and G.P.R. Métraux (eds) 2015. *Paradigm and Progeny: Roman Imperial Architecture and Its Legacy: Proceedings of a Conference Held at the American Academy in Rome on 6-7 December, 2011 in Honor of William L. MacDonald* (Journal of Roman Archaeology Suppl. 101).

Featherstone, M., J.-M. Spieser, G. Tanman and U. Wulf-Rheidt (eds) 2015. *The Emperor's House: Palaces from Augustus to the Age of Absolutism* (Urban Spaces 4). Berlin and Boston: De Gruyter.

Fertik, H. 2019. *The Ruler's House: Contesting Power and Privacy in Julio-Claudian Rome.* Baltimore: Johns Hopkins University Press.

Feyel, C. 2006. *Les artisans dans les sanctuaires grecs aux époques classique et hellénistique à travers la documentation financière en Grèce* (Bibliothèque des Écoles Françaises d'Athènes et de Rome 318). Athens: École Française d'Athènes.

Finley, M.I. 1973. *The Ancient Economy.* Berkeley: University of California Press.

Flohr, M. 2019. Artisans and Markets: The Economics of Roman Domestic Decoration. *AJA* 123 (1): 101–125.

Frank, T. 1924. *Roman Buildings of the Republic: An Attempt to Date them from Their Materials* (Papers and Monographs of the American Academy in Rome 3). Rome: American Academy in Rome.

Frank, T. 1933. *An Economic Survey of Ancient Rome, 1: Rome and Italy of the Republic.* Baltimore: The Johns Hopkins Press.

Frank, T. 1940. *An Economic Survey of Ancient Rome, 5: Rome and Italy of the Empire.* Baltimore: The Johns Hopkins Press.

Gerding, H. 2019. Public Building and Clientage: Social and Political Aspects of Roman Building Industry, in D. Möller (ed.) *Vetenskapssocieteten i Lund: Årsbok 2019*: 17–29. Lund: Vetenskapssocieteten i Lund.

Gerding, H. and P. Östborn 2015. The Diffusion of Fired Bricks in Hellenistic Europe: a Similarity Network Analysis. *Journal of Archaeological Method and Theory* 22 (1): 306–344.

Gerding, H. and P. Östborn 2016. Brick Makers, Muilders and Commissioners as Agents in the Diffusion of Hellenistic Fired Bricks: Choosing Social Models to Fit Archaeological Data. *Journal of Greek Archaeology* 1: 233–269.

Gerding, H. and P. Östborn 2017. The Diffusion of Architectural Innovations: Modelling Social Networks in the Ancient Building Trade, in E.H. Seland and H.F. Teigen (eds) *Sinews of Empire: Networks in the Roman Near East and Beyond*: 71–84. Oxford: Oxbow.

Ginouvès, R. (ed.) 1992. *Dictionnaire méthodique de l'architecture grecque et romaine 2: éléments constructifs:*

supports, couvertures, aménagements (Collection de l'École Française de Rome 84, 2). Rome: École Française de Rome.

Ginouvès, R. and R. Martin (eds) 1985. Dictionnaire méthodique de l'architecture grecque et romaine 1: matériaux, techniques de construction, techniques et formes du décor (Collection de l'École Française de Rome 84, 1). Rome: École Française de Rome.

Goldthwaite, R.A. 1980. The Building of Renaissance Florence: an Economic and Social History. Baltimore, MD: Johns Hopkins University Press.

Graham, S. 2006. Ex figlinis: the Network Dynamics of the Tiber Valley Brick Industry in the Hinterland of Rome (BAR Int. Ser. 1486). Oxford: J. and E. Hedges.

Greene, K. 2000. Technological Innovation and Economic Progress in the Ancient World: M. I. Finley Re-Considered. The Economic History Review 53 (1): 29–59.

Hales, S. 2003. The Roman House and Social Identity. Cambridge: Cambridge University Press.

Hirt, A.M. 2010. Imperial Mines and Quarries in the Roman World: Organizational Aspects, 27 BC-AD 235. Oxford: Oxford University Press.

Hopkins, J.N. 2016. The Genesis of Roman Architecture. New Haven: Yale University Press.

Hurst, J.T. 1886. A Handbook for Formulae, Tables and Memoranda for Architectural Surveyors. London: E. and F. N. Spon.

Jackson, M.D., P. Ciancio Rossetto, C.K. Kosso, M. Buonfiglio and F. Marra 2011. Building Materials of the Theatre of Marcellus, Rome. Archaeometry 53 (4): 728–742.

Jackson, M.D. and F. Marra 2006. Roman Stone Masonry: Volcanic Foundations of the Ancient City. AJA 110 (3): 403–436.

Kay, P. 2014. Rome's Economic Revolution. Oxford: Oxford University Press.

Kolb, M.J. 1997. Labor Mobilization, Ethnohistory, and the Archaeology of Community in Hawai'i. Journal of Archaeological Method and Theory 4: 265–285.

Korres, M. 2000. The Stones of the Parthenon. Los Angeles: J. Paul Getty Museum.

Korres, M. 2001. From Pentelicon to the Parthenon: Exhibition Catalogue: the Ancient Quarries and the Story of a Half-worked Column Capital of the First Marble Parthenon. Athens: Publishing House 'Melissa'.

Lancaster, L.C. 2005. Concrete Vaulted Construction in Imperial Rome: Innovations in Context. Cambridge: Cambridge University Press.

Lancaster, L.C. 2015. Innovative Vaulting in the Architecture of the Roman Empire: 1st to 4th centuries CE. New York: Cambridge University Press.

Lancaster, L.C., G. Sottili, F. Marra and G. Ventura 2011. Provenancing of Lightweight Volcanic Stones Used in Ancient Roman Concrete Vaulting: Evidence from Rome. Archaeometry 53 (4): 707–727.

Lancaster, L.C. and R.B. Ulrich 2014. Materials and Techniques, in R.B. Ulrich and C.K. Quenemoen (eds) A Companion to Roman Architecture: 157–192. Malden, MA: Blackwell.

Launaro, A. 2011. Peasants and Slaves: The Rural Population of Roman Italy (200 BC to AD 100). Cambridge: Cambridge University Press.

Launaro, A. 2015. The Nature of the Villa Economy, in P. Erdkamp, K. Verboven and A. Zuiderhoek (eds) Ownership and Exploitation of Land and Natural Resources in the Roman World: 173–186. Oxford: Oxford University Press.

Leach, E.W. 2000. Socially Responsible Books on Roman Architecture. CP 95 (1): 77–87.

Lipps, J. and D. Maschek 2014. Antike Bauornamentik: Bemerkungen zum Forschungsstand und zu den Absichten des vorliegenden Bandes, in J. Lipps and D. Maschek (eds) Antike Bauornamentik: Grenzen und Möglichkeiten ihrer Erforschung (Studien zur antiken Stadt 12): 9–24. Wiesbaden: Reichert.

Lugli, G. 1957. La tecnica edilizia romana: con particolare riguardo a Roma e Lazio. 2. Rome: G. Bardi.

MacDonald, W.L. 1982. The Architecture of the Roman Empire 1: An Introductory Study. 2 ed. New Haven: Yale University Press.

Marconi, C. (ed.) 2015. The Oxford Handbook of Greek and Roman Art and Architecture. Oxford: Oxford University Press.

Marra, F., E. D'Ambrosio, M. Gaeta and M. Mattei 2018. The Geochemical Fingerprint of Tufo Lionato Blocks from the Area Sacra di Largo Argentina: Implications for the Chronology of Volcanic Building Stones in Ancient Rome. Archaeometry 60 (4): 641–659.

Marra, F., E. D'Ambrosio, G. Sottili and G. Ventura 2013. Geochemical Fingerprints of Volcanic Materials: Identification of a Pumice Trade Route from Pompeii to Rome. GSA Bulletin 125 (3–4): 556–577.

Martin, S.D. 1989. The Roman Jurists and the Organization of Private Building in the Late Republic and Early Empire (Coll.Latomus 204). Brussels: Édition Latomus.

Marzano, A. 2007. Roman Villas in Central Italy: A Social and Economic History (Columbia Studies in the Classical Tradition 30). Leiden: Brill.

Maschek, D. 2013. Die ‚Nicchioni' von Todi: Ein Monument der legio XXXXI nach der Schlacht von Naulochus. RM 119: 139–168.

Maschek, D. 2016a. The Marble Stoa at Hierapolis: Materials, Labour Force and Building Costs, in T. Ismaelli and G. Scardozzi (eds) Ancient Quarries and Building Sites in Asia Minor: Research on Hierapolis in Phrygia and Other Cities in South-Western Anatolia: Archaeology, Archaeometry, Conservation (Bibliotheca archaeologica 45): 393–402. Bari: Edipuglia.

Maschek, D. 2016b. Quantifying Monumentality in a Time of Crisis: Building Materials, Labor Force and Building Costs in Late Republican Central Italy, in J. DeLaine, S. Camporeale and A. Pizzo (eds) Arqueología de la construcción V: Man-made Materials, Engineering and Infrastructure: Proceedings of the 5th International Workshop on the Archaeology of Roman Construction,

Oxford, April 11-12, 2015 (Anejos de Archivo Español de Arqueología 77): 317–330. Madrid: Consejo Superior de Investigaciones Científicas.

Maschek, D. 2017. Transfer, Rezeption, Adaption: Archäologische Erklärungsmodelle zur Verbreitung römischer Steinarchitektur zwischen Struktur und Prozess, in J. Lipps (ed.) *Transfer und Transformation römischer Architektur in den Nordwestprovinzen: Kolloquium vom 6. - 7. November 2015 in Tübingen*: 35–45. Rahden/Westf.: Marie Leidorf.

Maschek, D. 2018. Großbaustellen in Zeiten der Krise: Neue Überlegungen zu spätrepublikanischen Heiligtümern in Mittelitalien, in K. Rheidt and W. Lorenz (eds) *Groß Bauen: Historische Großbaustellen als kulturgeschichtliches Phänomen*: 168–180. Basel: Birkhäuser.

McCurdy, L. and E.M. Abrams (eds) 2019. *Architectural Energetics in Archaeology: Analytical Expansions and Global Explorations*. Abingdon: Routledge.

Mertens, D. 1999. Metaponto: L'evoluzione del centro urbano, in *Storia della Basilicata 1: L'antichità*. Bari: Laterza.

Mertens, D. 2006. *Städte und Bauten der Westgriechen: Von der Kolonisationszeit bis zur Krise um 400 vor Christus*. Munich: Hirmer.

Millett, M. 1990. *The Romanization of Britain: An Essay in Archaeological Interpretation*. Cambridge: Cambridge University Press.

Mogetta, M. 2019. Monumentality, Building Techniques, and Identity Construction in Roman Italy: the Remaking of Cosa, post-197 BCE, in F. Buccellati, S. Hageneuer, S. van der Heyden and F. Levenson (eds) *Size Matters: Understanding Monumentality Across Ancient Civilizations* (Histoire 146): 241–268. Bielefeld: transcript.

Pakkanen, J. 2018. Three-dimensional Documentation of Architecture and Archaeology in the Field: Combining Intensive Total Station Drawing and Photogrammetry, in A. Brysbaert, V. Klinkenberg, A. Gutiérrez García-M. and I. Vikatou (eds) *Constructing Monuments, Perceiving Monumentality and the Economics of Building: Theoretical and Methodological Approaches to the Built Environment*: 117–140. Leiden: Sidestone Press.

Patay-Horváth, A. 2020. Greek Temple Building from an Economic Perspective: Case Studies from the Western Peloponnesos, in P. Sapirstein and D. Scahill (eds) *New Directions and Paradigms for the Study of Greek Architecture: Interdisciplinary Dialogues in the Field* (Monumenta Graeca et Romana 25): 168–177. Leiden Brill.

Pegoretti, G. 1843. *Manuale pratico per l'estimazione dei lavori architettonici, stradali, idraulici e di fortificazione*. 2 vols. Milan: Editore Librajo Angelo Monti.

Pensabene, P. 2015. Marmi pubblici e marmi privati: note in margine ad un recente volume di Ben Russell. *ArchCl* 66: 575–593.

Peveler, E. 2018. The Supply of Building Materials to Construction Projects in Roman Oxfordshire: Logistics, Economics, and Social Significance. D.Phil Thesis, University of Oxford.

Pfanner, M. 1989. Über das Herstellen von Porträts: Ein Beitrag zu Rationalisierungsmaßnahmen und Produktionsmechanismen von Massenware im späten Hellenismus und in der römischen Kaiserzeit. *JdI* 104: 157–257.

Pirson, F. 1999. *Mietwohnungen in Pompeji und Herkulaneum. Untersuchungen zur Architektur, zum Wohnen und zur Sozial- und Wirtschaftsgeschichte der Vesuvstädte* (Studien zur antiken Stadt 5). München: Pfeil.

Pitt, R.K. 2016. Inscribing Construction: The Financing and Administration of Public Building in Greek Sanctuaries, in M.M. Miles (eds) *A Companion to Greek Architecture*: 194–205. Chichester: Wiley - Blackwell.

Platts, H. 2019. *Multisensory Living in Ancient Rome: Power and Space in Roman Houses*. London: Bloomsbury Publishing.

Prignitz, S. 2014. *Bauurkunden und Bauprogramm von Epidauros (400-350): Asklepiostempel, Tholos, Kultbild, Brunnenhaus* (Vestigia 67). Munich: C. H. Beck.

Rakob, F. 1967. Römische Architektur, in *Das römische Weltreich*, edited by T. Kraus, Propyläen Kunstgeschichte 2, 153–201. Berlin: Propyläen Verlag.

Rakob, F. 1983. Opus caementicium und die Folgen. *RM* 90: 359–372.

Renfrew, C. 1973. Monuments, Mobilization and Social Organization in Neolithic Wessex, in C. Renfrew (ed.) *The Explanation of Culture Change: Models in Prehistory*: 539–558. London: Duckworth.

Renfrew, C. 1983. The Social Archaeology of Megalithic Monuments. *Scientific American* 249 (5): 152–163.

Rice, C. 2016. Shipwreck Cargoes in the Western Mediterranean and the Organization of Roman Maritime Trade. *JRA* 29: 165–192.

Rostovtzeff, M. 1926. *The Social and Economic History of the Roman Empire*. Oxford: Oxford University Press.

Roth, U. 2007. *Thinking Tools: Agricultural Slavery Between Evidence and Models* (Bulletin of the Institute of Classical Studies Suppl. 92). London: School of Advanced Study, University of London.

Russell, B. 2013. *The Economics of the Roman Stone Trade*. Oxford: Oxford University Press.

Salmon, J. 1999. The Economic Role of the Greek City. *GaR* 46 (2): 147–167.

Sassu, R. 2013. Culti primari e secondari nel santuario di Metaponto. *Thiasos* 2 (1): 3–18.

Scheidel, W. (ed.) 2012. *The Cambridge Companion to the Roman Economy*. Cambridge: Cambridge University Press.

Schmidts, T. 2018. *Gestempelte Militärziegel außerhalb der Truppenstandorte: Untersuchungen zur Bautätigkeit der römischen Armee und zur Disposition ihres Baumaterials*

(Studia archaeologica palatina 3). Wiesbaden: Harrassowitz Verlag.

Scranton, R.L. 1960. Greek Architectural Inscriptions as Documents. *HLB* 14 (2): 159–182.

Sear, F.B. 1982. *Roman Architecture.* London: Batsford Academic and Educational.

Senseney, J.R. 2011. *The Art of Building in the Classical World: Vision, Craftsmanship, and Linear Perspective in Greek and Roman Architecture.* Cambridge: Cambridge University Press.

Shear, T.L. 2016. *Trophies of Victory: Public Building in Periklean Athens.* Princeton, NJ: Princeton University Press.

Sojc, N. (ed.) 2012. *Domus Augustana: neue Forschungen zum 'Versenkten Peristyl' auf dem Palatin: Investigating the 'Sunk Peristyle' on the Palatine Hill.* Leiden: Sidestone Press.

Sojc, N., A. Winterling and U. Wulf-Rheidt (eds) 2013. *Palast und Stadt im severischen Rom.* Stuttgart: Steiner.

Stöger, H. 2011. *Rethinking Ostia: a Spatial Enquiry into the Urban Society of Rome's Imperial Port-town* (Archaeological studies Leiden University 24). Leiden: Leiden University Press.

Taylor, R. 2007. *Roman Builders: A Study in Architectural Process.* Cambridge: Cambridge University Press.

Temin, P. 2013. *The Roman Market Economy.* Princeton, NJ: Princeton University Press.

Terpstra, T. 2019. *Trade in the Ancient Mediterranean: Private Order and Public Institutions.* Princeton, NJ: Princeton University Press.

Thomas, E. 2009. *Monumentality and the Roman Empire: Architecture in the Antonine Age.* Oxford: Oxford University Press.

Toma, N. 2018. Standardization and Mass Customization of Architectural Components: New Perspectives on the Imperial Marble Construction Industry. *JRA* 31: 161–191.

Toma, N. 2020. *Marmor - Maße - Monumente: Vorfertigung, Standardisierung und Massenproduktion marmorner Bauteile in der römischen Kaiserzeit* (Philippika 121). Wiesbaden: Harrassowitz Verlag.

Torelli, M. 1980. Innovazioni nelle tecniche edilizie romane tra il I sec. a.C. e il I sec. d.C., in *Tecnologia, economia e società nel mondo romano: Atti del convegno di Como, 27/28/29 settembre 1979*: 139–161. Como: Società Archeologica Comense.

Torelli, M. 1983. Edilizia pubblica in Italia centrale tra guerra sociale ed età augustea: ideologia e classi sociali, in M. Cébeillac-Gervasoni (ed.) *Les 'bourgeoisies' municipales italiennes aux IIe et Ier siècles av. J.-C. Colloque Centre Jean Bérard. Institut Français de Naples, 7-10 décembre 1981*: 241–250. Paris: Éd. du C.N.R.S.

Trigger, B.G. 1990. Monumental Architecture: A Thermodynamic Explanation of Symbolic Behaviour. *WorldArch* 22 (2): 119–132.

Ulrich, R.B. and C.K. Quenemoen (eds) 2014. *A Companion to Roman Architecture.* Malden, MA: Blackwell.

Van Oyen, A. 2017. Finding the Material in 'Material Culture': Form and Matter in Roman Concrete, in A. Van Oyen and M. Pitts (eds) *Materialising Roman Histories* (University of Cambridge Museum of Classical Archaeology Monographs 3): 133–152. Oxford: Oxbow.

Volpe, R. 2002. Un antico giornale di cantiere delle Terme di Traiano. *RM* 109: 377–394.

Volpe, R. 2008. Le iscrizioni parietali dipinte delle Terme di Traiano, in O. Brandt (ed.) *Unexpected Voices: the Graffiti in the Cryptoporticus of the Horti Sallustiani and Papers from a Conference on Graffiti at the Swedish Institute in Rome, 7 March 2003* (Skrifter utgivna av Svenska institutet i Rom 4° 59): 175–186. Stockholm: Svenska Institutet i Rom.

Volpe, R. 2010. Organizzazione e tempi di lavoro nel cantiere delle terme di Traiano sul colle Oppio, in S. Camporeale, H. Dessales and A. Pizzo (eds) *Arqueología de la construcción II: los procesos constructivos en el mundo romano: Italia y provincias orientales, Certosa di Pontignano, Siena, 13-15 de noviembre de 2008* (Anejos de Archivo Español de Arqueología 57): 81–91. Madrid: Consejo Superior de Investigaciones Científicas.

Volpe, R. 2012. Republican Villas in the Suburbium of Rome, in J.A. Becker and N. Terrenato (eds) *Roman Republican Villas: Architecture, Context, and Ideology* (Papers and Monographs of the American Academy in Rome 32): 94–110. Ann Arbor: University of Michigan Press.

Volpe, R. and F.M. Rossi 2012. Nuovi dati sull'esedra sud-ovest delle Terme di Traiano sul Colle Oppio: Percorsi, iscrizioni dipinte e tempi di costruzione, in S. Camporeale, H. Dessales and A. Pizzo (eds) *Arqueología de la construcción III: los procesos constructivos en el mundo romano: la economía de las obras, Ecole normale supérieure, Paris, 10-11 de diciembre de 2009* (Anejos de Archivo Español de Arqueología 64): 69–81. Madrid: Consejo Superior de Investigaciones Científicas.

von Hesberg, H. 2005. *Römische Baukunst.* Munich: C. H. Beck.

von Hesberg, H. and J. Lipps 2010-2011. L'architecture romaine, évolution d'un champ d'études depuis les années 1950. *Perspective: actualités de la recherche en histoire de l'Art: la revue de l'INHA* 2: 215–239.

Voutsaki, S., Y. van den Beld and Y. de Raaff 2018. Labour Mobilization and Architectural Energetics in the North Cemetery at Ayios Vasilios, Laconia, Greece, in A. Brysbaert, V. Klinkenberg, A. Gutiérrez García-M. and I. Vikatou (eds) *Constructing Monuments, Perceiving Monumentality and the Economics of Building: Theoretical and Methodological Approaches to the Built Environment*: 169–192. Leiden: Sidestone Press.

Wallace-Hadrill, A. 1994. *Houses and Society in Pompeii and Herculaneum.* Princeton, NJ: Princeton University Press.

Wheeler, R.E.M. 1964. *Roman Art and Architecture.* London: Thames and Hudson.

Wickham, C. 1988. Marx, Sherlock Holmes, and Late Roman Commerce. *JRS* 78: 183–193.

Wickham, C. 2004. The Mediterranean around 800: On the Brink of the Second Trade Cycle. *DOP* 58: 161–174.

Wickham, C. 2005. *Framing the Early Middle Ages: Europe and the Mediterranean 400-800*. Oxford: Oxford University Press.

Wilson, A. 2006. The Economic Impact of Technological Advances in the Roman Construction Industry, in E. Lo Cascio (ed.) *Innovazione tecnica e progresso economico nel mondo romano: Atti degli incontri capresi di storia dell'economia antica, Capri, 13-16 aprile 2003* (Pragmateiai 10): 225–236. Bari: Edipuglia.

Wilson, A. 2012. Raw Materials and Energy, in W. Scheidel (ed.) *The Cambridge Companion to the Roman Economy*: 133–155. Cambridge: Cambridge University Press.

Wilson Jones, M. 2003. *Principles of Roman Architecture*. 2 ed. New Haven: Yale University Press.

Wittenburg, A. 1978. Griechische Baukommissionen des 5. und 4. Jahrhunderts. Unpubl. PhD thesis, Ludwig-Maximilians-Universität München.

Wulf-Rheidt, U. 2014. '*Den Sternen und dem Himmel würdig': kaiserliche Palastbauten in Rom und Trier* (TrWPr 24). Wiesbaden: Harrassowitz Verlag.

Yegül, F.K. and D.G. Favro. 2019. *Roman Architecture and Urbanism: from the Origins to Late Antiquity*. Cambridge: Cambridge University Press.

Zarmakoupi, M. 2014. *Designing for Luxury on the Bay of Naples: Villas and Landscapes (c. 100 BCE-79 CE)*. Oxford: Oxford University Press.

Beyond Labour Figures:
The 'Hidden' Costs of Stoneworking and their Application in Architectural Energetics

Simon J. Barker

Department of Architecture and Urban Planning, Ghent University
simon.barker3@gmail.com

Ben Russell

School of History, Classics and Archaeology,
University of Edinburgh
ben.russell@ed.ac.uk

Abstract

A considerable amount of recent research on the economics of ancient construction has made use of architectural energetics, drawing primarily on 19th-century building manuals for useable labour constants. Such manuals are not the only source for understanding the Roman building economy, however, and indeed labour figures are only part of the equation. Focusing on stone carving, this paper highlights alternative comparative data, such as price-books, building and other accounts, and modern restoration projects, which can be used to better understand ancient practices. In particular, we explore a range of 'hidden' costs beyond labour and materials, revealed in these sources but rarely accounted for in architectural energetics. These include variation in wages, profit on the part of workers, incidental costs for tools and accommodation, and contingencies for wastage and supply issues. By considering these factors we can better define the parameters for energetic studies concerning stone construction.

Keywords: architectural energetics, stoneworking, building manuals, price-books, tools

1. Introduction

In his *Practical Masonry: A Guide to the Art of Stone Cutting*, the fourth edition of which was published in 1903, William Purchase notes 'there is perhaps a greater diversity of opinion as to the proper system to be adopted in estimating for stonework than is to be found in any other branch of the building trade'.[1] John Rea echoes this sentiment: 'there is considerable difference of opinion as to the description of various labours executed on stonework'.[2] Pietro Paolo Drei, a third generation member of one of the loyal families of the Fabbrica of St. Peter's in Rome during the 17th century, noted the difficulty he faced in estimating the value of work completed by the sculptors who executed Gian Lorenzo Bernini's designs for The Four Rivers Fountain in Piazza Navona (1651) due to the fact that: 'so many animals, trees, flowers and plants, all carved from a single mass of travertine supporting the obelisk required exceptional labour, labour that will not be

appreciated by those who did not watch it take place'.[3] For studies using architectural energetics to explore Roman architecture, for which reliable labour constants are the *sine qua non*, this is a problem: stoneworking, but also a range of other ancient building techniques, were (and remain) complicated, varied, and often highly regional. And indeed labour figures are only part of the puzzle. The organisation of the building site and the workforce, the supply and sharpening of tools, the provision of space, and the arrangement of transport all impacted on the cost of building projects, as did other incidental costs, accidents, errors, changes in plan, and even poor weather. These are the awkward little things that can add up, and for which we have little or no ancient data.[4] While scholars employing architectural energetics have tended to focus on labour figures, material requirements, and transport costs, the data relating to these others factors are harder to track

---

[1] Purchase 1903: 134.
[2] Rea 1904: 150.

[3] Excerpt from the *Biblioteca Corsiniana*, ms. 167,31.B.14.fol.102, translated in McPhee 2008: 352.
[4] For a discussion of what limited ancient evidence we have for a number of these issues, including building disasters, incompetent workers, and construction fraud, see Oleson 2011.

down, often more messy and anecdotal. 19th-century building manuals, which have proved vital for labour constants, do offer insights into these other costs, as do building accounts, company records, price-books, and even modern restoration projects. In this paper we draw on a range of datasets to consider these 'hidden' costs and how they can be integrated into studies using architectural energetics. We focus, in particular, on the evidence for 1) variation in wages, 2) profit on the part of workers, 3) incidental costs, such as for tools and working spaces, and 4) necessary contingencies to cover fluctuations in supply costs and lost or damaged materials. We end by suggesting a set of totals that should be added to material and labour costs in studies of Roman architecture employing architectural energetics.

2. Source materials

Before turning to the available datasets, a word on the source materials we use is necessary. In the absence of detailed Roman sources for the cost of architectural stonework, most scholars interested in this topic have responded by exploring cost not as a monetary figure but rather in terms of the labour it entailed.[5] This has involved using architectural energetics to 'quantify past architectural remains in terms of the labor force involved' in order to reach a labour 'cost' for the project.[6] For energetic studies looking at Roman architecture, the standard reference point for relevant labour constants has been the 19th-century building manual, *Manuale practico per l'estimazione dei lavori architettonici, stradali, idraulici e di fortificazione, per uso degli ingegneri ed architetti,* by Giovanni Pegoretti, originally published in two volumes in 1843 and 1844, with a second edition issued in the 1860s edited by Antonio Cantalupi.[7] Numerous comparable building manuals or price-books were published in Italy, France, Germany, Spain, Britain, and the United States throughout the 19th and early 20th centuries.[8] Useful data of a similar sort can be found in the under-used architectural encyclopaedias, such as Joseph Gwilt's *Encyclopædia of Architecture* and Edward Cresy's *Encyclopaedia of Civil Engineering*, both of which provide labour constants for various construction tasks.[9]

One of the criticisms often levelled at architectural energetics when applied to Antiquity is the reliability of these sources.[10] This is difficult to gauge with certainty, but close correspondence between manuals suggests that Pegoretti was by no means an outlier.[11] Other studies have also shown that his totals are in the right 'order of magnitude'.[12] Indeed, there is a close correlation between the average labour figures for various stoneworking tasks recorded in historical manuals and those recorded by modern restoration projects, on which distinctly ancient objects (such as Ionic or Corinthian capitals) were (re-)produced.[13] We should, of course, not expect pinpoint accuracy because such a goal is unachievable: time-labour values can only ever be an 'estimate of the scale of costs',[14] since they would have varied in reality depending on the skill of the individual workers and a range of other unquantifiable factors.[15] In the words of Richard Elsam, these manuals were 'to provide for architects, surveyors and builders, the wherewithal to competently judge the difficulties in the execution of the works, as well as of the different qualities of the materials and the goodness of workmanship, and thus be enabled to discharge

---

[5] For costs of whole buildings recorded epigraphically, see Duncan-Jones 1982: 64. Occasionally the costs of individual architectural elements are preserved, but this is rare, making any comparison difficult. For one example, *CIL* XIII 5416–5417, which refers to the cost of marble revetment for the baths at Mandeure (*Germania Superior*), see Blin 2012. On the general problems for the Roman period, see DeLaine 2017: 16–17. The situation is different for the Greek world, of course, from which several sets of building accounts are preserved. For example, at Epidauros, inscriptions list the building accounts for four separate structures in the sanctuary and list expenditures and incomes; see Burford 1969, and more recently, Prignitz 2014.
[6] Abrams and McCurdy 2019: 3. For a detailed review, see Dominik Maschek in this volume. For examples of scholarship exploring ancient stoneworking using an energetics-based methodology, see DeLaine 1997, 2001, 2015, and 2018; Barresi 2003; Soler 2012; Pensabene *et al.* 2016; and Russell and Leidwanger 2021.
[7] Pegoretti 1843–1844; 1868–1869. From a modern energetics perspective, the volume was first applied by Janet DeLaine for her book on the Baths of Caracalla; DeLaine 1997. For details, see Barker and Maschek in this volume.
[8] These other sources, without being exhaustive, include from Italy: Luigi Ponza di San Martino (1841); Antonio Cantalupi (1874); Francesco

Salmojraghi (1892); Alessandro Ricci (1895); from France: Joseph Morisot (1804, with revised edition in 1820–1824), Louis-Charles Boistard (1822), Claude-Jacques Toussaint (1834, with revised edition in 1853), Raymond Genieys (1835, with revised edition by Barthélémy Édouard Cousinery in 1846), Blottas (1839), Joseph Claudel and L. Laroque (1863), and Jean-Baptiste Rondelet (1867); from Germany: Carl Busch (1871); from Spain: Mariano Monasterio (1867); Francicso Nacente y Soler (1886), and Pascual Fernández Aceytuno y Gastero (1914); from Britain: Richard Elsam (1825), William Young (1896), John Hurst (1905), Banister Fletcher (1888), George Stephenson (1883), and Rea (1904); and for the United States, James Gallier (1836 and 1883), Frank Vogdes (1985), and Frederick Hodgson (1904). On comparing these manuals for stoneworking, see Barker and Russell 2012: 88–89. Pegoretti's work does seem to have been regarded as the industry standard in late 19th-century Italy; for references to it, see Salmojraghi 1892: 279; Ricci 1895; Cantalupi 1874. However, other countries produced equivalent volumes, such as Charles Mayes (1859, 1862), which evidently became the standard reference in Australia.
[9] Gwlit 1842; Cresy 1847.
[10] For the difficulties and problems, as well as a summary of recent developments, see DeLaine 2017.
[11] Pegoretti (1843: 8) quotes the following, mainly French, sources: Jean-Baptiste Anselin (1810), Hebert Gauthey (1832), Rondelet (1831), Toussaint (1834), Boistard (1822), Ponza (1841), Nicola Cavalieri San-Bertolo (1826–1827), Morisot (1820–1824), and Blottas (1839). French manuals were widely used in Italy in this period, and the sixth French edition of Rondelet's manual was translated into Italian in 1831 and quoted by Pegoretti.
[12] DeLaine 1997, 2001, and 2006; also Domingo 2012, 2014a, and 2014b.
[13] A series of examples are given in Barker and Russell 2012. For a similar test of the reliability and applicability for brick-laying, see DeLaine 1997: 295–296, n. 5.
[14] DeLaine 2017: 17.
[15] On this point, see Barker and Russell 2012: 86–89. For problems specifically related to marble, see Domingo 2012; DeLaine 2017.

their respective duties with honour and integrity'.[16] As noted in the preface to Pegoretti's first edition, detailed estimates made in advance of construction allowed architects, engineers, and their customers to predict the cost of projects, the benefits of or issues with certain design decisions, the quantities of materials and workers needed, and how long the whole thing might take, and then to make modifications to plans and seek out alternative solutions as required.[17]

Building manuals can be distinguished from so-called 'price-books', like Rea's or Elsam's. Where the former give labour constants measured in man-hours (with some daily wages and certain standard prices for materials), the latter provide the going rates, in monetary values, for a similar range of building tasks (with only a few labour constants). Although price-books are concerned with costs rather than time, it is still possible to infer labour times using the wage rates they list. For example, James Gallier's *American Price-book* estimates the cost of producing an 11–foot tall fluted Doric column at $101.74.[18] Using a mason's wage of $1.62 per day,[19] this amounts to 63 person-days of labour (excluding quarrying and roughing-out). Price-books were first published in Britain during the late 1700s[20] and then rapidly expanded through the 1800s.[21] Peter Nicholson's 1825 *The Practical Builders' Perpetual Price-book* is credited in Gwilt's 1842 *Encyclopædia of Architecture* as a key example in the development of this genre within Britain. Gwilt noted that Nicholson was: 'a gentleman to whom the architect as well as the practical man are more indebted than to any other author on this subject'.[22]

In his introduction, Joseph Morisot similarly reviews the history of French works concerning the estimation of building prices and costs, in each case giving details about both the author and the volume.[23] He notes that the earliest example to discuss prices is Louis Savot's *L'architecture françoise des bastimens particuliers*, published in 1642, which included prices for various building materials and a brief discussion of prices for excavating and moving earth.[24] Moreover, Morisot covers various notable price-books of the 1700s, some of which concerned specific building trades such as

carpentry,[25] while others aimed to be much more wide ranging, covering a wide range of building activities and materials.[26] Included in this review was his own original publication of 1804, which he argued achieved its main goal of providing a much clearer method for breaking construction tasks into their various parts and providing a straightforward means of estimating their respective costs.[27] Part of the catalyst behind Morisot's publication was the fault he found with previous work, and he sought to combat what he viewed as the 'pratiques arbitraires' and 'pratiques vicieuses' that had resulted from earlier guides to estimation.[28] Morisot's work stands as the first proper example of a building manual detailing labour-rates and prices. Indeed, French materials served as a major source for the later Italian manuals of Ponza and Pegoretti,[29] even if the British manuals seem to have developed without specific reference to these continental examples.

While scholarly attention has focused on these manuals and price-books—formally published texts, in other words—accounts from historic building projects or company records have received much less attention. These document actual work completed and the sums paid for it rather than hypothetical sums; they give us a better sense, in sum, of the kinds of costs that had to be accounted for on real projects. Building accounts, in particular, survive in large numbers. In Britain, for example, nearly 1500 building accounts are recorded in the Public Record Office that detail royal works from the reigns of Henry III to Charles I (1216–1649).[30] Additional records include the Fabric Rolls of cathedrals, such as York and Exeter (to name only a few),[31] and building accounts in public archives or private possession[32] in Britain, France, and Italy.[33] Most of the relevant accounts date from the 17th to 19th centuries, but earlier examples can also be found. Alongside these accounts of actual building projects, we can set records from companies supplying such projects, such as quarries, tool-makers, or hauliers.

The level of detail and information recorded in these historic accounts varies over time and between project and/or organisation. Some provide just summaries and

---

[16] Elsam 1826: v.
[17] Pegoretti 1843: 7–8.
[18] Gallier 1836: 23. The cost is for a column of the following size: 11 feet high, 18 inches diameter at the bottom, and 14 inches diameter at the top of the shaft; the capital is 9 inches deep and 1 foot 8 ½ inches square of abacus, with sunk neck and elliptic ends to the flutes. Assuming the block producing the shaft was 23 ft. 7 in³.
[19] Gallier 1836: 16.
[20] William Pain 1774.
[21] Cf. Nicholson 1823; Elsam 1825; William Laxton 1839; and William Skyring 1845.
[22] Gwilt 1842: chap. 3, sec. 2347.
[23] Morisot 1820: 5–82.
[24] Savot (1642: 401–11 and 420–34) for 'prix que la pierre' and 'la fouille des terres', respectively.

[25] Nicolas-Marie Potain 1749.
[26] For example, Nicolas Le Camus de Mézières (1786) and Jean Francois Monroy (1789).
[27] Morisot 1820: 142.
[28] Morisot 1820: 82.
[29] Ponza (1841: 12–3) referenced multiple French sources, including Ancelin (1810), Pierre Bergère (1799), Boistard (1822), Morisot (1820–1824), and Toussaint (1834). Likewise, Pegoretti (1863: 8) not only included these sources but also utilised the additional French works of Gauthey (1832), Rondelet (1810), and Blottas (1839).
[30] *Public Record Office Lists and Indexes*, no. 35: 272–305. See Knoop and Jones 1933a: 5, for the total number listed.
[31] Raine 1859 (York Minster); Findlay 1939; Erskine 1981 and 1983 (Exeter Cathedral).
[32] Salzman 1967.
[33] E.g. Klapish-Zuber 1969; Cailleaux 1997; Marconi 2004.

lists of total expenditure or selected expenses. Others provide detailed information about the quantities and costs of materials, their transport, and the number and wages of workmen. Occasionally, these accounts include weekly or monthly summaries of expenditure, including the amounts paid to (and the names of) the workmen employed and the cost of materials and tools. For a typical example of English accounts, we can turn to the journal of John Vady, who was clerk of works at Eton College near Windsor (founded in 1440 by King Henry VI).[34] In the entries for 1444–1445, for example, the name of every stonemason, carpenter, blacksmith, labourer, and other worker employed is listed along with the days of the week that each worked and the amount each worker was paid.[35]

The data provided in these accounts, however, needs to be treated with caution. They record expenditure, not estimates from which possible expenditure can be calculated. They also record the sums paid for the completion of certain tasks and not, or at least not typically, the times that these tasks took; accounts focus on money, while manuals focus on time. Moreover, since the totals listed in accounts cover everything, they record not simply the cost of labour but also often the costs of materials, as well as a range of other expenses associated with projects. These caveats aside, building and other accounts provide an insight into the *real* experience of project managing and financing. They show how unpredictable this activity was and also offer insights into the range of items of expenditure above and beyond simply the labour and materials required to complete the project.

3. Wages

Labour figures from building manuals tell us how long certain tasks could be expected to take. They are necessarily estimates, since the skill of individual workers would have had a large impact on the completion time for a given task. To translate these labour times into expense, we need to consider the costs for the time of specific workers. In most cases, studies of ancient construction projects have used the daily rates provided by Diocletian's Edict of Maximum Prices (*Edictum de pretiis rerum venalium*) of AD 301 and translated these into appropriate monetary sums for other periods.[36] The Edict gives maximum daily wages, and for stoneworking these consist of just three relevant sums: 60 *denarii* per day plus maintenance for a skilled marble worker (*marmorarius*), probably a specialist in *opus sectile*; 50 *denarii* per day plus maintenance for a stone carver (*lapidarius structor*); and 25 *denarii* per day plus maintenance for a labourer

(*operarius*).[37] Since it belongs to a distinctive historical and economic context, the totals from the Edict should be treated as highly approximate figures. In particular, we should be mindful here that both building manuals and accounts from later historical periods demonstrate that daily rates could vary quite considerably from period to period, from region to region, as well as between specialists.[38]

Dealing with these issues in reverse order, the building manuals as well as a range of accounts from later historical periods show that daily wages for workers could vary quite considerably, depending on their specialism. In **Table 1**, the base daily wages given by Ponza, Morisot, Rondelet, and Pegoretti (in the second edition) are provided. They show that the highest paid workers earned between two and three and a half times more than a basic labourer.

Accounts from the quarries of Carrara in Italy during the 1850s, furthermore, show that even within groups of specialists wages varied, presumably based on expertise or experience. Different workers also worked different hours. *Scultori* (sculptors), for instance, were paid 2.30–4.60 *lire* and *ornatiste* (ornament carvers) 2–3.50 *lire*, with both working eight-hour days. In contrast, a *sbozzatore* (rougher-outer) was paid 2.30–5 *lire* and a *scalpellino* (stone cutter), 1.50–2.50 *lire*; both worked nine-hour days.[39] Here the highest paid worker probably earned closer to five times more than a labourer (which is not listed), since we can expect labourers to have been paid less than the lowest end of the *scalpellino* scale (1.50 *lire*). We can see a similar wage gap between stonemasons and their servants or assistants in accounts from medieval Britain. An entry from 1480–1484 in the building accounts of Kirby Muxloe Castle in Leicestershire records the wages of both 'roughmasons' and 'servants of the said masons'.[40] The roughmasons are listed in three wage groups: W. Taillour, W. Wyso, and J. Paille were paid 18 pence (*d.*) for five days' work; T. Sandur was paid 6*d.* for two days' work; and J. Crosse was paid 6*d.* for three days' work. The 'servants' of these masons were paid 8*d.*, 4*d.*, and 4*d.*, respectively, for the same number of days' work as their masters. The roughmasons, therefore, earned roughly double (and sometimes more) that of their

---

[34] Knoop and Jones 1934a.

[35] Knoop and Jones 1934a.

[36] On the Edict, see Corcoran and DeLaine 1994; Russell 2013: 33–36.

[37] Polichetti 2002: 220–221; Bernard 2016: 81 f., Table 4.2; Groen-Vallinga and Tacoma 2016: 108 f., Appendix 1.

[38] On this point, see Pegoretti 1863: 13. Moreover, the review of medieval building accounts by Knoop and Jones (1933b: 474–476) shows a great diversity in wage rates for stoneworkers. For example, nine masons at seven different rates of pay worked at Ely Cathedral in Cambridgeshire in 1359–1360, while there were 29 masons at five different rates of pay at York Minster in North Yorkshire in 1372. At Vale Royal Abbey in Cheshire in 1280 and Caernarvon Castle in Gwynedd (north-west Wales) in October 1304, a total of 51 masons were employed at 13 different rates of pay and 53 masons were employed at 17 different rates of pay, respectively.

[39] Maini 1852: 96.

[40] Knoop and Jones 1933a: 70.

	Ponza (1841)	Morisot (1820–24)	Rondelet (1867)	Pegoretti (1868–1869)
	Francs	*Francs*	*Francs*	*Lire*
Marble worker (*marmista, marbrier*)	3.00	4.00	–	3.00 (*marmista riquadratore*)
Stone carver (*scarpellino, tailleur de pierre*)	2.70	3.50	3.60	3.00–3.80
Mason (*muratore, maçon*)	2.30	2.75–3.75	2.75–4.25	2.00
Sawyer (*segatore, scieur*)	2.50	4.00–4.50	4.50	–
Quarryman (*cavapietra, carrier*)	2.25	–	–	–
Labourer (*manovale, manoeuvre*)	1.00	1.90	2.20	1.15

Table 1. Base daily wages for various types of stoneworkers given by Ponza (1841), Morisot (1820–1824), Rondelet (1867), and Pegoretti (1868–1869).

		Worker Type/ Specialism	Wage (*d.* per week)
I.		Under-master	30
II.		Assistant under-master or warden	29
III.		Overseers or foremen	28
IV.		Masons skilled in arch moulds	27
V.	(a)	Masons skilled in straight moulded work	26
	(b)	Layers or setters of moulded work	24
VI.	(a)	Masons preparing ordinary square ashlar with a chisel	20
	(b)	Setters or layers of ashlar	18
VII.	(a)	Roughmasons preparing walling stone or 'rockies' with a scappling hammer	16
	(b)	Wallers of 'rockies' or of 'rubble'	15
VIII.		Rough wallers of 'backing'	12
XI.		Servants or labourer	8

Table 2. Proposal of the categories of masons at Vale Royal Abbey and respective wage rates. Based on Knoop and Jones (1934a: 20–23).

assistants. The same ratio can be found in the Vale Royal Abbey accounts, with roughmasons earning double what their servants earned, and the highest level masons (below management level) earning more than three times this (**Table 2**).

The gap apparent in the medieval and 19th-century figures between the highest and lowest paid workers in the stoneworking industry seems to narrow in the 20th century. **Tables 3–6** show wages from the 1930s for different quarry workers active in three areas of the Livorno (Leghorn in English) region, in the area around Turin and in the area around Milan. A full range of specialists is again listed, many of them on different wages. However, the spread of wages is much narrower than in earlier periods, especially if we ignore the apprentices and children recorded in

Turin and Milan (on which more below). What is more noticeable in these early 20th-century figures are the extent to which wages differ within the different quarry zones of Livorno, despite the close proximity of the quarries and the fact that in the region of Turin hourly wages were different inside and beyond the quarry.

The Turin and Milan figures also offer some insight into the economic implications of using apprentices and indeed children. In Milan apprentices were paid less than half what carvers were paid and indeed less than labourers, but no detail is given as to their experience. In Turin, apprentices were paid roughly half the wage of a second class marble 'designer', but only after three years of work; prior to this they were either paid much less, perhaps closer to the sum children were paid, or

Worker	Carrara and Valle del Lucido zones	Massa and Cave del Carchio Zones
	Lire per day	*Lire* per day
Quarrymen, chief (*capocava*)	26.10	24.85
Quarrymen, others (*sotto capo cava*)	23.85	23.00
Resquarer (*riguadratore*)	20.80	20.25
Blockmen (*uomini al masso*)	20.50	19.80
Cutters (*filista*)	19.50	19.80
Sledmen, head (*capo lizza*)	25.65	24.40
Sledmen, others (*sotto capo lizza*)	–	21.55
Rope slackers (*mollatori*)	21.95	20.85
Labourers	21.05	19.95

Table 3. Wage rates in the marble industry, in the Livorno (Leghorn) district of Italy, 1931. From Bureau of Labor Statistics 1932: 1173, Table 5.

Worker	Carrara and Valle del Lucido zones	Massa and Cave del Carchio Zones
	Lire per hour	*Lire* per hour
Sawyers (*segatori*)	2.20	2.12
Coppers and Squarers (*scapezzatori e ripassatori*)	2.05	2.12
Sculpturors (*scultori*)	3.28	3.12
Decorators or carvers (*ornastisti*)	3.07	2.87
Chisellers (*scalpellatori*)	2.66	2.54
Modelers (*smodellatori*)	2.36	2.19
Stampers (*scalpellini*)	2.26	2.10
Turners (*tornitori*)	2.26	2.10
Planers (*frsatori*)	2.26	2.10
Polishers (*lustratori*)	2.20	2.06
Cutters (*filisti*)	2.14	2.07
Bow drillers (*tiratori di violino*)	1.54	1.46
Labourers	2.25	2.12

Table 4. Wage rates in the marble industry, in the Livorno (Leghorn) district of Italy, 1931. From Bureau of Labor Statistics 1932: 1173, Table 5.

were simply provided with accommodation and food. In medieval Britain, these benefits were included alongside a small wage.[41] In 15th-century Venice, a qualified mason was paid 25 *soldi* per day (or about fifty ducats per year), while apprentices were paid

[41] This is clear from a number of medieval building accounts, which show masons' apprentices provided with housing, food, and clothing in addition to being taught the trade of stone carving. Payments from the Vale Royal Abbey accounts record over a period of several years payment to 'R. Winchecumbe and his apprentice', who received varying weekly wages of between 6 shilling (*s.*) 7*d.* and 4*s.* 10*d.* for the two. From this total, R. Winchecumbe paid out a wage to his

apprentice, with the latter receiving 2*s.* 3*d.*, then 2*s.* 6*d.*, and later 2*s.* 9*d.* as he became more skilled. See Knoop and Jones 1934a: 33–34. In some cases it is clear that the apprentice received this payment in addition to food and clothing. In 1480, Walter Byse, apprentice to John Gare for eight years, received meat, drink, clothing, and 3*d.* in wages in the first year of his apprenticeship, rising to 6*d.* in his second year, and so forth at a rate of 3*d.* a year, so that he received a wage 10*s.* after serving eight years. See Knoop and Jones 1934a: 33.

Worker	At the quarry	Away from the quarry
	Lire per hour	Lire per hour
Ornamental workers	4.11	3.60
Marble and stone cutters, first class	3.51	3.00
Marble and stone cutters, second class	3.10	2.60
Marble and stone designers, first class	3.51	3.00
Marble and stone designers, second class	3.00	2.50
Apprentices after 3 years	1.55	1.40
Labourers	2.30	1.90
Boys, under 16 years of age	0.85	0.75

Table 5. Wage rates in the marble industry, in the Turin district of Italy, 1931. From Bureau of Labor Statistics 1932: 1173, Table 5.

Worker	Lire per hour
Squarers and polishers (riguadratori e lucidatori)	3.75
Carvers (ornatisti)	4.55
Labourers	2.85
Apprentices	2.55
Boys	1.55

Table 6. Wage rates in the marble industry, in the Milan district of Italy, 1931. From Bureau of Labor Statistics 1932: 1173, Table 5.

Area/Worker	Wage (in d.)
Kent Wage Assessment, 1563	
Master freemason	13
Second sort of all artificers	9
The best apprentice of an artificer	7
Wiltshire Wage Assessment, 1604	
Master freemason	11
Master roughmason	11
Every common workman or journeyman of these sciences	8
For every apprentice of these sciences and for every labourer to attend to serve them	7
Kendal Wage Assessment, 1719	
A master freemason when working or walling freestone	12
A roughmason, waller	10
The journeymen servants that have formerly served apprenticeships to any of the above trades	8
The apprentices that have not served three years and more than one	7
The apprentices that have not served one year	5
Getters of stone	10

Table 7. Various Wage Assessments for different classes of worker from Britain. From Knoop and Jones 1932: 25.

between five and ten *soldi* per day, depending on age and training.[42] Similar wage differences are evident in medieval Britain, with apprentices of master masons sometimes paid as little as 33 per cent of the standard wage.[43] While apprentices' wages could sometimes be higher, in the order of 50+ per cent or 75+ per cent of the standard wage, it is unclear if these individuals were apprentice stonemasons or apprentice master masons.[44] **Table 7** shows the wages paid to apprentices in Britain from various periods and areas. As can be seen, in Kent in 1563 and in Wiltshire in 1604, apprentices were paid roughly half the wage of a master freemason.

---

[42] Connell 1988: 63–64.
[43] Knoop and Jones 1933a: 164–165.

[44] Knoop and Jones 1933a: 165 provide the caveat that it is unclear if these apprentices were training as stone cutters and carvers or in the planning, design, and organisation of building operations. Knoop and Jones suggest that the latter scenario would help to explain the relatively higher wages being paid, since these individuals would likely have been experienced stonemasons qualifying for 'higher branches of masonry ... rather than "raw recruits" learning the skill of stoneworking'.

The figures from Kendal in 1710 add the additional detail that wages of 5*d.* were paid to apprentices with less than one year's experience and 7*d.* for those with between one and three years' experience. The former category was less than half that of a master mason's wage (12*d.*) or exactly half that of a roughmason's wage (10*d.*). The wage for more experienced apprentices was just over half that of a master mason and about two-thirds that of a roughmason. If apprentices or junior carvers undertook the initial stages of roughing-out for architectural work, for example, then the cost ratios could look very different to those presented by simply applying basic figures for labour costs from the building manuals.[45]

Finally, while the modern concept of overtime does not seem to have existed in Antiquity, we might expect premiums to be added to jobs that needed to be completed in a rush. In 1932, higher wages were noted for overtime work at various quarries in Italy: near Rome, 20 per cent over the regular rate was paid for the first two hours of overtime and 25 per cent for each succeeding hour; 14 per cent extra was added for two hours of overtime in the Milan district; ten to 15 per cent extra was added according to the number of hours of overtime in the Livorno district; and, 20 per cent extra was added for the first two hours of overtime and 30 per cent thereafter for marble workers in the Turin district.[46]

Pre-20th-century material relating to wages therefore points towards a more pronouncedly graded scale of wages for different types of workers based on type of work performed as well as the level of experience and age of the worker. This division is also seen in wages from Roman Egypt (more so than in Diocletian's Edict of Maximum Prices). A papyrus dated to AD 105 for labourers engaged in agricultural work, for example, records boys receiving much lower wages than both men and 'young' men, between one and four obols compared to six and five obols, respectively.[47]

Moreover, the economic potential of apprentice labour revealed in later historical sources can also be seen in apprentice contracts from Roman Egypt. While there are no examples for stone carving,[48] there is evidence for other skilled professions,[49] including a builder's apprenticeship from the beginning of the 3rd century AD.[50] Routinely, apprentices provided labour in exchange for training, food, and clothing.[51] In the aforementioned builder's apprenticeship, Zoilos (the apprentice) was to be 'fed and clothed' and 'receive six *drachmas* (*dr.*) per month for the three years of the apprenticeship'.[52] This figure is much lower than the average wage of four *dr.* per day for builders during the 3rd century AD and for labourers, who typically earned half this amount.[53] Obviously the type of work the apprentice could undertake varied according to the stage of the training;[54] however, even when food and clothing costs are included, contemporary wages suggest that the apprentice (as a labourer or trainee builder) offered economic value for the master builder.[55] Such evidence demonstrates that we should be careful not to flatten the hierarchy of unskilled and

---

[45] Specialisation and division of labour were evidently part of the building and stone carving industries throughout Antiquity. Cicero (*Epist. ad Quint. frat.* 3.1.3) noted that apprentices (possibly slaves) worked alongside the building contractor Cillo. Lucian of Samostata based one of his satires on his own brief career as a stonemason's apprentice in his uncle's workshop (Lucian *Somn.* 1–4). See Tran 2011: 128–129 for funerary inscriptions related to apprentices. Boschung and Pfanner (1988: 13–15, fig. 7) assume the presence of both master carvers and assistants in the statue-carving process, with assistants undertaking all the carving until the final stages. This would entail the assistant carrying out the bulk of the work. Training pieces of apprentices were found at the Sculptor's workshop in Aphrodisias, confirming that the establishment was active in training marble sculptors; van Voorhis 1998. In this case, van Voorhis (2018: 41–47) has suggested that the workshop was a small family-run enterprise producing for the local market with at least three carvers: a portrait specialist, a generally trained sculptor, and an apprentice.
[46] Bureau of Labor Statistics 1932: 1173.
[47] Grenfell *et al.* 1900: 247–250, n. 102; West 1916: 304, Table II. Another farm account from AD 79 also records the daily wage of an ordinary labourer as 3 to 4 obols, and that of a boy as 2½ obols, cf. *P.Lond.* I.131 R (S. 166).

[48] While not an apprentice contract, *P.Oxy* 7.1029, datable to the 2nd century AD, shows that carvers of hieroglyphs took on apprentices. Similarly, contracts for four-year apprenticeships for stone cutting are known from earlier Babylonian contracts (*Cyr.* 248; Johns 1904: 181–182).
[49] E.g. weaving, hairdressing, and nail making. For discussion and examples of apprentice contracts, of which about 40 are known from the 1st through 3rd centuries AD, see Lewald 1910: 18–19; Berger 1911: 166ff.; Mitteis and Wilcken 1911: 261; Westermann 1914; Hermann 1957–1958; Bradley 1985; Bergamasco 1995: 144–150 and 162–167; Freu 2011; Russell 2019: 250–252.
[50] *P.Oxy* 38.2875, where Zoilos apprentices himself to the builder Apollonios to learn the 'craft of building'. For discussion, see Bagnall 1968: 135–139.
[51] Hawkins 2016: 176ff. In many contracts it is also evident that the apprentice continued to live at home, cf. *P.Oxy* 2.275.
[52] *P.Oxy* 38.2875; however, the apprentice Zoilos is responsible for paying the apprentice taxes himself. It also states that upon completion of the apprenticeship, Zoilos will receive 'clothes worth 60 *dr.* in return for those which he brings with him worth also 60 *dr.*', and also the 'tools of the builder's craft without cost'.
[53] See Bernard (2016: 78–79, Table 4.1) who uses Drexhage's (1991) catalogues of builders' wages, 13 of which record/provide a *per diem* wage.
[54] This would likely have been different depending on the type of craft and the skill of the apprentice. Plato (*Republic* 467a), for example, noted that potters' apprentices were not permitted to actually make pots until they had been apprenticing for a long period of time. Instead, they acted as servants or assistants in the shop until they had enough training.
[55] In other apprentice contracts, apprentices typically received between 4 and 5 *dr.* per month for food (cf. *P.Oxy* 2.275; *P. Tebt.* 2.385). Recent assessments of pre-modern apprenticeships have emphasised the value and economic potential of apprentices right from the start, providing unskilled labour for the master artisans in-between periods of training. See Wallis 2008: 845–851. As was the case in later periods, the apprentice could be expected to contribute to more skilled tasks over time, cf. Hawkins 2016: 176; De Munck and Soly 2007: 13–16. In the rare cases where apprentices received wages, the amount increased over the course of the apprenticeship. In one contract, an apprentice weaver, who was evidently sufficiently trained after two years and seven months, began to receive a wage: 12 *dr.* per month for the third year, 16 *dr.* per month for the fourth year, and 24 *dr.* per month for the fifth; *P.Oxy* 4.725. For another example, see also *P.Oxy* 41.2977.

skilled workers when considering wages in energetics figures (see below section 7.1).

4. Profit

The various wages listed in the section above consist of the sums paid to workers to cover their labour. On most historical building projects, however, various sums were usually added to these wages to cover the costs of employing workers, arranging contracts, and paying supervisors and other managers, the fees of which were not accounted for by the daily wages of actual workers. These sums are typically described as 'profit', and they effectively oiled the wheels of on-site human resourcing. In practice, most architects or project managers, especially on larger projects, would have contracted out the task of hiring and managing workers, as well as supplying materials, and it was the contractors they appointed who would have mostly consumed these profits.[56]

An example of just such an individual from a later period is John Prophete, who supplied stone for Westminster Palace in London and Windsor Castle in Berkshire during the 14th century. It seems that Prophete was also an entrepreneur, who owned or leased quarries, paid the wages of quarrymen and stone cutters, and sold both worked and unworked stone.[57] Master Thomas of Weldon, who supplied stone for Rockingham Castle in Northamptonshire, also appears to have employed a number of stone cutters, layers, quarrymen, and labourers.[58] Similarly, an agreement from 1434 by a mason to build the nave of Fotheringay Church in Northamptonshire records that all materials were to be provided by him and he was to be paid a total of £300, by instalments.[59] Out of this, he was to pay his men's wages, presumably making a profit along the way. Indeed, there was an expectation of profit on the part of such individuals. For example, an agreement by a mason, dated to 1511, for building the stone vault of the Lady Chapel of St. George's Chapel at Windsor Castle states that 'he is to provide all materials and to complete the work within 2¾ years, for a total of £326, 13s. 4d.'. The contract further adds that 'if at the end of the work he swears that he has not made £20 profit on the contract, he shall have another £11, 13s. 4d.'.[60] This £20 is equivalent to about 6 per cent of the total contract.

Larger contracts or bigger projects would have offered more scope for profit. During the 17th century in Britain, for example, payments for work were organised

in a number of ways.[61] One approach employed for the rebuilding of St Paul's Cathedral in London was work done 'by Great', where mason-contractors agreed to undertake a set piece of work for a fixed price.[62] This was typically either the whole building or part of the building. In the case of the rebuilding of St Paul's, Campbell has noted that this method sometimes ended with contractors getting themselves into financial trouble, because they had wrongly estimated the time the work would take, thereby jeopardizing the whole project.[63] As a result, more reliable contractors often charged a premium for working 'by Great', and, as Christopher Wren remarked, 'made great profit by it'.[64] The sum that the contractors would have quoted in this arrangement would have to have covered their own wages, the wages of any workers they engaged, and a profit of some sort.

If we turn to the Roman period, we can find some evidence from construction contracts for similar practices. A 2nd-century papyrus from Oxyrhynchus in Egypt provides an example for the supply of stone. It records a contract between Asklas and Appollonios, two stone cutters, who agreed to supply stone to Antonia Asklepias for the building of a house, at a price of 39 dr.[65] The contract included a variety of prices for 292 different sizes and types. We cannot assess how much profit these workers were making on these blocks, since we do not how long they had to produce them or whether they needed to pay someone else for the raw materials. However, it is striking that they also demanded four dr. per day and food should their services be required

---

[56] On this aspect of Roman building projects, see Duncan-Jones 1982: 75–76; Taylor 2003: 16–17; Mar 2008; Russell 2013: 202–207.
[57] Knoop and Jones 1933a: 10.
[58] Knoop and Jones 1993a: 10.
[59] Salzman 1967: 505–509, Appendix B, no. 66.
[60] Salzman 1967: 562–563, Appendix B, no. 106.

[61] See Campbell 2005: 33–339, for an overview of the methods of contracting used during the 17th century.
[62] Campbell 2009: 298–299 for the methods of payment and contracting used for rebuilding St Paul's Cathedral.
[63] Campbell 2009: 298.
[64] Campbell 2009: 298, quoting WS V: 20. In connection to his study of the Master Carpenter at St Paul's, Campbell (2005: 332–336) estimated that he would have likely made somewhere between 20 and 40 per cent profit. In this case, he was paid 'by Day', but importantly, he claimed that if had been paid either 'by Measure' or 'by Great' that he could have made higher profits for his work.
[65] P.Oxy 3.498: 'To Antonia Asklepias, also called Kyria, from Asklas, son of Alexandros, and Apollonios, son of Amois and Tauris, both from Oxyrhynchus. We undertake to cut the squared building stones, which are to be transported by camel from the northern quarry for your house, Antonia, in the quarter of Pammenes' Garden, at the following rate of payment: the outer squared camel stones at four *drachmas* for 16, the inner ones at four *drachmas* for 30, the *antiblemata* at three *drachmas* for 100 squared camel stones, oblong corner-stones at eight *drachmas* for 16 outer squared camel stones and at eight *drachmas* for 30 inner ones, axe-hewn squared camel stones at four *drachmas* for 50 and axe-hewn squared camel corner-stones at eight *drachmas* for 50. All of the previously mentioned stones we will cut, but no ornamentation will be expected of us. Each of us will also receive for each day that he works one loaf of bread and '*prosphagion*'. If the builders need assistance from the stone cutters, we or one of us will assist them, each man receiving four *drachmas* as wages for each day's assistance and each of us likewise one loaf of bread and '*prosphagion*' for each day. Until the 22nd of the present month of Epeiph you have the right to transfer to others this contract for cutting the previously mentioned squared camel stones from the northern quarry.... The agreement is valid.... Year....' Translation by Johnson 1936: 477–478, Nr. 304.

Mason-contractor	Sums received for individual projects			Total	Potential Profit (37%)
	St Paul's	Churches	Others		
Edward Strong (1652–1724)	£46,446	£19,548	£11,030	£77,004	£28,491
J. Marshall (1675–1678)	£5,543	£19,292	£26,646	£47,481	£17,568
T. Wise Jnr. and Thomas Hill (1686–1707)	£24,509	–	£13,571	£38,080	£14,090
Samuel Fulkes (1688–1708)	£23,115	£11,216	£447	£34,778	£12,868
John Thompson (1688–1700)	£8,089	£19,477	?	£27,566	£10,199
Edward Pearce	£13,494	£8,296	£2,664	£24,454	£9,048
Christopher Kempster (1625–1715) and Ephraim Beauchamp (1690–1707)	£15,132	£8,658	£608	£24,398	£9,027
Nathaniel Rawlins (1690–1707)	£15,751	–	?	£15,751	£5,828
Thomas Wise Senior (1678–1686)	£5,616	£6,818	£1,075	£13,509	£4,998
Jaspar Latham (1678–1690)	£10,537	£2,910	?	£13,447	£4,975
William Kemspter (1700–1716)	£9,019	–	?	£9,019	£3,337
Thomas Strong (1675–1681)	£7,918	–	?	£7,918	£2,930

Table 8. Incomes of the mason-contractors who worked on St Paul's in rank order. From Campbell 2009: 305, Table 3.

by the builders (presumably at the building site) after they had supplied the stone. This daily wage is roughly three to four times the average wage for workers recorded in the Nile Valley in this period and double that received by quarrymen at the imperial quarries at Mons Claudianus.[66] This would seem to indicate that in this part of the contract at least, Asklas and Appollonios were making a substantial profit.

Evidence from later periods certainly shows that specialists working at the very high end construction projects could make substantial profits. The contractors who worked on the rebuilding of St Paul's Cathedral in London are cases in point. Campbell has calculated that Edward Strong, the Master Mason on this project, was paid £690 for the work of 65 men over a period of 66 working days in September 1694.[67] If we assume a typical daily rate of 2s. per worker, a total of £6 12s. would have been paid to the workers over the 66 days, meaning a potential profit for Strong of 37 per cent of the total payment.[68] If the mason-contractors on the same project made a similar level of profit, their earnings would have been substantial (**Table 8**). Moreover, these were not the only projects undertaken by these individuals, and so these profits were only a portion of their overall income. The similar profitability of stonework in the ancient world is suggested by a series of inscriptions from tombs found in Phrygia, which testify to the wealth of individual stonemasons.[69]

Indeed epigraphic evidence does show that Roman stoneworkers sometimes achieved both wealth and, in some cases, high status through their work.[70]

5. Incidental costs

In addition to sums to cover the kind of profits outlined above, various historical sources offer a range of insights into the incidental costs associated with stoneworking beyond simply employing workers. Here we focus on two: tools, their purchase and maintenance, and the provision of accommodation or workshop space.

5.1 Tools

Historical building accounts show that it was common for the project itself to fund the purchase of tools and their maintenance, expenses which could add up to considerable sums. At Vale Royal Abbey in Cheshire, the building accounts from 1278–1280 record expenses for 'the purchase of 24 hatchets for the masons at 5d. each and 30 hatchets for the masons at 4½d. each, as well as hammers, wedges, picks, etc. purchased for use in the quarry'.[71] Considering that a smith's wage in the late 13th century was 2s. 8d. per week,[72] this is the equivalent to ten weeks of labour (or 21s. 3d.) for the purchase of tools alone. Further costs are recorded in other accounts.[73]

---

[66] Drexhage 1991; Serafino 2009: 47; Russell 2018: 737–738. See also, Alfred Hirt in this volume.
[67] Campbell (2009: 303) used the number of workers detailed in Knoop and Jones (1935: 73–77) and payments from the WS XIV: 137.
[68] Campbell 2009: 303.
[69] Waelkens 1986: nos. 417, 471, 486, 501, 502; Strubbe 1997: no. 256; Merkelbach and Stauber 2001: 200, no. 16/22/05.

[70] For more detail, see Russell 2020: 254–258. On the social position of craftsmen involved in the stone and marble trades generally, see Bosnić and Matulić 2018.
[71] Knoop and Jones 1933a: 62.
[72] Salzman 1967: 70.
[73] A further payment is recorded in the Vale Royal Abbey accounts for February 1277–1278 under 'necessary expenses', which show that a payment was made to 'Alexander de Norton for six 'pycons' (picks?)

The costs of repairing and sharpening tools, that is on-going rather than one-off costs, were also handled in a variety of ways on different projects. On the Vale Royal Abbey project described above, smithies were erected at both the quarry at Edisbury and the abbey to maintain the tools used by both the quarry workers and masons working on site. These were paid out of the project's accounts. Each smithy had six workers: a smith and his labourer (sometimes two smiths and two labourers), a charcoal burner, a labourer to work the bellows, a striker, and a further person to bring masons' tools back-and-forth to the smithy to be repaired.[74] Between 1278 and 1280, an average of seven workers worked at the smithies on the building site compared to 40 masons and 15 quarrymen, a ratio of roughly 1:8.[75] We should remember here that the ratio between those involved in tool sharpening and stoneworking in the granodiorite quarries at Mons Claudianus in the Roman period was about 1:4.[76] This discrepancy relates to the hardness of the stone.

Another solution to dealing with tool sharpening and maintenance is shown in the accounts of Kirby Muxloe Castle in Leicestershire, where a forge was erected in 1481. Here the smiths were paid by the number of tools sharpened, a total of 2d. per dozen.[77] Between August 1481 and November 1484, 46 entries are included in the accounts for a total of 318.5 dozen (3822) tools. In this period, there were 173 working weeks, and so an average of 22 tools were sharpened per week. If we accept an average of four masons working each week, this would equate to 5.4 axes and chisels sharpened per week for each mason or roughly one per day.[78] These figures also demonstrate the relative expense of tool-sharpening compared to the wages paid to the masons. The wage of each mason was 3s. per week in summer and 2s. 6d. in winter. The 1d. paid to the smith each week per mason for repairing tools is equivalent to just over 3–4 per cent of their wage bill, depending on the season.

Again, the stone being worked here was quite soft, and indeed in India it has been observed that carvers of the considerably harder granodiorite could sometimes blunt as many as six chisels in a single hour of carving, which would have had serious implications when it came to the provisions of metalworkers (if six chisels per day had needed repairing at Kirby Muxloe in the 15th century, this would have amounted to 18–24 per cent of a mason's weekly wage).[79] Granodiorite is a much harder material than most of the stones used in British building, but Knoop and Jones also note that smithies were more important at quarries than building sites due to the fact that quarrying, more than the dressing of stone, blunted the tools. They point to the fact that projects that included little quarrying—such as Eton College, where much of the stone was purchased rather than directly quarried—had relatively few smithies or payments for tool maintenance compared to Vale Royal Abbey and Caernarvon Castle in Wales (completed 1330).[80] Much later, Pegoretti notes that different types of carving also impact the rate at which tools need sharpening. Basing his figures on the experiments made in 1829 by the engineer Giuseppe Cadolini during the construction of the Barriera di Porta Orientale in Milan, he observes that each of the stoneworkers engaged in strenuous carving, such as carving columns, needed between 28 and 33 chisels to be sharpened daily, a task that consumed about 0.0136 kg of iron per chisel.[81] Carvers working on more fine carving, such as mouldings, however, only needed about half this number of chisels sharpened.[82] He further notes that for every 1000 chisels sharpened, a blacksmith, assisted by an apprentice, would need 30 to 32 hours and would consume about 6 kg of fuel.[83] This was presumably part of the work in which the smiths attested at the quarries of Mons Claudianus, discussed above, were engaged; indeed the metallurgical analysis of slag finds at this site points to continual reforging of the tips of chisels as they became dull from use (Hirt this volume).

During the Medieval period, it seems to have been generally assumed that tools would be maintained on-

---

for the quarry, 2s. 3d. at 4½d. each; for eight 'howis' (hoes?), 2s. at 3d. each; for ten 'bechis' and 'triwlis' (trowels?), 15d. at 1½d. each; Knoop and Jones 1934a: 16. In the building accounts of 1447 for Sheffield Castle, 13d. was paid for making one mallet, one stone-axe, two picks, and six iron wedges for use in the quarry for breaking and lifting stones; Knoop and Jones 1933a: 65. In addition, the accounts from Westminster Palace from 1532 record that 8d. and 16d were paid for 'stone sawis for masons' and 'a fyle for the said sawis', respectively; Salzman 1967: 330.
[74] Knoop and Jones 1933a: 63. The building accounts also include some of the costs of setting up the smith: two large bellows at 7s. 8d., two small bellows, one at 2s. and one 18d., two hammers at 10d., three hammers at 12d., and three pincers at 12d. See Knoop and Jones 1934a: 16.
[75] Knoop and Jones 1933a: 63.
[76] Russell 2018: 734.
[77] Knoop and Jones 1933a: 64.
[78] Knoop and Jones (1933a: 64–65) calculated the figure of 5.4 taking the total of 3822 tools being sharpened during the 706 mason-weeks worked between May 1841 and November 1484 and dividing it by the average number of masons including apprentices working each week, excluding the master mason. If the latter is included, the figure drops to 5.15 per mason-week.

[79] Pers. comm. Stephen Cox.
[80] Knoop and Jones 1933a: 63.
[81] Pegoretti (1863: 361–2) does not make it clear that the number of chisels being sharpened was per stoneworker per day; however, the later volume of Cantalupi (1874: 193), who referenced the experiments made by the engineer G. Cadolini, makes it clear that each carver working on flat or curved surfaces needs c. 30 chisels sharpened per day.
[82] Pegoretti 1863: 361–2. Cantalupi (1874: 193) added, 'per la lavoratura delle lastre di ardesia, denominate bevole, quantunque non si abbiano esperienze dirette onde poter desumere il tempo abbiso –. gnevole, ciò nonpertanto si può ritenere quanto si ammette dai pratici, cioè che siffatto lavoro richiede quanto si ammette dai pratici, cioè che siffatto lavoro richiede la metà od al più i 2/3 del tempo occorrente per la lavoratura del granito'.
[83] Pegoretti 1863: 361–2. This figure is also given by Cantalupi (1874: 193), who states 'che per acuminare n. 1000 subbie vi abbisognano ore 30 da fabbro col garzone, ettolitri 1,50 di carbone di legna, e circa un chilogrammo di ferro'.

site and that this would be paid for out of the project budget. When this was not the case and masons were expected to pay for the upkeep of their own tools, this fact was explicitly stated. In 1350, the Wage Regulations issued by the City of London, for example, included the following statement: 'In the first place, that the masons … shall take no more by the working day than 6*d*. … And for the making or mending of their implements they shall take nothing'; masons, in other words, were expected to pay for their own tools.[84] In some later periods, workers had sums extracted from their wages to cover the maintenance of their tools. Bill Mackie, for example, noted that his grandfather, a driller at Rubislaw Quarry in Aberdeen in the early 20th century, had money withheld from his wages (between 2*s*. and 2*s*. 6*d*. a fortnight) to pay for the repair and sharpening of his tools.[85] In modern Carrara the same kind of system still operates, with blacksmiths moving from workshop to workshop, collecting tools that need sharpening, repair, or altering.[86] Insight into this system (and the dissatisfaction the masons sometimes had with the end result) can be seen from the mid 1950s, when Fred Cargill related witnessing the blacksmith pushing his handcart up to Kincorth, near Aberdeen, where masons were constructing a housing estate:

'Lamont the blacksmith came with his handcart with big wheels, from Ashgrove Lane. He had a bag of sharps and took away your blanks, every few days. He was a slightly built wee chap and he pushed this big barrow. He had a squeaky voice. He used to come on to the site and say 'well boys how are the tools today'. We used to say just absolute shite, too hard, too brittle. He would say, okay, I'll let them know. Next day we would say too soft, just mushrooming. We would never say they were good. The tools didn't stand up to much, especially the puncheon, thumped with the 3 ½ pound hammer. The forge had rows and rows of puncheons being tempered. He took away their blunt tools and brought back sharpened ones he had collected a few days before. Tungsten was coming in at that time. It was too hard, it just burst. It is better now.'[87]

5.2 Accommodation and workshops

In addition to tools, a major incidental cost associated with the workforce on building projects related to the provision of workshop space and sometimes accommodation. The most basic form of workshop was a temporary shaded outdoor space; however, it is equally possible that temporary wooden structures were also built to accommodate workers. Unfortunately, both forms of temporary workspace are difficult to identify archaeologically except by the presence of noticeable layers of marble chippings and dust.[88]

We can get a sense of how such temporary workspaces may have looked by turning to 'The Stonemason's Yard' by Canaletto (1697–1768), which was painted *c.* 1725 and is now in the National Gallery in London (**Figure 1**). The painting depicts a temporary stonemason's yard situated in an open space known as the Campo San Vidal beside the Grand Canal in Venice, Italy. In the painting, several masons can be seen at work carving blocks for the reconstruction of the nearby church of San Vidal. A similar wooden structure, open along one side, with blocks set up on wooden workbenches, was erected for the stonemasons currently working to restore York Minster (**Figure 2**). The sheds used for stonework during the 19th and 20th centuries at the granite-yards and quarries around Aberdeen were also broadly similar. A description from an investigation into phthisis (tuberculosis) among granite workers carried out in 1876 by Dr. R. Beveridge from Aberdeen Infirmary described the working facilities as follows:

'The mason works in long, narrow sheds, completely open on one side; near the open side, he places the stone, and works his face towards the light and air, and stooping over his work. He is, therefore, practically in the open air, the shed serving simply to protect him from wet; the dust is almost entirely above and behind him; while the muscular exertion necessary to wield his heavy tools is such as to keep him physically warm to resist variations of external temperature.'[89]

In 1891, Charles Macdonald was the first to build a completely enclosed workshop for his workers. Macdonald's building was built of wood with a slated roof and ample air space; it housed 120 stone cutters and afforded them 'complete shelter in all kinds of weather'.[90] Sometimes roofed spaces had to be created at relatively short notice. The accounts of St Paul's cathedral in London, dating to the 17th and 18th centuries, show that special sheds had to be constructed by the carpenters in which to store the Reigate stone, so that it would not weather before use. Labourers were paid extra to collect the relevant blocks of stone and store them in these sheds,[91] as transport of stone by road for St Paul's could only be guaranteed between March and November due to the weather.

---

[84] Knoop and Jones 1933a: 66.
[85] Fiddes 2019.
[86] Wootton *et al.* 2013: 2.
[87] Fiddes 2019.

[88] On this point, see Claridge 2014. In Rome, such workspaces are suggested by thick deposits of marble debris, unworked quarry blocks, and unfinished sculpture in the area of the western Campus Martius; see Maischberger 1997: 108–156.
[89] Fiddes 2019: 122–123.
[90] Fiddes 2019: 124.
[91] Campbell 2013: 40; WS XIII: 156, 178, and 197 for details of the payments.

Figure 1. 'The Stonemason's Yard' by Canaletto, *c.* 1725, National Gallery, London. The painting depicts a temporary stonemason's yard situated in an open space known as the Campo San Vidal beside the Grand Canal in Venice, Italy.

Figure 2. Stonemasons working at York Minster Stoneyard's Masons' Lodge, located on the west side of York Minster, York, UK.

The financial implications for the provision of workshop space and accommodation for stonemasons are clearly visible in building accounts, and much of this cost of course needed to come early on in the project. For example, early entries in the Vale Royal accounts for 1278 include payments to 'carpenters for making the *logias* [lodges] and *mansiones* [dwelling houses] of the masons and other workmen, the smiths' forges at the quarry of Edisburi [Edisbury], and the site of the monastery [Vale Royal Abbey]', along with masons' workshops.[92] Similarly, a vacant piece of land was given to William of Cleve, clerk of works at Westminster Palace, London, in 1444, for the purpose of constructing worker accommodation and stores, such as the 'tymber-hawe' and 'trasiers' for the stone cutters.[93] At Dover in 1536, in order to save time a couple of old 'hales', or tents, were sought as workspace and dining areas in bad weather for the roughly 460 men so that they would not have to go into the town.[94] Moreover, the construction of a wall at Westminster Hall in 1395 required the king 'to find the lodgings for the masons and their mates during all the time they shall be occupied about the said work'.[95] Lodging was also provided at quarries, such as at Huddleton, used in the construction of York Minster, and Sandgate in Kent, used for the construction of Sandgate castle.[96]

It should be remembered that some accommodation for workers was necessarily large and therefore represented a substantial cost. At York Minster, the old lodge housed 20 masons with a second lodge erected in 1412 that housed 12 masons.[97] To put the erection of a lodge to accommodate the masons working at Vale Royal Abbey in some kind of context, the price of £4 16s. over two years accounted for only part of the costs related to these structures. Knoop and Jones suggest that by the end of the first two years, three lodges had been built to accommodate the average number of masons working on the project at that time (c. 41–51 masons), with an average of 17 masons accommodated in each building.[98] A fourth lodge seems to have been added by mid-1280. Two sets of payments in April 1280 record some of the costs related to its construction. Firstly, 'Nicholas the boarder with his fellows' was paid 20s. 'for making 1000 boards for the new masons' workshop and for others needed' and a further 40s. for making 2000 boards 'for covering the masons' workshop and other houses'.[99] In this same month, William le Daubour and his labourers were paid 34s. for 'plastering a certain workshop near the site of the monastery and covering certain houses with turves'.[100] The total, £4 14s. was equal to about 3½ weeks of a stonemason's wage, assuming a wage of 27d. per week.[101] Likewise, in 1448–1449 at Vale Royal Abbey, a hall '60 feet long and 18 feet broad with convenient height' was built as masons' accommodation at a cost of £9 paid to two carpenters (assuming an average wage of 6d. per day for a skilled labourer, this is equal to roughly 300 days of work).[102] Maintaining these structures could also add considerable cost to a project. The repair of two lodges at Westminster Abbey, London, in 1413, for example, cost 26s. 8d.[103] The importance of accommodation is evident in by-law VII, agreed between the Master Masons' Association and the Operatives Union in 1880 in Scotland, which stated that 'sufficient shed accommodation be provided to hewers where practical'.[104]

How projects dealt with these costs seems to have varied. Workers at the granite quarries in north-east Scotland were provided housing, but rent was deducted from their wages. We hear from an 1869 advertisement for the leasing of granite quarries at Cove that there were labourer's cottages 'beside and in the neighbourhood of the quarries which are chiefly tenanted by the quarry men'.[105] In a contract dated to 1457 for Corpus Christi College in Cambridge, however, a choice of arrangements is offered. The mason was either to be paid at a rate per rod (apparently equal to the rate he had been paid at Peterhouse College in Cambridge),[106] or else, 40s. in total for the whole project.[107] In the latter arrangement, the college provided lodgings for four men and the right of

---

[92] Knoop and Jones (1934a: 16–17) note the following payments: in January 1277–1278, a total of 45s. was paid to six carpenters for 'working and making huts (*logias*) and dwelling houses (*mansiones*) for the masons and other workmen' and for 'dwelling places where the master (*magister*) may be received and masons' workshops and other dwelling places'. In April 1278, two payments are recorded. Firstly, six carters were paid 24s. 'for carrying the boards and timber for making dwelling houses (*mansionibus*)', and secondly, 20 diggers were paid for six weeks' work for 'enclosing and ditching the places where they were making the dwellings of the masons and others'. In May, 1278, 40s. wages were paid to plasterers 'making and plastering the houses and other dwelling places in the site of the Abbey'. The following year in April 1279, four carpenters received wages for 'working on the masons' workshop'. In June of the same year, a boarder and his fellows were paid 28s. 'for making 14,000 boards' for the new masons' workshop. In addition, daily wages were paid to various carpenters 'felling tree for timber and preparing them there in the wood with their axes', as well as daily wages and piece rates to sawyers for timber.

[93] Salzman 1967: 39.
[94] Salzman 1967: 39.
[95] Salzman 1967: 39.
[96] Knoop and Jones 1933a: 76.
[97] Knoop and Jones 1933a: 57.

[98] Knoop and Jones 1933a: 57.
[99] Knoop and Jones 1934a: 17.
[100] Knoop and Jones 1934a: 17.
[101] For a discussion of masons' wages at Vale Royal Abbey, see Knoop and Jones 1934a: 18–19. Masons were paid different rates in summer and winter 'on account of the shorter days', with some receiving 30d. a week in summer, reduced to 25d. in winter (these are the highest wages paid to three workers in total). The average seems to have been 27d., reduced to 23d., with the lowest paid 12d. or less. It is possible that the highest paid were overseers supervising the cutters or hewerrs at 28d., 27d., 26d., and 24d., but this is far from certain, since the proportion paid compared to the others does not seem correct.
[102] Salzman 1967: 77.
[103] Knoop and Jones 1933a: 59.
[104] Fiddes 2019: 123.
[105] Fiddes 2019: 122.
[106] A *rod* is an old English measurement of length equal to roughly 5 m (or 16.5 feet).
[107] Salzman 1967: 531–532, Appendix B, no. 81.

using the college kitchen to cook their food. The mason took the latter option but also asked for the help of two of the college workmen in digging foundations.

Lodgings were often also used to store tools. For instance, at York Minster, the Fabric Rolls list 69 stone-axes, 96 iron chisels, 24 mallets, one compass, and two tracing boards, among other tools stored in the masons' lodge.[108] These tools were expensive items, and Ricci even suggests that for marble working the cost of supervision and security, to ensure that both valuable raw materials and tools are not stolen, needs to be factored into any accounting.[109]

6. Contingencies

In her 1860 book, *The Marble-Workers' Manual Designed for the Use of the Marble-Workers, Builders, and Owners of Houses*, Mary L. Booth lists a range of factors that could increase or decrease the cost of building, many of which were unpredictable: the talent and/or fame of the specialists involved, the 'scarcity or abundance' of a particular material at the time the work was undertaken, on-site accidents, and alterations by the client.[110] She goes so far as to state that 'it is impossible to indicate probable prices, since the price of today might be changed in a month or a year'.[111] To account for this unpredictability architects or project managers would have to have kept a contingency fund.

6.1. Fluctuations in material costs

While the Price Edict gives maximum prices for different types of marble in the early 4th century AD—probably panels per ft[2], though some have argued for blocks per ft[3]—it is by no means certain that there was ever a fixed price of stone in the Roman world.[112] Certainly a series of 2nd-century papyri from Heracleopolis in Egypt indicate great uncertainty over how much a consignment of porphyry panels would cost; and indeed they end up (as one might expect) being much more expensive than anticipated.[113] In connection to Greek building accounts, Burford noted that two consignments of plaster delivered to Delos in the same week differed in price by 25 per cent, while the cost of lead clamps at Epidauros rose 100 per cent within seven years.[114] This was certainly also the case in later periods, where the available data indicate that prices for building materials could fluctuate significantly from year to year and vary considerably depending on the quality of the block of stone and its dimensions.

Marble prices from early 19th-century Rome indicate that the same stone types not only varied in cost year by year but also that different versions of the same stone were priced differently, depending on grain size and colouring.[115] This is echoed in a 1902 report on prices at Carrara, where it is stated that 'so much depends upon color, quality, etc. of the various marbles produced at Carrara, that it is only possible to give the range of prices approximately'.[116] 19th-century valuations of individual quarries at Carrara support this with, for example, a quarry of first quality statuary marble estimated at 7500 *scudi*, while a quarry of veined marble was about half that; an 'ordinary' marble quarry sometimes had a value as low as 40 to 80 *scudi*.[117] However, the 1902 report goes on to also stress that in terms of cost, 'many things must necessarily be taken into account... location and proximity to the transport facilities, soundness, depth or thickness of the various veins, with consequent ability or inability to produce blocks of large size, amount of labor necessary to properly open the quarry, are all important factors'.[118] The impact of block size on price is particularly striking. An 1851 report shows that while the most expensive statuary marble cost 2.80 *lire* per cubic palm if between eight and 20 cubic palms in volume, the price rose to 11.20 *lire* per cubic palm for a block between 161 and 200 cubic palms in volume.[119] There was no such thing as a simple price per cubic metre (or palm), therefore. And this fact is reflected in the British sources. For example, under the terms agreed for the rebuilding of St. Paul's cathedral, Thomas Gilbert and Thomas Wise (the agents responsible for supplying Portland stone in 1680) were paid higher sums for delivering large stones due to the added difficulty in their quarrying and transport.[120] The rates paid for the stone are shown in **Table 9**. Likewise, a comprehensive pricelist for both 'pietre da taglio' and 'pietre lavorate' at Milan and Florence from the 1860s illustrates the remarkable variabilities of prices for stone and stonework.[121] Both categories were sold by different units of measurement (m[2], m[3], ft[2], linear metre, or per item), which changed depending on the form of the raw material being sold or the type of work being carried out.[122]

[108] Knoop and Jones 1933a: 60.
[109] Ricci 1895: 132.
[110] Booth 1860: 73–75.
[111] Booth 1860: 74.
[112] On the units used in the Price Edict, see Corcoran and DeLaine 1994; Russell 2013: 33–36.
[113] *C.P.Herm.* 86, 94; Russell 2013: 25.
[114] Burford 1965: 28. For the prices, see: IG XI, 2, 146A. 70–71; IG IV², I, 103.62 and 132.

[115] Pettinau 1983.
[116] *The Carrara Marble Industry* 1902: 22045–22046.
[117] Maini 1851: 95.
[118] *The Carrara Marble Industry* 1902: 22045–22046.
[119] Maini 1851: 95-96.
[120] Cambell 2013: 34. Figures approved at the meeting in Sept. 1680, London Metropolitan Archives, document: CLC/313/I/A/002/MS25622/1, f.44(r), and included in contract transcribed in full in WS XVI: 19.
[121] Cantalupi 1867: 795–804, Tavola CVI: 'costo della mano d'opera e dei materiali impiegati nelle costruzioni'.
[122] Payments to workers recorded in Greek building accounts seem to have operated in a similar manner with workers paid on the basis of time, measure, piece, or job. Sometimes the cost of labour and materials or labour and transport were combined. See Loomis 1998: 104–120 for a discussion of the Athenian evidence with numerous examples.

Quantity of stone	Price (s.)	Price (d.)	Percentage difference	Ratio of prices per ton
For ordinary blocks ten shillings and two pence per ton	10	2	0	1:1
Scapelled stones (i.e. roughly-squared), which are under 3 tons in a stone per ton	11	8	14	–
For all stones of 3 tons in a stone and under 4 tons	13	0	24	1:1.3
For stones of 4 tons in a stone	16	0	45	1:1.6
For stones of 5 tons in a stone	18	0	56	1:1.8
For stones of 6 tons in a stone	20	0	65	1:2
For stones of 7 tons in a stone	22	0	74	1:2.2
For all ashlar per ft. sup.	0	7	–	–

Table 9. Prices for the Portland stone used for the rebuilding of St. Paul's cathedral, London (1 ton of Portland stone = 15 cubic feet or 0.42 cubic metres of stone). From Campbell 2013: 34.

Sub-standard stone could also have impacted on the cost of projects. William Skyring, for instance, writing in the 1830s in Britain, complains that statuary marble 'is now from 30 to 50 shillings per foot cube, at the wharf; taking all chances for its opening, which nineteen times out of twenty turns out bad, it is not uncommon for one mason to give another from ten to 15 shilling per foot super for good slab;... these marbles are so various in value that it is impossible to ascertain the equitable price without inspection'.[123] For precisely this reason Booth encouraged all sculptors to select their own materials at the quarries: 'if the marble worker chooses to order his marbles ready cut, he must take such as are sent to him; and, instead of making his own choice in the quarry, he is never sure of obtaining the finest, and often chances to receive the most defective, for the simple reason that the finest blocks are often selected before they are cut'.[124] This was often done. Whenever possible, for example, Michelangelo preferred to select material himself at the quarries – he travelled to Carrara at least twenty times. If he could not go to the quarries himself, however, he was prepared to entrust the initial stages of work (quarrying and roughing-out) to other carvers, but these were always close associates, usually from his hometown of Settignano.[125] This kind of prospection would have cost: in 1442, William Hobbys was paid 6d. per day for eight days in which he rode to the quarries at Upton and Freme 'to choose and examine good stones called Cropston' for the repairs at Gloucester Castle.[126] Similarly, in 1448–1449, John Denma was paid travelling expenses to Huddleston quarry so that he could arrange for a supply of stone.[127] But for many British carvers in the 19th century who relied on imports of marble, travelling to the quarries

was unfeasible and would anyway have been expensive, and so a contingency fund was vital.

6.2. Supply issues

Transportation costs could similarly fluctuate. Sometimes this was connected to the price charged by the haulier. In a letter dated to March 1517 from the sculptor Domenico Buoninsegni, who was in Rome, to Michelangelo at Carrara, the former notes that for three to five cartloads of marble the price should be no more than two to two and half gold *scudi* per cartload, for five to eight cartloads no more than three *scudi* per cartload, and from eight to twelve cartloads no more than four *scudi* per cartload.[128] These low prices, which started at two *scudi* per cartload, are typical of prices at Carrara in this period.[129] Despite his knowledge of the regular price of Carrara marble, however, Buoninsegni himself had to pay above market rates in some instances: earlier, in 1505, for example, he paid 35 ducats for eight cartloads of marble, which was more than four *scudi* per cartload.

Bad weather and other unforeseen issues could also affect supplies of materials.[130] The 16th-century Sens cathedral accounts provide some insight into the potential vagaries of river transport.[131] One shipper is recorded as having brought two barges from the quarries upstream as far as Montereau without problem but struggled at the confluence of the Seine and the Yonne and was forced to unload one of the vessels at Montereau. The stone that remained loaded

[123] Skyring 1831: 82.
[124] Booth 1860: 57.
[125] Scigliano 2005: 74, 77, 162.
[126] Knoop and Jones 1933a: 47.
[127] Knoop and Jones 1933a: 48.

[128] Ristori *et al.* 1965: 261–262.
[129] Rapetti 2002: 42 f. Another note within Michelangelo's papers dated to July 9th 1517 penned by an unknown author, when Michelangelo was working in Carrara, also refers to prices starting from two *scudi* per cartload with a similar progression of prices for larger sized orders.
[130] With reference to this point, see also Burford 1965: 28.
[131] Cailleaux 1997.

was shipped the next month to Sens. A third of the cargo of the second barge, however, never arrived; this much stone had to be left behind in order for the ship to proceed upstream. Thomas Knight, who had a contract for the supply of Portland stone for the rebuilding of St Paul's,[132] regularly failed to provide stones needed, with others arriving damaged from transit and marked on delivery to the cathedral as unfit for use. Shipwrecks from both fluvial and maritime contexts show that consignments of stone were lost and never recovered.[133] A modern example shows that this kind of variability was not limited to pre-industrial contexts. Letters relating to the reconstruction of the Stoa of Attalos in the Athenian Agora in the 1950s show that quarrying and transport costs fluctuated wildly.[134] In a letter dated March 16 1954, Stuart Thompson records that while 'the estimated cost of Piraeus stone was $50.00 per m³... the actual delivered cost [was] $78.00 per m³. This means that [the] final costs will be exceeded by approximately $20,000'. Bad weather during the winter in the mountains had caused the quarries to shut down for three and a half months, which had apparently created a 'very great marble shortage resulting in much higher marble prices and greatly increased wages in the quarries'. As a result, Thompson had to find two new suppliers to fulfill the demands of the project, with the result that the total was (with delivery costs) $15,000 greater than the original estimated cost. However, Thompson also noted that the increase in stone price could be counteracted to some extent by the fact that the cost of work on site was running ten per cent below estimated costs.

6.3. Labour problems

Difficulties getting hold of both supplies and workers could also be caused by competing projects. This can be seen in 17th-century Rome during the large-scale projects carried out under Pope Alexander VII. In April 1661, Antonio del Grande (1625–1671), architect of the new wing of the Palazzo Pamphili, justified delays in this construction by noting difficulties acquiring both materials and workers due to the drain on such resources by the construction of Piazza S. Pietro.[135] These accounts echo the complaints of Bernardino Parenti, the elder statesman of the work crew, who was present on site in October 1659 and who stated that work was delayed because of '*mancanza di robba et hora per mancanza d'homini*' (shortage of materials and

now by a shortage of workmen).[136] The two-month delay in starting construction at the Palazzo Pamphili meant that the over 100 men who had originally been hired had moved on to work on Piazza S. Pietro.[137] This lack of workmen continued even during construction. Parenti had difficulties hiring workmen, especially *scarpellini* (stone cutters), who were in high demand for travertine projects, particularly because of Piazza S. Pietro.[138] In order to combat just such shortages in workers and the presence of workers without materials or vice versa, the Fabbrica of St. Peter's introduced a syndicate system and required in their contracts that each mason provided materials and workmen at the same time.[139] This system created a monopoly for the syndicate that guaranteed the supply of materials and a steady workforce resulting in lower construction costs and quicker construction rates.[140] Smaller contractors, on the other hand, did not have this same guarantee of materials and workers.

Other delays could be caused by labour issues at the quarries. Insurrection at the Portland quarries in the 17th century — a response to the awarding of exclusive rights to the Commission for Rebuilding St Paul's cathedral — caused significant delays in the shipment of stone.[141] Mismanagement at the quarries enflamed tensions. In March 1678, in fact, frustrated at the lack of communication from the quarries, the commissioners asked if someone living close to Portland could report back on what was happening.[142] They discovered the quarrymen were in open revolt and had smashed the piers used to load the stone in response to perceived poor work conditions and pay.[143] Comparable instances of lawlessness, including the theft of building stone and illicit dealings in stone, are a regular theme in building records too. For example, at Leicester several cases of theft and the sale of stone from town walls are recorded in the Municipal Records. In 1292, Richard of Thorpe, Canon of the Abbey, pleaded clemency for stone he purchased from Robert of the Dovecote, which he knew to have been stolen from the town wall.[144] In a report from York Minster compiled in 1344–1345, the master of works notes that 'timbers, stone, lime, cement, and so forth have frequently been made away with; and that there has been much misappropriation of stone from the quarry, and that almost nothing is fit for the

---

[132] Campbell 2013: 31; WS XVI: 11–13.
[133] Russell 2013: 95–140. On the impact of this on a building project, see Russell and Leidwanger 2021.
[134] The original letters are archived in the American School of Classical Studies in Athens. For this letter and the subsequent letters mentioned below, see Box 202/18, Folder I.
[135] Habel 2013: 85–86, with references to the original documents housed in the Archivio di Stato di Roma, Notai del Tribunale dell'Auditore Camerale, Ufficio 3 (H. Simoncellis).

[136] Habel 2013: 97–99.
[137] Habel 2013: 97–99.
[138] Habel 2013: 97–99.
[139] The Fabbrica subcontracted as many as seven firms. See Habel 2013: 105 and D'Amelio 2003: 702, n. 21.
[140] Habel (2013: 105) and McPhee (2008: 369–370 with references to the original documents) cite the example of S. Carlo al Corso, whose deputies petitioned the Fabbrica in 1665 to allow their purchase of travertine from the vendor of their choice.
[141] Campbell 2013: 31. The petition is reprinted in WS XVI: 11.
[142] Campbell 2013: 33, quoting the Minute Book housed in the London Metropolitan Archives, no. CLC/313/I/A/002/MS25622/1, f.29(v.).
[143] Campbell 2013: 33.
[144] Knoop and Jones 1933a: 55.

acting outside the prerogatives of a magistrate; or imperial, if the local curia was informed by the provincial governor. Presumably, the decurions would not hinder the proposal, although they should not have been exempt from some of the decision-making. In the latter case, the construction processes would have been the result of the interaction between different administrative spheres: local, state, or provincial.

A municipal case, the colonial law of *Urso* (Osuna, Seville),[20] states in chapter XCIX that the *IIviri* should propose in the curia where to build public aqueducts, while the decurions would approve or reject the proposal.[21] Similar stipulations are recorded in sections XXXIX and LXXXII of *Irni*'s municipal statute.[22] The first of these includes the obligation of the *IIviri* to present any proposal to the decurions, always seeking the benefit of the community.[23] The second, however, gives the *IIviri* the power to intervene in public works in the city, with the prior consent of the curia through a decurional decree.[24]

Hispanic epigraphic evidence provides little data when tracking building proposals in the local senate for private or imperial initiatives. However, we can draw on other sources. For example, we know that Pliny the Younger[25] asked the decurions of Como (Italy) to allocate a piece of land to build a temple at their expense. We also know that an individual could propose a building project to the Senate of Rome. In 51 BC, Faustus Silla carried out the reconstruction of the curia that L. Cornelius Sulla had already renovated in 81 BC.[26] This was made possible by the exceptionality of the situation, given the blood relationship between the two men: in this instance it was a relative of the *dictator* who guaranteed the good condition of the public building, even if he did so as a private person.

As noted above, there is no mention of similar episodes in Hispanic epigraphy and no explicit allusion to the proposal of a public building project by a *privatus* to the local curia. However, we can suppose that where inscriptions include an euergetic donation referring to the benefactor being responsible for the construction of the structure, they were also responsible for submitting the proposal to the local curia. Typically such inscriptions only register the benefactors's name, his *cursus honorum*, and the financed building through expressions such as *de suo*, *solo suo*, and *fecit*, *refecit*, or *dedit*. In fact, the presence of the formula *decreto decurionum* and its variants indicate that the matter was approved in the curia after the mentioned proposal. For instance, in an inscription of *Contributa Iulia Ugultunia* (Los Cercos, Badajoz), L. Valerius Amandus and L. Valerius Lucumo paid *de sua pecunia* part of the podium of the circus. All this was approved *ex decreto decurionum*.[27]

Imperial initiatives are also difficult to trace because in many instances the projects financed by emperors were in reality the result of the initial impulse of those holding provincial office such as *proconsules*, *legati Augusti*, or *praesides*. These high-ranking officials understood the needs of the city administration. The emperor's building activity was, in general, related to military and fiscal demands, to administratively important cities such as provincial capitals, or to cities intimately connected with the emperor.[28] Again Pliny the Younger provides clues as to how such high-ranking officials were able to influence the emperor's decisions. Specifically, Pliny[29] asks Trajan for his intervention in the construction of the *lacus sunonensis*, a work that according to the governor of *Bithynia* will enhance the emperor's name, despite the fact that the initiative was Pliny's own. Similarly, Philostratus[30] describes how Aristides asked the emperor Marcus Aurelius to rebuild Smyrna, which was left desolate by an earthquake in AD 177.

As with private initiatives, we need to understand the relationship between the imperial/provincial and local authorities in cases where emperors appear to be directly responsible for commissioning building work in the provinces. An example of this is the repair of the theatre at *Augusta Emerita* (Mérida) by order of Constantine I and his sons.[31] Later, a *comes* and a *praeses provinciae* took charge of the repair of the circus in the same city and honoured Constantine II, Constantius II, and Constantius I, by then emperors.[32] The similarity of both cases makes it impossible to differentiate whether the initiative of the repair should be awarded to the emperors themselves or to high-ranking provincial officials, as was the case in the episode of the *lacus sunonensis* in *Bithynia*.

Regarding approval of the building works, it is logical to suppose that in cases where the initiative was imperial, decurional acceptance was not necessary, although contact between the two administrative spheres must have existed, at least when deciding on the land on

---

20 Roman colony *Genetiva Iulia* - Osuna, Seville – dated 44 BC. *Vide* Rodríguez de Berlanga 1873, 1876; González 1989; Mangas 2001; Caballos 2006, 2008.
21 *Lex Ursonensis XCIX*.
22 *Municipium Flavium Irnitanum* – unknown, Seville – this is the most complete municipal *lex* from the Flavian period to date. See Rodríguez de Berlanga 1853; Caballos 2001; Mangas 2001; Andreu 2004a.
23 *Lex Irnitana XXXIX*.
24 *Lex Irnitana LXXXII*.
25 Plin. *Ep.* x, 8, 2.
26 Cass. Dio., XL, 50.

27 *CIL* II, 984.
28 Gros 1976; Jouffroy 1977, 1986.
29 Plin. *Ep.* X, 41–42.
30 Philost. *V.S.* II, 9.
31 *HEp* 13, 2003/2004, 111.
32 *AE* 1927, 165.

which to begin the work. However, for municipal and private initiatives, as explained above, the decurions' approval[33] was required, expressed epigraphically with the formula *ex decreto decurionum*,[34] *de decurionum sententia*,[35] *ex senates consulto*,[36] or *ex decreto ordinis*.[37]

Another element to take into account is the possible imperial authorisation prior to the construction of large public works in the provinces. Pliny the Younger's requests during his time as a magistrate in *Bithynia* suggest that the emperor's approval was essential before beginning a major construction project. However, the correspondence between Pliny and Trajan seems to be the product of exceptional measures resulting from concern about the financial disorder of some cities in the provinces.[38] The increasing interventionism of the Antonine emperors in municipal affairs[39] and the creation of new magistrates, such as the *curator rei publicae*, from the second century AD onwards (e.g. *vide infra*) suggests that in the provinces, imperial permission was not always required for the construction of a major public building.[40]

The land

The administrative foundations for a building project would have been established with the enactment of the decurional decree. One of the key elements to be resolved in the local senate would have been the choice of land for the construction site. In broad terms, there were several possibilities: that the land would be owned by the municipality, that a *privatus* would donate it as an euergetic act, or less probably, that the municipality would buy the land from the private individual.

Following a proposal made by magistrates, the local curia had to decide and approve the location of the construction work, unless the land was privately owned. This is made clear in the *Lex Ursonensis*,[41] which states that the decision to expropriate private land on which an aqueduct was to be constructed was a matter for the *ordo decurionum*.[42] On the other hand, if the land was provided by a benefactor, he would likely wish to include the land as part of his euergetic donations. Evidence for this kind of donation is given by Q. Torius

Culleonis,[43] who restored the walls of *Castulo* with his own money because they were *vetustate collapsos*. His involvement included the consolidation of a road that connected *Castulo* with *Sisapo*, the cancellation of a debt between himself and the city from an earlier contract, the placement of statues in the theatre and also the ceding of a piece of land that he owned to build a bath complex. It can be assumed that the construction of the baths was not paid for by Q. *Torius Culleonis*, since he presumably would have been concerned to report such a donation in the same dedication.[44]

There are no Hispanic examples where it is clearly registered that the municipal or colonial treasury paid for the construction of a public building on land owned by the local government.[45] This is due to the different motivations of municipal and private initiatives: the latter needed propaganda to achieve its objectives and the local government did not.[46] Therefore, it is logical that fewer epigraphic testimonies allude to public constructions by the municipality or the colony. The same would be true in those cases where we know that the construction of a building was financed by euergetic donations, but no mention of the land has been preserved. While it is possible that this was recorded in another inscription that has disappeared, it may be supposed that it was the city that contributed the land for the construction. This decision would have been taken during the discussion before the approval of the decurional decree and the subsequent building project.[47]

When the construction was provided by imperial initiative, as mentioned above, contact between the provincial governor and *ordo decurionum* would be constant. In this case, the city would provide the land necessary for the erection of the structure.

Funding organisation

After the approval of the project, the decurions would allocate the funds from the *arca publica* to be spent on the works.[48] In the case of a municipal initiative, the local *aerarium* could assume the whole cost or an euergetist could cover a part of the structure, resulting in mixed funding. In the latter case, the work would be divided into lots, often registered epigraphically with

---

[33] *Lex Irnitana LXXXIII.*
[34] *CIL* II, 3541
[35] *CIL* II, 3431
[36] *CIL* II²/14, 327
[37] *CIL* II, 1378.
[38] Melchor 1992–1993: 136–137.
[39] Melchor 2010: 40–42.
[40] Already in the 2nd century AD, the provincial governor had to approve all works financed with public money (*Dig.*, L, 10, 31), while evergetic donations had to have such permission in specific cases (*Dig.*, L, 10, 3, pr.).
[41] *Lex Ursonensis XCIX.*
[42] Again, the episode in which Pliny (*Ep.*, X, 8, 2) requested a piece of land from the decurions of Como to build a temple at their expense.

[43] *CIL* II, 3270.
[44] Other Hispanic cases of land donation by benefactors are: *CIL* II, 1649; 1956; 4509; 5488.
[45] The formula *solo empto ab re publica* present in *CIL* II²/7, 97 could indicate that the city bought the plot for the *tabernas et post horreum* erection (Melchor 1992–1993: 141; Rodríguez Neila 2003: 113) or that it was the *privatus* who bought it from the municipality (Goffaux 2003). The data available do not allow us to choose one option or the other.
[46] Eck 1997; Goffaux 2001.
[47] *Vide Lex Irnitana LXXXIII* and *Lex Ursonensis XCIX.*
[48] *Lex Irnitana LXXIX.*

the formula *per pedes*, which the different benefactors would undertake to pay.[49]

The construction of the wall of *Carthago Nova* (Cartagena) is an example of mixed funding. A dozen inscriptions have been found that refer to the erection of different sections with their respective towers. Some of these were apparently financed only by the colonial treasury, and the inscriptions include only *IIviri* and *aediles* supervising the works.[50] Other sections were presumably paid for by *privati* without specifying any positions;[51] these benefactors were involved in the construction of an important structure for their city and supported the public treasury financially. To these must be added the donations of the *IIviri* and *aediles* in charge of supervising the works.[52]

In two inscriptions from *Balsa* (Tavira, Portugal), some euergetists financed *per pedes* the podium of a circus.[53] In view of the size of the construction project, it is logical that the city motivated and accepted the participation of several private benefactors. Another inscription from *Italica* (Santiponce, Seville) in a mosaic from a Republican temple in the area of the forum[54] shows the construction of the temple (*aedem*) by popular subscription, *de stipe*, while a magistrate, *pr(aetor?)*, financed its gate *de sua pecunia*.[55] In another inscription from *Lucentum* (Alicante), the city (*res publica*) repaired a temple of Juno.[56] The peculiarity of this inscription is that it explicitly mentions that the work was entirely paid out of the municipal treasury –*sua pecunia*. Likewise, Aquiflavians were in charge of executing *de suo a pontem lapideum* in honour of Trajan,[57] and the Lusitanian *municipia* financed the bridge at Alcantara with common funds –*stipe conlata*.[58]

On other occasions, construction work could be financed exclusively by euergetists, except when the city granted, for example, the land for the structure. In *Emporiae* (Ampurias, L'Escala), C. Aemilius Montanus funded the construction of an *aedes* and a statue to the goddess Tutela.[59] The formula *de sua pecunia* suggests that it was an euergetic act and that the construction was not part of the prerogatives of his duumvirate. In *Oretum* (Ciudad Real), P. Baebius Venustus financed

the construction of a bridge with 200,000 *sesterces*.[60] He dedicated it to the *domus divinae* and made sure that the inscription reflected his help to the city. With the formula *petente ordine et populo*, he indicated that he responded to the request of both the *ordo decurionum* and the whole city, whose treasury did not have sufficient funds to cover this indispensable infrastructure.

When a structure was directly or indirectly paid for by the emperor, the inscription commemorating the construction does not usually provide explicit information about a possible division of funding. In *Hispania*, only a very fragmented inscription[61] at *Castulo* seems to record the association of the emperor Claudius with two members of the local elite, P. Cornelius Taurus and Valeria Verecunda, to finance an unknown public building. On other occasions, it seems clear that the costs were covered by the imperial *fiscus*. In *Pax Iulia* (Beja, Portugal), Augustus financed the erection of the walls, towers, and gates of the city.[62] Other inscriptions seem to reveal imperial intervention in a veiled way, providing for example building materials such as marble or specialised labour. This could be the case, for example, of some of the *Aqua Augusta*.[63] Archaeology can also provide data about the precise contribution of the imperial sphere in certain construction projects. Some studies point out that the use of certain prestigious materials, such as marble from Carrara, suggests imperial intervention,[64] since the emperor controlled these quarries. However, recent cost calculations from archaeological analysis seem to cast doubt on these claims, concluding that the total cost of some local marble may have been similar to imported material, as in the case of the theatre of *Carthago Nova*.[65]

Work organisation

The *IIviri*, *aediles*, and imperial *praefecti*[66] had full power over public construction; they were in charge of carrying out the work,[67] they built/repaired roads, channels, and sewers,[68] and above all, they had the authority to hire *redemptores* on behalf of the city.[69] These magistrates had to supervise so that the works were carried out in accordance with the conditions set out in the *lex locationis*.[70] The decurions would weigh up the terms during the presentation of the project, possibly with the support of experts and technicians,

---

49 As an example, the archaeological examination of some buildings in the forum at Ostia has revealed that their construction was carried out by different companies or *redemptores* (Steinby 1983: 219–220). We also know that at *Urso* (*Lex Ursonensis LXIX*) the necessary supplies for the *sacra* could be provided by several *redemptores*.
50 *CIL* II, 3425; 3426; *DECar* 4; *AE* 1975, 525.
51 *CIL* II, 3422.
52 *CIL* II, 3427=3518; *HEp* 7, 1997, 430.
53 *CIL* II, 5165 and 5166.
54 *CILA* II, 578.
55 We follow the reconstruction in the text of A. Caballos (1987–1988).
56 *CIL* II, 3557.
57 *CIL* II, 2478.
58 *CIL* II, 760.
59 *AE* 1981, 564.

60 *CIL* II, 3221.
61 *CIL* II, 3269.
62 *AE* 1989, 368.
63 See Sánchez de la Parra-Pérez (2020).
64 Mar 2008.
65 Soler 2012.
66 *Lex Irnitana - Salpensana XXV*.
67 *Lex Irnitana LXXXIII* and *Lex Ursonensis XCVIII*.
68 *Lex Irnitana LXXXII*, *Lex Ursonensis LXXVII*, and *Lex Tarentini* lin. 39–40.
69 *Lex Irnitana - Malacitana LXIII*
70 See *Lex Ursonensis LXIX*.

such as *architecti*.[71] These would be publicly revealed after their approval.

Subsequently, *redemptores* or private entrepreneurs would participate in a public contract by which, in a system of bids (*auctiones*), they would propose a cost for the execution of the part of the work that was being auctioned.[72] Once the *IIviri* assigned the project to a *redemptor*, the *lex locationis* would be published - a public legal text recording all the architectural, budgetary, and administrative terms that would limit the commission and that would be agreed upon during the curia session along with the outcome of the auction.[73] In this way, a contract was signed in the form of a *locatio-conductio redemptio operis*, that is to say, a work lease in which the *redemptor* promised to carry out the work in exchange for a certain fee.

The magistrates had the authority to contract on behalf of the city and to choose the project that best suited the public interest.[74] Before bidding for the contracts and in order to avoid awarding them to architects who offered excessively low prices,[75] the *redemptores* had to submit plans and budgets for the project,[76] on which the magistrates would decide during the auction. The results would be published in *tabulae publicae*, later exhibited in the city's forum.[77] We know some of the conditions of these *leges* and how they worked thanks to the *lex parieti faciundo* of *Puteoli* (Pozzuoli, Italy). Widely studied,[78] it is an inscription from 105 BC that commemorates the construction of a wall and the opening of a door in the temple of Serapis.[79] This document provides valuable information about the terms that included the *leges locationis* and the role of the *IIviri* as *curatores*. Similarly, in the *Tabula Heracleensis*,[80] the *aediles* appear as *curatores* in a public competition for road work. These *leges* had to include the payment to the *redemptor* for his work[81] and the guarantees they offered before the award,[82] the execution period, the days payments were made, and technical details about the work, such as the type of beams, roof tiles, and walls to be built.[83]

In turn, the local governments could reduce the cost on the municipal treasury by using the labour of the local population, who, according to the statutes of *Urso*[84] and *Irni*,[85] had to provide labour in the form of *munitiones*. According to the *lex Ursonensis*, inhabitants between 14 and 70 years of age and anyone who owned property in the colony had to contribute five days of personal work per year, plus three days if they owned beasts of burden. Apart from the *leges*, no epigraphic evidence has been found in *Hispania* that clearly records the construction of a building by these means. Only one inscription[86] could be a testimony of such *munitiones*[87]: those of the *Asanianc(enses)* who built (*fecerunt*) a *via(m)*.

However, in other parts of the empire, there are inscriptions that can provide data on mixed funding and the use of this type of *munitiones*. In *Auzia* (Mauretania), an inscription[88] dated AD 230 refers to the construction of a *macellum*, with porticos and all kinds of ornaments. It was the *res publica colonia Septimia Aurelia Auziensium* that dedicated and took charge of the works, which were carried out thanks to donations from the decurions -*ex sportulis decurionum*- and the people's labour – *operisque popularium*. On the one hand, the initiative was municipal, since it was *res publica fundamentis coeptum perfecit dedavitque*. On the other hand, the funding was mixed, since it was possible to pay for the work thanks to the *sportulae* donated by the decurions and the *munitiones* organised by the magistrates.

We assume that the same system of contracts would have been carried out in cases where private initiative paid on the construction. Obviously, the procedure and terms would not have been publicly stated, since the financing would not affect the city's treasury.[89] It would be the benefactor or a *curator* in their confidence who would decide to which *redemptor* or *societas publicanorum* to award the works.

In the Hispanic provinces, we know little about the types of contracts and *redemptores* who might have worked for imperial projects. In Rome, some specialists came to be known as *redemptores ab aerario* or *operum Caesaris* because of their special connection with the imperial house.[90] The *Haterii* can most likely be identified as such specialists. They were a family of builders active in Rome at the end of the 1st century AD and the beginning of the 2nd century AD. The family's tomb depicts some of the most emblematic monuments in the *Urbs*, such as the Flavian amphitheatre or the temple of Isis and Serapis in the *Campus Martius*, in the

---

71 Rodríguez Neila (2003: 119, note 22) recalls that L. Cornelius Balbus maior had a slave who was *architectus* (Cic., *Att.*, 14, 3, 1) and who possibly advised his nephew, who undertook as an *IIvir* the urban expansion of *Gades* (Str., III, 5, 3).
72 See Rodríguez Neila 2003: 127–130 and 155–158.
73 Rodríguez Neila 2009.
74 *Lex Irnitana - Malacitana LXIII.*
75 Vitr., *De Arch.*, 10.
76 Cic. *Ad. Q. Fr.*, 2, 6; Aul. Gell., *NA*, XIX, 10, 2–3; Front., *Aq*, XVII, 3.
77 *Lex Irnitana XCV* and *Lex UrsonensisCXV.*
78 Wiegand 1894.
79 *CIL* X, 1781.
80 *CIL* I², 593.
81 *Lex Irnitana – Malacitana LXIII* and *Lex Ursonensis LXIX.*
82 Submitting *cautiones* was widespread for anyone seeking access to public *locationes*, as evidenced by the *leges Irni-Malacitana LXIII-LXIV*, *Ursonensis LXXV* and XCIII. About the *cautiones*, see Rodríguez Neila 2003: 128–130 and 153–154.
83 *Lex Puteol. III*, 13 ss.

84 *Lex Ursonensis XCVIII.*
85 *LexIrnitana LXXXIII.*
86 *CIL* II, 5028.
87 Melchor 1992–1993: 139.
88 *CIL* VIII, 9062.
89 García Morcillo 2005.
90 Daguet-Gagey 1997.

construction of which the *Haterii* were likely involved.[91] In *Hispania* we must assume that the *redemptores* who worked in these contexts, although they probably could not be described as *ab aerario* or *operum Caesaris*, would have been well positioned politically and socially.

Likewise, *Hispania* provides very little epigraphic data about the labour force employed and the way in which it was organised. We know that cities had public slaves, *servi*, who could carry out specialised work. In this way, the local treasury would only allocate funds to their maintenance. The *fistulae* with cartouche of the *Caesaraugusta* (Zaragoza) aqueduct, for example, provide information about those in charge of supervising the works, the *aediles*, and the slaves of the colony who worked in the construction.[92] In addition to the *munitiones*[93] called for by the magistrates, free labour could be widely used in public construction.[94] On the other hand, cities would count on the obligatory contributions that the *servi publici* had to provide once they had been manumitted: the *operae libertorum*.[95]

Imperial initiatives would also take advantage of this labour as well as specialised workers,[96] often located in the legions.[97] In *Hispania*, a *strator*[98] from the *X Gemina*, whose functions were related to military roads, and a *praefectus alae* have been located in *Petavonium* (Rosinos de Vidriales, Zamora). The latter was in charge of the construction of some baths.[99] For other parts of the empire, we have references to individuals condemned to forced labour in public works, often requested for their use in construction undertaken on imperial initiative.[100] Finally, it may be supposed that private initiatives would also have employed slave labour, freedmen linked by clientele ties, and free workers, contracted in exchange for a *merces*.[101]

Supervision

As stated above, work had to be supervised by one or more *curatores*. Their names and responsibilities varied according to the type of initiative and the period of study (**Figures 1–3**). In projects of municipal or colonial initiative (**Figure 1**), the magistrates supervising the work - *IIviri*, *aediles*, or imperial *praefecti*[102] - had to ensure that projects were carried out in accordance

with the conditions set out in the *lex locationis*.[103] This *cura operum* was added to their duties for public construction, since, as mentioned above, they had to present the preliminary construction projects to the decurions, direct the public contracts, and summon the inhabitants of the city if the use of *munitiones* was required. In *Irni*,[104] it was established that the *aediles* could substitute for the *IIviri* in tasks related to the *curatio*. For example, the *aedilis* Maecius Vetus supervised the construction of 60 feet of the wall of *Carthago Nova*[105] and carried out the *probatio* (i.e., the verification that the architectural characteristics and conditions established in the *lex locationis* had been fulfilled after the work was completed).[106] Normally this was the prerogative of the *IIviri* as *curatores*, as in the case of another section of the same wall, supervised by Cn. Cornelius Cinna,[107] *IIvir* that *faciendum curavit idemque probavit*.

These *curatores* were intermediaries between the contractors and the cities.[108] On other occasions, specialists could also be appointed for specific works[109] because of their previous experience.[110] In *Hispania*, we find inscriptions that refer to this type of position, such as *curatores balinei*[111] or a *curator templi* who was also *praefectus murorum*.[112] A special mention should be made of an inscription from *Carthago Nova*,[113] which has been dated to the end of the Republic. In it, several *servi*, *mag(istri)* of a *collegium* of the city,[114] appear to be carrying out (*faci(undas) coeravere*) support structures in the port –*pilas III et fundament(a) ex caement(o)*.

When the expenses of the project were assumed by a benefactor, he could designate a person of trust to supervise the progress of the work to the pre-established conditions. For example, Quintus, Cicero's younger brother,[115] appointed a *curator* called Caesius to oversee the work in one of his villas, directed by Diphilos, architect and *redemptor*.[116] In projects of municipal initiative, the *curatores* chosen by the *privati* would supervise the work of the relevant lots. In turn, each euergetist and each *curator* appointed by them would be under the supervision of the official *curatores* (**Figure 2**).

---

[91] Martin 1989: 60.
[92] *CIL* II, 2992; *HEp* 2, 1990, 738–741.
[93] *Lex Ursonensis* XCVIII; *Lex Irnitana* LXXXIII.
[94] Brunt 1980; Steinby 1983: 219–222.
[95] *Lex Ursonensis* LXII; *Lex Irnitana* XIX, LXXII, and LXXIX.
[96] Vegetius, *De re militare* I, 7 alludes to some of these specialists.
[97] Shaw 1995:69–72.
[98] *CIL* II, 4114.
[99] *AE* 1937, 166.
[100] Cic., *Verr.*, II, 5, 48; Suet., *Nero*, XXXI, 3; 10; Plin., *Ep.*, X, 31, 2.
[101] Trisciuoglio 1998.
[102] In this case they held the honorary title of the highest local magistrate during that annuity. See *Lex Irnitana - Salpensana* XXV.

[103] *Lex Irnitana - Malacitana* XLVIII and LXIII.
[104] *Lex Irnitana* XIX.
[105] *AE* 1975, 525.
[106] Martin 1986.
[107] *CIL* II, 3425.
[108] *Dig.*, L, 10, 2, 1.
[109] Melchor 1992–1993: 137.
[110] Cases in which the *res publica* finances the works and appoints a *curator*, without further details as to his position, to supervise the works: *CIL* II²/7, 976; *CIL* II, 1946; *CIL* II, 963; *CIL* II²/5, 493.
[111] *CIL* II, 4610.
[112] *CIL* II²/14, 1124.
[113] *CIL* II, 3434 = *CIL* II, 5927.
[114] Abascal and Ramallo 1997: 71–77.
[115] Cic. *Ad. Q. fr.* III, 1, 1–2.
[116] Barresi 2003: 62.

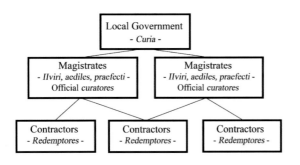

Figure 1. Simplified diagram showing the relationship between local government and contractors in public construction for projects of municipal initiative. Author's drawing.

An inscription[117] from the area near Elche de la Sierra (Albacete) records the construction of a *curiam* by *G. Allius Fuscianus*,[118] who paid for it at his own expense and carried out the *curatio* and probably also the *probatio*. This is an example of how a benefactor, without any administrative position, could completely finance a public work and follow the procedures of the construction promoted by the municipal initiative. The fact that G. Allius Fuscianus was both the *curator* and the euergetist suggests that he himself was in charge of controlling the works and presenting the *probatio* to the local administration, as proof that the new curia conformed to the official urban development plans. Another possibility is that, for further political propaganda, G. Allius Fuscianus decided not to mention the person he had appointed as *curator* of the works.

Another Hispanic inscription from *Legio VII*[119] refers to two freedmen who carried out the *curatio* of a bridge donated by their patroness. In this way, the benefactor would ensure that the work would be completed according to her interests, by appointing two people of her confidence as supervisors of the project. In *Nescania* (Abdalajís Valley, Malaga), we find the construction of a building of worship devoted to *Iupiter Pantheus Augustus*[120] whose *curatores* were not official magistrates but members of *collegia*, such as the *iuvenum Laurensium*. We know that it was the work of this community and not of the local government because L. Calpurnius Gallio and C. Marius Clemens carried out the *curatio* and offered and dedicated the stucture – *d(ederunt) et d(edicaverunt)*. Another inscription at *Carthago Nova*[121] includes a dedication to *Lares Augustales* and *Mercurium* by *piscatores et propalae* who, besides financing it (*de pecun(ia) sua*), supervised the work –*c(uraverunt) i(dem) q(ue) p(robaverunt)*.

With regard to the *probatio* in works financed by *privati*, again Cicero[122] refers to the supervision of the work once his brother's villa was completed. On this occasion, he states that Diphilos must remove the columns and put them back in the right place. That is, after supervising the work, the *redemptor* was ordered to modify those parts that did not conform to the terms of the contract.

Once the *probatio* was completed, the municipal *curator* had to present the *ratio operis* to the city.[123] As we have said, the *curator* had to coordinate the construction work and, therefore, make the payments to the different *redemptores*. To do so, he had to request money from the *quaestor* or person in charge of the municipal treasury.[124] The latter had to provide the amount as stipulated in the *lex locationis*. Once the project had been completed, the *ratio operis* consisted of declaring

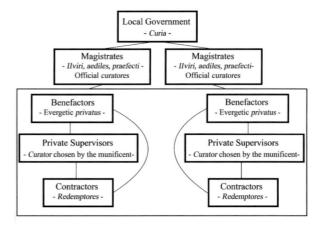

Figure 2. Simplified diagram showing the relationship between local government, euergetists, and contractors in public construction for projects of municipal initiative but with mixed financing. In the case of collaboration with the emperor, the scheme would be similar but with the participation of imperial *curatores*. Author's drawing.

what sums had been received from the *aerarium*, how much had been used and why. In *Hispania*, references to the justification of any public expenditure are found in the *Lex Irnitana*,[125] which mentions the *rationes comunes* that all magistrates had to deliver after the use of public money. In turn, specific episodes are known for public construction in the eastern part of the Empire. For example, Pliny the Younger[126] mentions the request made to Dio Chrysostom by the government of *Prusa* (Bursa, Turkey) asking him to present the *ratio operis* of a library.

117 *CIL* II, 3538.
118 I follow the proposal of Abascal (2019: 272–273).
119 *CIL* II, 5690.
120 *CIL* II²/5, 840.
121 *CIL* II, 5929.

122 Cic. *Ad Q. fr.* III, 1, 1–2
123 Rodríguez Neila 2003.
124 *Lex Irnitana XX.*
125 *Lex Irnitana XLV, LXVII,* and *XCVII.*
126 Plin. *Ep.* X, 81.

The *cura operum* in projects of imperial initiative was performed by members of the higher orders of the imperial administration. In the *Urbs* itself and in Italy, it was the *curatores operum publicorum*[127] and *curatores aedium sacrarum*[128] who were responsible for administering and controlling repairs, construction and land allocations through a body of workers called *statio operum publicorum*.[129] Both were under the order of the emperor, who controlled almost all public construction in Rome.

In the provinces, the governors acted as *curatores* in imperial work (**Figure 3**) until Gallienus's reform in AD 262,[130] when those in charge of supervising the works were *proconsules* and *legati Augusti pro praetore*, depending on whether they were senatorial or imperial provinces. Moreover, it is clear from Pliny's letters that the governor was also to ensure, at least at the beginning of the second century AD, that local government construction projects did not mean the ruin of the local treasury and that the *municipia* did not start a building project that remained unfinished.[131]

At *Pollentia* (Majorca) an inscription[132] was found in the north-eastern zone of the forum. It shows the construction – *f(aciendum) c(uravit)* – of a building[133] by a *legatus pro praetore*, that is, the governor of the province. The governor would designate a *legatus* who would finally dedicate –*dedicavit*– the work. The inscription has been dated to the first century AD[134] coinciding with the construction of Temple I of the forum, or to the second century AD.[135]

After Gallienus's reform of AD 262, many governors were replaced by *praesides* of equestrian rank. Later, Diocletian's provincial administrative reform modified the positions of the newly created districts.[136] Thus, the *vicarii* were in charge of the dioceses, the *praesides provinciae* were the provincial governors and the *comes*, another provincial administrative office, was created. At the beginning of the fourth century AD, the increase in the number of senators in the Constantinian reform meant that it was once again the senators, and not the equestrians, who became magistrates.[137] Broadly speaking, after the imperial building mandate the *comites provinciarum* would carry out the work through the *praesides provinciarum* and other subordinate offices.

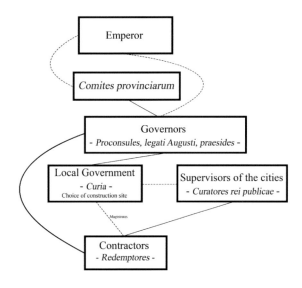

Figure 3. Simplified diagram showing the relationship between the imperial sphere, local government and contractors in public construction. The dotted lines express relationships existing only in a specific period of time. In cases with the collaboration of munifcents or municipalities, a similar scheme to that of Figure 1–2 should be added. Author's drawing.

In *Hispania*, inscriptions have been located that allude to some of these provincial offices. In *Tarraco* (Tarragona), Diocletian and Maximian ordered the construction of the porticos of a basilica. *Iulius Valens, v(ir) p(erfectissimus)* and *p(raeses) p(rovinciae) H(ispaniae) c(iterioris)*, was in charge of the supervision (*c(uravit)*) and dedicated the work –*de[dica]vit*.[138] In *Olisipo*[139] (Lisbon), *Numerius Albanus, vir clarissimus* and *praes provinciae Lusitaniae*, ordered the repair of the *Thermae Cassiorum*,[140] while *Aurelius Firmus* was in charge of supervising (*curante*) the repair of the baths. Moreover, we have already seen the participation of *comites* and *praesides* in the repairs of the theatre[141] and the circus[142] at *Augusta Emerita* in AD 337–340. Finally, in *Tarraco* another inscription[143], dated to the fourth century AD, included a dedication to *Marcus Aurelius Vicentius, vir perfectissimus* and *praes priovinciae Hispaniae Tarraconensis* for repairing other baths, the *Thermae Montanarum*. In this case, *Messius Marianus*, in his capacity as *curator rei publicae Tarraconensis*, was in charge of carrying out this honour and presumably was involved in the *cura operum* of the building.

---

127 *IRC* IV, 32; *IRC* IV, 34; *CIL* II, 1283; *CIL* IX, 1160; 2655; 1419.
128 *IRC* IV, 32; *IRC* IV, 34; *CIL* II, 4510; *CIL* XIV, 4091; *CIL* V, 7812; *CIL* VI, 36871.
129 Eck 1995; Kolb 1993.
130 Christol 1975; De Blois 1976.
131 Plin. *Ep*. X, 75–76; X, 91.
132 *HEp* 2, 1990, 62.
133 It has been associated with the erection of Temple I of the supposed capitolium of the city (Orfila *et al.* 2000: 56).
134 Orfila *et al.* 2000.
135 Mayer 2013.
136 Barnes 1982; Bravo 1991.
137 Barnes 1982; De Bonfils 1981.

138 *CIL* II²/14, 931.
139 *CIL* II, 191.
140 The inscription is dated after the reform of Diocletian, in AD 336, thanks to the consular dating formula *Nepotiano et Facundo consulibus*.
141 *HEp* 13, 2003/2004, 111.
142 *AE* 1927, 165.
143 *CIL* II²/14, 1004.

The functions and origin of the *curator rei publicae* should also be discussed.[144] Camodeca[145] states that *curatores rei publicae* had performed their functions at least from Hadrian's reign. They would have been exceptional magistrates sent by the emperor, for a limited time, to certain cities that needed administrative or financial supervision. The arrival of these imperial officials would not mean that the administrative bodies of the *res publica* would cease to function, but that they would have to supervise their management and good functioning.[146] Their prerogatives would include the control of the occupation and use of the city's own land or the concession, in consensus with the *ordo decurionum*, of *loca publica* in construction projects.[147]

Following Camodeca,[148] these positions would not perform exactly the same functions as the local *curator operis* but would be supervisors of all administrative and financial issues in the city, including public construction and urban planning. In *Hispania*, they appear punctually[149] associated with certain cities. Especially relevant, apart from the case of *Tarraco*,[150] is that of *Ucubi* (Espejo, Córdoba). In this inscription[151], the *curator rei publicae* is also *proc(urator) Aug(usti)* of a donation in honour of *Septimus Severus* made by the *ordo c(olonorum) c(oloniae) C(laritates) I(uliae)*. However, in *Tarraco* the *curator rei publicae* was in charge of the buildings together with the provincial governor, something which also occurred from the third century AD in other parts of the Empire.[152]

After the completion of the work

Once the *probatio* was resolved favourably and according to the terms of the *lex locationis*, the IIviri[153] had to order payment to the *redemptor*, requesting the sum from the quaestors.[154] In fact, if the duration of the work exceeded the annual period and others reached the duumvirate, they had to order the payment of the sums still pending.[155] The *solutio* would vary according to the terms of the *lex locationis*. Since advances were contemplated,[156] the *redemptor* had to present *cautiones* and *praedia*[157] to guarantee his economic solvency.

The inauguration of a public building was often accompanied by a solemn social event, where the main funders would bring together the city's inhabitants. When the financing was private, the euergetists would show themselves through the dedications[158] as civic benefactors, usually consisting with a speech. Sometimes they associated other donations with the construction, such as *epula*[159], money distributions[160], *sportulae*[161], donations of oil and ointments[162], free entrance to the baths[163], and the publication of games and shows.[164] These, although ephemeral gifts, accompanied the main donation and allowed benefactors to enjoy high social esteem in the short term together with the propaganda of the inscriptions on the buildings that lasted for generations.

There are several epigraphic references to this *dedication* in Hispanic epigraphic evidence, usually expressed with the verb *dedicavit, -erunt*. Many of them are linked to the placement of a statue in honour of a public figure.[165] Others commemorate the inauguration of a building. In the municipality of *Cartima* (Cártama, Málaga), *Iunia Rustica*,[166] *sacerdos perpetua et prima*, paid for building operations, financed civic events and paid taxes to the city: she repaired the porticoes, donated the land, added other porticoes to some baths, paid for the *vectigalia pulica*, raised statues, etc. She also added a banquet and the publication of some public shows. For her part, *Valeria Situllina*,[167] also from *Cartima*, organised another banquet on the day that she dedicated an unspecified donation.

Finally, another feature to be highlighted is the maintenance of structures. After the dedication, the ownership of the building became public, and even before that if the land had been contributed by the local government. Therefore, it was the responsibility of the *aediles* and IIviri to maintain the public structures in good condition, which meant a continuous expense on the municipal treasury. Thus, the state of the urban fabric would have been controlled by the local government. For example, the decurions had to give permission before the demolition of buildings or the reuse of their materials for other purposes[168]. We also suppose that if any euergetist wanted to remodel or restore any structure, the project had to be proposed in the curia in addition to *ex novo* constructions[169]. In fact,

[144] See Jacques 1983.
[145] Camodeca 2008: 520–521.
[146] Camodeca 2008: 511–512.
[147] Camodeca 2008: 517.
[148] Camodeca 1980; 2008.
[149] *CIL* II²/5, 441; *CIL* II, 1135; *AE* 2016, 848; *CIL* II²/14, 1004; *HEp* 2003/2004, 1036.
[150] *CIL* II²/14, 1004.
[151] *CIL* II²/5, 441.
[152] Barresi 2003: 40; Espluga and Pagan 1994: 1532.
[153] *Lex Ursonensis* LXIX.
[154] *Lex Irnitana* XX and LXVII.
[155] *Lex Ursonensis* LXIX.
[156] *Lex Puteol.* III, 14–15.
[157] *Leges Irnitana – Malacitana* LXIII-LXIV, *Ursonensis* LXXV and XCIII. About the *cautiones vide* Rodríguez Neila 2003: 128–130 and 153–154.

[158] Del Hoyo 1993; Mrozek 2004; Rodríguez Neila 2006.
[159] *CIL* II, 1956.
[160] *CIL* II, 5489.
[161] *CIL* II, 4511.
[162] *CIL* II, 4514.
[163] *CILA* II, 1209.
[164] *CIL* II²/5, 789.
[165] *CIL* II²/5, 737; *CIL* II²/5, 896.
[166] *CIL* II, 1956.
[167] *CIL* II, 5488.
[168] *Lex Ursonensis* XCVI and *Lex Irnitana* LXII.
[169] *Lex Ursonensis* XCIX and *Lex Irnitana* XXXIX - LXXXII.

the maintenance of structures must have been a long-term problem for the local treasury of municipalities or colonies that allowed the proliferation of constructions paid for by *privati*. The scarce interest[170] of the benefactors in providing funds for the maintenance of these structures led *Antoninus Pius* to encourage the repair of existing buildings[171]; however, the autonomy of cities meant that the terms for the maintenance of certain infrastructure differed from one city to another. For example[172], in Rome the maintenance of the aqueducts was first leased to individuals and later became the prerogative of the curator aquarum,[173] while in *Urso*[174] it was managed by the magistrates. We also have information about the maintenance of other parts of the urban fabric thanks to the *Tabula Heracleensis*.[175] Here, private inhabitants were responsible for maintaining the urban roads in the immediate vicinity of their properties, while the local government took care of the roads that ran alongside public buildings.

In *Hispania*, some euergetists, in addition to financing the construction of a building, donated sums of money to the city for maintenance of the structure. Alternatively donors could provide bequests and perpetual foundations: the donation of a specific sum which, placed at a certain interest, would relieve the burden on the local *aerarium* and allow the cities to guarantee the conservation of the structure.[176] As an example, *Voconia Avita* financed in *Tagili* (Tíjola, Almería) the construction of a public bath on a piece of land she owned.[177] She organised an event that would bring people together on the day of the dedication and donated 2,500 *denarii* to the city for the maintenance of the complex. Similarly, in *Murgi* (El Ejido, Almería), a benefactor promised to donate 150 *denarii* each year for the rest of his life for the maintenance of some baths whose construction he had paid for.[178] In another inscription, from *Baria* (Villaricos, Almería), the heirs of an euergetist donated 6,156 *sesterces* for the maintenance of a temple.[179]

Conclusions

It is clear that epigraphic evidence is not the only source of information when studying construction processes. The extant literature of some classical authors and the archaeological remains complement epigraphic data. Inscriptions provide the *tria nomina* of some of the protagonists, their institutional position, and their link to the construction process, and of the financiers of the public building, their social position, and their motivations, etc. However, it is impossible to completely reconstruct each phase without analysing the rest of the sources. Furthermore, we must remember that the number of inscriptions in Antiquity must have been much higher than those that are known today and that the nature of the information recorded depended directly on the intention with which the inscription was made.[180] In other words, the epigraphic habit can distort our conclusions,[181] so we must take into account the representativeness of the data in relation to the information provided by other types of sources.

In total, 39 inscriptions were analysed in this paper, and they record 44 agents involved in the construction process (see **Tables 1–3**). Roughly the same number of inscriptions mention agents in both the 1st century BC and the High Empire (from the beginning of the 1st through the 2nd century AD), 13 (29.5%) and 12 (27.2%), respectively. However, we must bear in mind that half of the examples datable to the 1st century BC correspond to the same construction project – the wall of *Carthago Nova*, a pre-eminent city in the Iberian Peninsula from the 2nd century BC due to its strategic position and the important role it played during the 2nd Punic War. We must also stress the randomness in the preservation of the epigraphic evidence.

Construction projects in *Hispania* were mainly developed during the 1st and 2nd centuries AD within the context of large-scale urban projects carried out under Augustus[182] or the Flavians[183] as well as notable interventions resulting from euergetism.[184] Thus it is logical that the greatest number of mentions of agents involved in the processes of public construction date from the High Empire. The similar number for the 1st century BC was directly influenced by the fortunate survival of a high number of inscriptions associated with the construction of the wall of *Carthago Nova*.

There are also ten (22.8%) mentions datable to between the 3rd and 4th centuries AD, with nine of these coming from large cities that were economically and politically pre-eminent in the Early Empire, such as *Tarraco*, *Augusta Emerita*, and *Olisipo*. This type of intervention was part of the revitalisation or continued urban maintenance of those cities of the empire that remained politically important.[185] During this period,

---

[170] The analysis of the evergetic phenomenon in *Hispania* shows that the local notables were little involved in these tasks (Melchor 1992–1993: 146 and 200).

[171] *Dig. L*, 10, 7.

[172] However, we cannot draw solid conclusions about this comparison given the chronological distance, the importance of both cities and the technical level of their aqueducts.

[173] Front., *Aq.*, 96.

[174] *Lex Ursonensis XCIX* and *C*.

[175] *CIL* I², 593.

[176] Melchor 1994–1995: 218.

[177] *IRAl* 48.

[178] *CIL* II, 5489.

[179] *IRAl* 31.

[180] Sartori 1999.

[181] Macmullen 1982.

[182] Pfanner 1990.

[183] Melchor 1992–1993.

[184] Melchor 1993b; Navarro 1997; Andreu 2004b.

[185] Fuentes 1997.

when most of the Hispanic theatres were in disuse,[186] provincial officials carried out repairs to two such building for public spectacles in *Augusta Emerita*, capital of the *diocesis Hispaniarum* in this period, and in *Tarraco*, capital of the *Hispania Tarraconensis* from the 1st century BC. Although the euergetic phenomenon declined from the reign of Caracalla onwards,[187] we find emperors beginning to intervene more frequently in the repair of public buildings.[188] As a result of both the biases in the epigraphic sample and a degree of randomness in survival, there are no statistically significant differences between the number of mentions of agents in the High Empire compared to the 3rd century AD onwards. The similar percentages of mentions of agents involved in public construction for the Republic, the High Empire, and the Late Empire suggest public construction in *Hispania* remained stable from the 1st century BC to the 4th century AD. However, public construction, and therefore the intervention of different agents, had its peak during the 1st century AD - something that has been demonstrated by studies on the development of the euergetic phenomenon and the different impulses behind urban development in *Hispania*.[189]

In contrast, we can identify chronological variations in the number of agents involved and their type. While the construction process remained practically unchanged from the Republic until the 2nd century AD,[190] in the Antonine period a series of provincial magistracies were created which, without diminishing the autonomy of the cities, tended towards stronger imperial intervention. These were the appearance of *curatores rei publicae*[191] and the greater participation during the late Roman Empire of the different magistracies related to provincial government – the *praesides* and *comites*.[192]

It is not possible to draw conclusions with regard to geographical differences or similarities. Although there is a scarcity of Hispanic inscriptions, we can look to inscriptions from other western provinces that exemplify what has already been observed in the *leges*[193] or that provide very specific data not present in Hispanic documentation.[194] This is very different to the eastern empire, where studies have revealed significant differences in the construction process.[195] Although the current study focuses only on the Hispanic provinces, it exemplifies general trends in public construction and

the different phases present in the rest of the western part of the empire.[196]

With regard to the type of structures in which we find the intervention of agents, we must highlight the greater relevance of essential infrastructure in a particular city. In total, we find 13 instances (29.5%) related to walls, gates, towers, and roads; ten (22.7%) related to structures linked to water such as ports, aqueducts, and baths; and five (11.4%) related to religious contexts such as temples. In total, four agents appear to be involved in the repair of buildings for public spectacles (9%), three intervene in the construction of structures such as temples and walls,[197] six manage or carry out dedications to the emperor or some deity (13.6%), one carried out the *curatio* of porticoes (2.3%), while the remaining two executed or supervised structures which are unknown (4.5%). Given the already-mentioned scarcity of the examples and the randomness of survival for the epigraphic record, we cannot draw solid conclusions about the types of structures favoured for the intervention of such agents. However, we can emphasise that they were active in the construction process of the most prominent and expensive structures of the urban environment, either because of the intervention of different promoters in their construction or because of the need to have specialists to carry out the *curatio operis*.

On the other hand, only five inscriptions[198] are without a direct reference to a specific structure. In such cases, the position of the individuals related to a *cursus honorum*, which was a specific characteristic that developed in honorary inscriptions. The remaining 39 mentions (88.6%) are found in inscriptions that expressly note the construction or repair of a specific building.

The analysis of the *ordines* and social strata involved in each phase of the construction process reveals greater representation of the local elite in the municipalities and colonies.[199] The building inscriptions, as public documents, were usually limited to the participation of the municipal officials,[200] who proposed, approved, and supervised the works, and of the euergetists. This can explain their overrepresentation in building epigraphy. The provincial authorities linked to extraordinary building projects or those carried out by imperial

---

[186] Fuentes 1997; Ceballos 2004.
[187] Melchor 1993b.
[188] See e.g. *Dig.* L, 10, 7.
[189] Melchor 1992–1993.
[190] We must remember that the *Lex Ursonensis* was promulgated by Mark Anthony in 44 BC, but there are no differences in terms of public construction with the *leges* of the Flavian period that we mention here – Iritana, Malacitana, and Salpensana.
[191] *CIL* II²/14, 1004; *CIL* II²/5, 441.
[192] *HEp* 13, 2003/2004, 111; *CIL* II²/14, 931; *CIL* II, 191; *AE* 1927, 165.
[193] *CIL* VIII, 9062 of *Auzia*.
[194] *CIL* I², 593.
[195] Barresi 2003.

[196] This work is part of a wider project on the in-depth study of Roman-era public construction in the West, covering North Africa and the Gallias.
[197] *CIL* II²/14, 1124.
[198] *CIL* II, 1283, 1371, 4610, and 4509; *CIL* II²/14, 1124.
[199] With regard to the frequencies with which each *ordo* appears, I refer to the conclusions of Melchor (1992-1993: 147-149; 1993b: 459-462), as they continue to be the reference works in this sense.
[200] See Tables 1–3, where the inscriptions analysed here have been collected. I have not collected the vast majority of inscriptions in which a magistrate or priest intervenes in the construction process as an euergetist. For the donations of public buildings in *Hispania*, see Melchor 1992-1993, 1993b; Navarro 1997; Andreu 2004.

initiative only appear in nine inscriptions. On the other hand, although they would undoubtedly always be involved in the construction process, the lower strata of society are represented by *servi*, *servi publici*, freedmen and those free persons who exceptionally appear in the inscriptions participating in some of the phases described: either as *curatores*,[201] as labourers,[202] or for example, serving as skilled workers.[203]

Overall, the epigraphic evidence suggests a predominance of magistrates belonging to a *cursus honorum decurionalis* (17 or 40.9%) – ten for *IIviri* (22.7%), six for *aediles* (13.6%), one *accensus* (2.3%), and one *praefecti operi faciundo* (2.3%). In total, 12 examples (27.3%) mention specialised *curatores* or those in charge of supervising a specific work. Positions linked to the control and government of the territory up to the 3rd century AD, such as *legati pro praetore*, are scarcely represented in public construction (2 in total, or 4.6%). Those involved in provincial administration during the 4th century AD, such as *praesides* and *comites*, appear seven times (15.9%) exercising functions related to the execution and control of public construction. During this period, *IIviri* and *aediles* were barely involved in the construction process, and it is clear that the euergetic phenomenon had been greatly modified by this time. Finally, there are two mentions of *curatores rei publicae* (4.5%), as well as another element of municipal administration at the service of the imperial spheres since the end of the 2nd century A.D – two (4.5%) *magistri collegii* and one inscription (2.3%) whose text does not retain the reference to the specific position of the individual who carried out the *curatio* and *probatio operis* of a temple.[204] Those holding these positions are exclusively responsible for supervising the construction (19 in total, or 43.2%) or they only carry out the work (10 cases, or 22.7%).

However, 15 (34.1%) of the individuals mentioned undertook several functions, either the *curatio* and *probatio* (4.5%), the execution and *curatio* (20.5%), or all three tasks (9.1%). The enormous presence of the *curatio* in Hispanic epigraphy can be explained by the greater intervention of specialised *curatores*, *IIviri*, and *aediles*, as municipal supervisors of public works in the city. While *legati*, *praetores*, and *comites*, due to the prerogatives inherent in their position, only carried out the works.[205]

In addition, as advocated throughout this paper, we must differentiate between the initiative for works and the source of funding. The detailed analysis of

the cases for which we have more information shows collaboration between the different agents involved, giving rise to mixed financing even if the initiative was only municipal, private, or imperial. Work by other researchers who have dealt with this type of issue[206] focuses on the reconstruction of the building process in a generic way or only for one of these initiatives. The comparison developed here arises from the aforementioned differentiation between funding and initiative.

When the initiative was municipal or private, a project had to be presented to the *curia*, which would accept and appoint local magistrates (*IIviri* and *aediles*) as *curatores* who would oversee that the project was carried out in accordance wih the established terms. The main difference between the two initiatives was whether the person in charge of announcing the project at that time held a position as a local magistrate (municipal initiative)[207] or was a *privatus* who did not act according to the prerogatives of a specific charge (private initiative). If the initiative was imperial,[208] a provincial governor (*proconsules*, *legati Augusti*, or *praesides*) or a person close to the emperor would inform the local senate of such a project, requesting the collaboration of local administration during the construction process. After the acceptance, the curia could appoint local magistrates as *curatores* of the project. From the 2nd century AD, the *curator rei publicae* could carry out the *curatio operis* in the cities where they were working. In the 4th century, provincial governors, such as the *praesides*, could also act as *curatores* for certain important works.

Once the project was accepted, the financing might be entirely municipal if the city treasury was able to cover all the expenses for the work. In this case,[209] the magistrates in charge of the *curatio operis* would assign the agreed public money for work through a system of public bids (*auctiones*) to one or more contractors (*redemptores*) who would then carry it out according to the terms of the *lex locationis*. After completion, and if the local magistrates had decided in favour of the *probatio*, they had to pay the due amount (*solutio*) to the various *redemptores*. On the other hand, the work could be divided into lots, which were then paid for by a combination of local benefactors and public funds. In this case, the financing would be mixed even if the initiative was municipal.[210] After the allocation of the lots, the different benefactors could assign both a specialised *curator* to supervise the fulfilment of the part they were going to pay and a *redemptor* to carry

---

[201] *CIL* II, 5690.
[202] *CIL* II, 2992.
[203] *ILSEG* 42.
[204] *CIL* II, 3557.
[205] Except on one occasion (*CILA* II, 578) when they also appear to be carrying out the *curation*.

[206] See, among others, Jouffroy 1977; Melchor 1992–1993; Barresi 2003: 15–94; Mar 2008; Rodríguez Neila 2009.
[207] See Figs. 1 and 2 above.
[208] See Fig. 3 above.
[209] See Fig. 1 above.
[210] See Fig. 2 above.

not have to invest the whole value of her share but in fact only 1/12 of the 400 *aurei* – 33$^{1/3}$ *aurei* – around 20% of her share of the estate, estimated at 150 *aurei*.

In the text authored by Publius Alfenus Varus in which we already came across a case of an *ad exemplum* estimation of a monument, we also find the similar albeit slightly different problem of deciding what amount of money the heirs should convey to build a monument. We remember that they were instructed on pain of a high penalty by the testator to build a monument like the one of Publius Septimius Demetrius which stood on the Salarian Way. Alfenus then reports on the issue which arose.

D. 35,1,27 Alfenus *libro quinto digestorum*

(...) et cum id monumentum Publii Septimii Demetrii nullum repperiebatur, sed Publii Septimii Damae erat, ad quod exemplum suspicabatur eum qui testamentum fecerat monumentum sibi fieri voluisse, quaerebant heredes, cuiusmodi monumentum se facere oporteret et, si ob eam rem nullum monumentum fecissent, quia non repperirent, ad quod exemplum facerent, num poena tenerentur. Respondit, si intellegeretur, quod monumentum demonstrare voluisset is qui testamentum fecisset, tametsi in scriptura mendum esset, tamen ad id, quod ille se demonstrare animo sensisset, fieri debere: sin autem voluntas eius ignoraretur, poenam quidem nullam vim habere, quoniam ad quod exemplum fieri iussisset, id nusquam exstaret, monumentum tamen omnimodo secundum substantiam et dignitatem defuncti exstruere debere.

The heirs were unable to find the monument of Publius Septimius Demetrius on the Salarian Way. There was only a monument of Publius Septimius Dama, which was conjectured to be the one to which the testator wished to refer. However, there was also doubt as to what kind of monument the heirs were actually supposed to build and whether they would have to pay the stipulated fine if they did not erect a monument due to the lack of a model to use. At this point Alfenus applies the classical interpretation of the testament. If the testator did not specify the monument – *in scriptura mendum esset* – but the will of the testator was known – *si intellegeretur, quod monumentum demonstrare voluisset* – then the heirs should build such monument as it was known that the testator desired – *quod ille se demonstrare animo sensisset, fieri debere*. However, if the will of the testator remains unknown then they will not have to pay the fine, but they still are obliged to build a monument. In such a case, the heirs should build a monument *secundum substantiam et dignitatem defuncti* – according to the wealth and rank of the deceased. So the jurist applied two criteria to the case which related directly to (1) the value of the estate

passed over to the heirs and (2) the social position of the testator, both of which should be reflected by the erected monument. The cost of the monument can neither be too big for the estate nor so little as to diminish the importance of the testator and the memory of the deceased.[23] This case gives us yet another perspective on how Roman monuments were created and how social circumstances might influence the estimation of Roman construction costs.

In fact, the aforementioned cases illustrate an issue which is connected with the analysis of testamentary dispositions concerning the financing of buildings: the costs of construction may not exceed the benefit of the heir or legatee or exceed a specific amount, as in the case of Cargillianus. This is why it is necessary to consider the possibility of a difference between the value of the bequest and the estimated value of the construction costs. What we have seen is that when the testator imposes a legal condition or a duty on the legatee, the testator needs to take into account both the value of the bequest and the estimated value of the construction. What is more, there arises the question, as in the case of the heirs of Cargilianus or in Seia's case, as to whether the beneficiary would be in fact a beneficiary *de facto* or if they should spend all their inherited wealth on the construction desired by the testator and be left with no surplus. The burden imposed by the testator should at the very least not exceed the value of the bequest or of the estate transferred to the heir or legatee. This is an indication that the amount dedicated to the construction project does not necessarily always equal the value of the construction costs. In the case of heirs, since the value of the estate would normally easily exceed the cost of the construction, testators would make specific indications as to how much an heir should invest in the construction, either by specifying a certain amount of money or by referring to the example to be used as a model for the monument.

Factors influencing construction costs: type of testamentary obligation and type of testamentary bequest

There are at least five factors that may have influenced construction costs: the type of obligation that requires the building of a monument out of a bequest, i.e. either duty (*modus*) or legal condition (*condicio*); the type of testamentary bequest concerned: *per damnationem* or *per vindicationem*; inheritance tax (*vicesima hereditatis*); the Falcidian quarter; and the delivery of the construction. The last is connected with the estimated costs of contracts – especially *locatio conductio* – that are required to erect the building.

---

[23] Miglietta 2018: 249.

First of all, it is important to recognise the difference between the formulation of a testamentary bequest in which 'someone received a gift if he built a tombstone' (*si monumentum fecerit*) and the formulation in which it was given simply 'to build a tombstone' (*ut monumentum faciat*).

D. 35,1,80 Scaevola *libro octavo quaestionum*

> *Eas causas, quae protinus agentem repellunt, in fideicommissis non pro condicionalibus observari oportet: eas vero, quae habent moram cum sumptu, admittemus cautione oblata: nec enim parem dicemus eum, cui ita datum sit, si monumentum fecerit, et eum, cui datum est, ut monumentum faciat.*

Examples of both formulas, which were differentiated in the quoted fragment of Scaevola, have already been presented in the above-mentioned fragments from Justinian's *Digest*. In the case of a testator imposing a duty on a beneficiary (*ut*), it is an order that obliges the beneficiary but does not withhold the effectiveness of the legacy.[24] The legatee receives the bequest and should erect a monument from this money. This was usually considered a moral duty which was difficult to enforce. Alternatively, it is a condition (*si*) – the bequest will become effective *when* the condition is met; a person will become a legatee or heir when they build the monument. It seems, therefore, that in this latter case the legatee will first have to cover the construction costs from their own funds, and then they will receive the bequest (or entire estate). There is, however, another way in Roman law to solve this situation, a way which seems less burdensome for the beneficiary. It is important to appreciate that if the purpose of such a bequest or disposition was to use the sum to commemorate the deceased, then it was paid out immediately to the legatees, and only a guarantee (promise) was taken from the legatees that they would return the sum if they subsequently failed to build the monument. Thus, when the legacy was burdened with such a condition, the money was paid out and would only have been returned if the condition which had been secured by the promise was not met – *satisdatio*. Moreover, the same legal mechanism started to be used to ensure that the imposed duty (*modus*) would be effectively fulfilled. This was the case, for example, with the already-analysed monument of Thermus Minor, who expressed in his will that he wanted to be commemorated by the building of the monument. It has been concluded in Roman legal scholarship on this case that the jurist Trebatius Testa introduced the interpretative rule 'to treat the instruction (*modus*) as the condition'.[25] However, this did not obstruct the

right of the legatees to receive the bequeathed amount immediately.

D. 35,1,40,5 Iavolenus *libro secundo ex posterioribus Labeonis*

> (...) *'Luciis Publiis Corneliis ad monumentum meum aedificandum mille heres meus dato'. Trebatius respondit pro eo [ea] habendum ac si ita legatum esset, si satisdedissent se ita id monumentum ex ea pecunia facturos. Labeo Trebatii sententiam probat, quia haec mens testantis fuisset, ut ea pecunia in monumentum consumeretur: idem et ego et Proculus probamus.*

The testator obliged his heir to give '1000' to the Lucii, Publii, and Cornelii for the erection of his monument. There arose the question of whether the legacy might be transferred immediately so as to be spent on the testator's monument. One might imagine that the heir could have waited to transfer money until the legatees had built the monument out of their own funds even though they had the right to these monies because they were not given under a condition but accompanied by a duty (*modus*). Four great Roman jurists - Trebatus and Labeo, active in the Augustan period, and Proculus and Iavolenus, from the next generation (1st century AD) - all resolved this issue in a similar way. They accepted that the provision could be interpreted to mean that the legatees should 'give security that they would erect the monument out of the sum bequeathed'; thus, the money would be transferred first, and the legatees would stipulate that they would give '1000' back if they did not fulfill the duty imposed by the testator. The reason for such a move 'was the testator's intention that the money should be expended upon the monument' – *quia haec mens testantis fuisset, ut ea pecunia in monumentum consumeretur*. In this case, therefore, '1000' should have been enough to erect the building and may have actually corresponded to the cost of the monument. Moreover, it would mean that the legatees would have to invest the entire bequest for the testator's sake – *ea pecunia in monumentum consumeretur*. That is why it was reasonable to allow them to use money from the estate. The right of the heir to withhold payment of the bequest before the duty (*modus*) had been completed was one of the ways of enforcing what was considered a merely moral obligation. The second way of guaranteeing that the *modus* was fulfilled was to demand a security from the beneficiaries that they would fulfill the duty imposed by the testator. In the case of the Thermus Minor monument, it was the heir who had the legal means to ensure that the legatees would fulfill their duty even though the requirement of such security had not been directly established by the testator.[26] A helpful hand was given in this by Trebatius, who came up with

---

[24] Longchamps de Bérier 2011: 213.
[25] Longchamps de Bérier 2011: 213; Di Salvo 1973: 40–41.
[26] Kaiser 1991: 165–166.

68

the idea of treating a duty like a condition, and obliging the legatees to give a security.

A more difficult case would be when the duty (*modus*) was imposed on a sole heir. Who would be able to demand from the heir the fulfilment of a duty of this kind? In fact, the placing of such duties on heirs was a very common practice, and a good record of this can be found in Justinian's *Digest*. In the text of Pomponius: (D. 33,1,7) *Si te heredem solum instituam et scribam, uti monumentum mihi certa pecunia facias....* – the testator appointed his sole heir and directed him (*uti...facias*) to erect a monument with a certain sum of money. In such a case, the praetor could have insisted on the heir fulfilling the duty by withholding a grant of action to secure his right to the estate, and so by treating the *modus* as if it were a condition (*si*). It could only have been the praetor – as a last resort – who enforced such a *modus,* particularly in the case analysed by Pomponius.

D. 33,1,7 Pomponius *libro octavo ad Quintum Mucium*

> *Si te heredem solum instituam et scribam, uti monumentum mihi certa pecunia facias... Ad auctoritatem scribentis hoc quoque pertinet, cum quis iussit in municipio imagines poni: nam si non honoris municipii gratia id fecisset, sed sua, actio eo nomine nulli competit.*

As Pomponius wrote, there could be no one entitled to bring an action against the heir if he were asked to erect statues (*imagines*) in the city not 'for the purpose of honoring the town, but to perpetuate his [the testator's] own memory'. If the purpose was to give glory to the city, then at least the city could have sued the heir to force him to fulfill his duty (*modus*), but if it was for the testator's glory alone, there was no one who could hold a legal claim to demand that the praetor enforce the testator's wishes. Perhaps, the praetor alone could have acted in favor of the *mens testatoris*.

A much more straightforward case was when the testator added a legal condition (*condicio*) to the appointment of an heir - which was also a well-known practice. Again, the Roman jurist Pomponius gives us an example of such a disposition.

D. 35,1,14. Pomponius *libro octavo ad Sabinum*

> *'Titius si statuas in municipio posuerit, heres esto'.*

Hence, Titius will become heir, 'if he erects statues in the city'. Here we have a different wording – *si* – which involves entirely different legal effects: it secures the fulfillment of the testator's wishes. Titius must erect statues in the city first, and only then his appointment is effective and he becomes the heir.

Of course, one can imagine that, having in mind the texts already analysed, a city could claim that it was full of statues and did not need another, or that there was a particular regulation that prohibited the erection of new monuments. This problem appeared in the fragment just quoted from Pomponius.

D. 35,1,14. Pomponius *libro octavo ad Sabinum*

> *(...) Si paratus est ponere, sed locus a municipibus ei non datur, Sabinus Proculus heredem eum fore et in legato idem iuris esse dicunt.*

Two great Roman jurists who usually held opposing views – Sabinus and Proculus – agreed that if the heir 'is ready to erect the statues, but the municipal authorities will not furnish him with a place for that purpose...he will become the heir, and that the same rule of law applies to a legacy'. This means that if the condition is not possible to be fulfilled because of a third party (a city), the person obliged to fulfill the condition who was prepared to complete the project would not face the negative consequences of the situation. The condition would be assumed to be fulfilled, and they could become heir. Both jurists apply the same rule to the cases of legacies left for the erection of a public work in a city. One might ask, how many constructions were not erected due to such denial by the public authorities if such cases are recorded in Justinian's *Digest*? We can now imagine that there was good reason for Antoninus Pius's legislation allowing cities to spend bequeathed money otherwise than for the erection of a new building or monument, e.g. for the maintenance of already existing structures.

However, another issue could arise, surrounding the question of whether the testator wanted the beneficiary to erect the monument himself or only to transfer money to the city which should erect it. In the quoted fragment of Pomponius the testator put the obligation on his heir, not on the city – 'if he erects statues'. That is why the city was only a recipient and thus was supposed only to provide the heir with a public space where the statues could be put. In the well-known case of the heirs of Cargilianus, they were only obliged to transfer the money to the city of Cirta, and the city itself was responsible for building the aqueduct. The money was given with a different testamentary disposition – *fideicommissum,* fiduciary bequest – which had a very similar legal characteristic to *legatum per damnationem* but was far more flexible and had a wider range of applications.[27] The city was thus not a mere recipient but a beneficiary who had to use the benefit for a specific purpose – *modus*. That is why the heirs of Cargilianus ensured that the city would spend the money only for the purpose of building aqueducts, and

---

[27] Longchamps de Bérier 2011: 196.

they received guarantees (*cautiones*) from the city that they would follow the duty (*modus*) imposed by the testator.

This is why the emperor Marcus Aurelius in another case issued a rescript in which he favored the will of the testator regarding the question as to who should erect a certain building.

D. 32,11,25 Ulpianus *libro secundo fideicommissorum*

> *Si quis opus facere iussus paratus sit pecuniam dare rei publicae, ut ipsa faciat, cum testator per ipsum id fieri voluerit, non audietur: et ita divus Marcus rescripsit.*

The famous Roman jurist Ulpian (2nd and 3rd centuries AD) recalled a case when someone 'was ordered to construct a public work and offers to furnish the money to the city in order that it may construct it itself'. The emperor stated that 'when the testator intended that the trustee himself should do so, he shall not be heard'. The case deals again with *fideicommissum,* which since the 1st century AD had become a very common instrument due to its flexibility both regarding the legal requirements of its validity and the wide range of persons enabled to be beneficiaries of such dispositions. As we can see, the same rules of interpretation apply in the case of bequests and *fideicommissa*. Moreover, from the 3rd century AD every duty imposed by a testator on an heir or legatee – *modus* – had to be interpreted as *fideicommissum* and thus received better legal protection than previously, fulfilling to a higher level the testator's will.[28]

Another point to be taken into account was the *type* of bequest that was used to transfer money in order to finance a construction project. Among different types of legacies there is one that is used more than any other in bequests transferring money for the erection of a building or monument – *legatum per damnationem.* This type of bequest meant that the heir was obliged to transfer a certain amount out of the estate to the legatees, even if he did not have it in cash at the time of succession.[29] It was the heir's debt to the legatees of the estate. That is why it was the best way to bequeath the sum of money – the most secure, both for the legatees and for the completion of the construction that the testator desired. We can discover examples of this type of bequest among the above-mentioned fragments, for instance: *Luciis Publiis Corneliis...mille heres meus dato.*[30] If the testator had used *legatum per vindicationem* – the secondmost popular type of bequest – the transfer of money could have been jeopardized if there had been a shortage of cash in the estate, and thus the erection of

the monument would not have been completed. Thus, it was an important issue for the testator to choose the proper type of bequest in order to make the transfer of money more probable and not dependent on the amount of cash in the estate at that particular time. If this was not done, there might have been a negative impact on the carrying out of the testator's will.

The amount of money received for erecting a building or monument by way of testamentary legacy could be subject to two other restrictions as well, which the testator needed to take into account. Firstly, it could be subject to inheritance tax. Secondly, it could be reduced because of the *lex Falcidia* – the right of the heir to retain one quarter of the inheritance. Moreover, I would like to suggest that a broader perspective should be taken, beyond that of the amounts received in the testament, and that we need to include the costs of the contracts concluded for the construction of particular buildings – first and foremost the contract for the specific work, *locatio conductio.*

Testamentary legacies and inheritance tax – a 5% variable

Some of the inscriptions which have survived on structures erected out of testamentary legacies specify how much money was transferred in the testament for their construction. In such cases this is assumed to be the value of the actual structure. However, there are also inscriptions which indicate that the inherited sum of money was subject to inheritance tax and the given amount was either gross or net – before or after deduction of the tax.

One example of this is the Victoria Parthica inscription (Thamugadi N, C. 2354) from AD 116 in modern Timgad in Algeria. The statue was erected from a bequest of 8000 *sesterces* (HS). From this bequest there was subtracted 5 per cent for inheritance tax (*vicesima*), giving HS 7600 net value of the bequest. To this amount HS 3000 was added by the donor's three freedmen, who would have probably contributed HS 1000 each.[31] This case illustrates two issues: first, there is another legal cost which needs to be taken into account – inheritance tax – which could diminish the effective value of the bequest; and second, the real cost of a construction project might have been higher than the amount of money bequeathed. In this particular case, the statue was co-financed by freedmen, as was specified on the inscription, which upgraded the value of the statue to HS 10,600. This example dates to the end of the reign of Trajan - a particularly appropriate time period for the current analysis, since Trajan introduced a reform of inheritance tax which will be discussed below.

---

[28] Longchamps de Bérier 2011: 214.
[29] Longchamps de Bérier 2011: 196.
[30] Longchamps de Bérier 2011: 196.
[31] Duncan-Jones 1962: n. 126.

The placing of such specific details on the monument itself helps us to understand the complexity of cost estimations and the legal costs that could come up when erecting a monument out of a testamentary legacy. It also shows us that writing down names and the amount of money which was contributed to a statue monument was considered important for the public life of a city and was customary before specific legislation on this subject was introduced by Antoninus Pius. Although this particular custom may be specific to elites in Roman Africa,[32] the presented case can nevertheless serve as a useful starting point for indicating the factors that need to be taken into account when estimating the value of a monument built out of a testamentary bequest. Even though a bequeathed sum was inscribed on a monument, one cannot simply assume that this sum was the actual final cost of construction.

Inheritance tax could be imposed on both the heir and the legatee. As we have seen in the example of the Victoria Parthica inscription, the testamentary legacy had to be reduced by the 5% inheritance tax, and only HS 7600 was spent on the construction desired by the testator. However, not all inscriptions which mention testamentary bequests as the source of their funding indicate whether the presented amount was the net value of the bequest after deducting the tax or the gross and hence the nominal value of the bequest provided by the testator.[33] This is an important factor in the estimation of construction costs and the value of the erected building or monument itself. It is yet another reason not to assume that the inscribed amount of money is equal to the value of the construction. One needs to remember to add 5% inheritance tax as a variable that may influence the final cost. If the inscription is as detailed as the one in the Thamugadi case, then the estimation is easier and closer to the actual costs. If however there is no reference to the *vicesima* (twentieth part of the estate – 5%) then it is better to introduce a +/– 5% variable in our estimations as we do not know whether the value is net or gross. In reality, it is probable that the inscription would match the nominal value indicated in the testament rather than the net value, as the legatee or heir obliged to erect a monument would want proof that he fulfilled the will of the testator. In such a case, one can expect the inscription to indicate gross value since the tax had to be subtracted before spending on the construction of the monument. Of course, everything depends on the way we define 'estimation of construction costs'. In broad terms, inheritance tax can be treated as one of the costs of construction, as can other necessary costs such as buying materials, employing workers, etc.

One can see the potential difference between the inscribed cost of a monument's construction and the nominal value mentioned in the testament in a fragment from the Roman jurist Alfenus contained in Justinian's *Digest*.

D. 50,16,202 Alfenus *libro secundo digestorum*

> *Cum in testamento scriptum esset, ut heres in funere aut in monumento 'dumtaxat aureos centum' consumeret, non licet minus consumere: si amplius vellet, licet neque ob eam rem contra testamentum facere videtur.*

The testator 'stated in a will that the heir shall only expend a hundred *aurei* for funeral expenses, or for the erection of a monument'. To this the jurist replied that 'he cannot spend any less than that amount'. On the other hand, if the heir wished to spend more, he was free to do so, and it would not be considered against the wording of the testament. In this case, if the testator wanted a legatee to spend a certain amount, then the legatee had to even if part of their own money was lost in the collection of the tax. A reasonable testator should have included the tax obligation as part of the value of the bequest. In any case, the inscription on such a monument would have confirmed that the heir had not spent less than was envisaged in the testament. That is why in the Victoria Parthica inscription both pieces of information were included: the value of the legacy and the tax subtracted from it. If such inscriptions served to prove the fulfillment of the testator's wishes, one might ask how reliable such texts really are, particularly if the value of the monument or building estimated on the basis of the material and labour dedicated to its erection substantially differed from the value inscribed on it. However, such a situation should be treated as exceptional, particularly in ancient Rome where the memory of the deceased was also manifest in their monument. We have seen that if a testator wished for a monument, then even if there were not any specific characteristics provided, the monument still had to be made according to the testator's dignity and wealth; otherwise, their heirs or legatees could face legal consequences.

It should be noted that inheritance tax was not always present in Roman law. That is why when we are estimating a specific construction we should take into account the inheritance tax applicable in the particular period. Inheritance tax should certainly be considered during the period from Augustus (AD 6)[34] to Constantine (early 4th century AD). Historical sources mention legal changes concerning inheritance tax during the time of Macrinus, but inheritance tax was still considered by the jurists Ulpianus and Marcianus (3rd century AD). Moreover, the tax regulation is mentioned in the

32 Duncan-Jones 1982: 64.
33 Duncan-Jones 1982: 64 and n. 6.
34 Günther: 2008: 31–32.

Sententiae of Paulus and *Lex Visigothorum* (6th century AD).[35] Certainly, Justinian confirms the revocation of inheritance tax and points out that it had already been abandoned for some time before his reign. Moreover, he points out legal acts imposed by certain emperors (e.g. Hadrian's rescript) and the substantial legal doctrine created around this matter. The whole issue was characterised by ambiguity and incomprehensibility, and this was the reason ultimately for the complete removal of this tax.[36]

Inheritance tax, although cloaked in a somewhat complicated doctrine, did not give rise to any doubts as to the *amount* to be calculated – it was called *vicesima hereditatis*, i.e. the twentieth part of the inheritance (5%). Only once in Roman history was inheritance tax increased beyond this – when Caracalla doubled the rate, i.e. to 10 percent (*decima*) and reduced exemptions from inheritance tax to a minimum. All this was done in order to increase revenues for the military budget – after all, inheritance tax since the time of Augustus had been feeding the *aerarium militare*. Military expenditure increased under Caracalla, and, with the expansion of Roman citizenship by his edict of 212 AD, so did inheritance tax. Immediately after Caracalla's death, his short-lived successor Macrinus returned to the regulation that had existed before Caracalla's reign, i.e. to the rate of 5%; perhaps it could be said that it was from that moment that the gradual erosion of inheritance tax from the legal system began.[37]

With regard to exemptions from inheritance tax, much of our information comes from the expert on the *aerarium militare*, i.e. Pliny the Younger, who devoted much space to inheritance tax in his Panegyric of Trajan. When assessing to what extent a recorded bequest was subject to tax, and therefore whether a 5% or 10% deduction was due, it is important to determine first of all whether the beneficiary was exempt or not. Tax exemptions can be divided into two categories: *subjective*, based on the personal relationship between testator and beneficiary; and *objective*, which was asset-related.

With regard to subjective exemptions, from the very beginning, i.e. since the times of Augustus, no tax had been paid by close relatives. In the doctrine it is recognised that this exemption applies to the so-called *decem personae* – father, mother, son, daughter, grandfather, grandmother, grandson, granddaughter, brother, and sister. So, the inheritance tax was imposed on people outside the family, on freedman with a bequest, or even those with an inheritance title. At the time of Nerva, an exemption was extended to relatives who were without connection by *agnatio* – i.e. they were

not legally related – especially to new citizens who did not have Roman *patria potestas* over their children. In the days of Trajan, the exemption envisaged by Augustus was fully extended to new citizens; this is also evidenced by the municipal laws of colonies that guaranteed inheritance tax relief for their inhabitants. And finally, Trajan introduced broader personal exemptions, as he exempted even distant relations – *remotus gradus.* In this case, it is even more difficult to understand what the term (*remotus*) means when it is read in opposition to the Augustan group of relatives. It could even mean exemption up to the 6th or 7th degree of kinship – that is, the farthest family related by blood (*cognatio*) that could inherit in the light of the Praetor's edict. For this reason, limiting to the Caracallan circle of statutory heirs would be equivalent to a limitation of the exemption from inheritance tax. In such a case, the tax would apply to the testamentary inheritance of people from outside the close family, i.e. from outside the restricted group of persons appointed to the statutory inheritance.[38]

The second type of exemption is based on the following grounds. First, certain inheritances or legacies are not taxed if they do not exceed a certain amount - under Augustus, this applies to the poor (either 'poor' inheritances/subscriptions or beneficiaries, i.e. 'poor' heirs and legatees); under Trajan, the exemption applies to small inheritances and legacies. As a consequence of this absence of taxation, we do not know the threshold exactly: it is generally thought that under Augustus inheritances up to HS 100,000 were not taxed. There are, however, several options in the doctrine – HS 200,000 or even the much lower sum of HS 20,000.[39] And what about legacies? We know that legacies worth HS 10,000 were taxed; moreover, information from the legionary camp at Nicopolis in Egypt (dated to AD 109–119) indicates that the tax was also paid on estates or legacies of 1900 drachmae (if considered as the Egyptian silver drachma it equaled HS 1900, if as a Greek silver drachma it amounted to HS 7600 so 1000 *denarii*).[40] Maybe the former restrictions on legacies were taken as the minimum amount above which tax was due, though in the case of legacies to construct a building these amounts are usually larger than this amount and thus subject to 5% tax. As was presented in the case of the Victoria Parthica inscription, the legacy of HS 8000 was subject to inheritance tax. Both cases of soldiers from Timgad call into question the meaning of Trajan's reform designed to free *modica pecunia* from tax obligations or else suggest that the term *modica* actually meant an amount below either HS 1900 or *c.* HS 7600.

In this respect, what is extremely important for the costs of buildings erected from testamentary legacies is that Trajan introduced a tax exemption if the inheritance/

[35] Blicharz 2016: 46.
[36] C. 6,33,3pr. Iustinianus (AD 531).
[37] Blicharz 2016: 78.
[38] Blicharz 2016: 78.
[39] Cass. Dio 55,25; Blicharz 2016: 49.
[40] Duncan-Jones 1998: 53.

bequest was used to commemorate the deceased and to offset funeral costs, i.e. ceremonies and the construction of a tombstone, due to the fact that legacies for construction purposes were usually connected to the construction of tombstones or funerary monuments (e.g. the pyramid of Cestius in Rome, etc.). This may be particularly interesting for those assessing the value of such structures.

Again, this exemption is not precisely specified, though at least the purpose for which the inherited benefit is to be used is quite clear, i.e. the deceased's commemoration and funeral costs. It is difficult to assess whether the taxable value of the inheritance was reduced by this amount or whether these costs were to exhaust the entire inheritance. All that is clear is that it seems these amounts were excluded from taxation. This is understandable because such purposes served both the common good - the public interest - with the burial of the deceased and the private interest - the fulfilment of family obligations, i.e. the memory of the deceased. This interpretation seems all the more justified because legacies of certain amounts, which the testator assigned to commemorate his own memory, should also be exempt. Nevertheless, this practice might well have given rise to the abuse of the envisaged exemption. According to Pliny, the heir was exempted from inheritance tax if *ita gratus heres volet, tota sepulcro, tota funeri serviet*. There are two possible readings of this passage. The first asserts that it is about spending the entire inherited wealth on the costs associated with the burial of the testator. Such an interpretation would apply to situations in which the costs of a funeral and a tomb exhaust the inheritance, and the emperor relieves the heirs of additional costs for the state. Then the tax exemption would be realised by investing the entire *mortis causa* benefit received for a specific purpose – funeral expenses, i.e. the ceremony and the monument.

A second reading would suggest an unusual solution in the form of a privilege permitting use of the amount of tax due for funeral expenses and not having to pay it to the state. In this way, the sum would serve to ensure the provision of funds for the burial of the deceased. Until now, in the literature the question of funeral expenses has been explained in such a way that they were deducted from the tax base before the *vicesimae* were established. This view is not based on the fragment above from the *Panegyric* itself but on the commentary of the jurist Macer, which we will analysed below. Both of these interpretations would be in line with the concept of 'deducting' funeral expenses as a concession for an understandable social need. It is not clear what the exemption mentioned in the *Panegyric* exactly meant to Pliny the Younger, but it undoubtedly formed part of the protection against the taxation of small amounts of property and entailed a complete exemption from

payment of the tax. On the other hand, the deduction of expenses from the tax base described by Macer was intended primarily to reduce the burden which large inheritances also had to face.

According to Pliny the Younger, the tax collectors were not to interfere in the use of the money allocated to commemorate the deceased. It is difficult to determine the scope of application of this tax exemption, as much depended on the size of the inheritance and the way the heirs wanted to commemorate the deceased. Undoubtedly, however, 'purpose-built expenses' became another way of avoiding taxation, probably already during the reign of Trajan. Disputes with the imperial administration were probably over determining whether the entire inheritance was actually used for erecting a monument for the deceased and for funeral ceremonies, and thus to assess the original value of the inherited goods. In addition, it was necessary to specify what the entire funeral costs meant in the context of tax exemption. The fact that the practice of circumventing tax obligations by expensive commemorations of the deceased proved to be a problem is evidenced by the rescript of Hadrian issued less than half a century later.

Hadrian introduced a very narrow definition of a sepulcher (*sepulchrum*) and associated funeral costs. It covered only the price of the place where the deceased was to be buried, the construction of a tomb of the size necessary to place a body in it, a sarcophagus, anything spent for the body before burial (ointment, for example), transport, and, finally, taxes (if any). Any other expenses, including those incurred for additional elements of the memorial, did not fall into this definition. The rescript had been issued as a result of a case in which a sepulcher was to be surrounded by a magnificent colonnade. Hadrian decided that the colonnade could not be classified as a *sepulchrum*. The need for defining this term arose from the dispute over inheritance tax, which the collectors wanted to obtain from an undoubtedly wealthy family, suspecting them of attempting tax evasion. This was indicated in Macer's reference to the rescript of Hadrian in the commentary to the statute on inheritance tax (*lex de vicesima hereditatum*). Hadrian's decision was a serious interference with the tax policy established by Trajan. From that point on, it was the Roman emperor who decided what was an acceptable form of celebrating the testator and what was the scope of tax exemption.

The issue of funeral expenses and their definition was a problem, and one that had many ramifications. It was evidenced especially in disputes about recovery of sums transferred for the purpose of a funeral (by means of *actio funeraria*), and it was related to the wider phenomenon of avoiding other inherited debts by disposing of inherited property, organising grand funeral ceremonies, or erecting expensive tombstones. That is why funeral expenses became the subject of regulation by the praetor, of the commentaries of jurists, and finally of imperial legislation.

Trajan's reforms of tax exemptions introduced two innovative solutions. First, a tax threshold was introduced, thus exempting small transfers of property from fiscal obligations, regardless of the stratified affiliation of heirs and legatees. Secondly, the source of tax privilege was to be the specific purpose for which the inherited wealth was to be used, in this case the commemoration of the deceased and provision of the necessary funeral, that is *funeris sumptus*.

As early as Hadrian's time, a legal definition had been established by the emperor of what should be regarded as a funerary monument and what costs should be regarded as funeral expenses. After all, these were also the subject of dispute in connection to reductions on the basis of the Falcidian quarter. As is evident, the understanding of these terms became significantly expanded, which meant that significant sums spent by heirs for these purposes reduced either the revenue from inheritance tax or the amount given in legacies to other beneficiaries for other purposes. It was therefore finally established by Hadrian that the amount spent on the grave – i.e. on a resting place necessary for the body of the deceased but not, as was previously the case, on a funerary statue proclaiming their glory – was not subject to tax; similarly, funeral expenses were to be limited to what was necessary but were not subject to the exclusion or exemption that applied to unnecessary expenses, because they were important for honouring the deceased.

Falcidian quarter: reduction of legacies

In addition to inheritance tax, when calculating the value of the legacies actually received, one needs to remember the right of the testamentary heir to a quarter of the inheritance, a right which was established by the *lex Falcidia* in 40 BC and which lasted until the end of the Roman Empire. The necessity of providing the heir with this quarter may mean that, if the value of the bequests exceeded 3/4 of the entire estate, then the legacies had to be reduced *pro rata*, by operation of the law (D. 35,2,73,5 Gaius *libro 18 ad edictum provinciale*). From this limitation were excluded the bequests covering the amount of the legitime; the bequests to the wife for the return of the dowry or items acquired for her; the bequest of a slave with added request for his liberation by the legatee.[41] If legacies exceeded 3/4 of the inheritance (which could have been the case if a large amount of money was transferred for a building), the legacies were reduced proportionally. This means that protection of the heirs could have influenced the final value of the bequest

transferred to a legatee and diminished the amount of money to be invested in the erection of a building or monument.

This is the situation described and analysed in the case of the aqueduct in Cirta and the heirs of Cargillianus which was discussed earlier. Taking into account the impact of the Falcidian quarter, we have reached a good position to revisit this text in order to present the whole scenario.

D. 22,6,9 Paulus *libro singulari de iuris et facti ignorantia*

> *Si quis ius ignorans lege Falcidia usus non sit, nocere ei dicit epistula divi Pii. Sed et imperatores Severus et Antoninus in haec verba rescripserunt: 'Quod ex causa fideicommissi indebitum datum est, si non per errorem solutum est, repeti non potest. Quamobrem Gargiliani heredes, qui, cum ex testamento eius pecuniam ad opus aquae ductus rei publicae cirtensium relictam solverint, non solum cautiones non exegerunt, quae interponi solent, ut quod amplius cepissent municipes quam per legem Falcidiam licuisset redderent, verum etiam stipulati sunt, ne ea summa in alios usus converteretur et scientes prudentesque passi sunt eam pecuniam in opus aquae ductus impendi, frustra postulant reddi sibi a re publica cirtensium, quasi plus debito dederint, cum sit utrumque iniquum pecuniam, quae ad opus aquae ductus data est, repeti et rem publicam ex corpore patrimonii sui impendere in id opus, quod totum alienae liberalitatis gloriam repraesentet. Quod si ideo repetitionem eius pecuniae habere credunt, quod imperitia lapsi legis Falcidiae beneficio usi non sunt, sciant ignorantiam facti, non iuris prodesse nec stultis solere succurri, sed errantibus.'*

The heirs transferred the money left by the testator in *fideicommissum* to the town to build an aqueduct in honour of the testator, but they did not realise that this sole disposition exceeded 3/4 of the entire estate. They could have deducted the Falcidian quarter and thus reduced the *fideicommissum* at the moment of payment, but they forgot to secure or to exercise their right from the *lex Falcidia*. The money which the heirs transferred to the city was entirely spent on the construction of the aqueduct, but but still the heirs wanted to reclaim some part from the city. The emperors did not grant them the right to reclaim a reduction of *fideicommissum* from the city treasury, because ignorance of the facts does not harm, but ignorance of the law does. They could have asked for a guarantee to make such a reduction at the moment of payment of the *fideicommissum* but failed to do so. In the case of *fideicommissa* there was set up, in AD 72, a similar portion to the Falcidian quarter, called the Pegasian quarter. Although this regulation was not a good piece of legislation, it was not abandoned until the times of Justinian. Due to the assimilation of *fideicommissa* with legacies in the times of Justinian,[42] in the case of the heirs

[41] Longchamps de Bérier 2011: 141–142.

[42] Longchamps de Bérier 2011: 208.

of Cargillianus the *lex Falcidia* is mentioned. This shows that the amount effectively received in the testamentary bequest or in *fideicommissum* may not always have been sufficient for a desired construction if one quarter of the *lex Falcidia* had been deducted. In fact, therefore, the testator would have needed to take into account a possible reduction of the legacy when bequeathing a certain amount.

We will now look more closely at the operation of the *lex Falcidia* in the case of one of the most popular buildings erected out of a testamentary bequest. A controversy arose as to whether even monuments for the commemoration of the deceased fall under the Falcidian quarter or if they are exempted from the reduction. If they *are* covered by the exemption, then in such cases we can assume that the value of the bequest was paid out in total. The Roman jurist Paulus provides a testimony about this controversy.

D. 35,2,1,19 Paulus *libro singulari ad legem Falcidiam*

> *De impensa monumenti nomine facta quaeritur, an deduci debeat. Et Sabinus ita deducendum putat, si necessarium fuerit monumentum extruere. Marcellus consultus, an funeris monumentique impensa, quantum testator fieri iussit, in aere alieno deduci debeat, respondit non amplius eo nomine, quam quod funeris causa consumptum est, deducendum. Nam eius, quod in extructionem monumenti erogatum est, diversam esse causam: nec enim ita monumenti aedificationem necessariam esse, ut sit funus ac sepultura. Idcirco eum, cui pecunia ad faciendum monumentum legata sit, Falcidiam passurum.*

We have the opinions of three jurists on this: Sabinus, Marcellus, and Paulus. The most lenient is the opinion of Sabinus who 'thinks that expenses incurred for the erection of a monument should be deducted if it becomes necessary to erect the monument'. However, both Marcellus and Paulus rejected the possibility of exempting such expenses. Marcellus argued that if the testator wished that certain expenses for a monument and funeral should be spent, then they can be deducted, but that a monument 'is not necessary, as the funeral and the burial are – *funus ac sepultura*'. As he elegantly argued, there may be various reasons for erecting a monument – *in extructionem monumenti erogatum est, diversam esse causam*. If the monument was not made *funeris causa* – necessary for burial purposes – then Marcellus would not grant the deduction from the Falicidian quarter. Thus, Paulus concludes, if someone received a legacy of money *ad faciendum monumentum* –for 'the erection of a monument' - such legacy 'must suffer the reduction under the Falcidian Law' - *Falcidiam passurum* - if the total value of all bequests exceeds 3/4 of the estate. However, in the following fragment of Justinian's *Digest* the very same Marcellus gives a slightly different opinion about

the operation of the Falcidian quarter in the case of the erection of a monument.

D. 35,2,2 Marcellus *libro 22 digestorum*

> *Nec amplius concedendum erit, quam quod sufficiat ad speciem modicam monumenti.*

The jurist thus allowed the spending of no more than would be sufficient for the erection of an ordinary monument (*modicam monumenti*). Both fragments deal with the expenses of an heir or legatee from an estate for funeral purposes and the erection of a monument. From Paulus's first text we can extract a principle: deduction is possible, if a monument is necessary; deduction is not possible, if it is not necessary. Paulus applies the latter rule to money bequeathed for the erection of a monument – not, therefore, for *funeris causa*. Moreover, in Marcellus's second fragment we can observe a new criterion, that of 'an ordinary monument'. Thus, the heir can deduct an amount sufficient for a simple monument. This fragment follows the fragment of Paulus, which means it expands on Paulus, giving more details, and it seems that heirs were allowed to deduct a small sum which they could spend or pay to legatees for the erection of a monument. Such an opinion by Marcellus was a modification of Sabinus's viewpoint, which allowed expenses for a necessary monument to be freed from the operation of the Falcidian portion. Paulus, in the 3rd century AD, returned to Marcellus's opinion that a monument is not a necessary expense, although he accepted an expense for the erection of an ordinary monument. He also rejected the deduction of such expenses and allowed them to be reduced for the benefit of the Falcidian portion. As the 16th-century jurist Cujacius rightly observed, interpreting this fragment, if the testator bequeathed money sufficient only for a small monument then such a legacy would not be reduced by the *lex Falcidia*. However, if the amount bequeathed was higher, it could not be entirely spent on the *monumentum*, but what exceeded the cost of an ordinary monument would be reduced by the *lex Falcidia*.[43] The opinion of Marcellus can also be understood in another way: that after the reduction of a bequest, only a sum for an ordinary monument might be allowed, so perhaps this bequest could have been reduced to a greater extent than other bequests. Nevertheless, just as in the case of inheritance tax, a *modica pecunia* is freed from the burden. Thus, this confirms the concept of Trajan who excluded inheritance tax for amounts spent on *sepulchrum* and *funerum*, and the intervention of Hadrian who defined *sepulchrum* in a a very narrow way by limiting it only to *funeris causa* – a burial place. Once again, the doctrines around the *vicesima hereditatis* and the *lex Falcidia* conicide with each other, and thanks to

---

this we can learn more about inheritance tax despite its abolition before the times of Justinian.[44]

A controversy similar to this was confirmed by the constitution of Alexander Severus in AD 223 which is contained in Justinian's *Code*. It deals with the case of bequests 'intended to be expended in public works, or for the erection of statues'. The emperor was asked whether such legacies might be deducted, and so excluded from the operation of the *lex Falcidia*.

C. 6,50,6,1 Imperator Alexander Severus

Omnia autem legata, quamvis in operibus publicis conficiendis statuisque ponendis data sint, ad contributionem dodrantis pro rata suae cuiusque quantitatis revocantur.

According to the emperor, even such bequests with a public purpose should make up the Falcidian portion in proportion to their amount – *pro rata*. This means that in the case of both monuments and public works constructed out of testamentary bequest the effective amount paid out of the estate could have been reduced in order to cover the heirs' Falcidian quarter. Only small monuments were freed from the operation of the Falcidian quarter, i.e. those which were limited to the place of burial, a necessary sepulchre.

Locatio conductio. Preliminary remarks on contractual costs of erecting buildings

Apart from issues arising from testamentary dispositions and regulation of the law of succession, there are other legal issues that need to be taken into account when estimating the costs of Roman construction projects. Very important is the phase of actually physically erecting the monument. If this was not carried out by the heirs themselves together with their household, then it usually had to be done by contracting a professional workman to erect the monument and any other buildings involved. In this phase there are two issues of relevance, and these can both be highlighted by texts from Justinian's *Digest*, which also provide us with some data.

First, even for Romans it was difficult to estimate the actual value of a building. This is a common occurrence nowadays as well: prices can change, the scope of the project may change, and the final cost of construction may differ from the one calculated at the beginning or even from the one in the testamentary bequest. We can find testimony of this in a text of the jurist Labeo.

D. 19,2,60,4 Labeo *libro quinto posteriorum a Iavoleno epitomatorum*

---

[44] Blicharz 2016: 110–111.

Mandavi tibi ut excuteres, quanti villam aedificare velles: renuntiasti mihi ducentorum impensam excutere: certa mercede opus tibi locavi, postea comperi non posse minoris trecentorum eam villam constare: data autem tibi erant centum, ex quibus cum partem impendisses, vetui te opus facere. Dixi, si opus facere perseveraveris, ex locato tecum agere, ut pecuniae mihi reliquum restituas.

The person who wanted to set up a *locatio conductio* contract first asked a professional to estimate the amount for the completion of the work to build a house. The price was set at 200 *aurei*, and the contract was agreed. However, in the course of time the owner of the land realised that the house would cost him at least 300 *aurei*, and so he forbade the hired person to proceed with the work.

The change of estimate was very high in this case – 50% –, which perhaps can tell us much about the hired professional, or maybe about the difficulty of estimating the costs of construction of that particular *villa*, or about fluctuations of prices in the construction market. Nevertheless, the owner had already incurred some expenses: he had given the workman 100 *aurei* in advance, and some of this sum had actually already been spent on erecting the house - this money he would not be able to recover. The change in the estimate thus influenced the whole process of erecting the building.

In Justinian's *Digest*, there is also an example of a more detailed estimation of costs before the commencement of work. The jurist Alfenus presents a contractual provision which sets up very precise contract terms.

D. 19,2,30,3 Alfenus *libro tertio a Paulo epitomarum*

Qui aedem faciendam locaverat, in lege dixerat: 'quoad in opus lapidis opus erit, pro lapide et manupretio dominus redemptori in pedes singulos septem dabit': quaesitum est, utrum factum opus an etiam imperfectum metiri oporteret. Respondit etiam imperfectum.

According to the contract: 'To the extent that stone is needed for this job, the owner will pay to the contractor seven per foot for his stone and remuneration'. The man who was hired to build the house agreed to deliver the material on his own and set the price for the material at 'seven per foot'. There is no currency indicated, though Mommsen suggested adding *sesterces* at this point. Besides this detail we may look at yet another aspect of this example – the calculation of work and material. The issue in this case is whether 'the job be measured [only] when it is finished or while still incomplete'. and the response here is: 'while still incomplete'. This illustrates one of the possible ways of setting up the payment: not in installments but *per pedes mensurasve*, and that is probably why it refers to a more skilled stonemason who was needed to give final shape to the structure.[45] The solution that it should be measured while still incomplete proves that it was an important task which should rather be kept under control. Moreover, measuring work by foot gives more flexibility to the owner to replace the workers if their skills are not up to delivering the final product desired.[46]

The second issue deals with the allocation of risk in the case of a contract for the erection of a building. Among other texts concerning *locatio conductio* contracts, there is one authored by Iavolenus.

D. 19,2,59, Iavolenus *libro quinto ex posterioribus Labeonis*

> *Marcius domum faciendam a Flacco conduxerat: deinde operis parte effecta terrae motu concussum erat aedificium. Massurius Sabinus, si vi naturali, veluti terrae motu hoc acciderit, Flacci esse periculum.*

Flaccus employed Marcius to build his house (*domus*). The work was partially done, but then came an earthquake which destroyed it. It was Flaccus who had to incur the loss and bear the financial loss of materials and work that were destroyed by force of nature (*vis naturalis*). The occurrence of accidents may also influence the final cost of construction works, and nowadays, as in Roman times, it is necessary to take such variables into account, particularly when we know the character of the place where a particular building was to be erected.

Conclusions

A map of legal issues connected with construction projects financed out of testamentary legacies would range from inheritance tax to the Falcidian portion, from the type of legacies (and their wording) to estimation of the estate's value, whilst also taking into account the costs of contracts set up to erect a monument or building. These five issues were identified as crucial factors influencing the costs of construction. As we have seen, an analysis of cases from Justinian's Digest can give a flavor of the legal costs that could be taken into account when estimating the value of a construction project to be financed out of a testament.

The first conclusion to be drawn is that construction costs may not be equal to the amount of money bequeathed. Secondly, the money bequeathed may not be equal to the benefit effectively received. One should take into account the 5% inheritance tax (or, in the short period applicable, 10%) as a variable that could influence these figures at least in the period from AD 6 to the 4th century AD (since inheritance tax was not a permanent solution in ancient Rome). Next, one must be aware of the possibility of both subjective and objective tax exemptions. If there is information about the personal bond between testator and legatee, we may expect the bequest to be exempted from tax. If the building was a monument to the testator it might have been exempt, at least from the time of Trajan, though this may be doubtful during Hadrian's reign. Finally, one cannot forget the Falcidian quarter, which could influence the value of the received benefit. From 40 BC onwards, the law allowed a reduction of all bequests to 3/4 of the inheritance so that at least 1/4 of the estate would remain with the heir. This particular factor shows that it is quite difficult to judge *ex post* whether the testamentary legacy was transferred in full or whether it had been reduced by operation of the Falcidian quarter. Moreover, it shows how carefully testaments had to be drafted in order to calculate additional costs after the death of the testator which might influence the fulfillment of the testator's wishes to erect a monument. A more predictable variable would appear to be inheritance tax, which also might be added to the estimation of costs. However, one should bear in mind that the evolving doctrine of tax exemptions and the lack of many details due to the abolition of the tax before Justinian means that it is possible that not every monument or building erected out of a testamentary legacy was in fact taxed with *vicesima*. The picture is even cloudier, because inscriptions which do mention the value of bequests which financed a construction project rarely indicate the deduction of inheritance tax. So it is probably better to assume that the tax was due and in fact collected rather than that *vicesima* was exempted in these cases. Finally, the cases collected in Justinian's *Digest* which refer to the appointment of heirs or to testamentary legacies in connection with details about erecting a building or estimating construction costs could reveal further data relevant for archaeological studies of extant architecture. Besides numerical data, the legal texts deal with all sorts of issues driving the estimation of construction work, such as the motives of individuals and even public interest in managing the erection of new buildings. All of these provide a different kind of qualitative data which could help deepen the methodology of the estimation of Roman construction costs.

Bibliography

Blicharz, G. 2016. *Udział państwa w spadku. Rzymska myśl prawna w perspektywie prawnoporównawczej.* Kraków: OdNowa.

Buckland, W.W. 1908 (reprint 1970). *The Roman Law of Slavery: The Condition of the Slave in Private Law from Augustus to Justinian.* Cambridge University Press.

Coleman, K.M. 2008. Exchanging gladiators for an aqueduct at Aphrodisias (SEG 50.1096). *Acta Classica* 51: 31–46.

---

[45] Martin 1989: 115–116; du Plessis 2012: 77–78.
[46] Martin 1989: 124.

Cujacii, J. 1837. *IC. Tolosatis Opera ad Parisiensem Fabrotianam Editionem*, vol. 4 of 13: Diligentissime Exacta in Tomos 13. Distributa, Auctiora Atque Emendatiora, Pars Tertia, Giachetti, Prati.

Di Salvo, S. 1973. *Il legato modale in diritto romano: elaborazioni dommatiche e realtà sociali*. Napoli: Jovene.

du Plessis, P. 2012. *Letting and Hiring in Roman Legal Thought: 27 BCE - 284 CE*. Leiden-Boston-Koln: Brill.

Duncan-Jones, R. 1962. Costs, Outlays and Summae Honorariae from Roman Africa. *Papers of the British School at Rome* 30: 47–115.

Duncan-Jones, R. 1982. *The Economy of the Roman Empire. Quantitative Studies*. 2nd edition. Cambridge-New York-Melbourne: Cambridge University Press.

Duncan-Jones, R. 1998. *Money and Government in the Roman Empire*. New York: Cambridge University Press.

Guarducci, M. 1971. L'iscrizione di Aberico e Roma. *Ancient Society* 2: 174–203.

Günther, S. 2008. *Vectigalia nervos esse rei publicae. Die indirekten Steuern in der Römischen Kaiserzeit von Augustus bis Diokletian*. Wiesbaden: Harrassowitz Verlag.

Honoré, T. 'Cervidius Scaevola, Quintus', Oxford Classical Dictionary, March 07, 2016, Oxford University Press, Date of access 9 May. 2020, <https://oxfordre.com/classics/view/10.1093/acrefore/9780199381135.001.0001/acrefore-9780199381135-e-1492>.

Johnston, D. 1985. Munificence and Municipia: Bequests to Towns in Classical Roman Law. *The Journal of Roman Studies* 75: 105–125.

Kaiser, W. 1991. Streit wegen einer satisdatio für einen Fideikommiss: Bemerkungen zu einer Inschrift aus Prusias ad Hypium (IK 27, 139). *Zeitschrift für Papyrologie und Epigraphik* 86: 163–181.

Katsari, C. 2011. *The Roman Monetary System: The Eastern Provinces from the First to the Third Century AD*. Cambridge University Press.

Longchamps de Bérier, F. 2000. *Nec stultis solere succurri*, in M. Zabłocka *et al.* (eds) *Mélanges de droit romain offerts à Witold Wołodkiewicz* 1: 470–475. Warszawa: Liber.

Longchamps de Bérier, F. 2011. *Law of Succession. Roman Legal Framework and Comparative Law Perspective*. Warszawa: Wolters Kluwer.

Martin, S.D. 1989. *The Roman Jurists and the Organization of Private Building in the Late Republic and Early Empire* (Collection Latomus 204). Tournai: Societé d'Etudes Latines.

Marucchi, O. 1912. *Christian Epigraphy; an Elementary Treatise, with a Collection of Ancient Christian Inscriptions Mainly of Roman Origin*, translated by J. Armine Willis. Cambridge University Press.

Miglietta, M. 2018. Emblematic Cases of Logical Conflict between *Quaesito* and *Responsum* in the Digesta of Publius Alfenus Varus, in F. Zuccotti and M.A. Fenocchio (eds) *A Pierluigi Zannini. Scritti di diritto romano e giusantichistici* (Quaderni del Dipartimento di Giurisprudenza dell'Università di Torino 6): 207–265. Torino.

Patrone, M. 2016. Il *modus* nel quadro dei vincoli testamentari, tesi di Dottorato in Diritto Privato, Diritto Romano e Cultura Giuridica Europea. Pavia.

Phillips, E.J. 1973. The Roman Law on the Demolition of Buildings. *Latomus* 32/1: 86–95.

Taylor, T.S. 2016. Social Status, Legal Status and Legal Privilege, in P.J. du Plessis, C. Ando and K. Tuori (eds) *The Oxford Handbook of Roman Law and Society*: 349–361. Oxford.

Tellegen, J.W. 2012. The Immortality of the Soul and Roman Law, in O. Tellegen-Couperus (ed.) *Law and Religion in the Roman Republic*: 181–202. Leiden-Boston: Brill.

van den Hout, M.P.J. 1999. *A Commentary on the Letters of M. Cornelius Fronto*. Leiden-Boston-Koln: Brill.

Winkel, L. 1996. L'Aqueduc de Cirta (Numidie). *Revue d'Histoire du Droit* 64/1: 141–144.

Yakobson, A. 1999. *Elections and Electioneering in Rome: A Study in the Political System of the Late Republic* (Historia Einzelschriften 128). Sttugart: Franz Steiner Verlag.

Ancient sources and inscriptions

Cicero
  Paradoxa Stoicorum 49

Pliny the Younger
  Plin. *Ep.* 1,19

Inscription of Abericus, Phryg. — Hieropolis (Koçhisar):
  Hüdāi Kaplicasi — bef. 216 AD — IChUR(1) II,1.xv —
  SEG 30.147
Victoria Parthica inscription (Thamugadi N, C. 2354)
  from 116 AD
Lucius Cassius Dio
  Cass. Dio 55,25

Digesta Iustiniani
  D. 19,2,30,3
  D. 19,2,59
  D. 19,2,60,4
  D. 22,6,9,5
  D. 32,11,23
  D. 32,11,25
  D. 32,42
  D. 33,1,7
  D. 35,1,14
  D. 35,1,27
  D. 35,1,40,5
  D. 35,1,80
  D. 35,2,1,19
  D. 35,2,73,5
  D. 50,10,5
  D. 50,10,7 pr.
  D. 50,10,7,1
  D. 50,16,202

Codex Iustinianus
  C. 6,33,3pr.
  C. 6,50,6,1

5.

Demolitions, Collapses, and the Control of the Housing Market in Rome

Marguerite Ronin

Centre national de la recherche scientifique (CNRS), Paris
marguerite.ronin@cnrs.fr

Abstract

The development of the housing business in Rome and in Roman cities from the 1st c. BC onwards is linked to the considerable expansion of urban markets throughout the empire. In this context, the literary sources draw our attention towards the practice of deliberate destruction of houses. The attempts to regulate this practice raise questions related to the need for new houses, the profitability of the construction business, and the distribution of risks between different classes of actors, namely the owners and the middlemen, a class of entrepreneurs making their living out of the sublease market. Public authorities probably tried, to a certain extent, to provide responses, for example by limiting the height of new buildings. The Roman system, however, seemed to have mostly favoured procedures of reciprocal control by private individuals, like the *cautio damni infecti*, a security given to the neighbours in case damage was foreseen from a house threatening to collapse. Between the end of the Republic and the beginning of the Empire, the construction sector and the housing market did not only represent a world of opportunities but were also subject to a set of legal constraints that are explored in this paper. Opportunities did not only lie in the construction of buildings but also in the salvaging market where entrepreneurs could prosper by recycling valuable materials from demolished houses. In the case of accidental collapses, however, it is likely that many owners were reluctant to deal with the least valuable rubble. Finally, landlords also had to consider the rights of their tenants when planning the demolition of an inhabited building.

Keywords: Urban risks, Roman law, *cautio damni infecti*, recycling, lease contracts

Introduction

The development of the housing business in Rome in the last centuries of the Republic was linked to the considerable expansion of urban markets throughout the empire.[1] A characteristic feature of this flourishing activity is the development of high buildings, often called *insulae*, intended for the rental market.[2] In this context, sources draw our attention towards the frequent destruction of private buildings, either accidental or deliberate.

> **Strabo, *Geograph.* 5.3.7.** τῇ δ' ἀρετῇ καὶ τῷ πόνῳ τῆς χώρας οἰκείας γενομένης, ἐφάνη συνδρομή τις ἀγαθῶν ἅπασαν εὐφυΐαν ὑπερβάλλουσα· δι' ἣν ἐπὶ τοσοῦτον αὐξηθεῖσα ἡ πόλις ἀντέχει τοῦτο μὲν τροφῇ, τοῦτο δὲ ξύλοις καὶ λίθοις πρὸς τὰς οἰκοδομίας, ἃς ἀδιαλείπτως ποιοῦσιν αἱ συμπτώσεις καὶ ἐμπρήσεις καὶ μεταπράσεις, ἀδιάλειπτοι καὶ αὗται οὖσαι· καὶ γὰρ αἱ μεταπράσεις ἑκούσιοί τινες συμπτώσεις εἰσί, καταβαλλόντων καὶ ἀνοικοδομούντων πρὸς τὰς ἐπιθυμίας ἕτερα ἐξ ἑτέρων.

When by their valour and their toil they had made the country their own property, there was obviously a concourse, so to speak, of blessings that surpassed all natural advantages; and it is because of this concourse of blessings that the city, although it has grown to such an extent, holds out in the way it does, not only in respect to food, but also in respect to timber and stones for the building of houses, which goes on unceasingly in consequence of the collapses and fires and repeated sales (these last, too, going on unceasingly); and indeed the sales are intentional collapses, as it were, since the purchasers keep tearing down the houses and building new ones, one after another, to suit their wishes. (Text and transl. Loeb Classical Library 50, Jones 1923)

These unceasing collapses (συμπτώσεις) can be explained by the poor quality of the buildings relegated to lower class housing and by the lack of urban space in Rome, where buildings were torn down, possibly to reconstruct them at a greater height, thus feeding an active market of raw and recycled materials. Demolitions thus directly or indirectly constituted business opportunities on the one hand, but also, on the other hand, posed urban risks which could conflict with public or private interests. Solutions were therefore developed to control the risks without

---

[1] Property ownership has been thoroughly studied by Dubouloz 2011. See also the classic, Garnsey 1976.
[2] Liv. 21.62.3: mentions a three-storey building in 218 BC. Plin. *HN* 3.67 describes how the majestic impression of the City is enhanced by the height of the buildings (*quod si quis altitudinem tectorum addat*).

impairing opportunities. But, because many dwellings were rented accommodations, tenants and subtenants also claimed a right to be protected from a peril that Strabo describes as commonplace.[3]

The attempts, by different authorities, to regulate the activities of the construction market raise questions related to the need for new houses, the profitability of the construction business, and the distribution of risks between different categories of economic actors, specifically between the owners and the middlemen, a class of entrepreneurs making their living out of the sublease market. Roman authorities also tried to control the risks caused by the poor construction quality. Emperors like Augustus or Nero tried, from the 1st c. AD, to restrict the poor quality of buildings by adopting measures like the limitation of a building's height. Legal mechanisms were also enacted, like the *cautio damni infecti*, a kind of insurance given to the neighbours in case of imminent damage from a house threatening to collapse. Between the end of the Republic and the beginning of the Empire, the construction sector and the housing market did not only represent a world of opportunities but were also subject to legal constraints that this paper proposes to explore.

Although issues related to the development of the housing market in Rome frequently appear in the literary and epigraphical evidence, they cannot be properly discussed without the help of Roman legal texts, which are instrumental in nuancing the complexities of the issues at stake for owners and entrepreneurs seeking to achieve a balance between economic opportunities and risks. The papers in this volume explore in depth the economic opportunities of the construction sector in what Dominik Maschek has called an 'architectural turn' in studies of the ancient economy. This paper aims not only to investigate how these opportunities could compete with each other but also to examine how legal rules, set to limit potential conflicts, could represent significant constraints for the economic actors.

Controlling urban risks by limiting the height of buildings

Stories of faulty constructions and public buildings threatening to collapse are frequent in Latin literature: a classic example is the theatre of Nicea whose walls, even before completion of the work in the early 2nd century AD, were 'sinking and cracked from top to bottom' according to Pliny the Younger.[4] Archaeological studies confirm how arduous and hazardous some construction projects were, like that of the Cahors aqueduct at the

beginning of the 1st century AD.[5] In the years following their completion, the preservation of such buildings was undoubtedly a challenge, although maintenance was also crucial for soundly constructed buildings, given their exposure to environmental effects and due to natural ageing, as inscriptions plainly show.[6] Private buildings naturally encountered similar constructional defects. If a landowner decided not to resort to his own staff to build a house, he could choose to hire a contractor. Different types of construction contracts are accounted for in the private sector between the end of the Republic and throughout the imperial period, like the *locatio conductio operis faciendi* or the *stipulatio*.[7] The builder was then legally liable for the defects until the approval of the work, a procedure called *probatio* in the case of the *locatio conductio*.[8] After the approval, the risk of deterioration passed to the developer.[9]

Rapid decay of private buildings seems to have been abundantly caused by the widespread use of so-called *opus craticium*, a building technique consisting of filling in a wooden lattice with *opus incertum*, or with a combination of straw and earth, and plastering over it. Although universally criticised by ancient authors for the serious fire risk it posed and for not being durable, this type of construction was widespread in the empire.[10] It was fast and easy to build. Moreover, it was cheap and provided more space because the lightness of the structure meant that buildings could be built higher and could include balconies and rooms projecting above the street.[11] Besides the fire risk, *opus craticium* was prone to cracks and could cause buildings

---

[3] On the rental market and its different actors, see in the first place Frier 1980. For an archaeological approach to the subject: Pirson 1999.
[4] Plin. *Ep.* 10.39.2: *Ingentibus enim rimis desedit et hiat.*

[5] Rigal 2011.
[6] See various contributions on restoration and maintenance in Ronin and Möller 2019. On ageing of public buildings and roads, see Thomas and Witschel 1992; Davoine 2019. Our written documentation on the maintenance of private properties is more limited, although legal sources inform us of imperial decisions on mutual obligations of co-owners, for example (*Dig.* 17.2.52.10; *Cod. Iust.* 8.10.4). For a discussion on these fragments, see Dubouloz 2011: 353-363.
[7] The *Digest*'s title on the *locatio conductio* (*Dig.* 19.2) contains a high number of opinions from Servius, prominent jurist from the 1st c. BC. This is indicative of the issues at stake in this period of intense activity in the construction sector. See Saliou 2012.
[8] *Dig.* 19.2.60.3.
[9] The building technique, type, and quantity of material used for the construction was also the responsibility of the owner, who could therefore not blame the entrepreneur for the low quality of a house if he had satisfied the terms of the contract. See Vitr. *De arch.* 6.8.9: *Quibus autem copiarum generibus oporteat uti, non est architecti potestas, ideo quod non in omnibus locis omnia genera copiarum nascuntur, ut in proximo volumine est expositum; praeterea in domini est potestate, utrum latericio an caementicio an saxo quadrato velit aedificare* (An architect cannot control the kinds of material necessary to use, for the reason that not all kinds of material occur in all places, as was explained in the last book. Besides, the client decides whether he is to build in brick or rubble or ashlar). (Text and transl. Loeb Classical Library 280, Granger 1934).
[10] Vitr. *De arch.* 2.8.20; Catull. 23.8-10; Juv. 3.190-204; Gell. *NA* 15.1. Full review of the latest studies on *opus craticium* in Stellacci and Rato 2019.
[11] The Vesuvian cities have preserved houses and buildings in *opus craticium*, for example the the structures of III.13-15 at Herculaneum. See Monteix 2009 about the mistaken reconstruction of Maiuri in the 1930s.

to collapse. It therefore created not only a possible private discomfort but also a real public danger and a threat to the neighbouring private properties. As Strabo points out for the city of Rome, construction of new houses was always necessary because they frequently burned down or collapsed.[12] To contain the damage, imperial authorities repeatedly tried to impose a standard by limiting thebuilding heights, although nothing indicates how binding the standards were.

The interventions that Augustus carried out to make Rome the capital worthy of his prestige fall into different categories. The embellishment of the city and the maintenance of public buildings naturally played a role in the definition of a unified urban image and in the self-celebration of the ruler.[13] Magnificence was, however, not the only priority, and a fair number of decisions clearly also aimed at better controlling what are now called 'urban risks'. In this second category, we not only find the cleaning up of the Tiber to tackle the flood risk and the reorganisation of the firefighting force but also the limitation of new buildings' height.[14] No such provision had been taken before Augustus, and most of the previous attempts to restrict the dimensions of private houses were, in fact, part of a broader movement of sumptuary laws.[15] Strabo states, on the other hand, that the decision taken around 7 BC to forbid any construction on a public street to rise above seventy feet (20 m) was made specifically to prevent collapse.

Strabo, *Geographia*, 5.3.7. Ἐπεμελήθη μὲν οὖν ὁ Σεβαστὸς Καῖσαρ τῶν τοιούτων ἐλαττωμάτων τῆς πόλεως, πρὸς μὲν τὰς ἐμπρήσεις συντάξας στρατιωτικὸν ἐκ τῶν ἀπελευθεριωτῶν τὸ βοηθῆσον, πρὸς δὲ τὰς συμπτώσεις τὰ ὕψη τῶν καινῶν οἰκοδομημάτων καθελών, καὶ κωλύσας ἐξαίρειν ποδῶν ἑβδομήκοντα τὸ πρὸς ταῖς ὁδοῖς ταῖς δημοσίαις.

Now Augustus Caesar concerned himself about such impairments of the city, organising for protection against fires a militia composed of freedmen, whose duty it was to render assistance, and also to provide against collapses, reducing the heights of the new buildings and forbidding that any structure on the public streets should rise as high as seventy feet. (Text and transl. Loeb Classical Library 50, Jones 1923)

This example was followed by other emperors. The reconstruction programme decided upon by Nero, after the Great Fire of AD 64, addressed the fire risk by combining the creation of open spaces to slow the spread of flames with restrictions on building heights to minimise the damage in case of a collapse.

Tacitus, *Ann.* 15.43. *Ceterum urbis quae domui supererant non, ut post Gallica incendia, nulla distinctione nec passim erecta, sed dimensis vicorum ordinibus et latis viarum spatiis cohibitaque aedificiorum altitudine ac patefactis areis additisque porticibus, quae frontem insularum protegerent.*

In the capital, however, the districts spared by the palace were rebuilt, not, as after the Gallic fire, indiscriminately and piecemeal, but in measured lines of streets, with broad thoroughfares, buildings of restricted height, and open spaces, while colonnades were added as a protection to the front of the tenement-blocks. (Text and transl. Loeb Classical Library 322, Jackson 1937)

Finally, a later source, the *Epitome de Caesaribus*, indicates that Trajan added a similar limitation, this time to sixty feet (17 m). His decision is said by the *Epitome* to have been taken after a series of public disasters had struck Rome and the empire (a particularly devastating surge of the Tiber, earthquakes in several provinces, a famine, epidemics, and fires).

Epit. de Caes., 13. *12. Eo tempore, multo perniciosius quam sub Nerva, Tiberis inundavit magna clade aedium proximarum; et terrae motus gravis per provincias multas, atroxque pestilentia famesque et incendia facta sunt. 13. Quibus omnibus Traianus per exquisita remedia plurimum opitulatus est, statuens ne domorum altitudo sexaginta superaret pedes ob ruinas faciles et sumptus, si quando talia contingerent, exitiosos.*

At that time, more destructively by far than under Nerva, the Tiber flooded with great devastation of close-by buildings; and there occurred a serious earthquake through many provinces and a dreadful plague and famines and fires. To all these things Trajan brought relief through remedies usually excellent, decreeing that the height of houses do not exceed sixty feet on account of proneness to collapse and deadly expenses if ever things such as this should come to pass. (Text Les Belles Lettres, Festy, 1999; Transl. Canisius College Translated Texts, Banchich 2018)

While these sources are well known and routinely cited in studies on the legal constraints of the construction

---
[12] *Geograph.* 5.3.7.
[13] Favro 1996.
[14] On the cleaning of the Tiber, Suet. *Aug.* 30; on the vigils, Cass. Dio 55.8.6–7. Teams of firemen were privately maintained, in addition to the insufficient public force placed under the authority of a triumvirate, at the end of the Republic. See *Dig.* 1.15.1. Three centuries after the time of Crassus, an imperial edict reminds that *insularii* have a responsibility in preventing fire from burning down *insulae* (*Dig.* 1.15.4).
[15] Summing up the main arguments, see Saliou 1994: 211.

82

business, they still raise important questions.[16] They concern the efficiency and enforcement of such pieces of imperial legislation, undoubtedly a thorny matter which would require a longer and more thorough study than the present one, but to which it is possible to give some quick thoughts.

It must first be noted that the emperors' decisions seem very stereotypical, corresponding to the sort of responses expected of them in cases of public disasters emanating from urban living conditions. This impression is particularly patent in the last text, the *Epitome*. Besides the fact that it was written some three centuries after the events described, the author enumerates a series of calamities to which the single response was to legislate on the height of houses, a supposedly excellent remedy (*per exquisita remedia*). The reasons why Augustus and Nero decided to take public action are more precisely related, by the texts, to the recurring problems of fire and collapse. This situation was not new in the imperial period. On the contrary, these problems were very common throughout the last centuries of the Republic, although we do not know of any similar piece of regulation before Augustus. It would, however, be excessive to associate the silence of our sources with a potential lack of interest of the Republican elite in the matter.[17] Indeed, many examples tell us that urban risks, directly impacting the living conditions of the urban population, were a real concern to those in charge of public offices in Republican times.[18] It is nevertheless interesting to note that we only hear of these construction laws with the advent of the imperial regime. A fundamental difference to the previous era was, indeed, that action was now expected from one single ruler. As such, the emperor had to show he was responding decisively to a critical situation and was living up to the people's expectation: imposing a rule was part of the process.[19]

As to the actual efficiency of the measure, limiting the height of such frail structures, as we are told some *insulae* were, obviously seems like common sense. If we follow Strabo and Tacitus, such regulation was valid only in Rome. On the other hand, although it remains quite imprecise, the text of the *Epitome* seems to indicate that the height limitation was applicable throughout the empire. It is certainly a possibility: scattered fragments of the *Digest* and of the *Code of Justinian* indeed refer to construction laws that applied more broadly than in Rome alone.[20] It remains, however, difficult to estimate how well these decisions were really applied and enforced. Seventy or sixty feet of height are roughly coherent with the few elements we can gather about the elevation of imperial apartment buildings. Preserved rooms in the Casa a Graticcio (III.1315) at Herculaneum are 2.95 m high on the ground floor and 2.90 m on the first floor.[21] Working areas may measure as high as 4.06 m in Pompeii, where archaeologists studied a bakery whose ground-floor room was presumably joined together with the upper floor.[22] An interpretation of some symbols on the *Forma Vrbis Romae*, although some two centuries later, proposes a maximum of eight storeys.[23] An average height of 3m by floor would give us a 24-m high building, but it is very likely that the uppermost floors (intended for lower class housing) also had lower ceilings. It follows that the buildings of the Severan era depicted on the *Forma Vrbis* would hypothetically match the seventy foot (20m) requirements of the Augustan legal provision. It is, however, challenging to ascertain whether this height resulted from the laws of the emperor or from the laws of physics.

To estimate the efficiency of imperial decisions is indeed an ambitious and rarely undertaken task. In addition, it is possible that the problem might actually lie more with the capacity of the Roman administration to impose these decrees on private owners and contractors. The fragments gathered by Saliou show that imperial regulation of building practices existed and was regularly referred to by jurists and presumably in court too, but it is probably not a coincidence that these fragments appear in the body of private law texts. Indeed, they constitute a larger set of solutions to which private individuals were entitled to resort. In fact, the private owners whose property was threatened by a collapsing house were probably more efficient than the costly public administration because they were determined to see their rights respected. To protect their assets from such peril, Roman private law developed and instituted specific mechanisms.

The *cautio damni infecti* and the neighbours' liability

A very prominent feature of the Roman legal system was favouring procedures of reciprocal control

---

[16] Catherine Saliou discusses another text, also referring to the limitation of building heights: *Cod. Iust.* 8.10.12.4. It could refer to a building height limitation in Constantinople, but Saliou argues that the text has been traditionally incorrectly translated and that it actually deals with the distance between houses (Saliou 1994: 215-216).

[17] As expressed, for example, by Van den Bergh 2003.

[18] Without being too optimistic about the interest of the senatorial class into the fate of their less wealthy fellow citizens, it was at least an electoral concern. A firefighting force already existed before the creation of the vigils by Augustus in AD 6: it was placed under the authority of the *triumuiri nocturni* (*Dig.* 1.15.1). During his censorship, Cato had the cisterns paved and the sewers cleaned (Liv. 39.44.4–6).

[19] Paul Veyne sums up the idea in one sentence: « Tout empereur doit continuer, sous peine de mort, à mériter le consensus qui l'a désigné » (Veyne 2002: 54).

[20] The texts, gathered by Saliou, refer to construction laws in general and do not specifically mention a height limitation (*Cod. Iust.* 8.10.1; *Dig.* 39. 1. 1. 17; *Dig.* 39. 1.5.9; *Dig.* 32. 1 1. 14). Saliou 1994: 212-216.

[21] Stellacci and Rato 2019: 15.

[22] Monteix *et al.* 2013.

[23] Pedroni 1992; and more recently Madeleine 2008.

between private individuals over the implementation of general legislation.[24] Alongside imperial decisions on the height of buildings, mechanisms of protection against the urban risk of collapse were thus developed by praetorian law and were undertaken by townspeople themselves. A property owner, fearing that an adjacent house might damage his own by falling down, could obtain a 'guarantee against anticipated injury' (a *cautio damni infecti*) from the owner of the threatening building.[25] As a result, he was given assurances to be indemnified for his loss in the event of a collapse.[26] Although this *cautio* took the shape of a type of contract called *stipulatio*, it was evidently not always a voluntary contract but could be forced on a party by the *praetor*.[27]

Accidental collapses naturally constituted a great threat on private properties, because of the reconstruction costs they potentially incurred and because of the financial loss they could induce if deterioration forced tenants to flee.[28] For this reason, at least from the end of the 1st century BC, *cautiones* were not only granted to property owners but also to the tenants of the individual apartments within a block of flats.[29]

It has been suggested that the *cautio damni infecti* was probably regularly (if not systematically) used in the business of selling and buying houses.[30] It seems likely that prospective investors preferred to acquire buildings for which a *cautio* had already been granted. Sellers had therefore more chances to make a good deal if they negotiated *cautiones* with their neighbours, especially if they suspected damage from the surrounding houses.[31] The importance of the *cautio damni infecti* in the contracts for the sale of immovable properties can be traced back to sometime between the 1st and the 3rd

centuries AD. In his comment on the work of Plautius (second half of the 1st century AD), the jurist Paul (beginning of the 3rd century AD) considered that the *cautio* was essential to the sale contract, whether or not a threat was suspected from the adjacent building.

Dig. 19.1.36. Paulus libro septimo ad Plautium. *Venditor domus antequam eam tradat, damni infecti stipulationem interponere debet, quia, antequam vacuam possessionem tradat, custodiam et diligentiam praestare debet et pars est custodiae diligentiaeque hanc interponere stipulationem: et ideo si id neglexerit, tenebitur emptori.*

It is the seller of a house who, before its delivery, should obtain the stipulation on threatened damage (*stipulatio damni infecti*); he has a duty to exercise safekeeping and care before delivering vacant possession, and obtaining this stipulation is a part of safekeeping and care. Therefore, if he neglected this, he will be liable to the buyer.

It is notable in this text that the ability to secure a *cautio* is seen, by the jurist, as part of the due care that an owner had to exercise to keep a property safe.[32] Does this mean that every house in Roman cities, and in Rome in the first place, was threatening to collapse on the adjacent properties? That is not what we learn from the legal texts. As a matter of fact, owners did not have to suspect a threat to seek a *cautio* (at least from the time of Paulus until the 6th century), as long as they swore that they were not trying to slander anybody.[33] Neither do our sources show that a *cautio* was a mandatory term of the sale contract. Nevertheless, in the absence of an insurance system, it is likely that a mechanism like the *cautio damni infecti* was routinely applied by private owners to protect their property against an unforeseeable but undoubtedly common urban risk. This practice is confirmed by a literary mention. In his famous speech held in 70 BC, Cicero states that a clause on the *damnum infectum* was inserted by Verres in a fraudulent construction contract, to keep up appearances and make it look genuinely lawful.[34]

Theoretically, owners freely enjoyed their own property and could dispose of it, obviously by selling it, but even by destroying it or letting it fall into ruin. It should consequently have been perfectly lawful for building owners to neglect their property to the point that it no longer served its original purpose. The *cautio damni*

[24] Similar views are expressed in different contexts by Dubouloz 2011: 71; Maganzani 2014: 67.
[25] The mechanism is detailed in the *Digest's* title 39.2 *De damno infecto et de suggrundis et proiectionibus* (Anticipated injury and house-eaves and projections). Burckhard 1875; MacCormack 1971.
[26] Jurists, however, remind that the compensation must be proportionate to the loss and remain moderate, as Ulpian puts it in a fragment where he, incidentally, condemns the 'immoderate luxury' (*immoderata luxuria*) of some houses adorned with pictures and carved stucco: *Dig.* 39.2.40 pr., Ulp. *Ad Sab.* 43.
[27] On the different *stipulationes praetoriae*, see Buckland 1921: 721-722.
[28] Tenants were indeed justified in fleeing and were not liable for any outstanding rent if there was a 'justified fear of collapse' (*iusto metu ruinae*), as Cassius (first half 1st c. AD) puts it (*Dig.* 39.2.28, Ulp. *Ad Ed.* 81). The fear could concern the building they were living in or even a neighbouring one. This is a case of justified abandonment, studied by Frier 1985: 92-105.
[29] *Dig.* 39.2.13.5, Ulp. *Ed.* 53: *Vicinis plane inquilinisque eorum et inquilinorum uxoribus cavendum esse ait Labeo, item his qui cum his morentur* (Labeo says that a cautio must obviously be given to neighbors, their tenants, and their tenants' wives as well as to those who reside with them). All texts from the *Digest*: Mommsen et al. 1886. Translation: Watson 1998.
[30] MacCormack 1971.
[31] Several texts in *Dig.* 39.2.40 detail how negotiations on the estimated amount of financial compensation can be complicated by the intervention of different parties, each possibly claiming a different portion of the final amount, depending on their exposure to the risk.

[32] Also see *Dig.* 39.2.18.8, Paul *Ad Ed.* 48. Although from the same author, the two texts differ slightly on the issue of the liability of the vendor. On both texts and the debate upon their authenticity, see MacCormack 1971: 301-309.
[33] *Dig.* 39.2.7 pr.
[34] Cic. *Ver.* 2.1.56 (146): *At ut videatur tamen res agi et non eripi pupillo* (to give it the appearance of a business arrangement and not a robbery of that boy [i.e. the underage son of the late contractor]). (Text and transl. Loeb Classical Library 221, Greenwood 1928).

infecti therefore constituted a serious restriction upon property rights.[35] However, the aim of this restriction was not only to achieve peaceful neighbourly relations but also to control an urban risk that potentially weighed heavily on the public interest and on everyone else's property as well. That is the reason why the *cautio damni infecti* was not a remedial but a precautionary measure, an aspect clearly illustrated by the fact that it applied to future damage only and that it could possibly be subject to an emergency procedure.

Dig. 39.2.2. Gaius libro 28 ad Edictum provinciale. *Damnum infectum est damnum nondum factum, quod futurum veremur.*

Anticipated injury is injury that has not yet occurred but which we fear may occur in the future.

Dig. 39.2.1 Ulpianus libro primo ad Edictum. *Cum res damni infecti celeritatem desiderat et periculosa dilatio praetori videtur, si ex hac causa sibi iurisdictionem reservaret, magistratibus municipalibus delegandum hoc recte putavit.*

Since anticipated injury is a matter that requires speedy handling and the praetor views as dangerous the delay that would arise if he reserved jurisdiction in such a case to himself, he rightly thought that the matter should be delegated to municipal magistrates.

Damnum infectum is not an isolated example in the Roman legal system of a legal action granted before any harm was actually done. The *Digest*'s next title, 39.3 'Water and the action to ward off rainwater' (*De aqua et aquae pluviae arcendae*), details the lawsuit farmers could bring against neighbours altering rainwater runoff, thus creating a flood risk. This action, as in the case of the risk of collapse, explicitly depended on an anticipated damage, not on an actual one (for which other actions existed).[36]

In the absence of documents recording the activity of Roman judicial courts, what can we establish with regard to the actual use of such a legal mechanism? It is possible that a very early version of the *actio damni infecti* existed in the XII Tables, since it is well established that the original remedy was a *legis actio*, before it was superseded by the praetorian mechanism,

sometime during the 2nd or the 1st century BC.[37] The first indications of its geographical dissemination come, on the other hand, from the body of private law itself. The title on the *damnum infectum* in the *Digest* indeed contains an unusually high number of fragments from the Provincial Edict, cited by Gaius. In fact, we know from the same Gaius that there was a whole chapter of the Provincial Edict specifically dedicated to the *cautio*.[38] It is probably from that source that derives the chapter 20 on *formulae* for *damnum infectum* in the *Lex (Rubria) de Gallia Cisalpina*, a Roman statute issued in 49 or 48 BC, dealing with local jurisdictions in the context of the enfranchisement of Cisalpine Gaul by Julius Caesar.[39]

A further provision ensured that the *cautio damni infecti* was efficiently enforced. If the owner of the threatening building refused either to make some repairs or to give the *cautio*, in spite of the praetor's request, the magistrate would concede to the plaintiff a *missio in possessionem damni infecti causa*, which could end with the aggrieved person being granted actual possession of the dilapidated house.

Dig. 39.2.4, Ulpianus libro primo ad Edictum. (...) 1. *Si intra diem a praetore constituendum non caveatur, in possessionem eius rei mittendus est. 'Eius rei' sic accipe, sive tota res sit sive pars sit rei. 2. An tamen is, qui non admittit, etiam pignoribus a magistratibus coerceatur? Non puto, sed in factum actione tenebitur: nam et si a praetore missus non admittatur, eadem actione utendum est. (...) 4. Si forte duretur non caveri, ut possidere liceat (quod causa cognita fieri solet) non duumviros, sed praetorem vel praesidem permissuros: item ut ex causa decedatur de possessione.*

(...) 1. If a *cautio* is not given within the period laid down by the praetor, the plaintiff must be granted *missio in possessionem* of the property in question. 'The property in question' is understood to mean either the whole property or a part thereof. 2. Can a party who does not admit the plaintiff be constrained by the magistrates even by means of pledges? I think not; but he will be liable to an action *in factum*, since that is the action that we must employ in the event of the plaintiff not being admitted despite a grant of *missio in possessionem* from the praetor. (...) 4. If failure to give a *cautio* should persist, permission to

---

[35] See the categorisation of legal mechanisms by Girard 1929: 278 and Johnston 1999: 71–76.

[36] *Dig.* 39.3.1, Ulp. *Ad Ed.* 53. *pr. Si cui aqua pluvia damnum dabit, actione aquae pluviae arcendae avertetur aqua (...). 1. Haec autem actio locum habet in damno nondum facto, opere tamen iam facto, hoc est de eo opere, ex quo damnum timetur (...)* (If rainwater is going to cause one injury, it can be averted by means of an action to ward off rainwater. [...] 1. This action is appropriate where no injury has yet been caused, but work of some sort has been carried out, that is, work from which injury is apprehended [...]).

[37] Kaser and Knütel 2008: 125. Gaius (*Inst.* 4.31) explains that the praetorian solution is easier and more efficient (*commodius ius et plenius*) than the old civil procedure. It is also referred to by Cicero, in the first half of the 1st century AD, as a common procedure in the construction business (Cic. *Verr.* 2.1.66 (146); Cic. *Top.* 4.22). More on that topic in Nörr 1982.

[38] Example in *Dig.* 39.2.8, Gaius *ad Edictum praetoris urbani, titulo de damno infecto* (Urban Praetor's Edict, Chapter on Anticipated Injury).

[39] *CIL* 11.1146. On the jurisdictional aspects concerning the competent magistrate to grant a *cautio* in this specific context, see Rainer 2005: 260, who shows that the *Lex* is derived from the *Edict of the peregrine praetor*.

take possession (which normally comes after the case has been investigated) will be given not by the *duumviri* but by the praetor or governor; similarly, when possession is to be abandoned on cause shown.

The magistrate could not compel a rebellious neighbour to give the *cautio* (*An tamen is, qui non admittit, etiam pignoribus a magistratibus coerceatur? Non puto*). The praetor could, however, issue a decree *in possessionem ire*, which allowed the plaintiff (to whom the *cautio* was refused) to temporarily take possession of the land but without ejecting the owner. This first step did not confer actual *possessio* of the adjacent building, but a second step could be taken and the owner of the threatening building was then exposed to an *actio in factum* (*in factum actione tenebitur*), based on that from which his liability was derived: his refusal to give the *cautio*. In a last resort, a second decree would be issued by a magistrate with *imperium* (*non duumviros, sed praetorem vel praesidem*), giving the actual right of *possessio* to the plaintiff over the adjacent property, or at least over a part of it (*sive tota res sit sive pars sit rei*).[40] The threat of a *missio in possessionem* would undoubtedly have been a great incentive for property owners to grant their neighbours the *cautio* they desired.[41]

There were other legal solutions for private individuals to protect their property against urban risks. The *nuntiatio operis novi*, for example, was useful to someone who had concerns about the works undertaken by a neighbour on adjacent land.[42] He was then allowed to serve a notice on the builder to cease work. It was, like the *cautio damni infecti*, a limitation to property rights, and also, interestingly, a mechanism used in case damage was feared.[43] This is, of course, not a coincidence as legal principles bear some similarities with the risk management approach: notably, both the legal system and the control of risks are based on the anticipation that damage (or a conflict leading to damage) will occur, although it is not possible to predict exactly where, when, in which conditions, or of what magnitude. That is why Roman private law arguably played a key role in the procedures of risk control, alongside other sets of solutions, either technical or political. It is, indeed, worth remembering that political decisions made by the emperors and given legal force are not separate from the risk prevention system we can observe in the private law. Rather, they are very much embedded within it. One of the conditions for serving a *nuntiatio operis novi* was indeed an incompatibility with building regulations established by *senatus consulta* and imperial *constitutions*.[44] Although the praetorian law contains

many rules designed to regulate the construction business, as we just saw, emperors were probably also prompted to act in some cases because, if legal solutions were available to private individuals, they could choose to act or not, depending on their own interests. In case they did not, public interest could be jeopardised.[45]

House demolition, between opportunities and constraints

Accidental collapses were not the only cause for the destruction of urban buildings in the Roman world. Strabo's description points out that houses in Rome were continually torn down by their owners.[46] The geographer explains that such a practice was made possible by the admirable wealth in natural resources that were transferred to the city from its surrounding territory. The depiction of such an abundance of commodities is, however, partly misleading. Although resources were certainly available, entrepreneurs were not unconcerned by the cost of building materials, as the development of an active salvaging sector plainly shows. Similarly, stating that demolitions happened to suit the wishes (πρὸς τὰς ἐπιθυμίας) of the owners only partly reflects the reality: literary and legal sources show that such enterprises were often part of a larger commercial project to increase an owner's profits on the housing market. Opportunities nonetheless had to be weighed against the costs incurred by demolition plans.

A letter from Cicero to his close friend Atticus reveals that the poor condition of his possessions gave him but little cause for concern, because he was actually seeing it as an opportunity to improve his investment, presumably on the rental market.

> **Cic. Att. 363 (14.9).** Scr. in Puteolano xv Kal. Mai. an. 44. <Cicero Attico Sal.> §1.*De re publica multa cognovi ex tuis litteris, quas quidem multiiugis accepi uno tempore a Vestori liberto. Ad ea autem quae requiris brevi respondebo. Primum vehementer me Cluviana delectant. Sed quod quaeris quid arcessierim Chrysippum, tabernae mihi duae corruerunt reliquaeque rimas agunt; itaque non solum inquilini sed mures etiam migraverunt. Hanc ceteri calamitatem vocant, ego ne incommodum quidem. O Socrate et Socratici viri! Numquam vobis gratiam*

---

[40] On this procedure, see Buckland 1921: 721.
[41] On the difficulties of implementing such a decree when either one of the buildings is held in co-ownership, see Dubouloz 2011: 256-263.
[42] *Dig.* 39.1 'Notice of New Work'.
[43] Buckland 1921: 722; Johnston 1999: 74; Kaser and Knütel 2008: 125.
[44] *Dig.* 39.1.1.16–17, Ulp. *Ad Ed.* 52; *Dig.* 39.1.5.9, Ulp. *Ad Ed.* 52.

[45] This can be observed when Augustus decided to clear the Tiber from all the rubble and debris that contributed to flood risk (Suet. *Aug.* 30). Although the management of rivers and riverbeds is the object of four titles of the Digest (*Dig.* 43.12; *Dig.*43.13; *Dig.*43.14; *Dig.*43.15) and many provisions are set out to prevent the obstruction of rivers, the praetor had no authority to act on his own in this matter. If no member of the riverside communities was ready to bring a legal action against a fellow resident, none of these solutions was implemented. That is probably one of the reasons why Augustus had to act. See Ronin 2022.
[46] Strabo *Geograph.* 5.3.7: καταβαλλόντων καὶ ἀνοικοδομούντων πρὸς τὰς ἐπιθυμίας ἕτερα ἐξ ἑτέρων.

referam. Di immortales, quam mihi ista pro nihilo! Sed tamen ea ratio aedificandi initur, consiliario quidem et auctore Vestorio, ut hoc damnum quaestuosum sit. (...)§3. quod quaeris iamne ad cen<ten>a Cluvianum, adventare videtur; sed primo anno l̄xxx detersimus.

Puteoli, 17 April 44. Cicero to Atticus. 1. I have learned a variety of political news from your letters, of which I received several in a batch from Vestorius' freedman. Let me briefly answer your enquiries. First, I am quite delighted with the Cluvius property. But you ask me why I have sent for Chrysippus: two of my shops have collapsed and the others are showing cracks, so that even the mice have moved elsewhere, to say nothing of the tenants. Other people call this a disaster, I don't call it even a nuisance. Ah Socrates, Socratics, I can never repay you! Heavens above, how utterly trivial such things appear to me! However, there is a building scheme under way, Vestorius advising and instigating, which should turn this loss into a source of profit. (...) 3. You ask whether the Cluvian property comes to 100,000 a year yet. It looks as though it is going to, but in the first year I have cleared 80,000. (Text and transl. Loeb Classical Library 491, Shackleton Bailey 1999)

Cluvius died in 45 BC, and Cicero inherited from him, amongst other properties, some shops (*tabernae*) in Puteoli. At that period, Cicero was spending most of his time either in Arpinum or in Tusculum, and Vestorius, another businessman of Puteoli, had dealt with the details of the inheritance.[47] The shops were obviously neglected to the point that two of them collapsed (*tabernae mihi duae corruerunt*) and the rest were not far from suffering the same fate: obviously a case of 'justified abandonment' since the tenants had fled.[48] Cicero, however, was taking the whole matter so light-heartedly because he saw in it a good opportunity to improve his position on the rental market. A construction project (*ratio aedificandi*) was on its way. Instrumental to that plan was the same Vestorius who was already involved in many different business transactions.[49] What is even more interesting for us is Cicero's insistence, in his next letter, that the collapse had not lowered the value of the estate.

Cic. Att. 365 (14.11) Scr. in Puteolano(?) XI Kal. Mai. an. 44. *§2. Cicero Attico Sal. de Cluviano, quoniam in re mea me ipsum diligentia vincis, res ad centena*

perducitur. Ruina rem non fecit deteriorem, haud scio an iam fructuosiorem.

Puteoli (?), 21 April 44. Cicero to Atticus. 2. As regards the Cluvius property, since your care for my interests exceeds my own, it's getting up to the 100,000 mark. The collapse of the buildings has not lowered the returns, indeed I rather think it may actually have increased them. (Text and transl. Loeb Classical Library 491, Shackleton Bailey 1999)

How exactly could the collapse of his buildings, and probably the demolition of the others whose walls were full of cracks, have helped Cicero improve his profits? It is likely that the 'building scheme' mentioned in the previous letter was intended to replace the original *tabernae* with larger buildings, allowing Cicero to lease to more tenants, maybe at a higher price, thus increasing the benefits from HS 80,000 to HS 100,000 a year.[50] This practice is reminiscent of Crassus, as reported by Plutarch.[51] Observing the damage inflicted by the frequent fires and collapses, he would purchase burnt houses and the adjacent ones at a trifling price and would then rebuild them.[52] Such a scheme probably required appropriate connections to the construction and/or demolition industry (indeed, Cicero explains that he had already called on the architect Chrysippus) and to have adequate access to building materials.[53] The costs could be appreciably offset through recycling and/or salvaging by sourcing second-hand materials, by reinvesting elements of the demolished building into a new project on the same site, or by reselling valuable pieces, such as bricks, stone, and even demolition debris.

The salvaging and recycling trade was indeed a prominent business in the construction sector, especially in the context of the exceptional urban growth of Rome and other Roman cities from the 2nd century BC onwards.[54] The activity was evidently well organised since dismantling requires specific equipment (scaffolding, lifting machines, rope, and pulleys) as well

---

[47] Cicero's share in Cluvius' inheritance additionally comprised the *horti Cluviani*, also situated in Puteoli. On the business relationship between Cluvius, Vestorius, and Cicero, see Andreau 1983.

[48] See note 28.

[49] Vestorius is also known for his role in the dyeing industry (Vitr. *De arch.* 7.11.1; Plin. *HN* 33.57.163) and was a successful financier and trader. More on this personality in Verboven 2012: 918–919, 930.

[50] D'Arms 1981: 49. On the profit surprisingly expected after a demolition, see Juvenal's and Martial's mockeries (Juv. 3. 220–223; Mart. *Epigrams* 3. 52).

[51] Plut. *Vit. Crass.* 2.3–4.

[52] Bruce Frier's analysis points out that Crassus' story, if we believe it, seems to be a very isolated example, from which much has been extrapolated, often without any real ground (Frier 1980: 32–34). Furthermore, it is not known if Crassus intended to resell the houses acquired at a very low price, which would make him a real speculator, or if he simply intended to reconstruct and lease them.

[53] According to Plutarch (*Vit. Crass.* 2.3–4), Crassus had a small army of 500 slaves, architects, and masons at his command.

[54] Recycling materials has always been common practice in construction. For a theoretical approach to recycling and case studies in different periods, see Brysbaert 2011; Kinney 2006. Concerning the Roman period, recycling and salvaging have long been associated with Late Antiquity, which is now widely questioned. For a new evaluation throughout the Roman period, see a comprehensive synthesis in Barker 2018.

as skilled labour. Materials had to be sorted according to what could be salvaged or just used as fill to level sites. In some cases, they were stored for subsequent use. All these operations required competence, capital, and networks, and the evidence clearly points towards a 'much more developed recycling economy than the casual reclamation of material following the demolition projects'.[55] Epigraphical evidence reveals not only that entrepreneurs could specialise in this line of business, as a painted sign for a shop in Pompeii shows,[56] but also that the profession itself was well established, as the mention of a *collegium subrutorum* in Rome, dated between AD 79 and 81, indicates.[57]

From imperial projects and the redevelopment of urban areas to specialised entrepreneurs acting at a local or regional level, or simply patrons refurbishing their respective houses, numerous and varied supply channels were exploited. The main reason for this was that second-hand materials had an economic value. This is of course evident in the case of skilfully carved capitals or marble decoration, but stones, bricks, wood, or metal elements also seem to have been systematically reclaimed and reused.[58] Indeed, second-hand materials were needed and, in some cases, probably much sought after. The study of marble-clad bars in Vesuvian cities remarkably demonstrates that the salvaging of marble was instrumental in bringing an elite fashion and taste for exotic stone to lower classes of Roman society.[59] More critically though, Roman construction techniques depended on recycled materials: much-needed lime was naturally obtained by burning limestone or marble, and the famous *opus caementicium* necessitated an aggregate composed of reused stones, broken tile, or brick rubble, thus making wide use of demolition debris.[60]

This picture of a flourishing salvaging market should not, however, overshadow the probably frequent occasions when building owners were reluctant to deal with rubble. If it could not acquire a certain value because recycled materials of that nature were needed nearby, evidence in some cases shows that debris mostly represented a hindrance.[61] Famously, the Ostian marshes were used to get rid of destruction debris after Rome's Great Fire of AD 64.[62] This was a very exceptional event, which required exceptional measures, but day-to-day solutions had to be found too. It has therefore been suggested by DeLaine and Barker that the boom in *opus caementicium*, in Rome, might partly be explained by the convenient solution it offered to dispose of rubble.[63]

Of course, in the collapse of a building, valuable materials were mingled together with more or less worthless debris. Landlords could thus be reluctant to pay for the cost of carefully sorting the crushed materials and be tempted to retrieve what was valuable and leave the rest on the site, irrespective of all the damage it was causing to public and private interests. To prevent that sort of situation from happening, jurists developed a 'take it or leave it' solution.

39.2.7, *Ulpianus libro 53 ad edictum.* 2. *Unde quaeritur, si ante, quam caveretur, aedes deciderunt neque dominus rudera velit egerere eaque derelinquat, an sit aliqua adversus eum actio. Et Iulianus consultus, si prius, quam damni infecti stipulatio interponeretur, aedes vitiosae corruissent, quid facere deberet is, in cuius aedes rudera decidissent, ut damnum sarciretur, respondit, si dominus aedium, quae ruerunt, vellet tollere, non aliter permittendum, quam ut omnia, id est et quae inutilia essent, auferret, nec solum de futuro, sed et de praeterito damno cavere eum debere: quod si dominus aedium, quae deciderunt, nihil facit, interdictum reddendum ei, in cuius aedes rudera decidissent, per quod vicinus compelletur aut tollere aut totas aedes pro derelicto habere.*

2. Therefore, there arises the question whether, if a house falls down before a *cautio* is given and the owner does not wish to remove the rubble, but abandons it, there is any action that can be brought against him. The case in which a ruinous house collapsed before a stipulation against anticipated injury had been introduced was put to Julian, and he was asked what the person onto whose house the rubble had fallen ought to do to secure reparation. He replied that if the owner of the house that had collapsed wished to take away the rubble, this should be permitted only if he took away everything, that is, including the useless material, and that he should give a *cautio* about not only future but also past injury; but that if the owner of the house which

---

[55] Barker 2018: 69.

[56] The late-Republican sign in *Insula* III.7, advertises for second-hand roof tiles (*CIL* 4. 7124). For more references, see Barker 2018: 60, n. 73.

[57] *CIL* 6. 940. As noted by Mommsen, *subruere* can mean 'demolish a house' but also 'cut down a tree'. Simon J. Barker follows the first meaning to deduce the existence of a category of entrepreneurs specialised in demolition (Barker 2011: 128; *contra* Davoine 2021: 104–105).

[58] Barker 2018: 79.

[59] Much of the marble used in the bars at Pompeii and Herculaneum was second-hand. Some might have come from left-overs from the production of flooring or revetment, but most of it seems to have been second-hand, generated by refurbishment of demolition projects of either public building of private houses (Fant *et al.* 2013).

[60] Vitruvius reminds that the strongest walls were made of old roofing tiles because they were weather-tested; Vitruv. *Arch.* 2.8.19.

[61] Jurists advocate against the demolition of a building illegally erected on a public ground for fear of the amount of debris it can generate (*Dig.* 43.8.2.17; *Dig.* 43.8.7). On debris, rubble, and ruins in general, see Davoine 2021. On the issue of managing demolition material for the continuation of construction in urban contexts, see Barker 2018: 51.

[62] Tac. *Ann.* 15.43.

[63] DeLaine 2001: 241–246; Barker 2018: 48.

had fallen down did nothing, an interdict should be granted to the person onto whose house the rubble had fallen by means of which his neighbor would be compelled either to remove the rubble or to regard the whole house as abandoned.

The owners of a collapsed building who wanted to avoid the costs of clearing the site could therefore do so by abandoning their entire property, valuable and worthless materials all jumbled up together.[64] In the case presented here to the 2nd-century jurist Julian and considered by Ulpian a century later, this option can constitute a compensation for the wronged neighbour who could look for valuable material in the debris pile since it was considered a *res derelicta*.[65] Alternatively, if the original owner wanted to recover the valuable material, he had to clear the site entirely, as the pile in its entirety belonged to him.[66]

Legal solutions demonstrate that some owners were reluctant to sort the debris, either because it did not contain anything valuable or because a sudden collapse made the salvaging of valuable pieces complicated and would therefore have consumed a lot of time and money.[67] Incidentally, the legal texts also address the issue of landlords, throughout Rome and the empire, who were wealthy enough not only to abandon their building materials but also to renounce, at least temporarily, the enjoyment of their land that could be cluttered up for a long period. In the meantime, piles of debris generated by the collapse were clearly hampering the traffic and creating a risk for adjacent properties, especially if only parts of the building had collapsed and the rest was threatening to do the same.

Finally, developers were acting and making their decisions within a normative framework which, albeit not as extensive as today's, could have represented a further constraint. The legal dossier contains a series of much-discussed *senatus-consulta*, rescripts

and municipal charters, amongst which the most significant are the *SC Hosidianum* from AD 47 and *Volusianum* from AD 56.[68] Inspired by emperor Claudius, the *SC Hosidianum* forbids the purchase of a house with the intention of dismantling it and making a profit by selling the building materials. The *SC Volusianum* complements this but contains a derogating provision in favour of the owner of a villa near Modena, where the disruption of the local market deprived the estate of commercial outlets. While the effects of the texts are quite clear, their purpose has been much debated. It has been thought for a long time that they were aimed at combating speculation, and especially the activity of *equites* and freedmen, against whom senators would have stood for upholding traditional values and the preservation of the urban landscape.[69] Although a commitment to protect the aesthetic aspects of the city (explicitly claimed by the senators) cannot be ruled out, a more convincing explanation, based on Roman inheritance and property law, has been proposed since.[70] The objective of the *senatus consultum* was in fact to keep together the different assets of one estate. Dismantling a house's building materials for commercial purposes was therefore forbidden, but owners retained the right to remove the different elements of the property as long as they kept them within the same patrimony, possibly for subsequent reuse. Such a piece of legislation could therefore, in effect, not prevent owners from demolishing a house, but it clearly constituted a constraint for entrepreneurs whose business depended, even partly, on the trade in materials.

The problem with the rental market...

The examples discussed so far only involve a limited number of actors: landlords and their neighbours. Potentially, the urban community at large was affected too, in the sense that ruins and piles of rubble could constitute a nuisance and a risk. Accidental collapses and deliberate demolitions brought further complications when buildings were occupied by tenants. Yet, amongst the studies on collapses, the evidence of the *locatio conductio* has so far failed to receive the consideration it deserves, despite the potential implications and far-reaching economic consequences the practice of demolition could entail when the property was leased.

[64] On this text and its interpretation, see Davoine 2021: 126–127 and 203.
[65] Around Julian's period, a similar solution is produced by Gaius (*Ad ed. Prov.* 1, *Dig.* 39.2.6) who reports that it is commonly accepted, although maybe not unanimously. Here it must be emphasised that the rubble does not become automatically a *res derelicta* that anyone can freely appropriate but needs to be legally abandoned, which implies the will (*animus*) of the original owner to abandon it, obviously to avoid the cost of clearing it. It seems, however, that the owner's will can be implicit, like a prolonged silence (*longo silentio*). That is what we can gather from Ulpian, *Ad ed.* 53 (*Dig.* 39.2.15.21).
[66] Further costs could accrue since the owner of the collapsed building, who had decided to retain (and therefore remove) the rubble, could also be compelled to rehabilitate the adjacent property damaged by the fall of building materials to its prior state. There is, however, no certainty that such an obligation existed. It depends entirely on whether the interdict *de ruderibus tollendi* was 'restitutory' or 'prohibitory', something about which our sources remain silent. For a synthesis of the different arguments, see De Castro-Camero 2017: 39-41.
[67] Barker provides some figures for the overcosts of recycling (and site clearing): Barker 2018: 84.

[68] The *senatus-consulta Hosidianum* and *Volusianum* are both published in *CIL* 10.1401. Alongside them must be cited the municipal charters of Tarentum (89–62 BC – *CIL* 1.590), of Urso (Caesarian time, published by Crawford 1996: 393-454), Malaca (Flavian time, published by Spitzl 1984), and Irni (Flavian time, published by González and Crawford 1986), and a rescript of Severus Alexander from AD 222 (*Cod. Iust.* 8.10.2), which are all conveniently gathered and discussed in two recent articles: Marano and Barker 2017; Davoine 2018.
[69] Phillips 1973; Garnsey 1976, in the first place. More references in Davoine 2018: 269-270.
[70] Thomas 1998, followed by Dubouloz 2011: 66-79 and Davoine 2018.

de la urbe tiene la ventaja de poder manejar tanto el registro arqueológico como la abundante información procedente de las fuentes textuales árabes, mientras que las investigaciones de los edificios de la Antigüedad suelen basarse exclusivamente en el registro material y en manuales del siglo XIX, de los cuales la referencia principal es Giovanni Pegoretti.[3]

El manejo conjunto de los registros textual y arqueológico: un diálogo necesario, pero no exento de incongruencias

Madīnat al-Zahrā' cuenta con más de un siglo de intervenciones arqueológicas, desde que en 1911 Ricardo Velázquez Bosco iniciase las excavaciones y comprobase que las ruinas de la hasta entonces denominada "Córdoba la Vieja" pertenecían a la ciudad palatina omeya. En las próximas siete décadas, los directores del yacimiento —el citado arquitecto (1911–1923), Félix Hernández (1923–1975) y Rafael Manzano (1975–1982)— destacaron por excavar la zona central del alcázar y restaurar algunos de los edificios allí encontrados, caso del célebre Salón de ʿAbd al-Raḥmān III (vid. **Figuras 1–2**). Asimismo, Basilio Pavón Maldonado excavó la mezquita aljama a partir de 1964.[4]

Los mayores avances en la investigación sobre el proceso constructivo de la ciudad palatina se han efectuado a partir de la creación del Conjunto Arqueológico de Madinat al-Zahra en 1985, especialmente durante el periodo de dirección de Antonio Vallejo (1985–2013; 2020-Actualidad). Si bien su equipo ha realizado alguna excavación, caso de la que permitió encontrar un tramo oriental del lienzo sur de la muralla urbana y una mezquita contigua a dicho muro,[5] la mayoría de las intervenciones se han destinado a la puesta en valor de la zona ya excavada —en total, alrededor del 10% de la ciudad— y a interpretar su relación con el resto de la urbe y con la articulación del territorio circundante. En este sentido, las fotografías aéreas y con película infrarroja y las prospecciones geofísicas han ayudado a conocer la distribución general del extenso tramo de la ciudad que aún no se ha exhumado.

Si atendemos a la puesta en valor de la zona excavada, la vertiente investigadora ha desempeñado un papel fundamental. Por un lado, el citado equipo ha llevado a cabo el análisis estratigráfico de las estructuras y sectores, interpretando las fases constructivas más importantes de la ciudad palatina. Por otro lado, se ha manejado conjuntamente la información procedente tanto del registro material como de las fuentes textuales, logrando, con hipótesis muy plausibles, identificar los edificios más importantes excavados

en la zona palatina con los nombres aparecidos en los textos árabes: la vivienda más alta del alcázar con la Dār al-Mulk "Casa del Poder"; la Vivienda de la Alberca con la casa del príncipe heredero; el Salón de ʿAbd al-Raḥmān III con al-Maŷlis al-Šarqī "el Salón Oriental"; y la vivienda del extremo suroriental del sector privado del alcázar con la dār "casa" de Ŷaʿfar.[6]

Si nos centramos en el análisis de las fuentes textuales árabes, aquellas coetáneas a la existencia de Madīnat al-Zahrā' en el siglo IVh./X contienen escasa información sobre la ciudad. Por ejemplo, la obra geográfica de Ibn Ḥawqal, viajero oriental que visitó al-Andalus entre 337h./948 y 340h./951–952, ofrece una somera descripción de la urbe palatina, enumerando algunos de los elementos de la infraestructura urbana que ya se habían construido para esa época.[7] Una segunda fuente del siglo IVh./X es el diccionario biográfico de Ibn al-Faraḍī, quien recopila las biografías de los ulemas de al-Andalus, incluidos aquellos nacidos, residentes y muertos en Madīnat al-Zahrā'. Si bien los datos sobre las edificaciones de la ciudad palatina se reducen a la mención del qaṣr "alcázar" y del ŷāmiʿ "mezquita aljama", la obra es un claro indicador cronológico de la vigencia de la urbe entre la década de 330h./941–951 y finales del siglo IVh./X, periodo en el que residieron allí todos los biografiados.[8]

El autor coetáneo a Madīnat al-Zahrā' que mayor información aporta sobre la urbe palatina es ʿĪsà b. Aḥmad al-Rāzī, un cronista de la corte omeya de quien conservamos su detallada narración de los años de gobierno del segundo califa omeya al-Ḥakam II entre 360h./970–971 y 364h./974–975.[9] Entonces, la ciudad palatina era la principal sede de la administración califal y la residencia del soberano, por lo que se trataba del escenario en el que se desarrollaron los acontecimientos políticos más relevantes de aquella época: el recorrido de las delegaciones de poderes extranjeros desde Córdoba hasta ser recibidos en audiencia por el califa dentro de la ciudad palatina; la celebración en el alcázar de al-Zahrā' de las dos festividades musulmanas más importantes —la fiesta de la Ruptura del Ayuno y la fiesta del Sacrificio—; etc. Estas referencias a la ciudad y especialmente a la zona palatina, si bien son poco descriptivas —al-Rāzī escribía para un entorno cortesano familiarizado con la urbe—, han posibilitado que el Conjunto Arqueológico de Madinat al-Zahra identificase ciertas estructuras excavadas con edificios del alcázar mencionados en la crónica.

---

[3] Pegoretti 1843; 1869.
[4] López Martínez de Marigorta, Manzano Moreno 2018: 28–29, 50–51.
[5] Vallejo Triano 2009: 214–223.

[6] Vallejo Triano 2010a: 130, 221, 465, 468, figs 9, 41, 44, 59; 2016: 437–440, 447–450.
[7] Ibn Ḥawqal 1967: 108, 111–113.
[8] Ibn al-Faraḍī 1954: I, 28 (Nº 47), 271–272 (Nº 707), 332–333 (Nº 857); 1988: II, 57–59 (Nº 1245).
[9] El testimonio de al-Rāzī lo reprodujo íntegramente el autor del siglo Vh./XI Ibn Ḥayyān en el *Muqtabis VII*, obra cronística que consistió en el texto de ʿĪsà b. Aḥmad y en unos escasos pasajes añadidos por Ibn Ḥayyān: Ibn Ḥayyān 1965; Manzano Moreno 2019: 24–28.

Ciudad   Alcázar:

Mezquita sudoriental   Sector oficial

_{149.93} Cota   Sector privado

--- Muralla

0   100 m.   200 m.

Figura 1. Plano de Madīnat al-Zahrā'. Elaborado a partir de: Vallejo Triano, 2010a, fig. 7.

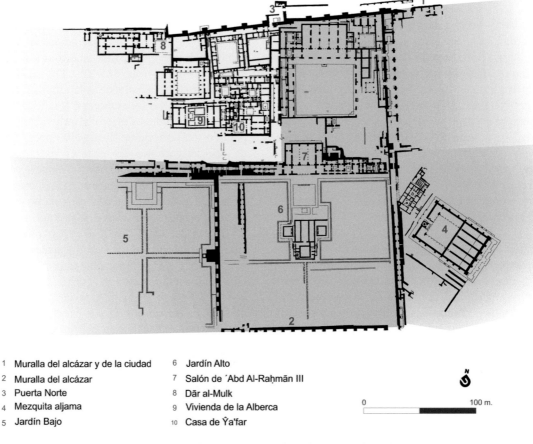

1	Muralla del alcázar y de la ciudad	6	Jardín Alto
2	Muralla del alcázar	7	Salón de ´Abd Al-Raḥmān III
3	Puerta Norte	8	Dār al-Mulk
4	Mezquita aljama	9	Vivienda de la Alberca
5	Jardín Bajo	10	Casa de Ŷa'far

0   100 m.

Figura 2. Plano del alcázar de Madīnat al-Zahrā'. Elaborado a partir de: Vallejo Triano, 2004, 72.

Si atendemos a las obras árabes que a partir del siglo VIh./XII tratan sobre Madīnat al-Zahrā', los arabistas Ana Labarta, Carmen Barceló y Mohamed Meouak han analizado el proceso de transmisión de los datos supuestamente de época califal que contienen. Los investigadores advierten sobre la necesaria crítica textual de dicha información antes de su uso en las interpretaciones históricas, pues algunas de estas fuentes tardías compilan datos históricos junto a leyendas e incorrecciones de copia y atribución —generalmente, adjudicando pasajes a prestigiosos escritores cercanos al periodo califal, caso de Ibn Ḥayyān—. También se produce una tendencia hacia el creciente uso de datos cuantitativos a medida que la obra es más lejana al periodo omeya. Los citados arabistas destacan igualmente la importancia de conocer el objetivo de la redacción de cada fuente tardía. Por ejemplo, el autor del siglo XIh./XVII al-Maqqarī escribió dos obras, tituladas *Nafḥ al-ṭīb* y *Azhār al-riyāḍ*, con el propósito de recopilar toda la información sobre la literatura de al-Andalus y el Magreb existente hasta su época, independientemente del origen histórico o legendario de dichos datos.[10]

Otra vía que está contribuyendo a problematizar la información aportada por las obras textuales tardías es la comparación de sus datos con los obtenidos a través del registro arqueológico. Si nos centramos en el mármol empleado en el levantamiento de Madīnat al-Zahrā', las fuentes a partir del siglo VIh./XII exponen que una significativa proporción de la piedra marmórea provenía de fuera de al-Andalus, específicamente, del imperio bizantino, Ifrīqiya[11] y el territorio franco. Sin embargo, no existen indicios materiales de ese lejano origen. Al contrario, los análisis químicos y petrográficos impulsados por el Conjunto Arqueológico de Madinat al-Zahra apuntan a que las losas de mármol usadas como pavimento en las estancias del alcázar procedieron de canteras de Estremoz (Portugal) y Almadén de la Plata (Sevilla).[12]

El presente trabajo es una primera aproximación al tiempo y el coste de la construcción de Madīnat al-Zahrā', centrándonos en el proceso de edificación vinculado al uso de la piedra calcarenita. Justamente, este fue el material constructivo más empleado en la ciudad palatina, al menos en las áreas que se han excavado hasta la actualidad: tanto las cimentaciones de los edificios como sus muros se levantaron con sillares de calcarenita, siendo también la piedra más utilizada en las losas de los pavimentos.[13] Este

Figura 3. Marcas de cajas de extracción de una cantera de Santa Ana de la Albaida.

material se habría obtenido mayoritariamente en las canteras de Santa Ana de la Albaida (*vid.* **Figura 3**).[14] A la par, las fuentes textuales a partir del siglo VIh./XII aportan datos numéricos en relación con el uso de la piedra como elemento constructivo. En las próximas líneas realizaremos la crítica textual de estos datos cuantitativos, de cara a conocer las cadenas de transmisión de la información; mientras que, en los próximos apartados, compararemos los datos numéricos con el análisis del registro material e interpretaremos las incongruencias que puedan existir entre ambos.

Centrándonos en el estudio de los datos cuantitativos relacionados con el empleo constructivo de la

---

[10] Labarta Gómez, Barceló Torres 1987: 93–94, 101–102, 104–105; Meouak 2004: 54–58.

[11] Circunscripción que, durante el periodo medieval, coincidía aproximadamente con la superficie actual de Túnez, el noreste de Argelia y Tripolitana.

[12] Vallejo Triano 2010a: 116–117, 359–360.

[13] *Op. cit.*, 86, 104, 295–296, 308–310, 313–314 (figs 255–256), 344–346 (fig. 289).

[14] Santa Ana de la Albaida forma, junto con Castillo de Maimón, Peñatejada y Cuevas Romanas, las canteras de piedra calcarenita situadas en las faldas de Sierra Morena, a una distancia de 2 a 5 km respecto a la ciudad de Córdoba. Todas ellas estaban ya activas en época romana, en el caso de las canteras del Castillo de Maimón en torno al s. I d.C., tal y como lo atestigua la presencia de una cisterna construida a base de *opus caementicium y signinum*; en tanto que la explotación de Santa Ana y Peñatejada se inició mediante galerías: Courault 2015: 39; 2016a: 329–330; 2016b; Penco Valenzuela 2002; Penco Valenzuela, Moreno Almenara, Gutiérrez Deza 2004: 242; Courault, Ruiz Arrebola, Borrego, en prensa. Centrándonos en el periodo andalusí, Santa Ana de Albaida, que ofrecía una gran cantidad de recursos pétreos, abasteció la práctica totalidad del ambicioso proyecto *ex novo* de Madīnat al-Zahrā': Vallejo Triano, Fernández Barba 2010. Las canteras localizadas al noreste de Córdoba, por su parte, suministraron a esta última ciudad. Muestra de ello es que las piedras de la reconstrucción omeya de la muralla romana que han recibido una analítica —obtenidas en el tramo de Paseo de Colón Nº 9— procedan de las Cuevas Romanas: Courault, Ruiz Arrebola 2019.

calcarenita, los hemos dividido en 4 grupos de información:

I. El periodo de ejecución del proyecto urbanístico de Madīnat al-Zahrā'.

II. Los recursos logísticos (materiales, animales y humanos) diarios en la construcción de la ciudad palatina.

III. Los medios humanos diarios en el levantamiento de la mezquita aljama.

IV. El gasto anual y total de la creación de la urbe palatina.

En cuanto al primer grupo de información, relativa al periodo de construcción de al-Zahrā', contamos con dos versiones. La primera indica que el levantamiento acaeció durante el califato de 'Abd al-Raḥmān III, iniciándose en 325h./936 y alargándose hasta el fallecimiento de este soberano en 350h./961. Esta versión se incluye en un pasaje de Maslama b. 'Abd Allāh, transmitido por los autores Ibn Gālib y al-Maqqarī de los siglos VIh./XII y XIh./XVII, respectivamente. Los datos de estos autores apuntan a que el citado Maslama desempeñó un relevante papel en la edificación de Madīnat al-Zahrā', pues Ibn Gālib lo describe como el *muhandis nāẓir* "arquitecto supervisor" de la construcción de la ciudad palatina, mientras que al-Maqqarī lo califica de *'arīf* "alarife" y *muhandis* "arquitecto". Desgraciadamente, carecemos de más datos en las fuentes que traten sobre Maslama y señalen claramente hacia su historicidad. En el caso de al-Maqqarī, precisa la procedencia de la información con la siguiente oración: *qāla* Ibn Ḥayyān: *Alfaytu bi-jaṭṭ* Ibn Daḥḥūn *al-faqīh, qāla* Maslama b. 'Abd Allāh *al-'arīf al-muhandis* "dijo Ibn Ḥayyān: Encontré escrito de puño y letra del alfaquí Ibn Daḥḥūn, que había dicho el alarife y arquitecto Maslama b. 'Abd Allāh".[15] Según ello, la cadena de transmisión habría sido: Maslama b. 'Abd Allāh → Ibn Daḥḥūn → Ibn Ḥayyān → al-Maqqarī. En el caso del alfaquí Ibn Daḥḥūn, tampoco disponemos de más información sobre él que permita contextualizarlo.

Si atendemos a la segunda versión sobre el periodo de ejecución de la ciudad palatina, se recoge en dos pasajes trasmitidos por al-Maqqarī. De acuerdo con ellos, si bien el califa 'Abd al-Raḥmān III inició el proyecto urbanístico en 325h./936, las obras se habrían extendido al gobierno de su hijo y califa al-Ḥakam II hasta su muerte en 366h./976, de modo que la construcción habría durado alrededor de 40 años.[16]

El segundo grupo de información se centra en los recursos materiales, animales y humanos diarios que fueron necesarios para el levantamiento de Madīnat al-Zahrā'. Estos datos también proceden del ya citado pasaje del arquitecto supervisor de las obras, Maslama b. 'Abd Allāh, transmitido por Ibn Gālib y al-Maqqarī. Variantes del mismo pasaje las reproducen otros autores —la obra anónima *Ḏikr bilād al-Andalus*, Ibn 'Iḏārī, Ibn al-Jaṭīb y al-Nuwayrī, todos ellos del siglo VIIIh./XIV—, pero sin atribuírselo al arquitecto Maslama. A continuación, enumeramos los medios gastados diariamente en el levantamiento de la ciudad, poniendo en negrita la información de Ibn Gālib[17] y sin negrita los datos del resto de los autores que difieren respecto a los del primero:

- **6.000 sillares, que Ibn Gālib denomina como** *ṣajr manḥūt muḥkam mu'addal* **"piedra tallada, perfeccionada e igualada".** La obra *Ḏikr bilād al-Andalus* también aporta la cifra de 6.000 sillares, en este caso describiéndolos como *ṣajr manŷūr* "piedra alisada" e igualada.[18] Ibn 'Iḏārī expone que, además de 6.000 sillares o piedras alisadas, se utilizaban otras para el *tablīṭ fī l-asās* "empedrado de la cimentación".[19] Ibn al-Jaṭīb, por su parte, fija la cantidad de sillares o piedras alisadas en 5.000, a las que habría que sumar el *ṣajr al-balīṭ wa-l-ta'sīs* "piedra del pavimento y de la cimentación".[20] Por último, al-Maqqarī sitúa nuevamente en 6.000 el número de sillares o piedras talladas, alisadas e igualadas, a los que añade las piedras sin igualar y las empleadas en el *tablīṭ* "pavimentación".[21] En definitiva, los datos de las distintas fuentes textuales apuntan a que, a diario, se utilizaron entre 5.000 y 6.000 sillares destinados al levantamiento de los muros de los edificios, a los que sumar la piedra usada en la pavimentación y la cimentación, parte de ella sin igualar. Toda esta piedra aludiría a la calcarenita. Ciertamente, en líneas anteriores hemos explicado que las excavaciones arqueológicas han permitido constatar el uso de sillares de calcarenita tanto en los muros como en las cimentaciones, así como la abundante presencia de losas de calcarenita en los pavimentos. En el caso de los cimientos, Antonio Vallejo informa que «se emplearon sillares de labra tosca, sin aristar ni carear, de dimensiones muy variables»,[22] lo cual señala en la misma dirección que las piedras sin igualar citadas por al-Maqqarī.

- *Murtil* **"mortero".** El registro material permite constatar que se trataba de un mortero rico en cal.[23]

---

[15] Ibn Gālib 1956: 31; al-Maqqarī 1968: I, 567–568; 1940: II, 269.
[16] Al-Maqqarī 1968: I, 565, 569; 1940: II, 267, 271. Existe una tercera versión sobre la duración de la construcción de Madīnat al-Zahrā', transmitida por el autor del siglo VIIIh./XIV al-Nuwayrī. Según él, el levantamiento de la urbe costó 12 años: al-Nuwayrī 1917: 61–62. Sin embargo, todas las cifras recogidas en este pasaje contienen el número 12, por lo que apunta hacia el redondeo de al menos algunas de ellas para la inclusión de dicho número, que tiene un cierto carácter simbólico dentro del Islam.

[17] Ibn Gālib 1956: 31–32.
[18] *Ḏikr bilād al-Andalus* 1983: 162.
[19] Ibn 'Iḏārī 1980: II, 209, 231.
[20] Ibn al-Jaṭīb 2003: II, 38.
[21] Al-Maqqarī 1968: I, 526, 567; 1940: II, 269.
[22] Vallejo Triano 2010a: 308.
[23] *Op. cit.*, 296.

- **1.400 *zawāmil* "acémilas, mulos".** De ellas, 400 eran propiedad del *sulṭān* "Estado [omeya]", mientras que las otras 1.000 pertenecían a *akriyā'* "arrendadores" por cuya *uŷra* "alquiler" se pagaban mensualmente 3.000 dinares de oro *ŷa'farí*,[24] es decir, 3 dinares por cada mulo. La obra *Ḏikr bilād al-Andalus* sitúa la cifra de *dawābb* "acémilas" en 1.500, indicando que por cada mulo alquilado se pagaban al día 2 dírhams.[25] Teniendo en cuenta que la mayoría de los meses del calendario musulmán tienen 30 días, se destinarían 60 dírhams al mes por el alquiler de cada mulo. A su vez, considerando que un dinar *ŷa'farí* equivale a 17 dírhams,[26] se abonarían 3 dinares y medio al mes por un mulo alquilado. Si atendemos a al-Maqqarī, reproduce dos variantes distintas del número de animales de carga: en un caso, lo fija en 1.500 acémilas, al igual que el *Ḏikr bilād al-Andalus*; en el otro caso, se transmiten los mismos datos que Ibn Gālib, de modo que los mulos son 1.400, 400 pertenecientes al poder omeya y 1.000 a los arrendadores.[27] En conclusión, el califato emplearía diariamente entre 1.400 y 1.500 bestias de carga en la construcción de la ciudad palatina, pagando por alrededor de 1.000 de ellas un alquiler de 3.000 a 3.500 dinares mensuales.

- **1.000 trabajadores.**[28] Estos se dividían en 300 *bunā* "albañiles" hábiles, 200 *naŷŷārūn* "carpinteros" diestros y 500 *uŷarā'* "asalariados". Junto con estos 1.000 trabajadores, en la construcción se utilizaban *'abīd* "esclavos" que eran *a'lāŷ al-naṣārà* "cristianos extranjeros". En cuanto a la información transmitida por el *Ḏikr bilād al-Andalus* y al-Maqqarī, podría proceder de un testimonio distinto al del arquitecto Maslama b. 'Abd Allāh. Indicio de ello es que al-Maqqarī no incluya dichos datos dentro del pasaje de Maslama que recoge, sino que se los atribuye a un genérico cronista de al-Andalus. Por un lado, el *Ḏikr bilād al-Andalus* expone que, diariamente en la construcción de al-Zahrā', los hombres[29] con una *uŷra* "salario" ganaban un dírham y medio y los *mu'allimūn* "maestros [artesanos]" 3 dírhams, además de emplearse 10.000 *juddām* "esclavos" hombres.[30] Por otro lado, al-Maqqarī indica que al levantamiento de la ciudad palatina se destinaron al día 10.000 *juddām* y *fa'ala* "trabajadores". Se les pagaba diariamente 1 dírham

y medio, 2 dírhams o 3 dírhams.[31] En definitiva, los autores árabes señalan hacia el uso diario de 9.000 a 10.000 esclavos cristianos de fuera del mundo islámico y 1.000 trabajadores asalariados. Dentro de estos últimos, había 300 albañiles y 200 carpinteros que son descritos como especialmente hábiles, por lo que una hipótesis plausible es que se tratase de maestros artesanos a los que se pagaba 3 dírhams diarios, en tanto que los 500 trabajadores restantes, que son definidos genéricamente como asalariados, podrían ser quienes recibiesen 1 dírham y medio al día.[32]

- **500 cargas**[33] de *ŷīr* "cal" y otras tantas de *ŷibs* "yeso". Al-Maqqarī, por su parte, plantea que cada 3 días se empleaban 1.100 cargas de cal y el mismo número de las de yeso,[34] es decir, 367 cargas diarias de cada una. En síntesis, se utilizarían diariamente entre 367 y 500 cargas de cal y la misma cantidad de yeso. Los datos del registro material indican que, además de utilizar la cal para el mortero, los dos citados materiales eran esenciales en los enlucidos que cubrían la gran mayoría de los paramentos de los edificios excavados.[35] Precisamente, existían tres tipos de enlucidos: los de cal, que se solían priorizar en los paramentos exteriores por su gran resistencia a la humedad; los de yeso, que se tendían a usar en el interior de las estancias; y bastardos de cal y yeso.[36]

Respecto al tercer grupo de información, al-Maqqarī reproduce un pasaje del biógrafo Ibn al-Faraḍī, en el que trata sobre los medios humanos existentes en la construcción de la mezquita aljama de Madīnat al-Zahrā'. De acuerdo con él, en el levantamiento del oratorio se habrían empleado diariamente 1.000 trabajadores hábiles, divididos en 300 albañiles, 200 carpinteros, y 500 asalariados y de otras *ṣanā'i'* "oficios". Completaron esta mezquita de 5 *abhā* "naves" en 48 días, en 329h./941.[37] Centrándonos en el análisis de dichos datos, uno de ellos sería la propia atribución del pasaje a Ibn al-Faraḍī: el diccionario biográfico titulado *Tārīj 'ulamā' al-Andalus*, consistente en la obra del

---

[24] En árabe, se denominan *danānīr min al-ḏahab al-ŷa'farí* "dinares de oro ŷa'farí".

[25] Dicha moneda de plata se designa *darāhim* "dírhams": *Ḏikr bilād al-Andalus* 1983: 162.

[26] Esta equivalencia es explicada por: Manzano Moreno 2015: 152–155.

[27] Al-Maqqarī 1968: I, 526, 567–568; 1940: II, 269.

[28] Ibn Gālib los cita en singular, como *'āmil* "trabajador".

[29] Se mencionan en singular, como *raŷul* "hombre".

[30] *Ḏikr bilād al-Andalus* 1983: 162.

[31] Al-Maqqarī 1968: I, 526.

[32] El autor oriental al-Nuwayrī transmite un pasaje que expone que, en la construcción de al-Zahrā', se emplearon diariamente 1.000 albañiles, cada uno de los cuales tenía a su cargo 12 *raqqāṣ* "peones". Ello aporta una cifra de 12.000 personas involucradas en las obras, coincidente con el número de 12.000 *ṣanā'i'* "trabajadores manuales" que, según el autor, el califa 'Abd al-Raḥmān III obtuvo en las expediciones que realizó contra los *rūm* "cristianos de fuera del mundo islámico": al-Nuwayrī 1917: 61–62; Castejón Calderón 1961–1962: 154. Tal y como hemos señalado anteriormente, tomamos las cifras aportadas por al-Nuwayrī con suma cautela, pues todas ellas, incluidas otras que no citamos, contienen el número 12, apuntando hacia el redondeo de al menos ciertas cifras.

[33] Se citan en singular, como *ḥiml* "carga".

[34] Al-Maqqarī 1968: I, 568; 1940: II, 269.

[35] Vallejo Triano 2010a: 321–322.

[36] Blanco-Varela, Puertas Maroto, Palomo Sánchez 1997: 29–43.

[37] Al-Maqqarī 1968: I, 564; 1940: II, 265–266.

citado autor que se ha conservado hasta la actualidad, no contiene el pasaje estudiado, por lo que no hemos podido confirmar su atribución al biógrafo. En cuanto al número tanto de trabajadores en general como de artesanos de cada oficio empleados en la creación de la aljama, son los mismos que los aportados por el ya examinado testimonio de Maslama b. 'Abd Allāh, si bien él relaciona la cifra con la construcción del conjunto de la ciudad y no del oratorio. Ante ello, existen dos opciones. Una primera posibilidad es que la citada cantidad de trabajadores fuese originaria de un pasaje que tratase sobre la urbe palatina, pero que las incorrecciones de transmisión hubiesen provocado la creación de una variante del pasaje en el que se atribuyese dicho número de constructores a la aljama. La segunda opción —teniendo en cuenta que en el siguiente apartado explicaré que la aljama y otras grandes obras de al-Zahrā', caso de la muralla urbana, no se levantaron de un modo coetáneo, sino a lo largo de un proceso constructivo que duró décadas— es que los 1.000 trabajadores representasen el número aproximado de constructores asalariados que la ciudad dispuso en la ejecución de todo el proyecto urbanístico de la ciudad, de modo que en ocasiones se emplearían en un edificio como la mezquita aljama, y en otras ocasiones en obras como la de la muralla. Finalmente, si comparamos la información del pasaje sobre la creación del oratorio con la obtenida a través de la excavación de dicha mezquita, hay datos que coinciden y otros que no: en cuanto a los primeros, el edificio hallado también dispone de 5 naves;[38] respecto a los segundos, la lápida fundacional encontrada informa que el oratorio se habría construido en 333h./944–945, en vez de en la fecha de 329h./941 citada por al-Maqqarī.[39]

El cuarto grupo de información versa sobre el gasto anual y total de la construcción de la ciudad palatina. Procede de la narración de un miembro de la *ahl al-jidma* "gente de la servidumbre" de al-Zahrā' que recogió el cronista Ibn Ḥayyān, siendo transmitido por Ibn Gālib y al-Maqqarī. Variantes de dicho pasaje han sido también reproducidos por otros autores, pero sin atribuírselo al citado sirviente de la ciudad palatina. A continuación, expondremos en negrita la información aportada por Ibn Gālib,[40] en tanto que los datos discordantes del resto de los autores los apuntaremos sin negrita:

• **Cada año, la *nafaqa* "gasto" en el levantamiento de Madīnat al-Zahrā' fue de 300.000 dinares metálicos de oro.[41] La financiación anual suponía un tercio de la *ŷibāya* "recaudación tributaria" del califa 'Abd al-Raḥmān III, destinándose otro tercio al mantenimiento del *ŷund* "ejército" y el último tercio a los *jazā'in* "tesoros [del Estado]".** El dato de 300.000 dinares anuales de gasto es

igualmente transmitido por al-Maqqarī,[42] mientras que la reserva de un tercio de la tributación califal a la financiación de la construcción de la ciudad palatina también la recoge Yāqūt.[43] En cuanto a Ibn 'Iḏārī, Ibn Jallikān —que transmite un pasaje de Ibn Baškuwāl—, el *Ḏikr bilād al-Andalus* y dos testimonios de la obra de al-Maqqarī, coinciden en señalar que la recaudación anual del califato de 'Abd al-Raḥmān III estuvo formada por 5.480.000 dinares procedentes de las *kuwar* "coras, circunscripciones provinciales" y *qurà* "alquerías",[44] además de 765.000 dinares provenientes del *mustajlaṣ* "patrimonio del soberano" y de las *aswāq* "zocos".[45] Ello supondría que, en total, la tributación del citado soberano sería de 6.245.000 dinares al año, un tercio de lo cual se correspondería con 2.081.667 dinares. En cuanto a estos dinares, no se especifica que se trate de una moneda metálica, por lo que lo más probable es que se refiera al *dīnār darāhīm* "dinar de dírhams", esto es, la moneda de cuenta en la que la hacienda omeya solía valorar su recaudación. Teniendo en cuenta que este dinar equivalía a 8 dírhams,[46] ello supondría que los 2.081.667 dinares de dírhams se convertirían en 979.608 dinares de oro. Otro dato a tener en cuenta es que existen dos variantes dentro de la información que los autores transmiten sobre el tercio de la tributación dedicado a la actividad edilicia: si bien Ibn Jallikān —tanto su obra como el pasaje que le atribuye al-Maqqarī—, Yāqūt e Ibn Gālib indican que el tercio de la recaudación se destinaba a la *'imāra* "construcción" de al-Zahrā';[47] Ibn 'Iḏārī y un testimonio de al-Maqqarī se refieren a que dicha proporción de la tributación se destinó a la *binā'* "construcción" en general.[48] Por consiguiente, los dos últimos autores apuntan a que los 979.608 dinares de oro anuales se emplearían, además de en el proyecto urbanístico de Madīnat al-Zahrā', en la articulación y mantenimiento del resto de las infraestructuras del califato omeya. Los registros textual y material ofrecen numerosos datos sobre la gran inversión de la administración califal en la construcción y reparación de fortalezas, puentes, caminos, ciudades, etc. a lo largo de los extensos dominios omeyas. Por consiguiente, si aproximadamente los otros dos tercios de la recaudación se destinaban al ejército y al tesoro

---

[38] Pavón Maldonado 1967: 223.
[39] Martínez Núñez, Acién Almansa 2004: 111, 117–118, 158 (lám. 10).
[40] Ibn Gālib 1956: 32.
[41] Se citan en singular, como *dīnār 'uyūn^(an) ḏahab^(an)* "dinar metálico aúreo".

[42] Al-Maqqarī 1968: I, 568; 1940: II, 269.
[43] Yāqūt 1977: III, 161.
[44] La alquería era la mínima unidad impositiva del mundo rural: López Martínez de Marigorta 2020: 362.
[45] Ibn 'Iḏārī y uno de los testimonios de al-Maqqarī son quienes precisan que los 5.480.000 dinares se percibían en las coras y las alquerías, mientras que los otros autores ofrecen la cifra sin indicar su origen: Ibn Jallikān 1977: V, 26; Ibn 'Iḏārī 1980: II, 231–232; *Ḏikr bilād al-Andalus* 1983: 164; al-Maqqarī 1968: I, 524–525, 569; 1940: II, 271.
[46] Manzano Moreno 2015: 150–154.
[47] Ibn Jallikān 1977: V, 26; al-Maqqarī 1968: I, 524; Yāqūt 1977: III, 161; Ibn Gālib 1956: 32.
[48] Ibn 'Iḏārī 1980: II, 232; al-Maqqarī 1968: I, 569; 1940: II, 271.

del Estado,[49] lo más plausible es que la partida de 979.608 dinares incluyese todas las obras del califato. Con todo, los 300.000 dinares que, según el pasaje del miembro de la servidumbre de al-Zahrāʾ, se destinaron a la ciudad palatina continuaría siendo una proporción muy relevante del gasto anual del califato en infraestructuras, consistiendo en algo menos de su tercio.

- El *infāq* "gasto" total de la construcción de la ciudad palatina fue de 15 erarios, denominados en singular *bayt māl* "erario". Al-Maqqarī transmite la misma información.[50] Si atendemos al significado del término *bayt māl* en el contexto de la valoración del gasto edilicio de la urbe palatina, hay dos posibilidades. Por un lado, ciertos autores lo emplean para indicar el valor del erario omeya durante el gobierno de un determinado soberano. En el caso de ʿAbd al-Raḥmān III, Ibn Ḥawqal señala que el erario de este califa era de alrededor de 20.000.000 dinares en 340h./951–952,[51] mientras que Ibn Jaldūn expone que cuando falleció dicho soberano en 350h./961 se situaba en 15.000.000 dinares.[52] Teniendo en cuenta que ambas cifras aludan a dinares de dírhams, es decir, a la moneda de cuenta manejada por la hacienda omeya, se traducirían en 9.411.765 y 7.058.824 dinares de oro, respectivamente. Por otro lado, el *Ḏikr bilād al-Andalus* describe la *bayt māl* como una unidad de cuenta equivalente a 1.000.000 dinares de peso legal y justo,[53] por lo que se tratarían de dinares de oro.[54]

Una ciudad palatina con dos grandes fases constructivas en un breve espacio de tiempo

Madīnat al-Zahrāʾ se emplazó 7 km al oeste de Córdoba, donde confluyen las laderas inferiores de Sierra Morena y el valle del Guadalquivir. Esta orografía posibilitó que la ciudad palatina se organizase en tres plataformas, tal y como el geógrafo al-Idrīsī describe: la terraza superior consistía en la zona palatina; la intermedia en los jardines y huertos; mientras que la inferior contenía la mezquita aljama y el caserío.[55] Las intervenciones arqueológicas

han confirmado esta distribución. Ciertamente, el califato construyó la ciudad como una escenificación del orden social existente en al-Andalus, en el que la alta jerarquía de la administración omeya, residente en el alcázar, gobernaba sobre los súbditos, representados por los habitantes de la plataforma inferior de la ciudad.

El análisis estratigráfico de las zonas excavadas ha llevado a Antonio Vallejo a interpretar que el citado paisaje urbano, más que a un programa unitario, responde a la suma de dos grandes fases constructivas: una primera, de la época de la fundación de la ciudad, desarrollada a principios de la década de 330h./941–951; y la segunda, a partir de la década de 340h./951–961.[56]

Las fechas que enmarcan dichas fases se han propuesto de acuerdo con los datos de las fuentes textuales y la epigrafía. Si atendemos a la etapa fundacional de al-Zahrāʾ, en el apartado anterior hemos indicado que la mayoría de los autores árabes datan el comienzo de su construcción en 325h./936–937.[57] No obstante, Ibn Ḥayyān, el cronista más cercano al periodo califal y el único del que tenemos la certeza de que obtuvo su información directamente de la corte omeya, retrasa dicho inicio: según él, el primer califa ʿAbd al-Raḥmān III erigió el alcázar de al-Zahrāʾ en 329h./940–941, pues el soberano se dedicó a su levantamiento como consecuencia de la derrota de la batalla de Alhándega en 327h./939.[58] Por consiguiente, coincidimos con Ana Labarta y Carmen Barceló en dar un mayor crédito al año 329h./940–941 como comienzo de la obra,[59] sobre un terreno que sería propiedad de la dinastía omeya.[60] En los años siguientes, el soberano trasladó su residencia y las sedes de los principales órganos de la administración califal al nuevo alcázar, que a partir de entonces comenzaría a ser denominado como *madīna* "ciudad".[61]

---

[49] La división en tres partes iguales del destino de los ingresos fiscales es una simplificación simétrica de una gestión económica omeya que contó sin duda con una mayor complejidad: Manzano Moreno 2019: 77–78.

[50] Al-Maqqarī 1968: I, 568; 1940: II, 269. El *Ḏikr bilād al-Andalus* expone que fueron 15.000 los erarios destinados a la financiación del levantamiento de Madīnat al-Zahrāʾ, una enorme cifra que apunta hacia un error de copia: *Ḏikr bilād al-Andalus* 1983: 164.

[51] Ibn Ḥawqal 1967: 108, 112.

[52] Ibn Jaldūn 2004: I, 350.

[53] Se mencionan en singular, como *dīnār bi-l-ḥaqq wa-l-ʿadl* "dinar legal y justo": *Ḏikr bilād al-Andalus* 1983: 34.

[54] Joaquín Vallvé propuso identificar dicha unidad de cuenta con 1.000.000 de dinares de dírhams, después de establecer diversas equivalencias entre monedas y pesos andalusíes: Vallvé Bermejo 1984: 164–167. Con todo, las palabras del *Ḏikr bilād al-Andalus* señalan claramente hacia la identificación de la *bayt māl* con 1.000.000 de dinares áureos.

[55] Al-Idrīsī 1968: 212.

[56] Vallejo Triano 2010a: 72, 465.

[57] Ibn Gālib 1956: 31; Ibn Jallikān 1977: V, 26; Yāqūt 1977: III, 161; Ibn ʿIḏārī 1980: II, 209, 231; Ibn al-Jaṭīb 2003: II, 38; *Ḏikr bilād al-Andalus* 1983: 162–163; al-Maqqarī 1968: I, 524, 526, 565, 567; 1940: II, 267, 269.

[58] Ibn Ḥayyān 1979: 437, 478–479.

[59] Ambas investigadoras sugieren que los autores más tardíos apostaron por el año 325h./936–937 como fecha de inicio porque, teniendo en cuenta que ʿAbd al-Raḥmān III gobernó entre 300h./912 y 350h./961, servía para dividir dicho periodo en dos mitades iguales de 25 años lunares, una primera caracterizada por una política exterior bélica y una segunda en la que destacó la actividad diplomática desarrollada en Madīnat al-Zahrāʾ: Labarta Gómez, Barceló Torres 1987: 95–96.

[60] Ibn Ḥayyān, al narrar la creación del alcázar de al-Zahrāʾ, describe el lugar como una *munya* "explotación agropecuaria suburbana de carácter aristocrático": Ibn Ḥayyān 1979: 478–479. Esta *munya* habría estado en manos de los Omeyas desde que el emir al-Munḏir (273h./886–275h./888) asesinó al visir Hāšim b. ʿAbd al-ʿAzīz, el antiguo propietario de la explotación, según la interpretación de Eduardo Manzano, basada en la información de Ibn Ḥayyān: Manzano Moreno 2019: 321, 425; Ibn Ḥayyān 1973: 190, 551.

[61] ʿAbd al-Raḥmān III ya recibía audiencias en el alcázar de al-Zahrāʾ en 333h./944, además de que trasladó la *sikka* "ceca" desde Córdoba hasta allí en 336h./947: Ibn ʿIḏārī 1980: II, 212, 215. En 338h./949, la ciudad palatina también contaba con la *dār al-ṣināʿāt* "casa de las manufacturas" y la *dār al-ʿudda* "casa de los pertrechos militares": al-Maqqarī 1940: II, 260–261.

El registro material, analizado por el Conjunto Arqueológico de Madinat al-Zahra, también apunta hacia la identificación del alcázar con el origen de la ciudad. De hecho, en la primera fase constructiva de la urbe, la zona palatina fue la única que estuvo rodeada por una muralla. El alcázar, que ocupaba una extensión de 19 ha,[62] disponía de dos ámbitos. Por un lado, el sector oficial, que se extendía por la plataforma intermedia y la mitad oriental de la plataforma superior. No obstante, las estructuras halladas en este sector forman parte de la segunda fase constructiva, teniendo una escasa información de las edificaciones previas a dicha reforma. Por otro lado, el sector privado del alcázar ocupaba la mitad occidental de la plataforma superior. Allí se situaban las viviendas de la familia del califa y de los máximos dignatarios de la administración omeya, además de los edificios desde los que se prestaban los servicios con los que asegurar el lujoso modo de vida de la corte: los ḥammāmāt "baños", las cocinas, etc. Ciertas estructuras de este sector privado sí que pertenecieron a su fase inicial, caso de la Dār al-Mulk y la Vivienda de la Alberca, esto es, las hipotéticas casas del califa 'Abd al-Raḥmān III y del príncipe heredero al-Ḥakam II, respectivamente. Centrándonos en la Dār al-Mulk, se ubicaba en el extremo septentrional del sector privado, concretamente en el punto más alto de la plataforma superior, siendo un modo de representar visualmente la jerarquía política existente en al-Andalus, encabezada por el califa. De hecho, esta residencia habría sido el referente a partir del cual se trazó y construyó el alcázar y el resto de la ciudad.[63]

La primera fase constructiva de al-Zahrā' también conllevó el inicio de la creación de espacios urbanos fuera del alcázar amurallado. Justamente, en la plataforma inferior se fueron construyendo áreas de uso religioso, económico y residencial que, directa o indirectamente, daban servicio al complejo aparato puesto en marcha por el Estado omeya. Esta urbanización extramuros fue fomentada por la propia administración desde la primera fase constructiva, cuando, según el geógrafo Ibn Ḥawqal, el califa gratificó con 400 dírhams a los súbditos de las distintas regiones de al-Andalus que trasladaron su residencia a la nueva ciudad.[64]

La mezquita aljama fue uno de los edificios más tempranamente construidos en la plataforma inferior, pues la lápida fundacional excavada en este oratorio señala que se levantó en 333h./944–945.[65] Consistía en la mezquita principal de la ciudad, aquella en la que se reunían sus habitantes, incluido el califa, para el rezo del viernes. De este modo, sería capaz de acoger a alrededor de 1.500 personas en sus 2.350 m² de superficie.[66] El oratorio tenía un muro perimetral con contrafuertes exteriores, acogiendo en su interior un patio de planta cuadrada y la sala de oración de disposición rectangular. Esta última estaba formada por 5 naves, trazadas por las arquerías de 8 arcos de herradura sobre columnas.[67]

La otra mezquita excavada en Madīnat al-Zahrā', emplazada 600 m al sudeste de la anterior, también se habría erigido en la primera fase de la ciudad. Por un lado, al igual que la aljama, tuvo una orientación precisa hacia La Meca, lo cual no sucede en las mezquitas andalusíes previas a la ciudad palatina, dato que apunta hacia su construcción coetánea o posterior a la fundación de al-Zahrā'. Por otro lado, el citado oratorio es anterior a la muralla urbana construida en la segunda fase, pues, al llegar a la altura de la mezquita, el trazado del cerco realiza un quiebro para evitar atravesarla, retomando tras ella la dirección original. La extensión de este oratorio, de 388 m², es mucho más reducida que la de la mezquita aljama. Las fotografías aéreas y con película infrarroja han permitido constatar que en esa misma zona al sudeste del alcázar hubo una extensa área residencial, por lo que a la mezquita acudirían los habitantes de esa zona.[68]

Si atendemos a la segunda fase constructiva de Madīnat al-Zahrā', se desarrolló a partir de la década de 340h./951–961. Uno de sus elementos más característicos fue la construcción de la muralla que rodeó el conjunto de la ciudad. La fecha post quem de la finalización del cerco se ha establecido en ese primer año de la década gracias a la información del geógrafo Ibn Ḥawqal, quien visitó al-Andalus entre 337h./948 y 340h./951–952 e indicó que la urbe no había logrado aún tener una muralla completa.[69]

Antonio Vallejo ha efectuado un detallado análisis de este cerco, que sirvió para delimitar la planta rectangular de la ciudad, con 1.518 m de eje norte-sur y 745 m en dirección oeste-este. De hecho, los cuatro lienzos de la muralla eran rectilíneos, a excepción del septentrional, pues su construcción sobre la ladera provocó pequeñas variaciones en el trazado. El cerco, que tuvo un grosor aproximado de 2,6 m, contó con torres rectangulares erigidas regularmente a lo largo de su alineación. Los lienzos occidental y oriental, por ejemplo, habrían contado con 41 o 42 torres cada uno.

[62] Vallejo Triano 2010a: 170–171, 223, 466, figs 10–12.
[63] Vallejo Triano, Montilla-Torres 2019: 2–11 (figs 1–2, 4, 7), 14–23 (figs 13, 18).
[64] Ibn Ḥawqal 1967: 111, 113.
[65] Martínez Núñez, Acién Almansa 2004: 111, 117–118, 158 (lám. 10). Si bien al-Maqqarī, reproduciendo un pasaje del biógrafo Ibn al-Faraḍī, indica que esta mezquita se habría realizado en 329h./941, el hallazgo del citado epígrafe durante la excavación del oratorio apunta claramente hacia la finalización de la obra en 333h./944–945: al-Maqqarī 1968: I, 564.
[66] Acién Almansa 1987: 19–20 (fig. 1); Vallejo Triano 2010a: 197, fig. 14.
[67] Pavón Maldonado 1967: 218–222; 1974: 325–328.
[68] Vallejo Triano 2009: 215–216, 219–223; 2010a: 186–187, 197, 217–218, fig. 7.
[69] Ibn Ḥawqal 1967: 108, 112–113.

A estas habría que sumar una mayor torre de ángulo que se construyó en cada vértice. Es muy probable que el cerco contase con un camino de ronda. Los muros se enfoscaron con cal y arena, encima de lo cual se dibujó la disposición de los sillares, empleando el color almagra para delinear los sillares, el ocre para rellenarlos y el blanco para marcar las juntas entre los sillares.

La ciudad amurallada tendría una superficie de 106 ha, pues sumó 87 ha intramuros de la plataforma inferior a las 19 ha aproximadamente que el alcázar ya tendría desde la primera fase. Los datos conocidos apuntan a que gran parte de la zona central de la terraza inferior permaneció sin edificar, siendo la mitad oriental y el extremo occidental las áreas que se urbanizaron durante los apenas 70 años de vida de la ciudad. Esta plataforma inferior permaneció aislada respecto a las terrazas alta e intermedia, pues el alcázar situado en estas últimas continuó teniendo una muralla propia que lo rodeaba, como en la fase anterior. En este sentido, el muro septentrional del alcázar coincidió con parte del lienzo norte del cerco de la ciudad, si bien este último tuvo una longitud bastante mayor por los extremos oriental y occidental. En el citado lienzo septentrional de la muralla del alcázar se sitúa la usualmente denominada Puerta Norte, esto es, la única entrada a la ciudad que se ha excavado hasta la actualidad, consistente en un zaguán en recodo flanqueado por una torre. Pese a su ubicación palatina, esta puerta no se habría erigido en la fase de construcción del alcázar, sino en la del levantamiento del cerco urbano.[70]

Otra de las grandes reformas de la década de 340h./951–961 se efectuó en el sector oficial del alcázar, formado por la plataforma intermedia y la mitad oriental de la terraza superior. Antonio Vallejo plantea que, en esa época, el Estado omeya puso en marcha un nuevo programa constructivo que tenía el propósito de que el sector oficial, además de acoger las sedes de los principales cuerpos de la administración, adquiriese una relevante función protocolaria y ceremonial. Dentro de la reorganización llevada a cabo en ese sector, destacó la de la plataforma intermedia: se dividía en dos mitades, la occidental denominándose Jardín Bajo y la oriental Jardín Alto. El edificio más emblemático del Jardín Alto, emplazado en su extremo septentrional, fue el Salón de 'Abd al-Raḥmān III, que habría que identificar con al-Maŷlis al-Šarqī "el Salón Oriental" que citan los autores árabes.[71] Las inscripciones que se hallaron durante su excavación posibilitaron datar la construcción entre 342h./953–954 y 345h./956–957,[72] fecha que apunta a que fuese uno de los primeros edificios de la reforma

del sector oficial, reflejo de su enorme importancia. Precisamente, el cronista 'Īsà b. Aḥmad al-Rāzī, reproducido por Ibn Ḥayyān, informa que este salón se convirtió en el centro del ceremonial omeya, donde el califa celebraba las dos festividades musulmanas más importantes —la fiesta de la Ruptura del Ayuno y la fiesta del Sacrificio— y llevaba a cabo las audiencias de las delegaciones.[73]

Respecto a la fecha de terminación de la construcción de Madīnat al-Zahrā', en el apartado anterior hemos explicado que los autores árabes la sitúan bien en el fallecimiento del califa 'Abd al-Raḥmān III en 350h./961, bien en el fin del gobierno de su hijo y califa al-Ḥakam II en 366h./976. El registro arqueológico apunta hacia la segunda opción, pues las reformas continuaron con al-Ḥakam II, teniendo constancia de ellas especialmente en el sector privado del alcázar. En su extremo suroriental, por ejemplo, tres viviendas de la fase fundacional se reestructuraron entonces para configurar una única casa, la supuesta residencia del ḥāŷib "chambelán" Ŷa'far.[74] Este último había sido designado para el cargo por el califa al-Ḥakam II, ejerciéndolo entre 350h./961 y su fallecimiento en 360h./970–971.[75]

El inicio del gobierno del tercer califa Hišām II implicó el fin de las reformas. A la muerte de al-Ḥakam II en 366h./976, su hijo y sucesor era un niño de 11 años, contexto que fue aprovechado por una facción de la corte omeya para empezar a acaparar todos los poderes del califato. Dicho grupo estaba encabezado por al-Manṣūr —el célebre Almanzor—, quien, a partir de que asumiese el cargo de ḥāŷib en 367h./978, se convirtió en el líder indiscutible del Estado omeya. Reflejo de ello es que, a continuación, iniciase la construcción de Madīnat al-Zāhira, una nueva ciudad palatina que se situaría al este de Córdoba y a la que el chambelán trasladó las sedes de los órganos de la administración. De este modo, los recursos del califato se emplearon a partir de entonces en la nueva urbe, en tanto que el califa Hišām II permaneció recluido en Madīnat al-Zahrā', como símbolo de la legitimidad califal que Almanzor requería para gobernar, pero sin que el Omeya tuviese de facto ningún poder político ni económico.[76]

---

[70] Vallejo Triano 2010a: 165–168, 177–189, 486, 503, fig. 7.

[71] Op. cit., 155–157, 485–492, 497, figs 57.

[72] Martínez Núñez 1995: 110–112 (N° 1, lám. I, fig. II), 116–118 (N° 9, fig. IX), 136.

[73] Ibn Ḥayyān 1965: 21, 28, 59, 81, 93–94, 136, 155, 184.

[74] Vallejo Triano, Montejo Córdoba, García Cortés 2004: 202–206. La información textual sobre esta vivienda la ofrece 'Īsà b. Aḥmad al-Rāzī, reproducido por Ibn Ḥayyān. Según él, en 360h./970–971 el citado chambelán residía en una dār "casa" de alto rango situada en el maṣāff garbī "flanco occidental" del alcázar: Ibn Ḥayyān 1965: 66.

[75] Ocaña Jiménez 1976: 219–221.

[76] Ballestín Navarro 2004: 109–114, 133–136.

7.

How to Define the 'Status' of Stonemasons Employed in a Rock-Hewn Worksite in the Medieval Period: Reflections and Hypotheses

Anaïs Lamesa

DIM-Matériaux anciens et patrimoniaux/CNRS
anaislamesa@yahoo.fr

Michael Gervers

University of Toronto
m.gervers@utoronto.ca

Abstract

The purpose of this paper is to question the status of masons on the worksites of rock-hewn monuments, a reverse architecture in which space is carved out rather than enclosed. Indeed, little attention has been paid to this issue especially for medieval worksites. Who were the people involved in a specific site? Had they exclusively high skill levels? If not, who were the amateurs? How do we identify them? What can we deduce in terms of the economics of construction? Can we compare the organisation of labour forces with worksites for built monuments?

J.-C. Bessac and L. Nehmé have dealt with this subject for the Mediterranean area by setting up a multidisciplinary methodology. One may, therefore, take their conclusions as a starting point for our own reflections. We start with a review of recent studies carried out on the Nabataean sites of Petra and Hegra where rock-cut tombs were carved. The intersection of epigraphy and the archaeology of techniques has made it possible to determine who participated at these sites.

We will then turn to Cappadocia to look at a specific case study: Mazıköy, where tombs from the Hellenistic and Roman periods and Byzantine churches were carved into the rock. With the help of such archaeological techniques as the traceology method (i.e. the reading of toolmarks) and the analysis of the *chaîne opératoire*, we will question the skill level of the masons. In this second part, we will discuss the four known inscriptions mentioning people who worked on worksites of rock-hewn monuments and the two works written by Neophyte the Reclus (from the Island of Cyprus) at the turn of the 12th-13th centuries in which the process by which a cell is carved is described.

Finally, our hypotheses will be tested against contemporary data. Indeed, there are people in Ethiopia who still carve rock-hewn churches using non-mechanised tools. Their testimonies seem to confirm the hypotheses formulated in the technical analyses and epigraphic review. Crossing archaeology, ethnoarchaeology, and history, the economics of building a rock-hewn monument will be addressed through the study of the status of the workers.

Keywords: stonemasons, rock-cut crafting, Turkey, Ethiopia, medieval

Introduction

This paper is a reflection on the socio-economic status of stone cutters working on a rock-hewn worksite between the 4th century BC and the 9th century AD. This question, better studied for traditional 'built' building sites, has not been addressed for monuments carved directly inside the stone.[1] This methodological gap conceals an entire area of research, particularly in the economics of construction outside traditional stone 'built' architecture. Our purpose is to ask who the masons were who might have been involved in the carving and finishing processes of rock-hewn churches during the medieval period. We provide examples from Mazıköy, a site located in the Central Anatolian region of Cappadocia, Turkey, and compare them with other examples in Ethiopia and Cyprus.

In terms of vocabulary, we choose to speak of rock-hewn practice rather than troglodytic. Digging directly into the rock to establish one's habitat, place of worship, or grave can be observed at different times throughout the world (Indian temples of Ellora, the Aztec temples of Malinalco, prehistoric hypogea of Sardinia, Etruscan tombs, or houses of the modern era in the Loire region).

---

[1] We mention the recent book (Dehejia and Rockwell 2016) on rock-hewn shrines in India. However, these authors do not seem to question the status of masons.

This chronological and geographical diversity prevents us from seeing rock-hewn practice as a specific cultural marker; we will therefore not refer to communities and monuments carved into the rock by the term 'troglodytic', which reflects an unusual way of life, often perceived negatively.[2] The term 'rock-hewn', which refers to the action of digging, cutting, or executing an element on a rock face, is preferred.

The rock-hewn practice is the adaptation of a community to its environment. People imitate, in a rock environment suitable for carving, built forms with some adaptations.[3] Thus, the study of rock-hewn monuments must be considered as a means to understand societies through a technical, economic, and anthropological prism.

Methodology and limits of the study

As with any building project, the creation of architecture carved directly into the bedrock itself required a specific organisation of workers. It should be noted that the study of rock-hewn worksites is not well developed, and data are often disparate and relatively rare. This explains our methodological choice to rely on multiple types of data (texts, inscriptions, toolmark observations, interviews) in several contexts and periods. To do so, we will begin our study in Antiquity, then continue with the medieval period and end with the present. Thanks to this long time span, different hypotheses emerge and help to shape two schemes in our conclusion.

The first part thus takes up the work of Leïla Nehmé and Jean-Claude Bessac in Petra (Jordan) and Hegra (Saudi Arabia).[4] The interest of this research lies in the comparison of the epigraphic inscriptions found on site with the technical analysis of the monumental rock-hewn tombs carved during the Nabataean kingdom between the 1st century BC and the 1st century AD. This has enabled them to link the economic context of the commission – more or less prestigious depending on the tombs – to the constitution of the teams working on the site.

Unlike the Nabataean sites, where the epigraphic and technical information is collected together, the Cappadocian (Turkey) data are disparate and concern funerary structures, housing, and religious monuments. We have chosen to focus our study on the site of Mazıköy (Turkey). It has the advantage of presenting a long period of occupation, from the 4th century BC to the 9th century AD.[5] Since the entire site

cannot be presented, only one monumental tomb and one church are the subject of an in-depth technical study. They are used to highlight the similarities and differences between these two types of structures. These technical analyses confirm the hypothesis put forward thanks to the work of Nehmé and Bessac: there is a strong correlation between the economic context and the composition of the work team. They also bring to light the dichotomy between commissions for prestige (monumental tombs) and commissions of necessity (the village church) that affected the composition of the work-team in the medieval period: experts and people who had no formal training in stone carving. We will not use the term professional which is a 'changing historic concept'.[6]

However, these new data raise the question of the socio-economic status of workers who were not formally trained in a rock-hewn church worksite and could call into question the idea of a team of experts working on this type of site. For this reason, in the third part of this paper, four inscriptions, interpreted as testimonies of rock-hewn practice in Cappadocia, will be discussed.[7] The epigraphic corpus is extremely thin in the region for the medieval period, as in the Byzantine Empire in general, but these inscriptions, three of which are from private and luxurious commissions, corroborate the original hypothesis: a team of highly skilled workers could participate in rock-hewn worksites when the commission was prestigious. These inscriptions could also explain the participation of unskilled workers, but some of them are questionable. Therefore, we use interviews collected in Tǝgray, the northern region of Ethiopia, with professional and non-professional stonemasons who participated in the carving of churches in the 2000s. These testimonies resonate with the hypotheses presented in this study. They help to define the 'status' of non-professional workers and confirm the strong link between worksite economics and the composition of the work team.

This work faces several challenges. The first, and perhaps the most difficult to justify, is having to use examples from different geographical regions and from different historical periods. Indeed, stoneworking is a craft learned in a particular location, with stoneworkers generally carving specific forms (architectural, sculptural, etc.). These constraints make comparison difficult, and we could have been content with our work on Cappadocia only. The pioneering work of Nehmé and Bessac opens up a whole range of research on the economics of construction but is restricted to a single site. Nevertheless, we think that some connections can be identified between sites

² On the origin and the meaning of this term: Lamesa 2019.
³ Ousterhout 2017: 10.
⁴ Bessac 2007, 2015; Nehmé 2007, 2015.
⁵ Thierry 2002: f. 1; Lamesa 2016.
⁶ Freidson 1983: 22 ; Stewart et al. 2020: 2–13; Russell 2020: 245–249.
⁷ Jerphanion 1925–1942; Jolivet-Lévy 2015.

used as examples in our study. Indeed, beyond the techniques, the qualifications of stoneworkers and composition of their team depends on the investments of patrons as well as the function of the monument. In other words, we assume that there is a very close relationship between worksite economics and team composition. Given this, the comparison between Hegra, Petra, and Mazıköy is made possible thanks to the presence of monumental tombs which result, in all three cases, from prestigious commissions whose function was mainly to show the power of the patrons. In these examples, we assume that patrons followed a similar scale of economics, i.e. high budget, and the employment of highly skilled workers. Similarly, the churches of Mazıköy and those currently being carved in the Təgray region seem to result from the same need, giving the village community a shelter for their worship. In Mazıköy, the absence of paintings in the churches suggests that commissions were not from the upper ranks of Byzantine society.[8] One church dating from the 9th century AD, unfortunately completely destroyed today, had painted decoration and could perhaps have been the result of another type of commission;[9] but it was not possible to carry out research on this specific church.

The second limitation, associated with the first, is the disparate nature of the outcrops where tombs and churches are carved from the rock. The sites of Hegra, Petra, and Təgray were excavated in sandstone, while ignimbrite, much softer than sandstone, was the stone in Cappadocia. Geology helps determine the process of tool selection or the *chaîne opératoire*. It appears that carvers use the same basic range of tools (no matter what the period) when the nature of the rock is the same. For instance, at Petra and in the Təgray region, picks for quarrymen and iron points to carve and shape tombs and churches were used during the medieval period.[10] Likewise, different geographical areas might have a tradition of stone carving based on the local geology. But the geological factors are not an issue here insofar as our purpose is to identify the stonemasons and consider their level of technical ability, instead of defining the carving process. As we pointed out previously, the tradition of stone carving is composed mostly by the empirical knowledge of the nature of the rock.[11] A highly qualified stonemason knows exactly how the rock will behave when he shapes it.

A third limitation is the choice of examples. Tombs and churches are specific commissions that do not necessarily reflect the daily life of the societies

being addressed. In Cappadocia, for instance, some medieval rock-hewn complexes have been identified as habitations,[12] but these complexes have not been subjected to the methods of archaeology or technology. Therefore, we do not include them in this paper. The reason for choosing these rock-hewn tombs and churches is also the need to define a chronological framework, i.e. from the 3rd century BC to the 9th century AD for our study: only these structures can be placed in a chronological range. Unlike the sites of Petra and Hegra, Cappadocian rock-hewn sites have not been excavated by archaeologists, so we have to restrict ourselves to structures that could be dated to the ancient and medieval periods. Moreover, the easiest way to study the qualifications of those working on rock-hewn structures is a method called traceology which requires the ability to inspect the toolmarks visually; only monuments without painting or plaster can be examined from this point of view. Other information, however, leads us to understand the level of workers' ability like the regularity of the plan, the sculpted decoration, and the final appearance of the monument. Indeed, some Cappadocian churches may have their columns carved at an angle, revealing the difficulty on the part of the stone cutter to visualise while he was carving it.

Finally, can it be assumed that the configuration of a team of stonemasons was stable from ancient times to the present day? Certainly not. However, this study does not define the different roles of workers by attributing to them such functions as quarryman, stonemason, sculptor, etc. Indeed, it is plausible that workers were multi-purpose. But certain constants seem to be present. Our purpose is also not to make a list of the trades employed on a rock-hewn monument worksite but to ask about the socio-economic status of workers involved in the process during the medieval period.[13] We also want to submit some general frameworks and some methodological guidelines, and raise questions about the economics of worksites for rock-hewn monuments.

Methodological examples: the Nabatean rock-hewn tombs of Hegra and Petra sites

Unlike the medieval period, the ancient period is rich in inscriptions in the Mediterranean Basin.[14] They tell us about the stone craftsmen and their organisation within the site. This is accurate to a lesser extent for masons working on a rock-hewn site. Almost twenty Nabataean inscriptions, discovered mainly at the Hegra site and dated between the 1st century BC and

---

[8] On the identification of a village at 'Mazıköy in medieval times, see Lamesa 2016: 484–493.
[9] Jolivet 1991: 177–178; Jolivet-Lévy and Lemaigre Demesnil 2015: 224.
[10] Lamesa and Hailay Atsba 2020.
[11] Dehejia and Rockwell 2016: 223–226.

[12] Ousterhout 2017: chapter 3.
[13] See for this kind of research Dehejia and Rockwell 2016: chapter 6.
[14] Unlike Indian shrines dating from ancient to modern times: see Dehejia and Rockwell 2016: 83–113.

the 1st century AD, refer to masons engaged in the carving of rock-hewn tombs.[15]

Four professions are attested in these inscriptions: the first and most widely represented is the term 'stonemason', which appears in twenty inscriptions from Hegra. Nehmé identifies eleven examples of stonemasons (*psl'*) as site managers based on their function as indicated in legal texts. She further identifies a second profession, that of the sculptor, which appears in an inscription engraved inside a rock-hewn chamber in Petra.[16] The third profession *ḥwy'* is a Nabataean hapax and is attested in a single example from the site of Hegra. In this case, Nehmé, with reference to a Phoenician inscription at Byblos, translates the term as restorer.[17] Finally, a fourth profession is more problematic. It is known as *bny'*. It is found in three inscriptions at Petra and two at Hegra. In the inscription JSNab 171, the profession *bny'* is associated with *psl'*.[18] The context of this inscription, engraved near the IGN 95 tomb and not directly on its façade, attracted the attention of Nehmé. The author first identified Karnū as the prime contractor for the IGN 95 tomb, while directing its 'inferior' status to stonemasons (*psl'*).[19] More recently, Nehmé considers this Karnū as a subordinate whose profession 'prevented him from saying that he was the main artisan [of this grave]'.[20] This epigraphic evidence suggests that the stoneworkers in Petra and Hegra seem to have a well-defined function. Furthermore, the workers are hierarchical since some stonemasons, or rather project managers, are legally engaged alongside the clients or officially designated project managers.

From the archaeological work of Bessac, the hierarchy of the team looks simpler and depends mainly on the importance of the monument to be carved. This author also demonstrates how in a rock-cut worksite, hierarchical distance is reduced since the slightest mistake during the carving process is unacceptable. It was, therefore, necessary for the site manager to be present during all the carving and finishing phases.[21] However, in the peculiar case of Hegra, Bessac notes that the tombs, whose façades are more than 5 m high, were carved by several stonemasons who divided the

work into zones. This analysis suggests a peculiar management of the teams: the site manager was not continuously present on site and the distribution by zone allowed him to check the work of his team from time to time.[22] The tombs whose façades do not exceed 4 m in height seem to have been carved by a single hand.[23] Apprentices could also work in parallel with experienced craftsmen, but unfortunately, it is impossible to confirm this through archaeology or epigraphy.[24]

An important technical detail also concerns the organisation of the teams: the shaping of tombs in Hegra and Petra was carried out by means of extracting blocks (**Figure 1**). Quarrymen had to work before the stonemasons to create a straight rock wall before beginning the façade.[25] In the case of small monuments, the same person might perform both functions.[26] The archaeological analysis therefore made it possible to enhance the data obtained from the epigraphic sources. In these examples it appears that the creation of large-scale rock-carved tomb sites necessitated a more hierarchical organisation of the workforce. In this case, a stonemason worked as the master craftsman and/or the project manager responsible for a team of between two and four stonemasons and quarrymen. This scheme might also include different levels of skilled workers such as apprentices and sculptors.[27]

These examples also show that the stoneworkers involved in these rock-hewn worksites must have been mostly stonemasons with a long-standing practice of carving. This conclusion is due to the high level of technical skills required to extract the blocks in order to create a straight rock wall and to shape it thereafter. Was this also the case with medieval rock-hewn sites; and more precisely with the rock-hewn church sites presented in this study?

Technical study

In order to answer this question, we focused on the rock-hewn structures at the site of Mazıköy. The settlement has been the subject of scattered publications and, in 2010, firsthand study.[28] The main valley is Davutlu Bucağı. Eight ancient tombs and

[15] Nehmé 2007: 15–26; 2015: 141–155. For references and archaeological and epigraphic contexts: Nehmé 2007: 22–26 annexe 1; 2015: 42–143, table 22. For the site of Petra, McKenzie 1990: 14. She translates the term *psl'* as a stone cutter for the first time: 'The Nabataean word (*psl'*) describing the maker of the tomb is most accurately translated into English as 'stone cutters' rather than a 'stonemason' or 'sculptor'; Nehmé 2007: 17.
[16] Nehmé 2007: inscription no. 9.
[17] Nehmé 2015: 141.
[18] 'May Karnū the builder (*bny'*), son of Abd'ubdat the stonemason (*psl'*), be safe and sound' (translation by L. Nehmé [Nehmé 2015: 142]).
[19] Nehmé 2007: 16.
[20] Nehmé 2015: 141.
[21] Bessac 2007: 143.

[22] Bessac 2015: 183.
[23] Bessac 2015: 183.
[24] Bessac 2007: 143; 2015: 183.
[25] Bessac 2007: 93; 2015: 180–182.
[26] Bessac 2015: 183–184.
[27] Bessac 2015: 183–184. On the notions of expertise and learning: Bril 2019.
[28] The publication of this PhD thesis is in progress: Lamesa 2016: 484–493 and all the appendices of Area 4. On the settlement identification, see Hild and Restle 1981: 230 and associated bibliography. On Mazıköy monuments: Grégoire 1909: 92; Thierry 1977: 108 and 137; 2002: f.1; Jolivet-Lévy 1987: 38–40; Equini-Schneider *et al.* 1997: 172–173; Jolivet-Lévy and Lemaigre Demesnil 2015: 224.

Figure 1. Petra, Tomb 765. The technique of extracting blocks to start the rock-hewn tomb (© J. -C. Bessac).

six churches are carved into two cliffs that form the canyon where the village is currently located. A chapel was carved in the large four-storey excavation or the 'underground city' below the village. Thanks to stylistic analysis, the rock-hewn tombs could be dated to the end of the Hellenistic period and the Roman period (4th century BC to 1st century AD). As Nicole Thierry notes, no monuments have characteristics from the Middle Byzantine period, indicating that the site might have been abandoned before that time.[29] The research of Anaïs Lamesa considerably expanded the knowledge of this settlement, restricted initially to the main valley of Davutlu Bucağı. Besides the well-known main valley, a second valley called Damlar Önü, perpendicular to the village, contains two inaccessible ancient tombs and three churches set side by side. A third valley, Göynük Dere, to the north-west at the entrance to the village, contains a vast Roman necropolis with fourteen tombs and a monumental façade. Less than two kilometres south-west of the village, a fourth valley, Keşlik Dere, comprises a medieval complex (five churches and several mostly buried rooms). This study pinpoints the evolution of the techniques used to shape rock-hewn monuments. We assume that the transformation of techniques reveals also the evolution of the status of

the workers and, more importantly, their skill level. To illustrate this observation, we will take two examples.

The first monument is T03 DB, an unfinished tomb located in the main valley of Davutlu Bucağı. It is dated to the Hellenistic period (**Figure 2**).[30] Its façade has the characteristics of a temple tomb: it consists of two columns, two antes, and a rectangular entablature. A flat-ceilinged *pronaos* opens onto a burial chamber where three benches form a return. These benches are carved with mouldings reminiscent of wooden furniture decorations. The technical observations point to the worker or workers being endowed with remarkable technical mastery. Indeed, the worker was able to anticipate all the problems relating to the carving process:

1. He perfectly integrated his structure into the rock face; the monument lies between two fractures that do not have a direct impact on the tomb itself (**Figure 3**). In this manner, he was able to prevent the possible destruction of the monument during the carving due to cracks.
2. He also took into consideration the obliqueness of the rock wall in playing with the depth

[29] Thierry 1977: 137.

[30] For T03 DB, see Thierry 1977: 108 and fig. 7; 1981: 41; 2002: f.1 (tomb no. 5); Equini-Schneider *et al.* 1997: 172–173 and table 160.

Figure 2. Mazıköy, T03 DB, Hellenistic rock-hewn tomb
(© A. Lamesa).

Figure 3. Mazıköy, T03 DB. The crack used by the stonemason
(© A. Lamesa).

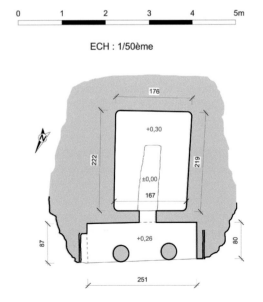

Figure 4. Mazıköy, T03 DB plan (© A. Lamesa and V. Dubois).

between the west and east walls of the *pronaos*. This behaviour highlights the capacity of the stone cutter to visualise in an abstract way the entire structure before and during the carving process by taking into account the slant of the cliff. He corrected the offset and thus was able to create a wall perfectly perpendicular to the two western and eastern walls.

3. The burial chamber has three perfectly perpendicular walls (**Figure 4**) as well as the *pronaos*, precisely reproducing the built model (i.e. regularity of columns with the same diameter, the presence of right angles) which is extremely rare in a rock-hewn site from any period.

4. The worker voluntarily chose to place the tomb between two cracks, giving the impression that the façade is detached from the rock wall when one looks at the monument from the valley below. This effect not only shows how the conception of the whole monument was determined before its realisation but also highlights the skill of the worker who succeeded in producing the expected effect.

The second monument is a rock-hewn church (E01 DB) carved at the bottom of the south cliff of Davutlu Bucağı. Its façade is a simple door topped by a *lunula* (**Figure 5**). It has a double *naos* that ended in two apses; however, the northern apse was destroyed. Two low chancel barriers delimit the southern apse. A single rectangular pillar, decorated with various types of crosses, supports the central separation of the two vaults (**Figure 6**). A capital has been added. Thierry attributes one of the crosses to the modern period.[31] In view of the damage, the mason did not seem to consider the fractures and cracks in the cliff: the walls of the two naves are on the verge of collapsing. Besides, only the toolmarks of an adze appear on the walls. Strangely, this tool seems to have been used for finishing and making architectural elements, such as the cornice. Its impacts are uneven in depth but evenly distributed over the walls (**Figure 7**). Finally, one notes the difficulties faced by the worker to create the internal space. For instance, the south apse is not circular because the worker was not able to create first a rectangular piece and then round it off evenly. These observations suggest the participation of workers with a low level of technical training. Indeed, the use of tools of various strengths and the various irregularities observed in the church prove that the worker had not mastered the art of creating a rock-hewn monument.

More generally, these observations can be made for all the rock-hewn excavations at Davutlu Bucağı. The rock-hewn tombs are carved with care, the workers

---

[31] Thierry 1977: 137.

Figure 5. Mazıköy, façade of the Byzantine rock-hewn church E01 DB (© A. Lamesa).

Figure 6. Mazıköy, unique pillar of E01 DB (© A. Lamesa).

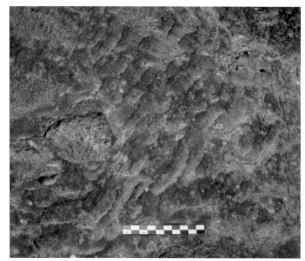

Figure 7. Mazıköy, toolmarks of the adze on the nave wall of E01 DB (© A. Lamesa).

seem technically much superior to those who carved the churches.

Finally, a last element must be mentioned: the disappearance of toothed tools (an axe with pointed teeth i.e. *marteau grain d'orge oriental* in French and an axe with flat teeth i.e. *bretture* in French) in Byzantine times throughout the site of Mazıköy.[32] This phenomenon has already been observed for construction sites in the medieval period in both the East and West,[33] and the toothed axe has not been observed in the hands of contemporary Cappadocian stonemasons.[34] The axe with pointed teeth was used in a tomb in the Göynük Dere, and the axe with flat teeth in five tombs in the Davutlu Bucağı. Using these tools for ignimbrites seems odd because the ignimbrite is a very soft and abrasive rock. Even so, this type of stone does not require the kinds of tools traditionally used for hard stones.[35] Furthermore, it compels a restoration to be carried out when the stone is abrasive.[36]

We can consider several hypotheses, which are not exclusive to each other, to explain this phenomenon. The first hypothesis could be the difficulty in supplying the worksites with iron between the 7th and 9th centuries due to the instability of the Cappadocian area.[37] The manufacture of toothed tools required 'excellent hardening and good steel', as Bessac reminds us.[38] To support or put into perspective this idea, we

---

[32] Lamesa 2018: 81.
[33] Bessac 1986: 21.
[34] Unlike the oriental diamond point hammer: Öztürk 2009; Lamesa 2011.
[35] Bessac 1986: 69.
[36] Bessac 1986: 62.
[37] Lamesa 2016: 468–469.
[38] Bessac 1986: 61.

need more studies on the quality of iron and steel in the Byzantine period. The second hypothesis would be that these tools were no longer useful from the stoneworker's point of view. At Mazıköy, selected tools are clearly different for the finishing stage of hewing out a tomb or a church. We assume that the abandonment of toothed tools illustrates a change in the *chaîne opératoire* and may be linked with a change in architectural tradition. For the Hellenistic and Roman periods, the worker carved inside the monument using a quarryman's pick. He then used a 'polka' or an axe (with flat cutting edges either aligned with the axe's handle or at 90 degrees to it, sometimes called an adze) to straighten up the wall. At the end of the process, he corrected wall imperfections with a toothed tool. This stage seems necessary for the wall at the Mazıköy site before starting the sculptural stage with chisels to create fluted columns or cornices. For the Byzantine period, the mason used exclusively a short pick or axe (i.e. a carver's pick with a short handle with one or two pointed cutting edges) to sculpt cornices and columns, as is apparent for instance in church E01 carved in the valley of Davutlu Bucağı. The disappearance of fine sculptures like fluted columns or imitations of wood furniture between the Hellenistic period and the Byzantine period could have impacted the technical skill of workers by diminishing the number of stages in the finishing process. Indeed, the disappearance of the sculpted façade or ornaments which require a straight wall and specific tools may have led to a reduction in the mason's versatility. This observation is also visible for the carving process. For the Hellenistic and Roman periods, even the technique of extracting blocks to start a rock-hewn tomb was not clearly observed on the settlement of Mazıköy; however, the presence of a large terrace near monumental tombs T07 and T08 DB and the morphology of the entablature of tomb T08 GD could result from the process of extracting blocks (**Figure 8**). In Byzantine rock-hewn churches, no technique of extracting blocks was ever observed leading to the hypothesis that it was no longer employed. The evolution of the carving process could be a social indicator, as also the changes in the habits of medieval stonemasons, since they no longer fulfilled the role of quarrymen.

Differences in technical skills between the workers who carved the ancient tombs and those employed to create medieval churches are obvious at Mazıköy. The teams making rock-hewn churches no longer seem exclusively to consist of stoneworkers with high technical skills. As explained above, medieval masons used shortcuts in their practices (like using tools for carving instead of tools for sculpting), did not have a good knowledge of their environmental and geological context, and were not able to reproduce the built models perfectly (for instance, the right angle or cornice). Some habits

also indicate that most of the medieval workers did not extract blocks when they shaped rock-hewn churches. We think that this reveals a change in the stonemason's status, i.e. he is no longer a quarryman or sculptor, leading us to think that he may have been an amateur rather than a professional. Finally, it should be noted that for the Hellenistic and Roman periods in the settlement of Mazıköy, it is possible to talk from a technical point of view about 'expert' stonemasons. For the medieval period, this aspect seems more delicate, since there is a clear decline in technical knowledge.

Stonemasons at rock-hewn worksites from written and epigraphic sources

We propose that a change in the type of workers took place between the ancient and medieval periods. Can this hypothesis be supported by Byzantine written and epigraphic sources? Robert Ousterhout made a few remarks about the terms used in the textual sources from the beginning of the 9th century. He noted the disappearance of the term *mechanikos* or architect and the spread of the terms *oikonomos* and *maïstor* or master mason.[39] Similarly, Ousterhout recalls that associated with these two terms, others are mentioned in the sources, such as *technites* for skilled workers and *ergates* for unskilled workers, *lithoxoon* for stonemasons and *tekton* for carpenters. From the 10th century onwards, all these terms referring to a particular profession (stonemason, carpenter, etc.) seem to merge together.[40] He also notes their absence in miniatures or mid-Byzantine mosaics.[41] Finally, he makes the following hypothesis: 'There must have been considerable variation in the organisation of a Byzantine workshop, depending on the size and the lavishness of each project and the source of funding. Sometimes it is possible to envision a single master mason, perhaps with an assistant, taking charge of the construction of a small or medium-sized church, conducting a team of unskilled workers'.[42] Data from written sources seems to confirm our archaeological and technical study.

What is particularly interesting is that some terms like *maïstor* also appear in Cappadocian inscriptions and seem to refer to the same type of stoneworkers. Two inscriptions thus refer to a *maïstor*: the first is in the New Church of Tokalı (Göreme E07) dated from the 10th century,[43] and the second one is in the vestibule of

[39] Ousterhout 1999: 44; 2019: 181.
[40] Kazhdan, *Sv.* Mason III: 1311–1312 quoted by Ousterhout 1999: 44, n. 26.
[41] Ousterhout 1999: 45.
[42] Ousterhout 1999: 52.
[43] Jerphanion 1925–1942: I.2, 301, inscription no. 31. From Tokalı kilise at Göreme: 'The church was completed on June 15. Lord, help the *maïstor*' (translation taken over from Jolivet-Lévy and Lemaigre Demesnil 2015: 73).

Figure 8. Mazıköy, tombs T07 and T08 DB and the terrace in front of them (© A. Lamesa).

Bezirhane (Avcılar E04a) and is difficult to date.[44] The *maïstor* has been identified as the contractor or master craftsman,[45] the person most often responsible for managing the team involved in the rock-hewn worksite or construction site.

The first occurrence can be easily explained insofar as the inscription lies within a remarkable church, the New Church of Tokalı. This stands out from the other churches at the Göreme site for its layout, proportions, and level of sculpted finish.[46] It is worth noting the regularity of the barrier separating the *naos* from the *bêma* and the geometric rigour of the niches on the eastern wall of the nave (**Figure 9**). The placement

of the church was also thought out in advance of the carving process. Indeed, the old church apse – destroyed during the digging process for the New Church of Tokalı – was used as a point of reference for the New Tokalı nave vault. This lavish commission, certainly ordered by relatives of the imperial court, explains the intervention of a *maïstor* leading a highly technically skilled team.[47]

The second inscription is more difficult to interpret. Now destroyed, it was not carved inside a church but in a now-ruined rock-hewn portico. It was covered by a barrel vault which opened onto four rooms – including a large three-aisled basilica hall – and a church.[48] The inscription was placed high on the wall and could well have been made by the master mason or his workman at the start of the operation, when they would have been working from the top down.[49] Guillaume de Jerphanion compares the two inscriptions, which use the same wording, and attributes them to the

---

[44] Jerphanion 1925–1942: I.2, 499–500, inscription no. 79. From Bezirhane located in the village of Göreme: 'In the name of God this passage was completed by the Maistor Nikitas, *chorion* (estate or village?) of Saint Theodore'. (Translation by Rodley 1985:32).
[45] Ousterhout 1999: 50.
[46] Many publications have appeared about this church, which is exceptional for its rich, painted decoration. See the bibliography in Jolivet-Lévy and Lemaigre Demesnil 2015: 73. See also Warland 2013: 80–84 who dates the church to the 13th century; and the review of this work by Jolivet-Lévy (2014), which reaffirms the 10th century dating of the church. In addition, see the note devoted to this church in the recent book by Ousterhout (2017: 226).

[47] On the commission of this church: Epstein and Schwartzbaum 1986; Thierry 1989.
[48] Rodley 1985: 27. See the bibliography in Jolivet-Lévy and Lemaigre Demesnil 2015: 104; Ousterhout 2017: 281–283.
[49] Rodley 1985: 32.

Figure 9. Göreme, the church of New Tokalı. The regular arches before the three apses (© J.-P. Gély).

same period.[50] Several indications could confirm this hypothesis: according to Lyn Rodley, the unity in the vocabulary of the sculpted decoration throughout the complex would suggest that it was created in a single phase.[51] The presence of a cross-in-square rock-hewn church indicates, if we follow the hypothesis of a single digging phase, that the complex would have been carved after the beginning of the 10th century. Indeed, this style of church plan appeared in Cappadocia at the beginning of the 10th century.[52] Finally, the style of execution dates the church's paintings between the 10th and 11th centuries.[53] Although it was impossible to visit the church, the perfectly-executed sculpted decoration of the basilica hall and the portico are clear (**Figure 10**). de Jerphanion also noted the care taken with the mouldings of the basilica space.[54] The complex therefore seems to have been a luxurious commission, in which a hierarchical team of masons could have worked.

These two inscriptions, the only instances found in Cappadocia, are striking. They limit the conclusions drawn from the technical analysis presented above since the inscriptions demonstrate the existence of experts who led hierarchical teams at rock-hewn church worksites. However, these two inscriptions appear in exceptional monuments. Even though the way they are written cannot be used as a determinant of a scribe's identity, it is remarkable that the term is mentioned in two complexes about ten kilometres from each other and within a relatively narrow chronological range. This observation suggests the existence of at least two master craftsmen who, in this case, took the opportunity to sign their work. Is this the mark of their contemporary activity? Could it be a form of competition? Why did such inscriptions appear only at this time? The discovery of other inscriptions could help to answer these questions.

Apart from these two secular testimonies, two epitaphs seem to attest to the participation of monks in the realisation of rock-hewn spaces. The first is a long text in verse painted in an *arcosolium* inside the narthex of

---

[50] Jerphanion 1925–1942: I.2, 499–500.
[51] Rodley 1985: 33. It has not been possible to see the paintings.
[52] Ousterhout 2017: 84.
[53] Rodley 1985: 33; Jolivet-Lévy and Lemaigre Demesnil 2015: 104.
[54] Jerphanion 1925–1942: I.2, 48–49.

a small church:[55] 'In my lifetime, I prepared a grave carved out of stone. So receive me also, Sepulchre, as you received the Stylite'.[56] The epitaph, attributed to the monk Simeon, has been interpreted literally: the monk would have made his grave.[57] However, the author of these lines refers to the Septuagint on many occasions. The act of digging a tomb in the rock is explicitly mentioned in Isaiah (XXII, 16): 'What do you have here that you have cut out a tomb here for yourself and made yourself a tomb on the height and inscribed a tent for yourself in a rock?'.[58] Although the hypothesis is very interesting, the shape of the epitaph does not validate the idea of Cappadocian monks digging their own graves.

If we look at the second epitaph, its interpretation is even less clear. It is in the fourth nave of Karabaş kilise at Soğanlı, painted near a portrait of an abbot: 'I, Bathystrokos Abbas, who have laboured a lot for this church and then died, I remain here. I died in the month of...'.[59] The epitaph is incomplete, which suggests that it was painted during the abbot's lifetime.[60] The term κάμνω is difficult to explain. It can be understood effectively as 'digging'.[61] Bathystrokos would then have dug the burial chamber in which the epitaph is painted. However, the term can also mean 'to exert oneself/to work hard'. One might as well consider this epitaph as an image: the monk would have worked all his life for the church and for his salvation.

Looking at hagiographic sources, only the autobiographical stories of the monk Neophytos of Cyprus seem to bear witness to the digging of two rock-hewn cells in his monastery in Paphos (Cyprus) at the end of the 12th century.[62] We will not go back over the content of these writings here. It is simply interesting to mention that in view of the *realia* contained in the texts, the story seems authentic and the monk Neophytos could have really dug his two rock-hewn cells. Thanks to these sources, we can legitimately ask ourselves: did a monk simply dig his cell, or could he also participate in the carving of a rock-hewn church? There is no evidence of such activity in the sources collected here. It should be recalled, however, that written sources have not been studied in the specific perspective of rock-

Figure 10. In the village of Göreme, the basilica hall of Bezir Hane (© A. Lamesa).

hewn worksite activities and a thorough investigation has yet to be carried out. Indeed, we can mention the *gädl* of Abuna Abrəham (priest and legendary founder of the monastery of Däbrä Ṣəyon) written in the 15th century.[63] The text is as yet unedited, but it seems that Abrəham led a team of stonemasons to carve his monastery.[64] Similarly, in medieval France and England, monks were actively involved in the building process – mentioned in the sources when accidents happened.[65]

Contemporary testimonies of stonemasons carving rock-hewn churches as evidence for earlier practices

If we look at all the elements that have been highlighted up to now, we can see the following: when it comes to monumental rock-hewn tombs, whether they are located in Nabataean or Cappadocian regions, the teams of stonemasons seem to consist mainly of experts, i.e. workers operating at a high technical level. The teams appear to have been led by a manager in overall charge of the whole project. When it comes to rock-hewn churches, there seem to be two options. The first option is the participation of workers whose technical skills do not appear to be very well developed. The second option is the presence of highly qualified stonemasons for the realisation of richly ornamented churches from a prestigious commission. In this second option, however, it cannot be ruled out that the excavation was carried out with the help of labourers. In both cases, the presence of a project manager seems mandatory. Project managers are attested in the inscriptions from luxury commissions and seem necessary for the guidance of unskilled workers.

[55] On this room and the identification of this stylite monk: Jerphanion 1925–1942: I 570–571. Following this identification: Jolivet-Lévy 2015: 219–220.
[56] Translation into English from the French translation of Thierry 2002: 201. See also Jerphanion 1925–1942: I.2, 575–582; Rodley 1985: 225; Thierry 1994: 323; Jolivet-Lévy 2015: 219–220. For the study of this inscription, see: Rhoby 2009: 299–302.
[57] Jolivet-Lévy 2015: 219.
[58] Translation from Pietersma and Wright 2007.
[59] Translation from de Jolivet-Lévy 2015: 237. On this inscription, see Jerphanion 1925–1942: II.1, 356 no. 200; Rodley 1985: 197; Thierry 2002: fiche 47; Jolivet-Lévy 2015: 237.
[60] Jolivet-Lévy 2015: 237.
[61] Jolivet-Lévy 2015: 237.
[62] On these texts: Congourdeau 1993; Lamesa 2010.

[63] Schneider 1983: 107.
[64] Lepage and Mercier 2005: 153. Anaïs Lamesa led two missions in 2020 to collect all manuscripts of this *gädl*, and on-going research on this text is being conducted with Dr. Daniel Assefa (Addis Ababa University).
[65] Blary and Gély 2020: 120 and 187.

However, some doubts remain as to the identification of the unskilled workers' status. Some data would tend to identify them as religious figures, but it has been shown that the two Cappadocian inscriptions mentioning the participation of monks are questionable. Also, would monks have been the only ones to be used as labourers in the digging of a church and the removal of rubble? To attempt to answer these questions, we would therefore like to turn to the testimonies of contemporary stonemasons.

The comparison of anthropological data with hypotheses drawn from ancient texts to explain a technical phenomenon and its organisation is common. It has long since acquired its validity in the world of prehistorians and among medievalists and modernists working in countries where sources are scarce.[66] It is therefore not inappropriate to use this method to move forward in our thinking. However, we must justify the choice of this change of study. Conducting ethnographical surveys in Cappadocia is limited. Only professionals still carry out the renovation of rock-hewn hotels, most often using mechanised tools.[67] Moreover, rural communities with a large Muslim majority have long since abandoned the digging of churches in the rock. This specific practice may still be alive in the Syriac communities of south-eastern Turkey, but the current situation prevents a thorough study from being carried out. We must therefore look to other regions of the world. In Ethiopia, carving a church in the traditional way is still perennial and therefore deserves attention. The fact that the geological formation is different is not an *a priori* constraint; indeed, it is not the *chaîne opératoire* on which our analysis focuses but the social organisation of a rock-hewn church worksite.

In order to preserve the memory of this traditional skill, gradually replaced by mechanisation, Michael Gervers and his team have, for five years, collected over forty testimonies. They are from people who participated in rock-hewn church worksites in various regions of Ethiopia.[68] Four cases located in Təgray (Gär'alta region) provide some additional answers to our initial question. The first case concerns the extension of the church of Däbrä Kidanä Məhrät Dəgum, in which Halaqa Gəbräägzi'abəher and Wäldä Gäbrə'el participated. It consisted of opening a door to the south and creating a new sanctuary.[69] The second case concerns the enlargement of the Mikael Haregwa church, as witnessed by Gəday Yəḫeyyəs Ӡmbayyä who

has also worked on three other churches.[70] The third case concerns the church of Dabra Sahəl. Tsegay Abera worked on its realisation with Täsfaye Fitwi.[71] Finally, the fourth case concerns a monk Aba Gəbrämädḫan Asbəh Gəbrämäsqäl who dug his cell, which will also be his grave when he dies.[72]

Of the five people recorded, all qualify as farmers and only two recognise themselves as craftsmen: Gəday Yəḫeyyəs Ӡmbayyä and Tsegay Abera. The other three men describe themselves as merchants and priests in the case of Täsfaye Fitwi and monks for Halaqa Gəbräägzi'abəher, Wäldä Gäbrə'el, and Aba Gəbrämädḫan Asbəh Gəbrämäsqäl. These four churchmen have not been solicited to carry out other projects, and they remain in their community. They were paid by the task or simply volunteered, working for the salvation of their souls. This is not the case for Gəday Yəḫeyyəs Ӡmbayyä and Tsegay Abera who travel around the Hawzen region, according to their contracts. The two craftsmen are paid for their work as contractors. They make an oral or written contract, depending on whether they are engaged in the village community until the contract is completed or whether they lack funds – which seems to happen most often. Gəday Yəḫeyyəs Ӡmbayyä nevertheless notes that the time he spends digging or repairing churches is punctuated by agricultural activities. It stops between October and November for harvesting and in June and July for sowing. Different seasonal occupations are evident in both the Roman and Medieval periods in building worksites.[73] A good example can be recalled from Late Antiquity. The village of Dara was fortified between AD 505 and 507 by the will of the emperor Anastasius.[74] Several sources described its worksite and one, the Chronical of Pseudo-Zacharia mentioned:

'So the craftsmen and slaves and peasants who were required for the collection of material there gained and were blessed. He (Anastasius) sent many stonecutters and masons, and he ordered that no man should be cheated of the wages of his labor, because he rightly perceived and cleverly understood that by the agreement a city would quickly be built upon the frontier'.[75]

---

[66] See for instance Leroi-Gourhan 1945–1971; Balfet 1991. For a theoretical reflection on ethnoarchaeology: Gallay 2011.

[67] We refer to the two studies based on interviews with contemporary stonemasons: Öztürk 2009; Lamesa 2011.

[68] These interviews, sponsored by the Arcadia Fund, are available online at: https://www.utsc.utoronto.ca/projects/ethiopic-churches/.

[69] https://www.utsc.utoronto.ca/projects/ethiopic-churches/dabra-kidana-m%c7%9d%e1%b8%a5rat-d%c7%9dgum-t%c9%99gray-region/

[70] https://www.utsc.utoronto.ca/projects/ethiopic-churches/mikael-haregwa/

[71] https://www.utsc.utoronto.ca/projects/ethiopic-churches/agwaza/

[72] https://www.utsc.utoronto.ca/projects/ethiopic-churches/mikael-m%c7%9dr%c7%9dro/

[73] Bernard 2018: 15.

[74] A lot of research has been conducted on this site: see especially for the most recent archaeological studies: Keser-Kayaalp and Erdoğan 2017; Lamesa and Erdoğan 2020.

[75] Ps. Zacharia, VII.6 ; Translation from Phenix et al. 2011: 75.

This testimony proves that several kinds of masons worked in the same time at a building worksite.[76] This being the case, a parallel with our ethnographic data can be considered. The recognition of the two craftsmen seems to be based on their knowledge and leads them to work more than half the year as project managers. We can therefore consider them as professionals. Indeed, unlike farmers who are paid by the task or by the day, these two experts make a contract with the patrons. They are the ones who take responsibility for the site, its organisation, and the execution of the contract. They may, if funds permit, decide to involve other professionals, but their rate of pay seems much higher since these experts also directly sign a contract with the community, as noted by Gəday Yəḥeyyəs Əmbayyä. In the light of these interviews, it can therefore be seen that the teams working on a rock-hewn church worksite in contemporary times are heterogeneous. They are made up of skilled people, considered professionals by village communities, who guide workforces who simply call themselves farmers and clergymen.

The farmer/craftsman association in a rock-hewn church worksite in Ethiopia echoes the epigraphic sources found in Cappadocia. These two craftsmen can be defined as maïstor who guide the workers, showing them the actions to be taken, as the monk Halaqa Gəbräəgzi'abəher testifies. They carry out the most delicate parts, especially the arches and ceilings as well as the finishing touches. The workforce was charged with simply carving the walls and clearing the monument.

Some hypotheses by way of conclusion

This study on the status of stoneworkers employed in a rock-hewn worksite suggest a number of hypotheses. Methodologically, it introduces the idea that the combining of historical, archaeological, and anthropological sources is necessary to move forward in the field of site economics in the case of rock-cut monuments. It also seems that we cannot limit ourselves to a simple period of time if we want to be able to formulate hypotheses. Indeed, from Antiquity to the present day, two schemes have emerged, most certainly connected with the needs of the patrons and according to their financial investment.[77] A first socio-economic context concerns large-scale rock-hewn worksites. The patrons seem to finance their creation for prestige as well as for the space as such. In this specific context, within hierarchical teams, the workers seem to be mainly experienced experts. This hypothesis is based on the epigraphic studies of

Nehmé associated with technical analyses by Bessac. The archaeo-technical analyses of the monumental tombs of Mazıköy as well as the examination of the New Church of Tokalı and the presence of its inscription tend to confirm this hypothesis. Would this be the case at the Bezirhane complex where the mention of maïstor and the care taken in the sculpted decoration would suggest a prestigious commission?

The second socio-economic context corresponds to a project commissioned not for prestige but out of necessity. This could be a single man who dug his own tomb or a hierarchical team composed mainly of locally recruited workers, whose daily remuneration distinguished them from the project managers and craftsmen employed on a contractual basis who traveled according to their contracts. This aspect is demonstrated by the interviews of professional stonemasons and the churches studied at Mazıköy where 'doing' takes precedence over 'doing well'. Perhaps this situation is indicative of a village community's development and its need to increase the number of places of worship at its disposal. It is also important to think about the funds allocated for the construction of the rock-hewn church and what impact this would have had on the project.

These two main models then make it possible to propose different approaches to rock-hewn tombs or churches and their worksites on a case-by-case basis. For example, in the case of Bezirhane, the technical analysis of the site – which has not been done yet – could specify whether the carving was carried out by professionals or by task workers. In the latter case, we would be faced with a variant of the second model where only the sculpted decoration would have been undertaken by an 'expert', specifically for the occasion.

In her study of rock-hewn architecture and carved decoration in Cappadocia between the 6th and 9th centuries, Nicole Lemaigre Demesnil proposed that workshops of sculptors/excavators could have been set up on sites within a radius of about ten kilometres.[78] The hypothesis that such 'workshops' (and thus craftsmen forming a defined social group) could exist in medieval Cappadocia seems difficult to demonstrate. By developing Lemaigre Demesnil's hypothesis differently, we believe that autonomous craftsmen whose skills were recognised within communities at the local or even regional level were able to move and work at different rock-hewn worksites. We are convinced that the two main models presented here could serve as a basis for reflections on the economics of rock-hewn worksites, their cost, and their social organisation.

More importantly this study makes it possible to propose hypotheses about the status of the inexperienced

---

[76] Zanini 2007: 386–387.
[77] As noted by Lemaigre Demesnil (2010: 165) who points out that interventions of sculptors/excavators were reserved for the eastern part of the church if the investment by its patron were limited.
[78] Lemaigre Demesnil 2010: 165.

workers who seem to be found both on construction sites and on rock-hewn sites. Two categories of people can be distinguished: secular farmers and clergymen, with the autobiographical accounts of Neophytos of Cyprus proving that monks could practice rock carving. Similarly, contemporary interviews in Ethiopia show that clergy members of all ages want to dig their own tombs and participate in the realisation of their place of worship for the salvation of their souls. The participation of monks in digging their own churches in the Medieval period is possible, based on the data gathered in this paper.[79] However, an individual with a high technical knowledge was needed to lead the process of carving a significant rock-hewn tomb or church. Finally, we would like to reiterate the need for the systematic collection of textual, archaeological, and anthropological data to further the study of medieval stonemasons and the importance of addressing this area of research in the future. As we stated at the start of this paper, the economics of construction for rock-hewn architecture still needs to be studied.

Acknowledgment

We would like to extend our sincere gratitude to the Turkish Ministry of Culture and Tourism for having authorised the survey in the province of Nevşehir in 2010 (n°07375590); to the members of the French Institute of Anatolian Studies for their logistical support; the Ethiopian Authority for Research and Conservation of Cultural Heritage for having authorised the ethnoarchaeological research conducted in Ethiopia between 2015 and 2020; and the University of Addigrat for their valuable administrative support and the French Center for Ethiopian Studies for their operative support. The data collection in Turkey was made possible thanks to a TÜBITAK fellowship, while the data in Ethiopia were gathered thanks to a joint DIM-Matériaux anciens et patrimoniaux/Region Île-de-France fellowship conducted under the supervision of Prof M.-L. Derat (CNRS/Laboratoire des Mondes séminitiques) and the Arcadia Fund in London. For their assistance during field work in Ethiopia, we are indebted to Dr. Hagos Abrha, Hailay Atsba, Tesfay Tsegay, Mezgebe Girmay, Bayene Melaku, Solomon Belay, and Priest Kassay; architects Tarn Philipp and Mario Di Salvo; videographers David Tonks and Iacopo Patierno; Sindayo Robel for data management; and Luigi Cantamessa for his valuable support.

The authors would like to thank warmly J.-C. Bessac, J.-P. Gély, and M.-L. Derat for their proofreading and permission to publish their photographs. We also thank Simon J. Barker, Christopher Courault, Javier Á. Domingo, and Dominik Maschek for their editing work, as well as the peer-reviewers for their constructive remarks and comments. Any errors are the responsibility of the authors.

Bibliography

Source

Ps. Zacharia: Brooks, E.W. (éd.) 1924. *Historia Ecclesiastica Zachariae Rhetori vulgo adscripta*, Paris ; Greatex, G. (ed.), Phenix R. R., Horn C. B., Brock S. P. and W. Witakowski (trad.), 2011. *The Chronicle of Pseudo-Zachariah Rhetor. Church and War in Late Antiquity*, Liverpool: Liverpool University Press.

Studies

Balfet, H. (dir.) 1991. *Observer l'action technique: des chaînes opératoires, pour quoi faire?* Paris: Édition du CNRS.

Bessac, J.-Cl. 2015. Artisans, techniques et économie des chantiers rupestres de Hégra, in L. Nehmé (dir.) *Les tombeaux nabatéens de Hégra* I: 163–201. Paris: Académie des Inscriptions et Belles-Lettres.

Bessac, J.-Cl. 2007. *Le travail de la pierre à Pétra*. Paris: Édition du CNRS.

Bessac, J.-Cl. 1986. *L'outillage traditionnel du tailleur de pierre: de l'Antiquité à nos jours*. Paris: Édition du CNRS.

Bernard, S. 2018. *Building Mid-Republican Rome. Labor, Architecture, and the Urban Economy*. New York: Oxford University Press.

Blary, Fr. and J.-P. Gély 2020. *Pierres de construction. De la carrière au bâtiment...* Paris: Éditions du Comité des travaux historiques et scientifiques.

Bril, B. 2019. Comment aborder la question du geste technique pour en comprendre l'expertise et l'apprentissage ?. *Techniques & Culture* 71: online. DOI: https://doi.org/10.4000/tc.11373

Congourdeau, M.-H. 1993. *L'Enkleistra* dans les écrits de Néophytos le Reclus, in C. Jolivet-Lévy, M. Kaplan and J.-P. Sodini (dir.) *Les saints et leur sanctuaire à Byzance. Textes, images et monuments*: 137–149. Paris: Publications de la Sorbonne.

Dehejia, V. and P. Rockwell 2016. *The Unfinished: Stone Carvers at Work on the Indian Subcontinent*. New Dehli: Rooli Books.

Epstein, A. W. and P. M. Schwartzbaum 1986. *Tokali kilise tenth-century metropolitan art in Byzantine Cappadocia*. Washington D.C.: Dumbarton Oaks Research Library and collection.

Equini-Schneider, E., M. Spanu, C. Morselli and C. Vismara 1997. Varia Cappadocia. *Archeologia classica* 49: 101–209.

Freidson, E. 1983. The theory of professions: state of the art, in R. Dingwall and P. Lewis (eds) *The Sociology of the Professions. Lawyers, Doctors and Others*: 19–37. London: Macmillan.

Gallay, A. 2011. *Pour une ethnoarchéologie théorique*. Paris: Éditions errance.

---

[79] Hypothesis formulated by Jolivet-Lévy 2015: 237.

Grégoire, H. 1909. Voyage dans le Pont et la Cappadoce. *Bulletin de correspondance hellénique* 33-1: 3–169.

Hild, F. and M. Restle 1981. *Kappadokien: Kappadokia, Charsianon, Sebasteia und Lykandos.* Vienne: Verlag der Österreichischen Akademie der Wissenschaften.

Jerphanion, G. de 1925–1942. *Une nouvelle province de l'art byzantin: Les églises rupestres de Cappadoce* I-II. Paris: P. Geuthner.

Jolivet-Lévy, C. 2015. La vie des moines en Cappadoce (VIe-Xe siècle): contribution à un inventaire des sources archéologiques, in O. Delouis and M. Mossakowska-Gaubert (eds) *La vie quotidienne des moines en Orient et en Occident (IVe-Xe siècle) I. L'état des sources*: 215–249. Le Caire-Athènes: Institut français d'archéologie orientale.

Jolivet-Lévy, C. 2014. Byzantinisches Kappadokien. (Zaberns Bildbände zur Archäologie), *Bryn Mawr Classical Review*. January, online. Consulted on 2 October 2019.

Jolivet, C. 1991. *Les églises byzantines de Cappadoce: le programme iconographique de l'abside et de ses abords.* Paris: Éditions du CNRS.

Jolivet, C. 1987. Peintures byzantines inédites de Cappadoce: un décor du haut Moyen Âge à Mazıköy. *Archeologia* 229: 36–46.

Jolivet-Lévy, C. and N. Lemaigre Demesnil 2015. *La Cappadoce. Un siècle après G. de Jerphanion* I-II. Paris: Geuthner.

Kazhdan, A. 1991. Mason, in A. Kazhdan (ed.) *Oxford Dictionary of Byzantium*: 1311–1312. Oxford: Oxford University Press.

Keser-Kayaalp, E. and N. Erdoğan 2017. Recent research on Dara/Anastasiopolis, in E. Rizos (ed.) *New Cities in Late Antiquity. Documents and Archaeology*: 151–172. Turnhout: Brepols.

Lamesa, A. 2019. Les barbares Troglodytes: évolution de leur représentation à l'époque antique, in C. Noacco and S. Duhem (eds) *L'homme sauvage dans les lettres et les arts*: 37–48. Rennes: Presses universitaires de Rennes.

Lamesa, A. 2018. Rock-cut tombs and churches in Cappadocia during the Roman and Byzantine periods. The analysis of *chaines opératoires* to understand the economy and sociology of the building sites, in M. Godon (ed.) *Merging Techniques and Cultures. IFEA Archaeological Meeting, 24-25 novembre 2015*: 75–83. Istanbul: Institut français d'études anatoliennes Georges Dumézil.

Lamesa, A. 2016. D'une Cappadoce à l'autre (Ve siècle av. J-C. — Xe siècle apr. J.-C.): problèmes historiques, géographiques et archéologiques. Unpublished PhD dissertation, University of Paris, Sorbonne.

Lamesa, A. 2011. Détermination des intervenants lors de chantiers d'églises rupestres en Cappadoce médiévale (VIIe-XIIIe siècle): méthodes d'analyses croisées, in J. Lorenz and J.-P. Gély (eds) *Carriers et bâtisseurs de la période préindustrielle: Europe et régions limitrophes. Actes du 134e Congrès national des sociétés historiques et scientifiques «Célèbres ou obscurs, hommes et femmes dans leurs territoires et leur histoire», Bordeaux, 20-24 avril 2009*: 177–190. Paris: Édition du comité des travaux historiques et scientifiques.

Lamesa, A. 2010. Processus techniques et *realia*: une histoire de creusement proposée par Néophyte le Reclus, in J. Boivin, V. Lapointe Gagnon, P.-M. Noël and M. Morin (eds) *Actes du 9e colloque étudiant du département d'Histoire de l'université de Laval*: 149–161. Québec: Artefact.

Lamesa, A. and N. Erdoğan 2020. La nécropole rupestre de Dara (Turquie). De nouvelles perspectives de recherche, in D. Moreau, C. S. Snively, A. Guiglia Baldini, L. Milanović, I. Popović, N. Beaudry and O. Heinrich-Tamáska (eds) *Archaeology of a world of changes: Late Roman and Early Byzantine architecture, sculpture and landscapes. Selected papers from the 23rd International Congress of Byzantine Studies (Belgrade 22-27 August 2016 in memoriam Claudiae Barsanti)*: 105–116. Oxford: BAR.

Lamesa, A. and Haylay Atsbəha Haylu 2020. Church Worksites in Eastern Təgray (from the Middle Ages to the 21st Century): Technical-economic and Ethno-archaeological Analyses of local Rock-hewn Practices. *Un œil sur la Corne. Blog scientifique du CFEE* <https://cfee.hypotheses.org/7349>.

Lemaigre Demesnil, N. 2010. *Architecture rupestre et décor sculpté en Cappadoce (Ve-IXe siècle).* Oxford: Archeopress.

Lepage, Cl. and J. Mercier 2005. *Les églises historiques du Tigray: art éthiopien. The Ancient Churches of Tigrai: Ethiopian Art.* Paris: Éditions Recherches sur les Civilisations.

Leroi-Gourhan, A. 1945–1971. *Évolution et technique.* Paris: A. Michel.

McKenzie, J.S. 1990. *The architecture of Petra.* Oxford: Oxford University Press.

Nehmé, L. (dir.) 2015. *Les tombeaux nabatéens de Hégra* I. Paris: Académie des Inscriptions et Belles-Lettres.

Nehmé, L. 2007. Qui sont les artisans des monuments rupestres?, in J.-Cl. Bessac (ed.) *Le travail de la pierre à Pétra*: 15–26. Paris: Édition du CNRS.

Ousterhout, R. 2019. *Eastern Medieval Architecture. The Building Traditions of Byzantium and Neighboring Lands.* New York, Oxford: Oxford University Press.

Ousterhout, R. 2017. *Visualizing community: art, material culture, and settlement in Byzantine Cappadocia.* Washington D.C.: Dumbarton Oaks Research Library and Collection.

Ousterhout, R. 1999. *Master Builders of Byzantium.* Princeton: Princeton University Press.

Öztürk, F. G. 2009. *Kapadokya'da dünden bugüne kaya oymacılığı.* Istanbul: Arkeoloji ve Sanat Yayınları.

Pietersma, A. and B. G. Wright 2007. *A new English translation of the Septuagint: and the other Greek translations traditionally included under that title.* New York, Oxford: Oxford University Press.

Rhoby, A. (dir.) 2009. *Byzantinische Epigramme in inschriftlicher Überlieferung I*, Vienne: Österreichische Akademie der Wissenschaften.

Rodley, L. 1985. *Cave Monasteries of Byzantine Cappadocia.* Cambridge: Cambridge University Press.

Russell, B. 2020. Roman Sculptors at Work: Professionnal Practitioners?, in E. Stewart and D. Lewis (eds) *Skilled Labour and Professionalism in Ancient Greece and Rome*: 243–265. Cambridge: Cambridge University Press.

Schneider, R. 1983. Notes éthiopiennes. *Journal of Ethiopian Studies*, 16: 105–114.

Stewart, E., E. Harris and D. Lewis 2020. Introduction, in E. Stewart and D. Lewis (eds) *Skilled Labour and Professionalism in Ancient Greece and Rome*: 1–25, Cambridge: Cambridge University Press.

Thierry, N. 2002. *La Cappadoce de l'Antiquité au Moyen Âge.* Turnhout: Brepols.

Thierry, N. 1994. *Haut Moyen Âge en Cappadoce: les églises de la région de* Çavuşin. Paris: P. Geuthner.

Thierry, N. 1989. La peinture de Cappadoce au Xe siècle. Recherches sur les commanditaires de la Nouvelle Église de Tokalı et autres monuments, in A. Markopoulos (ed.), *Constantine VII Porphyrogenitus and his age. Second International Byzantine Conference*: 217–246. Athènes: Eurōpaïkó Politistikó Kéntro Delphṓn.

Thierry, N. 1981. Monuments de Cappadoce de l'Antiquité romaine au Moyen Âge byzantin, in C. D. Fonseca (ed.) *Le aree omogenee della civiltà rupestre nell'ambito dell'Impero Bizantino: la Cappadocia, Atti del Quinto Convegno Internazionale di studio sulla civiltà rupestre medioevale nel Mezzogiorno d'Italia (Lecce-Nardo, 12-16 ottobre 1979)*: 39–73. Galatina: Galatina congedo editore.

Thierry, N. 1977. Un problème de continuité ou de rupture, la Cappadoce entre Rome, Byzance et les Arabes. *Comptes rendus de l'Académie des inscriptions et belles-lettres* 121/1: 98–145.

Warland, R. 2013. *Byzantinisches Kappadokien.* Darmstadt: P. von Zabern.

Zanini, E. 2007. Technology and Ideas: Architects and Master-Builders in the Early Byzantine World, in L. Lavan, E. Zanini and A. Sarantis (eds) *Technology in Transition A. D. 300-650*: 379–405. Leiden: Brill.

The Energetics of Earth and Turf Construction in the Roman World

J. Riley Snyder
School of Engineering,
University of Edinburgh
Riley.Snyder@ed.ac.uk

Ben Russell
School of History, Classics and Archaeology,
University of Edinburgh
Ben.Russell@ed.ac.uk

Tanja Romankiewicz
School of History, Classics and Archaeology,
University of Edinburgh
T.Romankiewicz@ed.ac.uk

Christopher T.S. Beckett
School of Engineering,
University of Edinburgh
Christopher.Beckett@ed.ac.uk

Abstract

The vast majority of studies incorporating architectural energetics in Classical Archaeology have focused on building in stone and brick/concrete. Other forms of construction that were ubiquitous in the Roman world have been less explored using this methodology, however. Notable among these neglected materials are earth and turf. These were used in different ways and for different types of structures throughout the Roman world, often for everyday, mostly domestic, projects but also occasionally for massive structures - most obviously the linear walls of Hadrian (the western end of which was originally turf) and of Antoninus Pius in northern Britain. Although Pegoretti and other sources typically used by Classical archaeologists working with architectural energetics rarely discuss earth, a range of other sources and the results of experimental archaeology projects can be used to explore the labour requirements of earth and turf construction. This work forms a key element of the Leverhulme-funded *Earthen Empire: Earth and Turf Building in the Roman North-West* project, some of the initial results of which will be presented here.

Keywords: Earth building materials, turf, energetics, labour rates, Antonine Wall

Introduction

Beyond the necessary examination of the form and function of architectural projects, discussions of their construction have become central themes in scholarship on Roman architecture over the last few decades. The prevalence of physical remains in the archaeological record and discussion of building practices in historical texts has allowed for some direct knowledge of Roman building practices. However, it is the addition of quantitative methods of analysis that have provided a means of modelling material and labour resource management — aspects of building practices that are less evident in traditional data sources. This is why energetics has now become a major strand of architectural history.

While the remains of stone and brick masonry buildings make up the majority of extant Roman architectural remains, earthen construction is widely attested throughout the empire. Unfortunately, due to poor preservation or a selective focus in scholarship on the more 'classical' definition of Roman stone, brick, or concrete architecture, the scale of the use of earthen building materials in the Roman world has yet to be fully explored. The tendency to relegate earthen architecture to a purely vernacular practice fails to account for examples of large-scale construction projects that are almost entirely built of earth or turf: in Britain, the initial phase of the western sector of Hadrian's Wall and the entirety of the Antonine Wall being cases in point. Similarly, the misconception that earthen construction was limited to specific climatic zones or restricted to certain social groups in the Roman period tends to create a 'classical' bias in interpretation.

With this in mind, the *Earthen Empire* project, funded by the Leverhulme Trust (RPG-2018-223), aims to encourage a discussion of the importance of earthen architecture within the Roman world, highlighting its architectural and geotechnical properties and the extent and nature of its use. Although the project (and consequently, this paper) focuses on the north-western provinces, the resulting labour rates and discussion are applicable empire-wide. This paper will begin by discussing different examples of earthen architecture— namely mudbrick, rammed earth, cob, and turf— found throughout the Roman Empire,

IQR for each method reflects the influence that a range of variables (i.e. skill level, environmental conditions, size of the workforce) may have on the rate at which they can be completed.

The range of rates provided in **Table 5** show the typical optimistic (upper quartile), pessimistic (lower quartile), and average (interquartile mean or IQM, calculated as the average of the data between the upper and lower quartiles) values for each earthen construction type. This range should not be viewed as the minimum and maximum rates at which these can be undertaken but as the average rates under good and bad conditions. For example, if a three-metre-high wall of rammed earth was being constructed by a group of five people familiar with the technique, the optimistic rate could be chosen. On the other hand, if the wall was being constructed by fewer people and to a height greater than three metres, the pessimistic value could be chosen. Neither the optimistic nor the pessimistic values reflect the best or worst possible rates and instead provide a conservative range to be used when some conditions are known. In an archaeological context, this range provides some leeway when aspects like soil condition, size of workforce, or season of building is known: important factors that have tangible effects on rates for earthen construction techniques.

Material		Rate (m³/p-day*)	Rate (m³/p-hour)
Mudbrick	Optimistic	0.48	0.060
	Pessimistic	0.29	0.036
	Average	**0.39**	**0.049**
Cob	Optimistic	0.81	0.101
	Pessimistic	0.48	0.060
	Average	**0.64**	**0.080**
Rammed Earth	Optimistic	0.53	0.066
	Pessimistic	0.26	0.033
	Average	**0.39**	**0.049**
Turf	Optimistic	1.31	0.164
	Pessimistic	0.67	0.084
	Average	**0.99**	**0.12**

Table 5. Selected optimistic, pessimistic and average rates for building in mudbrick, rammed earth, cob, and turf. The rates provided for mudbrick and turf factor in the rates for both material production/acquisition and construction. *Rates in person-days account for a working day of eight full hours of labour.

The majority of rates provided in the assessed literature for cob and rammed earth encompass both the preparation and application of the material, though not its extraction. In the case of turf and mudbrick, rates are typically provided separately for the production of the mudbricks and cutting of the turf on the one hand, and the construction of the walls on the other. For the purposes of this paper, these separate rates for turf and mudbrick have been combined where possible to make comparison between building techniques easier. The mudbrick totals, therefore, include the labour that was involved in the manufacture of the bricks (though not the extraction of the soil) and their use. A range of 0.45 to 0.81 m³ per person-day for erecting mudbrick wall has been combined with the optimistic, pessimistic, and average values for producing mudbricks.[103] These totals were combined by converting both figures – production and construction – to person-days per cubic metre, adding these values, and converting them back into cubic metres per person-day. This is represented by the following formula, Equation 1:

$$\text{Rate}_{a+b} = \frac{1}{\left(\frac{1}{\text{Rate}_a} + \frac{1}{\text{Rate}_b}\right)} \qquad [1]$$

For turf, we include the cutting totals, since no processing of the material was required. Similarly, the two rates provided for erecting a structure of turf blocks – 2.22 m³ per person-day and 3.2 m³ per person-day – have been combined with the rates for cutting turf.[104] The lower rates for building in mudbrick compared to building in turf likely come down to the major difference in application. While turf, if placed while still wet and malleable, can be applied to a structure as-is, or with minimal manipulation, mudbrick typically requires additional steps. For instance, a mud 'mortar' would be used to bond each brick and the mudbricks would need to be wetted before application so as not to dry out the bond too quickly – both similar processes to fired brick masonry.

Using the average rates, constructing one cubic metre of material would require the input of roughly 2.6 person-days for mudbrick, 2.6 person-days for rammed earth, 1.6 person-days for cob, and 1.0 person-day for turf. It should be noted, however, that rammed earth had one major advantage over both mudbrick and cob. In the case of mudbrick, the bricks used in construction would have needed to try for at least ten days prior to construction.[105] Cob also requires drying time for each vertical section of roughly 0.5 metres before continuing construction, although this can be as little as half a day if thinner lifts or a drier mix is applied.[106] Rammed earth walls, in contrast, can be worked on continuously and then used immediately, much like turf structures, something that is distinct from even masonry construction.

---

[103] This range is based on Smailes 2019; the much higher rate from Lancaster 2019 was discounted as an outlier.
[104] War Office 1911; Gillette 1920.
[105] Remise 2019: 86.
[106] Evens et al. 2002: 210.

Case study of Roman monumental earthen construction: building a stretch of the Antonine Wall

The Antonine Wall was built around AD 140, with planning apparently already underway as early as AD 139, and the victory of Antoninus Pius over the area celebrated with official diploma and coin issues by AD 142.[107] It runs across Scotland's Midland Valley, cut by the rivers Carron and Kelvin between the firths of the Forth and the Clyde. Its eastern end sits at Carriden near Bo'ness on the shore of the Firth of Forth; its western end lies at Old Kilpatrick on the Clyde. A new comprehensive summary of this impressive turf monument has recently been provided by Hanson and Breeze,[108] with further detail to be found in the individual contributions in the same volume.[109]

The Antonine Wall, although cutting across some of Scotland's most populated areas, is still well preserved in places, with the ditch to the north of the Wall and its upcast mound in front recognisable over large stretches, especially in the central section. Similarly, the Wall survives in places as an upstanding mound of around 1.5m, typically following north-facing, elevated locations, overlooking the wetter areas around the river courses and the territory beyond. The Wall is constructed on a stone base, the superstructure generally utilising turf blocks laid in horizontal layers; this is the *murus caespiticius* ('turf wall') referred to in the *Historia Augusta*.[110] Numerous excavations which cut across the main Wall structure, however, have identified a variety of construction methods and soil-based materials with different architectural detailing, as well as phases of repair and rebuilding. What once appeared as a unitary monument has been argued to be a complex set of architectural elements, including the base, the wall core, and different facing types, and potentially variable methods of capping the wall at the top. Considering all of this evidence, the Antonine Wall is still the Roman Empire's largest turf-based monument, but its complexities are perhaps more accurately described by the term 'earthen structure'.[111]

Anatomy of the Wall

The archaeological excavations across the Antonine Wall, undertaken in earnest since the end of the 19th century, have indicated its heterogeneity in materials used, construction type, and time-depth in construction and repair. Together with the current state of preservation, this makes it very difficult to understand the full structure as it once stood or as originally planned. In particular, this has led to many theories about its original profile. There are, however, aspects of the Antonine Wall that seem to be consistent. First, the Wall was built on a base made of a single layer of un-mortared cobble or rubble stone flanked on each side by larger, worked kerb stones; this was placed, in most (but not all) cases, on subsoil that had been stripped of turf. The function of this stone base is a matter of some debate, but in a recent study we have argued that its primary purpose was connected to moisture management.[112] A second feature that is common throughout the Wall is that the bulk of its superstructure was built of earthen materials, mostly stacked turf or earth fill cladded by faces, the so-called cheeks, of turf or possibly clay-rich soils. It has been proposed that 'clay' cheeks could have been made of puddled clay – a wet plastic waterproofing material of high clay content.[113] Since this material has not been analysed, we will refer to 'clay' cheeks, acknowledging that the exact composition of these elements is uncertain.

Archaeological excavations have shown that there are four basic modes of superstructure construction along the line of the Wall, which can vary over even short distances. First, a stacked turf core with cheeks of what appears to be a different, more clay-rich turf. The best example of this was found at Croy.[114] A second construction type also consisted of a stacked turf core but potentially with what the excavators called 'clay' cheeks. This type has been proposed for parts of the Wall at Inveravon and at Beancross, both sites in the eastern sector.[115] The third type of construction has mostly been identified around Falkirk and further east, and has been reconstructed as an earth core and 'clay' cheeks, most convincingly at Callendar Park.[116] The fourth construction type is an earthen core with turf cheeks, suggested for certain areas at the eastern end of the Wall, at Polmont Park for example, and also, to some extent, at Inveravon.[117] More variety in construction materials is apparent east of the site at Watling Lodge, perhaps as a result of different land use; however, turf remained an important construction material along the line of the Wall and probably always the dominant one.[118]

With little of the Wall surviving vertically and nothing past a height of roughly 1.50 m, at and around Rough Castle for example, there have been many interpretations of its profile.[119] These can be grouped into three basic

[107] Keppie 1974: 151; Hanson and Breeze 2020: 28.
[108] Hanson and Breeze 2020.
[109] Breeze and Hanson 2020.
[110] Ant.Pius, SHA, 5.4.
[111] Romankiewicz *et al.* 2020: 121, 138.
[112] Romankiewicz *et al.* 2020.
[113] Bailey 1995: 586; see discussion in Romankiewicz *et al.* 2020: 131–132.
[114] Glasgow Archaeology Society 1899: 73; Robertson 1969: 39. The current authors have excavated a section of the Wall at Laurieston that shows similar features, the publication of which is forthcoming.
[115] Inveravon: Dunwell and Ralston 1995: 526; Beancross: Bailey 1995a: 612.
[116] Bailey 1995b.
[117] See discussion in Bailey 1995b: 594; Inveravon: Dunwell and Ralston 1995: 526.
[118] Macdonald 1921: 22; Keppie 1974: 71, 78; Hanson and Maxwell 1983.
[119] GAS 1899: 129; Robertson 1967.

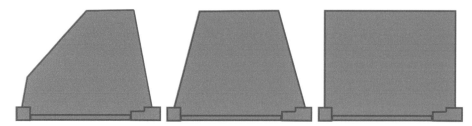

Figure 8. Examples of profile types that have been suggested for the Antonine Wall: 'rampart' type (left), 'battered' type (middle), and vertical type (right).

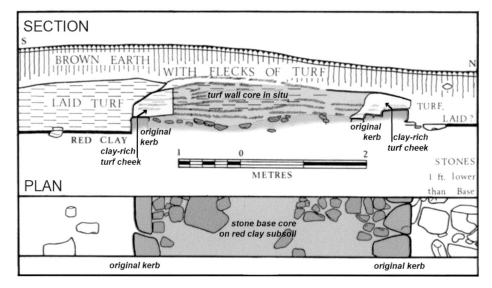

Figure 9. Section drawing and plan of excavation through the Antonine Wall at Croy Hill by Anne Robertson, 1967 (Section No. 11). Drawing by Tanja Romankiewicz after Robertson 1969: Fig 1. Compare colour-coding of different elements with Figure 12.

types (see **Figure 8**). The first is a typical Roman earthen rampart: steep battering rising to the top on the outside (northern side) of the Wall with the inside (southern side) having a near-vertical rise for a third of the way up with a much shallower batter continuing the rest of the way.[120] The second takes the form of a battered wall with an equally steep slope on both sides, similar to the outer face of the rampart profile, which has been put forward in numerous reconstruction images.[121] The third profile is a vertical wall on both sides with a top as wide as its base.[122] However, due to the limited evidence, only the first two more widely accepted profiles will be considered for this paper; these will be referred to as the 'battered' and the 'rampart' profiles. Most scholars agree that the Wall would have been between 3 and 4 m in height, with arguments for and against wall walks and battlements, which do not survive in the archaeological record. The *Earthen Empire* project seeks to examine aspects of the Antonine Wall's structure further, such as its profile shape and likely full original height using geotechnical and structural engineering analytical methods.

Hypothetical model and assumptions

For the purposes of this paper, a hypothetical 100-m stretch of the Antonine Wall has been modelled. Because of its preservation, this model has been based on the averages of measurements taken over the full distance of the Wall. The width of the stone base measures on average 4.25 m, a figure that is commonly reported from interventions across the length of the Wall. Kerb stones were made of a variety of hard stones, such as crystaline sandstone, basalt, or greywacke. They average about 0.5 m deep with the outward face dressed flush along the line of the Wall. The internal stone layer is primarily made of smaller irregular and broken cobbles (up to 0.25 m in diameter) and occasional boulders, all forming a mostly-level, unmortared surface between the kerbs.

Using this stone base as a constant, the four different modes of construction mentioned above will be volumetrically quantified and broken down into material components. They are listed as follows: turf core with turf cheeks (T/T), turf core with clay cheeks (T/C), earth core with clay cheeks (E/C), and earth core with turf cheeks (E/T). The cross-sectional area

---

[120] Hanson and Maxwell 1983: 81–82.
[121] E.g. Breeze 2006: 75, Fig. 5.11; 88, Fig. 5.17.
[122] Bailey 1995: 586; ScARF 2012: 18, Fig. 8.

Process	Rate (m³/p-d)	Source
Collect cobbles	5.49	Abrams, 1984
Lay cobble base	12.00 (m²/p-d)*	Abrams, 1984
Cut kerb stones	0.31	O'Donnell, 2020
Lay kerb stones	6.00 (m²/p-d)*	*Half the rate for laying cobbles (2 workers per stone)*
Cut and stack turf (core)	1.64	This study (optimistic rate)
Cut and stack turf (cheek)	1.24	This study (average rate)
Apply clay (cheek)	1.02	This study (optimistic rate)
Excavate earth (core)	3.30	DeLaine 1997
Fill/pile earth (core)	8.38	Murakami 2015
Build and secure wattle hurdles for battlements and wall walk	6.4 (m²/p-d)**	Coles and Darrah 1977

Table 6. Selected labour rates applied to the model of a 100-m stretch of the Antonine Wall. Grey highlighted rows reflect the rates that have been derived in this paper (see Table 5). All rates have been adjusted to reflect a ten-hour working day.

*Surface area covered by cobbles/kerb stones; **surface area of wattle hurdles.

of both of the above-proposed profiles has been calculated based on the following assumptions:

- The height of the Wall rises 3 m above the stone base.
- All dimensions remain constant over the 100-m distance.
- The 'battered' profile model has an angle of incline of 75 degrees above horizontal, creating a platform, which could, in theory, support a wall walk at the top of the Wall 2.5 m wide.
- The 'rampart' profile model has an 80 degree incline on the outer face[123] as well as for the first metre of the inner face, which then becomes a shallower angle of 45 degrees. The top platform of this model is 1.5 m wide, which, theoretically, could also support a wall walk.
- 'Clay' and turf cheeks are both designated as 0.50 m thick for direct comparison, which is the average value of all recorded instances. It should be noted that the documented thicknesses range from c. 0.30–0.70 for 'clay' cheeks and c. 0.30–1.00 m for turf cheeks.
- The dimensions of the model's stone base are taken from the plan of the excavation of Section No. 11 at Croy Hill (see **Figure 9**).

Additional assumptions built into the energetics model of these profiles are:

- The wall walk is assumed to consist of wattle hurdles measuring 2.9 m long and 1.1 m wide for each construction type and wall profile.[124] While the wall walk is purely hypothetical, having not been identified along the Antonine

Wall, it has regularly been proposed because of evidence of its use in other Roman earthen fortifications. Timber planking has also been identified, but a conservative estimate for the wall walk is preferred in the absence of evidence.
- Wattle hurdles of the same size are also assumed to have been used as battlements, requiring upright posts to be placed every few metres.[125] The justification is the same as above. The orientation is a full hurdle (merlon) alternating with half of a hurdle (crenel).
- For this exercise, transport of materials is not taken into consideration beyond the movement of materials within the construction site, as these are already built into the labour rates. While the *Earthen Empire* project aims at clarifying the provenance of materials used to construct the Wall using micromorphological analysis, there is not enough evidence to positively conclude the origins of the turf, clay, or earth fill.
- In instances where 'clay' cheeks might have been used, it is assumed that this was a lightly processed earthen material, similar to cob in consistency and application. While this material could have been puddled clay or even cob rammed between shutters, and thus required a greater labour investment, a more conservative rate has been chosen to reflect the current absence of evidence.
- Rates for cutting and building with turf and applying 'clay' cheeks (see **Table 6**) have been scaled from per-hour (rightmost column of **Table 5**) to per-day rates, assuming here

---

[123] See discussion of Croy Hill by Hanson and Maxwell 1983: 81.
[124] Coles and Darrah 1977; Shirley 2000.

[125] Coles and Darrah 1977.

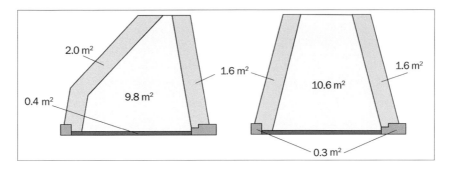

Figure 10. Cross-section of 'rampart' (left) and 'battered' (right) profiles of the Antonine Wall showing the area of cheeks, core, kerb stones, and cobble base.

ten hours per day. This has been done in part to facilitate comparisons with studies of Hadrian's Wall, which all use a ten-hour workday, but also to reflect the fact that soldiers would have worked long days. Indeed, it should be noted that while the working day for Roman military projects would likely have been considerably longer for each worker than for builders employed on typical building projects, it is also possible that soldiers may have been required to work in shifts all day and night when necessary.

- Rates chosen for the turf (**Table 6**) differ between those stacked in the core and those used as cheeks. This is reflected by the selection of the most optimistic rate for the core, assuming the builders' skill level to be high and that the turf used was of satisfactory quality for building (that is, the turf blocks could be removed from the ground whole and transported to the site without breaking). The same assumptions are made for the cheeks, yet with the condition that cutting and building would be done with greater care and precision to maintain even courses and a secure link with the core of the Wall. It has also been suggested that a different type of turf was used for the cheeks, at least for some sections,[126] possibly requiring more care than the turves stacked in the core. Thus, the average rate has been selected for the turf cheek construction.

Material volumes and labour investment

The two examined Wall profiles were broken down further into individual components – kerb stones and cobbles for the stone base, the cheeks and core for the Wall's superstructure (**Figure 10**) – to determine their constitutive cross-sectional areas. These areas were multiplied by 100 m to calculate their volumes over the length of the hypothetical stretch of the model. The labour rates given in **Table 6** were then

applied to these volumes (or surface area in the case of laying cobbles and building wattle hurdles).

Stone base

The stone base, being equivalent for both profiles and each construction technique, was calculated as comprising 27 m³ (surface area of 90 m²) of kerb stones and 35 m³ (covering a surface area of 350 m²) of cobbles. Applying the labour rates above, it would take 86.4 person-days to cut the kerb stones with an additional 18.8 person-days to lay them. The cobbles would require 6.4 person-days to collect and 29.2 person-days to put in place. In total, the stone base required the labour input of just over 137 person-days for this hypothetical 100-m stretch.

Battlements

Along this 100-m stretch of wall, 34.5 wattle hurdles measuring 2.9 m in length (c. 110 m²) would be required to form the wall walk and 40 wattle hurdles (c. 128 m²) for the battlements. It would have taken roughly 37 person-days to produce and place the hurdles for the wall walk and battlements.

Superstructure

The superstructure (the wall above the stone base) consists of a cross-sectional area measuring 9.8 m² for the 'rampart' profile and 10.6 m² for the 'battered' profile. When broken down into the core and cheeks and applied to the length of the wall, the area of the 'rampart' profile yielded volumes of 200 m³ for the inner cheek, 160 m³ for the outer cheek, and 627 m³ for the wall's core. The 'battered' profile was made up of 160 m³ for both the inner and outer cheeks respectively and 735 m³ for the core. The labour input for each mode of construction and profile type of the superstructure is listed in **Table 7**.

---

[126] Romankiewicz *et al.* 2020: 133, 136.

	'Rampart' Profile (in person-days)					'Battered' Profile (in person-days)			
	T/T	T/C	E/T	E/C		T/T	T/C	E/T	E/C
Cheeks	285	351	285	351		259	319	259	319
Core	382	382	265	265		447	447	310	311
Superstructure	*667*	*733*	*550*	*616*		*706*	*766*	*569*	*630*

Table 7. Labour input for each profile and construction technique used to build the superstructure of a 100-metre stretch of the Antonine Wall. T/T = Turf Core with Turf Cheeks, T/C = Turf Core with 'Clay' Cheeks, E/C = Earth Core with 'Clay' Cheeks, and E/T = Earth Core with Turf Cheeks.

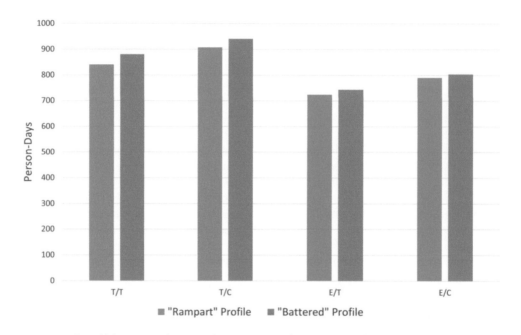

Figure 11. Comparison of total labour input between the 'rampart' and 'battered' profiles for the hypothetical 100-m stretch of the Antonine Wall. T/T = Turf Core with Turf Cheeks, T/C = Turf Core with 'Clay' Cheeks, E/C = Earth Core with 'Clay' Cheeks, and E/T = Earth Core with Turf Cheeks.

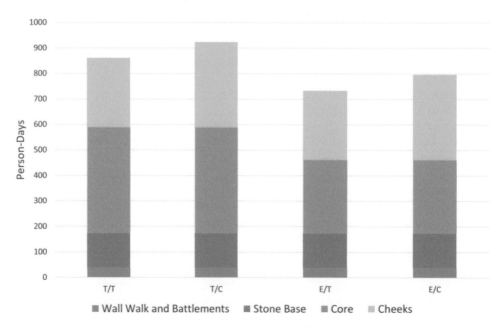

Figure 12. Comparison of labour input between the different modes of construction of the Antonine Wall, broken down by element (core, cheeks, stone base, and wall walk and battlements) using an average of the two profile types. T/T = Turf Core with Turf Cheeks, T/C = Turf Core with 'Clay' Cheeks, E/C = Earth Core with 'Clay' Cheeks, and E/T = Earth Core with Turf Cheek.

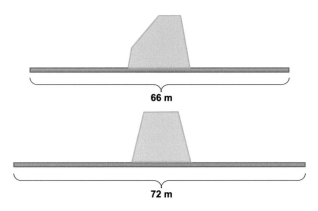

Figure 13. Example of the distance on either side of the Wall that would need to be stripped of turf along its length to construct a superstructure made of turf cheeks and turf core (T/T).

Totals

Combining the labour input necessary for the stone base, superstructure, wall walk, and battlements for each profile and construction technique (**Figure 11**), it is clear that there is little overall difference between profiles; only from 4.5% at the greatest (turf core with turf cheeks) to as low as 1.6% (earth core with 'clay' cheeks). Because of this small difference in labour input and the hypothetical nature of these profiles, the sums of all labour tasks can be averaged for comparison: 860 person-days for turf core with turf cheeks (T/T), 924 person-days for turf core with 'clay' cheeks (T/C), 733 person-days for earth core with turf cheeks, and 797 person-days for earth core with 'clay' cheeks.

Figure 12 shows the breakdown in person-days per construction component using the averaged values of these profiles. It is clear that the variation in the person-days across the different modes of construction is, unsurprisingly, linked to the type of material being applied. The application of clay cheeks requires a 19% increase in labour input compared to turf cheeks. Similarly, digging and piling earth for the core is almost 31% less labour intensive than cutting and stacking turf. While this may seem to suggest that the 'preferred' method of construction would have been a superstructure comprising an earth core and turf cheeks, the currently available archaeological evidence instead suggests that a solid turf wall (here, the turf core with turf cheeks, i.e. the second most labour intensive option in **Figure 11**) was the most widely used mode of construction. This may be due to factors such as the structural nature of turf block construction compared to an earth core, the traditions familiar to those tasked with building different segments of the wall, or the terrain on which the wall was built. For instance, we do know that in contrast to marching camps that used excavated material from the

ditch to build ramparts, the Antonine Wall created a separate upcast mound on the north side of the ditch out of this same excavated material, creating a need for additional digging and piling up of earth to build an earth core of the wall itself. These are issues that require further investigation in order to realise their full impact.

It is important to reiterate that the results (**Figures 11 and 12**) do not reflect the labour required to transport materials to the building site. The source of the kerb stones, for instance, is a point of uncertainty that could have a marked impact on required labour. However, since in many cases local stone was used, the average totals for transport across the full length are still likely to be low, even if in some cases outcrops further afield, at a distance of 1–2 km, had to be exploited.[127] Similarly, the cobbles could have been acquired from the immediate ground surface or from the digging of the ditch in front of the wall. In the case of the turf itself, this could mostly have been taken from the immediate vicinity of the Wall. In the case of a superstructure of both turf core and cheeks (T/T) with turf blocks the size described by Vegetius, an area of 33–36 m wide would have to be stripped from both sides of the centre of the wall, depending on the profile type (**Figure 13**). While this assumes that the entire area around the wall would have yielded viable turf material for constructing the wall, even twice or three times the distance could still be considered immediate to the building works. In the rare cases when good turf was not available, material could have been brought in from further afield or a different mode of construction employed, such as the E/C method.

Discussion

If it is assumed that the Antonine Wall was made of roughly equal proportions of the four modes of construction (T/T, T/C, E/T, E/C), the labour input of the hypothetical model, acting as a proxy, could be thought of as an average of the values presented in **Figure 12**. This would be roughly 829 person-days to construct the 100-m stretch. In practice, since the T/T and T/C modes of construction seem to have been the most common, an average of closer to 900 person-days might be more representative.

How does this compare to that other northern British linear structure, Hadrian's Wall? The recent work of O'Donnell comprehensively investigates the energetics of quarrying stone for the construction of Hadrian's Wall.[128] The results showed that the total labour input for the 117 km-long, 2.5 m-wide, and roughly 4.4 m-high wall was over 3 million person-days – equivalent to

---

[127] E.g. Dunwell and Ralston 1995: 526.
[128] O'Donnell 2020.

roughly 2745 person-days per 100 m. Using the work of Hill, Hodgson estimates that the construction of 100 m of Hadrian's Wall would have taken 1140 person-days.[129] Adding the totals by O'Donnell and Hodgson together results in 3895 person-days for quarrying and construction.

At face value, a 100-m length of Hadrian's Wall, therefore, would require over four times more labour than the equivalent length of the Antonine Wall. In addition, considerable extra labour would have been needed to transport the quantities of stone needed for the former, which on average came from 1 km away.[130] Furthermore, it is likely that construction would have taken considerably more labour than suggested by Hodgson since his estimates have been extrapolated from Hill's assessment of only the first four courses (0.75 m) of the wall and do not consider in detail important aspects such as lime production, scaffolding, and lifting materials to a height. It is very likely, in fact, that a 100-m length of Hadrian's Wall actually took closer to five or six times more labour, in person-days, to complete than an equivalent stretch of the Antonine Wall.

In one of the few other studies to attempt to integrate architectural energetics into an analysis of the Antonine Wall, Flügel and Obmann have recently used figures from experimental archaeological work at the Lunt fort in the 1960s for turf rampart construction.[131] These are the same totals on which Shirley based her analysis for Inchtuthil.[132] For Flügel and Obmann these totals from the Lunt emphasise how expeditious Roman military architecture in turf and timber could be. In practice, however, the rates proposed by Hobley for cutting turf at the Lunt fort are considerably lower than the average values that we use in this paper, which draw on a much wider range of sources.[133] If the figures from the Lunt fort were used in the calculations above, in fact, the total labour necessary for building a wall of solid turf (T/T) or turf core with 'clay' cheeks (T/C), would increase from 900 to over 1400 person-days, i.e. an increase of over 50%. While Flügel and Obmann are correct, therefore, that in the hands of experienced military builders turf construction could be undertaken extremely quickly, the figures that we have detailed above indicate that it could be completed *even* faster than they propose. While it is not the purpose of this paper to calculate the speed of construction and related aspects (project management, size and makeup of the labour force, logistical operations, etc.), it is important to acknowledge that these topics can be addressed using energetics. A full study of all of these aspects of

the Antonine Wall's construction history is in progress by the authors.

Conclusion

Earthen building materials held the same set of advantages for Roman builders as they do for those who continue to practice earthen architecture throughout the world today. The rate at which an earthen structure could be constructed in comparison with structures in stone masonry clearly illustrates the advantages of such architecture. This is especially evident in large building projects like earthen fortifications, where quick building with local materials was essential in hostile environments. Not only did Vegetius recall the suitability of turf for Roman soldiers on the move but it was also still being recommended in the construction of trench revetments only 80 years ago in military engineering manuals.[134]

Possibly the most considerable benefit of earthen architecture is the ubiquity of immediately-available raw materials in almost any geographical location. Furthermore, the adaptability of building techniques to suit the local soil type, environmental conditions, function of the intended building, and skill set of the workers allows for greater adaptability in construction. Where the wet climate of somewhere like Scotland does not provide the means to produce dependable mudbrick or rammed earth buildings, it has clear advantages for constructing in turf or cob.[135]

While buildings of brick, stone, and mortar are typically thought of as having more permanence, earthen structures were not necessarily built to be temporary. Roman structures built of earth that have been found in the archaeological record are often associated with plaster with intricate frescos or marble veneer, therefore confirming an intended permanence in an arguably higher status architectural context. However, one aspect of earthen architecture that has not been factored into the labour rates discussed in this paper is the regular maintenance needed for exposed earthen walls. No matter the type of technique used, or the climactic conditions faced, deterioration will occur if these structures are exposed to the elements. Despite this also being a concern for stone or brick masonry structures and one that has yet to be fully explored in architectural energetic studies, the frequentness of interventions following the initial construction would have been much greater for earthen architecture. This is another topic worthy of further exploration.

The somewhat recent addition of architectural energetics into the study of Roman construction has

[129] Hill 2010: 121–124; Hodgson 2017: App. II.
[130] O'Donnell 2020.
[131] Flügel and Obmann 2020.
[132] Shirley 2000.
[133] Hobley 1971.
[134] United States War Department 1940.
[135] Walker and McGregor 1996a; Walker 2006; Romankiewicz 2019.

broadened our understanding of the capabilities of, and investment made by, Roman builders. Ultimately, however, the role of earth and turf has continued to be understated in the corpus of Roman architecture, especially when compared to prehistoric and medieval archaeology. This paper's aim has not been to elucidate the prevalence of these forms of earthen architecture in the Roman period: this will be published elsewhere. What it has shown, however, is that this prevalence is based, at least in part, on the pronounced efficiency and versatility of earth and turf construction.

Acknowledgements

The authors would like to thank the Leverhulme Trust for the generous support of their research presented here as part of the *Earthen Empire* project (RPG-2018-223). The drawing underlay for **Figure 9** has been provided courtesy of the Glasgow Archaeological Society. The authors would also like to give a special thanks to the reviewers of this paper and editors of this volume for their helpful feedback.

Bibliography

Abrams, E.M. 1984. *The Organization of Labor in Late Classic Copan, Honduras: The Energetics of Construction.* PhD dissertation. Pennsylvania State University, University Park.

Abrams, E.M. 1994. *How the Maya Built Their World: Energetics and Ancient Architecture.* Austin TX: University of Texas Press.

Abrams, E.M. and L. McCurdy 2019. Massive assumptions and moundbuilders: The history, method, and relevance of architectural energetics, in L. McCurdy and E. Abrams (eds) *Architectural Energetics in Archaeology.* London: Routledge.

Alcindor, M. and O. Roselló 2012. Cob, a handy technique for a new self-builder, in C. Mileto, F. Vegas and V. Cristini (eds) *Rammed Earth Conservation.* London: CRC Press.

Bailey, G. 1995a. 4 Beancross (NS 924796), (pp. 611–619), in L.F.J. Keppie, G.B. Bailey, A.J. Dunwell, J.H. McBrien and K. Speller. Some excavations on the line of the Antonine Wall, 1985–93. *Proceedings of the Society of Antiquaries of Scotland* 125: 601–671.

Bailey, G. 1995b. The Antonine frontier in Callendar Park, Falkirk: its form and structural sequence. *Proceedings of the Society of Antiquaries of Scotland* 125: 577–600.

Barker, S. and B. Russell 2012. Labour figures for Roman stone-working: pitfalls and potential, in S. Camporeale, H. Dessales and A. Pizzo (eds) *Arqueología de la Construcción III. Los procesos constructivos en el mundo romano: la economía de las obras.* Madrid and Merida: Anejos de Archivo Español de Arqueologa.

Beckett, C.T.S., P.A. Jaquin and J.-C. Morel 2020. Weathering the storm: A framework to assess the resistance of earthen structures to water damage. *Construction and Building Materials* 242(10): 118098.

Bergère, P. 1820. *Devis-modèle des travaux dépendant du service du génie, contenant l'indication des conditions qui doivent être imposées aux entrepreneurs, ainsi que des détails sur les constructions de chaque nature d'ouvrage, et sur les qualités des matériaux à y employer; suivi d'observations sur la manière de régler, par l'analyse, les prix des ouvrages,* Vol. 3. Paris: De l'imprimerie de la République, Messidor an VII.

Binding, G. 2001. *Medieval Building Techniques,* Tempus, Stroud.

Bourgeois, J. 1987. The History of the Great Mosques of Djenné. *African Arts,* 20(3): 54–92.

Breeze, D.J. 2006. *The Antonine Wall.* Edinburgh: John Donald.

Breeze, D.J. and W.S. Hanson 2020. *The Antonine Wall: Papers in honour of Professor Lawrence Keppie* (Archaeopress Roman Archaeology 64). Oxford: Archaeopress.

Cammas, C. 2018. Micromorphology of earth building materials: toward the reconstruction of former technological processes (Protohistoric and Historic Periods). *Quaternary International* 483: 160–179.

Cato, Varro 1934. *On Agriculture.* Translated by W.D. Hooper and H.B. Ash. Loeb Classical Library 283. Cambridge, MA: Harvard University Press.

Coles, J.M., and R.J. Darrah 1977. Experimental investigations in hurdle making. *Somerset Levels Papers* 3: 32–38.

de Chazelles, C.-A. 1990. Les constructions en terre crue d'Empúrias à l'époque romaine. *Cypsela* 8: 101–118.

de Chazelles, C.-A. 1997. *Les maisons en terre de la Gaule méridionale.* Montagnac: Editions Monique Mergoil.

de Chazelles, C.-A. 2011. La construction en brique crue moulée dans les pays de la Méditerranée, du Néolithique à l'époque romaine. Réflexions sur la question du oulage de la terre, in C.-A. de Chazelles, A. Klein and N. Pousthomis (eds) *Les cultures constructives de la brique crue. Echanges transdisciplinaires sur les constructions en terre crue, 3:* 153–165. Toulouse: Editions de l'Espérou.

DeLaine, J. 1997. *The Baths of Caracalla. A Study in the Design, Construction, and Economics of Large-scale Building Projects in Imperial Rome* (JRA Supplemental Series No. 25). Portsmouth, RI: Journal of Roman Archaeology.

DeLaine, J. 2001. Bricks and mortar: exploring the economics of building techniques at Rome and Ostia, in D.J. Mattingly and J. Salmon (eds) *Economies beyond agriculture in the classical world:* 230–268. New York: Routledge.

Dunwell, A. and I. Ralston 1995. Excavations at Inveravon on the Antonine Wall, 1991. *Proceedings of the Society of Antiquaries of Scotland* 125: 521–576.

Erasmus, C. 1965. Monumental building: Some field experiments. *Southwest Journal of Anthropology* 12: 444–471.

Evans, I., L. Smiley and M.G. Smith 2002. *The hand-sculpted house: a philosophical and practical guide to building a cob cottage*. Vermont: Chelsea Green Publishing.

Flügel, C. and J. Obmann 2020. The power of vivid images in Antonine Wall reconstructions: re-examining the archaeological evidence, in D.J. Breeze and W.S. Hanson (eds) *The Antonine Wall: Papers in honour of Professor Lawrence Keppie* (Archaeopress Roman Archaeology 64): 420–431. Oxford: Archaeopress.

French, C.A.I. 1984. A sediments analysis of mud brick and natural features at el-Amarna, in B.J. Kemp (ed.) *Amarna Reports I*: 189–201. London: Egypt Exploration Society.

Glasgow Archaeological Society (GAS) 1899. *The Antonine Wall Report. Being an Account of Excavations, etc. made under the Direction of the Glasgow Archaeological Society during 1890-1893*. Glasgow: James Maclehose and Sons.

Gillette, H.P. 1907. *Handbook of Cost Data for Contractors and Engineers: A Reference Book Giving Methods of Construction and Actual Costs of Materials and Labor on Numerous Engineering Works*. New York: The Myron C. Clark Publishing Co.

Gillette, H.P. 1920. *Earthwork and its Cost, a Handbook of Earth Excavation*. New York: McGraw-Hill Book Company, Inc.

Hamard, E., B. Cazacliu, A. Razakamanantsoa and J.-C. Morel 2016. Cob, a vernacular earth construction process in the context of modern sustainable building. *Building and Environment* 106: 103–119.

Hanson, W.S. and D.J. Breeze. 2020. The Antonine Wall: the current state of knowledge, in D.J. Breeze and W.S. Hanson (eds) *The Antonine Wall: Papers in honour of Professor Lawrence Keppie* (Archaeopress Roman Archaeology 64): 9–37. Oxford: Archaeopress.

Hanson, W.S. and G.S. Maxwell, G.S. 1983. *Rome's north west frontier: the Antonine Wall*. Edinburgh: Edinburgh University Press.

He, N. 2015. *How to Study Ancient Mind: the Theory and Practices of Cognitive Archaeology* (怎探古人何所思——精神文化考古理论与实践探索). Beijing: Science Press.

Hill, P. 2010. *The Construction of Hadrian's Wall*. Stroud: The History Press.

Hobley, B., 1971. An experimental reconstruction of a Roman military turf rampart. *Roman Frontier Studies 1967*: 21–33.

Hobley, B. 1982. Roman military structures at The Lunt Roman fort: Experimental simulations 1966–1977, in P J. Drury (ed.) *Structural Reconstruction*,

BAR British Series no. 110: 21–33. Oxford: British Archaeological Reports.

Hodder, I. (ed.) 2013. Çatalhöyük *excavations: the 2000-2008 seasons*. Çatal Research Project vol. 7. British Institute at Ankara Monograph 46. Monumenta Archaeologica 29. Los Angeles: Cotsen Institute of Archaeology Press.

Hodder, I. (ed.) 2014. *Integrating Çatalhöyük: themes from the 2000-2008 seasons* (Çatal Research Project vol. 10, British Institute at Ankara Monograph 49. Monumenta Archaeologica 32). Los Angeles: Cotsen Institute of Archaeology Press.

Hodgson, N. 2017. *Hadrian's Wall: Archaeology and history at the limit of Rome's empire*. London: Robert Hale.

Hodgson, N. 2020. Why was the Antonine Wall made of turf rather than stone?, in D.J. Breeze and W.S. Hanson (eds), *The Antonine Wall: Papers in honour of Professor Lawrence Keppie* (Archaeopress Roman Archaeology 64): 300–331. Oxford: Archaeopress.

Holden, T. and L. Baker. 2004. *The Blackhouses of Arnol*. Research Report. Edinburgh: Historic Scotland.

Homsher, R. 2012. Mud bricks and the process of construction in the Middle Bronze Age southern Levant. *Bulletin of the American Schools of Oriental Research* 368: 1–27.

Houben, H. and H. Guillaud 1994. *Earth Construction: A Comprehensive Guide*. London: Intermediate Technology Publications.

International Labour Office 1963. *Men Who Move Mountains: An Account of a Research Project Concerned with Manual Methods of Earthmoving*. ILO Management Development and Productivity Mission to India. Bombay: R. Leslie Mitchell.

Jaquin, P.A., C.E. Augarde, D. Gallipoli and D.G. Toll 2009. The strength of unstabilised rammed earth materials. *Géotechnique* 59 (5): 487–490.

Jimenez, R.A. and D. O'Dwyer 2018. Earthen buildings in Ireland, in I. Wouters, S. van de Voorde, I. Bertels, B. Espion, K. de Jonge and D. Zastavani (eds) *Proceedings of the 6th International Congress on Construction History (6ICCH 2018). Brussels, Belgium, vol. 2*: 787–794. Boca Raton FL: CRC Press.

Kemp, B. 2000. Soil (including mud-brick architecture), in P.T. Nicholson and I. Shaw (eds) *Ancient Egyptian Materials and Technology*: 78–103. Cambridge: Cambridge University Press.

Keppie, L.F.J. 1974. The building of the Antonine Wall: archaeological and epigraphic evidence. *Proceedings of the Society of Antiquaries of Scotland* 105: 151–165.

Kuhnle, G. 2018. *Argentorate. Le Camp de la VIIIe Legion et la Presence militaire romaine à Strasbourg*. Vol. 1. Monographien Band 141,1 and 141.2. Mainz: Römisch-Germanisches Zentral Museum.

Lancaster, J. 2019. To house and defend: The application of architectural energetics to southeast Archaic Greek Sicily, in L. McCurdy and E. Abrams (eds)

Architectural Energetics in Archaeology: 95–113. London: Routledge.

Little, B. and T. Morton 2001. *Building with Earth in Scotland: Innovative Design and Sustainability*. Scottish Executive Central Research Unit. Edinburgh: Her Majesty's Stationary Office.

Lorenzon, M., J. Nitschke, R. Littman and J. Silverstein 2020. Mudbricks, Construction Methods, and Stratigraphic Analysis: A Case Study at Tell Timai (Ancient Thmuis) in the Egyptian Delta. *American Journal of Archaeology*,124(1):105–131.

Macdonald, G. 1921. The building of the Antonine Wall: a fresh study of the inscriptions. *Journal of Roman Studies* 11: 1–24.

Maniatidis, V. and P. Walker 2003. *A Review of Rammed Earth Construction*, Report for DTi Partners in Innovation Project 'Developing Rammed Earth for UK Housing', Bath.

McHenry, P.G. 1984. *Adobe and Rammed Earth Buildings: Design and Construction*, Tucson: University of Arizona Press.

Michel, P. 1985. Les expériences contemporaines au service d'archéologie, in J. Lasfargues (ed.) *Architecture de terre et de bois. L'habitat privé des provinces occidentales du monde romain. Antécédents et prolongements: Protohistoire, Moyen Age, et quelques experiences contemporaines*: 169–176. Paris: Editions de la Maison des Sciences de l'Homme.

Milek, K.B. 2012. Floor formation processes and the interpretation of site activity areas: an ethnoarchaeological study of turf buildings at Thverá, northeast Iceland. *Journal of Anthropological Archaeology* 31: 119–137.

Miller, F.T.W. 1901. *Lockwood's Builder's and Contractor's Price Book.* London: Crosby Lockwood.

Moulherat, C., M. Tengberg, J.F. Haquet and B. Mille 2002. First evidence of cotton at Neolithic Mehrgarh, Pakistan: analysis of mineralized fibres from a copper bead. *Journal of Archaeological Science*, 29(12): 1393–1401.

Murakami, T. 2015. Replicative construction experiments at Teotihuacan, Mexico: Assessing the duration and timing of monumental construction. *Journal of Field Archaeology* 40(3): 263–282.

Noble, R. 1983. Turf-walled houses of the Central Highlands. An experiment in reconstruction. *Folk Life* 22: 68–83.

O'Donnell, K. 2020. The quarries of Hadrian's Wall Labour Costs and Material Requirements, in C. Courault and C.M. Moreno (eds) *Quantitative Studies and Production Cost of Roman Public Construction*. Cordoba: Universidad de Córdoba, UCOPress.

Perring, D. 2002. *The Roman House in Britain*, London and New York: Routledge.

Phelps Brown, E.H and S. Hopkins 1955. Seven Centuries of Building Wages. *Economica, 22*(87): 195–206.

Pickett, J., J. Schreck, R. Holod, Y. Rassamakin, O. Halenko, and W. Woodfin 2016. Architectural energetics for tumuli construction: The case of the medieval Chungul Kurgan on the Eurasian steppe. *Journal of Archaeological Science* 75: 101–114.

Pliny 1961. *Natural History, Volume 9: Books 33–35.* Translated by H. Rackham. Loeb Classical Library 394. Cambridge, MA: Harvard University Press.

Quagliarini, E. and S. Lenci 2010. The influence of natural stabilizers and natural fibres on the mechanical properties of ancient Roman adobe bricks. *Journal of Cultural Heritage* 11: 309–314.

Rees, A. 1819. *The Cyclopaedia: Universal Dictionary of Arts, Sciences, and Literature.* Vol. 27. London: A. Strahan Printer.

Remise, F. 2019. An energetics approach to the construction of the Heuneburg: Thoughts on Celtic labour cost choices, in L. McCurdy and E. Abrams (eds) *Architectural Energetics in Archaeology*: 76–94. London: Routledge.

Robertson, A.S. 1969. Recent work on the Antonine Wall. *Glasgow Archaeological Journal* 1: 37–42.

Romankiewicz, T., K. Milek, C. Beckett, B. Russell and J.R. Snyder 2020. New perspectives on the structure of the Antonine Wall, in D.J. Breeze and W.S. Hanson (eds) *The Antonine Wall: Papers in honour of Professor Lawrence Keppie* (Archaeopress Roman Archaeology 64): 121–141. Oxford: Archaeopress.

Roux, J.-C. and C. Cammas 2007. La bauge coffrée: apprehension d'un mode de construction inédit dans la ville protohistorique de Lattes, Hérault (deuxième quart du IVe s. av. n. è.), in H. Guillaud, H. de Chazelles and A. Klein (eds) *Les constructions en terre massive: pisé et bauge, échanges transdisciplinaires sur les constructions en terre crue 2*: 87–98. Montpellier: de l'Espérou.

Roux, J.-C. and C. Cammas 2010. Les techniques constructives en bauge dans l'architecture protohistorique de Lattara, Lattes, Héault (milieu V^e - IVe s. av. n. è.), in T. Janin (ed.) *Premières données sur le cinquième siècle avant notre ère dans la ville de Lattara* (Lattara 21): 219–288. Lattes: Association pour le Développement de l'Archéologie en Languedoc.

Russell, B. 2018. 'Difficult and costly': stone transport, its constraints, and its impact, in C. Coquelet, G. Creemers, R. Dreesen, É. Goemaere (eds) *Roman Ornamental Stones in North-Western Europe*: 131–150. Namur: Agence Wallone du Patrimoine.

Russell, B. and E. Fentress 2016. Mud brick and pisé de terre between Punic and Roman North Africa, in J. DeLaine, A. Albuerne and A. Pizzo (eds) *Arqueología de la construcción, V. Man-made materials, engineering and infrastructure.* Madrid: Consejo Superior de Investigaciones Científicas: 131–143

Russell, M. 2002. *A Different Country. The Photographs of Werner Kissling.* Birlinn: Edinburgh.

SAMPU and HPICHA (School of Archaeology and Museology Peking University and Henan Provincial Institute of Cultural Heritage and Archaeology), 2007. *Discovery and Study in Wangchenggang, Dengfeng during 2002-2005 (登封王城岗考古发现与研究 (2002-2005))*. Zhengzhou: Daxiang Press.

ScARF 2012. F. Hunter and M. Carruthers (eds) *Scotland: The Roman Presence*, Scottish Archaeology Research Framework: Society of Antiquaries of Scotland. <http://tinyurl.com/d24fbpr>. Accessed 23/04/2020>.

Shen, K., J.N. Crossley, A.W.-C. Lun 1999. *The Nine Chapters on the Mathematical Art: Companion and Commentary*. Oxford: Oxford University Press/ Beijing: Science Press.

Shillito, L.-M. 2017. Multivocality and multiproxy approaches to the use of space: lessons from 25 years of research at Çatalhöyük. *World Archaeology* 49(2): 237–259.

Shirley, E.A.M. 2000. *The Construction of the Roman Legionary Fortress at Inchtuthil*, BAR British Series no. 298. Oxford: Archaeopress.

Smailes, R.L. 2011. Building Chan Chan: A project management perspective. *Latin American Antiquity* 22(1): 37–63.

Smailes, R.L. 2019. A construction management approach to building the monumental adobe ciudadelas at Chan Chan, Peru, in L. McCurdy and E. Abrams (eds) *Architectural Energetics in Archaeology*. London: Routledge.

Snyder, J.R. 2019. Bricks in the wall: an examination of brick procurement in fifth-century Ravenna, in E. Cirelli, E. Giorhi and G. Lepore (eds) *Economia e Territorio: L'Adriatico centrale tra tarda Antichità e alto Medioevo* (BAR International Series 2926): 83–89. Oxford: BAR.

Stefánsson, H. 2019. *From Earth. Earth Architecture in Iceland. Transl. A. Yates*. Reykjavík: Gullinsnið.

Trumm, J. and M. Flück 2013. *Am Südtor von Vindonissa. Die Steinbauten der Grabung Windisch-Spillmannwiese 2003-2006 im Süden des Legionslagers*. Veröffentlichungen der Gesellschaft Pro Vindonissa 22. Brugg: Kantonsarchäologie Aargau.

United States Commission of Fish and Fisheries 1886. *Report of the Commissioner for 1884*, Part XII. Washington, DC: Government Printing Office.

Unites States War Department 1940. *FM 5-15 Engineering Field Manual of Field Fortifications*. Washington, DC: United States Government Printing Office.

Vegetius 1996. *Epitome of Military Science*. Translated by N.P. Milner. Translated Texts for Historians 16. Liverpool: Liverpool University Press.

Vitruvius 1931. *On Architecture, Volume I: Books 1-5*. Translated by F. Granger. Loeb Classical Library 251. Cambridge, MA: Harvard University Press.

Vitruvius 1934. *On Architecture, Volume II: Books 6-10* (Loeb Classical Library 280). Translated by F. Granger. Cambridge, MA: Harvard University Press.

Walker, B. and C. McGregor, with R. Little. 1996a. *Earth structures and construction in Scotland. A guide to the recognition and conservation of earth technology in Scottish buildings* (Technical Advice Note 6). Edinburgh: Historic Scotland.

Walker, B., and C. McGregor, 1996b. *The Hebridean Blackhouse. A Guide to Materials, Construction and Maintenance* (Technical Advice Note 5). Edinburgh: Historic Scotland.

Walker, B. 2006. *Scottish Turf Construction* (Technical Advice Note 30). Edinburgh: Historic Scotland.

Walker, P., R. Keable, J. Martin, and V. Maniatidis 2003. *Rammed Earth: Design and Construction Guidelines*. Watford: BRE.

War Office 1911. *Manual of Field Engineering, 1911*. London: His Majesty's Stationery Office.

Williams-Ellis, C. 1920. *Cottage Building in Cob, Pisé, Chalk and Clay: a Renaissance,* (second edition). London: Country Life Limited.

Williams-Ellis, C., J. Eastwick-Field and E. Eastwick-Field 1947. *Building in Cob, Pisé and Stabilized Earth* (revised and enlarged edition). London: Country Life Limited.

Wilson, P. 2012. Archaeology in the Delta, in C. Riggs (ed.) *The Oxford Handbook of Roman Egypt*. Oxford: Oxford University Press.

Xie, L., D. Wang, H. Zhao, J. Gao and T. Gallo 2021. Architectural energetics for rammed-earth compaction in the context of Neolithic to early Bronze Age urban sites in Middle Yellow River Valley, China. *Journal of Archaeological Science, 126*, 105303.

Yuan, Z. 1983. Addressing the corvee labour of the Qin from the archaeological data of the mausoleum of the first emperor of Qin (从秦始皇陵的考古资料看秦王朝的徭役), in *Monograph on Peasant Wars in Chinese History*, vol. 3 (中国农民战争史研究集刊(第三辑)). Shanghai: Shanghai People's Press: 42–55.

Ziyaeifar, M., H. Meshki and M.A. Morovat 2005. Arg-e-Bam (Bam Citadel) and Its History. *Earthquake Spectra*, 21(1 suppl): 13–28.

'perch, n.1.' *Oxford English Dictionary Online*, Oxford University Press, December 2019, <www.oed.com/view/Entry/140575>. Accessed 15 December 2019.

Quarrying Megaliths in Heliopolis (Baalbek, Lebanon): The Jupiter Temple and the Hajjar al Hibla Quarry

Jeanine Abdul Massih

Lebanese University
abdulmassih.j@gmail.com

Abstract

The study of stone exploitation in Baalbek, conducted by the Lebanese University within the framework of a program initiated by the German Archaeological Mission (DAI), and in particular the Hajjar al Hibla quarry, offered a unique opportunity to analyse an extraction area where the destination and use of stone are well-defined in a monument: the Jupiter Temple. The main objectives of this study are to reconstruct the chronology of the extraction phases and to establish a sequence of quarrying operations in relation to the monument. The close examination of the organisation in the quarrying area, the extraction and transportation techniques used, and the daily life in the quarry broadened our observations and made it possible to propose a reconstruction of the sequence from the quarry to the temple.

Keywords: Quarry, stone exploitation, Baalbek, Jupiter Temple, economy of construction

Introduction

In 16 BC two legions of veterans, the 5th Macedonian and the 8th Augusta, were ordered by the emperor Augustus to be stationed for the first time in Beirut and Baalbek.[1] The city of Heliopolis had just been annexed to the *Colonia Iulia Augusta Felix Berytus* under Julius Cesar's reign. It was most probably around the same period that the construction of Heliopolis's temple of Jupiter was ordered by Augustus, in an attempt to spread Roman culture and to secure the inland cities. In AD 193, the city was granted *ius italicum* rights by the emperor Septimus Severus and became known as *Colonia Iulia Augusta Felix Heliopolitana.*[2]

Prior to the Roman conquest, Heliopolis was an important religious centre well-installed along the Beqaa valley's major circulation routes; it continuously held this role during Hellenistic times[3] and through the reigns of Iturean princes. Local Arab rulers were identified as client kings to Rome; they had titles such as tetrarch or high priest inscribed on their coinage testifying to the presence of an important pilgrimage centre in the city.[4] Heliopolis was therefore chosen by the emperor Augustus to receive the great temple of Jupiter. It was to be constructed directly above the earlier sacred buildings and to integrate all the previous religious traditions within its design.

It was on this artificial mound that the construction of the gigantic temple started. A Greek inscription dedicated to Fortuna is engraved on the top of the shaft of one of the great court's columns, dating to the reign of Nero. It is the only existing inscription that certifies the continuity of construction up until AD 60 and that testifies to its unfinished state.[5] The building project continued throughout the reigns of successive emperors and was finally inaugurated, in its unfinished form, in the 3rd century AD, along with the temples of Bacchus, Venus, and Mercury, which were mainly built during that same century.

Jupiter temple

Workshops of architects, masons, stonemasons, sculptors, blacksmiths, carpenters, and quarrymen were involved in the construction of the temple of Jupiter. It was a Corinthian peripteral temple that was initially planned with huge dimensions (106 × 69 m) that were reduced (88 × 48 m), but it was still one of the largest, if not the largest, temples of the Roman world. The massiveness of the architecture is instantly noticeable from the gigantic building material used for the podium and the entire elevation.

Constructed on a prominent podium 13 m high that overlooks the Beqaa valley, the temple was surrounded by no less than 54 columns of which only six remain on the southern façade. Ten columns constitute the temple front, 19 run along each side, and ten stand on the west

---

[1] Strabo 16.2.19.
[2] Aliquot 2009: 39; Sawaya 2009: 26.
[3] Coquais 1967: 2990; Hajjar 1977: 4-7, n. 1.
[4] Rey-Coquais 1967: 2851.

[5] Seyrig 1937: 95–97; Rey-Coquais 1967: 2733.

Figure 1. Aerial view of the temple of Jupiter (© Bassem El Zeim).

side. The columns were 20 m tall, had a diameter of 2.2 m, and were composed of three drums. They were raised on bases of 3 m by 2.2 m high installed directly on the platform's upper face (**Figure 1**).

The Corinthian capitals ornamenting the upper part of the columns were carved from blocks of the same size as the bases, with a weight of approximatively 70 tonnes. Placed above the columns, some 35 m above the Beqaa level, the capitals carried the entablature, which was another 5 m high and was composed of 58 tonnes of sculpted architrave/frieze and 75 tonnes of pediment. Tall walls and more columns inside the temple must have supported the massive roof, which was made of cedar wood.

The podium

This gigantic sanctuary dedicated to Jupiter Heliopolitan is elevated on a massive podium built with huge megalithic blocks. The construction of the podium employed massive shaped stones that we will call 'megaliths' in order to differentiate them from the huge 'monolithic stones' also used in the construction.

The podium of the temple of Jupiter was designed to incorporate the Hellenistic temple and all the earlier remains within the base structure of its foundation. The archaeological sounding performed in the

courtyard of the religious building[6] has revealed that the Hellenistic temple was directly installed above the remains of earlier occupations dating from the Chalcolithic Age to the Bronze Age. The instability of the *tell* on which the earlier sanctuary was built meant that the Roman builders had to reinforce the podium in order to ensure its structural stability and its ability to support the future weight of the gigantic temple. This is important due to the seismic nature of the Beqaa plain that stretches between two Lebanese mountain ranges. The seismic activity is mainly related to the so-called Yamouneh fault, which extends from south to north through Baalbek.

Megalithic, shaped stones extracted from the nearby quarry, located 800 m south-east of the sanctuaries, were used to compose the structural shell of the podium. The temple's huge structure was supported by a characteristic two- or three-row megalith design. The first row is composed of 30 shaped, megalithic blocks with an average dimension of 9.50 m in length, 4.20 m in height, and about 4 m in width, each weighing about 400 tonnes. These rows encircle the monument on its northern, western, and southern sides. The eastern side, embedded in the construction of the sacred courtyard, could not be observed. The northern and southern faces of the podium are

---

[6] van Ess 2008: 99–120.

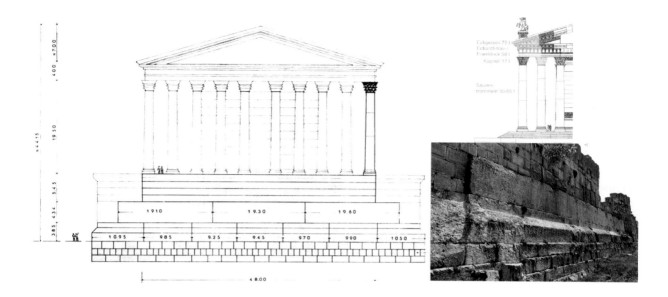

Figure 2. Left: drawing of the podium's western façade (Adam 1977: fig. 13); Right: view of the trilithon (bottom) and drawing of the elevation of the temple (above) (van Ess and Rheidt 2014: 163).

composed of megalithic stones that were used to enlarge the platform by about 10 m on each side. They were abandoned after the original plan of the building was reduced, at which point the Hellenistic walls delimited the building on its longest façades. The reason for these changes is not clear, but it was probably related to financial or time constraints.

A second course of megaliths was planned above the first layer of construction but was aborted after three megalithic stones on the western façade were erected. Known as the trilithon, these gigantic stones measure 19.10 m, 19.30 m, and 19.56 m long, 4.20 m high, and about 4 m wide, and they weigh approximately 800 tonnes each (**Figure 2**). Two other megaliths of the same size were found abandoned in situ in the south-east quarry commonly known as the quarry of Hajjar al Hibla. This name was given by the local inhabitants to the oldest and most famous megalith, Hajjar al Hibla (stone of the pregnant woman or 'pierre de l'enceinte'). In the 1970s, a second megalith of the same size was unearthed during construction work in the western extraction area. The similarity in size of these two stones and the trilithon led the German scholar Ruprechtsberger to conclude that these two megaliths were meant to be the two angle stones of the podium (north and south corners. These stones would have completed the construction of the trilithon course.[7]

The phases of the podium construction

The western façade offers a unique opportunity to observe the nearly-completed enlargement of the podium. It therefore reveals the different stages of its construction. The preparation phase or 'foundation layers' consist of three rows of monolithic stones. They were assembled alternately using two headers and one stretcher. The choice of using smaller sized blocks as the foundation for the megalithic construction is due to the irregular bedrock of the Beqaa Valley, which is known from geophysical surveys and geological studies. The three rows of stone masonry composed of monolithic blocks are in fact an adjustment layer, made to create a regular and horizontal level on which the megaliths could be placed. The foundation was planned to be invisible, embedded in the earth under the ancient walking level.

The upper surface of the foundation holds the first row of megaliths, which is approximately 4 m high. The second row of megaliths is represented by the trilithon, composed of three large stones of 4.20 m high, identical to the megaliths of the first row. At this stage, the megalithic construction was interrupted, and the remaining height of about 5.5 m to reach the platform's surface was completed with reused stones. A column base belonging to the temple colonnade and other monolithic stones were incorporated into the construction of the last courses in the monument's western façade. The north and south façades were realigned to the boundaries of the Hellenistic temple.

---

[7] Ruprechtsberger 1998: 333–339; 1999: 7–56.

The quarry of Hajjar al Hibla

The south-eastern limestone quarry presents a more or less compact conglomerate that develops in a slope of approximately 15.5 degrees north-west.[8] According to the geological map, this limestone is both from the Upper Lutetian (a compact marmorean) and Lower Lutetian (a marly composition). This conglomerate is made of fine, compact limestone elements with an average length of a few centimetres bonded by a calcareous and iron oxide cement; it highlights the fragmented aspect of the rock and reflects both its colour and the dissolution of the cement during prolonged exposure to water. The actions of water and natural elements eroded the surface of the exposed faces producing the natural rock's fragmentation as seen on all the upper layers of the geological formation.

Due to its fragmented composition, the rock was not suitable for sculpture or decoration and was therefore used for the extraction of the podium's massive elements. A more homogeneous limestone was found in the quarry known as Al-Kayale, which probably provided all of the stone used for the decorative elements. The diversity of limestone observed in the construction of the temple of Jupiter led us to undertake a survey around the city of Baalbek, which revealed several stone exploitation sites situated mainly within a radius of 2 km around the city. Nevertheless, the most important and most exploited area is the south-eastern quarry that extends from Hajjar al Hibla to more than 2 km southward. The furthest megalith, known as the Machnaqa Stone, is 1.5 km south of Hajjar al Hibla and corresponds in size to the first row of megaliths observed at the sanctuary.[9] The megalithic construction required, above all, a proximity between the monument and the quarries. Most megalithic extraction areas are located less than one kilometre from the monuments for which the stones are destined.[10]

Areas of extraction

The research on the Hajjar al Hibla quarry started in 2004 with a general survey of the entire stone exploitation area of Baalbek along with the study, documentation, and mapping of the Hajjar al Hibla quarry. The exploitation areas, the extraction techniques, and the elements regarding the organisation of the operations in the megalithic quarry were documented.[11]

From 2014 to 2018 excavation works and site presentation were carried out on the deep extraction pit of Hajjar al Hibla. The research program aimed to explore the stratigraphic layers in order to propose a chronology for the occupation of the heritage site. Through the clearance of the layers from the quarry floor and the quarry faces, a more accurate analysis of extraction techniques was realised by identifying toolmarks and evidence for transport, such as ropes and traces of machinery.

The surface area of the Hajjar al Hibla quarry covers about 14 hectares, stretching from the Hill of Cheikh Abdallah to the west, to the great depression south of the modern road to Beirut (**Figure 3**). This vast exploitation is divided into several areas of extraction and occupation. Two types of quarrying technique were identified. The first, widespread on the surface of the hill, is an opencast extraction quarried in steps. The second type is a deep extraction pit opened in the substratum's lower levels. The 4.2-m natural geological stratum from which the megaliths were extracted has been identified in these deep layers.

The hilltop quarry

The exploitation of Cheikh Abdallah's Hill is distinguished by the extraction of ridges in the bedrock surface. Thus, the extraction of the stone was carried out by the simple use of a crowbar operating on the natural cracks of the rock. In this flattened surface, several cavities were dug using the natural geological cracks to initiate their opening. Several toolmarks left on unfinished natural cracks allowed us to reconstruct the stages and process of creating these cavities. A total of 11 caves overlooking the quarry and the entire city of Baalbek were excavated into the hillside and opened towards the west. The entrances are organised along a long trench dug into the slope, leading to the cave doors (**Figure 4**). Some are equipped with a locking system and others are, today, in a poor state of conservation, which makes it difficult to identify whether or not they were similarly equipped.

Attributed to the installation of the necropolis in the quarry during the Roman and Byzantine periods, the caves were used as carved tombs. They consisted of an entrance leading to a central room with carved sarcophagi on its three sides that were placed under shaped *arcosolia*. Observation suggests an earlier phase of occupation in some of the caves. This evidence is of a structural nature; an opening in the ceiling of the central room for ventilation and light was found in one of the caves in addition to a latch on door locking systems that can only be operated from the inside. These elements led us to consider an earlier phase of

[8] Dubertret 1950.
[9] Abdul Massih 2014: 56.
[10] Bessac 2010: 176.
[11] Abdul Massih 2008: 77–96.

Figure 3. General map of the quarry showing the circulation and different installations (J. Abdul Massih and N. Chahine).

Figure 5. Quarrying monoliths in the upper quarry (© Archive Bonfils).

Figure 4. Above: the entrance to one of the carved cave dwellings on the hilltop; below: a second opening located in the western quarried face of Hajjar al Hibla (Photo J. Abdul Massih).

occupation probably related to extraction activities, such as the use of a simple room as a shelter for workers. These installations have been widespread in stone quarries from ancient times to the present day.[12]

The entire upper part of the hill is now separated from the rest of the quarry by a modern road. On the west side of this modern asphalt road is an opencast quarry where monolithic stones were extracted in steps following the natural slope of the hill. Today, the entire extraction area is filled with gravel, accumulation, and waste, which reduces the scope of our observation. Fortunately, an archived photo published by Bonfils (**Figure 5**) depicts a quarry of large stones delimited by wide extraction trenches. The extraction techniques observed in this quarried area correspond to the type of extraction activities spread over the entire upper layer above the thick geological strata from which the megaliths were extracted. About one hectare of quarry overlooks the edge of the deep extraction pit of Hajjar al Hibla. The southern edges of the quarry feature long, sinuous, 0.13-m wide trenches dug into the bedrock surface and forming a system of narrow channels used to collect rainwater that was then stored in a large cistern created down the hill. On the western edge of the cistern and coming from the upper level, a series of stair levels from the step extraction led to the lower extraction pit.

---

[12] Schmidt-Colinet 1990: 87-92; 1995: 53-58; Abdul Massih *et al.* 1997: 159–197; Bessac 2002: 29-51.

The megalithic Hajjar al Hibla extraction pit

The area of the megalithic quarry of Hajjar al Hibla was excavated in a deep extraction pit. The eastern quarry face is 6 to 8 m high and approximately 255 m in length. The delimited area, carved in the north-west slope of the hill, covers a surface of two hectares of extraction, creating a steep rocky angle at the junction of the south and east quarry faces. The western modern limit of this exploitation is marked by the asphalt road. In its southern half, the rocky boundary is completely embedded in gravel under the cemetery structures. The northern half, covered by the modern road, was completely cleared on its eastern façade. A rock-cut face of approximately 3 m in depth was uncovered, showing large monolithic blocks similar to the ones observed on the upper slope of the hill. The presence of wide trenches of extraction and many stones left on site offer a unique chance to study this material alongside the blocks used on the construction site.

Later, in the Roman and Byzantine periods, the necropolis of the city spread to the western quarry face (**Figure 6**). Carved tombs were dug in the rock using natural, weakened cracks in the bedrock similar in shape and type to the ones observed on the upper area of Cheikh Abdallah's hill. The entrance to these tombs, preceded by a corridor, reused the wide extraction trenches to reproduce the long passage that characterises this type of installation in the upper caves (**Figure 4**). The tombs had decorated stone doors with a locking system. These stone doors were quarried on site in the only small-scale post-Roman quarry area, located just south of the tombs carved into the quarry's western face. Narrow extraction trenches were uncovered that defined blocks of the same size as the tomb doors (**Figure 7**).

The extraction pit of the megalithic quarry of Hajjar al Hibla is divided in two by the modern cemetery wall. This wall was built on an ancient rock boundary that marked different levels of extraction between the two sectors. The quarry's northern boundary is marked on its western limit by two 'witness stones', stones left on site in order to demonstrate the original height of the quarried area (see below). In the north-east corner of the quarry, a second rocky outcrop is left along the eastern face of the quarry.

This sector of Hajjar al Hibla is an extraction pit of about 2300 m^2. It is probably the first sector that was exploited by the Roman quarrymen. Under the surface rock stratum, there was a second geological layer, 4.2 m high and delimited by two stratification joints (**Figure 8**).

The width of this geological layer dictated the heights of the first megaliths and therefore the entire

Figure 6. A view of the caves reused for inhumation in the western quarry face (Photo J. Abdul Massih).

Figure 7. The extraction layer used for necropolis doors and the witness stone in the northern edge of the quarry (Photo J. Abdul Massih).

construction of the first and second podium courses. Considering that this was the first sector of extraction, these megaliths' dimensions must have corresponded to those of the podium's first row; that is to say half the size of Hajjar al Hibla. This would be unless large megaliths were extracted and then divided in two, which would correspond perfectly to the dimensions. The extraction sector would have been exploited first in its northern part, starting from the witness stone and gradually descending towards the south in order to ensure the passage and the transportation of the megalith to the temple. Considering the area between the northern boundary and the megalith, the extraction of at least four megaliths similar in size to Hajjar al Hibla or eight smaller ones could have been carried out in the geological layer of Hajjar al Hibla. Archaeological research has been carried out in the northern sector at the base of Hajjar al Hibla within the limits of the present site, revealing the quarry floor with the hope of finding the negative imprints of extracted megaliths

Figure 8. Hajjar al Hibla and the excavation of the new megalith. On the edge of Hajjar al Hibla the megalith with narrow separation trenches visible and a karst cavity in the middle of the stone (Photo J. Abdul Massih).

Figure 9. Hajjar al Hibla and the new megalith viewed from the north (Photo J. Abdul Massih).

and uncovering traces of extraction techniques and transport machinery.

The excavation of the northern sector did not reveal the quarry floor as expected but rather the upper face of a second megalith extracted from a lower geological layer. Delimited by extraction trenches on all four sides, its vertical faces are well shaped; only the northern face seems unfinished. A reference line carved into the rock remains visible to this day along the entire length and edge of the stone. The uncovered megalith measures 19.6 m long and 6.1 m wide, with a depth of 5.6 m. It weighs approximately 1600 tonnes and rests directly on the quarry floor as revealed by the northern sounding. Abandoned in the quarry due to changes in the original plan of the podium, the new megalith was probably intended to be placed on the last course of the temple of Jupiter's podium (**Figure 9**).

The study of these two megaliths was undertaken after the excavation of the entire area, revealing the reasons why the Hajjar al Hibla stone was left in place. The change in the building plan of the temple is the reason commonly given for this; however, the observation of the northern and western faces of the megalith showed the presence of a karst cavity that developed in the north-west corner of the stone. This discovery could explain the slightly off-centre position (a few degrees north) of the new megalith that sought to avoid the karst formation of the north-western corner of Hajjar al Hibla that extends deep into the rock. The observation of the northern face also revealed the development of two cracks at the base of the stone running along the face of the megalith, thus restricting the height of the extracted block. The horizontal cracks were probably not visible when the stone was hewn and shaped. They may have been formed naturally, as the rock emerged from the substrate, through the drying and widening of micro cracks that came in contact with open air. This phenomenon is very often observed on stones extracted from deep homogeneous layers where invisible micro cracks are formed once the stones have been removed from their natural environment. For the quarrymen of Hajjar al Hibla, this phenomenon condemned the megalith and made it unusable. Thus it was left in situ. The Hajjar al Hibla stone is therefore a perfect example of accidents and consequent loss of money and time that quarrymen could encounter during extraction.

The observation of the upper face of the megalith shows a small trench dug in the middle of the stone, an aborted attempt to split the block in two. The block was then left on site, the extraction of megaliths stopped, and the Hajjar al Hibla sector was used for monolithic stones that were extracted and transported to the temple. It is possible that the upper face of the megalith was used as a platform for lifting machines operating around the block. Traces of quarried stone have been found on the quarry floor south of Hajjar al Hibla. The size of the extracted blocks, revealed in negative, corresponds to the measurements of the temple of Jupiter's column bases.

The modern cemetery

The southern sector of the Hajjar al Hibla extraction pit is occupied by the modern cemetery. The survey and studies in this area of the quarry (area III, **Figure 3**) were carried out only on the eastern and southern sides of the pit, as the rest of the quarry is the cemetery. On the eastern face of the quarry, a few metres from the modern wall, a large cave was carved in the rock with an opening 3.50 m high (**Figure 10**). The installation inside is divided into two occupation areas, north and south, of the same size, separated by a passage formed by the entrance and a central pillar-shaped rock with a cistern dug into its northern face. The two parts of the cave

Figure 10. The blacksmith's cave (Photo J. Abdul Massih).

are each equipped with two platforms established at different levels overlooking the entrance. The northern side is identified as a dwelling area. The southern side, not as well finished in its hewing, must have been occupied by an artisanal installation, probably a workshop related to a forge. The central pillar directly relates to the southern installation and includes several holes dug into the rock, revealing traces of rope wear likely related to a manually operated furnace blower installed outside the cave. Currently, only the lower part of the furnace is preserved. Built outside against the rock face of the cave, it was filled with layers of carbonized lime, probably from recent use. Archaeological strata in the vicinity are characterised by waste from continuous cleanings of the furnace. The archaeological material collected from these strata includes pottery sherds and numerous pieces of light-density iron slag. It testifies to the presence of a blacksmith shop which was probably installed in the quarry for the maintenance of extraction tools.[13]

The presence of workshops, such as those for blacksmiths, has been revealed in excavations of many Roman quarries.[14] These workshops are directly linked to extraction activities. In Baalbek, they are part of a complete operating network related to the hilltop housing facilities, rainwater collection system, and cisterns used for daily life at the quarry. All these

13 Abdul Massih 2015: 313–329.
14 Bessac 2002: 29–51.

facilities are connected by a circulation path, adapted to the topography of the quarry, that runs from the hillside dwellings to the south, via a stairway included in the extraction levels, alongside the rainwater harvesting cistern (**Figure 3**). Once at ground level, a slight slope develops to the north, creating a ramp most likely used to transport the extracted blocks. The slope links the extraction pit of Hajjar al Hibla with the main ramp running towards the temple. The quantity of stone extracted from this part of the quarry could not be determined. Nevertheless, the south-east corner offers a deep quarry face more than 5 m high, with Lewis holes dug at its base at regular intervals; this is evidence of a system probably related to the transportation of blocks. The imposing rocky face extends along the southern edge of the quarry and runs westward, below the modern road. This delimits the western extraction pit installed in the large depression (**Figure 11**).

The exploitation of the western quarry area

The western quarry area (area IV, **Figure 3**) included a large depression from which megaliths were extracted. The exploitation area is more than three hectares and extends to the west following the slope of the hill. Several extraction sectors have been distinguished in the western quarry, including the south-east extraction pit, delimited on its southern limit by the quarry face that extends from the Christian cemetery towards west. It constitutes the southern limit of the extraction pit in which the megalith, similar in size to the Hajjar al Hibla megalith, was discovered. This extraction pit, whose eastern boundary is currently buried under the modern road, is bordered by an impressive quarry face of more than 10 m high in its northern boundary. Observations of this northern face confirm the extraction of monolithic blocks in the upper layer of the hill over the entire exploitation area. Beneath the surface layer, the megaliths were extracted from a thick geological stratum composed of homogeneous limestone that does not show any faults or stratification joints. It is very likely that this thick limestone layer allowed the extraction, from its depth, of two rows of megaliths one of which remains in situ in the lower layer attached to the substratum. The height of the uncovered megalith (4.2 m) must have been dictated by the geological stratum from which the Hajjar al Hibla stone was extracted.

The south-east extraction pit extends over an area of about 3450 m², now completely filled with gravel and waste. The megalith was discovered in the 1970s when bulldozing revealed the megalith in its entirety. This work also revealed a stratigraphic section of the successive occupations that followed the abandonment of the quarry (**Figure 12**). A sounding was therefore carried out in these layers, near the southern face of the megalith, that revealed two major phases of

Figure 11. Drone image of the entire Hajjar al Hibla quarry (© S. Nishiyama).

Figure 12. The megalith from the western extraction pit (Photo J. Abdul Massih).

Figure 13. Left: Quarrying large trenches with a pick; Right: the technique of splitting a stone in two using wedges
(© J. Abdul Massih).

Islamic occupation. The first occupation extends from the 9th to the 10th centuries. It is followed by a phase of abandonment and then a second occupation from the 12th to the early 15th centuries, according to ceramic studies.[15] The nature of the later occupation could not be determined. A wider investigation must be conducted in the future; however, it is likely that it involved artisanal activities as can be seen from the ashen black colour of the occupation layers and the location outside the city boundaries.

The remaining sectors of the western quarry could not be explored due to the enormous amount of gravel covering it. It has, however, been fully surveyed and documented revealing the presence of a rocky massif that was carved and probably left as a witness stone in the middle of the large depression. Only the upper part of the rocky massif is visible, revealing a carved space of more than 4 to 5 m high that reveals the thickness of the rubble covering the quarry floor.

The extraction techniques

The extraction techniques of the entire quarry of Hajjar al Hibla can be identified from all the quarry faces, the upper surface of the Cheikh Abdallah, the Christian cemetery, and the extraction pit of the western exploitation area. However, the main study of these techniques was carried out during the excavation of the Hajjar al Hibla extraction pit which highlighted

the similar techniques for exploitation, extraction, and organisation throughout the quarry.

The extraction of a monolithic or megalithic stone entailed marking the dimensions of the block according to the client requirements. These were marked by vertical extraction trenches carved with quarry picks. Usually three sides were excavated and the fourth side, already cleared and exposed, was used to bring out the extracted stone. The width of the trenches varies from 10–15 cm for stones less than 70 cm high and 40 to 80 cm for blocks with greater height. The most widely used technique for delimiting and extracting both monolithic and megalithic blocks from the Hajjar al Hibla quarry consisted of wide trenches (also known as enjarrot) **(Figure 13)**. The use of wide extraction trenches allowed the quarryman to enter the trench and quarry the full height of the block. While the height was dictated by the natural thickness of the geological stratum, the width of the trench was determined by the number of quarrymen working in it. A reduced trench size diminished the amount of waste and saved working time.

Once the block was completely delineated by the trenches, a reference line was engraved along the edge of the upper face of the block and used by the stonemasons to shape the four vertical faces. Traces of these lines can be seen on the western edge of the upper face of Hajjar al Hibla and on the northern edge of the newly uncovered megalith's upper face.

Detaching the megalith from the bedrock was achieved by digging a trench at the base of the stone with a height that allowed the quarrymen, probably on their

---

[15] Vezzoli (forthcoming).

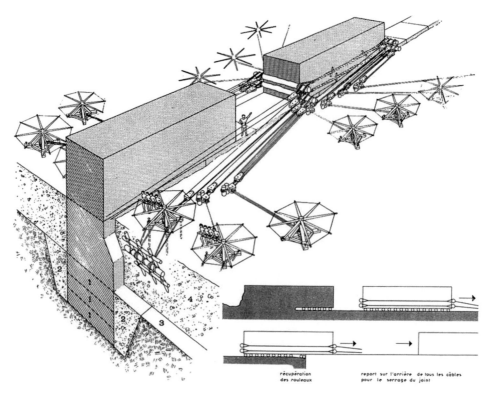

Figure 14. Transportation of the megaliths: technique using rope, pulleys, and capstans (J.-P. Adam 1977: 54, fig. 14).

knees, to quarry the rock with a quarry pick. A series of pick marks are visible along the entire length of surviving trenches, reflecting the simultaneous work of several quarrymen within a single trench. The large amount of rubble from the excavation of the trench was immediately moved to the surrounding area and probably directly reused for the construction of the access ramp. The trench under the megalith was gradually dug from east to west, following the natural slope, and was synchronised with the transport process. Logs were placed under the block as the trench was excavated. The megalith was secured by fixing ropes anchored in chiselled holes scattered all over the stone and the quarry faces (**Figure 14**).

Transportation and number of workers

Once the block rested with its full weight on the logs, it was released from its original position and placed on a prepared track, most likely consisting of a succession of layers of packed gravel. The advantage of using layers of packed gravels as the foundation of the transportation system was the availability of the material, as it consisted of quarry waste. This provides a new perspective on the management of rubble and quarry waste, and the clearing of the extraction space.

The track was then adapted to the location of the quarry, which was slightly higher then the podium platform and at a distance of 800 m from the construction site. The megaliths were dragged the whole way on this

designed track to the level of each course, thus avoiding any lifting.

The path and the transportation machinery

The importance of this ramp led us to carry out archaeological investigations on the entire length of the path in order to uncover some traces of the track. Geophysical and archaeological investigation were conducted without any success. However, an estimate of the width can be proposed based on calculations and observations made in the extraction pit of the Hajjar al Hibla megalith. From this evidence and the distance between the witness stones bordering the only exit from the quarry, we can propose a width of at least 20 m to accommodate all the facilities necessary for the transport operation.

On the gravel path, long pieces of wood would have been placed longitudinally to form a hard surface for the passage of the rollers. 'The beam carriageway receiving the convoy offers a flat and firm running surface enabling the initial load to be reduced to 1/12th of its value, i.e. 66,600 kg'.[16] The megalith would have been dragged out of the quarry by a system of ropes and pulleys attached to capstans that were in motion all the

---

[16] Adam 1977: 55. The figure is based on the studies of Rondelet (1802-1817) and Morin (1832), who determined the coefficients of friction for different materials in static and dynamic contact, either with simple friction or with the interposition of a bearing.

Figure 15. Trace of a capstan in the Hajjar al Hibla quarry (Photo J. Abdul Massih).

way to the construction area. 'The moving of a megalith of approximately 800 tons needed sixteen capstans, each operated by 32 men, which adds up to a total of 512 men with a draught force power of more than 10 tons which when multiplied by the pulley systems including four pulleys each (and affected by a large coefficient of friction) sums up to a 557 tons draught power, representing approximatively 2/3 of the load'.[17]

Lewis holes for hanging ropes were used to secure the megalith or to fix the capstans, and they are observed on the quarry floor around the megalith of Hajjar al Hibla and again on the quarry faces of this area. A circular trace of wear was uncovered on the rock during the excavation of 2014 (**Figure 15**). An analysis of the eroded face shows traces of rope friction around the remains of an anchor point for the capstan. In the opposite corner, along the south-eastern boundary of Hajjar al Hibla, traces of anchor ropes were found on the floor of the quarry and might have been used to secure a capstan. This evidence supports the theory of using this type of machinery for transport. Nevertheless, we hope and expect to discover further evidence by extending the investigated area.

Thus, the transport of the megaliths from the quarry to the construction site would have involved complex organisation and therefore had to be precisely planned by the quarrymen responsible for transportation. It is

clear that Baalbek's quarrymen directed the transport of more than 33 megaliths to the podium of the temple of Jupiter. The weight and mass of the stones, the constraint of the sloping topography of the quarry, the extraction of the megaliths, their transportation to the temple, and their placement in their final location in the construction made this a very demanding and precise undertaking. Any mistake could have led to the complete loss of the block and certainly to fatal accidents.

Estimated transportation time

The time required to transport a megalith from the quarry of Hajjar al Hibla to the podium of the temple of Jupiter could be estimated based on similar cases.[18] Here, we will consider only the example of the megalith of St. Petersburg for its similarity in form and dimension to the megalith of Hajjar al Hibla. The granite megalith, commissioned by Catherine the Great, empress of Russia (1762–1796), to serve as a pedestal for the statue of Peter the Great, was 11 m long, 6 m wide, 7 m high, and weighed about 1200 tonnes.[19] Larger than the megaliths left in the quarry and the trilithon on the podium of the temple of Jupiter, it can only be compared to the new limestone megalith discovered in the pit of Hajjar al

---

[17] Adam 1995: 32.

[18] Adam 1977: 43.

[19] It should be noted that there were factors involved in this calculation that could be analysed in this study and that could slightly modify the results obtained.

Revealing is the use of comparatives like 'more quickly' (ταχύτε[ρον]) or 'finish faster without hindrance'(ταχύ[τερ]ον, ἀπαρτίσωμεν); it suggests a certain urgency underlying the requests for equipment and reports on the progress of works. This sense of urgency also surfaces in the archive of Athenodorus, a *tabularius* in charge of distributing materials from the stores at Mons Claudianus in the Antonine period (c. AD 150–154). Some letters from this archive reveal the frustration of those waiting for supplies, as in the case of Socrates, a foreman at Tiberiane / mod. Wadi Barud, a subsidiary quarry to Mons Claudianus. He repeatedly requests *stómōma*, 'steel', and wants smiths to be seconded to Tiberiane to refit the chisels with *stómōma*. He becomes increasingly irate when his requests go unanswered:

O.Claud. 877

Σωκράτης ἐργοδότης Ἀθηνοδώ-
ρῳ καὶ Ἀμμωνίῳ τοῖς τιμιωτάτοις
vac. χαίρειν.
καλῶς ποιήσετε ἐπὶ οἱ σκληρουργοὶ λέ-
5 γουσίν μοι ὅτι 'οὐχ ἰσερχόμε\σ/θα ἔσω στ[ο-]
μ[ῶντες] ἐξελθόντες στομώσατε.› καὶ
[γρ]άφητε ἡμᾶς ἀργεῖν. ἐκ δύο τ[ὸ]
[.] ἓ\ν/ δρᾶ, εἵνα στομώσητ[ε ἢ πε-]
[ρ]ισσώτερα κεφάλια ἐνέν[κητε .]
10 πέμψετε τὴν σφύραν, ἐ[πεὶ]
λέγουσει οἱ ὀνηλάται ‹οὐ-
κ ἰρήχετε ἡμῖν ἆραι οὔτ'
ἔσω ἐστὶ παρ' αὐτούς .'
ἐρρῶσθαι ἡμᾶς
15 εὔχομαι

'Sokrates *ergodotes* to Athenodoros and Ammonios, most honoured, greetings. Please, since the stonemasons say to me "we do not come in to get *stómōma*, come out here to make *stómōma*." And you write that we are idle! Do one of two: make *stómōma* or bring some more heads. Send the hammer, since the donkey-drivers say "You have not told us to bring it and it is not with them down there." I hope you are well.'

The letter makes it clear that Sokrates is not best pleased about the accusation of doing nothing (ἀργεῖν <ἀργέω). The problem of not being able to progress with work, due to logistical failures, also emerges elsewhere. Hieronymos, the architect, reports of quarries being unworked:

O.Claud. 891

Ἰερώνυμος Ἀθηνωδώρῳ τῶι
τιμιωτάτῳ χαίρειν.
καλῶς ποιήσις ἐξαυτῆς πέμψας
τὰς ἀγόνας διὰ τῶν ὄνων ἐπὶ
5 διὰ τοῦτο τὸ ἔργον καταργῖται.
ἐρρῶσθ(αί) σε εὔχομ(αι).

'Hieronymos to Athenodoros, most honoured, greetings. Please send the whetstones at once through the donkeys, since the work is lying idle because of this. I hope you are well!'

Here again we find concern about doing nothing, about lying idle (καταργῖται < κατ-αργέω), clearly expressed; the demand to send whetstones 'at once' (ἐξαυτῆς) emphasises the time sensitivity of the delivery.[34]

The unease over the temporary cessation of work, or the threat thereof, fits well with the notion of a time efficient line of production. We might, however, consider other motives than efficiency for a speedy completion of work orders. After all, idle workers might just wander off without leave if not put to work, or the quarry teams might fall victim to an attack by the beduin.[35] The ostraca from military sites throughout the Eastern Desert of Egypt repeatedly flag the threat of attacks by sizeable forces of beduin. This perhaps presented one incentive to complete work quickly.[36] At Mons Claudianus, the threat from marauding beduin is reflected in the lists of soldiers and members of the *familia* on guard duty and assigned to what appear to be four shifts throughout the night, suggesting some form of time measurement.[37] As for daylight hours, the published texts so far make almost no mention of them outside the military context, with one exception:

O.Claud. 872

Ἰησοῦς Οὐερνᾶτι τῷ
τειμιωτάτῳ χαίρειν.
ὁ στύλος τετέλεσται καὶ ὥραν
πρώτην εἰς κρηπεῖδα ἐστὶν
5 ἐνάτῃ καὶ εἰκάδι. τὸ λοιπὸν,
[ὅτα]ν σο[ι] δόξῃ.
vac. ? lines
[ἐρ]ρῶσθαί σε εὔχομαι.

'Iesous to Vernas, the most honoured, greetings. The column is finished and is on the loading-ramp

---

34 *O.Claud.* 132.
35 *O.Claud.* 851.
36 E.g. *O. Krok.* 87. *O.Claud.* inv. 4888; *O.Claud.* 851.
37 *O.Claud.* 309–356.

at the first hour on the twenty-ninth. Well, when you please. I hope you are well.'

This reference to the first hour of day could easily be ignored were it not for a find of a planar sundial near the slipway leading to quarry 90.[38] The sundial divides daytime into 10 hours. The occurrence of a sundial in the context of an ancient quarry is not unique: vertical sundials are also attested in the quarries of Kertassi and Debod in Roman Nubia.[39] What the purpose of these sundials was is not clear, but a connection to the structuring of daily work, be that the marking of breaks or shifts seems possible, especially in combination with reference to hours being observed in order to better coordinate the collection of quarried items.

Conclusion

So, where does all of this lead us? Although we do not learn much about the costs and time expended on the production of a quarried item, the information and data collected within the quarry organisation and related to quarry operations seem to chime with the aim of controlling waste of finite resources through the detailed account of equipment and materials distributed. Moreover, the lists of quarrying personnel and their deployment are perhaps best understood as reflecting the process of a flexible and efficient deployment of a highly specialised workforce. The lists of named personnel and the notation of ill workers enabled the authorities to check whether individual quarrymen complied with their contractual obligations and actually showed up for work. Finally, the letters and reports exchanged between different actors within the quarrying administration appear to show their concern about the timely execution of their tasks. This all seems to point towards the objective of the quarrying organisation as a whole, namely the production of the columns, blocks, basins, etc. ordered by the emperor, as quickly and as efficiently as possible.

Other concerns needed to be factored in as well: the *P.Panop.Beatty* 2 papyrus contains the incoming correspondence to the *strategos* of the Panopolite nome for AD 300 from the office of the procurator of the Lower Thebaid. Lines 43–50 render the letter of Aurelius Isidorus, procurator of the Lower Thebaid, who writes to the *strategoi* within his procuratorial district; Isidorus reminds the *strategoi* of the urgency with which columns from Syene are to be transported down river. The ten state ships sent are not sufficient to complete the task, more are required and quickly. The procurator is at pains to explain that the transport needs to happen speedily, especially as the 'fall in the level of the water

is increasing daily (*l*.46)', and 'the time limit by which the columns must be brought to Alexandria' (*l*. 45; tr. C.E.P. Adams) will be exceeded. Even if the winds are unfavourable, considering the 'absolute necessity of this task', the ships going up the Nile are to be towed by their crews (?) and by the inhabitants of the villages and river ports along the way.[40] The letter is issued on Mecheir 2nd, i.e. January 28th, very close to the end of the sailing season on the Nile for boats with a draft of 100t (from mid-August to mid-February) and a month and half away from the end of season for boats with a draft of 40t (mid-July to mid-March).[41]

The navigability of the Nile, together with deadlines set by the imperial authorities by which columns, blocks, and other items needed to be at Alexandria to be shipped out to Rome, were also relevant to the imperial quarries in the Eastern Egyptian Desert: two texts note the requisition of camels for hauling columns from Porphyrites on the order of the *praefectus Aegypti* Annius Syriacus in AD 163; they date to the 29th and 30th of January respectively.[42] The evidence is not substantive enough to argue that stone transports from the quarries in the Eastern Egyptian Desert were subjected to similar deadlines and concerns about the navigability of the river; however, the few dates we have for the completion of columns seem to fall within November and December, which would fit with transport arrangements to the Nile and beyond organised for January of the following year.[43] The transport of stone across the Mediterranean Sea was possible throughout the year but the peak for sea transport of marble from Carrara in later periods falls in the spring and summer months.[44] Should this apply to stones from the Egyptian quarries as well, a deadline in spring for the transhipment of stone in Alexandria seems possible.

To conclude, the sense of pressure emerging from the texts might well have been driven by concerns about the navigability of the Nile and onward shipment to and deadlines imposed by building programmes in Rome. The close reading of the letters and reports on pottery sherds has not only brought concerns to light about the timely completion of columns and blocks: the existence of lists of equipment and tools provided to individuals and gangs of workmen in named quarries suggests that waste and costs were important to the quarry supervisors as well. The lists and reports on ill or absent quarrymen indicate that the availability of hired workers was strictly monitored, ultimately with labour

---

[38] Peacock and Maxfield 1997: 226 with fig. 6.65.
[39] Roeder 1911: 3, 174 f.

[40] For translation and comments, see Skeat 1964; Adams forthcoming.
[41] Cooper 2014: 183, fig. 11.6.
[42] *BGU* III 762. *P.Lond* II 328, cf. Adams 2001: 175.
[43] The texts *O.Claud.* 850 and 853 report completion of a column for 26 Hathyr (i.e. 22 November), whereas *O.Claud.* 856 notes a finished column on 14 Choiak (i.e. 10 December).
[44] Russell 2013: 110 f.

costs and efficiency in mind. The detailed reports on the secondment of various specialists and workmen to specified quarries provided the information required for a targeted deployment of the available workforce, implying again the concern with the efficient use of labour. How successful those with responsibility were in coordinating the efforts of various quarry crews and their adequate and timely supply is questionable in light of the repeated complaints about delayed supplies.

Bibliography

Adams, C.E.P. 2001. Who bore the burden? The Organization of Stone Transport in Roman Egypt, in D.J. Mattingly and J. Salmon (eds) *Economies Beyond Agriculture in the Classical* World: 171–192. London and New York: Routledge.

Adams, C.E.P. forthcoming. *Administration and Bureaucracy in Later Roman Egypt: The Chester Beatty Papyri from Panopolis.*

Bingen, J. *et al.* 1992. *Mons Claudianus. Ostraca Graeca et Latina I (O. Claud. 1 à 190).* Cairo: Archeolog Caire.

Bingen, J. *et al.* 1997. *Mons Claudianus. Ostraca Graeca et Latina II. O.Claud. 191 à 416.* Cairo: Archeolog Caire.

Bülow-Jacobsen, A. 2009. *Mons Claudianus. Ostraca Graeca et Latina IV. The Quarry Texts. O.Claud. 632-896.* Cairo: Archeolog Caire.

Bülow-Jacobsen, A. 2016. Stomoma. Why, what, when, and how?, in Chr. Freu *et al.* (eds) *Mélanges d'historie romaine et d'antiquité tardive offerts à Jean-Michel Carrié*: 183–189. Turnhout: Brepols.

Cech, B. (ed.) 2017. *Die Produktion von Ferrum Noricum am Hüttenberger Erzberg. Die Ergebnisse der interdisziplinäaren Forschungen auf der Fundstellen Semlach/Eisner in den Jahren 2006-2009.* Graz: Unipress Verlag.

Cooper, J.P. 2014. *The Medieval Nile: Route, Navigation and Landscape in Islamic Egypt.* Cairo: The American University in Cairo Press.

Cuvigny, H. 1996. The Amount of Wages Paid to the Quarry-Workers at Mons Claudianus. *Journal of Roman Studies* 86: 139–145.

Cuvigny, H. 2000. *Mons Claudianus. Ostraca Graeca et Latina. III. Les reçus pour avances à la familia O. Claud. 417 à 631.* Cairo: Archeolog Caire.

Cuvigny, H. 2005. L'organigramme du personnel d'une carrière impériale d'après un ostracon du Mons Claudianus. *Chiron* 35: 309–353.

Cuvigny, H. 2019. Poste publique, renseignement militaire et citernes à sec. Les lettre de Diourdanos à Archibios, curator Claudiani. *Chiron* 49: 271–297.

Cuvigny, H. 1998. Kainè, ville nouvelle. Une expérience de regroupement familial au II e s. è. Chr, in O.E. Kaper (ed.) *Life on the Fringe. Living in the Southern Egyptian Deserts during the Roman and early-Byzantine Periods. Proceedings of a Colloquium held on the Occasion of the 25th Anniversary of the Netherlands Institute of Archaeology and Arabic Studies in Cairo 9–12 December 1996*: 87–94. Leiden: Research School CNWS.

Flück, H. and R. Gautschy 2016. Zwei Sonnenuhren aus Vindonissa – archäologisch, archivalisch und astronomisch betrachtet. *Gesellschaft Pro Vindonissa. Jahresbericht*: 3–13.

Maxfield, V.A. and D.P.S. Peacock 2001. *Mons Claudianus. Survey and Excavation. 1987-1993. Volume II. Excavations. Part 1.* Cairo: Archeolog Caire.

Peacock, D.P.S. and V.A. Maxfield 1997. *Mons Claudianus. Survey and Excavation. 1987-1993. Volume I. Topography and Quarries.* Cairo: Archeolog Caire.

Roeder, G. 1911. *Debod bis Bab Kalabsche.* Cairo: Impr. de l'Institut français d'archéologie orientale.

Russell, B. 2013. *The Economics of the Roman Stone Trade.* Oxford: University Press.

Russell, B. 2018. Labour forces at Roman imperial quarries, in D. Matetić Poljak and K. Marasović (eds) *ASMOSIA IX. Interdisciplinary Studies on Ancient Stone*: 733–739. Split.

Skeat, T.C. 1964. *Papyri from Panopolis in the Chester Beatty Library Dublin.* Dublin: Hodges Figgis and Co. LTD.

Speidel, M.A. 2009. Einheit und Vielfalt in der römischen Heeresverwaltung, in M.A. Speidel (Hrsg.) *Heer und Herrschaft im Römischen Reich der Hohen Kaiserzeit*: 283–304. Stuttgart: Franz Steiner Verlag.

Tomber, R. 2006. The pottery, in V.A. Maxfield and D.P.S. Peacock (eds) *Mons Claudianus 1987-1993. Survey and Excavations. Vol. III. Ceramic Vessels and Related Objects from Mons Claudianus (FIFAO 54)*: 1–236. Cairo: Archeolog Caire.

Townley, B. 2008. *Reason's Neglect. Rationality and Organizing.* Oxford: Oxford University Press.

11.

From Extraction to Transport: Technical and Management Aspects of Quarries of Building Stone

Anna Gutiérrez Garcia-M.

RyC Researcher and Head of the Archaeometric Studies Unit,
Catalan Institute of Classical Archaeology-ICAC
agutierrez@icac.cat

Abstract

The Roman world was highly urbanised, and as such, building stone was one of the most extensively employed materials. In addition, compared to other building materials that were widely used in the Roman period (e.g. timber, mortar, or plaster), stone has a much higher degree of preservation in the archaeological record. Despite this, more ordinary, everyday building stone and the quarries from which it was extracted often have been overlooked with a few notable exceptions, such as the comprehensive studies of A. Dworakowska and Jean-Claude Bessac;[1] however, the topic has recently started to attract attention from researchers. It is vital therefore to understand the procurement and supply of ordinary, less expensive, and everyday stone, which was used for the bulk of Roman building projects. The cost of this building stone obviously formed a key part of construction costs alongside the highly luxurious and costly marbles and ornamental stones that often were used for decorative elements. This paper seeks to contribute to the issue by examining the production of non-decorative stone during the Roman period. Rather than providing a definitive conclusion on the topic, this is intended as a preliminary discussion of the large core of data currently available on building stone quarries around the Roman town of Tarraco (modern Tarragona, NE Spain) and which has significantly increased in the last decade.

Keywords: stone extraction, procurement, transport, Tarraco, *Hispania*

Introduction

This paper is divided into three parts: firstly, it presents an up-to-date overview of stone studies related to the Iberian Peninsula, addressing the various interdisciplinary approaches that have been adopted thus far and reviewing aspects related to the primary phases of the industry in stone for building material, sculpture, epigraphy, and other commodities. Secondly, the main focus of this paper is on the technical and management aspects related to the initial phase of any construction project – the extraction and supply of building stone. This is approached from an archaeological perspective through the use of specific case studies of the limestone quarries opened in the territory around Tarraco. The territory's urban development, which included numerous monumental architectural projects intended to provide Tarraco, the capital of the largest province within the western Roman Empire, with the appropriate architectural image it deserved, meant that an extremely large quantity of building stone was needed. As a result, Tarraco's local stone resources were heavily exploited and transported to the town. This left a rich panorama

of quarry sites that allow for an examination of the Roman stone industry and the dynamics behind it in this part of the western Mediterranean. Yet, not all of the building stone quarried around Tarraco was destined for large-scale public programs; an important part of these quarry operations was used to meet the needs of a broad spectrum of other smaller-scale or minor building projects. Following a review of the different types of stone employed in the town's monumental building programmes, villas, infrastructure, and other monumental landmarks within the town's *territorium*, the possible factors behind their selection, exploitation, and procurement will be addressed. Then, in the final part of this paper, some consideration will be given to the catchment area, production, and supply mechanisms that were put in motion in order to bring the much-needed building stone from the quarry site to the workshop or building sites. These are aspects of the building process that tend to go unnoticed but are key to understanding the intensive exploitation of the lithic resources within territories and the dynamics behind the implementation of certain procurement concepts for specific architectural buildings or complexes of buildings.

---

[1] Dworakowska 1975, 1983; Bessac 1996, 2018, among other works.

The study of stone as a natural resource and its procurement in Roman Spain: up-to-date overview and some thoughts

In recent years, the study of stone and its use as a fundamental raw material for construction (both for decoration and ordinary building work) as well as for artistic and epigraphic uses has gained increasing emphasis in line with its importance in Antiquity. Stone, after all, was one of the most extensively employed raw materials of the Classical world, and in the highly urbanised Roman society, building represented a major economic activity.[2] In addition, compared to other building materials that were widely used in the Roman period (e.g. timber, mortar, or plaster), stone has a much higher degree of preservation in the archaeological record.

In the last decades, one of the most outstanding lines of research in Spanish academia has focused on identifying the quarry provenance of stones from the Iberian Peninsula that were exploited in Antiquity. In particular, focus has been on the quarries or quarry districts across the territory that supplied raw materials to different urban centres and workshops. This research topic has become part of the wider dialogue surrounding the archaeology of construction[3] and the economics of Roman building activity, as can be seen by the frequent presence of Spanish case studies and scholars in symposia held in Venice,[4] Rome,[5] Edinburgh,[6] Bonn,[7] Berlin,[8] and Oxford,[9] as well

as from the scientific meetings conducted in Madrid[10] and Murcia,[11] which focused specifically on ancient quarries. In connection with these studies, we can also mention the recent meetings held in Barcelona,[12] Irún,[13] and Segovia,[14] which not only included studies focused on quarries but also emphasised the value of marmora as a status symbol for architectural decoration, sculpture, and monumental epigraphy, among other uses.

This boom of scientific meetings is part of a number of research projects aimed at unravelling the exploitation and distribution of specific Spanish stones that have been carried out during the last decade. Aside from occasional archaeological excavations at certain quarry sites, such as those at La Encarnación and its surroundings,[15] at L'Ènova, near the Villa of Cornelius,[16] and initial work on the quarries near Vrso,[17] Corduba,[18] Posadas,[19] and Labitolosa,[20] there are a significant number of teams now conducting larger-scope projects. The Roman province of Baetica and its marmora are well covered by the University of Seville,[21] and for Lusitania, the native marbles have for a long time been the object of study from an archaeometric standpoint.[22] Here, the

---

[2] As noted by Jongman (2007: 609), building was the most important non-food related production activity in most pre-industrial societies, and this was also the case during the Roman period.

[3] See, for example, the series of scientific meetings organised by the Instituto de Arqueología de Mérida (IAM-CSIC), the University of Siena, the École Normale Supérieure de Paris, and the University of Padova that focused on ancient construction, in which Hispania had an important place from the outset (Camporeale et al. 2008, 2010, 2012; Bonetto et al. 2014; DeLaine et al. 2016).

[4] 'Le marché des matières premières dans l'Antiquité et au Moyen Âge. La circulation des matières premières. Les acteurs et l'organisation des marchés. Journées d'études internationales' organisé par Casa de Velázquez – Universitá Ca Foscari – École Française à Rome and held in November 12th-13th 2015 (Boisseuil et al. 2021).

[5] Workshop 'Aspectos económicos de la construcción de edificios públicos en el Occidente romano' hosted by the Escuela Española de Historia y Arqueología en Roma (Rome, May 9th 2017).

[6] Celebrated as a panel within the Roman Archaeology Conference (RAC) and the Theoretical Roman Archaeology Conference (TRAC) both held at the University of Edinburgh between the 12th and 14th of April 2018 (the name of the panel was 'Quantifying Public Construction: Figure Labour, Territory Exploitation and Production Cost'). The results of this meeting and of that held in Rome (see above, footnote 5) have been published in Courault and Márquez 2020.

[7] Also held as a conference panel under the title 'Constructing monuments, perceiving monumentality and the economics of building' within the XIX International Congress of Classical Archaeology (Cologne/Bonn, 22nd-26th May 2018) (Pakkanen and Brysbaert 2021).

[8] Conference 'Architecture and the Ancient Economy' held at the Freie Universität Berlin between the 26th and 28th September 2019 (Maschek and Trümper 2022).

[9] Workshop 'From concept to monument: time and cost of construction in the ancient world' held at Wolfson College-University

of Oxford between the 16th and 18th January 2020, the result of which is the present volume.

[10] Colloquium 'Carrières Antiques de la Péninsule ibérique' hosted at the Casa de Velázquez the 8th-9th February 2016 (Gutiérrez Garcia-M. and Rouillard 2018), the workshop 'Paisajes e historias en torno a la piedra. La ocupación y explotación del territorio minero y las estrategias de distribución, consumo y reutilización de los materiales lapídeos desde la Antigüedad' co-hosted at the MAN and the UNED the 13th–14th December 2017 (García-Entero et al. 2020), and the workshop 'Espacios de Canteras Históricas' organised by the IGME the 27th November 2018 (Álvarez Areces et al. 2019).

[11] Workshop 'Las canteras históricas y su valor patrimonial. Acciones para su conservación y puesta en valor' held at the University of Murcia 19th–21st September 2019.

[12] Colloquium 'Barcino-Tarraco-Roma. Power and prestige in marble' in honour of Prof. I. Rodà and organised by the ICAC, the University Rovira i Virgili, and the MUHBA (Museu d'Història de Barcelona). This meeting took place between the 21st and 23rd November 2019, and a volume compiling not only the presented contributions but also some additional papers will be published in Gorostidi and Gutiérrez Garcia-M. forthcoming.

[13] Course, 'Un imperio de mármol: piedras decorativas y canteras en la Península ibérica en época romana', organised by the University of the Basque Country (EHU) and the Oiasso Museum (30th September – 2nd October 2020).

[14] Workshop, 'Lapides et marmora: la construcción de un imperio. Recursos lapídeos de la Hispania romana', organised by the Museo de Segovia and held via video conference (due to the COVID-19 pandemic), the 11th–12th November 2020.

[15] Brotons Yagüe and Ramallo Asensio 2018.

[16] Despite the lack of specific publications, this very interesting quarry has received successive attention by several researchers.

[17] López Garcia 2014.

[18] Undertaken by M.I. Gutiérrez Deza (2012) and C. Courault (see his contribution in this volume).

[19] García Arrabal and Peña Cervantes 2017.

[20] Albeit with a non-conclusive result (cf. Cisneros and Gisbert 2019).

[21] Cf. Beltrán Fortes and Rodriguez Oliva 2010; Beltrán Fortes et al. 2012; Taylor 2018; Rodríguez Gutiérrez and Jiménez Madroñal 2019, among many others.

[22] Studies undertaken within the framework of several projects of the Museo Nacional de Arte Romano (MNAR), Mérida by T. Nogales-Basarrate, now the museum director, and P. Lapuente (University of Zaragoza), lecturer of Geology cf. Lapuente et al. 2014, 2018 for their latest publications.

local granite sources used to build the capital town of Augusta Emerita have also been specifically addressed.[23] For *Hispania Tarraconensis*, the most recent projects have focused on the north-western corner (modern Galicia) and the quarries near present-day Espejón, in the central Meseta: the former started in 2012 under the name of '*Marmora* Galicia'[24] and has uncovered a much more complex panorama than anticipated,[25] while the latter[26] has provided a significant body of data over the last five years.[27] Alongside these studies and the long-standing work of the University of Murcia (focused on the south-east)[28] and the group ICAC-Autonomous University of Barcelona (focused on the north-east),[29] the Franco-Spanish team working on the El Ferriol quarries has provided a unique approach, integrating an in-depth spatial study.[30] Moreover, and in spite of its wider chronological range, the efforts by the Instituto Geológico Minero de España (IGME) to create an inventory of Spanish historical quarries[31] and the research carried out by T. Anderson[32] must also be mentioned as they obviously affect the ancient material. All of this intense activity has resulted in two very positive, concrete outcomes: a non-negligible number of PhD theses focused on quarries and their stone from these regions,[33]

as well as the creation of a national research network encompassing most of the aforementioned teams.[34]

A fundamental part of this research has been its archaeometric approach and the development of analytical protocols, including scientific techniques,[35] to identify the provenance of both white marbles and ornamental coloured stones (*marmora*), which were used for the highest level of Roman projects, as well as what we might term, 'lesser stones', which, while not regarded as important in terms of their prestige, were nonetheless essential in the Roman economy due to their wide distribution and use. The increasing adoption of scientific techniques and methods in archaeological circles has meant that such interdisciplinary approaches to the study of quarries and their stones are a vital component to the subject.[36] One of the most important consequences of this recent interdisciplinary trend has been the discovery of an ever increasing number of quarries or quarry areas that were exploited in Antiquity but were previously unknown. The discovery of these ancient quarries stems from a very simple principle, that is, in order to positively identify the quarry origin of a stone through analytical techniques, it is mandatory to have reference samples taken from the geological outcrops with which to compare the archaeological pieces or artefacts. In turn, this process entails, once the geological profile of ancient stones are recognised, further reference to existing geological documentation to correctly pinpoint outcrops with analogous characteristics. Field survey is then necessary in order to identify ancient quarries directly and to verify the presence (or absence) of traces of ancient quarrying.

In spite of having been generally neglected in the overall picture of archaeological research, quarries are an outstanding source of information on past societies. The pioneering papers of J. Röder for

[23] Pizzo 2010; Pizzo and Cordero Ruiz 2014; Pizzo *et al.* 2018.

[24] Undertaken within the framework of several R+D projects funded by the Spanish Government (HAR2011-25011, HAR2015-65319-P y PGC2018-099851-A-I00) and the LabEx LaScArBx (n° ANR-10-LABX-52; projects *Marmora et lapides Hispaniae*: exploitation, usages et distribution des ressources lithiques de l'Espagne romaine' and 'Graver dans le marbre: Routes et Origine des Marbres antiques d'Aquitaine et d'Espagne -ROMAE' between 2013 and 2018).

[25] González Soutelo *et al.* 2014; González Soutelo and Gutiérrez Garcia-M. 2020; Gutiérrez Garcia-M. *et al.* 2016, 2018; Lapuente *et al.* 2019, among others.

[26] R+D projects HAR2013-44971-P ('*Marmora Hispaniae*. Explotación, uso y difusión de la caliza de Espejón en la Hispania romana y tardoantigua') and PGC2018-096854-BI00 ('Arqueología e historia de un paisaje de la piedra: la explotación del *marmor* de Espejón (Soria) y las formas de ocupación de su territorio desde la Antigüedad al siglo XX'), both funded by the Spanish Government (MICINN/AEI/FEDER, EU) and directed by V. García-Entero (UNED).

[27] García-Entero 2020; García-Entero *et al.* 2018a, 2018b.

[28] Cf. Antolinos *et al.* 2018; Soler 2019; Soler Huertas *et al.* 2014 for their latest publications.

[29] Of which the author of this paper is a part; this research has recently focused on the Roman quarry of El Mèdol, which will be part of the discussion here, as well as the quarries around Dertosa (cf. Gutiérrez Garcia-M. 2010, 2011, 2012, 2014, 2020; Gutiérrez Garcia-M. and López Vilar 2018; Gutiérrez Garcia-M. *et al.* 2015, 2019; López Vilar and Gutiérrez Garcia-M. 2016, 2017), Gerunda (in collaboration with J. Oliver Vert), and at Formentera (in collaboration with A. Artina).

[30] Gagnaison *et al.* 2006, 2007; Costa *et al.* 2018; Rouillard *et al.* 2020.

[31] Baltuille Martín and Fernández Suárez 2019.

[32] His research has focused on quern and millstone quarries (cf. Anderson and Scarrow 2011; Anderson *et al.* 2014)

[33] After the publication of a monograph on the Roman quarries of north-eastern Spain (Gutiérrez Garcia-M. 2009), four other PhD theses covering the different geographical areas of the Iberian Peninsula have been carried out: two of them on the quarries of Almadén de la Plata, near Seville (Taylor 2015) and the Pyreneean marbles (Royo 2016); a third one, submitted in early 2021, focusing on the marbles of the north-western corner of Spain (ancient *Gallaecia*) by M.-C. Savin (University of Bordeaux Montaigne, France - Univeristy of Zaragoza, Spain); and a fourth one, on the quarries and stone supply of Gerunda (modern Girona) from Roman times to the early Middle Ages (Oliver Vert 2022).

[34] Red de investigación 'El ciclo productivo del *marmor* en la Peninsula Ibérica desde la Antigüedad: extracción, elaboración, comercialización, usos, reutilización, reelaboración y amortización' (RED2018-102722-T) under the auspices of the MCIU/AEI of the Spanish Government. This thematic network is led and coordinated by V. García-Entero (UNED).

[35] For a summary of the multi-method approaches and the different analytical techniques that are currently the most commonly applied to pinpoint the provenance of ancient stones and with specific reference to Spanish cases, see Lapuente 2014, 2019.

[36] The studies are so numerous that it would be too long and tedious to mention them all, but it is worth mentioning the role of the *Association for the Study of Marbles and Other Stones in Antiquity* (ASMOSIA; http://asmosia.willamette.edu/) and its triennial conferences, the proceedings of which are published: Herz and Waelkens 1988; Waelkens *et al.* 1992; Maniatis *et al.* 1995; Schvoerer 1999; Herrmann *et al.* 2002; Lazzarini 2002; Jockey 2009; Maniatis 2009; Gutiérrez Garcia-M. *et al.* 2012; Pensabene and Gasparini 2015; Matétić Poljak and Marasović 2018. For the specific case of Roman Spain and the importance of interdisciplinary studies combining archaeological and archaeometric approaches: Gutiérrez Garcia-M. 2019; Lapuente 2019.

Germany and Turkey,[37] A. Dworakowska for Greek and Roman quarries,[38] and the ground-breaking work by J.-C. Bessac[39] demonstrate the clear potential for this quarry evidence. Moreover, further confirmation is evident from the numerous studies concerning Spanish quarrying and the building industry that have already been mentioned above. Examining quarries *per se* will not only help in our understanding of the quarry site itself but also will allow a whole set of important, interrelated aspects to be linked to the economic, social, and political history of the society that exploited them. Indeed, their study allows for a greater understanding of the scope and variety of Roman exploitation of natural resources and raw materials, the technology and 'chaîne opératoire' used to obtain these materials, the amount of material extracted, and therefore the scale of production at individual quarries. Taken as a whole, this allows us to examine the strategies employed by the Romans in the exploitation, circulation, and distribution of stone for building projects, providing insight into the role of quarry activity and the stone industry within the micro- and macro-economics of the Roman Empire.

In addition, the study of quarries or quarry districts from a comprehensive perspective can also shed light on other topics, such as the creation of man-made landscapes. Despite their intangible nature, quarries have an undeniable cultural value and are therefore increasingly valued and protected. Without a doubt, quarries are one of the best examples of how the natural topography can be directly and substantially modified by human action, irreversibly altering it, even if the area is reclaimed by vegetation after the quarry has been abandoned. Moreover, both the location of ancient quarries—nearly always outside the urban environment—and the total absence of built infrastructure at such sites (or at least the complete disappearance of structures due to construction in perishable material) has meant that quarries have generally remained 'invisible' when compared to other types of archaeological sites. Notwithstanding the above, the analysis of both the specific stoneworking techniques and the whole extracting process can provide insights into the connectivity between craftsmen and territories. Indeed, the mobility of craftsmen, who moved from one region to another, and the transfer of specific skills can sometimes be inferred through the study of stoneworking techniques and methods.[40]

Ultimately, we should not forget that the location of outcrops supplying certain types of stones and their exploitation were a direct response to the demand for raw materials created by local needs,[41] which was driven not only by practical concerns but also by the desire to materially represent concepts linked to self-presentation and self-image within Roman society. Such concerns became ever more important with the adoption of these stones in newly incorporated territories, which increased significantly all across the empire and for all kinds of stones, especially between the last century BC and the first three centuries AD.[42]

Quarrying for building materials

Archaeological evidence for the quarrying - building relationship at Tarraco

As already mentioned, rather than providing a final or definitive statement, this paper is intended to provide an initial discussion on the subject, addressing the production of everyday building stone with a specific focus on the initial stages of quarrying and transport. In order to do this, the paper will examine archaeological cases from Tarraco and its territory. Tarraco was one of the first Roman *praesidia* on the north-eastern shores of the Iberian Peninsula, founded shortly after the landing of the Roman troops in 218 BC in the midst of the Second Punic War. Thanks to its abundant natural resources as well as its strategic location on a hill next to the sea and at the mouth of a small river, with easy access to both to the Spanish coast and the inland territories, it soon developed into an important urban settlement during the late Republic. By the end of the 1st century BC, the town had received the status of colony and was the provincial capital of *Hispania Citerior*, which was, following Augustus' administrative reorganisation, renamed after the town itself, *Hispania Tarraconensis* (**Figure 1**).[43]

The numerous remains of large-scale complexes, buildings, and architectural projects demonstrate the wealth and power of Tarraco, especially during the late Republican and early imperial periods. Indeed, as the political and economic centre of the largest province in the western Roman Empire,[44] the city's dominion and status was shown by these projects. The monumental building program was not only confined to Tarraco itself but was also extended to its territory, both of

---

[37] Röder 1957, 1959, 1965, 1971.
[38] Dworakowska 1975, 1983.
[39] His extremely extensive work on the subject includes the interpretation of toolmarks, in-depth studies of the quarries at the Bois des Lens and in *Gallia* in general, as well as the categorisation of extraction strategies and methods, among many others topics; cf. Bessac 1988a, 1988b, 1993, 1996, 2003, 2018; Bessac and Sablayrolles 2002.
[40] A very interesting example of this phenomenon has been identified by C. Previato in her study on the quarries of Nora (Sardinia), where finds of semi-extracted blocks using Punic units of measure have been interpreted as the result of the presence of Punic quarrymen still working in the Roman period (Previato 2016: 56).

[41] This included buildings, infrastructure, art, inscriptions, and other commodities, as stated at the beginning of this text.
[42] Cf. Russell 2013: 16.
[43] The literature on the evolution and urban development of Tarraco is too extensive to be comprehensively mentioned here, so we need only refer to a number of the existing monographs (Dupré 2006; Macias *et al.* 2007; Mar *et al.* 2012) and a useful paper summarising the state of the research, which only excluded the most recent work (Macias and Rodà 2015).
[44] Alföldy 2001.

Figure 1. Schematic map with the location of Tarraco (upper left corner) and view of the Roman wall, showing the megalithic base made with Jurassic breccia blocks and the upper part made with Miocene limestones ashlars (photo by the author).

which have been studied albeit to different degrees. Moreover, most sites have been included in the city's wider ensemble, which was declared a World Heritage by UNESCO in 2000. One of the first and most admired remains of ancient Tarraco is the town's defensive wall, which was the first architectural project built by Rome outside Italy[45] and still remains, enclosing most of the original acropolis of the ancient town, locally identified as the 'upper part' (**Figure 1**). The early date of this large-scale building project and the sheer amount of stone employed in its construction serve to make it a unique and highly interesting monument.[46]

Within the walled area of the town, this monumental 'upper part' consisted of an area of 12 ha in size that was divided into three large terraces: a circus was erected in the lower one, the so-called Provincial Forum was in the middle one, and a temple and its porticoes stand above the rest on the upper terrace. This part of the town stood out and dominated the urban landscape of the ancient town (as it still does even today), but there are also several Roman remains in the town's 'lower part', including the colonial forum.[47] Other important architectural remains of Roman Tarraco include the theatre,[48] located not far from the colonial forum, the amphitheatre, built immediately *extramuros* between the town walls and the seashore, the Visigothic

---

[45] The first wall was built *c.* 200 BC and enclosed only part of the top of the hill. It probably replaced the *praesidium* defences. Later on, between 150 and 125 BC, the wall's circuit was enlarged both in its dimensions, with the wall now reaching 10–12 m in height and 5–6 m in width, and in its overall length. For a brief description of its main features, see Menchón 2017: 47–50.

[46] The wall was largely modified in post-Classical periods and with significant additions in the 16th – 18th centuries, which explains why this defensive structure is commonly referred to in the plural ('the walls'; cf. Menchón 2017: 41–42). It has been the subject of study and discussion since the mid-1970s (see Hauschild 1975, 1983; Menchón 2009; Mar *et al.* 2012: 51-52, among others).

[47] There have been several excavations and projects focused on the better known 'upper part' of the town. This has included excavations inside the cathedral, undertaken within the framework of an agreement between the Tarragona City Council, the Catalan Institute of Classical Archaeology (ICAC), and the Archbishopric of Tarragona, and several projects related to the architecture and construction. This has been fostered by the ICAC and Rovira i Virgili University (URV). The resulting literature is extensive; however, for a brief overview of these two *fora*, see Gutiérrez Garcia-M. and Vinci 2018.

[48] The theatre is currently being partly re-excavated under the auspices of the Museu Nacional Arqueològic de Tarragona (MNAT) and is also the subject of a PhD thesis by J. Sánchez, who is also the director of the archaeological excavation. For a summary of the principal publications on this building, see Rodà 2016: 253, fn.36; Remolà 2019.

Figure 2. View of the Roman Amphiteatre (left; photo by Alberto-g-rovi available at Wikipedia Commons, CC BY-SA 3.0) and the Roman aqueduct known as Pont de les Ferreres, or del Diable (right; photo by Gpatgn available at Wikipedia Commons, GNU FDL).

church built in its arena[49] (**Figure 2**), and the early Christian basilicas and necropolis, erected on the western *suburbium*.[50] The town's ancient remains also include structures vital to Tarraco's urban life, such as infrastructure for water distribution and sewers, and terracing structures to level the slopes of the terrain and ensure the grid design of the town (**Figure 2**). Amongst these important public works was also the port of Tarraco. Its function as the first point of entry to the Iberian peninsula provided a network hub for all kinds of imported goods and luxury merchandise as well as for the export of Spanish materials and products to Rome and the rest of the empire. The importance and magnitude of this infrastructure and its adjacent quarter has been highlighted recently in several studies.[51]

The rich archaeological remains of the town are paralleled in its surrounding territory. Despite the difficulty in establishing the precise limits of the town's area,[52] it seems that Tarraco probably had a quite large *territorium*. This would have been vital to fulfil the requirements of an urban centre with the status and size of Tarraco. Within a *c.* 25 km radius, and particularly in its direct surroundings, are numerous Roman remains attesting to the extremely intense occupation and use of the land. Several research projects have provided a much better understanding of various aspects of this

area, including how the *ager* was distributed,[53] wine production,[54] water supply[55] and the evolution and role of the numerous large and luxurious villas scattered in this area. Indeed, the high density of villas was a notable feature of *ager Tarraconensis*,[56] and a number of these villas stand out for their grandeur in terms of both architecture and ornament. This is the case with the Roman villa of Els Antigons, which has been the subject of an in-depth study within the framework of the aforementioned *Ager Tarraconensis* project but unfortunately of which only very scant remains still survive.[57] The much better preserved villa of Els Munts was one of the most luxurious and splendid villas from early imperial times and was probably used by the emperor Hadrian during his visit to *Tarraco*.[58] Equally, the villa of Centcelles, with its renowned dome with

[49] A number of studies have focused on the Roman amphitheatre. The most significant is the excavation carried out between 2009 and 2012, the results of which were the publication of a monograph (Ciurana *et al.* 2013).

[50] The ten-year comprehensive study by J. López Vilar (2006) remains the standard reference work on the basilicas; however, several parts of this area and the necropolis, which is one of the best preserved late Roman cemeteries, has been more recently studied and renovated as part of the modernisation of the Early Christian Museum and Necropolis of the MNAT (Remolà and Lasheras 2019).

[51] Macias and Remolà 2005; Terrado 2017; Lasheras 2018. The port of Tarraco has also been one of the elements integrated into parts of the ERC project 'Portus Limen – Rome's Mediterranean Ports', directed by S. J. Keay (University of Southampton/British School at Rome).

[52] Arrayás 2005: 121–124.

[53] Such studies from different perspectives are thanks to research led by J. Guitart and M. Prevosti from the ICAC, within the 'Ager Tarraconensis project' (for an updated list of the published works resulting from this project, see http://www.icac.cat/en/recerca/ projectes-de-recerca/projecte/projecte-ager-tarraconensis-pat-el-paisatge-arqueologic-antic-a-la-dreta-del-riu-francoli/) and by I. Arrayás and O. Olesti from the UAB (within the framework of several research projects, see, for example, Arrayás 2005; Olesti and Olesti 2013).

[54] Approached through the study of *amphorae* and through a number of studies, such as those undertaken by J.A. Remolà (2000) and those included within the aforementioned 'Ager Tarraconensis project' and the 'Amphorae ex Hispania' project, led by R. Járrega (ICAC) (for a list of the published works, see http://www.icac.cat/en/recerca/ projectes-de-recerca/projecte/amphorae-ex-hispania/ and http:// www.icac.cat/en/recerca/projectes-de-recerca/projecte/amphorae-ex-hispania-sistematizacion-y-accesibilidad-en-red-de-los-centros-de-produccion-id-har2015-68554-p/).

[55] Recently studied within the 'Aqua Augusta' project, led by J. López Vilar (ICAC) with support from the regional goverment (Diputació de Tarragona), Tarragona's water consortium (Consorcio de Aguas de Tarragona), ICAC and Mútua Catalana Private Foundation (see http:// www.icac.cat/en/recerca/projectes-de-recerca/projecte/auqua-augusta/).

[56] For a summary of the most relevant examples, see Remolà 2007 and, more recently García Noguera *et al.* 2013; Gorostidi *et al.* 2013; López Vilar and Puche 2013.

[57] Járrega and Prevosti 2014.

[58] Tarrats *et al.* 2000 and Remolà 2009. A monograh detailing new data on this site is currently in preparation by Remolà and others and is expected to appear soon.

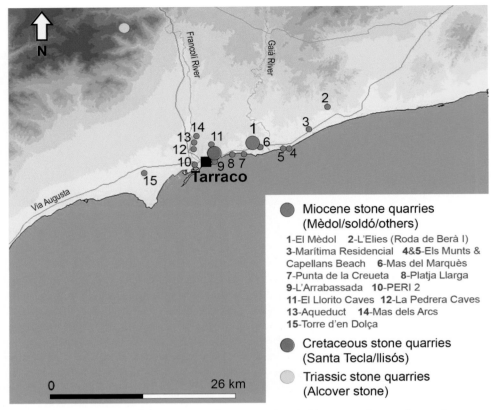

Figure 3. Map showing the location of the quarries of Roman and probable Roman date in the territory around Tarraco (map by the author).

mosaic decorations, has recently been interpreted as possessing links with the late Roman military camp on the outskirts of the town.[59] The territory's intense land occupancy and the vast amount of stone it required right from its foundation and throughout the growth and monumentalisation of Tarraco, undoubtedly necessitated the mobilisation of significant resources and labour in order to sustain the intense building activity this entailed.

Suitable geological bedrock of building stone within the territory near Tarraco was unsurprisingly intensely exploited as a result of this construction activity. Local exploitation had the added advantage of significantly reducing transport expenses.[60] The remains of this quarrying activity represent the largest concentration of archaeological evidence related to stone extraction in the whole of the north-eastern corner of the Iberian Peninsula. Following the studies of A. Dworakowska and J.-C. Bessac,[61] publications by the present author, now more than ten years ago, sought to study and draw attention to the importance of quarries and stone

extraction within the wider Roman archaeology of this part of *Hispania*.[62] As a result, a detailed inventory of quarries opened and exploited in this territory during Antiquity has now been well-established. In total, 17 quarries (or quarry districts) can be identified, where Roman exploitation can be definitively established or at least for which exploitation is highly likely during this period, given the stones used in Roman times (**Figure 3**).

The majority of the quarries were located to the north or north-east of Tarraco and still retain enough evidence to provide a wide corpus of data for building stone extraction methods and techniques:

Marítima Residencial (**Figure 4**, **Table 1**) is a small, trench-type[63] quarry that is now partly covered by modern houses. The currently visible remains of the quarry show half-cut/delimited blocks, trenches, orthogonal working surfaces as well as toolmarks and ledges stemming from ancient extraction. It is a rather small site—about 300 m³ of stone can be estimated to have been extracted from the visible section of the quarry. The quarry's location suggests that it was used to supply building stone for the nearby Roman villas of

---

[59] Remolà and Pérez 2013 and the upcoming proceedings of the International Conference held in June 2022.
[60] It is worth remembering that regardless of the means (sea, river, or land), transport had a direct impact on the overall cost of products, sometimes accounting for a large proportion of the total cost. On this point, DeLaine 1997: 217–19.
[61] See above, footnotes 38 and 39.

[62] Gutiérrez Garcia-M. 2009, 2011.
[63] Bessac 2003: 26, Fig. 7c.

Figure 4. Different views of Marítima Residencial quarry and a map showing its location in relation to the Roman villas in its vicinity (photos by the author; Google Earth with modifications by the author).

La Clota[64] and El Moro.[65] However, an interesting feature of the quarry is that it consists of three consecutive small trench-type fronts separated from each other by stone walls of about 1 m or less. This division does not seem to be a result of the stone itself, which does not show any fractures or faults that would have presented during extraction, and may therefore be linked to the division of the working space into smaller areas[66] or *loci*.

Capellans Beach and Els Munts quarries (**Figure 5, Table 1**) are two small-size quarries opened to meet the needs of the large and sumptuous Roman villa of Els Munts, *c.* 14 km north-east from Tarraco. The former one consists of two trench-type[67] extraction points (or fronts) opened next to each other along and just to the right of the coast line. The location enabled direct sea-borne transport from the quarry site to the building site. The latter quarry is a single extraction front approximately 70 m long and 3 m deep, of an 'in terraces' quarry type.[68] It was opened right next to the location where the villa was being erected. In both sites, the terraces show that blocks were extracted in a planned, systematic way and present visible traces of ancient working. This consisted of small trenches or channels, wedge sockets, and pick marks, revealing the extraction technique commonly employed in Roman times; however, some intermittent modern quarrying has occurred at the Els Munts quarry during the 20th century.[69]

---

[64] The late Republican villa of corridor-type had a short lifespan. It was built on a site known as Rincón del César and is best known for its abundance of pottery that points towards the existence of a pottery workshop at the site producing common ware, *tegulae/imbrex,* and *amphorae* Dr-2-4 (IPAC 2006).

[65] Despite evidence of an earlier building, the main villa was built in the mid-1st century AD and consisted of a rectangular building of about 2500 m³ that comprised a large, columned *peristylum*, a number of other rooms, and a bath complex. It may have been abandoned between the end of the 2nd and the early 3rd centuries AD, perhaps due to its inclusion in a larger *fundus* (cf. Remolà 2007: 119–132).

[66] This can be seen, for example, at L'Arquet quarry (La Couronne, near Marseille), where small stone walls up to 1 m high and 20 cm wide were recorded during the rescue excavations (Pedini 2018: 112). However, it must also be noted that this quarry is linked to modern extraction and therefore the interpretation of these 'division walls' at the Marítima Residencial quarry still remains uncertain, pending archaeological excavation.

[67] Bessac 2003: 26, fig. 7c.

[68] Bessac 2003: 26, fig. 7a.

[69] Gutiérrez Garcia-M. 2009: 135–141.

Figure 5. View of the main front of Els Munts quarry (top left) and of the two fronts at Capellans beach quarry (right); map showing the locations of the quarries and the Roman villa of Els Munts (photos by the author; Google Earth with modifications by the author).

Mas del Marquès consists of a series of small to relatively large quarry sites scattered across the slopes of the Punta de la Mora promontory (c. 10 km north from Tarraco). The quarries reveal evidence of extensive extraction[70] and probably belonged to the same quarrying complex of El Mèdol, which is the largest quarry in this territory and which is located close by, across from Mas del Marquès (**Figure 6**, **Table 1**). Six of the eleven sites or small fronts recorded are likely to be of Roman date, but later use is also very plausible since the nearby medieval castle of Tamarit and its adjacent quarry demonstrate further evidence of building activity in this area. Moreover, a number of the quarry sites show evidence of modern extraction.[71]

La Creueta Point quarry was small but extensively worked with 'wearing down' quarrying.[72] This was mainly surface quarrying, occupying a considerable area without going very deep into the bedrock. The quarry is now partially underwater. The most common evidence of extraction is delimited rectangular, half-cut blocks and negative traces on the horizontal surfaces of the site, sometimes preserved in groups of two to three

blocks perhaps delimited and detached simultaneously (**Figure 6**, **Table 1**). Probably short-lived, this quarry seems to have been mostly intended to supply blocks to build the nearby 1st-century funerary monument known as Scipio's Tower and, perhaps, the nearby Roman villa.[73]

El Llorito Caves are a series of three underground quarries located on the south-western slope of a low hill, only c. 2 km north-north=east from Tarraco. Although the quarries reveal different approaches (i.e. gallery-type and pillar-type quarries),[74] they are probably different fronts of the same area of extraction, which was not overly large and the main favourable traits of which were its proximity to the town and the workability of its stone. While not all of the remaining traces of working (e.g. vertical walls with orthogonal cuts in the bedrock, numerous parallel pick marks, trenches, several wedge sockets, and scattered abandoned blocks) can be associated with Roman quarrying activity, ashlar blocks matching the stone were used to build the Roman wall (**Table 1**),[75] suggesting some extraction during this period.

[70] Bessac 2003: 24, fig. 3b.
[71] Gutiérrez Garcia-M. 2009:159–166.
[72] Bessac 2003:26, fig. 7b.
[73] Gutiérrez Garcia-M. 2009: 166–169.
[74] Bessac 2003: 30, fig. 14b and 14c.
[75] Gutiérrez Garcia-M. 2009: 185–191.

Figure 6. General view and detail of the quarry at La Creueta Point (left) and view of two sites at Mas del Marquès (right); map showing the locations of the quarries and the funerary monument (Scipio's Tower) as well as the El Mèdol quarry and the loading dock at Roca Plana (photos by the author; Google Earth with modifications by the author).

The Aqueduct and Mas dels Arcs quarries represent two different quarry zones located about 4 km north from Tarragona and distributed over a relatively wide area around Tarraco's Roman aqueduct.[76] The quarries show abundant evidence for extraction using the common Roman working methods (e.g. parallel toolmarks, trenches, wedge sockets, abandoned blocks, orthogonal working surfaces, and right-angle cuts in the bedrock). The first group includes ten fairly well-preserved, opencast quarries in the small valley and on the hill slopes in the area surrounding the aqueduct. These were undoubtedly opened to supply the aqueduct's construction or later repair, since some of the quarries are extremely small, with c. 4 – 30 m³ of stone extracted compared to c. 500 – 1000 m³ from the larger quarries (**Figure 7**, **Table 1**). The second quarry zone of Mas dels Arcs, located slightly further north, comprises only 4 quarry fronts where use in Roman times seems plausible but where the evidence is less clear-cut.[77]

La Pedrera Caves are a group of eight quarries closely linked with the previous ones, as they are located only a few hundred metres to the south of the Aqueduct and Mas dels Arcs quarries and the Roman aqueduct. They all show the same evidence of working methods (e.g. trenches, toolmarks, wedge sockets, and the negative imprint of extracted blocks, which were almost square to rectangular) but are nonetheless diverse both in terms of the type of extraction (with opencast and

underground quarries) and size (some of them are the result of intensive extraction, with c. 1000 to almost 7000 m³ of stone extracted, whereas others seem to be the result of occasional, short-term use) (**Table 1**).[78]

Tarragona - Peri 2, Plots 18–21 and L'Arrabassada Beach are the only two quarries found in the immediate outskirts of the Roman town. The latter consists of trench-type extraction[79] on the south-western limit of L'Arrabassada beach (**Figure 8**, **Table 1**), and the former was discovered during several rescue excavations carried out between 1995 and 2006. It showed mixed traits of both 'in-terraces' and pit-type quarries.[80] The quarries were probably intended to supply the adjacent buildings and/or infrastructure. This was especially the case for the latter quarry.[81]

Evidence of ancient quarrying is no longer visible at other areas due to later and modern industrial extraction, but there is abundant proof of their stone being used in Roman Tarraco. This is the case for quarries located in the La Budallera and La Savinosa areas, i.e. El Llorito, La Salut, and La Savinosa quarries, located just a few kilometres north-east of Tarraco. This is also the case for the quarry at La Lloera, located near the current town of Alcover, c. 20 km north-north-west of Tarraco.[82]

---

[76] Today it is known as *Aqueducte de les Ferreres* or *Pont del Diable*. The total length of this infrastructure is currently being studied, alongside a second aqueduct which brought water from the Gaià river. The study is under the direction of J. López Vilar (ICAC; see above footnote 55).
[77] Gutiérrez Garcia-M. 2009: 197–208.

[78] Gutiérrez Garcia-M. 2009: 191–197.
[79] Bessac 2003: 26, fig. 7c.
[80] Bessac 2003: 26, fig. 7a, 28, fig. 11c.
[81] Gutiérrez Garcia-M. 2009: 174–179.
[82] Gutiérrez Garcia-M. 2009: 208–223, 180–185, and 223–226, respectively.

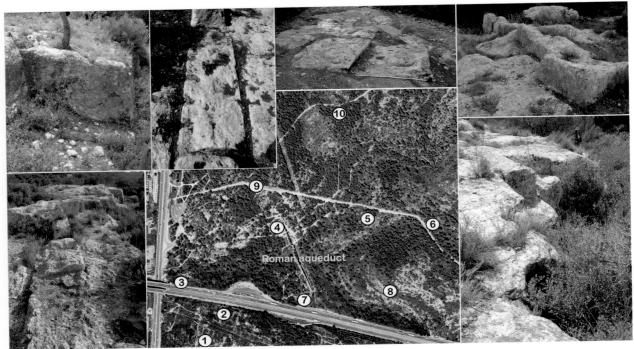

Figure 7. Map showing the location of the Roman aqueduct and the ten quarries near it; and views of six of the quarries (photos by the author; Ortophoto by the Institut Cartogràfic de Catalunya with modifications by the author).

Figure 8. Views of the quarries at L'Arrabassada (left) and Platja Llarga beaches (right) (photos by the author).

Nevertheless, recent advances in archaeological fieldwork during the last decade have led to several new discoveries, including the identification of new sites, such as the one uncovered at Platja Llarga beach in January 2020 (**Figure 8**, **Table 1**)[83] or the previously unknown quarry fronts at Torre d'en Dolça.[84] Moreover, archaeological research on previously known, non-ornamental stone quarries has also yielded important

results. This included work carried out at the L'Elies and El Mèdol quarries.

L'Elies (or Roda de Berà 1) quarry is *c.* 25 km north of Tarraco, and despite being the object of intense exploitation in modern times, it has nevertheless preserved limited evidence for Roman extraction. This was most likely for stone blocks used to build the nearby Roman arch[85] (**Table 1**). A small but very restricted archaeological excavation was undertaken in 2012. It was undertaken in the upper area of the quarry where a significant difference in the extraction pattern was

[83] Unfortunately, part of the deck of a nearby restaurant was built on top of it, so it is not possible to determine its full extent.
[84] They are still currently the subject of study and as such a Roman date cannot be entirely ruled out. For the already-known quarry fronts at Torre d'en Dolça, see Gutiérrez Garcia-M. 2009: 169–173.

[85] Gutiérrez Garcia-M. 2008, 2009: 113–120.

visible, which points to a probable early date for the use of this particular part of the quarry. Unfortunately, the absence of pottery remains prevented precise dating of this activity, but analysis of the remaining toolmarks indicates three different periods of activity.[86]

El Mèdol quarry holds a pre-eminent position among the quarries around Tarraco, not only due to its very large size but also because of its very exceptional features, such as the monolithic pinnacle standing at its centre.[87] In-depth study has been undertaken both at the site itself and its surrounding landscape following the outbreak of a fire in 2010.[88] The work consisted of field surveys, the detailed recording of the quarry fronts, quarry debris, and other quarrying-related features, and eight test-pits in the central and eastern sectors of the quarry.[89] The results provided substantial insights into our understanding of this site, which included both the first detailed plan of all the quarry fronts and sectors, and the discovery of a new small area in the north-eastern corner of the quarry area (**Figure 9**). The estimated volume of extraction is substantial – *c.* 150,000m³, equivalent to 350,000 tonnes of stone (**Table 1**).[90] The in-depth study was also able to demonstrate that the initial quarry extraction should be dated to the late Republican/early imperial period, which is much earlier than had previously been suggested.[91] It also revealed important evidence for the quarry's management process thanks to the discovery of what seems to be the remains of a hut with wooden roof beams. This was located at the entrance to the main area of extraction, midway up the ramp descending towards the lower part of the pit. This was not far from the quarry entrance and where a large number of discarded blocks with carved and painted inscriptions was discovered.[92] This suggests that the hut might have been a post controlling the entrance and exit to the main area of extraction. Altogether, this evidence provides extremely interesting insight

into the complex organisation of the supply of stone (**Figure 10**).

The large-scale extraction of stone at El Mèdol can be explained by the size of the outcrop, the quality of the stone, and its location relatively near the seashore, which allowed for a constant supply of blocks to the town. The location of a loading dock on a nearby beach provided interesting evidence related to the transportation of this stone (**Figure 6**). This infrastructure is about 40 m long and 11 m wide and takes advantage of the natural features of the rock in which it is carved to provide a flat platform acting as a natural breakwater. The sea level has risen here since Roman times, but the presence of square post-holes near the rectilinear channel (**Figure 11**), together with the location of this dock in relation to the sea currents, strongly point to this being the place from which the blocks were loaded and transported to the town. The effort involved in creating this infrastructure points towards intensive use. Moreover, the existence of a nearby small Roman site (c. 150 m away), where pottery from the mid-1st century AD has been found, suggests that it was in use when the Provincial Forum was under construction. The comprehensive study of the quarry and this infrastructure has therefore shed much light on the extent, chronology, and dynamics of the exploitation of local resources. Moreover, this can be directly connected to the town's greatest phase of construction activity and urban renovation. As such, its study has allowed substantial advances in our knowledge, revealing complex logistical activity and evidence for a direct link between the quarry and the building of large-scale public projects in the capital of *Tarraconensis*.

Additionally, work concerning the petrographic characterisation of the stone outcrops at El Mèdol and Coves del Llorito has been undertaken in recent years.[93] Overall, work on the quarries in the vicinity of Tarraco has significantly improved and revised previous assumptions and provided new thoughts on the extraction process and the initial stages in the procurement of ancient building stone in this area. The combination of significant past and on-going archaeological investigation of the ancient quarries and the monuments in Tarragona and its surroundings makes Tarraco and its hinterland an ideal case study of the initial stages of procuring raw materials in the quarry and how this was connected to the material's subsequent use.

---

[86] Artina and Benimeli 2013; Artina 2014.
[87] The literature about this site is vast; see Gutiérrez Garcia-M. 2009: 146–158 for the pre-2009 bibliography.
[88] Gutiérrez Garcia-M. *et al.* 2015.
[89] López Vilar and Gutiérrez Garcia-M. 2016, 2017; Gutiérrez Garcia-M. and López Vilar 2018; Gutiérrez Garcia-M. *et al.* 2019. Part of this research was conducted within a larger architectural project under the auspices of ABERTIS-ACESA, while part of it was also undertaken within the framework of several I+D projects funded by the Spanish Government (HAR2008-046000/HIST, HAR2011-25011 and HAR2015-65319-P: http://www.icac.cat/en/recerca/projectes-de-recerca/projecte/pedrera-del-medol/)
[90] The final amount must have been much higher, as this figure corresponds only to the central part of the quarry (known locally as *El Clot del Mèdol*).
[91] Evidence comes from a charred piece of wood that was uncovered at the base of the central pinnacle during archaeological excavations in 2013. Its ¹⁴C analysis provided a date range of between 27 BC and AD 19 (López Vilar and Gutiérrez Garcia-M. 2016: 185, 191).
[92] The study of these marks was carried out by S. Vinci in collaboration with M. Navarro (AUSONIUS UMR 5067 CNRS/UBM) and D. Gorostidi (ICAC/URV). For the results, see Vinci 2018, 2019.

[93] These were directed by Dr Ll. Casas, who is a lecturer at the Geology Department of the Autonomous University of Barcelona (UAB), and who has helped contribute to a better description of the specific features of each outcrop. It is also worth mentioning the current PhD thesis on Roman sculpture made in local stone, which is being undertaken by M. Moreno under the supervision of M. Claveria from the Art History Department of this same university.

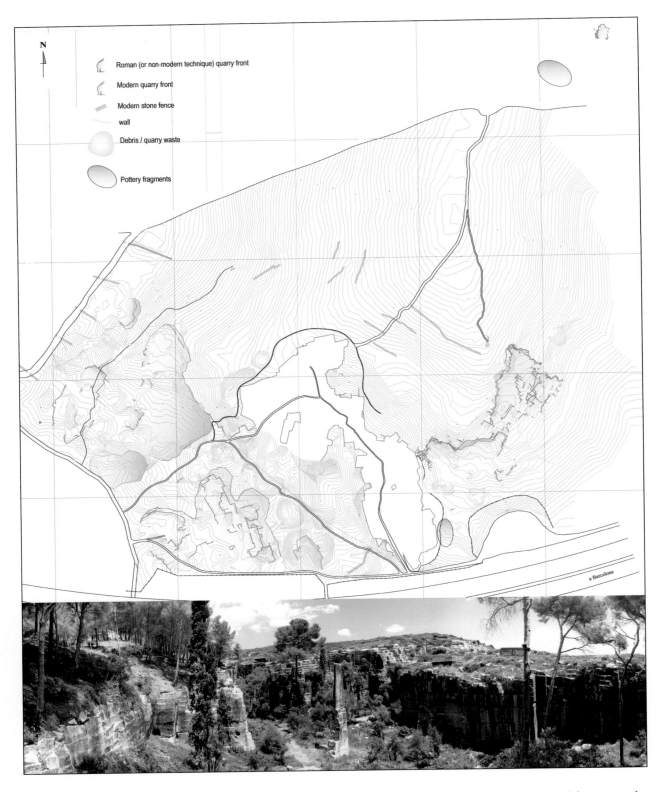

Figure 9. Plan of El Mèdol quarry (top) and general view of its central area (*Clot*) (plan by UDG/ICAC, with modifications and photos by the author).

Figure 10. View of El Mèdol quarry: detail of the small, newly discovered site at the north-easternmost limit (top left), negative traces of extremely regular blocks (right), and section at the base of the pinnacle in the central region (*Clot*) showing the three consecutive floors (marked with arrows) established on quarry debris (bottom left) (photos by the author).

Figure 11. View of the rectilinear channel at Roca Plana, with Tarragona -ancient Tarraco- at the horizon (right) and details of the square post-holes (left) (photos by the author).

Quarry	Sites / fronts	Approximate volume of extraction	Location	Significant monument/ building nearby	Close (<3 km) to Tarraco
Roda de Berà	1	6875 m³	interior	Roman arch of Berà	-
Marítima Residencial		300 m³	coast	Roman villas (Rincón del Cesar and El Moro)	-
Capellans beach		190 m³	shoreline	Roman villa (Els Munts)	-
Els Munts		6385 m³	coast	Roman villa (Els Munts)	-
El Mèdol		150000 m³	coast	-	-
Mas del Marquès	1,2, 5,6, 9, 10	2670 m³	coast	-	-
La Creueta point		1560 m³	shoreline	Funerary monument (Scipio's Tower)	-
El Llorito Caves	1–3	10010 m³	interior	-	yes
L'Arrabassada beach		480 m³	shoreline	-	yes
PERI 2 –lots 21 and 18		110 m³	coast	-	yes
La Pedrera Caves	1–3, 5–7	2993 m³	interior – next to main road	-	yes
Aqueduct	1,3,4,7–9	1789 m³	interior – next to main road	Roman aqueduct	-
Mas dels Arcs	1–4	13690 m³	interior –next to main road	Roman aqueduct and Roman villa (Centcelles)	-
Mas d'en Dolça		2160 m³	interior – next to main road	Roman villa (La Pineda-Calípolis)	-
Platja Llarga beach		? m³	shoreline	-	-

Table 1. Approximate volume of stone extracted from the quarries discussed (only Roman and probable Roman fronts have been considered, while those of uncertain date have not been included) and their locations (defined as 'shoreline' - quarries directly on the seashore; 'coast' - quarries near the coast but not on the shoreline; and 'interior' - inland quarries).

Range of materials, selection of sources, and the chaîne opératoire

Thanks to an abundance of suitable geological outcrops, the territory of Tarraco was favourably located in terms of access to building stone. The outcrops on which the quarries were opened consist of Cretaceous, Miocene, and Triassic geological layers, which provided a relatively wide range of stones.

Not all of the stones used for building at Tarraco came from quarries specifically opened during the Roman period. This is the case of the Jurassic dolomitic breccia which forms Tarraco's bedrock. This stone was used—due to its extreme hardness—for the large, irregular megalithic blocks of the lower courses of the town's defensive wall, which as noted above, was the first major structure of Tarraco (**Figure 1**). However, the vast majority of building stone used in Tarraco was Miocene limestone, which was extracted in a more systematic and organised manner, as evident from the array of surviving ancient quarries discussed in the previous section. It goes without saying that the reconstruction of the 'chaîne opératoire' is essential for estimating the cost and time needed to complete specific tasks (aspects not addressed in this paper) and for recognising the inherent complexity of the overall extraction process. For example, this would have included the need to adapt to individual cases based on stone characteristics, availability, and source location.

The Miocene limestones are not overly hard and are therefore relatively workable. This made them both ideal for use as building stone and highly sought-after materials. They come from a geological formation that extends mainly south-west to north-east from the city, explaining the high concentration of quarries in this part of the territory (**Figure 3**). From this group of quarries, the most common stones were El Mèdol stone and *soldó* (two different varieties of the same material depending on the amount of bioclasts), although these were not the only stones extracted.[94] The overall similarity in terms of petrography and hardness of these limestones meant that the process of cutting the stone from the bedrock did not significantly differ from site to site. Remains of the first steps of opening a new quarry (i.e. the initial location of a usable outcrop and the removal of topsoil and the covering rock layer, which was typically of poor quality) rarely survive and are difficult to trace archaeologically due to the very nature of the extraction process, which typically removes any traces of this initial phase. However, a possible example of these first steps is preserved in a small site in the north-easternmost limit of the El Mèdol quarry (**Figure 10**). This area seems to be the result of work undertaken to check the quality of the stone at this site.

---

[94] See Gutiérrez Garcia-M. 2009: 106–113 for a detailed description of these and other Miocene stones, as well as local building stones used in Tarraco and its surroundings.

Once the first surface was located, extraction *per se* began and consisted of the gradual removing of blocks, thus creating the quarry front. Traces of this stage are frequent and show that the most common extraction technique consisted of detaching the blocks by making vertical cuts (trenches) with a quarryman's pick (*dolabra*) that delimited their shape to a depth corresponding approximately to the intended height. Iron wedges (*cunei*) were subsequently placed horizontally into small holes specifically carved at the bottom of the block and were sometimes used to separate the blocks from the substratum through percussion (hammering) with mallets or other instruments (*mallei*). Continued extraction using this method leaves very characteristic traces that are found in most of the aforementioned quarries. This can be seen especially at El Mèdol,[95] where the amount of simultaneous working levels and terraces, and the lifespan of extraction activity was much higher than in any of the other quarries around Tarraco (**Figure 10**). The only exception in terms of extraction technique is found at the La Lloera quarries, where the strongly bedded Triassic geological layers providing Alcover stone made the use of trenches and even wedge sockets almost superfluous.

After the fire at El Mèdol, it was possible to uncover a main feature of quarrying at this site that had been previously unknown. The clearance of dense vegetation revealed a series of heaps and dumps of quarry debris covering specific areas of the quarry, especially in the western sector but also in the northern half of the central region. They give a remarkable insight into the operations linked with waste management and the progression of quarrying at the site, as exhausted quarry fronts were used as dump sites while areas where extraction was to continue remained clear of debris. Moreover, quarry debris, which was a by-product of the main activity (extraction of blocks), provided material for important logistical elements, such as ramps to give access to the central pit (*Clot*) and very hard debris floors for flat transit and working areas (**Figure 10**). Debris was also used for the construction of auxiliary premises, such as the very coarse floor and walls of the small hut which acted as a control post located midway up the ramp and which led out of the main quarry area.

This control post was strongly linked to the discarded blocks that were located right next to the entrance (or exit) of the *Clot*. This seems to be a natural area to implement all intermediate control tasks (e.g. quality control checks and any necessary further working of rough-hewn blocks) as well as a suitable location to temporarily store blocks before they were transported from the quarry to their places of use. Most of the blocks which make up the debris had faults and cracks and therefore appear to have been discarded/rejected in Antiquity. It has not been possible to determine the date of their accumulation,[96] but there can be no doubt that at least a large number of the blocks were amassed from the Roman period onwards thanks to the extraordinary collection of inscriptions (carved and painted) on the blocks themselves.[97]

In fact, a precise date for extraction is extremely difficult to identify except in a few very specific cases, such as El Mèdol and PERI 2, where archaeological excavations have been carried out. In other cases, only informed guesses can be made either on the relative chronology of the specific site(s), such as in the central area (*Clot*) of El Mèdol, where the uniformity and regularity of the negative impressions left from the extracted rows of blocks suggest that they were part of the same intervention. The overall period in which these quarries were active can also be estimated by looking at the date of the objects and buildings constructed using Miocene, Cretaceous, and Triassic stones. Obviously, the specific processes and rates of extraction differed depending on the circumstances of each quarry and the quality of the stone; however, the overall picture suggests the start of quarrying in the late Republican period, with a peak during early imperial times, especially under the Flavian emperors and later under Hadrian, when massive monumentalisation and refurbishments of the upper part of the town took place. After this point, a progressive decline started, probably from the 3rd century onwards, when the reuse of earlier stone began to increase until it became common practice[98] during Late Antiquity.

The vast size and quantity of material extracted at the El Mèdol quarry equal those of the largest quarries in the empire[99] and clearly indicate that it was the main source of building stone within the territory. In contrast, the rest of the quarries that exploited outcrops with Miocenic layers appear to have been modest operations, frequently opened to supply the construction of a nearby monument or project. Such is the case with the quarries of Els Munts and Capellans Beach, the Marítima Residencial quarry, the L'Elies (or Roda de Berà 1) quarry, the Punta de la Creueta quarry, and the small quarry found at PERI 2-Sector Tabacalera de Tarragona, in the western *suburbium* of Tarraco. Most of these quarries are the result of specific building site dynamics and were opened in order to use the most locally available and suitable building stone to the area

---

95 The technical aspects of quarrying at this and the other quarries has already been presented in other publications, see Gutiérrez Garcia-M. 2009, 261–274; 2011, 2014.

96 See Roig *et al.* 2011.
97 See above, footnote 92.
98 This phenomenon is most clear with regard to decorative stones, but it also applies to stones used for general building purposes.
99 That is, sites where more than 120,000 m³ of stone was extracted (cf. Russell 2013: 63).

where the specific buildings or monuments[100] were to be erected. The same dynamic probably explains the existence of two small quarries opened immediately along the coastline, at L'Arrabassada and at Platja Llarga beaches. Here, we see the deliberate intent to shorten (as far as possible) the distance from the point of extraction to the point of use. This is most evident for the case of the small quarries opened around the *arcuationes* of the aqueduct that transported water from the Francolí river towards Tarraco. Erected, probably under Augustus' reign, this stretch of the conduit was built not with stone from El Mèdol, which was located relatively nearby (only *c.* 7 km away and certainly fully functioning by this point), but using an array of smaller quarries specifically opened for the purpose and located immediately adjacent to it. Some of these quarries (the smallest and closest) are probably attributable to different phases of repair that this infrastructure underwent in the following centuries and during the early medieval period, but the rest are certainly the result of a number of specific choices. In these cases there was a preference not to use the common calcisiltite stone outcropping in the nearby quarries of La Pedrera Caves[101] and to find suitable building stone as close as possible to the site of construction in order to avoid as much land transport as possible. Attention to the impact of transport is shown by the fact that by this time stone from El Mèdol was already arriving in Tarraco by sea – remarkable since the town is only *c.* 4 km away from the aqueduct.

Stones coming from Mesozoic geological formations, i.e. the Cretaceous Santa Tecla and *llisós* stones and the Triassic Alcover stone (also known as La Lloera stone),[102] were only used for building as secondary products. These stones were used for decorative and epigraphic purposes. In fact, the hinterland of *Tarraco* was also the source of stones with high aesthetic value, from the smooth Alcover stone used for important inscriptions and wall revetment in late Republican-Augustan Tarraco[103] to the outstandingly beautiful Santa Tecla stone, whose colours resemble those of the highly appreciated *marmor Numidicum* (*giallo antico*) and *marmor Chium* (*portasanta*).[104] Small chips and irregular chunks of Santa Tecla stone are sometimes found as *rudus* within the *caementicium* of structures in Tarraco. Apart from its aesthetic qualities, the most significant

advantage of this material was its close proximity to Tarraco, since the quarries, also the source of the grey/dark brown llisós limestone, are only a few hundred metres from the town with easy access to the coastline (**Figure 12**). In addition, the location of the quarry near the coast allowed this stone to be marketed elsewhere. It is likely that without these favourable circumstances with regard to transport, this local *marmor* would probably have been relegated to local use only. These same factors probably explain the use of debris and other secondary products from the Santa Tecla stone quarries as rubble core in the structures of Tarraco's public buildings, for temporary structures on construction sites, such as ramps or platforms, and most likely also in the production of lime.

Procurement dynamics: some considerations on management and transport

The landscape of stone extraction at both intra-site and territory-wide levels was based on several factors, including the strategies and methods of extraction used throughout the life-span of the quarries,[105] the accessibility of the site, and the ease of transport from the quarry to the intended destination. Obviously, each case had its own particularities, but thanks to surviving evidence we are able go beyond mere speculation. Again, we can to turn to evidence from El Mèdol. Its pre-eminence within the quarries supplying projects in Tarraco was the result of a number of favourable aspects among which was is location. Coastal transport was a major advantage in moving material as quickly and cost-effectively as possible to the town and undoubtedly helps to explain the extensive extraction at this quarry. The proximity of the quarry to the coastline, therefore, was an essential factor in the quarry' success. The loading dock at Roca Plana beach discussed above played a major role in the distribution of the material extracted from this quarry and, probably, from the nearby Mas del Marquès quarries as well.

The stone intended for the construction of the Provincial Forum and the buildings of the town's upper area was loaded onto barges and most likely arrived at Punta del Miracle, next to Playa del Miracle beach, which is located immediately below this part of the town (**Figure 12**). This was the closest point to the location in which the stone was used, and mooring there would have avoided disrupting the harbour and the town's inner circulation with constant shipments of building blocks.[106] The practicality of this point in terms

---

[100] E.g. the Roman arch of Berà or the large funerary monument knowns as Scipio's Tower.
[101] They supply the calcisiltite known as Coves stone (*pedra de les Coves*) as well as the calcarenite; see Gutiérrez Garcia-M. 2009: 112, 192.
[102] Àlvarez *et al.* 2009; Gutiérrez Garcia-M. 2009: 109–112.
[103] Gutiérrez Garcia-M. 2009: 223–226; Gorostidi *et al.* 2018.
[104] Santa Tecla stone had an important role in the decorative and epigraphic programs of the towns in the northern half of *conventus Tarraconensis* (cf. Gutiérrez Garcia-M. 2009: 109–112, 208-222; and especially Àlvarez *et al.* 2009: 71–80) and sporadically in the *conventi Carthaginsensis* and *Caesaraugustanus* (see Soler 2003, 2004; Lapuente 2014: 151–153; Lapuente *et al.* 2015; Royo *et al.* 2015).

[105] Other factors that also influenced the method of extraction are the characteristics of the material, the nature of the ownership of the quarry or the quarry district, the infrastructure and transport nodes, the client and/or market demand(s), and the type of object being produced; cf. Russell 2013: 6.
[106] For a useful example, although on a larger scale, of the disruption to urban life and circulation, see Pensabene and Domingo 2017.

Figure 12. Location and probable transport routes from El Mèdol and the Cretaceous quarries to Tarraco (Google Maps with modifications by the author).

of seafaring is reinforced by the discovery of a series of cuts at the shoreline and at sea level that were interpreted as holes for large beams, possibly part of a wooden dock. The date of this feature, however, remains unclear despite the discovery of Troad granite column drums and Samian pottery underwater, which at the very least point towards this area being used in Antiquity.[107] As for the stone used in the colonial forum, the theatre, and the other public buildings and spaces in the lower part of the town, we cannot dismiss the actual harbour as the unloading point due to its closer proximity. Thus, a sort of 'double system' of unloading might have been in place during periods when more intense building activity was taking place.

Less clear, however, is how land transport was implemented. To-date, no evidence has been preserved in the archaeological record or survives from inscriptions and historical sources. Stone must have been moved by land in most cases, albeit at varying distances. Shorter distances did not require complex mechanisms, but the fact that many of the quarries are directly located along the coastline, or nearby, confirms that the usual preference was avoiding the high cost/effort of land transport whenever and wherever possible. This was the case even for very short-lived sites, such as the funerary monument called Scipio's Tower, which was supplied by its own quarry opened at Punta de la Creueta despite its proximity to El Mèdol. (**Figure 6**).

Another main factor in the transport of building stone was the desire to minimise the distances that stone was moved as much as possible. This seems to apply for stone used in both private and public buildings. The quarries of Marítima Residencial and Els Munts, which provided building stone for the nearby villas, testify to the former, while the best example for the latter are the quarries surrounding the aqueduct. Despite being a public project, the erection of the *arcuationes* was not supplied by El Mèdol –with stone moved by a combination of sea and land transport- but by opening several smaller quarries in the surroundings, perhaps allowing the monument to also profit from the best quality stone in this specific area.

Proximity was also an important factor in the use of large quantities of non-dimensional fragments and debris from the Cretaceous ornamental stone quarries. They arrived at construction sites in Tarraco to be used as *rudus* and, as we have seen at El Mèdol, as basic material for ramps, working platforms, and maybe even to produce lime.

[107] Gutiérrez Garcia-M. *et al.* 2019.

Considering these observations, several remarks can be made about the dynamics of quarrying building stone near Tarraco and its supply to the town. First, there was a system, with the quarry of El Mèdol at the centre, that was catalysed by large-scale public works. The recent discoveries at this quarry allow us to corroborate different aspects that were, until this point, a matter of (albeit educated) speculation and which we can now understand more accurately. This allows for a much more nuanced consideration of the internal mechanisms of a large and long-lasting quarry, which provided building material for the monumental projects that developed during the late Republican and (especially) the early imperial periods in Tarraco.[108]

In addition, there were quarries that probably operated under the same technical and management dynamics, albeit on a much smaller scale and appropriately adapted to their own particularities. Although they might also have supplied construction works in the town, their main purpose was to provide stone to smaller building projects, and therefore, their life-span was either typically very short or episodic. In both cases, a very close link can be established between the quarry and the site of construction (or the destination of the stone) that allowed quarries to directly respond to local demands, including the need for immediacy and adaptation. This entailed working on demand (i.e. it is safe to assume that large, long-term stocks were not required) and with few intermediaries, if any, between the source and the structure (especially when compared, for example, with the long-distance transport and delivery of marbles from Italy, Greece, and other eastern territories to Tarraco). In addition, areas for temporary storage, quality control, and loading (both land-based and sea-based) were needed, even for short distances within the *territorium* of Tarraco. We need, therefore, to try to overcome the difficulties and somehow bring into our models these kinds of ephemeral auxiliary infrastructures, most of which leave little or no trace in the archaeological record.

Another aspect worth mentioning is the importance of quarry debris and other quarry waste. Often neglected in overall analyses of quarrying, except maybe when quantifying the volume of stone extracted, they were always present both at the quarry itself and at the construction site. Unfortunately, it is not always possible to identify and quantify quarry debris and waste, as they tend to become 'invisible' once the quarry is abandoned, being made inaccessible by vegetation or being destroyed through use as secondary products (*rudus*, lime, etc.), especially for large-scale projects or those in very close proximity to the quarries. Hauling ramps, such as the ones recreated by Korres

for the construction of the Parthenon in Athens,[109] as well as in-site kilns and working platforms were often required, and such structures could make use of quarry debris in addition to large quantities of stone. Typically, such structures were dismantled or reused once a construction project was finished. Furthermore, the presence of Santa Tecla stone chips as *rudus* in the *caementicium* of buildings clad with El Mèdol and soldó stone demonstrates that the mechanisms for procuring ordinary building stone and ornamental stone were not completely separate from each other, but they tended to logically coalesce.

Despite these observations, there are still many unanswered questions, especially concerning intermediate phases and mechanisms for large-scale public building projects at Tarraco. Apart from the first roughing-out of blocks at the quarry site, were there also on-site workshops at the quarry for carving more elaborate elements (i.e. the capitals, mouldings, and columns made in local Miocene stone)? Or, since Tarraco was nearby, were the roughed-out elements processed directly at the urban workshops or construction sites? If at workshops, where were these located? And, in the case of those works not related to public architectural projects, did they have their own direct procurement of material, as we see in some cases, or were they also supplied by El Mèdol, since it probably had enough capacity to accommodate more demand? In regard to transport, how was this managed, and where were the intermediate depots or temporary storage areas located that would have been required along the route? Other questions have to be added to these in relation to quarry ownership: were the quarries under the control of the local government, as has been suggested by several authors for El Mèdol,[110] or was the opposite the case? And, can we postulate private ownership for some of the quarries, as has also been previously documented for some city quarries, for example at Aphrodisias?[111]

The lack of evidence regarding these aspects forces us to be cautious, since there is ample room for speculation. This applies equally to questions about the amount of time and work required to remove and clean off all the rubble, stone chips, and fragments from working areas,[112] as well as those surrounding

---

[108] Gutiérrez Garcia-M. and Vinci 2018.

[109] Korres 1995: 48.
[110] This hypothesis was originally suggested by the interpretation of the quarry marks engraved on the rejected blocks (cf. Mar and Pensabene 2010, 513–515, fig. 6); however, this has recently been revised, with the marks now proven to represent work-teams (cf. Vinci 2019).
[111] It has been suggested that town benefactors could have been the owners of the quarries or the lands on which they were located (Russell 2013: 53–55).
[112] This is evident from the *c.* 4 m filling that covers the bottom of the *Clot* and the numerous mounds that characterise the topography of the rest of the exploitation areas.

the necessary existence of temporary storage areas. These may have been close to the Roca Plana loading dock, where the stone blocks from the quarry waited to be shipped, or as in the case of Miracle beach, where material accumulated prior to loading for its final destination.

Nonetheless, the evidence around Tarraco, especially that provided by the quarry of El Mèdol, provides a complex picture. This complexity significantly increases when we take into consideration the multiple types of non-ornamental stone employed both in the town and throughout its territory, as well as the fact that continued working (until very recently, or in some cases on-going)[113] at ancient quarries has resulted in the loss of ancient evidence for extraction. In any case, what is absolutely clear is the extraordinary capacity of the Roman stone industry to adapt to both technical and logistic problems related to stone extraction. The adaptability and capacity to overcome these issues are reflected in the wide variability of strategies used in the extraction of stone in the quarries around Tarraco.[114] Despite using the same techniques, different quarries created different action plans and infrastructure in order to ensure an uninterrupted supply of building stone to the city.

Acknowledgements

This research is part of the objectives of the Ramón y Cajal contract RYC-2017-22936 and the project 'El mensaje del mármol: prestigio, simbolismo y materiales locales en las provincias occidentales del imperio romano... (PGC2018-099851-A-I00, MINECO/FEDER, UE)', both funded by the Spanish *Ministerio de Ciencia, Innovación y Universidades*. It is also the result of collaboration with the project 'SULMARE: *Sulcato marmore ferro*. Canteras, talleres, artesanos y comitentes... (PID2019-106967GB-I00, MINECO/FEDER, UE) and has been carried out within the framework of the ArPA –Archaeometry and Artistic Productions research team (https://www.icac.cat/en/research/research-teams/arqueometria-i-produccions-artistiques-arpa/). The author would like to express her gratitude to J.López Vilar, D. Gorostidi, P. Lapuente, I. Rodà, L. Galan, A. Collado, the members of the excavation and survey team working at El Mèdol and Roca Plana, to the Graphic Documentation Unit at the ICAC for El Mèdol plan, and to S. Barker for his insightful comments and reviewing of the text.

Bibliography

Alföldy, G. 2001. Tarraco, capital de la província més gran de l'Imperi romà, in I. Rodà (ed.) *Tarraco porta de Roma (Catàleg de l'exposició)*: 26–31. Tarragona: Fundació La Caixa.

Àlvarez, A., V. García-Entero, A. Gutiérrez Garcia-M. and I. Rodà 2009. *El marmor de Tarraco. Explotació, utilització i comercialització de la pedra de Santa Tecla en època romana / Tarraco Marmor. The Quarrying, Use and Trade of Santa Tecla Stone in Roman Times* (Hic et Nunc 6). Tarragona: ICAC.

Álvarez Areces, E., J.M. Baltuille Martín, J. Fernández Suárez, J. Martínez Martínez and M.A. Utrero Agudo (eds) 2019. *Espacios de canteras históricas. Jornada interdisciplinar sobre Espacios de Canteras Históricas* (Publicaciones del Instituto Geológico Minero de España / Serie: Recursos Minerales nº 10): 69–74. Madrid: Instituto Geológico Minero de España.

Anderson, T.J. and J.H. Scarrow 2011. Millstone quarries in Southern Spain: preliminary pinpointing of provenance and production - exploiting the Internet, in D. Williams and D. Peacock (eds) *Bread for the people: the archaeology of mills and milling. Proceedings of a colloquium held in the British School at Rome 4th–7th November 2009* (University of Southampton Series in Archaeology 3, British Archaeological Reports International Series 2274): 259–275. Oxford: Archaeopress.

Anderson, T.J., J.H. Scarrow and A. Cambeses 2014. Continued characterisation of querns and quern quarries in Southern Spain, *Arkeologisk museum i Stavanger -Skrifter* 24: 111–131.

Antolinos, J.A., J.M. Noguera and B. Soler Huertas 2018. La actividad extractiva en las canteras del entorno de Carthago Nova, in A. Gutiérrez Garcia-M. and P. Rouillard (eds) *Lapidum natura restat. Canteras antiguas de la península Ibérica en su contexto (cronología, técnicas y organización de la explotación)* (Documenta 31/Colección de la Casa de Velázquez 170): 37–48. Tarragona/Madrid: Institut Català d'Arqueologia Clàssica-Casa de Velázquez.

Arrayás, I. 2005. *Morfología histórica del territorio de Tarraco (ss. III-I a.C.)* (col·lecció Instrumenta 19). Barcelona: Publicacions i Edicions UB.

Artina, A. 2014. La cantera de Roda de Berà I (Tarragona), in J.M. Àlvarez, T. Nogales-Basarrate and I. Rodà (eds) *CIAC: Actas XVIII Congreso Internacional Arqueología Clásica. Centro y periferia en el mundo clásico*: 319–322. Mérida: Museo Nacional de Arte Romano.

Artina, A. and R. Benimeli 2013. La pedrera de l'Elies: passat, present i futur, *BOI*: 30.

Baltuille Martín, J.M. and J. Fernández Suárez 2019. Inventario Nacional de Canteras Históricas asociadas al Patrimonio Arquitectónico: metodología para la localización de canteras históricas, in E. Álvarez Areces, J. M. Baltuille Martín, J. Fernández Suárez,

---

[113] For the complete list of quarries in the area, regardless of their chronology, see Gutiérrez Garcia-M. 2009: 112–113.
[114] As seen through the different types of quarries identified by following the classification proposed by J.-C. Bessac (2003).

J. Martínez Martínez and M.A. Utrero Agudo (eds), *Espacios de canteras históricas. Jornada interdisciplinar sobre Espacios de Canteras Históricas* (Serie: Recursos Minerales nº 10): 35–42. Madrid: Publicaciones del Instituto Geológico Minero de España.

Beltrán Fortes, J. and O. Rodríguez Gutiérrez 2010. Los materiales lapídeos de la provincia *Baetica*: estado de la cuestión y líneas actuales de investigación, in S. Camporeale, H. Dessales and A. Pizzo (eds) *Arqueología de la Construcción II. Los Procesos constructivos en el mundo romano: Italia y las provincias occidentales* (*Siena, 13-15/11/2008*) (Anejos de AespA 57): 555–570. Madrid-Mérida: Instituto de Arqueología de Mérida - Consejo Superior de Investigaciones Científicas.

Beltrán Fortes, J., O. Rodríguez Gutiérrez, P. López Aldana, E. Ontiveros Ortega and R. Taylor 2012. Las canteras romanas de mármol de Almadén de la Plata (Sevilla)/The Roman marble quarries of Almadén de la Plata (Sevilla), in V. García-Entero (ed.) *El marmor en Hispania. Explotación, uso y difusión en época romana*: 253–276. Madrid: Universidad Nacional de Educación a Distancia.

Bessac, J.-C. 1988a. Problems of identification and interpretation of tool marks on ancient marbles and decorative stones, in N. Herz and M. Waelkens (eds) 1988. *Classical Marble: Geochemistry, Technology, Trade. Proceedings of the NATO Advanced Research Workshop on Marble in Ancient Greece and Rome: Geology, Quarries, Commerce, Artifacts*, (II Ciocco, Lucca, Italy, May 9–13, 1988): 41–53. Dordrecht/Boston: Kluwer Academic Publishers.

Bessac, J.-C. 1988b. Influences de la conquête romaine sur le travail de la pierre en Gaule méditerannée, *Journal of Roman Archaeology* 1: 57–72.

Bessac, J.-C. 1993. Traces d'outils sur la pierre : méthodes d'étude et interpretation, in R. Francovich (ed.) *Archeologia delle attività estrative e metallurgiche. V ciclo di lezioni sulla ricerca applicata in archeologia, Cretosa di Pontignano (SI) - Campiglia Maritima (LI), 9–12 settembre 1991*: 143–176. Firenze: Consiglio Nazionale delle Ricerche-Università di Siena.

Bessac, J.-C. 1996. *La pierre en Gaule Narbonnaise et les carrières du Bois des Lens (Nîmes): Histoire, Archéologie, Ethnographie et Techniques* (Journal of Roman Archaeology, supplementary serie number 16). Michigan: Ann Arbor.

Bessac, J.-C. 2003. L'extraction des pierres de taille et des roches marbrières dans l'Antiquité : les principales stratégies d'éxploitation, in L. Poupard and A. Richard (eds) *Marbres en Franche-Comté : actes des journées d'étude, Besançon 10–12 juin 1999*: 21–34. Besançon: Association pour la Promotion et le Développement de l'Inventaire comtois.

Bessac, J.-C. 2018. Carrières antiques méditerranéennes : élaboration d'une recherche, in A. Gutiérrez Garcia-M. and P. Rouillard (eds) *Lapidum natura restat. Canteras antiguas de la península Ibérica en su contexto (cronología, técnicas y organización de la explotación)* (Documenta 31/Colección de la Casa de Velázquez 170): 9–21. Tarragona-Madrid: Institut Català d'Arqueologia Clàssica-Casa de Velázquez.

Bessac, J.-C. and R. Sablayrolles 2002. Problématique archéologiques des carrières antiques en Gaule, *Gallia. Archéologie de la France Antique* 59: 3–9.

Boisseuil, D., C. Rico and S. Gelichi (eds) 2021. *Le marché des matières premières dans l'Antiquité et au Moyen Âge* (Collection de l'École Française de Rome 563). Roma: École Française de Rome.

Bonetto, J, S. Camporeale and A. Pizzo (eds) 2014. *Arqueología de la Construcción IV. Las canteras en el mundo antiguo: sistemas de explotación y procesos productivos. Padova, 22–24/11/2012* (Anejos de AespA 69). Madrid-Mérida: Instituto de Arqueología de Mérida - Consejo Superior de Investigaciones Científicas.

Brotons Yagüe, F. and S.F. Ramallo Asensio 2018. Canteras antiguas en la Cuenca de Caravaca (Caravaca de la Cruz, región de Murcia, España), in A. Gutiérrez Garcia-M. and P. Rouillard (eds) *Lapidum natura restat. Canteras antiguas de la península Ibérica en su contexto (cronología, técnicas y organización de la explotación)* (Documenta 31/Colección de la Casa de Velázquez 170): 81–94. Tarragona-Madrid: Institut Català d'Arqueologia Clàssica-Casa de Velázquez.

Camporeale, S., H. Dessales and A. Pizzo (eds) 2008. *Arqueología de la Construcción I. Los Procesos constructivos en el mundo romano: Italia y las provincias orientales, Mérida, 25–26/10/2007* (Anejos de AespA 50). Mérida: Instituto de Arqueología de Mérida - Consejo Superior de Investigaciones Científicas.

Camporeale, S., H. Dessales and A. Pizzo (eds) 2010. *Arqueología de la Construcción II. Los Procesos constructivos en el mundo romano: Italia y las provincias occidentales. Siena, 13–15/11/2008* (Anejos de AespA 57). Madrid-Mérida: Instituto de Arqueología de Mérida - Consejo Superior de Investigaciones Científicas.

Camporeale, S., H. Dessales and A. Pizzo (eds) 2012. *Arqueología de la Construcción III. Los procesos constructivos en el mundo romano: la economía de las obras. Paris, 10–11/12/2009* (Anejos de AespA 64). Madrid-Mérida: Instituto de Arqueología de Mérida - Consejo Superior de Investigaciones Científicas

Cisneros, M. and J. Gisbert 2019. Canteras locales y rocas ornamentales empleadas en la arquitectura y epigrafía de *Labitolosa* (*conventus Caesaraugustanus*, provincia Hispania Citerior), *Anales de Arqueología Cordobesa* 30: 105–132.

Ciurana, J., J.M. Macias, A. Muñoz, I. Teixell, and J.M. Todrà 2013. *Amphiteatrum, memoria martyrum et ecclesiae*. Tarragona: Generalitat de Catalunya – Ajuntament de Tarragona – Institut Català d'Arqueologia Clàssica – Museu Bíblic Tarraconense – Associació Cultural Sant Fructuós.

Costa, L., J. Moratalla and P. Rouillard 2018. Elche (Alicante): des pierres et des chemins. Une démarche multi-scalaire pour comprendre l'organisation et la structure des carrières d'El Ferrol, in A. Gutiérrez Garcia-M. and P. Rouillard (eds) *Lapidum natura restat. Canteras antiguas de la península Ibérica en su contexto (cronología, técnicas y organización de la explotación)* (Documenta 31/Colección de la Casa de Velázquez 170): 25–36. Tarragona-Madrid: ICAC-Casa de Velázquez.

Courault, Ch. and C. Márquez (eds) 2020. *Quantitative studies and production cost of Roman public construction.* Córdoba: UCOPress.

DeLaine, J. 1997. *The Baths of Caracalla: a Study in the Design, Construction and Economics of Large-Scale Building projects in Imperial Rome* (JRA Supplementary Series 25). Portsmouth, Rhode Island: Journal of Roman Archaeology.

DeLaine, J., S. Camporeale and A. Pizzo (eds) 2016. *Arqueología de la Construcción V. Man-made materials, engeneering and infrastructure (Oxford, 11–12/04/2015)* (Anejos de AespA 76). Madrid-Mérida: Instituto de Arqueología de Mérida - Consejo Superior de Investigaciones Científicas.

Dupré, X. (ed.) 2006. *Colonia Iulia Urbs Triumphalis Tarraco* (Forum 12). Tarragona: Museu Arqueològic de Tarragona.

Dworakowska, A. 1975. *Quarries in Ancient Greece.* Wroclaw: Polish Academy of Sciences, Institute of the History of Material Culture.

Dworakowska, A. 1983. *Quarries in Roman provinces.* Wroclaw: Polish Academy of Sciences, Institute of the History of Material Culture.

Gagnaison, C., Ch. Montenat, J. Moratalla, P. Rouillard and E. Truszkowsi 2006. Un ébauche de sculpture ibérique dans les carrières de la Dame d'Elche. Le buste d'El Ferriol (Elche, Alicante), *Mélanges de la Casa de Vélázquez* 36(1): 153–172.

Gagnaison, C., Ch. Montenat, P. Barrier and P. Rouillard 2007. L'environnement du site ibérique de La Alcudia et les carrières antiques de la Dame d'Elche (province d'Alicante, Espagne), *ArchéoSciences* 31: 2–33.

García Arrabal, D. and Y. Peña Cervantes 2017. Cantera honda de Posadas (Córdoba): una extracción de material lapídeo presumiblemente vinculada a la explotación olivarera del curso medio del Guadalquivir en época romana, *Romvla* 16: 195–218

García-Entero, V. 2020 Poniendo el marmor Cluniensis en el mapa de Hispania. El uso de la principal roca ornamental de color de procedencia ibérica en el interior peninsular en época romana, in V. García-Entero, S. Vidal, A. Gutiérrez Garcia-M. and R. Aranda (eds) *Paisajes e historias en torno a la piedra. Ocupación, explotación del territorio, distribución, consumo y reutilización de los materiales lapídeos desde la Antigüedad*: 117- 190. Madrid: Universidad Nacional de Educación a Distancia.

García-Entero, V., A. Gutiérrez Garcia-M., S. Vidal Álvarez, M.J. Pérez Agorreta and E. Zarco Martínez 2018a. Espejón limestone and conglomerate (Soria, Spain): archaeometric characterization, quarrying and use in Roman times, in D. Matetić Poljak and K. Marasović (eds) 2018. *Interdisciplinary Studies on Ancient Stone: Proceedings of the XI International Conference of ASMOSIA (Split, Croatia, May 18–22, 2015)*: 567–576. Split: University of Split and Arts Academy of Split.

García-Entero, V., A. Gutiérrez Garcia-M. and E. Zarco Martínez 2018b. Las canteras de calizas y conglomerados de Espejón (Soria). Evidencias arqueológicas y la documentación escrita, in A. Gutiérrez Garcia-M. and P. Rouillard (eds) *Lapidum natura restat. Canteras antiguas de la península Ibérica en su contexto (cronología, técnicas y organización de la explotación)* (Documenta 31/Colección de la Casa de Velázquez 170): 185–197. Tarragona-Madrid: Institut Català d'Arqueologia Clàssica-Casa de Velázquez.

García-Entero, V., S. Vidal, A. Gutiérrez Garcia-M. and R. Aranda (eds) 2020. *Paisajes e historias en torno a la piedra. Ocupación, explotación del territorio, distribución, consumo y reutilización de los materiales lapídeos desde la Antigüedad.* Madrid: Universidad Nacional de Educación a Distancia.

García Noguera, M., J.F. Roig Pérez and I. Teixell 2013. Darreres aportacions en l'estudi de la vil·la romana de la Llosa (Cambrils, Baix Camp): l'edifici septentrional, in M. Prevosti, J. López Vilar and J. Guitart (eds) *Ager Tarraconensis 5. Paisatge, poblament, cultura material i història. Actes del Simposi internacional / Landscape, Settlement, Material Culture and History. Proceddings of the International Symposium*: 281–294. Tarragona: Institut Català d'Arqueologia Clàssica.

González Soutelo, S. and A. Gutiérrez Garcia-M. 2020. El proyecto 'Marmora Galicia': identificación y estudio de la explotación, empleo y circulación de los mármoles en el NW peninsular en época romana y tardorromana', in V. García-Entero, S. Vidal, A. Gutiérrez Garcia-M. and R. Aranda, R. (eds) *Paisajes e historias en torno a la piedra. La ocupación y explotación del territorio de la cantería y las estrategias de distribución, consumo y reutilización de los materiales lapídeos desde la Antigüedad*: 125–197. Madrid: UNED-Arte y Humanidades.

González Soutelo, S., A. Gutiérrez Garcia-M. and H. Royo Plumed 2014. El mármol de O Incio: proyecto de caracterización, estudio de la explotación y uso de un marmor local en la Galicia romana, in J.M. Álvarez, T. Nogales-Basarrate and I. Rodà (eds) *CIAC: Actas XVIII Congreso Internacional Arqueología Clásica. Centro y periferia en el mundo clásico*: 323–326. Mérida: Museo Nacional de Arte Romano.

Gorostidi, D., J. López Vilar and A. Gutiérrez Garcia-M. 2018. The Use of Alcover Stone in Roman Times (Tarraco, Hispania Citerior). Contributions to the Officina Lapidaria Tarraconensis, in D. Matetić Poljak and K. Marasović (eds) *ASMOSIA XI Interdisciplinary Studies on Ancient Stone. Proceedings of the Eleventh International Conference of ASMOSIA, Split 18-22 May 2015*: 577–582. Split: University of Split and Arts Academy of Split.

Gorostidi, D., J. López Vila, M. Prevosti and I. Fiz 2013. Propietaris de les vil·les de l'ager Tarraconensis (meitat occidental del Camp de Tarragona). Proposta per a un catàleg, in M. Prevosti, J. López Vilar and J. Guitart (eds) *Ager Tarraconensis 5. Paisatge, poblament, cultura material i història. Actes del Simposi internacional / Landscape, Settlement, Material Culture and History. Proceddings of the International Symposium*: 401–424. Tarragona: Institut Català d'Arqueologia Clàssica.

Gorostidi, D. and A. Gutiérrez Garcia-M. (eds) forthcoming. *Tituli, imagines, marmora. Poder y prestigio en mármol. Homenaje a Isabel Rodà de Llanza*. Anejos de AEspA, in press.

Gutiérrez Deza, M.I. 2012. Aproximación a los materiales pétreos de la gran arquitectura de Colonia Patricia Corduba, in V. García-Entero (ed.) *El marmor en Hispania. Explotación, uso y difusión en época romana*: 299–314. Madrid: Universidad Nacional de Educación a Distancia.

Gutiérrez Garcia-M., A. 2008. Aproximació a l'explotació de la pedra en època romana: les pedreres de Roda de Berà, *BOI 20*: 9–14.

Gutiérrez Garcia-M., A. 2009. *Roman quarries in the northeast of Hispania (modern Catalonia)* (Documenta 10). Tarragona: Institut Català d'Arqueologia Clàssica.

Gutiérrez Garcia-M., A. 2010. Recursos lapídeos del noreste de la península ibérica en época romana: canteras y ciudades, *Bolletino di Archeologia online*, volume speciale A/A8/2: 13–33.

Gutiérrez Garcia-M., A. 2011. The exploitation of local stone in Roman times: the case of north-eastern Spain, *World Archaeology* 43(2): 313–336.

Guitérrez Garcia-M., A. 2012. Los marmora de las canteras de Tarragona: uso y difusión, in V. García-Entero (ed.) *El marmor en Hispania. Explotación, uso y difusión en época romana*: 97–114. Madrid: Universidad Nacional de Educación a Distancia.

Gutiérrez Garcia-M., A. 2014. La producción de material lapídeo en el norte del conventus Tarraconensis: extracción, organización y gestión de las canteras, in J. Bonetto, S. Camporeale and A. Pizzo (eds) *Arqueología de la Construcción IV. Las canteras en el mundo antiguo: sistemas de explotación y procesos productivos* (Anejos de AespA 69): 311–328. Madrid-MéridaInstituto de Arqueología de Mérida - Consejo Superior de Investigaciones Científicas.

Gutiérrez Garcia-M., A. 2019. El estudio de las canteras de época romana: de la arqueología a la interdisciplinariedad, in E. Álvarez Areces, J. M. Baltuille Martín, J. Fernández Suárez, J. Martínez Martínez and M.A. Utrero Agudo (eds), *Espacios de canteras históricas. Jornada interdisciplinar sobre Espacios de Canteras Históricas*, Publicaciones del Instituto Geológico Minero de España / Serie: Recursos Minerales nº 10): 69–74. Madrid: Instituto Geológico Minero Español.

Gutiérrez Garcia-M., A. 2020. Canteras y materiales. Panorama actual y reflexiones sobre los modelos y mecanismos de explotación y abastecimiento en zonas costero-fluviales del NE hispano, in S. Vinci, A. Ottati and D. Gorostidi (eds) *La cava e il monumento. Materiali, officine, sistemi di costruzione e produzione nei cantieri edilizi di età imperiale*: 15–30. Roma: Quasar.

Gutiérrez Garcia-M., A., S. Huelin, J. López Vilar and I. Rodà de Llanza 2015. Can a fire broaden our understanding of a Roman quarry? The case of El Mèdol (Tarragona, Spain), in P. Pensabene and E. Gasparini (eds) *Interdisciplinary Studies on Ancient Stone. Proceedings of the Tenth International Conference of ASMOSIA (Rome 21-26 May 2012)*: 779–789. Roma: L'Erma di Bretschneider.

Gutiérrez Garcia-M., A., P. Lapuente and I. Roda (eds) 2012. *Interdisciplinary Studies on Ancient Stone. Proceedings of the IX ASMOSIA Conference (Tarragona, Spain, June 8-13, 2009)* (Documenta 23). Tarragona: Institut Català d'Arqueologia Clàssica.

Gutiérrez Garcia-M., A. and J. López Vilar 2018. La cantera de El Mèdol (Tarragona). Técnicas, organización y propuesta de evolución de la extracción del material lapídeo, in A. Gutiérrez Garcia-M. and P. Rouillard (eds) *Lapidum natura restat. Canteras antiguas de la península Ibérica en su contexto (cronología, técnicas y organización de la explotación)* (Documenta 31/ Colección de la Casa de Velázquez 170): 67–79. Tarragona-Madrid: Institut Català d'Arqueologia Clàssica-Casa de Velázquez.

Gutiérrez Garcia-M., A., J. López Vilar, G. Martí, P. Terrado 2019. Evidències de dues antigues infraestructures portuàries: els embarcadors de la Roca Plana i del Miracle a Tarragona, *Butlletí Arqueològic* V/41: 127–142.

Gutiérrez Garcia-M., A. and P. Rouillard (eds) 2018. *Lapidum natura restat. canteras antiguas de la península Ibérica en su contexto (cronología, técnicas y organización de la explotación)* (Documenta 31/Colección de la Casa de Velázquez 170). Tarragona-Madrid: Institut Català d'Arqueologia Clàssica-Casa de Velázquez.

Gutiérrez Garcia-M., A., H. Royo Plumed, S. González Soutelo, M.-C. Savin, P. Lapuente and R. Chapoulie 2016. The marble of O Incio (Galicia, Spain): Quarries and first archaeometric characterisation of a material used since Roman times, *ArcheoSciences. Revue d'archéométrie* 40: 103–117

Gutiérrez Garcia-M., A., H. Royo Plumed, S. González Soutelo 2018. New data on Spanish marbles: the case of Gallaecia (NW Spain), in D. Matetić Poljak and K. Marasović (eds) *Interdisciplinary Studies on Ancient Stone: Proceedings of the XI International Conference of ASMOSIA (Split, Croatia, May 18-22, 2015)*: 365- 375. Split: University of Split and Arts Academy of Split.

Gutiérrez Garcia-M., A. and S. Vinci 2018. Large-scale building in Early Imperial Tarraco (Tarragona, Spain) and the dynamics behind the creation of a Roman provincial capital landscape, in A. Brysbaert, V. Klinkenberg, A. Gutiérrez Garcia-M. and I. Vikatou (eds) *Constructing monuments, percieving monumentality and the economics of building: Theoretical and methodological approaches to the built environment*: 271-294. Leiden: Sidestone press.

Hauschild, Th. 1975. Torre de Minerva (San Magín). Ein Turm der römischen Stadtmauer von Tarragona', *Madrider Mittelungen* 16: 246-262.

Hauschild, Th. 1983. *Arquitectura romana de Tarragona*. Tarragona: Ajuntament de Tarragona.

Herrmann, J., N. Herz and R. Newman (eds) 2002. *ASMOSIA 5, Interdisciplinary Studies on Ancient Stone: Proceedings of the Fifth International Conference of the Association for the Study of Marble and Other Stones in Antiquity (Museum of Fine Arts, Boston, June 1998)*. London: Archetype Publications.

Herz, N. and M. Waelkens (eds) 1988. *Classical Marble: Geochemistry, Technology, Trade. Proceedings of the NATO Advanced Research Workshop on Marble in Ancient Greece and Rome: Geology, Quarries, Commerce, Artifacts*, (II Ciocco, Lucca, Italy, May 9-13, 1988). Dordrecht/Boston: Kluwer Academic Publishers

IPAC 2006. Carta arqueològica: Tarragonès, in *Inventari del Patrimoni Arqueològic*. Barcelona: Generalitat de Catalunya.

Járrega, R. and M. Prevosti (eds) 2014. *Ager Tarraconensis 4. Els Antigons, una vil·la senyorial del Camp de Tarragona*. Tarragona: Institut Català d'Arqueologia Clàssica.

Jockey, Ph. (dir.) 2009. *Levkos Lithos: Marbres et autres roches de la Méditerranée antique: études interdisciplinaires. ASMOSIA VIII. Proceedings of the 8th International Conference of the Association for the Study of Marble and Other Stones in Antiquity*. (Aix-en-Provence, June 12-18, 2006). Paris: Maisonnueve and Larose.

Jongman, W. 2007. The early Roman Empire: consumption, in W. Sceidel, E.L. Moris and R. P. Saller (eds) *The Cambridge Economic History of the Greco-Roman World*: 592-618. Cambridge: Cambridge University Press.

Korres, M. 1995. From Pentelicon to the Parthenon: the ancient quarries and the story of a half-worked column capital of the first marble Parthenon. Athens: Melissa

Lapuente, P. 2014. Archaeometry on stones. multi-method approach to investigate stone provenance. Studied cases from Roman Hispanic *marmora*, *Archaeometry Workshop* XI/3: 149-158. Hungarian National Museum.

Lapuente, P. 2019. Arqueometría para la determinación del origen de materiales, in E. Álvarez Areces, J. M. Baltuille Martín, J. Fernández Suárez, J. Martínez Martínez and M.A. Utrero Agudo (eds) *Espacios de canteras históricas. Jornada interdisciplinar sobre Espacios de Canteras Históricas* (Publicaciones del Instituto Geológico Minero de España / Serie: Recursos Minerales nº 10): 69-74. Madrid: Instituto Geológico Minero Español.

Lapuente, P., T. Nogales-Basarrate, H. Royo and M. Brilli 2014. White marble sculptures from the National Museum of Roman Art (Mérida, Spain): sources of local and imported marbles, *European Journal of Mineralogy* 26: 333-354.

Lapuente, P., H. Royo, J.A. Cuchí, J. Justes and M. Preite-Martínez 2015. Local stones and marbles found in the territory of 'Alto Aragón' (Hispania), in Roman times, in P. Pensabene and E. Gasparini (eds) *Interdisciplinary Studies on Ancient Stone. Proceedings of the Tenth International Conference of ASMOSIA, Rome 21-26 May 2012*: 191-200. Roma: L'Erma di Bretschneider.

Lapuente, P., T. Nogales-Basarrate, H. Royo Plumed, M. Brilli and M.-C. Savin 2018. Grey and greyish banded marbles from the Estremoz Anticline in Lusitania, in D. Matetić Poljak and K. Marasović (eds) *Interdisciplinary Studies on Ancient Stone: Proceedings of the XI International Conference of ASMOSIA (Split, Croatia, May 18-22, 2015)*: 391-399. Split: University of Split and Arts Academy of Split.

Lapuente Mercadal, P., M.-C. Savin, S. González Soutelo, A. Gutiérrez Garcia-M., R. Chapoulie, A. Laborde Marqueze and P.P. Pérez García 2019. Marble Pieces in the Romanesque Portal of Glory of the Santiago de Compostela Cathedral. New Data through a Multi-Analytical Approach, *International Journal of Architectural Heritage*, DOI: 10.1080/15583058.2019.1602683.

Lasheras, A. 2018. El suburbi portuari de Tàrraco a l'Antiguitat tardana. Unpublished PhD dissertation, Universitat Rovira i Virgili.

Lazzarini, L. (ed.) 2002. *Interdisciplinary Studies on Ancient Stone: ASMOSIA VI, Proceedings of the Sixth International Conference of the Association for the Study of Marble and Other Stones in Antiquity (Venice, June 15-18, 2000)*. Padova: Bottega d'Erasmo Aldo Ausilio Editore.

López Garcia, I. 2014. Identificación de las canteras de piedra de explotación antigua en el área de Vrso, in J.M. Álvarez, T. Nogales-Basarrate and I. Rodà (eds) *CIAC: Actas XVIII Congreso Internacional Arqueología Clásica. Centro y periferia en el mundo clásico*: 1325-1328. Mérida: Museo Nacional de Arte Romano.

López Vilar, J. 2006. *Les basíliques paleocristianes del suburbi occidental de Tarraco. El temple septentrional i el complex martirial de Sant Fructuós*. Tarragona: Institut Català d'Arqueologia Clàssica.

López Vilar, J. and A. Gutiérrez Garcia-M. 2016. Intervencions arqueològiques a la Pedrera del Mèdol (Tarragona), *Tribuna d'Arqueologia 2013-2014*: 177–195.

López Vilar, J. and A. Gutiérrez Garcia-M. 2017. L'embarcador romà de la Roca Plana (Tarragona), *Auriga* 88: 15–17.

López Vilar, J. and J.M. Puche 2013. El balneum de la vil·la romana de la Llosa (Cambrils): una nova interpretació, in M. Prevosti, J. López Vilar and J. Guitart (eds) *Ager Tarraconensis 5. Paisatge, poblament, cultura material i història. Actes del Simposi internacional / Landscape, Settlement, Material Culture and History. Proceddings of the International Symposium*: 295–302. Tarragona: Institut Català d'Arqueologia Clàssica.

Macias, J.M., I. Fiz, Ll. Piñol, M.T. Miró and J. Guitart 2007. *Planimetria Arqueològica de Tarraco* (Documenta 7). Tarragona: Institut Català d'Arqueologia Clàssica.

Macias, J. M. and I. Rodà 2015. Tarraco, the First Capital. *Catalan Historical Review* 8: 9–28. Barcelona: Institut d'Estudis Catalans.

Macias, J.M. and J.A. Remolà. 2005. *El port de Tarraco a l'Antiguitat tardana*, in J.M. Gurt and A. Ribera (eds) *VI reunió d'arqueologia cristiana hispana. Les ciutats tardoantigues d'Hispania: cristianització i topografía: Valencia 8,9 i 10 de maig de 2003* (Monografies de la Secció Històrico-Arqueològica, 9): 175–187. Barcelona: Institut d'Estudis Catalans.

Maniatis, Y. (ed.) 2009. *ASMOSIA VII: Actes du VIIe colloque international de l'Association for the Study of Marble and Other Stones in Antiquity (Thasos 15-20 Septembre 2003)* (Bulletin de Correspondance Héllenique Supplément 51). Athens: École française d'Athènes.

Maniatis, Y., N. Herz and Y. Basiakos (eds) 1995. *The Study of Marble and Other Stones Used in Antiquity*. London: Archetype Publications.

Mar, R., J. De Arbulo, D. Vivó and J.A. Beltrán-Caballero 2012. *Tarraco. Arquitectura y urbanismo de una capital provincial romana. Volumen I. De la Tarragona ibérica a la construcción del templo de Augusto* (Documents d'Arqueologia Clàssica, 5). Tarragona: Universitat Rovira i Virgili-Institut Català d'Arqueologia Clàssica.

Mar, R. and P. Pensabene 2010. Finanziameno dell'edilizia pubblica e calcolo dei costi dei materiali lapidei: il caso del foro superiore di Tarraco, in S. Camporeale, H. Dessales and A. Pizzo (eds) *Arqueología de la Construcción II. Los Procesos constructivos en el mundo romano: Italia y las provincias occidentales. Siena, 13-15/11/2008* (Anejos de AespA 57): 509–537. Madrid-Mérida: Instituto de Arqueología de Mérida - Consejo Superior de Investigaciones Científicas.

Maschek, D. and M. Trümper (eds) 2022. *Architecture and the Ancient Economy* (Analysis Archaeologica Monograph Series 5). Roma: Edizioni Quasar.

Matetić Poljak, D., and K. Marasović (eds) 2018. *Interdisciplinary Studies on Ancient Stone: Proceedings of the XI International Conference of ASMOSIA (Split, Croatia, May 18-22, 2015)*. Split: University of Split and Arts Academy of Split.

Menchón, J. 2009. *La muralla romana de Tarragona: una aproximació*. Barcelona: Societat Catalana d'Arqueologia.

Menchón, J. 2017. Murallas de Tarragona, algunas reflexiones en torno a su conservación y puesta en valor, in *Simposium Internacional de Murallas*: 41–98. Ávila: Grupo Ciudades Patrimonio de la Humanidad de España, Comisión de Ciudad y Patrimonio (UNESCO)-Ministerio de Cultura y Deporte.

Olesti, O. and F. Olesti 2013. L'ager Tarraconensis i les muntanyes de Prades. Un espai colonial mal conegut, in M. Prevosti, J. López Vilar and J. Guitart (eds) *Ager Tarraconensis 5. Paisatge, poblament, cultura material i història. Actes del Simposi internacional / Landscape, Settlement, Material Culture and History. Proceddings of the International Symposium*: 45–56. Tarragona: Institut Català d'Arqueologia Clàssica.

Oliver Vert, J. 2022. L'aprovisionament i ús de les roques constructives i ornamentals a la ciutat de Girona. Unpublished PhD dissertation, Universitat Rovira i Virgili - Institut Català d'Arqueologia Clàssica.

Pakkanen, J. and A. Brysbaert (eds) *Building BIG - Constructing Economies: from design to long-term impact of large-scale building projects. Proceedings of the 19th International Congress of Classical Archaeology (Cologne/Bonn, 22-25 May 2018)*, vol. 10, Propylaeum / Heidelberg University online Publishing, Heidelberg, in press.

Pedini, C. 2018. L'étude des carrières: une approche nécessairement pluridisciplinaire. L'exemple des carrières de La Couronne (Martigues, Bouches-d-Rhône), in A. Gutiérrez Garcia-M. and P. Rouillard (eds) *Lapidum natura restat. Canteras antiguas de la península Ibérica en su contexto (cronología, técnicas y organización de la explotación)* (Documenta 31/ Colección de la Casa de Velázquez 170): 109–119. Tarragona-Madrid: ICAC-Casa de Velázquez.

Pensabene, P. and J.Á. Domingo 2017. El transporte de grandes fustes monolíticos por el interior de la trama urbana de Roma, *Arqueología de la Arquitectura* 13: 1–14.

Pensabene, P. and E. Gasparini (eds) 2015. *Proceedings of the Tenth International Conference of ASMOSIA (Rome, Italy, May 21-26, 2012)*. Rome: L'Erma di Bretschneider.

Pizzo, A. 2010. El aprovisionamiento de los materiales constructivos en la arquitectura de Augusta Emerita: las canteras de granito, in S. Camporeale, A. Pizzo and E. Dessales (eds) *Atti del Workshop I cantieri edili dell'Italia e delle provincie romane. Italia e provincie orientale* (Anejos de AEspA LVII): 571–588. Madrid-Mérida: Instituto de Arqueología de Mérida - Consejo Superior de Investigaciones Científicas.

Pizzo, A. and T. Cordero Ruiz 2014. El paisaje de las cantera emeritenses. Poblamiento y áreas de producción, in J. Bonetto, S. Camporeale and A. Pizzo (eds) *Arqueología de la Construcción IV. Las canteras en el mundo antiguo: sistemas de explotación y procesos productivos* (Anejos de AespA 69): 329–340. Madrid-Mérida: Instituto de Arqueología de Mérida - Consejo Superior de Investigaciones Científicas.

Pizzo, A., M.I. Mota, R. Fort and M. Álvarez de Buergo 2018. Las canteras de Augusta Emerita. Identificación de los materiales y primeros datos sobre la relación con los edificios de espectáculo: el teatro romano, in A. Gutiérrez Garcia-M. and P. Rouillard (eds) *Lapidum natura restat. Canteras antiguas de la península Ibérica en su contexto (cronología, técnicas y organización de la explotación)* (Documenta 31/Colección de la Casa de Velázquez 170): 149–160. Tarragona-Madrid: Institut Català d'Arqueologia Clàssica-Casa de Velázquez.

Previato, C. 2016. *Nora. Le cave di pietra della città antica* (Scavi di Nora VI). Padova: Padova University Press.

Remolá, J.A. 2000. *Las ánforas tardo-antiguas en Tarraco (Hispania Tarraconensis). Siglos IV-VII d.C* (Instrumenta 7). Barcelona: Publicacions i Edicions UB.

Remolà, J.A. (coord) 2007. *El territorio de Tarraco: vil·les romanes del Camp de Tarragona* (Forum 13): 19–132. Tarragona: MNAT.

Remolà, J.A. 2009. Mithra en la villa romana dels Munts (*ager Tarraconensis*). Lecture presented at the I Jornadas mitraicas de Cabra 29–30 de maig de 2009. Online publication: <https://www.academia.edu/1976086/Mithra_en_la_villa_romana_dels_Munts_ager_Tarraconensis_> (last viewed 10/07/2020).

Remolà, J.A. 2019 (ed cient) *Troballes arqueològiques al teatre romà de Tarragona. Diari de Francesc Carbó (1919).* Tarragona: MNAT.

Remolà, J.A. and A. Lasheras 2019. Ad suburbanum Tarraconis. Del área portuaria al conjunto eclesiástico del Francolí, in López Vilar (ed.) *Tarraco Biennal. 4rt congrés internacional d'Arqueologia i Món antic. VII Reunió d'Arqueologia Cristiana Hispanica. El cristianisme a l'Antiguitat Tardana. Noves perspectives*: 75–82. Tarragona: Universitat Rovira i Virgini-Institut d'Estudis Catalans.

Remolà, J.A. and M. Pérez 2013. Centcelles y el praetorium del comes Hispaniarum Asterio en Tarraco, *Archivo Español de Arqueología* 86: 161–186.

Rodà, I. 2016. Tarraco y Barcino en el Alto Imperio. *Revista de Historiografía* 25: 245–272. Madrid: Instituto de Historiografía Julio Caro Baroja.

Roig, J.F., M. Sirisi, E. Solà and J. Trenor 2011. El dipòsit de carreus del Mèdol (Tarragona). Resultats preliminars, *Tribuna d'Arqueologia 2009–2010*: 383–405.

Röder, J. 1957. Die antiken Tuffsteinbrüche der Pellenz, *Bonner Jahrbücher* 157: 213–271.

Röder, J. 1959. Zur Steinbruchgeschichte des Pellenz – und Brohltaltuffs, *Bonner Jahrbücher* 159: 47–88.

Röder, J. 1965. Zur Steinbruchgeshichte des Rosengranits von Assuan, *Archäologischen Anzeiger*, 1965: 467–552.

Röder, J. 1971. Marmor Phrygium. Die antiken Marmorbrüche von Iscehisar in Westanatolien, *Jahrbuch des Deutschen Archäologischen Instituts* 86: 252–312.

Rodríguez Gutiérrez, O. and D. Jiménez Madroñal 2019. Caracterización de un nuevo *marmor* polícromo bético explotado en época romana, *Lvcentvm* 37: 255–280.

Roig Pérez, J.F., Sirisi Parreu, M., Solà Agudo, E. and J. Trenor Allen 2011. 'El dipòsit de carreus del Mèdol (Tarragona). Resultats preliminars, *Tribuna d'Arqueologia 2009–2010*: 383–405.

Rouillard, P., L. Costa, J. Moratalla, Ch. Montenat, C. Blondeau, C. Gagnaison, C. Verdú and J. de Jonghe 2020. *Les carrières d'Èlche (Alicante, Espagne). Le territoire du pays de la Dame, d'elche à Aspe.* Madrid-Paris: Casa de Velázquez.

Royo, H., F.J. Ruiz, J.L. Cebolla, J.A. Cuchí and P. Lapuente 2015. Estudio arqueométrico de mármoles procedentes del teatro romano de Huesca, *Lucas Mallada* 17: 45–57. Huesca: Instituto de Estudios Altoaragoneses.

Royo, H. 2016. Mármoles de la Cordillera Pirenaica: afloramientos norpirenaicos y asociados al 'Nappe des Marbres'. Caracterización y uso en época romana. Unpublished PhD dissertation, Universidad de Zaragoza.

Russell, B. 2013. *The economics of the Roman stone trade.* Oxford: Oxford University Press.

Schvoerer, M. (ed.) 1999. *Archeomateriaux: Marbres et autres roches utilises dans le passe. ASMOSIA IV, actes de la IVème Conference internationale de l'Association for the Study of Marble and Other Stones used in Antiquity (Bordeaux-Talence, 9-13 octobre 1995).* Bordeaux-Talence: Publications Université de Bordeaux.

Soler, B. 2003. Algunas consideraciones sobre el empleo privado del mármol en Carthago Nova, *Mastia* 2: 149–187. Cartagena: Museo Arqueológico Municipal de Cartagena.

Soler, B. 2004. El uso de rocas ornamentales en los programas decorativos de la Carthago Nova altoimperial: edilicia pública y evergetismo, in S.F. Ramallo (ed.) *La decoración arquitectónica en las ciudades romanas de occidente: actas del Congreso Internacional celebrado en Cartagena entre los días 8 y 10 de octubre de 2003*: 455–483. Murcia: Universidad de Murcia.

Soler, B. 2019. Canteras históricas de la Región de Murcia. Balance y perspectiva de la investigación, in E. Álvarez Areces, J. M. Baltuille Martín, J. Fernández Suárez, J. Martínez Martínez and M.A. Utrero Agudo (eds), *Espacios de canteras históricas. Jornada interdisciplinar sobre Espacios de Canteras Históricas* (Serie: Recursos Minerales nº 10): 57–66. Madrid:

Publicaciones del Instituto Geológico Minero de España.

Soler Huertas, B., J.A. Antolinos Marín, J.M. Noguera Celdrán and A.A. Linares 2014. Producción, aprovisionamiento y empleo de materiales constructivos en Carthago Nova, in J. Bonetto, S. Camporeale and A. Pizzo (eds) *Arqueología de la Construcción IV. Las canteras en el mundo antiguo: sistemas de explotación y procesos productivos* (Anejos de AespA 69): 285–310. Madrid-Mérida: Instituto de Arqueología de Mérida - Consejo Superior de Investigaciones Científicas.

Tarrats, F., J.M. Macias, F. Ramón and J.A. Remolà 2000. Nuevas actuaciones en el área residencial de la villa romana de 'Els Munts' (Altafulla, Ager Tarraconensis). Estudio preliminar, *Madrider Mitteilungen* 41: 358–379.

Taylor, R. 2015. Las canteras romanas de mármol de Almadén de la Plata (Sevilla, España): un análisis arqueológico. Unpublished PhD dissertation, University of Seville.

Taylor, R. 2018. Análisis formal de las evidencias de explotación antigua en la Loma de los Castillejos de Almadén de la Plata (Sevilla), in A. Gutiérrez Garcia-M. and P. Rouillard (eds) *Lapidum natura restat. canteras antiguas de la península Ibérica en su contexto (cronología, técnicas y organización de la explotación)* (Documenta 31/Colección de la Casa de Velázquez 170): 95–108. Tarragona-Madrid: Institut Català d'Arqueologia Clàssica-Casa de Velázquez.

Terrado, P. 2017. *Portus Tarraconis*. El puerto de Tarraco en época tardorrepublicana y altoimperial. Fuentes, historiografía y arqueología. Unpublished PhD dissertation, Universitat Rovira i Virgili.

Vinci, S. 2018. Marci di cava e sigle di construzione : nota preliminare sul materiale epigrafico proveniente dall'area di Tarraco, *Aquitania* 34: 145–170.

Vinci, S. 2019. Painted marks at El Mèdol quarry near Tarragona: observations on the logistics and organisation of a Roman limestone quarry, *Journal of Roman Archaeology* 32: 251–278.

Waelkens, M., N. Herz and L. Moens (eds) 1992. *Ancient Stones: Quarrying, Trade and Provenance: Interdisciplinary Studies on Stones and Stone Technology in Europe and Near East from the Prehistoric to the Early Christian Period* (Acta Archaeologica Lovaniensia, Monographiae 4). Leuven: Leuven University Press.

L'evoluzione costruttiva della "parte alta" di *Tarraco* in epoca romana: alcune osservazioni sulla costruzione del cosiddetto Foro Provinciale

Maria Serena Vinci

Universidad Nacional de Educación a Distancia (UNED, Madrid)

svinci@geo.uned.es

Abstract

The construction of a large monumental complex such as the so-called Provincial Forum of Tarraco (*Hispania Citerior*) undoubtedly involved a building site (*cantiere di costruzione*) with work over a long period, a time frame that is still difficult to quantify even today. Given the lack of a dating stratigraphy associated with the ancient structures, the construction chronology of Tarraco's monumental complex is a question still open to debate. It is made even more complicated by the several different phases in the construction of the Provincial Forum and the changes made as they were being carried out. However, it remains interesting to reflect on the evolution of construction on Tarraco's acropolis, the most emblematic sector of the town, where the Romans probably established a military *castrum* during the Second Punic War. Unfortunately, with the exception of the city walls, the available data do not allow us to reconstruct the architectural aspect or human activity of the area at any time during the Republican and late Republican periods. Starting from the Augustan period, there is more explicit evidence of building activities aimed at monumentalising the highest part of the Tarragona hill. This continued until the Julio-Claudian era and resulted in the construction of the large monumental complex that still shapes the image of the town today. The aim of this article is to attempt to identify the main stages in the construction of the Tarraco monumental complex and to reflect on some aspects of the building site that influenced its management, organisation, and construction times.

Keywords: Provincial Forum, *Tarraco*, building site, building processes, Roman construction

Sebbene il cosiddetto Foro Provinciale rappresenti uno dei monumenti più emblematici delle province occidentali dell'impero, risulta ancora complesso stabilire con precisione la cronologia della sua evoluzione costruttiva. Il cantiere edilizio del monumento tarragonese fu attivo certamente per un lungo periodo di tempo. Purtroppo scarsa è la stratigrafia associata alle strutture e, in assenza di esplicite fonti epigrafiche e letterarie, è possibile solo ipotizzare, tanto l'effettivo inizio dei lavori come l'inquadramento cronologico delle varie fasi costruttive. La difficoltà nello stabilire le tempistiche delle operazioni edilizie sta inoltre in quella pluralità di fattori difficilmente identificabili che dovettero intervenire nella costruzione, come ad esempio tipologia e quantità dei finanziamenti e dunque quantità di manodopera a disposizione, possibili interruzioni e riprese delle attività, etc. Nonostante ciò, riflettere sulle testimonianze a disposizione riferibili alle attività antropiche dell'acropoli di *Tarraco* permette di comprendere in maniera più coerente il contesto in cui ebbero inizio i lavori di costruzione del Foro Provinciale. Allo stesso tempo, analizzare alcuni degli aspetti del cantiere che influenzarono le varie operazioni edilizie fornisce ulteriori dati sui fattori che ne determinarono la gestione, l'organizzazione e le tempistiche.

L'epoca repubblicana e tardo-repubblicana

L'inizio dell'attività costruttiva e dell'occupazione antropica della cosiddetta "parte alta" di *Tarraco* rappresenta una questione difficile da approfondire a causa della scarsa presenza di dati archeologici conservati. Seppur in totale assenza di testimonianze o fonti storico-letterarie, è plausibile supporre che, a partire dalla fine del III secolo a.C., durante la Seconda Guerra Punica, che portò al primo sbarco delle truppe romane a *Kesse*[1], e per tutta l'epoca repubblicana, la città avesse attraversato una fase di coesistenza di un duplice nucleo insediativo, una sorta di *dipolis*: nella cosiddetta "parte bassa", in prossimità della foce del fiume *Francolí*[2], almeno dal VI secolo a.C. si attesta la presenza di un insediamento iberico; la parte più alta, invece, sarebbe stata occupata dalle truppe romane[3] che vi stabilirono un *praesidium* e successivamente i *castra hibernae*[4]. Si trattava certamente di un ottimo punto per organizzare le attività militari. La cosiddetta "parta alta" è infatti una collina, dal sostrato geologico

---

[1] Otiña e Ruiz de Arbulo 2000: 109; Panosa 2009.
[2] Miró 1994; Adeserias *et al.* 2000; Asensio *et al.* 2000.
[3] Sebbene non vi sia alcuna testimonianza archeologica, si potrebbe comunque pensare a una presenza iberica anche nella "parte alta" della città, previa all'ocupazione romana (Menchon 2009).
[4] Ruiz de Arbulo 1991.

eterogeneo composta da rocce calcaree e argilla, che si eleva a 80 m s.l.m., con il versante orientale che scende bruscamente verso la costa e quello sud-occidentale dal rilievo molto meno accentuato. Fu dunque la stessa topografia del sito a determinare, in maniera abbastanza naturale, lo sviluppo urbanistico e architettonico della colonia romana.

La prima attività edilizia di cui ci è giunta testimonianza con riferimento alla "parte alta" della città è, come è noto, la realizzazione delle mura urbiche. Una prima fase di costruzione, con paramenti realizzati con grandi blocchi megalici, potrebbe essere contemporanea agli avvenimenti della Guerra Punica o relazionabile alla trasformazione della città in capitale di provincia nel 197 a.C. o alle campagne repressive di Catone del 195 a.C.[5]. È possibile difatti attribuire alla struttura solo una cronologia *ante quem*, che deriva dalla datazione del materiale ceramico associato alla successiva fase edilizia[6]: una seconda fase di costruzione, tra il 150 e il 125 a.C., fu caratterizzata dall'ampliamento delle mura urbiche e portò a includere anche la "parte bassa" della città, fino alla zona portuaria (**Figura 1**).

A eccezione delle mura, per ciò che riguarda l'epoca repubblicana, i dati archeologici della "parte alta" restituiscono tracce di attività antropica, sebbene in un numero molto esiguo di casi queste facciano riferimento a strutture vere e proprie. Si tratta infatti, nella quasi totalità delle testimonianze, di attività di regolarizzazione del banco roccioso che denotano comunque una volontà di sfruttare questa zona dal punto di vista costruttivo[7]. Resti di questo tipo di attività si riferiscono principalmente all'area che, in età imperiale, sarà occupata dalla terrazza intermedia del cosiddetto Foro Provinciale[8]. Anche nella zona nord-orientale della futura Piazza di Rappresentazione (C/*Merceria* 11) si rinvengono strati repubblicani che sembrano essere associati a una struttura realizzata con blocchi megalitici[9]. Si tratta in realtà di blocchi erratici

che però si rinvengono posizionati lungo quello che lo studioso B. Hernández Sanahuja[10] identifica come un muro ciclopico[11].

Infine, nella zona corrispondente al circo, si documenta, anche se in maniera non uniforme, stratigrafia datata tra la fine del II secolo a.C. e i primi anni del I secolo d.C., oltre a un canale scavato nella roccia. I resti si inseriscono in un contesto in cui l'attività di epoca repubblicana sembra restituire altre evidenze, come un muro in *opus incertum* e una cisterna rivestita in cocciopesto entrambi datati alla prima metà del II secolo a.C. e rinvenuti in corrispondenza del settore meridionale del circo (presso la *Rambla Vella* 29)[12].

In base alle notizie storiche note, le evidenze rinvenute nella "parte alta" della città facenti riferimento ad epoca repubblicana/tardo-repubblicana potrebbero dunque essere ricollegate alla prima occupazione romana della zona. Tra la fine del II secolo e l'inizio del I secolo a.C. la città attraversa un periodo di importanti cambiamenti, primo tra tutti la divisione amministrativa delle province ispaniche nel 197 a.C. che converte *Kesse/Tarraco* in un centro di controllo fiscale e finaziario della provincia Citeriore. Nella metà del I secolo a.C. gli viene concesso il rango di colonia probabilmente per mano dello stesso Giulio Cesare che nel 49 a.C. celebra una "riunione provinciale" a *Tarraco*[13]. La riunione ebbe la finalità di ripartire ricompense e castighi a seguito della battaglia di *Ilerda* durante la quale G. Cesare aveva sconfitto le truppe di Gn. Pompeo anche grazie all'appoggio di numerose comunità ispaniche della valle dell'Ebro, tra cui *Tarraco* che aveva rifornito le truppe di alimenti[14].

La "parte alta" in epoca augustea

Altrettanto complesso risulta ricostruire l'attività di epoca augustea, sebbene si disponga di un maggior numero di informazioni.

Sappiamo che il settore della città maggiormente interessato dalle riforme costruttive di questa epoca fu quello della "parte bassa": in epoca augustea si assiste a una trasformazione dell'antico foro repubblicano o Foro della Colonia[15] e del settore marittimo[16], alla costruzione

---

[5] Mar *et al.* 2015: 51–52; Menchón 2009: 48–49.
[6] Sull'interpretazione delle fasi costruttive delle mura si veda: Hauschild 1975: 246–262; 1979: 204–250; 1983.
[7] Nella terrazza superiore si rinvengono tracce di epoca repubblicana nel settore orientale: nella zona attualmente occupata dal *Consell Comarcal del Tarragonès* (COAC) con riferimento a uno strato disposto al di sopra del banco roccioso, attestato durante gli scavi condotti nel 1977 (Ferrer 1985: 283); un canale scavato nella roccia nel settore dell'*Antic Hospital de Santa Tecla* (rinvenuto durante gli scavi realizzati dal Ted'a nel 1989) forse attribuibile ad un sistema di smaltimento delle acque.
[8] Nella zona sud-occidentale (corrispondente alla *Torre de la Antiga Audiència*) è stato attestato un rudimentale pavimento che definisce un piano di calpestio datato alla seconda metà del II secolo a.C. Nella stessa zona si rinviene anche una cisterna dalla cronologia non definita, sebbene, in base alle notizie di scavo, sembra fosse contemporanea o posteriore alla seconda metà del II secolo a.C. e precedente ai primi anni del I secolo d.C. (Dupré e Carreté 1993: 78). Anche in quello che sarà l'angolo opposto della terrazza intermedia, occupato dalla *Torre del Pretori*, si attestano attività di regolarizzazione degli affioramenti rocciosi (Balil 1969).
[9] Piñol 1993a: 259–261.

[10] Hernández Sanahuja 1877: 104–105 e 107–108.
[11] Blocchi megalitici associati ad attività di regolarizzazione del terreno si rinvengono anche nel settore nord-occidentale del circo, inclusi nelle fasi di costruzione successive, all'interno della galleria parallela al muro di contenimento della terrazza. I blocchi per fattura e dimensione sono stati tipologicamente associati a quelli delle mura repubblicane (Fernández *et al.* 2017: 130–131).
[12] Foguet e López 1993: 162.
[13] Per una discussione storica sugli avvenimenti vincolati alla concessione a *Tarraco* del rango di colonia si veda: Mar *et al.* 2012: 211–217.
[14] *Bell. Civ.* 1.59.
[15] Ruiz de Arbulo 1990; Mar *et al.* 2012: 238–249.
[16] Adserias *et al.* 2000; Pociña e Remolà 2000.

Figura 1. Tracciato delle mura urbiche nella *Tarraco* di epoca tardo-repubblicana (Macias *et al.* 2007: 27, fig. 17).

del teatro[17] e all'installazione di un nuovo modello urbano. Con riferimento alla "parte alta" esistono invece indizi che, storicamente contestualizzati, fanno pensare che non fosse inverosimile che, a partire da epoca augustea, la zona potesse essere stata oggetto di una volontà di monumentalizzazione. Con questo non si vuole affermare che l'area fosse già dotata di spazi monumentali ben definiti, bensì che fosse in atto una progettualità che la predisponesse a tali finalità[18].

Un dato importante a questo proposito sembra essere la costruzione dei due acquedotti della città, quello del *Francolì* e del *Gaià*[19]. Quest'ultimo presenta due diramazioni che raggiungono il Foro Provinciale entrando uno in corrispondenza della terrazza intermedia e l'altro poco a sud del circo (**Figura 2**). La presenza di un acquedotto e quindi la pianificazione di un sistema idrico di questa parte della città che oltretutto offriva, grazie alle condizioni topografiche, uno spazio dalla scenograficità naturale, permette quantomeno di

ipotizzare che la zona fosse stata prescelta per essere monumentalizzata come simbolo e riflesso, tra le altre cose, del nuovo *status* di capitale della maggiore provincia ispanica[20]. È noto che nel 27 a.C. il governatore dell'*Hispania Citerior* si insedia definitivamente a *Tarraco*[21], e che tra il 26 e il 25 a.C. Augusto soggiorna nella città. Quest'ultima si converte così nel centro di propulsione della riforma politica e amministrativa della provincia romana che si concluderà, qualche anno più tardi, con la riorganizzazione di tutta la provincia ispana con *Tarraco* eletta, non a caso, capitale dell'intera *Hispania Citerior*.

Esistono inoltre anche varie ipotesi sulla possibilità che fosse stata proprio la "parte alta" a essere la zona prescelta per erigere il famoso altare dedicato dai tarragonesi ad Augusto quando l'imperatore era ancora in vita[22]. Della sua costruzione si ha notizia unicamente grazie a rappresentazioni monetali di epoca tiberiana[23] e all'aneddoto tramandatoci da Quintiliano[24], ma non esiste alcuna prova archeologica che possa confermarne l'ubicazione in un settore specifico della città. La presenza di suddetto altare viene inoltre messa

---

[17] Ruiz de Arbulo *et al.* 2004; Mar *et al.* 2012: 286–322 con bibliografia precedente.
[18] Vinci e Ottati 2018: 173–174.
[19] Recenti scavi hanno localizzato un settore del suddetto acquedotto in un'area appena fuori dalle mura, a nord-ovest del promontorio cittadino, confermandone la costruzione in epoca augustea (Mesas 2015: 249). La datazione è stata avvalorata inoltre dal ritrovamento di un blocco di pietra, nei pressi di uno dei settori documentati dell'acquedotto (nei pressi del centro di *Els Pallaresos* a km 6,5 a nord di Tarragona), sulla cui faccia principale restano visibili tracce di alcune lettere di un'iscrizione che riporterebbe il nome del monumento come A[QV]AM [AVGVS]TA[M] (López e Gorostidi 2015: 253).

[20] Vinci e Ottati 2018: 173.
[21] Ruiz de Arbulo 1992: 124–128; Alföldy 1999: 7–12; Arrayás 2004: 291–303; Ruiz de Arbulo 2009.
[22] Mar *et al.* 2012: 345–348.
[23] *RPC*, I, 218.
[24] Quint., *Inst. Orat.*, 6.3.77.

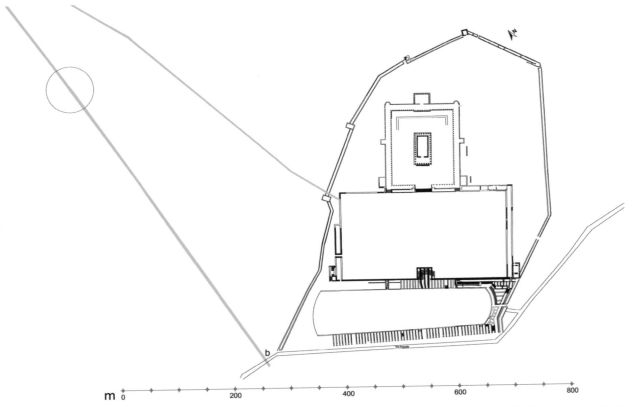

Figura 2. Ricostruzione planimetrica del Foro Provinciale di *Tarraco* in epoca imperiale con indicazione delle due diramazioni dell'acquedotto di epoca augustea che si immettono rispettivamente nella terrazza intermedia e a sud del circo (rielaborazione autore da Macias *et al.* 2007: 29, fig. 19).

in relazione ai resti di una struttura in *opus quadratum* (**Figura 3**), corrispondente al settore sud-orientale della terrazza intermedia, previa alla realizzazione tanto della *Torre del Pretori* che del circo, associata al rinvenimento di un pavimento datato ad epoca augusteo-tiberiana[25]. Se così fosse si tratterebbe di un'azione costruttiva che sembra prevedesse quantomeno un recinto delimitato da una muratura in blocchi con relativi snodi di accesso[26].

Infine, a un momento precedente al soggiorno del *Princeps* a *Tarraco*, probabilmente immediatamente successivo al termine delle Guerre Cantabriche, è da inquadrare anche la riorganizzazione viaria da lui

stesso incentivata. Modificando l'antico percorso della *Via Heraclea* e il suo ingresso nella parte nord-orientale delle mura urbiche, viene prevista una ripianificazione degli accessi alla città e dunque il passaggio della *Via Augusta* a sud del futuro edificio circense[27]. A contatto con l'estremo sud-orientale del circo si conservano ancora resti di una porta di accesso alla città dalla *Via Augusta*, realizzata in blocchi, decorata con lesene[28] e probabilmente pavimentata con grandi lastre come sembra confermare la toponimia di epoca medievale di *vicus losatus*[29]. In questo modo la riforma veniva a delineare una separazione ancora più marcata tra il nucleo urbano di epoca repubblicana nella "parte bassa" e quello che era stato il *castrum* militare nella "parte alta".

È possibile dunque affermare, sebbene siano scarsi i dati archeologici, che in epoca augustea nella

[25] Anche nel lato opposto della terrazza, nella zona che sarà occupata dalla cosiddetta *Torre de la Antiga Audiència*, si documentano livelli di riempimento, un pavimento con il corrispondente strato di preparazione e tagli nella stratigrafia dei precedenti livelli repubblicani. Il volume dei materiali rinvenuti ha permesso di datare quest'attività ai primi anni di epoca tiberiana (Dupré e Carreté 1993: 81).

[26] Si tratta del cosiddetto settore della *Volta Llarga* (Vinci *et al.* 2014: 5–8; Vinci 2020: 98–99). Parte della struttura in opera quadrata, successivamente reimpiegata all'interno del muro di terrazzamento meridionale della piazza intermedia, conserva nell'estremo orientale l'imposta e le reni di un arco, anch'esso realizzato in blocchi, che marca un passaggio da nord a sud. Nel paramento interno del piedritto conservato si osserva la presenza su due blocchi di due marchi di cava incisi (Vinci 2018: 702–705).

[27] Anche nell'organizzazione urbana si documenta un modello differente rispetto a quello di epoca repubblicana nell'area attualmente compresa tra la *Rambla Vella* e la *Rambla Nova*. È probabile che la zona fosse già urbanizzata ma che fino a quel momento non fosse stata interessata da una precisa organizzazione viaria, elemento che ne determina una modifica (Fiz e Macias 2007: 33–34).

[28] Dupré *et al.* 1988: 45–47.

[29] La menzione si rinviene in una lettera inviata a *Pedro III* (Arnall 1984: 113–114, doc. 26).

Figura 3. Struttura in *opus quadratum* previa alla realizzazione della *Torre del Pretori*.

parte più alta della città furono realizzati interventi costruttivi probabilmente previ alla realizzazione di un più ampio progetto di monumentalizzazione del sito. L'intento sembra essere quello di voler modellare quell'immagine di forte impatto visivo e simbolico che sarà poi raggiunta con la costruzione del Foro Provinciale.

La costruzione del Foro Provinciale

Come già menzionato poc'anzi, sembra quantomeno plausibile ipotizzare a partire da epoca augustea l'esistenza di un progetto teso a monumentalizzare la "parte alta" della città. Tuttavia, è a età giulio-claudia che sembra possibile ricondurre attività di costruzione vincolate alla realizzazione del cosiddetto Foro Provinciale.

Come è noto, l'enorme complesso monumentale si articola in tre grandi spazi a ognuno dei quali viene attribuita una specifica valenza al tempo stesso funzionale e celebrativa (**Figura 2**): nella zona inferiore un grande circo funzionava da punto di raccolta della popolazione durante le manifestazioni e quindi da cerniera tra spazio amministrativo-religioso e la città; la terrazza intermedia era occupata da una grande piazza dalla valenza politico-amministrativa per tutta la provincia Citeriore, denominata appunto Piazza di Rappresentazione; la terza, la più alta, ospitava il luogo religioso votato al culto imperiale, una grande piazza porticata che conchiudeva il tempio probabilmente dedicato ad Augusto, denominata Recinto di Culto.

Sappiamo che a epoca tiberiana sembrerebbe datarsi la realizzazione dell'edificio templare, posto al centro della terrazza superiore, la cui costruzione, in base alla testimonianza di Tacito[30], sarebbe stata concessa dall'imperatore su richiesta degli stessi tarragonesi, convertendosi in un'iniziativa che doveva essere da esempio per tutte le altre province dell'impero[31]. È noto, inoltre, come tale edificio sia rappresentato su emissioni monetali di epoca tiberiana in due varianti[32], tempio ottastilo su podio con scalinata centrale e tempio ottastilo su crepidoma di tipo greco. Naturalmente non è noto né quando ebbero inizio i lavori di costruzione né tantomeno quando terminarono. Si suppone che se il permesso per la sua realizzazione fu richiesto nel 15 d.C., le operazioni sarebbero iniziate negli anni subito successivi a questa data. L'esistenza di un edificio di epoca giulio-claudia sarebbe altresì confermata dagli elementi di decorazione architettonica che a questo sono stati associati, nonostante siano stati rinvenuti fuori contesto[33]. Purtroppo tentare un calcolo approssimativo dei tempi di costruzione dell'edificio templare, come indizio ulteriore alla discussione, risulterebbe in questo caso poco utile. Ne è stata ricostruita la planimetria, ma in realtà non conosciamo le caratteristiche dell'alzato dell'edificio[34] e, a parte frammenti di decorazione architettonica, i resti rinvenuti, a parere di chi scrive, sono troppo scarsi anche solo per poter fare delle ipotesi su una volumetria realmente attendibile del monumento[35].

Ad ogni modo, la realizzazione del tempio avrebbe imposto importanti operazioni previe di preparazione del terreno per la sistemazione della terrazza superiore. Anche in questo caso, non possiamo definire in che modo fosse già stata modificata l'orografia della collina considerando, come è già stato sottolineato, le poche notizie note sull'attività costruttiva nella "parte alta" tra epoca repubblicana e età augustea. Sappiamo che per la costruzione di almeno una parte delle mura urbiche tardo-repubblicane era stato impiegato il

materiale estratto dal sottosuolo roccioso, la roccia cosiddetta *fetge de gat*[36], e che in epoca augustea esistono indizi che fanno intuire l'esistenza di un progetto di monumentalizzare questa parte della città. Tuttavia, non è possibile ricostruire con certezza la topografia del sito in quest'epoca e non esistono sufficienti dati che permettano di ipotizzare un'inizio delle operazioni di preparazione del terreno in epoca augustea.

Al contrario appare plausibile immaginare che tali operazioni abbiano avuto avvio almeno in epoca tiberiana, quando si decise la costruzione del tempio e dunque la sistemazione del complesso architettonico in terrazze. Difatti, per la realizzazione della quasi totalità della terrazza superiore e della parte nord-ovest della piazza intermedia fu necessario abbassare notevolmente la quota degli affioramenti rocciosi. Per ciò che riguarda il Recinto di Culto, la parte occidentale e settentrionale richiese un'intensa attività di sbancamento del terreno roccioso che ancora oggi in alcuni punti raggiunge un livello di quota molto elevato (**Figura 4**). Nella parte orientale, invece, dove la pendenza collinare aumenta gradatamente procedendo da nord a sud, furono necessarie opere di terrazzamento per creare il piano di circolazione della piazza. Con riferimento alla Piazza di Rappresentazione si ricorre per la maggior parte della sua superficie alla creazione di un terrapieno artificiale che implica la realizzazione di imponenti strutture sostruttive. Tuttavia, gli affioramenti rocciosi presenti nel settore nord-occidentale della terrazza imposero, anche in questo caso, attività particolarmente impegnative di sbancamento del terreno. Proprio le caratteristiche orografiche della collina in questo punto determinarono una planimetria della piazza che non è perfettamente speculare nei due lati lunghi: nel braccio orientale erano previsti almeno tre livelli di circolazione, ovvero due gallerie a due quote differenti e un ultimo livello di cui si ipotizza l'esistenza; nel braccio occidentale era invece un unico ambiente voltato (a cui si sovrapponeva un ulteriore piano di circolazione) che si sviluppava solo per circa metà del lato, a causa appunto della presenza della roccia a una quota elevata[37].

La sistemazione della collina in terrazze avrebbe dunque implicato ingenti lavori, includendo lo scavo della roccia, la gestione dei detriti e il probabile utilizzo di questi per innalzare il livello di quota nel lato orientale della piazza superiore. È stato stimato, in base a un calcolo approssimativo, che fu necessario spostare circa 500.000 m[3] di terra[38] per lo scavo della roccia in entrambe le terrazze. È stato dunque ipotizzato che, con una media di estrazione da parte di un gruppo di 3/4 operai di 1 m[3] di terra al giorno e un totale di

---

[30] Tac., *Ann.*, 1.78.
[31] Un'interpretazione differente del passo di Tacito farebbe del *Princeps* non la persona in onore della quale si erige l'edificio templare, ma colui al quale se ne richiede l'autorizzazione per la sua costruzione (Castillo Ramírez 2015: 176–180.).
[32] RPC, 1, 219, 222, 224, 226; Beltrán 1953: 39–66; Villaronga 1979: 273–274.
[33] Gli elementi decorativi forse più noti datati ad epoca giulio-claudia sono i due frammenti di fregio in marmo di Luni/Carrara decorati con girali d'acanto, uno rinvenuto nei dintorni del *Carrer de Sant Lorenç* e uno presso la *Plaça del Forum* (Pensabene e Mar 2004: 73–88), corrispondenti grosso modo al settore orientale esterno alla terrazza superiore. Per una descrizione dettagliata di tutti i frammenti di decorazione architettonica riferibili al Tempio di Augusto si veda da ultimo Pensabene e Domingo 2019: 66–70.
[34] Una ricostruzione tridimensionale dell'edificio è comunque presente in Mar *et al.* 2012: 365, fig. 223; Mar *et al.* 2015: 122, fig. 83b. Le varie proposte ricostruttive della planimetria sono presenti in: Pensabene e Mar 2010: 257, fig. 10; Macias *et al.* 2012b 155, fig. 1; Mar *et al.* 2012a: 367, fig. 224; Pensabene e Domingo 2019: 73.
[35] I dati archeologici relativi all'edificio, documentati durante gli scavi archeologici condotti tra il 2010 e il 2011 all'interno della cattedrale di Tarragona, farebbero riferimento a parte della fondazione in conglomerato dell'edificio, profonda circa 2,30 m, a cui si addosserebbero resti di *opus caementicium* della scalinata (Macias *et al.* 2012b; 2014).

[36] Menchon 2009: 27.
[37] Vinci 2020: 89 e fig. 73.
[38] Puche 2010: 37.

3000 / 4000 operai, le operazioni di scavo della collina sarebbero state completate nell'arco di 10 anni circa. In realtà se tenessimo conto dei dati proposti, lo scavo di 500.000 m³ di terreno sarebbero stati effettuati in almeno 2 anni e mezzo circa[39]. Definire i tempi delle diverse fasi di costruzione, in questo caso della sistemazione del terreno calcareo per l'abbassamento del livello di quota, rientra in un campo della ricerca particolarmente rischioso, che va affrontato con la giusta cautela e coscienti del valore spesso puramente approssimativo dei dati[40]. Tuttavia, in alcuni contesti una stima anche solo generica dei tempi di esecuzione delle operazioni edilizie può fornire un'idea delle tempistiche del lavoro. Nel caso della collina di *Tarraco*, se teniamo in considerazione il dato di 500.000 m³ da rimuovere e le informazioni fornite dal manuale di Pegoretti[41] sulle tempistiche del lavoro per un terreno di tipo calcareo, sarebbero state necessarie 17,5h per il taglio di 1m³ di roccia. Il problema principale resta quello di definire la quantità di operai non specializzati che si occuparono di questa fase del lavoro. La cifra di almeno 3000/4000 operai già proposta[42] sembra essere accettabile[43]. Questi sarebbero stati organizzati in gruppi di almeno tre persone[44] che avrebbero lavorato per circa 10h al giorno[45]. In base a tali dati il lavoro sarebbe stato svolto in almeno 875 giorni, dunque in circa 4 anni.

Terminato lo scavo della collina e la sistemazione della terrazza sarebbe stato innalzato il tempio e solo in un secondo momento avrebbe avuto inizio lo scavo della trincea di fondazione del muro perimetrale della

Figura 4. Paramento esterno del lato settentrionale della terrazza superiore (attualmente nel chiostro della cattedrale) in cui si apprezza il livello del banco roccioso rispetto alle strutture di epoca romana.

terrazza. La realizzazione delle strutture del recinto sacro successiva a quella del tempio avrebbe permesso naturalmente uno svolgimento più agile di tutte le operazioni di cantiere per la costruzione dell'edificio sacro.

Per ciò che riguarda le strutture in alzato della terrazza, è noto il rinvenimento di una trincea di fondazione, poi ampliata nel progetto finale del monumento, a cui si associano materiali di riempimento di epoca giulio-claudia. In diversi settori della terrazza superiore si documenta un tracciato con forma a U che ricalca quella del successivo Recinto di Culto, seppur con dimensioni inferiori (**Figura 5**). Già a partire dagli anni '60, alcuni saggi effettuati da Sánchez Real[46] avevano portato alla luce parte di queste evidenze. Interventi archeologici successivi, realizzati negli anni '70 da Th. Hauschild[47] nel chiostro della cattedrale (corrispondente alla zona occidentale della terrazza) e alla fine degli anni '80 dal TED'A all'interno del *Consell Comarcal del Tarragonès*[48] (in corrispondenza del lato orientale della piazza), confermarono l'esistenza di una trincea parallela al portico, interpretata come traccia di un primo progetto construttivo poi abbandonato. La trincea in questione è ampia circa m 3, profonda m 2,50 e lunga circa m 88,80 (3 piedi)[49]. La stratigrafia del riempimento ha restituito due fasi: uno strato inferiore interpretato come apporto di terra dopo la regolarizzazione del livello di roccia finalizzato a creare un piano su cui disporre i blocchi databile grazie al rinvenimento di una moneta di epoca claudia del 41 d.C. a un momento posteriore a questa

[39] Si tiene in considerazione il numero di 220 giorni lavorativi per anno, ovvero da aprile a Novembre, come proposto da J. DeLaine (1997: 105–106) per la costruzione delle Terme di Caracalla a Roma.
[40] Recentemente un filone di studi, derivato dalla disciplina di Archeologia della Costruzione e sfociato già in numerosi incontri scientifici, si sta ocupando di indagare gli aspetti più propriamente economici e di quantificazione delle tempistiche della costruzione definito *Architectural Energetics* (un'opera di prossima uscita che raccoglie lavori che utilizzano questo approccio è a cura di C. Couralt e C. Márquez).
[41] Pegoretti 1843: 78. Si ringrazia il Dr. C. Courault per il suggerimento. Per una raccolta bibliografica sulle diverse formule applicate dagli studiosi nel calcolo delle tempistiche nelle varie fasi del lavoro della pietra si veda: Courault e Domingo 2020: 40–41.
[42] Puche 2010: 37.
[43] C. Courault e J. Domingo (2020: 47) ipotizzano per il lavoro di estrazione in cava, con riferimento alla cava di *Castillo de Maimón* presso Cordova, la presenza di un operaio almeno ogni 5m², disposti lungo i vari fronti di estrazione. Nel caso di *Tarraco* si tratta di un'operazione di tipo differente, ma l'esempio può comunque servire a dare un'idea della distribuzione del personale. Nella stima quantitativa dei lavori necessari per la realizzazione del Foro di Cesare, invece, si calcola che per la sistemazione del terreno, per cui sarebbe stato necessario rimuovere circa 5388 m³ di terra, sarebbe stati impiegati 55 operai divisi in cinque gruppi (Oraschewski c.d.s.: 72).
[44] Pegoretti 1843: 78.
[45] Dodici ore totali con 2 ore di pausa come riportato da DeLaine (1997: 107) in base a Pegoretti (1843: 13). Si segnala come alcuni autori (Voutsaki *et al.* 2018: 174; Domingo 2012: 390–391) abbiano messo in evidenza come questo valore dovrebbe essere ricalibrato a seconda di alcuni fattori come la stagione dell'anno, la regione e dunque il clima in cui i lavori si svolgono e altri aspetti socio-culturali (Courault e Domingo 2020: 36).

[46] Sánchez Real 1969: 278.
[47] Hauschild 1974.
[48] Dupré 1995: 20–33.
[49] Il livello di quota è di 65 m s.l.m.

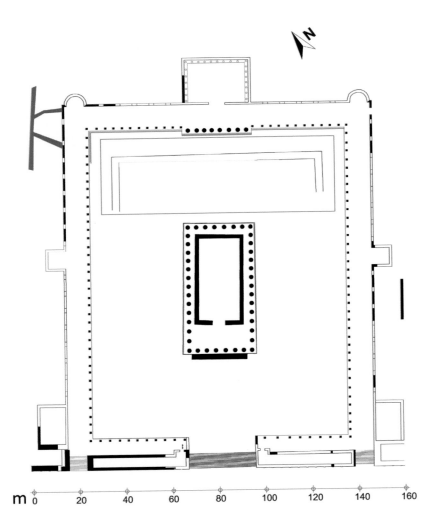

data[50]; lo strato superiore si data invece tra epoca neroniana e l'inizio di età vespasianea, identificato come pertinente al momento costruttivo[51]. Uno studio dei materiali ceramici tuttavia definì che entrambi gli strati potevano essere ascritti a epoca neroniana[52].

Come già menzionato, la trincea era stata interpretata in un primo momento come il risultato di un progetto costruttivo non portato a termine, abbandonato e poi ripreso in epoca flavia, un'ipotesi che era chiaro riflesso di una maniera di concepire l'architettura antica, oggi ormai superata, come istantanea di un momento cronologico preciso, ignorando la dinamicità e la lunga vita che invece caratterizzavano i cantieri edilizi.

Definire se la prima trincea di fondazione fosse mai giunta a essere associata a una qualche struttura o se invece si tratti di una modifica di progetto in corso d'opera, risulta ancora una questione complessa.

Se suddetta trincea non fosse stata associata ad alcuna struttura prima di epoca neroniana, momento in cui ne avviene il riempimento, ci troveremmo effettivamente davanti a un lasso di tempo, forse troppo lungo, che va da età tiberiana a età neroniana, durante il quale sarebbe stati realizzati soltanto i lavori di preparazione e regolarizzazione del terreno, la costruzione del tempio e l'inizio della costruzione delle fondazioni di un primo recinto sacro. Vari autori[53] hanno recentemente ipotizzato, invece, che la trincea di fondazione sia la testimonianza della costruzione del primo recinto che circondava l'area sacra intorno al Tempio di Augusto. La struttura sarebbe poi stata smantellata a partire da epoca neroniana, considerando la datazione dei materiali di riempimento, per essere ampliata tra la fine dell'epoca giulio-claudia e l'età flavia. Lo smantellamento di queste strutture avrebbe

---

50 In un primo momento lo strato era stato datato a epoca tiberiana/neroniana.
51 Hauschild 1983: 125.
52 Rüger 1968: 239.

53 Mar *et al.* 2015 e da ultimo Pensabene e Domingo 2019: 57.

però implicato il riutilizzo dei materiali, soprattutto i blocchi di calcarenite con cui sarebbero stati realizzati alzati e fondazioni. È certo che negli strati costruttivi di alcuni settori del Recinto di Culto, come ad esempio in corrispondenza dell'ala orientale della piazza, si rinvengono numerosi frammenti marmorei e di pietra di *El Mèdol*, così come scarti di lavorazione o veri e propri pezzi inclusi negli strati di riempimento. Tuttavia, più che di reimpiego sembrerebbe trattarsi del risultato di operazioni svolte in cantiere e di scarti dovuti a errori di elaborazione[54]. Inoltre resterebbe da definire, in merito all'eventuale realizzazione del primo recinto sacro che ipotizziamo dotato di un portico, se la trincea facesse riferimento alla fondazione del muro perimetrale o del colonnato. La realizzazione del muro d'alzato in grandi blocchi del recinto, corrispondente alla seconda fase costruttiva, poggia su una fondazione anch'essa in blocchi, almeno per la maggior parte del perimetro, disposti di testa dall'ampiezza massima di circa m 1,50/1,70. La fondazione del colonnato, dall'ampiezza di m 2,50, è realizzata invece con uno strato di conglomerato su cui poggiavano blocchi oggi spoliati. Usando questi dati come confronto, la dimensione della trincea più antica, pari a circa m 3, risulterebbe eccessiva per corrispondere alla fondazione del muro perimetrale. Si può considerare che le attività di spoliazione avrebbero implicato un'ampliamento delle sue dimensioni originali, ma la documentazione di scavo in nessun caso riporta informazioni o tracce che possano riferirsi a questo tipo di attività. La dimensione sembra invece corrispondere a quella della fondazione del colonnato, ma in questo caso si sarebbe dovuto documentare il tracciato di un'ulteriore trincea pertinente al muro perimetrale, elemento che invece non è stato riscontrato. Va certamente considerato che l'area della piazza superiore non è stata scavata in tutta la sua superfice, tuttavia zone come quella occidentale, occupata dal chiostro della cattedrale, sono state oggetto di numerosi interventi archeologici.

Risulta dunque evidente come sia ancora complesso stabilire con certezza la cronologia assoluta di ognuna delle operazioni di costruzione, sebbene resti fondamentale continuare a dibattere la questione. Forse si potrebbe tenere in considerazione l'ipotesi secondo cui la prima trincea di fondazione non sia mai stata associata a una struttura, ma che possa riferirsi invece a una modifica di progetto in corso d'opera. In fin dei conti non sappiamo con certezza quando ebbero inizio i lavori di sistemazione del terreno e costruzione del tempio. Certo è che almeno a partire da epoca

neroniana anche nell'area che verrà successivamente occupata dal circo, vengono smantellate le installazioni della *figlina*, confermando un momento di particolare attività dei lavori nella "parte alta". Suddette installazioni, che fanno riferimento a bacini per la decantazione dell'argilla[55] e probabilmente a un *horreum* per la conservazione di *tegulae*[56], sono in pieno uso in epoca tiberiana (tra il 15 e il 30 d.C.) come sembrano attestare i materiali ceramici rinvenuti negli strati di regolarizzazione del terreno o nei livelli di circolazione[57]. In un recente articolo P. Pensabene e J. Domingo suggeriscono che la seconda fase di progetto sarebbe stata messa in atto in epoca neroniana, concretamente tra il 61 e il 68 d.C., periodo in cui Servio Sulpicio Galba era governatore dell'*Hispania Citerior*[58]. Si potrebbe forse ritenere che i lavori più che avere origine in questo periodo avrebbero trovato, sotto il governo di Galba, un rinnovato impulso. Gli autori difatti, a ragione, rilevano come tradizionalmente si dati a epoca vespasianea una rimodellazione del complesso architettonico tarragonese, in concomitanza con il conferimento, proprio a opera di Vespasiano, del *Latium "uniuersae Hispaniae"*[59]. Tuttavia, le prime epigrafi dedicatorie ai *flamines* provinciali provenienti dal Foro Provinciale si datano tra il 72-73 d.C. supponendo dunque che a questa data almeno una parte del monumento fosse già in uso. Tutto ciò ovviamente non implica che i lavori di costruzione fossero stati terminati, anzi se consideriamo che l'erezione delle strutture aveva avuto inizio a partire da epoca neroniana, supponiamo in una forbice tra il 55 e il 61 d.C., negli anni 70 del I secolo d.C. i lavori sarebbero già stati in corso per un periodo che va tra i 9 e 15 anni. Non esiste un calcolo preciso sulle tempistiche della costruzione del complesso tarragonese, ma considerando che non doveva trattarsi di un'opera finanziata completamente dal governo centrale e che gli investimenti imperiali nella colonia di *Tarraco* non potrebbero certamente essere comparati con quelli realizzati a Roma, immaginare un lasso temporale di 10-15 anni per l'erezione di un monumento dalle caratteristiche eccezionali come il Foro Provinciale appare irreale. Il protrarsi dei lavori almeno fino alla fine del I secolo d.C., se non oltre, comunque non avrebbe precluso l'utilizzo degli spazi del complesso architettonico già realizzato[60].

In epoca flavia poi il progetto monumentale dovette subire ancora una volta una trasformazione. Ne sono prova almeno la cosiddetta sala assiale, certamente

---

[54] Tra i materiali marmorei si rinvengono per la maggior parte frammenti di pavonazzetto. In minor quantità si attestano scarti di lavorazione e frammenti di elementi elaborati in marmo di Luni/Carrara (frammento di capitello, di fusto di colonna e cornici modanate). In giallo antico si documenta solo un'unica placca di rivestimento, mentre i materiali in marmo di *Santa Tecla* sono costituiti solo da frammenti informi (Aquilué 1993: 95).

[55] López e Piñol 2008: 15.
[56] Gebellí 2017: 294–296.
[57] Gebellí 2017: 293–296.
[58] Pensabene e Domingo 2019: 59–60.
[59] Dalla notizia di Plinio il Vecchio: *Uniuersae Hispaniae Vespasianus imperator Augustus iactatum procellis rei publicae Latium tribuit* (Plin., *Nat.*, 3.3.30).
[60] Si veda, solo per citare un esempio, il caso del Colosseo che venne inaugurato nel 79 d.C. sebbene i lavori non fossero ancora stati terminati (Rea *el al.* 2002: 352–353).

ispirata al modello del *Forum Pacis* di Roma e la decorazione architettonica del suo pronao colonnato, di cui sembra essere stato identificato il fregio decorato con ghirlande e bucranei. A questo momento è stata anche attribuita una modifica costruttiva e dell'apparato decorativo della zona della *Torre del Pretori*[61]. Difatti durante gli scavi effettuati nel patio dell'edificio negli anni '60 la stratigrafia aveva restituito numerosi frammenti di schegge e scarti di lavorazione tanto in pietra calcarea che in marmo così come frammenti di elementi marmorei, alcuni dei quali sembrano presentare tracce di rielaborazione.

Infine, un'ulteriore fase del processo costruttivo del monumento sarebbe da attribuire al restauro voluto dall'imperatore Adriano. Questo riguardò il Tempio di Augusto[62] e forse la terrazza intermedia, se consideriamo i fusti di colonna in marmo della Troade rinvenuti nell'area di Tarragona come appartenenti al foro della provincia[63]. È questo un momento di rinnovato impulso in cui Adriano, rifacendosi alla figura di Augusto, opera un restauro del culto imperiale utilizzandolo in chiave ideologica. Il culto imperiale, già fondamentale nella politica giulio-claudia, ora ne sottolinea la continuità. Adriano soggiorna a Tarragona nell'inverno 122–123 d.C. e in questo periodo gli viene attribuita la convocazione di un *conventus* per regolare una delicata questione di arruolamento di soldati, ma soprattutto il restauro del Tempio di Augusto. È specialmente questa seconda attività, testimoniata archeologicamente da materiali decorativi, soprattutto capitelli in marmo proconnesio[64], a contenere un significato particolare all'interno di un preciso progetto ideologico. La presenza di Adriano a Tarragona e la sua attività evergetica, rientrano infatti in un più ampio programma messo in opera dall'imperatore nell'intento di dare una nuova forma a un impero ormai inadeguato e bisognoso di riforme strutturali[65].

Considerazioni sul cantiere di costruzione del Foro Provinciale

L'ubicazione topografica del complesso monumentale sulla parte più alta del promontorio cittadino dovette certamente influire anche sul funzionamento e sulle tempistiche del cantiere di costruzione, generando non poche problematiche logistiche e organizzative.

È plausibile pensare che i lavori ebbero inizio nelle zone occidentale e settentrionale del recinto sacro che, come si è visto, implicarono operazioni di preparazione del terreno particolarmente consistenti e impegnative. I materiali, derivanti dalle attività di sbancamento del sottosuolo roccioso sarebbero poi potuti essere sfruttati per la realizzazione del terrazzamento della parte orientale della piazza.

Naturalmente sono numerose le attività che influirono sulla gestione del cantiere edilizio. Tra queste, ad esempio, possiamo citare la questione della disposizione delle aree di stoccaggio dei materiali lapidei, che dovettero giungere in grandi quantità[66] considerando che in gran parte del monumento l'opera quadrata costituisce la tecnica edilizia principalmente impiegata. Le aree di stoccaggio di suddetti materiali si sarebbero ubicate plausibilmente in prossimità del monumento, anche tenendo in considerazione quello che poteva essere il loro punto d'arrivo. Recenti ricerche archeologiche hanno infatti fornito alcuni dati che suggeriscono come possibilità che i materiali che partivano dalla cava di *El Mèdol* arrivassero in cantiere per via marittima. La zona estrattiva infatti è prossima alla costa e si situa a circa 1 km dalla cosiddetta *Roca Plana*, a est della denominata *Platja de Calabecs*[67] **(Figura 6)**. L'approdo, dalla posizione particolarmente favorevole e protetto da correnti e venti di nord-ovest e sud-ovest, avrebbe potuto costituire il punto di carico dei materiali estratti presso la cava di *El Mèdol*. Questi sarebbero dunque arrivati via mare a uno dei porti o approdi siti sul litorale tarragonese, per poi essere trasportati fino alla parte più alta della città. Risulta questionabile infatti che i materiali arrivassero a quello che conosciamo come il porto della città. Questo avrebbe imposto un tragitto marittimo più lungo, nonché l'arrivo alla "parte bassa", implicando poi il trasporto terrestre fino alla "parte alta", operazione che avrebbe innanzitutto imposto costi più elevati[68]. La

---

[61] Mar *et al.* 2012: 366–368.

[62] *HA*, Spart., 12.

[63] Sulle colonne in granito della Troade attribuite al Foro Provinciale si veda: Pérez Martín 2007: 201–206; Rodà *et al.* 2012. Sull'aspetto architettonico della terrazza intermedia vedi: Pociña e Remolà 2000: 32–43; Mar *et al.* 2015 con blibliografia precedente; Pensabene e Domingo 2019: 88–93; Vinci 2020.

[64] Si tratta di due capitelli corinzi di colonna in proconnesio, di provenienza sconosciuta (Pensabene 1993: cat. 1–2, 33–35); una cornice con soffitto decorato a cassettoni e un cassettone, in marmo proconnesio, rinvenuti all'interno della cattedrale di Tarragona (Macias *et al.* 2012a: cat. 1.2.10 e 1.2.11, 30).

[65] Sull'argomento si veda: Ottati 2016: 239–253.

[66] Un tentativo di quantificare la pietra calcarea impiegata per la costruzione della terrazza superiore fu realizzato da R. Mar e P. Pensabene (2008: 526–527). Lo scopo principale dei calcoli effettuati era però quello di stabilire i costi della costruzione e non le tempistiche. Ad ogni modo, fu calcolato che erano stati necessari 7128.4 m^3 della locale pietra de *El Mèdol*, definendo una quantità di 0,37 m^3 per blocco. In realtà si può stabilire che ogni blocco corrisponde almeno a 0,51 m^3 e che dunque per la costruzione del Recinto di Culto (tempio, lo spazio porticato e la sala assiale) furono necessari 14.000 blocchi circa.

[67] Si tratta di un promontorio che presenta una superficie liscia e circa m 75 di lunghezza, di cui almeno m 50 restano sommersi a poca profondità. La parte in acqua assume la conformazione di una sorta di canale che se da una parte sembra essere un approdo di origine naturale, dall'altra presenta tagli antropici in entrambi i lati. I saggi effettuati (Gutiérrez Garcia-M. *et al.* 2015: 784–787.) hanno inoltre permesso di rilevare la presenza di incassi quadrangolari, per i quali si ipotizza la funzione di punti di appoggio per le macchine per il sollevamento dei materiali, nonché di un blocco in pietra di *El Mèdol* abbandonato (Gutiérrez Garcia-M. *et al.* 2019: 129). A circa m 150 dal sito è stata inoltre registrata la presenza di abbondante ceramica risalente al secondo terzo del I sec. d.C.

[68] Nel caso delle Terme di Caracalla J. DeLaine ha stimato che più del 50% del totale del costo della costruzione fu utilizzato per il trasporto sia terrestre che marittimo (DeLaine 1997: 216-217).

Figura 6. Localizzazione delle cave di pietra locali con indicazione dei possibili approdi della *Roca Plana* e della *Platja del Miracle* e tragitto marittimo dei materiali per giungere al cantiere del Foro Provinciale (Gutiérrez Garcia-M. e Vinci 2018: 285, fig. 12.7).

difficoltà e dunque il dispendio economico del trasporto terrestre dipende ovviamente da diverse variabili, come la distanza da realizzare, il tipo di terreno, i mezzi di trasporto impiegati e il peso del carico. Nel caso di Tarragona, sebbene la distanza risulti relativamente breve, circa km 1,6 tra le installazioni del porto e la cima della parte alta della collina, l'orografia del terreno con quasi 1% di pendenza avrebbe reso il trasporto più difficoltoso e pericoloso[69]. Inoltre, il conseguente attraversamento di tutta la città avrebbe implicato non pochi disagi[70]. Per il cantiere del Foro Provinciale risulta forse più coerente pensare all'uso di approdi alternativi certamente presenti lungo il litorale. Si potrebbe ipotizzare l'uso dell'attuale *Platja del Miracle*, sita ai piedi della collina su cui si costruisce il complesso di epoca imperiale. A questo proposito sono note mappe antiche che suggeriscono un possibile uso del sito come porto durante il XVII secolo[71]. Purtroppo ad oggi non si dispone di prove archeologiche, occultate o cancellate

da una costruzione degli anni '60 del secolo scorso. Esiste tuttavia un una descrizione previa dell'area[72], la quale include una pianta e la documentazione di tagli nella roccia, alcuni dei quali associabili a incassi quadrangolari, che farebbero pensare alla presenza di un molo. L'archeologo tedesco A. Schulten sosteneva che l'antico porto di *Tarraco* si sarebbe situato proprio nella baia della *Punta del Milagro*, essendo più interna e per questo più protetta dal vento di levante[73]. Con questo non si vuole affermare l'esistenza di un porto, tuttavia esistono rinvenimenti provenienti dal fondale marino che lasciano aperte alcune considerazioni. Si tratta delle colonne in granito rinvenute al largo della spiaggia[74] le quali fanno riferimento probabilmente a un momento di reimpiego di questi materiali, in quanto alcuni degli elementi presentano tracce di rilavorazione. Sebbene non si possa definire a che periodo faccia riferimento l'attività di reimpiego, i resti mettono in evidenza come in qualche momento la zona fosse stata utilizzata come installazione portuaria. Certamente c'è da considerare anche la questione di tutte le infrastrutture di cui un eventuale approdo sarebbe stato dotato per sopperire alle necessità di un cantiere di grande entità e di lunga durata. Non è da escludere che una parte o la totalità

---

[69] Russell 2013: 100–101.

[70] Sebbene non costituisca un parallelo stringente, si veda: Pensabene e Domingo 2016 per il trasporto di grandi fusti monolitici all'interno della trama urbana di Roma, in cui mettono in evidenza come gli stessi autori antichi ricordano i disagi che comportava il passaggio di grandi blocchi o elementi in marmo attraverso la città. Plino ad esempio cita come il trasporto di una serie di colonne alte circa 38 piedi avesse provocato danni alle cloache (Plin., *Nat.*, 36.6–7), mentre Giovenale riporta come il passaggio di grandi blocchi in marmo poteva rappresentare un pericolo per i pedoni, oltre che produrre un insopportabile rumore (Giovenale, *Satire*, 3.236–237).

[71] Gutiérrez Garcia-M. 2019: 131.

[72] Serres 1951. Si tratta di un documento realizzato da Eduard Serres, membro della *Reial Societat Arqueològica Tarraconense* (notizia presente in Gutiérrez García *et al.* 2019: 131).

[73] Schulten 1921: 23.

[74] Pérez Martín 2007.

di queste infrastrutture potesse essere stata messa a disposizione dal governo centrale come forma di finanziamento del monumento[75].

Se il punto d'arrivo dei materiali lapidei locali fosse stata la *Platja del Miracle*, le aree di stoccaggio, almeno per ciò che riguarda la costruzione della terrazza superiore, non si sarebbero potute ubicare al di fuori del lato settentrionale e occidentale del cosiddetto Recinto di Culto a causa della ravvicinata presenza della roccia. Si potrebbe ipotizzare che i materiali si accumulassero all'interno del perimetro della piazza, tuttavia bisogna considerare la presenza dell'edificio templare al centro di questa. Forse un'ipotesi più plausibile è che un'area di stoccaggio si ubicasse al di fuori del portico orientale. Per la realizzazione del resto del complesso, invece, oltre alla grande superficie della terrazza intermedia, la vasta area che sarà poi occupata dal circo sarebbe stata senza dubbio un settore utile a gestire alcune delle attività del cantiere.

I grandi blocchi di pietra calcarea provenienti dalle cave site nei dintorni della città[76] sarebbero giunti al monumento già squadrati e praticamente pronti per la messa in opera. I dati provenienti dalla cava di *El Mèdol* e facenti riferimento soprattutto all'accumulo di blocchi abbandonati rinvenuti davanti all'accesso al sito estrattivo[77], restituiscono informazioni interessanti a questo proposito. Gli elementi lapidei del cumulo si riferiscono probabilmente a scarti dell'attività di estrazione vincolata alla realizzazione del Foro Provinciale[78]. I blocchi rinvenuti non conservano l'originaria forma parallelepipeda, ma appaiono danneggiati, circostanza che ne giustifica un'interpretazione come elementi di scarto, abbandonati dopo l'estrazione probabilmente perché difettosi[79]. Il momento dello scarto potrebbe essere avvenuto immediatamente dopo l'estrazione o nelle

Figura 7. Blocco in corso di lavorazione con uno dei bordi scalpellati e superficie lasciata a bugnato.

prime fasi di lavorazione quando il *quadratarius*, iniziato il lavoro di sbozzatura/squadratura del pezzo, si sarebbe reso conto dell'esistenza di problemi strutturali al suo interno. L'analisi del grado di lavorazione dei pezzi ne conferma una fase di modellazione in alcuni casi non ancora iniziata[80], in altri non completata. Nel caso dei blocchi che presentano un primo stadio di lavorazione si attesta come una delle superfici venisse lasciata a bugnato, scalpellando solo i bordi (**Figura 7**), così come documentato nella maggior parte dei paramenti della terrazza superiore e intermedia del Foro Provinciale, e come la superficie d'attesa fosse già dotata della cavità necessaria all'utilizzo dell'olivella per il loro spostamento e sollevamento sia presso il sito estrattivo che in cantiere (**Figura 8a**). I blocchi destinati al complesso architettonico della "parte alta" sarebbero stati certamente prodotti in maniera standardizzata come oltretutto conferma la dimensione in altezza di questi, coerente per ognuna delle due terrazze (tra 0,56 e 0,59 cm per la terrazza superiore e tra 0,59 e 0,62 per la terrazza intermedia). Probabilmente sarebbero stati realizzati in cava anche elementi più complessi, come la modellazione di blocchi modanati (**Figura 8b**). Naturalmente in cantiere sarebbero poi state effettuate tutte quelle operazioni tese ad adattare gli elementi lapidei alle necessità della costruzione. Ad esempio, nei punti d'incontro del lavoro di maestranze diverse, i blocchi presentano gli angoli rilavorati per recuperare l'allineamento dei filari: si veda il muro meridionale della *Torre de la Antiga Audiència* in cui si apre la porta che da diretto accesso alla piattaforma superiore del circo (**Figura 9**). La fattura del complesso sistema di copertura della porta, con una sequenza di doppia piattabanda e arco di scarico, doveva aver richiesto

---

[75] P. Pensabene e J. Domingo (2014: 124) ipotizzano che oltre alla realizzazione del tempio, i tarragonesi avrebbero potuto fare anche richiesta di specifiche infrastrutture per la costruzione e il trasporto di elementi lapidei. Gli autori fanno specifico riferimento ai blocchi giganteschi in marmo, ma una parte delle infrastrutture sarebbe potuta essere utilizzata anche per la gestione dei materiali locali. Risulta, infatti, forse più coerente immaginare che i marmi di importazione sarebbero continuati a giungere al porto della città, considerando l'apparato amministrativo-burocratico necessario alla loro gestione.

[76] I materiali da costruzione principalmente impiegati per la costruzione del Foro Pronvinciale sono le biocalcareniti di origine miocenica: in particolar modo, le varietà del cosiddetto *soldó* o *saldó* (di cui non si identifica un preciso punto estrattivo, essendo attestata la sua presenza in concomitanza con altre varietà lapidee, Gutiérrez Garcia-M. 2009: 108) e la pietra di *El Mèdol* proveniente soprattutto dalla cava omonima (Gutiérrez Garcia-M. 2009: 146–158). Tra i materiali locali più pregiati spicca l'uso del cosiddetto marmo di *Tarraco* o pietra di *Santa Tecla* in associazione all'*llisós*, quest'ultimo ampiamente utilizzato come materiale da costruzione oltre che per funzioni puramente ornamentali (Álvarez *et al.* 1994: 23).

[77] Roig *et al.* 2011.

[78] Vinci 2019.

[79] L'ipotesi sembra essere confermata dalla documentazione di blocchi che presentano fratture naturali.

[80] Come confermerebbero le tracce di piccone non ancora rimosse su alcuni blocchi e corrispondenti alla fase di distacco del pezzo del filare superiore nel fronte di cava (Vinci 2019: 260–261).

Figura 8. A sinistra blocco con incasso per olivella (foto CODEX), a destra blocco in corso di lavorazione, probabilmente modanato. Entrambi provengono dall'accumulo di elementi lapidei rinvenuti di fronte alla cava di *El Mèdol*.

l'intervento di maestranze altamente specializzate, probabilmente differenti da quelle che realizzano il resto del paramento. Il punto d'incontro del lavoro delle distinte maestranze si rileva grazie alla presenza di blocchi i cui angoli sono rilavorati per permetterne l'incastro[81]. Oppure si osservi il muro occidentale dell'aula assiale realizzato in opera quadrata, sulla cui parte inferiore si addossava il podio anch'esso realizzato in blocchi, che circondava tutta la sala. La faccia a vista dei blocchi presenta una lavorazione differente rispetto al resto del paramento: è regolarizzata ad ascia e ribassata in maniera graduale a creare una superficie con una sorta di tre fasce[82]. La finalità potrebbe essere stata quella di garantire una migliore adesione dei blocchi del podio alla superficie del muro. Le tre fasce, infatti, corrisponderebbero grosso modo all'altezza dei tre filari di blocchi che avrebbero composto il podio. Dall'osservazione delle tracce di lavorazione sulla superficie dei blocchi è inoltre possibile notare la loro diversa orientazione, frutto delle differenti posizioni assunte dal *quadratarius* durante il lavoro di rifinitura, così come si può notare che la traccia dello strumento, determinata da uno stesso colpo di ascia, spesso prosegue su blocchi contigui (**Figura 10**). Considerando che la rifinitura dei blocchi doveva necessariamente avvenire prima della loro messa in posa, sembra plausibile ipotizzare che, nelle zone in cui la traccia dello strumento di lavoro prosegue su blocchi contigui, si tratta di elementi di grandi dimensioni rifiniti in cantiere e solo successivamente tagliati prima del loro posizionamento[83].

Conclusioni

La questione relativa a una possibile quantificazione dei tempi di costruzione del Foro Provinciale si vincola strettamente al dibattito, da decenni ormai esistente, sull'inquadramento cronologico della realizzazione del grande complesso architettonico tarragonese. Per tale ragione risulta interessante riflettere sull'evoluzione costruttiva della collina della città su cui il monumento si costruisce. Come è stato messo in evidenza, sebbene possiamo immaginare una volontà di monumentalizzare la "parte alta" della città già a partire da epoca augustea, le attività previe alla realizzazione del tempio dedicato ad Augusto sarebbero iniziate almeno a partire da età tiberiana. Resta difficile stabilire quando ebbero inizio i lavori per la realizzazione delle strutture della terrazza superiore e di conseguenza del resto del complesso architettonico. Le fonti letterarie riportano il 15 d.C. come data in cui sarebbe stato concesso il permesso per la realizzazione del tempio dedicato ad Augusto, lasciando ipotizzare che i lavori di preparazione del terreno della collina sarebbero iniziati almeno in epoca tiberiana. Scarse tuttavia solo le testimonianze archeologiche che non permettono di definire con chiarezza l'evoluzione costruttiva del monumento. A risultare però evidente è la dinamicità del cantiere di costruzione, denso di modifche e cambi in corso d'opera, che dovette protrarsi per un lungo periodo di tempo, probabilmente almeno un secolo.

Senza dubbio le caratteristiche dell'architettura del Foro Provinciale così come l'organizzazione e la gestione del cantiere furono influezate dal contesto urbano e dall'orografia del sito prescelto per la costruzione. Un contesto topografico che impose un ingente impegno nella preparazione del terreno e nell'adattare le strutture non solo all'ambiente naturale ma anche a quello antropico preesistente, soprattutto a causa della presenza del circuito murario previo. Certamente

---

[81] Vinci 2020: 94.

[82] Vinci 2020: 64–65, figg. 47 e 49.

[83] Le operazioni di rifinitura dei blocchi sarebbero avvenute probabilmente presso il cantiere di costruzione come attestano anche le numerose schegge e frammenti di pietra rinvenuti nelle fondazioni del Recinto di Culto (Vinci 2020: 61–62).

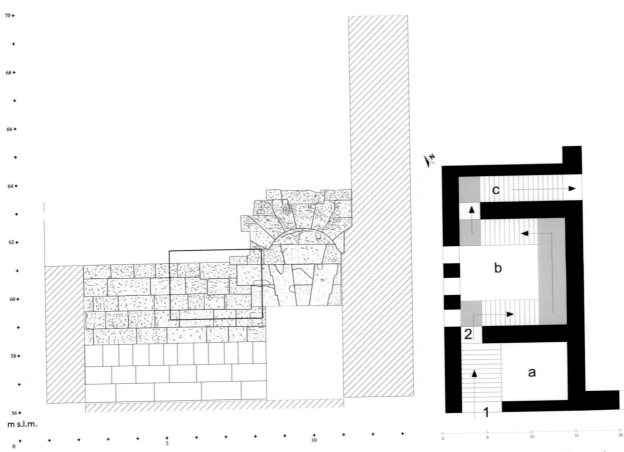

Figura 9. Paramento interno della porta di accesso alla *Torrre della Antiga Audiència* dalla piattaforma superiore del circo (in pianta porta n. 1) con dettaglio di blocchi rilavorati per permettere l'incastro del lavoro eseguito da due maestranze diverse.

Figura 10. Dettaglio di blocchi, corrispondenti alla superficie di appoggio del podio dell'aula assiale della terrazza superiore, con tracce di lavorazione ad ascia che proseguono sui due blocchi contingui.

numerosi furono i fattori che influenzarono il funzionamento e l'organizzazione del cantiere, a partire dalla gestione dei materiali lapidei utili alla costruzione, in primis la pietra locale. Ragionare sul possibile punto d'arrivo di questi materiali che giungevano dalla vicina cava di estrazione o sulle aree di stoccaggio site nei pressi del monumento, sono solo alcuni degli aspetti che lasciano intravedere quanto numerosi fossero gli ingranaggi e quanto complesso fosse il meccanismo che permetteva il funzionamento di un cantiere edilizio di questa entità.

Bibliografia

Adserias, M., C.A. Pociña e J.A. Remolà 2000. L'hàbitat suburbà portuari de l'antiga Tàrraco. Excavacions afectats pel PERI2 (Jaume I-Tabacalera), in J. Ruiz de Arbulo (ed.) *Tàrraco 99. Arqueologia d'una capital provincial romana. Tarragona 15, 16 i 17 d'abril de 1999*: 137–154. Tarragona: Universitat Rovira i Virgili.

Alföldy, G. 1999. Tàrraco, capital de la Hispània Citerior. *Kesse* 28: 7–12.

Àlvarez, A., J.L. Prada e C. Benet 1994. Canteras romanas de *Tarraco* y sus alrededores, in X. Dupré (ed.) *Actes XIV Congrés Internacional d'Arqueologia Clàssica. La ciutat en el món romà vol. 2*: 23–25. Barcelona: Institut d'Estudis Catalans.

Aquilué, X. 1993. *La seu del Col.legi d'Arquitectes. Una intervenció arqueològica en el centre històric de Tarragona*. Tarragona.

Arnall, M.J. 1984. Documents de Pere el Cerimoniós referents a Tarragona i conservats en el seu Arxiu Històric Provincial. *Quaderns d'història Tarraconense* IV: 51–130.

Arrayás, I. 2004. *Tarraco*, capital provincial. *Gerión* 22.1: 291–303.

Asensio, D., M. Ciuraneta, M. Martorell e P. Otiña 2000. L'assentament ibèric de Tarragona. L'excavació arqueològica al carrer dels Caputxins n. 24, l'any 1978, in J. Ruiz de Arbulo (ed.) *Tàrraco 99. Arqueologia d'una capital provincial romana. Tarragona 15, 16 i 17 d'abril de 1999*: 71–81. Tarragona: Universitat Rovira i Virgili.

Balil, A. 1969. *Excavaciones en la "Torre de Pilatos" (Tarragona). Campaña de excavaciones de 1962*. Madrid: Ministerio de Educación Nacional. Dirección General de Bellas Artes. Servicio Nacional de Excavaciones Arqueológicas.

Beltrán, A. 1953. Los monumentos en las monedas hispano-romanas. *Archivo Español de Arqueología* 26: 39–66.

Castillo Ramírez, E. 2015. Tácito y el templo de *Tarraco*: nueva propuesta de interpretación, in J. López (ed.) *Tarraco Biennal. Actes del 2on Congrés Internacional d'Arqueologia i Món Antic. August i les províncies occidentals. 2000 anniversari de la mort d'August (Tarragona, 26-29 de Noviembre de 2014)*: 171–180. Tarragona: Fundació Privada Mútua Catalana.

Courault, C. e J.Á. Domingo 2020. Problemáticas sobre la cuantificación de los esfuerzos de producción en canteras (piedras locales y mármol) y su repercusión en el coste de los edificios de época romana, in M.S. Vinci, A. Ottati e D. Gorostidi (eds) *La cava e il monumento: materiali, officine, sistema di costruzione e produzione nei cantieri edilizi di età imperiale*: 31–55. Roma: Quasar.

Courault, C. e C. Márquez 2020. *Quantitative studies and production cost of Roman public construction*. Córdoba: Editorial Universidad de Córdoba.

Delaine, J. 1997. *The Baths of Caracalla in Rome: a study in the design, construction and economics of large-scale building projects in imperial Rome*. Portsmouth: Journal of roman Archaeology, suppl. 25.

Domingo, J.Á. 2012. Los costes de la arquitectura romana: el capitolio de Volúbilis (Mauretania Tingitana). *Archeologia Classica* 63: 381–418.

Dupré, X. 1995. Recerques arqueològiques, in J.R. Costa i Pallejà (ed.) *El Consell Comarcal a l'antic hospital*: 20–33. Tarragona: Ajuntament de Barcelona. Delegació de Serveis de Cultura.

Dupré, X., M.J. Massó, M.Ll. Palanques e P.A. Verduchi 1988. *El circ romà de Tarragona. I. Les Voltes de Sant Ermenegild*. Barcelona: Generalitat de Catalunya.

Dupré, X. e J. M., Carreté 1993. *La "Antiga Audiència". Un acceso al Foro Provincial de Tarraco*. Madrid: Instituto de Conservación y Restauración de Bienes Culturales.

Fernández, I., J.M. Macias, J.M. Puche, P. Solà-Morales e J.M. Toldrà 2017. Metodología de análisis del circo romano de Tarragona y nuevos resultados, in L. Roldán, J.M. Macias, A. Pizzo e O. Rodríguez (ed.) *Modelos constructivos y urbanísticos de la arquitectura de Hispania*: 117–135. Tarragona: ICAC.

Ferrer, M. 1985. Tarragona. Excavaciones en la calle de San Lorenzo, 1977. *Noticiario Arqueológico Hispánico* 21: 221–297.

Fiz, I. e J.M. Macias 2007. *Forma Tarraconis*: una descoberta en evolució, in J.M. Macias, I. Fiz, Ll. Piñol, M.T. Miró e J.M. Guitart 2007. *Planimetria Arqueològica de Tarraco*: 25–40. Tarragona: ICAC.

Foguet, G. e J. López 1994. Alguns aspectes de l'urbanìsne romà de *Tarraco*: Delimitació d'espais monumentals i residencials a la llum de les darreres excavacions, in X. Dupré (ed.) *Actes XIV Congrés Internacional d'Arqueologia Clàssica. La ciutat en el món romà vol. 2*. Barcelona: Institut d'Estudis Catalans.

Gebellí, P. 2017. Una figlina al subsòl del circ de tàrraco: producció ceràmica intramurs de la ciutat en època julioclàudia, in J. López (ed.) *Tarraco Biennal. Actes del 3r Congrés Internacional d'arqueologia i món antic. La glòria del circ curses de carros i competicions circenses (Tarragona, 16-19 de novembre de 2016)*: 293–299. Tarragona: Fundación Privada Mútua Catalana.

Gutiérrez García-M., A. 2009. *Roman Quarries in the Northeast of Hispania (modern Catalonia)*. Tarragona: ICAC.

Gutiérrez García-M., A., S. Huelin, J. López e I. Rodà 2015. Can a fire broaden our understanding of a roman quarry? The case of el Mèdol (Tarragona, Spain), in P. Pensabene e E. Gasparini (eds) *Interdisciplinary Studies on Ancient Stone, Asmosia X. Proceedings of the Tenth International Conference of ASMOSIA (Rome, 21–26 May 2012)*: 779–789. Roma: L'Erma di Bretschneider.

Gutiérrez García-M., A., e M.S. Vinci 2018. Large-scale building in Early Imperial Tarraco (Tarragona, Spain) and the dynamics behind the creation of a Roman provincial capital landscape, in *Constructing Monuments, Perceiving Monumentality and the Economics of Building. Theoretical and Methodological Approaches to the Built Environment*: 271–294. Leiden: Sidestone Press.

Gutiérrez García-M., A., J. López, G. Martí e P. Terrado 2019. Evidències de dues antigues infraestructures portuàries: els embarcadors de la Roca Plana i del Miracle a Tarragona. *Butlletí Arqueològic* 41 èp. V: 127–142.

Hauschild, Th. 1974. Römische Konstruktionen auf de oberen Stadtterrasse des antiken Tarraco. *Archivo Español de Arqueología* 45–47: 3–44.

Hauschild, Th. 1975. Torre de Minerva (San Magín). Ein Turm der römischen Stadtmauer von Tarragona. *Madrider Mitteilungen* 16: 246–262.

Hauschild, Th. 1979. Die römische Stadtmauer von Tarragona. *Madrider Mitteilungen* 20: 204–250.

Hauschild, Th. 1983. *Arquitectura romana de Tarragona*. Tarragona: Ajuntament de Tarragona.

Hernández Sanahuja, B. 1877. *Recuerdos monumentales de Tarragona*. Tarragona.

López, J. e Ll. Piñol 2008. *Tarracotes arquitectòniques romanes. Les troballes de la Plaça de la Font (Tarragona)*. Tarragona: ICAC.

López, J. e D. Gorostidi 2015. Aqva Avgvsta a Tarraco?, in J. López (ed.) *Tarraco Biennal. Actes del 2on Congrés Internacional d'Arqueologia i Món Antic. August i les províncies occidentals. 2000 anniversari de la mort d'August (Tarragona, 26–29 de Noviembre de 2014)*: 251–255. Tarragona: Fundació Privada Mútua Catalana.

Macias, J.M., I. Fiz, Ll. Piñol, M.T. Miró e J.M. Guitart 2007. *Planimetria Arqueològica de Tarraco*. Tarragona: ICAC.

Macias, J.M., J. Menchón, A. Peña, M. Ramon e I. Teixell 2012a. *Praesidium, Templum et Ecclesia. Les intervencions arqueològiques a la Catedral de Tarragona 2010-2011*. Tarragona: Associació Cultural Sant Fuctuós.

Macias, J.M., A. Muñoz e I. Teixell 2012b. Arqueologia a la nau central de la Catedral de Tarragona. *Tribuna d'Arqueologia* 2010–2011: 151–174.

Macias, J.M., A. Muñoz, A. Peña e I. Teixell 2014. El templo de Augusto en Tarraco: últimas excavaciones y hallazgos, in J.M. Álvarez Martínez, T. Nogales e I. Rodà (ed.) *Actas del XVIII Congreso Internacional de Arqueología Clásica: centro y periferia en el mundo clásico*: 1539–1543. Mérida: Museo Nacional de Arte Romano.

Mar, R. e P. Pensabene 2008. Finanziamento dell'edilizia pubblica e calcolo dei costi dei materiali lapidei: il caso del foro superiore di Tarraco, in S. Camporeale, H. Dessalles e A. Pizzo (eds) *Los procesos constructivos en el mundo romano: Italia y las provincias orientales* (Anejos de Archivo Español de Arqueología 50): 509–553. Mérida: CSIC.

Mar, R., J. Ruiz de Arbulo, D. Vivó e J.A. Beltrán 2012. *Tarraco. Arquitectura y urbanismo de una capital provincial romana vol. I*. Tarragona: Universitat Rovira i Virgili.

Mar, R., J. Ruiz de Arbulo, D. Vivó e J.A. Beltrán 2015. *Tarraco. Arquitectura y urbanismo de una capital provincial romana vol. II*. Tarragona: Universitat Rovira i Virgili.

Mesas, I. 2015. Los acueductos romanos de *Tarraco*: cronología y nuevos tramos, in J., López (ed.) *Tarraco Biennal. Actes del 2on Congrés Internacional d'Arqueologia i Món Antic. August i les províncies occidentals. 2000 anniversari de la mort d'August (Tarragona, 26–29 de Noviembre de 2014)*: 245–250. Tarragona: Fundació Privada Mútua Catalana.

Miró, M.T. 1994. Dades per a un estudi de l'evolució urbanística de Tàrraco: el carrer dels Caputxins de Tarragona, in X. Dupré (ed.) *Actes XIV Congrés Internacional d'Arqueologia Clàssica. La ciutat en el món romà vol. 2*: 287–288. Barcelona: Institut d'Estudis Catalans.

Menchón, J. 2009. *La muralla romana de Tarragona: una aproximació*. Barcelona: Societat Catalana d'Arqueologia.

Oraschewski, S. 2020. The preparation of a new city-center: how the Forum Iulium, knows as Caesar's Forum, was commenced, in C. Courault e C. Márquez (eds) *Quantitative studies and production cost of Roman public construction*. Córdoba: Editorial Universidad de Córdoba.

Otiña, P. e J. Ruiz de Arbulo 2000. De Cese a Tárraco. Evidencias y reflexiones sobre la Tarragona ibérica y el proceso de romanización. *Empúries* 52: 107–136.

Ottati, A. 2016. Costruzione, ricostruzione e "restaurazione": l'ideologia del principato nell'edilizia della metà del II sec. d.C. in Argolide, in F. Longo, R. Di Cesare e S. Privitera (eds) *Dromoi. Studi in onore di E. Greco*: 239–253. Paestum: Pandemos.

Panosa, M.I. 2009. *De Kese a Tarraco. La población de la Tarragona romano republicana amb especial referència a l'epigrafia*. Tarragona: Arola.

Pegoretti, G. 1843. *Manuale pratico per l'estimazione dei lavori architettonici, stradali, idraulici e di fortificazione per uso degli ingegneri ed architetti*. Milano: Editore Libraio Angelo Monti.

Pensabene, P. 1993. La decorazione architettonica dei monumenti provinciali di Tarraco, in R. Mar (ed.) *Els monuments provincials de Tàrraco. Noves aportacions al seu coneixement*: 33- 105. Tarragona: Universitat Rovira i Virgili.

Pensabene, P. e R. Mar, R. 2004. Dos frisos marmóreos en el acrópolis de Tarraco, el templo de Augusto y el complejo provincial de culto imperial, in J. Ruiz de Arbulo (ed.) *Simulacra Romae. Roma y las capitales provinciales del Occidente Europeo*: 73–86. Tarragona: Consorcio Urbium Hispaniae Romanae.

Pensabene, P. e R. Mar 2010. Il tempio di Augusto a *Tarraco*: gigantismo e marmo lunense nei luoghi di culto imperiale in *Hispania* e *Gallia. Archeologia Classica* LXI, 11: 243–307.

Pensabene, P. e J.Á. Domingo 2016. El transporte de grandes fustes monolíticos por el interior de la trama urbana de Roma. *Arqueología de la Arquitectura* 13: 1–14.

Pensabene, P. e J.Á. Domingo 2014. Blocchi giganteschi di cava nell'architettura pubblica di Roma e delle province occidentali, in J. Bonetto, S. Camporeale e A. Pizzo (ed.) *Arqueología de la construcción IV. Las canteras en el mundo antiguo: sistemas de explotación y procesos productivos*: 117–134. Mérida: CSIC, Università degli Studi di Padova, École Normale Supérieure.

Pensabene, P. e J.Á. Domingo 2019. El *Concilium Provinciae Hispaniae Citerioris*: una lectura arquitectónica a la luz de los nuevos datos y de los conjuntos imperiales de Roma. *Butlletí Arqueològic* 41, ép. V: 41–126.

Pérez Martín, W. 2007. *Troballes arqueològiques al litoral tarragoní. 12 anys d'arqueologia subaquàtica (1968-1980).* Valls: Cossetània Edicions.

Piñol, Ll. 1993. Intervencions arqueològiques al Carrer Merceria, in R. Mar (ed.) *Els monuments provincials de Tàrraco. Noves aportacions al seu coneixement*: 257- 268. Tarragona: Universitat Roviri i Virgili.

Pociña, C.A. e J.A. Remolà 2000. La Plaza de Representación de Tarraco: intervenciones arqueológicas en la Plaza del Fòrum y la Calle d'en Compte, in J. Ruiz de Arbulo (ed.) *Tàrraco 99. Arqueologia d'una capital provincial romana. Tarragona 15, 16 i 17 d'abril de 1999*: 27–45. Tarragona: Universitat Rovira i Virgili.

Puche, J.M. 2010. Los procesos constructivos de la arquitectura clásica. De la proyección a la ejecución. El caso del *Concilium Provinciae Hispaniae Citerioris* de *Tarraco. Arqueología de la Arquitectura* 7: 13–41.

Rea, R., H.J. Beste e L. Lancaster 2002. Il cantiere del Colosseo. *Römische Mitteilungen* 109: 341–375.

Rodà, I., P. Pensabene e J.Á. Domingo 2012. Columns and rotae in Tarraco made with granite from the Troad. in A. Gutiérrez García-M. *et al.* (ed.) 2012: 210–227.

Roig, J.F., M. Siris, E. Solà e J. Trenor 2011. El dipòsit de carreus del Mèdol (Tarragona). Resultats preliminars. *Tribuna d'Arqueologia* 2009–2010: 383–405.

Rüger, Ch. 1968. Romische Keramik aus dem Kreuzgang der Katedrale von Tarragona. *Madrider Mitteilungen* 9: 237–258.

Ruiz de Arbulo, J. 1990. El foro de Tárraco. *Cypsela* 8: 119–138.

Ruiz de Arbulo, J. 1991. Los inicios de la romanización en Occidente: los casos de Emporion y Tárraco. *Athenaeum* 79: 459–493.

Ruiz de Arbulo, J. 1992. Tarraco, Carthago Nova y el problema de la capitalidad en la Hispania Citerior republicana, in Dupré, X. (ed.) *Miscel·lània Arqueològica a J. M. Recasens*: 115–128. Tarragona: Estarraco.

Ruiz de Arbulo, J. 2009. La *Legio Martia* i la fundació de la colònia Tarraco, in F. Tarrats (ed.) *Tarraco pedra a pedra*: 36–55. Tarragona: Museu Nacional Arqueològic de Tarragona. Barcelona: Generalitat de Catalunya, Departament de Cultura i Mitjans de Comunicació.

Ruiz de Arbulo, J., R. Mar, J.Á. Domingo e I. Fiz 2004. Etapas y elementos de la decoración arquitectónica en el desarrollo monumental de la ciudad de Tarraco, in S.F. Ramallo Asensio (ed.) *La decoración arquitectónica en las ciudades romanas de occidente. Actas del Congreso Internacional celebrado en Cartagena entre los días 8 y 10 de octubre de 2003*: 115–152. Murcia: Universidad de Murcia.

Russell, B.J. 2013. *The economics of Roman Stone trade.* Oxford: Oxford University Press.

Sánchez Real, J. 1969. Exploración arqueológica en el jardín de la Catedral de Tarragona. *Madrider Mitteilungen* 10: 276–301.

Serres, E. 1951. *El primitivo puerto de Tarraco.* Opera inedita presentata al "Premio Cronista José Maria Pujol" e conservato presso l'archivio della Reial Societat Arqueològica Tarraconense.

Schulten, A. 1921. *Tarraco.* Barcellona.

Villaronga, L. 1979. *Numismática Antigua de Hispania.* Barcelona: Cymys.

Vinci, M.S. 2018. Notae Lapicidinarum: documentation and analysis of quarry marks from the Provincial Forum of Tarraco, in D. Matetić Poljak e K. Marasović (eds) *Interdisciplinary Studies on Ancient Stone, Asmosia XI. Proceedings of the Eleventh International Conference of ASMOSIA. (Split 18-22 May 2015)*: 699–710. Split: University of Split.

Vinci, M.S. 2019. Painted marks at El Mèdol quarry near Tarragona: observations on the logistics and organisation of a Roman limestone quarry. *Journal of Roman Archaeology* 32: 251–278.

Vinci, M.S. 2020. *Il "Foro Provinciale" di Tarraco: tecniche e processi edilizi.* Bordeaux: Un@-Ausonius Éditions.

Vinci, M.S., J.M. Macias, J.M. Puche, P. Solà-Morales e J.M. Toldrà 2014. El subsuelo de la Torre del Pretorio: substructiones de tradición helenística bajo la sede del Concilium Prouinciae Hispaniae Citerioris (Tarraco). *Arqueología de la Arquitectura* 11: 1–20.

Vinci, M.S. e A. Ottati 2018. La monumentalizzazione delle Hispaniae: alcune riflessioni su progettualità e realizzazione del Foro Provinciale di Tarraco, in M. Livadiotti, R. Belli Pasqua, L.M. Caliò e G. Martines (ed.) *Theatroeideis. L'immagine della città, la città delle immagini, Thiasos Monografie 11, vol. II. L'immagine della città romana e medievale*: 169–182. Roma: Quasar.

Voutsaki, S., Y. Van den Beld e Y. de Raaff 2018. Labour mobilization and architectural energetics in the North Cemetery at Ayios Vasilios, Laconia, Greece, in A. Brybaert, V. Klinkenberg, A. Gutiérrez Garcia-M. e I. Vikatou (eds) *Constructing monuments, perceiving monumentality and the economics of building. Theorical and methodological approaches to the buildt environment*: 169–191. Leiden.

Labour and its Cost During the Aegean Late Bronze Age

Ann Brysbaert

Leiden University
a.n.brysbaert@arch.leidenuniv.nl

Abstract

In past pre-industrial societies whenever large-scale building projects took place, extensive manual labour was invested when materials were sourced, extracted, transported, employed, and subsequently maintained. For large expenditure of energy and sizeable undertakings, careful and strategic planning in advance was required. In this paper, I focus on a wide range of labour activities and their costs during the Aegean Late Bronze Age (LBA), specifically the 13th century BC. I review the status of labour studies in architecture for Aegean prehistory. In focusing on labour by humans and other animals, my goal is to illustrate how prehistoric people in the Aegean heartland of the Argolid achieved their multiple daily tasks, including construction work, while remaining resilient before the adverse events around 1200–1190 BC. The data discussed form a representative set against which the agricultural data can be compared since the latter is the most essential for the healthy survival and reproduction of the population as a whole. Monumental building, domestic house building, terrace construction, infrastructure provision, chamber tomb digging, pottery production, and agricultural activities including food processing all required significant labour input on a societal scale.

Estimating the hours of labour and thus the cost of each type of activity helps us to understand the burden that the different tasks may potentially have had on the population in the region, something not always well understood in previous scholarship. It is also possible to compare and discuss their implications for the society as a whole. In the LBA, the decision-making about long-term construction projects had to stand in relation to the constant needs of seasonally-driven subsistence provisions for both people and animals. The labour costs presented can be refined and corrected in future research, but here they force us to discuss the timeframe in which such tasks took place. The different tasks need to be fitted into the complete picture of the taskscape rather than seen as stand-alone activities.

Keywords: Aegean Prehistory, overhead costs, monumental and domestic building, craft production costs, ancient economy

Introduction

In past pre-industrial societies whenever large-scale building projects took place, extensive manual labour was invested when materials were sourced, extracted, transported, employed, and subsequently maintained. Any activity requires the expenditure of energy, and the larger the scale of the undertakings, the more careful and strategic the advanced planning that is required. In general, human resources could have been treated as regular workers, carrying out an acceptable workload per day, commensurate with their capability and depending on the socio-political structures of a given society.[1]

In this paper I focus on a wide range of labour activities and their costs during the Aegean Late Bronze Age (LBA), specifically the 13th century BC. I also review the status of labour studies in architecture for Aegean prehistory. Monumental building, domestic house building, terrace construction, infrastructure provision, chamber tomb digging, pottery production, and agricultural activities including food processing all required significant labour input on a societal scale. By estimating the hours of labour required for the different categories, it is possible to compare and discuss their joint implications to society as a whole. The decision-making about long-term construction projects always stands in relation to the constant needs of seasonally-driven subsistence provisions for both people and animals.[2] Following Janet DeLaine's example, this paper aims to move 'beyond the calculation of average and peak overall man-power requirements to consider the workforce as individuals, thereby allowing a closer estimation of the size and nature of the man-power'.[3] The calculated labour estimates only become useful when compared to other expenditure. Simplified comparisons between monumental and domestic projects, for example, are not sufficient since such comparative data only tell which took longer and required more people. Specific figures for labour estimates help us to understand the the potential burden that different tasks may have had

---

[1] E.g. Nakassis 2012 for building workers in Linear B tablets.

[2] See Brysbaert 2013.
[3] DeLaine 1997: 195

on the population in the region, something not always well understood in previous scholarship. These specific figures can be refined and corrected in future research, but they force us to discuss the timeframe in which such tasks took place. The different tasks need to be fitted into the complete picture of the taskscape. In a recent paper, I combined results for monumental building, domestic house building, and pottery production in the LBA 13th-century BC Argive Plain and compared them with farming, thus demonstrating the far more labour-intensive scale of agricultural activities.[4] However, comparison of the latter with only a few categories of production activities does not give the full picture, so this paper introduces several more labour-intensive task categories which were part and parcel of LBA life in the Argolid. As such, this paper aims to arrive at a more precise estimate for each task category than just an order of magnitude. The obtained estimates allow direct comparisons between the different tasks as well as the socio-political and economic contextualisation of these data.[5]

In focusing on labour by humans and other animals, the goal of this paper is to illustrate how prehistoric people in the Aegean heartland of the Argolid achieved their multiple daily tasks, including construction work, while remaining resilient before the adverse events around 1200–1190 BC. Presenting detailed labour estimates for all the tasks outlined below is beyond the scope of this paper. Instead, the data discussed below form a representative set against which the agricultural data can be compared, since the latter is the most essential for the healthy survival and reproduction of the population as a whole.

Background and context (Figure 1)

In the Aegean, large-scale building programmes took place from the 14th century until the end of the 13th century BC and resulted in awe-evoking citadels, burial monuments, waterworks, roads, and bridges.[6] It has often been expressed that these programmes must have mobilised substantial labour forces over sustained periods of time.[7] Simultaneously, since agriculture and animal husbandry were the predominant subsistence strategies for most people in the Aegean LBA, one can assume that such building efforts, requiring a consistent amount of human and material resources, may have affected local economies profoundly. Some scholars have expressed their concern that mobilising these workforces resulted in resource exhaustion and was detrimental, especially c. 1200 BC, to the sustainability of socio-political structures. The human impact on

dwindling resources and climatic changes have been seen as contributors to the Mycenaean socio-political 'collapse', even while the 'collapse' phenomenon itself is debated.[8] Warfare, epidemics, and many other factors have been proposed as factors,[9] while others have been refuted.[10] Despite attempts to explain the Mycenaean LBA crises or 'collapse' *around* 1200 BC in these terms, the extremely complex nature of the different factors that caused these societal upheavals is still poorly understood; however, progress is being made.[11] The suggestion that intense building programmes were detrimental to the LBA Mycenaean societies needs to be (re-)evaluated. It is most likely that each region in the Aegean and in the eastern Mediterranean suffered case-specific features that led to their demise on differing scales.[12]

The Aegean Bronze Age, spanning from 3300–1100 BC, is a relatively new period for the employment of architectural energetics and labour cost studies. We can count the number of studies that present systematic work employing this method almost on one hand, and most of these have been extensively used in later work.[13]

Since its start in 2015, the SETinSTONE project has assessed if and how monumental building activities in the LBA Argive Plain impacted on the political and socio-economic structures of the Mycenaean polities in the period between 1600 and 1100 BC, and how people responded to changes in these structures. An approach combining data collection in the field and labour cost studies to investigate several large monuments helps in understanding how humans and their resources could have achieved long-term and large-scale building alongside many other tasks in the 13th century BC. It also helps us to understand how different levels of mobility of people with their skills, knowledge, animals, and materials were part of these energy flows. For example, what were the minimum resource requirements for specific tasks? Did these resources become depleted towards 1200 BC, and if so, to what degree? How did people with a shorter life span and restricted diet than today's western standards manage monumental construction, domestic construction, and various craft activities within the rhythm of other daily tasks?

In a previous study, I collected the energetics data on several factors that were part of daily life in the LH III B Argive communities (c. 1300–1200 BC).[14] **Tables 1–6**

[4] Brysbaert 2020.
[5] Cf. DeLaine 1997
[6] E.g. Hope Simpson and Hagel 2006; Maran 2010.
[7] E.g. Shelmerdine 2001; Galaty and Parkinson 2007.

[8] E.g. Tainter 1988, 2006; Diamond 2005.
[9] E.g. Bennet 2013; Middleton 2017.
[10] Hinzen et al. 2018.
[11] Most recently: Knapp and Manning 2016; Maran and Wright 2020.
[12] E.g. Cline 2014.
[13] E.g. Loader 1998; Cavanagh and Mee 1999; Fitzsimons 2011; Devolder 2013; Brysbaert 2013, 2015; Harper 2016.
[14] For details, see Brysbaert 2020. The figure of 100 people is used regularly in the study and should be seen as a working figure rather than a real one; this was incorrectly used in Bintliff 2020. For more nuanced figures, see Brysbaert 2013.

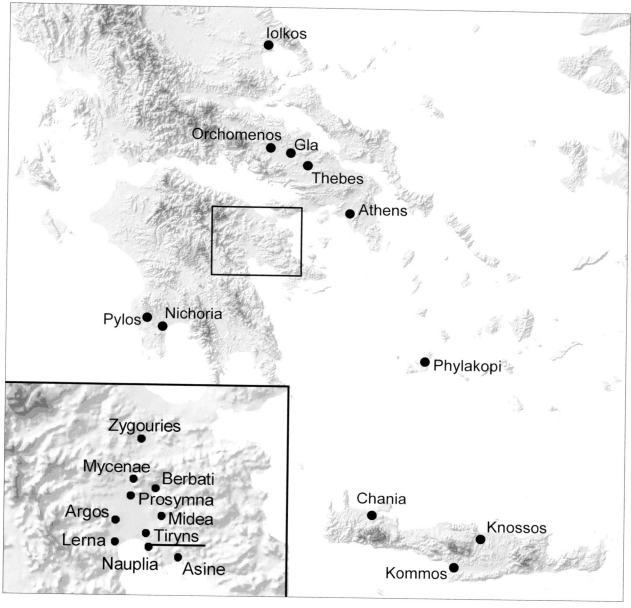

Figure 1. Map of Greece with inset of the Argolid indicating the most important sites discussed in this paper.

present the labour costs of the six largest monumental constructions in the region;[15] the level, amount, and cost of domestic house construction needed for the population of the region as currently published;[16] the cost of the domestic pottery required to sustain this population; and the labour that went into the agricultural activities needed to sustain the estimated population in the region during the LH IIIB period. The goal of this work was not to determine the exact cost or numbers of mobilised

workers but to understand, comparatively, the different labour input between the monuments themselves and domestic building and pottery production, on the one hand, and the agricultural efforts of the region, on the other. Since any detailed study of the demography in the region is hampered by the lack of intensive surveys,[17] population figures may change with new data for the region. These will influence the final figures, but until such a survey has been carried out and fully published,[18] useful suggestions can still be made about how people carried out specific activities and lived their daily

---

[15] The tholos tomb of the Genii is not included, because no study on its construction materials has been undertaken in detail, and so it is not possible to provide a full energetics costing. Moreover, its date to the LH III period is not free of debate; see Pelon 1976.
[16] E.g. Bintliff 2020.

[17] For extensive surveys, see Bintliff 1977; Hope Simpson and Dickinson 1979.
[18] However, see WARP, e.g. Gallimore et al. 2017.

Standard 100 m wall	People + oxen	‡Tiryns 725 m wall	†Tiryns Dam
Yr 1	25 + 10	180 + 22	50 + 2
Yr 2	30 + 10	210 + 22	50 + 2
Yr 3	33 + 10	236 + 22	50 + 2
‡Mycenae 980 m wall	***Mycenae Atreus**	***Mycenae Clytemnestra**	**‡Midea 462 m wall**
245 + 22	82 + 4	82 + 4	116 + 10
297 + 22	82 + 4	82 + 4	139 + 10
324 + 22			152 + 10/20?

Table 1. Simplified table of working teams of people and oxen calculated per year for two or three **full years** (365 days, 8hrs/day) and relating to the volume and masses of materials needed to complete each construction.

The grey cells refer to a standard set of calculations extracted from Brysbaert 2013 and 2015. The remaining data was adapted from *Cavanagh and Mee 1999, updated with Harper 2016; †Loader 1998, app. 4; ‡Loader 1998, app. 4, updated with Brysbaert 2013 and 2015.

	Dimensions	Work effort in individual person years (py)		Work effort of 100 people employed simultaneously(i.e. in 100 py)	
		Brysbaert based on Brysbaert 2013 and 2015	Loader 1998† / Cavanagh and Mee 1999*	Brysbaert 2013 and 2015 / Harper 2016æ	Loader 1998†† / Cavanagh and Mee 1999**
Tiryns Citadel	725 m L wall	c. 60 py	55.26 py†	6	0.55††
Tiryns Dam	100L x 9H x 65W(av.)		144 py†	1.45††	1.44††
Mycenae Citadel†††	980 m L wall	c. 75 py	-	7.5	-
Mycenae Atreus	13.5 H × 13.5 diam		20,000 pd* = 54.8 py**	267570 / 162240æ = 1.65 x larger than C.-M. = 0.9ææ	0.55**
Mycenae Clytemnestra**	13.5 H × 13.5 diam		20,000 pd** = 54.8 py**	267570 / 162240ææ = 1.65 x larger than C.-M. = 0.9ææ	0.55**
Midea Citadel	462 m L wall	c. 15 py	14.16 py†	1.5	0.14††
Total effort for 100 people				**18.25 years**	

Table 2. Labour costs for six major 13th-century BC building works in the Argive Plain, with basic dimensions of a simplified circumference or shape. These data do not include stone differentiation; specific masonry features; site clearance; the estimated 20% clay/soil infill found between the stones in Cyclopean-style construction Mylonas 1962; Wright 1978: 160; Küpper 1996: 33; Mundell *et al.* 2009: 205); or friction between transport vehicles and road surfaces.

Data combined from Brysbaert 2013 and 2015, Loader 1998†, Cavanagh and Mee 1999*, and Harper 2016æ. **Extrapolated data from Cavanagh and Mee 1999 by Brysbaert. ææExtrapolated from Harper 2016 by Brysbaert. ††Extrapolated from Loader 1998 by Brysbaert. When compared, the right two columns show a difference of 8–10 times in the scale of effort between Loader's and Brysbaert's work and a 1.65 times difference between Cavanagh and Mee's work and that of Harper.

lives. However, without including as many production categories as possible in which people were involved, the picture remains incomplete. Cost calculations of many other activities need to be calculated in order to place agricultural production in a more comprehensive context of craft and production. Only at that stage will it be possible to estimate which factors may have played a detrimental role *within* these societies around 1200–1190 BC, how, and to whom.

This paper takes the earlier data a step further by including additional labour activities. These include, first, the labour costs of constructing chamber tombs during the LH IIIB period based on the current data on these tombs. Second, providing transport and mobility infrastructure in the form of roads was an important factor to many social groups in the region in LH IIIB. These roads were used to transport building materials, to provide daily access to material resources (clay for

Estimated Argive Plain population: 20,000 people (13th c. BC) or 4,000 households of five members		
	Large houses	Small houses
Amount	1000	3000
Cost/unit	150 pd	75 pd
Cost for all	150,000 pd	225,000 pd
Cost for the whole 13th c. BC	300,000 pd	450,000 pd
4 builders/unit	75	36.5
4 builders for all/size	75,000 days (= 205 years)	112,500 days (= 308 years)
100 builders for all houses	7,500 days (= 20.6 years)	

Table 3. Cost of domestic house building for the Argive Plain households for an entire century.

Estimated pottery needed for 4,000 households in the Argive Plain per year		
	50 per household	100 per household
Amount	200,000	400,000
Cost/unit	6.7 pots/ph* = 54/pd	6.7 pots/ph* = 54/pd
Cost for all	3979 pd	7940 pd
Cost per year	11py or 11 potters	22py or 22 potters
Team of 5/ workshop	55 py or potters with team	110 py or potters with team
100 potters	2.75 py	5.5 py

Table 4. Yearly cost of pottery needs for the estimated households of the Argive Plain. Based on Whitelaw (2001) and Acton (2014).

*Refers only to the potter (see Whitelaw 2001). Acton suggests 5 people/workshop.

Task	Labour cost rate	Labour in person-days (pd)		
		1 ha	3 ha	5 ha
Tilling-sowing	0.01 – 0.03 ha/pd	34 – 100	102 – 300	170 – 500
Reaping	0.1 ha/pd	10 – 13	30 – 39	50 – 65
Manual threshing	100 – 300 kg/pd	3.75 – 10	11.25 – 30	18.75 – 50
Dehusking	100 – 300 kg/pd	3.75 – 10	11.25 – 30	18.75 – 50
Crop cleaning	Variable/person	25	75	125
Total without grinding		76.25 – 157.5	228.75 – 472.5	381.25 – 787.5
Grinding into flour	3 h/day (2 kg?)	162.6	487.8	813
Collecting water	1h /day			
Collecting wood/fuel	1h /day	162.6	487.8	813
Cooking	1 h/day			
Adult requirements for 365 days/yr		1.3	4	6.6

Table 5. Agricultural tasks in the Argive Plain for crop rearing including rates for production and preparation for consumption, labour cost rates, and labour efforts/task, with totals. Adapted from Halstead's figures (2014, table 4.1) and very similar to Bresson (2016: 409). 3 ha of cultivated land as the minimum needed for a 5-member household, 5 ha as a plot size to start using draught animals. Coloured cells represent food processing tasks.

Animal	Amount	Adult food need/month X 20 months (for nbr of animal type)	Individual cost/animal in kg of wheat
Cattle	2	12.5 – 16.6 × 20 (2)	125-166.6 kg
Sheep	16-20	12.5 – 16.6 × 20 (16-20)	15.6 – 20.75 kg (for 16) 12.5 – 16.6 kg (for 20)
Goat	16	12.5 – 16.6 × 20 (16)	15.6 – 20.75 (for 16)

Table 6. Animal cost related to the cost of a slave in Classical times; pig figures were not available (based on Gallant 1991: table 4.2).

pottery and mudbricks, limestone for quicklime, wood for domestic and monumental construction), and to facilitate traffic between home and places of work, including crop fields and meadows.[19] Third, evidence shows that the use of terraces increased significantly during the LBA, especially in the Argolid and its surroundings.[20] While these are notoriously difficult to date due to later reuse, it is possible to arrive at a range of estimates; terrace building was potentially an essential survival strategy for a growing population in the Argolid. Fourth, building costs themselves are not limited to the *chaînes opératoires* of quarrying, transport, and construction. Earlier studies have pointed to tools, facilities, equipment,[21] accommodation, food provisions for humans and animals that work on the construction,[22] and various additional factors required for a successful building project to be completed.[23] In prehistoric contexts, however, these have not yet been calculated as actual cost factors. Additionally, in her study of the costs of the building of the Baths of Caracalla, DeLaine noted that, compared with what the state paid the army on a yearly basis, building the Baths was a relatively small cost: by one if not two orders of magnitude.[24] Although they did not make cost estimates, Drennan and Kolb discuss the relationship between monumental building projects and warfare campaigns in Pharaonic Egypt. They observe that internal warfare *within* Egypt led to less and less impressive building projects than when warfare was attested with Egyptian troops involved *beyond* Egypt itself.[25] While evidence is limited, preliminary numbers on potential military costs are discussed here.

Tomb digging

As the most popular LBA tomb type in the south Aegean, chamber tombs were perhaps not used exclusively by elite members of the society,[26] however, the majority of the built chamber tombs seem to represent the social agendas of emerging elites who competed locally with one another through elaboration and experimentation in tomb architecture.[27] Chamber tombs resemble tholos tombs in layout and elevation, but they were dug into bedrock, not constructed with stone. They can range from small to relatively large. This tomb type required additional effort compared with smaller pit- and cist-type graves that are known from the MH period and common also in the LH Argolid.[28] Since many of the tomb clusters or cemeteries were excavated in the late 19th century and several were robbed in Antiquity, detailed

contextual data for secure dating is often lacking. Most of the dates published are ranges based on finds found inside the tombs. Many of the tombs were in continuous use for stretches of several centuries. Another limitation of employing these data is the focus on chamber tombs (excluding pits and cists), but calculating labour costs for all tomb types is beyond the scope of this paper. Since no intensive survey has been conducted in the region, we likely are still missing several tomb clusters. However, the known number of tombs can be compared with the population estimates. This suggests that the known tombs clearly provide a representative sample of the tombs once present in the Argolid. Therefore, the cost calculations provide figures which can be compared to other craft activities and agricultural labour costs.

Tables 7–8 bring together the published chamber tombs in the region of the Argive Plain and its surroundings. The right column in both tables indicates the minimum number of chamber tombs that were dug in LH IIIB and the number of chamber tombs that may have been reasonably in use during this same period. For single or multiple tomb clusters with a time range including LH IIIB, there is a chance that some of the tombs were constructed and/or in use in LH IIIB. For example, when the date of a tomb cluster is derived from a range 'LH II to IIIB', 1/6 of the total tombs of this range have been estimated *to have been in use* in LH IIIB. When the range starts at LH IIIA, 1/3 of this cluster is taken *to have been in use* in LH IIIB. Total numbers are rounded. When the range starts at LH IIIB and continues in LH IIIC or later, these are considered *to have been constructed* in LH IIIB. This is the only way to calculate the minimum numbers. Other types of tombs (cists, pits) cannot be taken into account in these numbers, because their data is even less secure.

The published data for Mycenae is taken from the Mycenaean Atlas since this is the most up-to-date source of information concerning Mycenae itself.[29] For the additional sites, data was collected from the regions of Tiryns, Berbati, Prosymna, Asine, Argos, Kokla, Nafplio, Dendra, and various smaller locations in the general area.[30] The individual chamber tombs varied greatly in size. The largest one near Mycenae (chamber tomb 505) had a volume of c. 250 m³,[31] while the largest one known from Voudeni cemetery (VT 75; Relative Index [TRex] 9.26, or 2313–3084 person hours (ph) = 62 days for 10 labourers, or 9 days for 70), was 257 m³.[32] Voudeni's smallest chamber tomb (VT 3) had a volume of 4.88 m³ and is 'far below the median and among the lowest recorded on site' (TRex 0.18, or 44–59 ph, 4 people for

[19] See Brysbaert et al. 2020; Brysbaert 2021.
[20] Kvapil 2012; Fallu 2017.
[21] E.g. Loader 1998; Blackwell 2014, 2018; Boleti 2020.
[22] Brysbaert 2013, 2020.
[23] See Barker and Russell, this volume.
[24] DeLaine 1997: 221.
[25] Drennan and Kolb 2019.
[26] Turner 2020: 31.
[27] Galanakis 2017–18: 89–92, 94.
[28] Alden 2000: 19–21; Fitzsimons 2011: 93.

[29] Iakovidis et al. 2003 with full references.
[30] See especially Alden 1981; Sjöberg 2004. See also **Table 8** in this paper.
[31] Mylonas 1957: 75.
[32] Turner 2020: 43, 100.

Chamber tomb cemetery	Range of dates†	Nbr of Tombs®*	Estimated LH IIIB tombs	
			Min.	Reasonable
Panagia	LH IIA-LH IIIC 1/6 = 2	Approx. 12, 4 unexcavated	0	2
Epano Pigadi/Fournodiaselo	LH II-LH IIIB 1/6 = 2.66	Approx. 16, at least 9 unexcavated	0	2.66
Bouzioti (Kalkani North Bank)	LH II-LH IIIB 1/6 = 1.5	9	0	1.5
Kalkani South Bank	East: LH I and LH II West: LH IIIC	15, probably some unexcavated	0	0
Aghios Georgios	Early LH II-LH III 1/6 = 1.66	10	0	1.66
3rd Kilometre	LH II-LH IIIC 1/6 = 1	6	0	1
Alepotrypa	LH IIB-LH IIIC 1/6 = 1.5	14, at least 5 unexcavated	0	1.5
Kalkani South West	LH IIIA1-LH IIIC 1/3 = 1.33	4	0	1.33
Kato Fournos	LH II-LH IIIB 1/6 = 1.33	10, at least 2 unexcavated	0	1.33
Asprokhoma/Agriosykia	LH II (?), LH III A1-LH IIIB 1/3= 2	7	0	2
Asprokhoma East	LH IIA-LH IIIC Middle 1/6 = 2.16	13	0	2.16
Asprokhoma West	LH III 1/3 = 3.66	11	0	3.66
Koutsoumbela*	-	4, several unexcavated	0	0
Loupounou*	-	8	0	0
Batsourorachi*	-	3, possibly more unexcavated	0	0
Souleimani	LH IIA-LH IIIC 1/6 (of 15) = 2.5	20, several unexcavated	0	2.5
Vythisma South*	Destroyed due to ploughing	5	0	0
Boliari (Outside map N)	LH IIIA2-LH IIIB, maybe LH IIIC	1, at least 2 unexcavated	0	0
Kapsala North/Vlakhostrata	LH IIIB	9	9	9
Kapsala South	-	1, at least 1 unexcavated	0	0
Paleogalaro West	LH II-LH III 1/6 = 0.66	4, 2 unexcavated	0	0.66
Paleogalaro East	LH IIIB	3, at least 3 unexcavated	3	3
Gortsoulia	LH IIIA-LH IIIC Middle 1/3 = 1.33	4, at least 2 unexcavated	0	1.33
Totals		164 dated 23 undated 31 unexcavated	12	37

Table 7. Chamber tombs of LH date from various cemeteries in and near Mycenae.

*Cemeteries excavated by E. Paleologou. †Dates refer both to the potential date of construction and dates of usage. Italic numbers correspond to reasonable numbers in right column. ®The majority was excavated by Tsountas, others by Wace, Mylonas, and Verdelis (Iakovidis *et al.* 2003 with full references). The table only indicates the total number of excavated and unexcavated tombs.

Chamber tomb cemetery	Range of dates†	Nbr of tombs^æ	Estimated LH IIIB Tombs	
			Min.	**Reasonable**
Prosymna	**LH I - LH III** (LH IIIA2- LH IIIB2) 8 tombs LH IIA - LH IIIB1 3 tombs LH IIA - LH IIIB2 5 tombs LH IIB - LH IIIB1 *1/6 = 2.66* 5 tombs LH IIIA1 - LH IIIB1 5 tombs LHIIIA2 - LH IIIB1 4 tombs LHIIIA2 - LH IIIB2 *1/3 = 4.66* *1 tomb LH IIIB1* *1 tomb LH IIIB1 - LH IIIB2* *1 tomb LH IIIB2* 1 tomb LH I 1 tomb LH I - LH IIIA1 1 tomb LH IIA - LH IIB 1 tomb LH IIA - LH IIIA1 3 tombs LH IIA - LH IIIA2 1 tomb LH IIIA1 2 tombs LH IIIA1 - LH IIIA2 4 tombs LHIIIA2 1 tomb LH IIB - LH IIIB2 2 tombs LH I - LH IIIB1 1 tomb LH IIIA1 - LH IIIB2	52 (Blegen 1937: 231-232) 53 (Sjöberg 2004: 118-119).	3	2.66 + 4.66 + 3 = **10.32**
Tiryns	**LH I - LH III** (LH IIIA – LH IIIC, well-represented; Sjöberg 2004: 111, table 8.3). 2 tombs LH IIA - LH IIIB1 1 tomb LH IIB - LH IIIC 1 tomb LH IIA - LH IIIC *1/6 = 0.66* 3 tombs LH IIIA2 - LH IIIC 1 tomb LH IIIA1 - LH IIIB1 1 tomb LH IIIA1 - LH IIIB2 1 tomb LH IIIA2 - LH IIIB2 *1/3 = 2* 1 tomb LH I - LH III A2 2 tombs LH IIA 1 tomb LH IIA - LH IIB 1 tomb LH IIA - LH IIIA1 1 tomb LH IIB - LH III A2 1 tomb LH IIIA1 3 tombs LH IIIA1 - LH IIIA2	Approx. 50. 20 published by Rudolph 1973. (Alden 1981: 233-235; Sjöberg 2004: 110-114).	0	0.66 + 2 = **2.66**
Berbati	LH IIA - LH IIIB: 1 tomb LH IIA – LH IIIB *1/6 = 0.16* 1 tomb LH IIIA1 - LH IIIB 1 tomb LH IIIA2 - LH IIIB *1/3 = 0.66* 3 tombs LH IIIA1 - LH IIIA2 2 tombs LH IIIA2	8 (Sjöberg 2004: 122)	0	0.16 + 0.66 = **0.82**
Asine	**LH IIA - LH IIIC:** 1 tomb LH IIA – LH IIIC 2 tombs LH IIB – LH IIIC *1/6 = 0.5* 1 tomb LH IIIA1 – LH IIIC 1 tomb LH IIIA2 – LH IIIC *1/3 = 0.66* 1 tomb LH IIIC 2 tombs LH IIIA1	> 50, 8 published (Sjöberg 2004: 91-106)	0	0.5 + 0.66 = **1.16**

Table 8. Chamber tombs of LH date from various cemeteries beyond Mycenae in the region of the Argive Plain and its surroundings.

†Dates refer both to the potential date of construction and dates of usage. Italic numbers correspond to reasonable numbers in right column. ^æMinimum number taken if authors differed in opinion; only published ones taken into account.

Argos	LH IIB - LH IIIC 8 tombs: LH IIB – LH IIIC 12 tombs: LH IIIA1- LH IIIC 14 tombs: LH III A2- LH IIIC 1 tomb LH IIB - LH IIIB 1 tomb LH IIB - LH IIIC *1/6 = 0.33* 1 tomb LH IIIA1 - LH IIIB 1 tomb LH IIIA1 - LH IIIC 3 tombs LH IIIA2 - LH IIIB 3 tombs LH IIIA2 - LH IIIC *1/3 = 2.66* *2 tombs LH IIIB - Sub-Myc.* *8 tombs LH IIIB* 3 tombs Sub-Myc. 1 tomb LH I 1 tomb LH IIA 1 tomb LH IIB - LH IIIA1 2 tombs LH IIIA1 4 tombs LH IIIA1 - LH IIIA2 6 tombs LH IIIA2	**34** (Sjöberg 2004: 115-118) **41** (Alden 1981: 185)	10	0.33 + 2.66 + 10 = **12.99**
Nafplio	Majority dates to the LH IIIA and LH IIIB. *1/3 of 40 (dated to LH IIIA-IIIB) = 13.33*	**Approx. 50** (Alden 1981: 295-296)	0	13.33
Dendra	**LH IIA - LH IIIC** 2 tombs LH IIB - LH IIIC *1/6 = 0.33* 2 tombs LH IIIA2 – LH IIIB *1/3 = 0.66* *3 tombs LH IIIB* 1 tomb LH IIA 1 tomb LH IIA - LH IIB 2 tombs LH IIA - LH IIIA1 1 tomb LH IIB - LH IIIA1	**12** (Sjöberg 2004: 111)	3	0.33 + 0.66 + 3 = **3.99**
Phychtia	**LH IIIB**	**1** (Béquignon 1931: 476); date estimated by Alden (1981: 163a)	1	1
Vraserka/Vreserka	**LH IIIA - LH IIIB** based on findings found in 3 unlooted tombs	**5** (Demakopoulou 1988)	0	1
Monastiraki (Priftiani)	1 tomb LH III A1-2 *1 tomb LH IIIB* 6 tombs: LH IIIA2 - LH IIIB *1/3 = 2*	**2** (Filadelfeus 1922: 35-38; Charitonidou 1952: 19-30) **6** (Alden 1981: 137)	1	1 + 2 = **3**
Schoinochori	**LH I - LH III A2** 1 tomb LH I - LH IIIA2 1 tomb LH IIB - LH IIIA2 1 tomb LH IIIA1 - LH IIIA2 2 tombs LH IIIA2	**8** in total **5 published** (Alden 1981: 289; Sjöberg 2004: 122-123)	-	-
Kokla	**LH I – LH IIIB** 5 tombs LH IIA - LH IIB 4 tombs LH IIIA – IIIB *1/3 = 1.33*	**9** (Demakopoulou 1989: 83-85; Sjöberg 2004: 123)	0	1.33
Kiveri	**7 tombs LH IIIA1 - LH III B** *1/3 = 2.33*	**7** (Simpson and Dickinson 1979: 47)	0	2.33
Panariti	1 tomb LH II - LH III B1 *1/6 = 0.16*	**2** (Piteros 1999: 151-152; Blackman 2000: 37; Sarri 2000: 101)	0	0.16
Totals		**219** **520** (including non-published and non-excavated ones, or different opinions)	18	54

Table 8 *cont.*: Chamber tombs of LH date from various cemeteries beyond Mycenae in the region of the Argive Plain and its surroundings.

long day or at most half a week).[33] VT 75 was 51 times costlier than VT 3. Since this paper represents a work in progress based on difficult-to-retrieve data, I employ Turner's TRex (27.75 m³) as representative for all tombs in the Argive Plain and its surroundings, fully realising that the range of different sizes may vary widely, irrespective of the range of variation noted at the Voudeni cemetery. The hours in a working day in Aegean prehistory vary from 5 h/day (top efficiency),[34] to 8 h/day,[35] to 10 h/day (based on Mediterranean farmers and 19th-century daily working hours).[36] Here, however, I employ an 8 h/day rate to continue with the same rate as employed in the other cost calculations brought together in **Tables 1–6**.[37]

Turner's idealised tomb benchmark places the digging of chamber tombs in a useful comparative light.[38] This idealised tomb has a total volume of 27.75 m³ and would cost 250–333 ph to excavate based on Turner's rate of 9–12 ph/m³ for digging compact earth or soft rock with the tools available in the LBA (with 4 ph/m³ for reopening and 2 ph/m³ for closing). Converting this rate to one based on the volume of compact earth (or soft stone), 0.08–0.11 m³ could be excavated per ph. In a day of 5 working hours, this rate amounts to 0.42–0.56 m³/day (or 0.83–1.1 m³/day for a 10-hour day). Turner employs 5 effective working hours per day (with longer, less effective hours possible) and 7 working days.[39] His ideal tomb digging job would take 10 tomb builders between 5 and 10 days of work, with smaller tombs taking under 5 days and larger ones taking more than 10 days of work. To compare, Claudel and Laroque give very detailed figures for digging 1 m³ of compact earth and throwing it up 1.6 m into a wheelbarrow, thus producing 5.25 m³ of loose earth (they use 10 h/day).[40] Soft rock removed by a pick would only collect 2 m³ of loose material if also thrown in a wheelbarrow. Elsam takes the depth of digging into account (e.g. well digging) and classifies a single load of earth as 27 ft³ or 1 yd³ (= 0.76 m³).[41] These figures can be applied to tomb digging. Fletcher differentiates between digging less than 6 feet deep, when earth can be thrown out manually, and digging deeper, when earth needs removal by a wheelbarrow or to be carted away. In the latter case, the cart distance is an important factor,[42] something which may also apply to tomb digging, especially in a tightly clustered cemetery. Moreover, Fletcher states that when digging greater depths, the cost increases with each yard dug. Fletcher's rates, converted to m³, for excavating clay/heavy ground or gravel/

hard ground are 1.3 ph or 2 ph/ m³, respectively.[43] These figures are higher than Turner's, but Turner deals with digging or even cutting in bedrock for the production of tombs and cannot be compared to (top) soil digging. Moreover, the 19th-century publications must have referred to iron or even steel tools, while effective tools in the LBA were in stone, bronze, or wood. Of the c. 75 chamber tombs which Turner studied at Voudeni,[44] 20 tombs were larger than his TRex, and 39 were smaller.[45] Turner's *rates* stand in contrast to Wright's *single constant* of one person digging 1 m³/day, although the length of this day is not specified in terms of hours.[46] Fitzsimons follows Wright's constant. Moreover, Fitzsimons did not calculate the labour cost for the stonework of the tholoi but only calculated the digging effort for shaft graves, chamber tombs, and tholoi based on the volume of soil.[47]

Turner's index provides a very useful yardstick against which other tombs can be compared and placed into a social ranking based on size, complexity, and therefore status. Moreover, with his study of Menidi's tholos, he also offers a reassessment of the effort needed for digging versus stone construction, the latter being far more labour-intensive. Papers prior to this, therefore, underestimate the work required for tholoi.[48]

If the total population of the Argive Plain was 20,000[49] and the average life-span was 40,[50] assuming a reasonably stable population, the number of people who died and were buried can be estimated as c. 50,000 during the century of LH IIIB. Graves of small children are rare, so child mortality is not taken into account here. Of the 50,000 people, we can estimate that 5–10 % belonged to the elite.[51] Therefore, it is reasonable that 2500 to 5000 elite members (male and female adults) of the region could have been buried in chamber tombs in LH IIIB, whether newly dug or reused. In the region of Mycenae, 164 chamber tombs (**Table 7**) have been discovered and plausibly dated to all of the LH sub-periods (23 additional tombs are undated, and another 31 were not excavated). In the rest of the Argolid, 219 chamber tombs have been excavated and published (another 83 are not published, see **Table 8**). Therefore, 383 of the estimated original 2500–5000 chamber tombs have been published, and a total of 520 are known. **Tables 7 and 8** show that of these 383 chamber tombs, at least 30 were most probably constructed in LH IIIB, and 91 were in use (some possibly

[33] Turner 2020: 87.
[34] Based on Erasmus 1965.
[35] E.g. Loader 1998; Devolder 2013: 50.
[36] Cf. Pegoretti 1863; DeLaine 1997; Barker and Russell 2009: 85; Brysbaert 2013, 2015; Pakkanen 2013.
[37] For details, see Brysbaert 2020.
[38] Turner 2020.
[39] Turner 2020: 65–66.
[40] Claudel and Laroque 1870: 237.
[41] Elsam 1825: 122–124.
[42] Fletcher 1888: 9–11.

[43] Fletcher 1888: 221.
[44] See Kolonas 2009: 8.
[45] Turner 2020: table 4.3.
[46] Wright 1987: 174.
[47] Fitzsimons 2011: 80.
[48] This is with the exception, perhaps, of Cavanagh and Mee (1999) and Harper (2016).
[49] See Timonen and Brysbaert 2021.
[50] Gallant 1991: 18–20.
[51] For Classical Athens, see Ober 1989: 127–129. For New Kingdom Egypt, see Baines 1996: 343, n. 11. For Classical Maya, see Chase and Chase 1992: 15.

Volume	Digging afresh: 9-12 ph/m³	Reopening: 4 ph/m³	Closing: 2 ph/m³
1 TRex = 27.75 m³	250-333	111	55.5
Freshly dug = 824	206,000-274,392		45,732
Reused = 1676		186,036	93,018
TOTAL Effort	Min = 530,786 ph or 5 labourers @ 8 h/day 13,270 working days for 5 people during one century 663.5 pd for 100 people 95 days for 700 (140 x 5) people 1.8 py for 100 people		
	Max = 599,178 ph or 5 labourers @ 8 h/day 14,979 working days for 5 people during one century 748.95 pd for 100 people 94 days for 800 (160 x 5) people 2 py for 100 people.		

Table 9. Efforts to dig afresh, reuse, and close chamber tombs during the LH IIIB period in the Argive Plain and its surroundings, based on an elite population of 5% or 2,500 tombs. If 10% of the elites were buried, numbers need to be doubled. Rates based on Turner 2020.

also constructed) in in this period. Ninety-one tombs out of a total of 2500 tombs forms a sample of c. 4%, so a substantial number of tombs has been studied. Extrapolating this to the estimated 2500 or 5000 tombs, 824 out of 2500 tombs would have been constructed in LH IIIB (= 30/91 × 2500; or 1648 out of 5000), and 1676 of 2500 (= 61/91 × 2500; or 3352 of 5000) would have reused an earlier tomb. When spread over the entire century, annually 8.2–16.5 tombs would have been freshly constructed and 16.8–33.5 would have been reused.

Taking the TRex median volume size of a chamber tomb as the average size for all of the assumed 2500 chamber tombs in the Argolid, we have a total volume of 22,866 m³ for the 824 freshly constructed tombs and 1676 reused tombs. Based on Turner's more nuanced figures for fresh digging, for reopening, and for closing, I calculate that all 2500 tombs could be dug, reopened, and closed in a minimum of 530,786 or a maximum of 599,178 ph (**Table 9**).

To compare this effort with the labour crews used in **Tables 1–4**,[52] 100 labourers would work a minimum of 663.5 and a maximum of 749 days, at 8 h/day, over the course of a century to dig, reopen, and close all 2500 tombs. 100 people could work on chamber tombs an average of 7–8 days/year for 100 years, or 140–160 teams of five people could have been involved in digging tombs for c. 94–95 days per year. From these figures, which should be doubled for 5000 tombs, it is clear that the effort of digging chamber tombs in LH IIIB in

relation to the population size was of a low order when compared to monumental stone construction and agricultural activities (see **Tables 1–4**). Again, it should be stressed that this only takes into account a percentage of the tombs. Pits, cists, and other grave types were not included, and the effort for the beautification of chamber tombs was not calculated as the data is too incomplete.[53]

Transport and infrastructure provision

Archaeological remains illustrate that mobility was practiced daily and extensively in prehistoric times. The Pylian Linear B tablets also attest to named individuals who were active in many different areas of work that were each located in different regions of the Pylian kingdom.[54] They thus required a road network. Roads were also linked to long-distance exchange networks of crafted goods such as finished metal items and textiles (e.g the export of textiles from Mycenae to Thebes[55] and dispersal of raw materials such as bronze and wool). Both Fitzsimons and Wright have argued that transport costs can be ignored in discussions of architecture, because most materials were extracted from nearby locations.[56] Rubble and simple field stones could have indeed been collected nearby (which nevertheless would have taken effort), but organised transport was essential when blocks with a mass of several hundred kilos or more had to be moved.[57] Equally, the topography of Greece

[52] See also Brysbaert 2020.
[53] However, see the very helpful update by Galanakis 2017–18.
[54] Nakassis 2013: 47; 2015: 587, 589.
[55] See Aura Jorro 1985: 353–354.
[56] Fitzsimons 2007: 110–112; Wright 1978: 229, n. 329.
[57] Brysbaert 2015.

Highway	Start – End	Materials	Technique(s)
M1	Mycenae-Tenea (Corinth)	Earth/bedrock (c. 1 km), stone terraces, bridges, culverts	Cut-and-terrace, Earth/bedrock removal
M2	Mycenae-Zygouries-Kleonai (Corinth)	Earth/bedrock	Earth/bedrock removal, Earth packing
M3	Mycenae-Corinth	Earth/bedrock, stone bridges	Earth/bedrock removal
M4	Mycenae-Tiryns	Earth/bedrock, stone bridges	Cut-and-terrace, Earth/bedrock removal, Earth packing
m5	M1-Tiryns	Earth	Earth trampling
M6	Aidonia-Heraion	Earth	Earth/bedrock removal, Earth packing
M7	Mycenae-Argos	Earth, bedrock (towards Larissa)	Earth/bedrock removal, Earth packing
M8	Mycenae-Fychtia	Earth	Earth packing

Table 10. Eight Mycenaean highways with construction materials, techniques, and the start and end of each road.

requires taking slopes into account as part of any movement. Different means of transport were possible, and they were carried out by people with or without the additional help of draught animals. Cavanagh and Mee suggest the use of wagons, possibly specially built by the palace to facilitate such transport.[58] This hypothesis is certainly plausible since more recent work has shown that the owners of most well-fed oxen were likely palace-based, and in addition there were oxen owned by the *dāmos*.[59] For large and awkward loads, such as Cyclopean blocks, wagons with four wheels would have been better able to carry heavier loads than two-wheeled carts. In addition, sledges would have been necessary for the heaviest items. The size and mass of the building materials (mud-bricks versus multi-tonne blocks), the distance to cross, the accessibility to the required type of draught animals, and significant slope gradients would have largely determined whether draught or pack animals came into the equation.

However, perhaps the most understudied aspect of transport in the Aegean LBA is the infrastructure itself. Eight Mycenaean highways have been recognised by various scholars for areas in and near Mycenae, all connecting the major sites in the Argolid.[60] Most of these roads were constructed in the LH IIIB period, although several may have had predecessors along the same trajectories in earlier periods when other roads and paths were also in use.[61] Because of the length of these highways, their construction techniques, their width, and their start and end points, it is certain that they were constructed under the order and supervision of the palatial authorities who had direct or indirect access to the needed labour forces. All together these highways would have covered a minimum length of c. 175–180 km while several highways also had stretches of overlap between them.[62]

For this paper, 175 km is used for all highways together. Many of the highways start at Mycenae and arrive at important sites with which the centre had close contact for various reasons (**Table 10**).[63] Several of these highways seem to have had a similar average *road* slope of 2.8 degrees (e.g. M1, M4, M6),[64] a very convenient slope for transport with heavy goods vehicles (HGV), which is one of the main reasons for their existence. The respective *hill* slopes into which most of these road stretches have been cut vary widely. These hill slopes are especially important in calculating the labour costs to create wide enough road surfaces to be useful for carts and wagons to pass. Moreover, the steeper the slope, the more stones that were needed to construct the terrace that kept the road surface in place, and consequently the higher the cost of construction. **Table 10** provides the start and end point of each road, its construction materials, and the techniques of construction.

For the majority of the highways so far studied, hill slopes seem to fall between 8% (e.g. parts of M4) and 25% (parts of M1), although some may turn out to be lower or higher when all data are collected. M7 and M8 ran

[58] Cavanagh and Mee 1999.
[59] Brysbaert 2013, with references.
[60] See especially, Lavery 1990, 1995; Jansen 1997, 2002; Brysbaert 2021; Brysbaert *et al.* 2020.
[61] Brysbaert *et al.* 2020.
[62] Brysbaert *et al.* 2020: 80–81.
[63] See Jansen 2002; Brysbaert *et al.* 2020.
[64] Brysbaert 2022.

on flat land apart from the climb to the Larissa Hill at Argos (M7). Several other stretches on other highways were almost flat: e.g. M4: Argive Heraion to Tiryns (12 km); M5: a length of *c*. 55 km in the Berbati valley; and several stretches along M1, M3, and M6. The cost of the construction of each highway was calculated based on varying hill slopes (flat stretches, and 8-degree and 25-degree stretches), the total length of all highways together, and the materials and techniques employed in their construction.

The tasks and the rates for road construction of all indicated M-highways are summarised in **Table 11** (for consistency, the labour rates are the same as in the following section). The two digging figures depend on the tools that would have been used: bronze versus non-metal digging tools.[65] These two rates indicate that both tool types, metal and non-metal,[66] could have been used for digging the road surface in the hill flank. Moreover, the difference between these two figures may not be that great when compared with the use of iron tools.[67] Specific experiments are thus needed to study the variation between the different metal types used for tools. Due to erosion, new terracing, and changes in the exact route of the road, most highways currently do not feature clearly recognisable stone terraces, which would have been needed to keep the soil in place, especially when heavily saturated by rain. Hill slopes of more than 8 degrees would have required terracing, so this has been calculated for road stretches cut into these slopes even if these are currently missing. More work is ongoing on the stone extraction for roads with bridges, culverts, and extensive terraces (e.g. M1).

The figures obtained show that road construction seems to have taken almost three times as much work as tomb digging. Constructing all highways would have taken 5 or 5.4 py for 100 people working 365 days each year. This is not that much less effort than the labour required for the citadels of Tiryns (6 py) and Mycenae (7.5 py).

Terrace construction

The final activity involving excavation of soil and bedrock brings us to the agricultural sphere. We cannot be sure how much terracing was carried out in the region around Mycenae and beyond (Nemea, Limnes, Stefani) in LH IIIB. Terracing is useful for the creation of more space for crop cultivation and to improve moisture retention and regulation of the soil, providing better root penetration for crops on slopes. It also avoids soil eroding downslope with rainfall or other erosive factors,[68] and it allows

manure to enrich these sloping plots of land.[69] Fallu's discussion of terracing in and near Mycenae is based on data from the Mycenaean Atlas Survey. He states that 48 terraces near and around Mycenae should be dated to LH III,[70] and another 278 were also used in Mycenaean times.

What is missing, however, is the surface area of these terraces in order to understand exactly how much these expand the current estimates of agricultural land in the Argive Plain, but Timonen is useful here. She has suggested, preliminarily, that a total of *c*. 52,700 ha of slopes in the Argive Plain region could have been terraced, about 3430 ha of which are near settlements. Terraced zones for agricultural production near a settlement resulted in 172 ha or 857 ha if 5% or 25% were in use, respectively. If all potential slopes were terraced, 5% in use for agricultural land would raise the total to *c*. 2640 ha, and if 25% was used for agricultural land the total would increase to 13,200 ha.[71]

For Kalamianos-Korphos, Kvapil notes a total of 150,000 m² (15 ha) of terraced surface or 154 terraces.[72] She calculated the labour cost of a sample of 20,000 m² (i.e. 2 ha) and found it difficult to date these closer than to the LH IIIB period; however, this is not a problem for the current paper. Kvapil employed labour rates from Erasmus, Cavanagh and Mee, and Burford and included the following tasks:[73] site clearing, stone quarrying and gathering, transport of stone in baskets, hammer dressing/shaping, riser construction,[74] placing of packing, and placing of tread fill.[75] In all her calculations, she adopted Erasmus's five-hour days. Kvapil estimated that it would have taken about 70,000 working hours to terrace 2 ha in the region of Kalamianos-Korphos, irrespective of how much of this would have been cultivated.[76] She equated this figure to the labour effort needed to construct the Treasury of Atreus in Mycenae.[77] A series of problems with these calculations were noted, however. First, Cavanagh and Mee's figure of *c*. 20,000 man-days does not specify the working hours in a day.[78] By equating the work of the 20,000 m² of terraces (*c*. 70,000 work *hours*) with *c*. 20,000 man-*days*, Kvapil seems to suggest that Cavanagh and Mee employed a rate of 3.5 working hours per day, which is highly unlikely;[79] they more likely employed 5- (after Erasmus 1965), 8-, or 10-hour working days. Second, Kvapil's table 2 reversed the labour rates from hr/m³ to m³/hr, thus arriving at

---

[65] After Turner 2018.
[66] After Turner 2018.
[67] Cf. Halstead 2014, who makes this distinction in relation to ploughing.
[68] Moody and Grove 1990: 183.
[69] E.g. Kvapil 2012: 240.
[70] Fallu 2017: 115–120.
[71] Timonen in prep.
[72] Kvapil 2012: 183, 220, appendix 1.
[73] Kvapil 2012: 199–200. See Erasmus 1965, Cavanagh and Mee 1999, and Burford 1969.
[74] Riser is the term for a terrace wall.
[75] Tread fill is the term for the terrace earth fill.
[76] Kvapil 2012: 200, table 2.
[77] Cf. Cavanagh and Mee 1999; contra Harper 2016.
[78] Cavanagh and Mee 1999: 100.
[79] Kvapil 2012: 201–202.

Task	Labour rate	Volume			Labour effort (ph)		
	(h/ m³)	Flat (m³)	8° (m³)	25° (m³)	Flat	8°	25°
Site clearing*	2.08	43,750 × 4.4 × 0.2 = 38,500	87,500 × 4.4 × 0.2 = 77,000	43,750 × 4.4 × 0.2 = 38,500	80,080	160,160	80,080
Digging soil = 50%	1.8 – 4.2 (Turner 2018)	-	87,500 × (2.2 × 0.31)/2 × 50% = 14,918.7	43,750 × (2.2 × 1.025)/2 × 50% = 24,664	-	26,854 – 62,658	44,395 – 103,589
Digging riser foundations = 50%			87,500 × 0.3 × 0.3 × 50% = 3,937.5	43,750 × 0.3 × 0.3 × 50% = 1,969		7,087.5 – 16,537.5	3,544 – 8,270
Stone quarrying = 50%	10 (Brysbaert 2015)	-	87,500 x (2.2 × 0.31)/2 × 50% =14,918.7	43,750 × (2.2 × 1.025)/2 × 50% = 24,664	-	149,187	246,640
Digging riser foundations = 50%			87,500 × 0.3 × 0.3 × 50% = 3,937.5	43,750 × 0.3 × 0.3 × 50% = 1,969		39,375	19,690
Soil-stone transport in basket	0.75 + 0.00178h/ trip✿	-	87,500 x (2.2 × 0.31)/2 =29,837 # trips: 29,837/0.03 = 994,580	43,750 × (2.2 × 1.025)/2 = 49,328 # trips: 49,328/0.03 = 1,644,267	-	22,378 + 1,770 h	36,996 + 2,927 h
Riser construction**	6.3 (Hurst 1902: 381; Pakkanen: 2021)	-	87,500 × 0.3 × 0.6 = 15,750	43,750 × 0.3 × 0.6 = 7,875	-	99,225	49,612.5
Packing placement	0.367h/ m³ (Hurst 1902: 377)	-	87,500 × 0.3 × 0.3 = 7,875	43,750 × 0.3 × 0.3 = 3,937.5	-	2,890	1,445
Tread fill placement***	2 h/ m³ (Turner 2020) ✿✿	43,750 × 4.4 × 0.2 = 38,500	83,212.4	76,015.5	77,000	166,425	152,031
SUB-TOTALS					157,080	675,351.5 or 720,605.5	637,360.5 or 701,280.5
TOTALS					1,469,792 or 1,578,966		
	@ 8h/day = **183,724 or 197,370.75 pd**						
	100 people together @ 365 days = **5 py or 5.4 py**						

Table 11. Calculations of the road construction process over a length of 175 km, following adapted rates from Kvapil (2012) for terrace construction (Brysbaert 2022, table 12).

* site clearing to a depth of 0.2 m; ✿ extrapolated from DeLaine (1997: 268, carrying over rate and basket rate of 0.03 m3) and Pegoretti 1863: 156 (0.000444 hr/trip) for 4 m (instead of 105 m in DeLaine 1997: 268); ✿✿Turner 2020's figure for closing/infilling tombs; **terrace construction (0.3 m x 0.3 m) in limestone (@2.7 tonnes/m3); *** tread fill = site clearing + (plus) stone quarrying + rubble gathering – (minus) riser construction – packing placement.

Task	Labour rate		Volume of material (m³)		Person hours	
	Kvapil (m³/h)	Author (h/ m³)	Kvapil	Author	Kvapil	Author
Site clearing	0.48	2.08	10,000*	8,000*	4,880.00	16,640.00
Stone quarrying	0.09	10 (Brysbaert 2015)	1,225	306ᵃᵉ	110.25	3,060.00
Rubble gathering	0.30	2 (Abrams 1994)	306	1,225ᵃᵉ	91.80	2,450.00
Rubble/stone transport/basket	0.60	0.75 + 0.00888h/ trip♣	306	1,225 + 306	183.60	1,148.25 + 453.17
Hammer dressing/ shaping	0.30	-	1,225	-	367.50	-
Riser construction	0.09	6.3 (Hurst 1902: 381; Pakkanen: 2021)	1,225	1,225 +306 = 1,531♣♣♣	110.25	9,645.30
Packing placement	1	0.367h/ m³ (Hurst 1902: 377)	1,225	1,225	1225.00	449.57
Tread fill placement	7.10	2 h/ m³ (Turner 2020) ♣♣	8,775**	6,775***	62,302.50	13,550.00
TOTAL			24,287		69,190.90	**47,396**

Table 12. Task assessment and rates for Kalamianos-Korphos employed by Kvapil (2012) versus Brysbaert.

*based on 20,000 m² terraced surface and cleared to an average depth of 0.5 m (Kvapil) and 0.4 m (Brysbaert); **tread fill = cleared site minus volume of terrace risers and packing placement (Kvapil 2012: table 2, n. 445–446); *** tread fill = site clearing +(plus) stone quarrying + rubble gathering – (minus) riser construction – packing placement (Brysbaert); ᵃᵉboth figures reversed by Brysbaert in relation to Kvapil. ♣ Extrapolated from DeLaine (1997: 268, carrying over rate and basket rate of 0.03 m³) and Pegoretti 1863: 156 (0.000444 hr/trip) for 20 m (instead of 105 m in DeLaine 1997: 268). ♣♣Turner 2020's figure for closing/infilling tombs; ♣♣♣ this volume would accommodate a terrace wall of H: 1.28 m × W: 0.60 m × total L: 2000 m. This includes wall foundations.

incorrect person hours or 'work hours' in her table's right column because she multiplied instead of divided. This is amended here by reversing these rates (**Table 12**, column 2 grey field: Author [h/m³]) and double-checking how these reversed rates compare to existing task rates. Third, several tasks and volumes outlined by Kvapil have been adapted to a more realistic set of tasks. I employed again the 8 h/day rate for the Argive Plain terracing calculations (in **Table 13**). Then, I calculated the labour effort for both 5% and 25% of the slopes for those near the settlements and for all those possible in the Argive Plain.

Table 13 (grey cells) indicates that if people in the Argive Plain terraced only a 5% sloping terrain near their settlements, 100 people working 365 days would take c. 14 years for these terraces. If they did the same for 25%, it would take c. 70 years. If they terraced 5% of any sloping ground in the region (25% seems too high), 100 people would work for 214 years, 200 people would work for 107 years, or 400 people would work for 53.5 years, all year round without a day break. These calculations, if the terracing figures are reliable, suggest either that more people than the hypothetical 100 were involved in terracing, which is likely considering that terracing was a household matter, or that terracing was done to a lesser extent than 5% of all possible sloping grounds. It is also possible that only those close to settlements were terraced. The only factor not taken into account here is the differences in the degree (see previous section) between the potentially different slopes that were terraced. This is beyond the scope of the current paper but is taken into account in ongoing calculations.

Overheads and incidental costs

Overhead, incidental, indirect, or fixed costs are those costs spent, by a business, on aspects other than those

Terraced land	Total labour cost (ph)	Labour (pd @ 8 hrs)	100 people's labour (pd)	100 people (py @ 365 days)
2 ha*	47,396	-	-	-
1 ha	23,698	2,962.25	29.62	0.081
13,200 ha	312,813,600	39,101,700	391,017	1,071.3
2,640 ha	62,562,720	7,820,340	78,203.4	214.25
860 ha	20,380,280	2,547,535	25,475.35	69.8
172 ha	4,076,056	509,507	5,095	13.95

Table 13. Overview of cost calculations for terracing in relation to size of terraced land, starting with the 2 ha sample (based on Kvapil 2012) and the **cost of 1 ha.**

*Based on results by Brysbaert in Table 12; Pink: Timonen's 25% and 5 % of all possible terraced slopes; Green: Timonen's 25% and 5% of terraced slopes near the settlements (all calculations by Brysbaert).

involved in the products they make.[80] These costs are fixed since, according to given contracts, they are to be covered whether there is production output or not. In the building industry, these can be, among many others, the costs of tool making and repair, equipment and installations needed for extracting and transporting materials, accommodation and food provisions for workers and animals, replacement of workers and animals due to illness or accidents, delay of supply delivery, bottlenecks of materials on site, taxes, supervision costs, indirect labour, and depreciation of tools and equipment.[81] In contrast, the variable costs are related to production output, and these refer to the materials and the labour needed to execute the job.[82] For example, the higher the pottery demand, the more clay and aggregate that is required, and thus the more labour and time. Several of the above-mentioned costs also existed in the past, but in prehistoric contexts we cannot rely on recorded cost figures.

The Linear B tablets, however, do provide useful insights. For example, workers with specific responsibilities noted in certain tablets (e.g. tablet PY Fn 7, see below) received more grain remuneration, perhaps because certain forms of supervision were understood as skilled work, or because certain better-paid individuals were in charge of hiring others with this grain resource. The tablets, though, do not give prices for tools, installations, or materials needed in construction. Such costings, thus, need to be carried out on the basis of combined sources: later sources dealing with the same region (Archaic and Classical Greece), ethnographic accounts and cross-cultural studies dealing with similar projects, and the knowledge that humans and animals have certain standard capacities in energy expenditure. It is of course important to be conscious of the differences when using values from later or different contexts in the prehistoric realm.

The section below describes and discusses, where possible, the indirect or fixed costs related to the building activities undertaken in the 13th century BC in the Argive Plain. These are subsequently contextualised in relation to other known variable costs for construction, other crafts, and agriculture.

Tools

Of great interest is the use of tools employed in construction and other labour processes. These tools not only helped shape materials but also provided additional job opportunities for those making them. In addition to stone and metal tools, strong ropes, woven baskets, buckets for water, and wooden aids (e.g. scaffolding, levers, mallets, wagons/carts, sledges, and rollers) were also in use. Woven materials are also known from negative imprints in unfired ceramics and as carved decoration on stone, such as a vase from Knossos.[83]

The cost of tools depends on their raw materials (type and origin), their production techniques, and the time it takes to produce them. Moreover, the production lines and who controls them are important to establish as well. No prehistoric texts help us with the above-mentioned aspects, but costing information can be gathered indirectly: archaeologically, textually, and ethnographically.

Stone tools

A number of scholars discuss tools used in construction at Tiryns (and beyond),[84] including the pendulum

---

[80]   https://dictionary.cambridge.org/dictionary/english/indirect-cost
[81]   After Barker and Russell 2009: 90, with references; Barker and Russell, this volume; Brysbaert 2015: 102; 2013: 85–86.
[82]   https://www.inc.com/encyclopedia/costs.html

[83]   See Evely 2000 and Evely 1993: pl. 46, respectively.
[84]   Cf. Schliemann and Dörpfeld 1886: 194–195, 300–303; Müller 1930: 183–184; Schwandner 1991: 219–223; Küpper 1996: 7, 31–52.

saw[85] and stone tools, such as granite hammers and diorite axes. Loader refers to the use of stone chisels, (wooden) wedges and mallets, hammers, axes, and picks to extract stone building materials and dress them.[86] Walberg mentions hard stone types used for hand stones (limestone, basalt, chert, and andesite).[87] According to Boleti, these could have been used for dressing limestone and conglomerate stone blocks in tholoi and citadels.[88] She stresses, however, the lack of contextual evidence for this assertion. Moreover, she emphasises the need to study toolmarks and to consider the original tool shape (edged versus rounded) rather than the fully-used or exhausted stone tools. Percussion toolmarks in architectural production are known from Akrotiri.[89] The use of percussive stone tools in Mycenaean architecture is also mentioned in several publications on the basis of toolmarks.[90]

Grossman and Küpper both refer to the use of diorite or basalt stone pounders to shape stone.[91] This seems based on their knowledge of such stone tools used in and accessible from Egypt and by Schliemann's mention of these for Tiryns and Mycenae.[92] Morero states that Aegean diorite stone vases were Egyptian in origin (in stone type and in manufacturing techniques) and were, therefore, imported.[93] Grossmann refers to Marinatos and Orlandos depicting a similar stone tool (associated with metalworking rather than stone dressing),[94] but nowhere is the type of stone nor a detailed description of the stone given in those two publications. Diorite is present in the Aegean but mainly in the north, for example on Samothrace.[95] Diorite-porphyry comes from the region of Sparta, but this stone, known as *Lapis Lacedaimonius*, was only employed to shape stone vessels.[96] Quartz-diorite seems to be present in the region of central and eastern Macedonia,[97] and granodiorite near Lavrio (Attica).[98]

However, there is no evidence that the sources for any of these stones were known, exploited, or transported for use elsewhere. In contrast, andesite, similar in appearance, strength, and many other properties as

diorite[99] and extensively used for saddle querns,[100] was extracted in Methana, Poros, and Aigina. Andesite ground stone tools, and especially grinding stones, are known from Tiryns,[101] Midea,[102] and likely also from Mycenae. According to Newhard,[103] it is possible that these andesite items were brought to Mycenae along the same routes as the Saronic Gulf pottery, which was present on the same sites,[104] and the chert tools whose source Newhard identified near Epidauros at Agia Eleni/Tracheia,[105] about 39 km on foot from Tiryns. Whether the stone pounders were perhaps andesite rather than diorite or diorite was used, both stones would have been imported to the Argolid, either *c.* 50-80 km from the Saronic Gulf[106] or much further away from Egypt.[107]

If the stone pounders were indeed diorite, how did this stone make it to the Aegean and how did the *knowledge of using it as a pounder* make it there too? This is relevant because Egyptian architecture in the Bronze Age does not resemble Aegean Cyclopean-style stonework known from fortification walls, terraces, Mycenaean highways, and bridges. Bevan and Bloxam did not discuss the diorite pounder from Tiryns in their discussion of stonemasons and craft mobility.[108] Boleti asserts that in Egypt hard stones were used as percussive stones for quarrying and dressing other stones.[109] They include dolerite, granite, basalt, and chert. These were substantially more robust in hardness and durability than metal tools, especially bronze, but obtained the same result. Boleti also indicates,[110] following Bessac,[111] that care needs to be taken in distinguishing between the marks made by stone picks and those made by metal pick since similarities between them have led to the misidentification of some of these toolmarks, especially on architectural stonework. Experiments indicate that grooves in quarrying zones can just as easily be produced by sharp-edged strong stone tools as by metal ones. Bessac also believes that the choice of stone instead of metal tools would make a lot of sense for hard stoneworking since stone would be far more durable than easily worn-out metal tools.[112]

Bevan and Bloxam refer to the use of diorite, granodiorite, gabbro, and Chephren gneiss stone tools in the Fayoum quarries during the Pharaonic period, some of which were transported to the site from as far

[85] See also Blackwell 2018a.
[86] Loader 1998: 47–48.
[87] Walberg 2007.
[88] Boleti 2020. See also Wace 1949: 34, 36, 44, 135; Mylonas 1966: 16–18; Wright 1978: 159, 189, 202, 217, 258; Loader 1998: 47.
[89] Palyvou 2005: 113, 130.
[90] E.g. Müller 1930: 178; Mylonas 1966: 16-18; Iakovidis 2006: 232, 239; Fitzsimons 2007: 90.
[91] Grossman 1967: 99; Küpper 1996: 32.
[92] Schliemann 1886: 194–195.
[93] Morero 2015: 140–141, 143–144.
[94] Grossmann 1980: 496, referencing Marinatos 1970: 44, fig. 37.1; Orlandos 1971.
[95] E.g. Hatzipanagiotou and Tsikouras 2001. For Delos: Pe-Piper *et al.* 2002.
[96] See Brysbaert and Vetters 2010; http://chc.sbg.ac.at/sri/thesaurus/node.php?id=90
[97] Tsoupas and Economou-Eliopoulos 2008; Yassoglou *et al.* 2017.
[98] See www.mindat.org

[99] Higgins and Higgins 1996: 217–218.
[100] E.g. Runnels 1994.
[101] Brysbaert and Vetters 2013: 195–196, TN 19.
[102] Wallberg 2007.
[103] Newhard 2003: 111, 121, 189.
[104] E.g. Lindblom 2001.
[105] This is in agreement with Higgins and Higgins 1996: 50.
[106] Brysbaert and Vetters 2013: 201.
[107] E.g. Bevan and Bloxam 2016: 83 on diorite from Aswan.
[108] Bevan and Bloxam 2016.
[109] Boleti 2020, with references.
[110] Boleti 2020.
[111] Bessac 1987: 21–23
[112] Bessac 1987.

away as 800 km.[113] This suggests that the stones were brought by their specialist users who traveled from project to project. If a diorite pounder traveled from Aswan to Tiryns, this would have taken a Roman sailing ship 6.1 days (1206 km overseas: Isthmia-Alexandria, the nearest harbour to the LBA Marsa Matruh harbour) and an additional 287 km overland (58 hours or *c.* 7 days), totalling about two weeks. This is based on the Roman World Orbis geospatial Network Sea Route on which the nearest harbour to Tiryns is Isthmia.[114] If done overland (1240 km: Aswan-Marsa Matruh), it would have taken 250 hours, or a full month at 8 h/day (based on google maps).

Bevan and Bloxam also emphasise the importance of the learning process and knowledge transfer between stoneworkers[115] as the most important catalysts for long-term traditions and potential changes between groups over larger distances. In discussing Hittite stone tools, Boleti does not indicate the type of stone or whether there was a transfer of stone tools from the Hittite region to the Aegean.[116] Bevan and Bloxam suggest that a limited transfer of techniques and know-how matched with an equally narrow site spread (e.g. only at Tiryns) may refer to mobile craftspeople.[117] In this scenario, stone tools may have traveled with them, as suggested for Egypt.

Boleti suggests that stone tools were used and reused until exhausted, and that they were potentially not always used for the same jobs, but used *across* crafts.[118] This may account, at least in part, for the dearth of evidence for stone tools in Mycenaean building or quarrying contexts but their presence in domestic and craft contexts.[119] Furthermore, Boleti demonstrates the use of Naxian emery and drilling on Crete, and the subsequent transfer of this material and technique to the Mycenaean mainland sites of Mycenae and possibly Tiryns.[120] The distance from Naxos to the Mycenaean port of Tiryns can be estimated at *c.* 260 km overseas.[121] The journey would have taken *c.* 1.5 days in total. **Table 14** shows the possible origins of production for different tool types. This highlights the complexity of the issue and the difficulty in costing these different types of tools.

Production Origin	Item
Elsewhere, imported	Diorite stone pounder, Worked fragment of diorite porphyry (TN 184)
Local, with imported materials, foreign or local style	Ivory points, spatulas, Metal tools (copper and tin imports; TN 83)
Local, with local materials, imitating foreign objects	Stone vases imitating Egyptian ones but adapted to local taste
Local, with imported/ local materials, by local/ forejign artisans, knowing foreign skills	-
Local, with local materials, by local artisans, with skills possibly learned elsewhere	Worked *Lapis Lacedaimonius* stone (TN 183; Sparta, *c.* 100 km), Andesite grinding stones (Aigina, Poros, Methana, *c.* 50-80 km)
Local, with local materials, by local artisans, with skills learned locally	Bone pin (e.g. TN 84, TN 193), Obsidian tools (Melos, *c.* 100 km; TN 112, TN 111, TN 107, TN 98, TN 105), Lead clamps (TN 59, TN 61, TN 62, TN 68)

Table 14. Production origin categories against tool types known from Tiryns (TN data from Brysbaert and Vetters 2010: 41–43: tables 1–3 and Brysbaert and Vetters 2013: 203, table 8).

Metal tools and their distribution

In discussing the relationship between stone and metal tools, Evely and Loader are both convinced that stone tools in the Aegean BA were never replaced by metal counterparts due to the ease of access to stone resources.[122] Both copper and tin had to be imported which implied a greater cost for making, resharpening, repairing, and replacing. Boleti suggests the same use of stone tools based on the use-wear traces on architectural stone of fortification walls.[123] These do not confirm the use of metal tools. Instead, some evidence for metal tool shows that they were used alongside stone tools but perhaps for different tasks, ranging from quarrying and rough shaping of stones (stone tools) to finer dressing and finishing stones (metal tools).

Linear B tablets provide information on only two tools likely used in the building industry: the saw[124] and potentially tongs or pincers used to hold and

---

[113] Bevan and Bloxam 2016: 83.
[114] http://orbis.stanford.edu/
[115] Bevan and Bloxam 2016: 70.
[116] Boleti 2020.
[117] Bevan and Bloxam 2016. See also Brysbaert and Vetters 2010; Brysbaert 2015: 84; 2018 on communities of practice.
[118] Boleti 2020.
[119] See Brysbaert and Vetters 2010, 2013, 2015.
[120] Boleti 2017, 2020.
[121] http://orbis.stanford.edu/: Naxos to Isthmia covers roughly the same distance overseas as it would from Naxos to Tiryns, see above.

[122] Evely 1993: 116; Loader 1998.
[123] Boleti 2020.
[124] Palaima 2015: 630–631.

move building stones.[125] The saw is also attested archaeologically, both as a tool and in traces (see below),[126] but bronze tongs/pincers are more problematic because these would be limited in the amount of weight they could lift/move before they would bend or break. While they are known from the Classical and Hellenistic periods in combination with pullies or lifting devices,[127] it is unclear if these were used in Mycenaean times and exactly how much they could lift.[128] Shaw reported seeing no protrusions or holes in stones to attach ropes for lifting in Minoan architecture.[129] Evely's suggestion of a sling combined with a lifting device, known from a well, and large bronze hooks could have been used but not for multi-tonne blocks, which would have required ropes and (wooden) levers.[130]

In the Hittite context, both the pendulum saw and the drill were used in similar ways to those noted at Tiryns.[131] The working of conglomerate, rather than limestone, required the use of both stone and metal tools (see below).[132] The concurrent use of stone and metal tools in the building industry is thus similar to the continuous use of flint, chert, and obsidian tools alongside metal ones throughout the BA in many crafts.[133] Blackwell observed a sharp increase in the quantity and variety of metal tool use from the MH to the LH periods.[134] Saws, axe-adzes, drills, socketed chisels, and axes make their entry in the LBA. Most can be associated with masonry/carpentry and are found in urban centres such as Mycenae, Tiryns, Athens, Orchomenos, and Midea.[135] Blackwell noted a strong correlation between the evolution of metal tools and masonry/carpentry, and this expressed itself in the presence of metal tools, especially for cutting stone and wood, increasing throughout the 2nd millennium BC.[136] Shaped conglomerate blocks were employed in the tholos tombs of Atreus and Klytemnestra, in various parts of several other Mycenaean tholoi, and in specific parts of fortification walls and gates. There is clear evidence of the use of chisels, saws, and possibly rasps to work both conglomerate and poros limestone into shaped blocks.

When it comes to costing the tools, Ugan *et al.* have shown that the length of the time of use of better technologies/ tools plays a crucial role in the cost benefit that can be obtained from them.[137] If the cost investment for a refined tool is higher that than of a crude tool, it will only bring profit if it is used for a longer period of time than the crude one. In this context, experiments are needed to find the difference in lifespan between metal and stone tools in both quarrying and stone dressing. Such experiments should include the time needed for resharpening both stone and metal tips or cutting/ striking edges. The lifespan of the tools, the availability of stone and metal, and the skills of the builders and carpenters were important. It is, therefore, possible to hypothesize that metal tools are potentially better in certain jobs, but blunt very fast in relation to the time they can be used versus the stone ones. The metal tools were thus not use-effective in the long run for specific jobs. This was already pointed out for the combined use of the metal-bladed pendulum saw with an abrasive.[138]

Blackwell has conducted useful experimental work on different pendulum saw blade types to cut limestone.[139] Two of his types cut at a speed of 3.75 cm and 4.5 cm per hour, respectively, with water and sand added every two minutes. He assumed that emery would have worked better. Also, the type of stone would have had a substantial influence on the cutting rate. For example, the Stoa of Attalos's rebuilders worked limestone five times faster than marble with the same tools.[140] Conglomerate, on which the pendulum saw was mostly used, may have been slower than sawing limestone especially since the hardness of conglomerate depends on the types of clasts and the strength of the cement.

In discussing the raw materials, the Cape Gelidonya shipwreck evidence points to freelance tinkers/smiths trading in bronze and undertaking repair work.[141] At the same time, the metal trade must have been partially under the control of the Mycenaean palaces in the 13th century BC to ensure access to at least some amount of the dwindling resource.[142] According to Linear B tablets, the Pylian palace employed about 400 smiths and their assistants but did not distribute much metal for them to work. Some received nothing, others a mere of 3.5–4 kg allotment per year,[143] an amount that any experienced smith could work through in a week.[144] Palatial control over metal distribution and the presence of bronze hoards, including scrap, broken, and finished tools, seem to suggest that the Mycenaean palaces distributed the same range of metal materials (i.e. scrap, broken, and complete items) to be recycled.[145] Their interest seems to have been mainly in weapon production (javelins, arrowheads). But why, then, were the Pylos palatial

[125] Melena 2014: 151–152; Palaima 2015: 630–631.
[126] Blackwell 2018a.
[127] Martin 1965: 201–219, figs 93–97.
[128] However, see perhaps Maran 2008: 47–48.
[129] Shaw 1973: 44, 164.
[130] Evely 1993: 217.
[131] Schwandner 1991: 220; Seeher 2011: 191–193.
[132] Blackwell 2018a and b.
[133] Evely 1993, 2000; Newhard 2003; Brysbaert and Vetters 2010.
[134] Blackwell 2011, 2014.
[135] Blackwell 2011: 120, 200, table 4.23.
[136] Blackwell 2011: 125.
[137] Ugan *et al.* 2003. See also Buonasera 2015 on the use of milling stones.

[138] Schwandner 1991: 220.
[139] Blackwell 2018a: 226–228.
[140] Burford 1969: 197, n. 2.
[141] Bass 1967.
[142] Blackwell 2018b: 514–515.
[143] Nakassis 2013: 169–170.
[144] Molloy: personal communication.
[145] Cf. Smith 1992–1993.

authorities employing *c.* 400 smiths and helpers? Understanding this issue in the context of the use of tools in various spheres of work (agriculture, masonry, carpentry) that were controlled in part by the palace, may provide some insights. Since many smiths did not receive an allotment, the question arises whether they actually *needed* an allotment to be a smith for palatial work. Some smiths may have been employed *only to repair* tools and weapons, for which they simply received the damaged items. We should also not forget that the Linear B tablets record a frozen moment in time. We can easily imagine that the palatially-distributed tools were in use all year and were thus regularly disbursed, used, damaged, or broken. They needed, therefore, to be regularly recollected, resharpened, and repaired. In particular, metal tools needed resharpening and repairing very often when used in building activities.[146] Such work (and its recording in tablets) could not wait a year before the logistical chain of collecting broken items was set in motion again, so this must have been a constant task.[147]

Blackwell shows how five specific types of tools (double axe, broad and narrow chisel, knife, and sickle) recur in hoards very regularly.[148] These were in use by carpenters, masons, and agricultural workers during harvesting and digging work. Digging work was of course also essential for constructing terraces, roads in hill flanks, canals, dams, and tombs. Many digging activities may have required similar tools and materials. Turner noted that it helps to differentiate tool use by material for digging activities, and he separated metal from non-metal tools in their efficiency.[149] For the context of agricultural tools and ploughing, Halstead refers to differential efficiency rates between wood/copper and iron tools.[150] Turner's different rates for employing metal tools (chisels, picks) and non-metal tools (digging sticks) were compared above for the digging of highways.[151]

Blackwell indicates a specific tool kit, valued for its combination. In some hoards, these are present in too large numbers to be personal property, so perhaps they were state-owned.[152] Both Palaima and Backwell have argued that the Pylian palace may have distributed and recollected metal agricultural tools, as well as raw material (to make more).[153] Tools, as state property, were likely loaned to semi-dependent workers and had to be returned for reworking, even when broken, to prove that they were in fact broken.[154]

It is likely that masons, carpenters, and farmers used the same tool sets and were involved in each other's work when need be.

In summary, the overhead cost of stone tools depended on the type of stone used. Any normal rounded hand stone can be employed as an expedient tool, as we still do today to hammer spikes in the ground when we go camping. The cost, therefore, of employing a local stone could be very minimal, but rarer and imported stone types (see the discussion of diorite from Egypt or andesite from the Saronic Gulf), like bronze tools, would have entailed a cost. In addition, the maintenance of tools plays a role in their cost. Repairs and resharpening of tools occurred alongside day-to-day care, such as cleaning, as can be seen for wagons, buckets, baskets, and woven material. That cleaning was included in cost estimates is clearly indicated by Claudel and Laroque who state that the cost of 20 hours of emptying and cleaning stretchers for soil transport is roughly the same as 12 hours of supervision for terrace digging.[155] It is difficult to estimate exact costs for imported tools, because it is impossible to estimate how many such tools were in use and for how long before abrasion, breakage, and exhaustion occurred. Therefore, only a certain percentage can be estimated alongside other overhead costs (see below).

Accommodation and food provision

Accommodation and food provision for labourers and animals are important factors in cost estimates, but context plays a crucial role. As I have indicated before, the Argive Plain seems to be a well-argued case to understand that labourers in construction were also the local farmers.[156] The majority of both groups of professionals were capable of carrying out each other's jobs, and both jobs fitted nicely in the same time schedule, if the workers were allowed to plant, look after, and collect harvests when and if needed. Moreover, as far as the current calculations are concerned, there would have been no need to invite or force people from elsewhere to move into the region to carry out building works.[157] Despite the fact that the LH IIIB demographic figures are ambiguous by themselves, it seems clear that people could deal with the estimated building demands. Even doubling the number of building projects would not pose a problem to the overall economic and thus socio-political situation leading up to 1200 BC. If this is indeed the case – future demographic figures based on intensive surveys may dictate otherwise – this fact also aids in calculating the impact of accommodation since no additional cost would be needed. Most people working in construction likely lived nearby and went

---

146 After Barker and Russell, this volume.
147 This is supported by Smith 1992–1993: 197.
148 Blackwell 2018b: table 2.
149 Turner 2018: tables 9.1–9.2.
150 Halstead 2014.
151 Turner 2018.
152 Blackwell 2018: 524.
153 Palaima 2015: 632–633; Backwell 2018b: 528.
154 See Postgate 1992: 228, for the Near East.

155 Claudel and Laroque 1870: 239.
156 Brysbaert 2013, 2020.
157 Cf. Brysbaert 2020.

home at the end of the day. If most of these were also farmers, living near their land was of great importance, and they would not have moved for work unless it was absolutely necessary. Such mobility was perhaps only the prerogative of a small group of professional builders such as the specialists needed on all sites: e.g. architects and master builders. These professionals would then have hired local labour forces.

Food provision, however, was a different matter. If local people were involved in building projects, they either had to be left free to carry out agricultural work when needed,[158] or others had to provide for them. This cost of additional food provision for humans and animals could have been required for several hundreds of people for large parts of the year. Linear B tablet PY Fn 7, for example, indirectly shows how various people were given rations of grain as payment for their work in construction. This was distributed in a hierarchical way: the standard daily rate for dependent male labourers was 1.2 litres of grain/day, but some received up to 3.2 litres/day, and two named individuals were given enough for a single person for an entire month.[159] Nakassis believes that these two may have been responsible for recruiting and paying (in food rations!) the unskilled labour forces needed in construction processes (see above).[160] Many workers on other tablets also had to be fed by foodstuffs produced by others than themselves. If Hiller is correct that about 4100 people at the Pylos palace were monitored by the palatial authorities,[161] it would be worthwhile, in a future study, to calculate the percentage of the population (if possible) that was provided with grain and other remuneration (land, figs). These provisions had to be produced on top of the usual household provisions or taxes to the palace. For example, female textile workers were given equal amounts of figs and wheat.[162] This certainly would have added an additional cost factor to the total required agricultural effort.

Additional overheads

Barker and Russell have noted that the level of incidental costs in a project depends on the type of stoneworking being done.[163] To them, it is clear that when marble, for instance, needed to be sawn, the incidental labour costs could be significant, varying between 20–25%. They divide the so-called 'hidden' costs into two categories: incidental expenses for stoneworking (i.e., the actual labour) estimated at 6% (soft stone), 20% (marble), or 30% (hardstone) of the cost of the whole project,

depending on the stone worked, with a further 10% taken up by the cost of supervision and security; and another 5% to ensure that valuable materials and tools were not stolen.[164] This figure range can increase to an additional 15% when unexpected developments and a level of profit margin is taken into account as well.

Considering all the overheads discussed above - the lower level of stoneworking *per se* (apart from conglomerate),[165] the use and repair of (perhaps) less-complex tools, the minimal accommodation provision, a certain level of additional food production required to feed artisans of many different types - a certain overhead percentage, charged to the overall costs of every project, would be justified. Simultaneously, replacement workers for factors such as illness, accidents, or absenteeism are difficult to estimate. Delays in supplies, mistakes made, and supply bottlenecks would have resulted in idling of workers and would have caused additional costs. On the basis of all these factors taken together, allowing for an additional 20–40% of the total cost per project would be a well-reasoned figure in a context where the written sources cannot help us.[166] **Table 15** gives an overview of these overheads and indicates a difference between the tasks that that include monumental projects, workshop activities, and public works and the tasks done within the household (terrace construction, house building, and agricultural work, including food processing). Overheads for the first group were calculated as 20% and 40%, but those within the household were calculated as 5% to a maximum of 10% since most of the incidental costs would have been assumed by the household itself and carried over to the next season or year if necessary. I did not calculate any percentage of overheads for agricultural work since this would have been ongoing as long as people were physically capable. However, overproduction was essential to their survival in bad years and to provide food for those who did other jobs.

The range of overhead costs (at 20 - 40%) for monumental construction and public works equates to 35.4 to 41.5 person years. This would mean that one person would work for 35.5 to 41.5 years in the 13th century BC to cover overheads alone. Taking the lower percentage for overheads into account for the household tasks, a very different range comes into view: several figures demand more than 100 people to be employed as soon as numbers go over 100 themselves. The 5% and 10% overheads for the lowest rates for terraces and house building together are in the same range as those for the highest public building overheads. Moreover, the other figures are at least double and up to six times higher than the highest cost estimates with 40% overhead

[158] Brysbaert 2020: table 4.
[159] Ventris and Chadwick 1973: 393, 420; Palmer 1989: 96–97.
[160] Nakassis 2015: 595–596.
[161] Hiller 1988.
[162] Ab series and others; cf. Killen 2004: 161–163.
[163] Barker 2020: personal communication. See also Barker and Russell, this volume.

[164] Barker and Russell, this volume.
[165] See Blackwell 2018b.
[166] I also inserted a low 10% for overheads, but considering the various factors mentioned by Barker and Russel (this volume), this figure will be likely too low.

Project	Cost time (py)	No. people	Overhead			Totals (py)		
Public and monumental efforts			10%	20%	40%	10%	20%	40%
Mycenae citadel	7.5	100	0.75	1.5	3	8.3	9	10.5
Tiryns citadel	6.0	100	0.6	1.2	2.4	6.6	7.2	8.4
Midea citadel	1.5	100	0.15	0.3	0.6	1.7	1.8	2.1
Tiryns dam	1.45	100	0.145	0.29	0.58	1.6	1.7	2
Treasury of Atreus	0.9	100	0.09	0.18	0.36	1.0	1.1	1.27
Tholos of Klytemnestra	0.9	100	0.09	0.18	0.36	1.0	1.1	1.27
Chamber tomb digging	1.8-2	100	0.18-0.2	0.36-0.4	0.72-0.8	2.0-2.2	2.2-2.4	2.52-2.8
Infrastructure provision	3.7-3.9	100	0.37-0.39	0.74-0.78	1.48-1.56	4.1-4.3	4.4-4.7	5.18-5.46
Pottery production	2.75-5.5	100	0.27-0.55	0.54-1.1	1.08-2.2	3.0-6.0	3.3-6.6	3.83-7.7
Totals						29.3-32.7	31.6-35.4	37.1-41.5
Household efforts			5%	10%		5%	10%	
Terrace construction	13.9 – 69.8 – 214.3	100	0.69-3.49-1.07	1.39-6.98-2.14		14,6-73.3-215.3	15,3-76,8-216.4	
House building	20.6	100	1.03	2.06		21.6	22.7	
Agricultural work	Year round	1.3–4–6.6*	-	-		-	-	
Totals						36.2-94.9-236.9	38-99.5-239.1	

Table 15. Overhead costs per project discussed in Brysbaert 2020 and in this paper.

* People per household in relation to 1 – 3 – 5 ha respectively, based on 365 days/year, counting in total an active adult population of c. 8,000–10,000 people (adapted from Brysbaert 2020, table 4; and Table 5 in this article, with food processing expanded).

on public and monumental building. This comparison shows clearly that most efforts were channeled into the agricultural sector, its land management, and the subsequent food processing and production.

The military and its cost

DeLaine noted that the Roman state paid the army on a yearly basis and that this formed a cost of one or two orders of magnitude compared to the construction of the Baths of Caracalla.[167] In Aegean prehistory, remarkably little study has been carried out on the LBA infantry in the Mycenaean world and beyond,[168] let alone its cost. Infantry could include runners, skermishers, archers, defense troops, foot soldiers, chariot fighters, and hand-to-hand fighters. Lejeune refers to the o-ka tablets in relation to the pe-di-je-we, likely the Linear B equivalent to pedieis (foot soldiers).[169]

These were the anonymous soldiers mentioned in larger numbers. They were recruited locally when needed and represented several types. The Linear B o-ka texts from Pylos mention coast guard operations together with 13 e-qe-ta who are understood to be aristocratic representatives of the central administration. They possibly headed troops and liased between the palace and their troops.[170] One military commander, ko-ma-we of a coast guard unit (PY An 519), was also a smith (of weapons?) for the palace and a pig herder.[171] Another example, a-tu-ko, seems to be a royal armourer who is also a landholder and a smith again (PY Ep 301, En 609.5).[172] Smithing seems to have been carried out part-time alongside other activities at Pylos.[173] Utchitel refers to several Pylian tablets (An 519, 614, 654, 656, 657, 661) in relation to coast guarding and referring to military men, named (unit commanders, officers, e-qe-

[167] DeLaine 1997: 221.
[168] Drews 1993: 135–139.
[169] Lejeune 1968: 41.
[170] Nakassis 2013: 7; 2015: 594.
[171] Nakassis 2013: 50, 58–59.
[172] Nakassis 2013: 62.
[173] Nakassis 2013: 167–168.

ta) and unnamed.[174] Some of these tablets list a series of such unnamed men (VIR) together with a numeral ranging from 10–110, likely referring to the foot soldiers that Nakassis refers to in relation to the *e-qe-ta*. From Utchitel's information,[175] I deducted a total of 640 VIR on tablets An 519 (VIR 110, 20, 30, 50), An 654 (VIR 50, 60 + 5 × VIR 10 and specifically called *pe-di-je-we*), An 657 (VIR 50, 20, 10, 30, 30), and An 661.1-7 (VIR 70, 30, 10, 20) together. An additional 160 VIR can be deducted from An 656 (VIR 20, 80, 20, 10) and An 661.9-13 (VIR 30), totaling to VIR 800. This number does not include higher ranking officers, followers, or other men.[176] We should keep in mind, though, that these are the tablets which survive and which registered the men in service, thus representing the need of the palace *at that point in time*. Of a population of 50,000, 8% of the male adult population, thus, were foot soldiers that year if 1/5 of the population was adult and male. Nakassis calculates 1/4 of the population as adult males,[177] making this figure 6.4% of the male population. In line with earlier work, I maintain 1/5 on the basis of a household composition of 5.[178]

Both offensive and defensive weapons are known from the tablets, and protective clothing such as helmets and cuirasses are mentioned as well.[179] The archaeological evidence of javelin production at Tiryns[180] complements evidence on pictorial pottery and on painted wall plaster from Pylos[181] of foot soldiers in protective clothing carrying weapons.[182] Additionally, ideograms of bronze cuirasses and boar tusk helmets have been attested on Linear B tablets from Mycenae (Sh series) and Tiryns (Si series).[183] One complete bronze cuirass was found at the Dendra cemetery, dating to the LH IIIA period,[184] and parts of several similar ones in Thebes, dating to LH IIIB.

The numbers of armed troops, their equipment, arms, food provisions, and by whom and how they were paid, however, cannot easily be reconstructed even for Pylos, which has the best documentation. Due to the dearth of information and the insecure numbers of people living in the Argive Plain region who could have potentially been (called) under arms,[185] the cost of running and maintaining troops cannot easily be reconstructed. Moreover, its nature cannot be deduced based on the Pylian information, because the socio-political

situation was very different in the Argive Plain than in Pylos. However, it is important here to point out the cost of such a force as it would have impacted the larger picture of costings and may help future studies.

Discussion

In a previous analysis, I demonstrated that the different parts of total economies (including the various forms of production and consumption) are codependent.[186] The *combined* efforts needed for the six main monuments analysed here, pottery-making, and domestic house building were many times less than that needed for agriculture on a yearly basis, even though it was not necessary to carry out all tasks full-time throughout the entire year.[187] While a broad-brush approach was prevalent throughout all calculations and thus an amount of underestimation is likely, this observation indicates that a large amount of additional labour would have to be assigned to all production tasks before their combined input would approach or equal agricultural labour efforts. Refinements in the labour cost calculations will lead to higher reliability and accuracy of the analysis, but a reversal in the order of magnitude between the combined production tasks versus the agricultural tasks is unlikely (**Tables 5 and 6**). It is possible, however, that at the end of the Bronze Age there could have been a critical point after which adding another task requiring more labour would not have been feasible and would have directly affected people's resilience against 'unforeseen' factors (epidemics, variations in climate, internal and external turmoil). This is true especially if these additional stresses endangered agriculture or, more generally, the available healthy adult labour pool. In this paper, I have introduced a range of additional labour factors into the equation to understand how any or all these factors combined could have changed the analyses I have previously put forward. While the conclusions presented here are still not the total picture of activities in the 13th century BC in the Argolid, this analysis provides a yardstick against which the different socio-political and economic hypotheses can be compared. For example, looking at the different categories of tasks, it is possible to distinguish different strategies for the organisation and control of the labour force. This is perhaps the best way to distinguish between labour (corvée or not) required by the elite for monumental building (largest tholoi, fortification walls) and a (potential) collective labour force from the agricultural population which was able to build at a similar scale (building terraces, their own houses) but was not driven by (in)direct elite organisation. Certain projects, such as the Dam at Tiryns, may have been ordered and organised from the top down, but at the same time, it

---

[174] Utchitel 1985: 60–63.
[175] Utchitel 1985: 63–65.
[176] 13 *e-qe-ta* in Pylos: Nakassis 2013: 7, 89; 13 at Knossos of 213 on Crete: Palaima 2015: 641.
[177] Nakassis 2013: 34, n. 24. This figure is based on Akrigg 2011: 54–55.
[178] Gallant 1991; Halstead 1995; Brysbaert 2020: 67, Table 4, n. 39.
[179] See Lejeune 1968 for an overview on the military in this period.
[180] E.g. Brysbaert and Vetters 2013: 185.
[181] Lang 1969.
[182] Vermeule and Karageorghis 1982: 108–109, pl. X.1.
[183] Snodgrass 1965.
[184] Åström 1977.
[185] Bintliff 2020.

[186] Brysbaert 2020; see also **Table 1–6** in this paper.
[187] Brysbaert 2020: table 4.

also benefited the community as a whole and not only the organiser. As such, the community at Tiryns may have been part of the organisation and support of these works, perhaps in conjunction with the palace. This would thus blur the distinction between top-down and bottom-up initiatives and organisational activities between the elites and the communities.

More specifically, when the efforts for elite chamber tomb digging are compared with the other figures, they turn out to be at the low end of the spectrum: only 1.8 to 2 py of constant digging by 100 people would have been required (or to reverse the calculations, only two people working continuously the whole century would have been needed to dig these elite tombs). Additional input would have been needed for the other smaller tombs, production of the burial gifts, ceremonial activities of burying someone, and carrying out the sacrifices at the grave. These other tasks are harder to quantify, but even with their inclusion, the overall picture presented in this paper would not change.

In comparison with tomb digging, the construction of 175 km of road seems to require almost triple the time, or the equivalent of at least two thirds of the construction of a large citadel in the Argive Plain. What has not been calculated yet is the (yearly?) maintenance and repairs to keep these roads open and functioning for HGVs all year round. HGVs in particular will have taken their toll on the surfaces with wheel tracks and ruts.

The terracing figures are best compared to other tasks carried out in the Argive Plain.[188] For example, the domestic house building for the region's population for a century would have taken 100 people approximately 21 years of labour, eclipsing the construction effort of all the major monuments at c. 18 years of constant building. Terracing 25% of the slopes nearby the settlements (70 py) would have taken almost four times as long as all of the monumental building (18 py) or the domestic house building (21 py). Terracing is an integral part of agricultural land management, again highlighting that far more labour effort was invested in agriculture and food processing than other complex tasks of society.[189] The agricultural activities for crop rearing also involve important figures for food processing (**Table 5**), such as grinding, bringing water and fuel, and cooking. The labour investment in grinding alone is at least as high as the entire agricultural crop production process combined. While this may be a surprising outcome, it also places all gender and age groups firmly at work. Moreover, one may expect that a similar ratio will emerge between animal rearing (**Table 6**) and animal processing for consumption (for which work is currently underway).

Overheads in prehistory are a difficult category to cost effectively, and the figures here are inevitably hypothetical. However, with figures that are realistic in relation to later, better-documented periods, these may not be too far removed from reality. They point to costs that are already high on a comparative scale, and that now stand out again. They could have easily put extra pressure on certain social groups responsible for activities such as agricultural work.

Equally ambiguous is the economic cost of the military sector of Mycenaean life. In contrast to the archaeological evidence, the Linear B tablets are problematic to use because the ideas and numbers relate to Pylos and not to the Argive Plain. How far such data can be applied to other Mycenaean societies remains to be studied. Again, this is a sector not studied in terms of labour or workforce estimates.

Energy-saving strategies to retain a high level of resilience were perhaps best visible when a range of adverse circumstances and factors occurred at the same time around 1200–1190 BC; however, these strategies were certainly not new at the time. One such strategy would have been the 'collapsing together' of several daily activities that then became embedded activities.[190] Under these circumstances, a single activity, such as fetching water or collecting fire wood, is carried out for several jobs in a manner that shares knowledge and saves resources and time. Such activities may have been particularly useful in reducing transport costs of material resources, digging in uneven topography, and using animals to carry out draught tasks. For example, for chert stone tool transport, Newhard refers to an embedded trade route system in which there was a level of exchange between two regions so that certain materials (pottery, mill stones in andesite, and chert) would have found their way from the Saronic Gulf into the Argolid, possibly together.[191] In this way, no journey would be wasted. This is also DeLaine's reasoning for removing building waste from the site, as these trips would be absorbed by bringing in other materials on the return.[192] A similar argument was used for the use of M4 from Mycenae to Tiryns and back.[193] Moreover, in addition to sharing tools and tasks, farmers and builders would have learned from each other as they likely even did each other's work when needed.[194] Nakassis mentions that people were active in several types of jobs, such as agricultural, pastoral, and military.[195] Sledges for heavy cargo transport, known in the Near East since the 4th millennium, may have been used as threshing tools as well - something that is known from pre-industrial

---

[188] Brysbaert 2020.
[189] Cf. Brysbaert 2020.
[190] Brysbaert 2012.
[191] Newhard 2003: 111, 121, 189.
[192] DeLaine 1997: 191.
[193] Brysbaert 2022.
[194] As argued in Brysbaert 2013, 2020.
[195] Nakassis 2013: 47, 167–168.

contexts in Greece until early in the last century.[196] The use of bovines for ploughing, for the transport of heavy and large crop loads, and for threshing requires several years of training and special care before the oxen are willing enough to follow the ox-guide. Ox-guides therefore were skilled workers, and their close collaboration with the animal on whose rhythm they relied was useful in transporting large blocks. Very likely, the use of oxen in agriculture led to their use in building; such mutually enhancing 'technology clusters' have also been recognised elsewhere.[197] Furthermore, when skilled people did not have the chance to grow their own crops because they were employed year round, they had to be fed through the work input of others.[198] Their specialisation thus created jobs for others, especially if they moved from one building project to another. Whether skilled builders brought their own tool sets or they were given tool sets by the palace,[199] they were likely not made by the builders themselves. Simultaneously, when work was slow during specific seasons, people could earn extra income by offering their hands and skills elsewhere.

It can be estimated that 80% of the total population was involved in agriculture one way or another *at crucial times*, including children and the elderly, the latter often in supportive roles and doing gentler tasks.[200] This means that agricultural workers would have spent between eight to nine months of the year in agriculture and would have been free for other jobs (crafting, building) at slower agricultural times (**Table 16**, right column). The spreadsheet model shows this schematically for tasks within the building industry,[201] and this is also applicable to the range of tasks discussed above (**Table 16**) since not all could be done simultaneously.

Independent from this, Mylonas suggests a specific sequence for construction activities at Mycenae,[202] starting with the construction of the Lion Gate and West Wall, followed by the Grave Circle A circumference, and finally the Great Ramp. This sequence, and others, will have distributed workers over the years alongside other more essential (agricultural) work.

Finally, seasonality plays a major role in the agricultural agenda which, if all parties were making rational decisions on priorities, would rule the overall calendar year for all activities (**Table 16**). Moreover, certain activities did not make sense in specific seasons: muddy road conditions in winter are not conducive to transporting large stone blocks.[203] Equally difficult would be the digging of tombs during heavy rain or in wet seasons, because the saturated soil would make the digging much more difficult.[204] Wet soil tends to stick much tighter to shovels or any digging tool and is much heavier for lifting. Moreover, a tomb at risk of flooding also causes higher risk of collapse for the diggers. However, the dead did not await dry seasons, and some tomb digging had to take place despite less favourable conditions.

Conclusion

In looking at the available adults of the Argive Plain, the presented labour figures seem to suggest a model of one central authority (Mycenae), who created and maintained alliances with less powerful citadels (Tiryns and Midea) and who centralised available resources such as the labour force. This creation and maintenance of alliances signifies both power and fragility in the bonds created. To me, this stands, for now, in contrast to a situation in which each citadel would be more independent and perhaps competitive, and in which each would have access to a more limited pool of people to carry out these series of large-scale building works. It should be clear from this paper that people had to work *together*, and with their animals, to make these monuments while also looking after each other for food, housing, clothing, and many other material needs. Pooling people and efforts from among all citadels thus seems to be the best way to achieve this. In my view, this needs a central organisation in charge. Around 1200 BC, the palatial centres in particular suffered setbacks while it seems that people in the Argolid just went on with their jobs as before. The three centres in the Argolid show several signs of continuity rather than total disruption.

Rural landscapes and their populace formed the backbone of pre-industrial societies, and this seems very much the case in the LBA Argive Plain. Analyses of the foci of cities and other central places (often with monumental architecture), the rural 'hinterland', *and* the communication between these are essential to the understanding of day-to-day rhythms, larger seasonal practices, and how each of these was interconnected. In an ideal situation, the balance created by the different parties would have resulted in a resilient society prepared for adverse times and events. These different agents and phenomena and their interconnections are crucial to our understanding of how political units functioned at several socially interconnected levels. Bottom-up approaches can dissolve a 'monolithic' understanding of a past society, because the many social groups can be shown to have been dependent on each other, albeit perhaps in unequal measures. The

[196] E.g. Cole 1954: 710.
[197] Ivanova 2017.
[198] Brysbaert 2013: 85. See also Linear B tablets, e.g. fn. 7 for builders.
[199] On this point, see Blackwell 2018.
[200] Brysbaert 2020; Timonen and Brysbaert 2021.
[201] Cf. Abrams 1994.
[202] Mylonas 1962, 1966, 1968.
[203] Brysbaert 2013.
[204] After Claudel and Laroque 1870: 238.

Month	Tilling, Ploughing	Sowing	Harvest*	Crop processing†	Land management	Animal husbandry/ gathering	Building (B), Ceramic production (C), Chamber tomb digging (Ch), Road construction (R), Terrace construction (T)
Jan.	*Ploughing for sowing*	Lentils, peas, bitter vetch			Weeding, Field clearing, extend/improve Fallow/Crop rotation/mix	*Lambing and kidding, Milking & processing milk*	Ch? – T
Feb.							Ch? – T
March		Pulses, beans			Weeding	*Shearing sheep Calving, milking & processing milk,*	Ch?
April					Cross-ploughing	*processing milk, Sheep to mountains*	C – Ch
May			Pulses, grain			Gathering leaves, shoots, fruits, seeds, nuts**	B? – C – Ch – R?
June					Weeding during harvest, Manuring after harvest, Ploughing of fallow fields, Watering young trees and vines	Gathering leaves, shoots, fruits, seeds, nuts, harvesting figs	C – Ch
July			*Grain, then pulses*	*Threshing grain, then pulses*			C – Ch
				Grind daily			
Aug.			Pulses/ beans			Culling old sheep, goat, cattle, harvesting figs	B – C – Ch – R
Sept.					Manuring before sowing, field clearing,	Spin, weave, hunt, fish, Harvesting figs/olives	B – C – Ch – R – T
Oct.	*Ploughing for sowing*	Wheat, barley, oat, rye			Felling timber & wood seasoning, Pruning, manuring and planting (fruit/ olive) trees		B – Ch – R – T
Nov.						*Milking new lambs, Lambing and kidding,* Harvesting olives	B – Ch – R – T
Dec							Ch? – T

Table 16. Life cycle calendar indicating which activities took place each month. Bold italic indicates most crucial task/period (based on Hesiod *Works and Days*, 420; Dahl and Hjort 1976; Koster 1977; Forbes 1989; Blitzer 1990; Foxhall 2007; Fitzjohn 2013; Halstead 2014). Last column indicates when non-agricultural activities were possible (based on Brysbaert 2020, table 2 and expanded with Ch – R – T as discussed in this paper).

* **Harvest** includes reaping, binding, drying, and transporting.
† **Crop processing** includes threshing, winnowing, transporting sheaves, sieving, grinding, and storing.
æ **Land management** includes fallowing/crop rotating, mixed cropping, manuring, weeding, and extending/improving.
** Emphasising the importance of this category: Gallant 1991: 68 with refs: 65-70% cereals, 20-25% fruits, pulses, and vegetables, 5-15% oils, meat, and wine, for the Classical period. But see Halstead (2014: 119) on pulses-cereals ratios for earlier periods.

Argive Plain societies showed remarkable resilience in the rapidly changing conditions during the 13th century BC, and their adaptive skills were remarkable. Understanding their energy expenditure from a bottom-up perspective suggests large levels of responsibility in the hands of the farmers and workers rather than the elites ruling the scene at all times. Additional stress undoubtedly would have been caused by successive bad harvests due to annual weather pattern fluctuations, but elsewhere I have argued that storage capacity for two years worth of provisions would most often have been enough to counter such events.[205]

_____
[205] Timonen and Brysbaert 2021.

Crucial subsistence activities could be badly disrupted by both natural and human-induced events and actions. The latter were especially important in relation to prolonged monumental building activities. Garnsey stated that the severity of subsistence crises would vary with the incidence of war, piracy, civil strife, and the non-economic heavy exploitation of labour, producers, and consumers by the powerful.[206] If the powerful were clever about it, they would respect the agricultural cycle and employ people at the right time for the right jobs.

According to Nakassis, people were active in several types of jobs.[207] He recognised a significant overlap between the personal names of metal smiths and the names of herders. This can only be interpreted as several of them having multiple job responsibilities for the palaces. He also asserts that some individuals also may have had a mixture of tasks beyond the palatial economic sphere too. This links in neatly with the fact that journeying was an important part of daily sedentary life. Motivation for moving and journeying between places was easy to find and indirectly documented by the Linear B tablets in terms of transporting local and exotic goods, and travelling craftspeople, farmers, and workers.

In political and geographic terms, the Mycenaean highways are perhaps the most indicative material expression of all interactions that went on in the region. All eight together show the extent of the potential connections and influences that the three major citadels had together, either under Mycenae or each in their own way as competitive entities. Their construction figures indicate efforts well beyond the local community level, in terms of coordination, execution, and sponsorship. Thus, this clearly illustrates a set of dependent relationships. The highways also highlight who benefited most. The grandeur of the roads demonstrated far-reaching territories, visible power due to their monumental character and scale, and access to (and perhaps control over) fit labour forces that could also be used for military efforts if needed. The choice between spreading monumental construction efforts over time or using more people to finish the jobs at hand would have had very different effects on the management of other large-scale projects. At the same time, other tasks, as outlined above, still needed to be undertaken. The concentration, then, of well-constructed highways to and from Mycenae may suggest its dominant political role in the region, and its exertion of political cohesion and authority, perhaps even over the other citadels, as suggested above. I have argued elsewhere that only *pooling* of human and animal resources under a strong central authority and

with healthy alliances would have allowed for building at such a scale in the region.[208] The road network in particular seems to confirm this picture.

In the LBA societies of mainland Greece, monumental architecture can be regarded as a clear reflection of power, socio-political organisation, and relationships, which can be studied through the lenses of labour investment and the symbolic meaning of the created monuments. In particular, the way energy sources are spent shows levels of inequality, for example the potential ownership of oxen.[209] Farmers without enough land of their own and who worked on other people's land for income were likely of lower status than those who owned their own oxen. The latter could collect far more harvest with oxen, and when it came to food shortage, animals of any type could be converted into meals or could be exchanged for other much-needed supplies. Understanding these processes and strategies of survival is essential to provide meaning for the produced labour cost calculations and further understanding of the roles of all social groups involved. Since most ancient societies were based on subsistence economies, important decision-making was a daily balancing act between building work, agriculture, and other craft activities. These decisions often influenced patterns of land use and may have also resulted in circular economic strategies. In such cases, undoubtedly the completed monuments in which human and other energy was expended – often risking lives – and the process of making them undoubtedly exuded power that would have rippled throughout the entire society *and* through individual people. While there would have been many weeks and months without specific events, an event like the cyclopean effort needed to move and place the 120-tonne lintel block over the entrance of the 'Treasury of Atreus', would have been a spectacle for everyone. Equally, the living and passed-on memory of such activities would have played a role in people's lives: in the perception of themselves as builders and workers, in the perception of others, and in the stories told to the next generations for years and decades.

The construction presented in this paper all took place within a period of 100 years which results in a slightly grainy timeframe. This also means that the people who carried out these multiple tasks represent at least five generations of active workers, and this will have its own implications. During some generations, pressure on people's capacities and thus their resilience may have been more pronounced than at other points in time when more numerous participants, perhaps also with better health, would have been able to carry out the work. Instability and unrest were just around the corner, and that was fatal for at least some of the

---

[206] Garnsey 1988.
[207] Nakassis 2013: 47, 167–168.
[208] Brysbaert 2020.
[209] After Halstead 2014. See also Brysbaert 2020: 73–75.

individuals involved in the various tasks discussed in this paper. This is also testified by the several ruinous monuments that were never rebuilt to their former standard.

Acknowledgements

I thank the conference organisers for their wide perspective regarding labour cost studies and for allowing me to slip in a presentation on the Greek Bronze Age. This paper was written in a very difficult period in my personal life early in 2020, and I would like to thank Dominik Maschek specifically for his kind help and Simon Barker for providing useful references and proofreading. Irini Vikatou kindly helped out with providing references and compiling data for the tomb digging section. I thank Jari Pakkanen for useful advice on energetics calculations and for his time in proofreading and commenting on an earlier draft. Last but not least, I would like to thank Janet DeLaine for being a constant inspiration. She has made the economics of the past a very exciting field indeed.

This research is part of the ERC-Consolidator SETinSTONE project under the direction of Prof. A. Brysbaert, Leiden University, and funded by the European Research Council under the European Union's Horizon 2020 Programme / ERC grant agreement n° 646667.

Bibliography

Abrams, E.M. 1994. *How the Maya Built their World. Energetics and Ancient Architecture*. Austin: University of Texas Press.

Acton, P. 2014. *Poiesis. Manufacturing in Classical Athens*. Oxford: Oxford University Press.

Akrigg, B. 2011. Demography and Classical Athens, in C. Holleran and A. Pudsey (eds) *Demography and the Graeco-Roman World. New Insights and Approaches*: 37–59. Cambridge: Cambridge University Press.

Alden, M.J. 1981. *Bronze Age Population Fluctuations in the Argolid from the Evidence of Mycenaean Tombs*. Göteborg: Paul Åströms Förlag.

Alden, M. 2000. *The Prehistoric Cementery: Pre-Mycenaean and Early Mycenaean Graves*. (Well Built Mycenae. The Helleno-British Excavations at Mycenae, 1959–1969, 7). Oxford: Oxbow Books.

Åström, P. 1977. *The Cuirass Tomb and Other Finds at Dendra* (Studies in Mediterranean Archaeology 4). Jonsered: Paul Åströms Förlag.

Aura Jorro, F. 1985. *Diccionario Micénico* I. Madrid: Instituto de Filología.

Baines, J. 1996. Contextualising Egyptian representations of society and ethnicity, in J.S. Cooper and G. Schwartz (eds) *The Study of the Ancient Near East in the 21st Century: The William Foxwell Albright Centennial Conference*: 339–384. Winona Lake: Eisenbrauns.

Barker, S. and B. Russell 2009. Labour figures for roman stone-working: pitfalls and potential, in *Les Chantiers de Construction de l'Italie et des Provinces Romaines. Cycle de Rencontres sur l'Archeologie de la Construction. 3. L'Economie des Chantiers, 10–11 Decembre 2009* : 83–94, 271–290. Paris: Ecole Normale Superieure.

Bass, G. 1967. *Cape Gelidonya: A Bronze Age Shipwreck*. Philadelphia: American Philosophical Society.

Bennet, J. 2013. Bronze Age Greece, in P.F. Bang and W. Scheidel (eds) *The Oxford Handbook of the State in the Ancient Near East and Mediterranean*: 235–258. Oxford: Oxford University Press.

Béquignon Y. 1931. Chronique des fouilles et découvertes archéologiques dans l'Orient hellénique (1931). *Bulletin de Correspondance Hellénique* 55: 450 – 522.

Bevan, A. and E. Bloxam 2019. Stonemasons and craft mobility in the Bronze Age Eastern Mediterranean, in E. Kiriatzi and C. Knappett (eds) *Human Mobility and Technological Transfer in the Prehistoric Mediterranean*: 68–93. Cambridge: Cambridge University Press.

Bintliff, J.L. 1977. *Natural Environment and Human Settlement in Prehistoric Greece*. Parts I and II. Oxford.

Bintliff, J.L. 2020. Natural and Human Ecology: Geography, Climate, and Demography, in I.S. Lemos and A. Kotsonas (eds) *A Companion to the Archaeology of Early Greece and the Mediterranean*: 3–32. Hoboken NJ: Wiley-Blackwell.

Blackman, D. 2000. Archaeology in Greece 1999–2000. *Archaeological Reports* (1999 - 2000) 46: 3–151.

Blackwell, N.G. 2011. Middle and Late Bronze Age Metal Tools from the Aegean, Eastern Mediterranean, and Anatolia: Implications for Cultural/Regional Interaction and Craftsmanship. PhD thesis, Bryn Mawr College.

Blackwell, N.G. 2018a. Contextualizing Mycenaean hoards: metal control on the Greek mainland at the end of the Bronze Age. *American Journal of Archaeology* 122(4): 509–539.

Blackwell, N.G. 2018b. Experimental stone-cutting with the Mycenaean pendulum saw. *Antiquity* 92(361): 217–232.

Blegen, C.W. 1937. *Prosymna. The Helladic Settlement Preceding the Argive Heraeum*. Cambridge: Cambridge University Press.

Boleti, A. 2017. *L'émeri. Modalités d'Exploitation dans le Monde Egéen Protohistorique et Antique*. Paris: Publication de la Sorbonne.

Boleti, A. 2020. Stone tools related to stone masonry techniques in the Bronze Age Eastern Mediterranean. An overview, in M. Devolder, I. Kreimerman and J. Driessen (eds) *ASHLAR. Exploring the materiality of Cut Stone Masonry in the Eastern Mediterranean Bronze Age. Proceedings of the workshop held at U.C. Louvain 8 -9 march 2018*: 241–264. Louvain-La-Neuve.

Bresson, A. 2016. *The Making of the Ancient Greek Economy. Institutions, Markets, and Growth in the City-States*. Princeton: Princeton University Press.

Brysbaert, A. 2012. People and their things. Integrating archaeological theory into Prehistoric Museum Displays, in S. Dudley, A.J. Barnes, J. Binnie, J. Petrov and J. Walklate (eds) *Narrating Objects, Collecting Stories. Essays in Honour of Professor Suzan M. Pearce*: 255–270. London: Routledge.

Brysbaert, A. 2013. Set in Stone? Socio-economic Reflections on Human and Animal Resources in Monumental Architecture of Late Bronze Age Tiryns in the Argos Plain, Greece. *Arctos* 47: 49–96.

Brysbaert, A. 2015. Set in stone? Constructed symbolism viewed through an architectural energetics' lens at Bronze Age Tiryns, Greece, in C. Bakels and H. Kamermans (eds) *Excerpta Archaeologica Leidensia* (Analecta Praehistorica Leidensia 45): 91–105. Leuven: Peeters.

Brysbaert, A. 2020. 'Forces of the hands, forces of the lands'. An awareness of physical and social multi-tasking in the agrarian and economic landscape of the Late Bronze Age Argive Plain. *Groniek* 223: 585–607.

Brysbaert, A. 2021. Logistics and Infrastructure in Support of Building BIG in the Late Bronze Age Argolid, Greece, in J. Pakkanen and A. Brysbaert (eds) *Building BIG – Constructing Economies: from Design to Long-Term Impact of Large-Scale Building Projects. Panel 3.6. (Archaeology and Economy in the Ancient World – Proceedings of the 19th International Congress of Classical Archaeology, Cologne/Bonn 2018, Vol. 10)*: 11–26. Heidelberg: Propylaeum.

Brysbaert, A. 2022. Mobility along prehistoric roads and Least Cost Paths in the Argolid, Greece, in S.W. Manning (ed.) *Critical Approaches to the Archaeology of Cyprus and the Wider Mediterranean*: 197–216. London: Equinox.

Brysbaert, A. and M. Vetters 2010. Practicing identity: a crafty ideal? *Mediterranean Archaeology and Archaeometry* 10(2): 25–43.

Brysbaert, A. and M. Vetters 2013. A Moving Story about 'exotica': objects' long-distance production chains and associated identities at Tiryns, Greece. *Opuscula* 6: 175–210.

Brysbaert, A. and M. Vetters 2015. Mirroring the Mediterranean. Self-image and artisanal networking in 12th century BCE Tiryns, Greece, in A. Babbi, F. Bubenheimer-Erhart, B. Marín-Aguilera and S. Mühl (eds) *The Mediterranean Mirror. Cultural Contacts in the Mediterranean Sea between 1200 and 750 B.C. Proceedings of the International Conference, Heidelberg, October 6th-8th, 2012*: 167–181. Mainz: RGMZ.

Brysbaert, A., I. Vikatou and H. Stöger 2020. Highways and byways in Mycenaean Greece. Human-environment interactions in dialogue. *Arctos* 54: 33–94.

Buonasera, T.Y. 2015. Modeling the costs and benefits of manufacturing expedient milling tools. *Journal of Archaeological Science* 57: 335–344.

Burford, A. 1969. *The Greek Temple Builders at Epidauros. A Social and Economic Study of Building in the Asklepian Sanctuary, During the Fourth and Early Third Centuries.* Liverpool: Liverpool University Press.

Cavanagh, W.G. and C.B. Mee 1999. Building the Treasury of Atreus, in P.P. Betancourt, V. Karageorghis, R. Laffineur and W.-D. Niemeier (eds) *Meletemata: Studies in Aegean Archaeology Presented to Malcolm H. Wiener*: 93–102. Liège – Austin: Université de Liège – University of Texas.

Charitonidou, S.I. 1952. Δύο Μυκηναϊκοί τάφοι εν τω χωρίω Πρίφτιανι παρά τας Μυκήνας. *Archaeologiki Ephemeris* 1952: 19 – 33.

Chase, A.F. and D.Z. Chase 1992. Mesoamerican elites. Assumptions, definitions, and models, in D.Z. Chase and A.F. Chase (eds) *Mesoamerican Elites: An Archaeological Assessment*: 3–17. Norman: University of Oklahoma Press.

Claudel, J. and L. Laroque 1970. *Pratique de l'Art de Construire. Maçonnerie, Terrace et Platrerie.* Paris: Dunod.

Cline, E.H. 2014. *1177 B.C. The Year that Civilization Collapsed.* Princeton: Princeton University Press.

Cole, S.M. 1954. Land transport without wheels, roads and bridges, in C. Singer, E.J. Holmyard and A.R. Hall (eds) *A History of Technology*: 704–715. Oxford: Clarendon Press.

de Fidio, P. 2001. Centralization and Its Limits in the Mycenaean Palatial System, in S. Voutsaki and J.T. Killen (eds) *Economy and Politics in the Mycenaean Palace States* (Cambridge Philol. Soc. Suppl. 27): 15–24. Cambridge: Cambridge Philological Society.

DeLaine, J. 1997. *The Baths of Caracalla: A Study in the Design, Construction, and Economics of Large-ScaleBuilding Projects in Imperial Rome* (JRA Supplement, 25). Portsmouth: Rhode Island.

Demakopoulou, K. 1988. Βρασέρκα. *Archaeologikon Deltion* 36 (1981) B1 Chronika: 97 - 99.

Demakopoulou, K. 1989. Kokla. *Archaeologiko Deltion* 37 (1982) B1, Chronika: 83–85.

Devolder, M. 2013. *Construire en Crète Minoenne. Une Approche Energétique de l'Architecture Néopalatiale* (Aegaeum, 35). Leuven – Liège: Peeters.

Diamond, J. 2005. *Collapse. How Societies Choose to Fail or Survive.* New York: Viking Press.

Drennan, M. and M.J. Kolb 2019. Pharaonic power and architectural labor investment at the Karnak Temple Complex, Egypt, in L. McCurdy and E.M. Abrams (eds) *Architectural Energetics in Archaeology. Analytical Expansions and Global Explorations*: 56–75. London: Routledge.

Drews, R. 1993. *The End of the Bronze Age. Changes in Warfare and the Catastrophe ca. 1200 B.C.* Princeton: Princeton University Press.

Elsam, R. 1825. *The Practical Builder's Perpetual Price-Book.* London: Thomas Kelly.

Erasmus, C. 1965. Monument building: some field experiments. *Southwestern Journal of Anthropology* 21: 277–301.

Evely, R.D.G. 1993. *Minoan Crafts: Tools and Techniques. An Introduction* (SIMA 92, 1). Göteborg: Paul Åströms Förlag.

Evely, R.D.G. 2000. *Minoan Crafts: Tools and Techniques. An Introduction* (SIMA92, 2). Göteborg: Paul Åströms Förlag.

Fallu, D.J. 2017. Bronze Age Landscape Degradation in the Northern Argolid: A Micromorphological Investigation of Anthropogenic Erosion in the Environs of Mycenae, Greece. PhD thesis, Boston University.

Filadelfeus, A. 1922. Ανόρυξις Θαλαμοειδών Τάφων εν Μυκήναις. *Archaeologikon Deltion* 5 (1919), Parartima: 34–38.

Fitzsimons, R.D. 2006. Monuments of Power and the Power of Monuments: The Evolution of Elite Architectural Styles at Bronze Age Mycenae. PhD thesis, University of Cincinnati.

Fitzsimons, R.D. 2007. Architecture and Power in the Bronze Age Argolid, in J. Bretschneider, J. Driessen and K. Van Lerberghe (eds) *Power and Architecture: Monumental Public Architecture in the Bronze Age Near East and Aegean*: 93–116. Leuven: Peeters.

Fitzsimons, R.D. 2011. Monumental Architecture and the Construction of the Mycenaean State, in N. Terrenato and D.C. Haggis (eds) *State Formation in Italy and Greece. Questioning the Neoevolutionist Paradigm*: 75–118. Oxford: Oxbow.

Fletcher, 1888. *Quantities. A Textbook for Surveyors in tabulated form*. London: B.T. Batsford.

Foxhall, L. 2007. *Olive Cultivation in Ancient Greece: Seeking the Ancient Economy*. Oxford: Oxford University Press.

Gallant, T. 1991. *Risk and survival in Ancient Greece. Reconstructing the Ancient Economy*. Oxford: Polity Press.

Gallimore, S., S. James, W. Caraher and D. Nakassis 2017. To Argos: Archaeological survey in the Western Argolid, 2014–2016, in D.W. Rupp and J.E. Tomlinson (eds) *From Maple to Olive. Proceedings of a Colloquium to Celebrate the 40th Anniversary of the Canadian Institute in Greece, Athens, 10–11 June 2016*: 421–438. Athens: Canadian Institute.

Grossmann, P. 1967. Zur Unterburg Mauer von Tiryns. *Archäologischer Anzeiger* 1967: 92–101.

Grossmann, P. 1980. Arbeiten an der Unterburgmauer von Tiryns in den Jahren 1969, 1971 und 1972. *Archäologischer Anzeiger* 1980: 477–98.

Halstead, P. 1995. Plough and power: the economic and social significance of cultivation with the ox-drawn ard in the Mediterranean. *Bulletin on Sumerian Agriculture* 8: 11–22.

Halstead, P. 2014. *Two Oxen Ahead. Pre-Mechanized Farming in the Mediterranean*. Oxford: Wiley-Blackwell.

Harper, C.R. 2016. Labouring with the economics of Mycenaean architecture. Theories, methods, and explorations of Mycenaean architectural production. PhD thesis, Florida State University, Tallahassee, Florida.

Hatzipanagiotou, K. and B. Tsikouras 2001. Rodingite formation from diorite in the Samothraki ophiolite, NE Aegean, Greece. *Geological Journal* 36: 93–109.

Higgins, M.D. and R. Higgins 1996. *A Geological Companion to Greece and the Aegean*. Ithaca: Cornell University Press.

Hiller, S. 1988. Dependent personnel in Mycenaean texts, in M. Heltzer and E. Lipinski (eds) *Society and Economy in the Eastern Mediterranean, c. 1500-1000 BC* (Orientalia Lovanensia Analecta, 23): 53–68. Leuven: Peeters.

Hinzen, K.-G., J. Maran, H. Hinojosa-Prieto, U. Damm-Meinhardt, S.K. Reamer, J. Tzislakis, K. Kemna, G. Schweppe, C. Fleischer and K. Demakopoulou 2018. Reassessing the Mycenaean earthquake hypothesis: results of the HERACLES project from Tiryns and Midea, Greece. *Bulletin of the Seismological Society of America* 108(3A): 1046–1070.

Hope Simpson, R. and O.T.P.K. Dickinson 1979. *A Gazetteer of Aegean Civilisation in the Bronze Age. Vol. 1. The Mainland and the Islands* (Studies in Mediterranean Archaeology 52). Göteborg: Paul Åströms Förlag.

Hurst, J.T. 1902. *A Hand-Book of Formulae, Tables, and Memoranda for Architectural Surveyors, and Others Engaged in Building*. London: E. and F. N Spon.

Iakovidis, S.E., E.B. French, K. Shelton, C. Ioannides, A. Jansen and J. Lavery 2003. *Archaeological atlas of Mycenae*. Athens: The Archaeological Society of Athens.

Ivanova, M. 2017. The 'green revolution' in Prehistory: Late Neolithic agricultural innovations as technological system, in P. Stockhammer and J. Maran (eds) *Appropriating Innovations. Entangled Knowledge in Eurasia, 5000-1500 BCE*: 40–49. Oxford: Oxbow Books.

Jansen, A.G. 1997. Bronze Highways at Mycenae. *EMC* 41(16): 1–16.

Jansen, A.G. 2002. *A study of the Remains of Mycenaean Roads and Stations of Bronze Age Greece* (Mellon Studies in Archaeology, 1). Lampeter: Edwin Mellen Press.

Killen, J.T. 2004. Wheat, barley, flour, olives and figs on Linear B tablets, in P. Halstead and J.C. Barrett (eds) *Food, Cuisine and Society in Prehistoric Greece* (Sheffield Studies in Aegean Archaeology, 5): 155–173. Oxford: Oxbow.

Knapp, A.B. and S.W. Manning 2016. Crisis in context: the end of the Late Bronze Age in the Eastern Mediterranean. *American Journal of Archaeology* 120(1): 99–149.

Kolonas, L. 2009. *Voudeni: An Important Site of Mycenaean Achaia*. Athens: Ministry of Culture.

Küpper, M. 1996. *Mykenische Architektur. Material, Bearbeitungstechnik, Konstruktion und Erscheinungsbild* (Internationale Archäologie, 25). Espelkamp: Marie Leidorf.

Kvapil, L.A. 2012. The Agricultural Terraces of Korphos-Kalamianos: A Case Study of the Dynamic

Relationship between Land Use and Socio-Political Organisation in Prehistoric Greece. PhD thesis, University of Cinncinnati.

Lang, M.L. 1969. *The palace of Nestor at Pylos in Western Messenia. Volume 2. The frescoes*. Princeton: Princeton University Press.

Lavery, J. 1990. Some Aspects of Mycenaean Topography. *Bulletin of the Institute of Classical Studies* 37: 165–71.

Lavery, J. 1995. Some 'New' Mycenaean Roads at Mycenae. *Bulletin of the Institute of Classical Studies* 40: 264–65.

Lejeune, M. 1968. Le civilization Mycénienne et la guerre, in J.-P. Vernant (ed.) *Problèmes de la Guerre en Grèce Ancienne* : 31–51. Paris: Mouton.

Lindblom, M. 2001. *Marks and Makers: Appearance, Distribution, and Function of Middle and Late Helladic Manufacturer's Marks on Aeginetan Pottery* (SIMA, 128). Jonsered: Paul Åströms Förlag.

Loader, C.N. 1998. *Building in Cyclopean Masonry with Special Reference to Mycenaean Fortifications on Mainland Greece*. Jonsered: P. Åström Förlag.

Maran, J. 2008. Forschungen in der Unterburg von Tiryns 2000–2003. *Archäologischer Anzeiger* 2008: 35–111.

Maran, J. and J.C. Wright 2020. The rise of the Mycenaean culture, palatial administration and its collapse, in I.S. Lemos and A. Kotsonas (eds) *A Companion to the Archaeology of Early Greece and the Mediterranean*: 99–132. Hoboken NJ: Wiley-Blackwell.

Marinatos, S. 1970. *Excavations at Thera III: 1967-1969 Seasons*. Athens: The Archaeological Society of Athens.

Martin, R. 1965. *Manuel d'Architecture Grecque I. Matériaux et Techniques*. Paris: Editions A. et J. Picard et Cie.

Melena, J.L. 2014. Mycenaean writing, in Y. Duhoux and A. Morpurgo Davies (eds) *A Companion to Linear B: Mycenaean Greek Texts and Their World. Volume 3* (Bibliothèque des Cahiers de l'Institut de Linguistique de Louvain, 133) : 1–186. Louvain-la-Neuve/Dudley, Mass: Peeters.

Middleton, G.D. 2017. *Understanding Collapse. Ancient History and Modern Myth*. Cambridge: Cambridge University Press.

Moody, J. and A.T. Grove 1990. Terraces and enclosure walls in the Cretan landscape, in S. Bottema, G. Entjes-Nieborg and W. van Zeist (eds) *Man's Role in the Shaping of the Eastern Mediterranean Landscape*: 183–191. Rotterdam: Balkema.

Morero, E. 2015. Mycenaean lapidary craftsmanship: the manufacturing process of stone vases. *The Annual of the British School at Athens* 110(1): 121–146.

Müller, K. 1930. *Die Architektur der Burg und des Palastes* (Tiryns, III). Augsburg: Dr. B. Filser.

Mundell, C., P. Walker, C. Bailey, A. Heath and P. McCombie 2009. Limit-equilibrium assessment of drystone retaining structures. *Proceedings of the Institution of Civil Engineers - Geotechnical Engineering* 162(4): 203–212.

Mylonas, G.E. 1957. *Ancient Mycenae. The Capital City of Agamemnon*. Princeton: Princeton University Press.

Mylonas, G.E. 1962. Το διασωθέν δυτικόν κυκλώπειον τείχος. *Αρχαιολογική Εφημερίς* 101: 101–109.

Mylonas, G.E. 1966. The East Wing of the Palace at Mycenae. *Hesperia* 35: 419–426.

Mylonas, G.E. 1968. *Mycenae's Last Century of Greatness* (Australian Humanities Research Council. Occasional Paper, 13). London: Methuen.

Nakassis, D. 2012. Labour Mobilization in Mycenaean Pylos, in P. Carlier, C. de Lamberterie, M. Egetmeyer, N. Guilleux, F. Rougemont and J. Zurbach (eds) *Etudes Mycéniennes 2010. Actes du XIIIe Colloque International sur les Textes Egéens* (Biblioteca di Pasiphae, 10) : 269–283. Pisa: F. Serra.

Nakassis, D. 2013. *Individuals and Society in Mycenaean Pylos*. Leiden: Brill.

Nakassis, D. 2015. Labor and individuals in Late Bronze Age Pylos, in P. Steinkeller and M. Hudson (eds) *Labor in the Ancient World* (The International Scholars Conference on Ancient Near Eastern Economies, 5): 583–616. Dresden: ISLET-Verlag.

Newhard, J.M.L. 2003. Aspects of Local Bronze Age Economics: Chipped Stone Acquisition and Production Strategies in the Argolid, Greece. PhD thesis, University of Cinncinnati.

Ober, J. 1989. *Mass and Elite in Democratic Athens. Rhetoric, Ideology, and the Power of the People*. Princeton: Princeton University Press.

Orlandos, A.K. 1970. To Ergon tis Archaeologikis Etaireias kata to etos 1969. *Ergon* 1969: 150–164.

Pakkanen, J. 2013. The economics of shipshed complexes: Zea, a case study, in D. Blackman and B. Rankov (eds) *Shipsheds of the Ancient Mediterranean*: 55–75. Cambridge: Cambridge University Press.

Pakkanen, J. 2021. Building big and Greek Classical and Hellenistic houses? Estimating total costs of private housing in Attica, in J. Pakkanen and A. Brysbaert (eds) *Building BIG – Constructing Economies: from Design to Long-Term Impact of Large-Scale Building Projects (Panel 3.6)* (Archaeology and Economy in the Ancient World - Proceedings of the 19th International Congress of Classical Archaeology, Cologne/Bonn 2018, Vol. 10): 59–75. Heidelberg: Propylaeum.

Palaima, T.G. 1989. Perspectives on the Pylos oxen tablets: textual (and archaeological) evidence for the use and management of oxen in Late Bronze Age Messenia (and Crete), in T.G. Palaima, C.W. Shelmerdine and P.H. Ilievski (eds) *Studia Mycenaea* (Živa Antika Monogr., 7): 85–124. Skopje: Dept. of Classical Philology of the University of Skopje.

Palaima, T. 2015. The Mycenaean mobilization of labor in agriculture and building projects: institutions, individuals, compensation and status in the Linear B tablets, in P. Steinkeller and M. Hudson (eds) *Labor in the Ancient World* (The International Scholars Conference on Ancient Near Eastern Economies, 5): 617–648. Dresden: ISLET-Verlag.

Palmer, R. 1989. Subsistence rations at Pylos and Knossos. *Minos* 24: 89–124.

Palyvou, C. 2005. *Akrotiri Thera. An Architecture of Affluence 3500 years Old*. Philadelphia: INSTAP Press.

Pegoretti, G. 1863. *Manuale Pratico per l'Estimazione dei Lavori Architettonici, Stradali, Idraulici e di Fortificazione. Per Uso degli Ingegneri ed Architetti*. Milano: Presso l'Editore Librajo Angelo Monti.

Pelon, O. 1976. Tholoi, Tumuli et Cercles Funéraires. Recherches sur les Monuments Funéraires de Plan Circulaire dans l'Égée de l'Âge du Bronze. IIIe et IIe millénaires av. J. –C. (Bibliothèques de l'Ecole Française d'Athènes et de Rome – Série Athènes 229), Paris : Diffusion de Boccard.

Pe-Piper, G., D.J.W. Piper and D. Matarangas 2002. Regional implications of geochemistry and style of emplacement of Miocene I-type diorite and granite, Delos, Cyclades, Greece. *Lithos* 60(1): 47–66.

Piteros, Ch. 1999. Παναρίτι δήμου Μιδέας. Περιοχή Μάζι – 'Σχολείο' (κτήμα Δ. Κατσαλούλη – Παναγ. Δανομάρα). *Archaeologikon Deltion* 49 (1994) Chronika B1: 151 – 152.

Postgate, J.N. 1992. *Early Mesopotamia: Society and Economy at the Dawn of History*. London – New York: Routledge.

Rudolph, W. 1973. Die Nekropole am Prophitis Elias bei Tiryns, in U. Jantzen (ed.) *Tiryns: Forschungen und Berichte VI*: 23–126. Mainz: Philipp von Zabern.

Runnels, C.N. 1994. On lithic studies in Greece, in P.N. Kardulias (ed.) *Beyond the Site. Regional Studies in the Aegean Area*: 161–172. London: Lanham.

Sarri, E. 2000. Μιδέα. Παναρίτης, θέση Μάζι (οικόπεδο αφών Κατσαλούλη). *Archaeologikon Deltion* 50 (1995) Chronika B1: 101.

Schliemann, H. 1886. *Tiryns. Der Prähistorische Palast der Könige von Tiryns. With Contributions by W. Dörpfeld*. Leipzig: F.A. Brockhaus.

Schwandner, E.-L. 1991. Der Schnitt im Stein. Beobachtungen zum Gebrauch der Steinsäge in der Antike, in A. Hoffmann, E.-L. Schwandner, W. Hoepfner and G. Brands (eds) *Bautechnik der Antike. Internationales Kolloquium in Berlin vom 15.-17. Februar 1990. Veranstaltet vom Architekturreferat des DAI in Zusammenarbeit mit dem Seminar für Klassische Archäologie der Freien Universität Berlin* (Diskussionen zur Archäologischen Bauforschung, 5): 219–223. Mainz: Philipp von Zabern.

Seeher, J. 2011. *Gods Carved in Stone. The Hittite Rock Sanctuary at Yazılıkaya*. Istanbul: Ege Yayinlari.

Shaw, J.W. 1973. *Minoan Architecture. Materials and Techniques* (Annuario della Scuola Archaeologica di Atene, 49). Roma: Istituto Poligrafico dello Stato.

Shaw, J.W. 2009. *Minoan Architecture. Materials and Techniques* (Studi di Archeologia Cretese, 7). Padova: Centro di Archeologia Cretese – Bottega d'Erasmo.

Shelmerdine, C.W. 1997. Review of Aegean prehistory VI: the palatial Bronze Age of the southern and central Greek Mainland. *American Journal of Archaeology* 101(3): 537–85.

Sjöberg, B. 2004. Asine and the Argolid in the Late Helladic III Period. A Socio-Economic Study (British Archaeological Reports, International Series 1225). Oxford: Archaeopress.

Smith, J. 1992-1993. The Pylos Jn series. *Minos* 27–28: 167–260.

Snodgrass, A. 1965. The Linear B Arms and Armour Tablets— Again. *Kadmos* 4: 97–98.

Tainter, J.A. 1988. *The Collapse of Complex Societies*. Cambridge: Cambridge University Press.

Tainter, J.A. 2006. Social complexity and sustainability. *Ecological Complexity* 3: 91–103.

Timonen, R. in prep. Plain of Plenty. Farming practices, food production, and the agricultural potential of the Late Bronze Age Argive Plain, Greece. PhD thesis, Leiden University.

Timonen, R. and A. Brysbaert 2021. Saving up for a rainy day? Climate events, human-induced processes, and their potential effects on people's coping strategies in the Late Bronze Age Mycenaean Argive Plain, Greece, in P. Erdkamp, J.G. Manning and K. Verboven (eds) *Climate and Society in Ancient Worlds Diversity in Collapse and Resilience*: 243–276. London: Palgrave.

Tsoupas, G. and M. Economou-Eliopoulos 2008. High PGE contents and extremely abundant PGE-minerals hosted in chromitites from the Veria ophiolite complex, northern Greece. *Ore Geology Reviews* 33(1): 3–19.

Turner, D.R. 2018. Comparative Labour Rates in Cross-cultural Contexts, in A. Brysbaert, V. Klinkenberg, A. Gutiérrez García-M. and I. Vikatou (eds) *Constructing Monuments, Perceiving Monumentality and the Economics of Building. Theoretical and Methodological Approaches to the Built Environment*: 195–218. Leiden: Sidestone Press.

Turner, D.R. 2020. *Grave Reminders. Comparing Mycenaean Tomb Building with Labour and Memory*. Leiden: Sidestone Press.

Ugan, A., J. Bright and A. Rogers 2003. When is technology worth the trouble? *Journal of Archaeological Science* 30 (10): 1315–1329.

Utchitel, A. 1985. Mycenaean and Near Eastern Economic Archives. PhD Thesis, University College London, UK.

Ventris, M. and J. Chadwick 1973. *Documents in Mycenaean Greek*. Cambridge: Cambridge University Press.

Vermeule, E.D.T. and V. Karageorghis 1982. *Mycenaean Pictorial Vase Painting*. Cambridge MA: Harvard University Press.

Wace, A.J.B. 1949. *Mycenae. An Archaeological History and Guide*. Princeton: Princeton University Press.

Walberg, G. 2007. *Midea. The Megaron Complex and the Shrine Area. Excavations on the Lower Terraces, 1994-1997*. Philadelphia: INSTAP Academic Press.

Whitelaw, T. 2001. Reading between the tablets: assessing Mycenaean palatial involvement in ceramic production and consumption, in S. Voutsaki and J. Killen (eds) *Economy and Politics in the Mycenaean Palace States. Proceedings of a Conference held on 1–3 July 1999 in the Faculty of Classics, Cambridge* (Cambridge Philological Society, supplementary volume 27): 51–79. Cambridge: Cambridge Philological Society.

Wright, J.C. 1978. Mycenaean Masonry Practices and Elements of Construction. PhD thesis: Bryn Mawr College.

Wright, J.C. 1987. Death and power at Mycenae: changing symbols in mortuary practice, in R. Laffineur (ed.) *Thanatos. Les coutûmes funéraires en Egée à l'age du Bronze* (Aegaeum, 1): 171–184. Liège: Université de Liège.

Yassoglou, N., C. Tsalidas and C. Kosmas 2017. *The Soils of Greece* (World Soils Book Series). Cham: Springer International.

14.

Building Accounts, Monumental Construction Projects, and Labour Rates in the Classical and Hellenistic Periods

Jari Pakkanen

Royal Holloway, University of London
J.Pakkanen@rhul.ac.uk

Abstract

The potential of Greek building accounts for estimating building costs of monumental architecture has been recognised for a long time. An early labour rate study on the cost of quarrying, transport, and construction of a single column of the colossal Hellenistic temple of Apollo at Didyma was published in 1926 by Bernard Haussoullier. However, the full potential of building inscriptions has not been fully utilised in labour rate studies, as will be demonstrated in the case studies of this paper and comparison of ancient data with Giovanni Pegoretti's 19th-century cost rates. Analyses of the actual block sizes of the temple of Apollo compared to the dimensions listed in the inscriptions allow for the calculation of different rates for ordered and delivered building blocks. The suggested daily wage of two Attic (Alexandrian) drachmas for a skilled workman make possible direct comparisons of the Didyma rates with other building projects. Further case studies discussed in the paper include the quarry, transport and construction costs of the Late Classical temple of Asklepios at Epidauros, land transport of Pentelic marble to Eleusis, and the cost of stonework for the Parthenon.

Keywords: Building cost, Hellenistic temple, transport, stonework, labour figures

Introduction

The conservative design of Classical and Hellenistic buildings and the use of durable materials mean that the volumes of construction materials can often be reconstructed reliably enough to be used as the basis of labour cost calculations.[1] In addition, a range of preserved detailed building accounts provide a wealth of information which can be used for studying the *chaîne opératoire* and economics of Greek construction.[2] Following Janet DeLaine's ground-breaking *The Baths of Caracalla* (1997), there has been a tendency to incorporate and compare data and labour rates in a considered way from a range of different contexts. This has also been taken up in the sphere of ancient Greek construction.[3] Ann Brysbaert's SETinSTONE project has already moved the field of building cost analyses of Greek Late Bronze Age architecture to a new level. The project's publications demonstrate the importance of collecting labour rates from different contexts to analyse prehistoric construction projects and the use of three-dimensional digital documentation techniques

for calculating the building material volumes in econometric studies of ancient construction.[4] The evaluation of the costs of the Classical shipshed complexes at Zea, one of the two military harbours of Athens, was part of my contribution to the project 'Shipsheds of the Ancient Mediterranean', and it presents a range of comparative labour rates from Greek, Roman, and New World contexts.[5] These trends are also evident in a series of papers presented in 2018 at the 19th International Congress of Classical Archaeology with the theme 'Archaeology and Economy in the Ancient World'.[6]

In this paper, I analyse in detail how a comparison between the unfinished column blocks of the colossal Hellenistic temple of Apollo at Didyma and the information from the building accounts can be used to gain a detailed picture of the labour rates and costs of the project. The principal places mentioned in this study are

---

[1] Pakkanen 2013: 56–72. Cf. also Salmon 2001: 195.
[2] For example, series of building accounts have been preserved related to Classical projects in Attica, Delphi, and Epidauros and Hellenistic building on Delos and at Didyma and Lebadeia. For overviews of Greek building inscriptions, see Scranton 1960; Hellmann 1999; Feyel 2006; Pitt 2016. For economic studies using the accounts, see e.g. Haussoullier 1926: 127–138; Stanier 1953; Rehm 1958: 62–64; Burford 1969; Haselberger 1985a; Clark 1993; Davies 2001; Pakkanen 2013.
[3] Brysbaert 2013, 2015; Pakkanen 2013; Lancaster 2019.

[4] For overviews of the project and further references, see Brysbaert 2017; Chapter 13 in this volume; Brysbaert *et al.* 2018. On the role of three-dimensional digital field documentation methods employed in the project, see the contributions by Brysbaert and her two project members in Pakkanen *et al.* 2020: 4–9.
[5] Pakkanen 2013. For further information on the project, see the Acknowledgements at the end of this paper.
[6] See publication of the panel 'Building BIG – constructing economies: from design to long-term impact of large-scale building projects' in Pakkanen and Brysbaert 2021. The experimental work carried out by Jean-Claude Bessac and Silke Müth on quarrying and constructing the city walls of Messene as part the project on the city wall is an important contribution to the field; Müth and Bessac 2018.

Figure 1. Map of principal sites mentioned in the text.

presented in **Figure 1**. Bernard Haussoullier's analysis of the expenses of constructing a column of the temple of Apollo is an early example of how the cost rates from early 2nd-century BC inscriptions can be used to estimate building costs of ancient architecture.[7] In the full publication of the Didyma building accounts, Albert Rehm presented a revised version of the calculations,[8] and his study is the basis of the analysis presented below. From the point of view of labour cost studies, perhaps the most important aspect of the inscriptions is that they give the precise actual costs of the early 2nd-century BC building phase. Study of the blocks makes possible comparison of the volume of the stone ordered from the quarries with the actually delivered blocks. The level of daily wages of skilled craftsmen at Didyma is not known with certainty, so a wider appraisal of wage and price levels in the Classical and Hellenistic periods provides a framework for comparing the costs of construction projects.

The remains and accounts of the temple of Asklepios at Epidauros provide a good comparative basis for a smaller building using less expensive limestone. Alison Burford's monograph on the building accounts demonstrates the scale of economic and social information that can be derived from the inscriptions, but rather curiously, she ignores the relevant data in Georges Roux's architectural study of the temple of Asklepios.[9] Therefore, Sebastian Prignitz's new study of the building accounts and rereading of several of

the prices from the contracts gives an opportunity to restudy the labour rates for quarrying, transport, and construction of the temple.[10]

Basing econometric calculations on the principle of estimating minimum costs is a sensible approach since in many cases the sources are not able to provide an exact date or duration of a project, and delays would have easily been created by bottlenecks in the delivery of materials and construction.[11] However, since the Greek building accounts record the actual costs of monumental building projects, it is possible to compare the labour rates derived from the inscriptions with estimates for minimum costs as is done in this paper.[12] Giovanni Pegoretti's 19th-century handbook of architectural labour rates has been used extensively in estimating the manpower requirements of ancient Roman construction,[13] and I compare his production rates with Greek architectural and inscriptional data from the Classical and Hellenistic periods. In the concluding section of this paper, R.S. Stanier's estimate for the cost of stonework for the Parthenon at Athens[14] is revaluated in light of the analyses on quarry and construction rates presented in this paper. Even though the labour rates here are mainly expressed in terms of drachmas because they are derived from the building accounts, I have given the silver weights of the different standards and the probable daily wages of skilled

---

[7] Haussoullier 1926: 127–138.
[8] Rehm 1958: 62–64.
[9] Roux 1961; Burford 1969. Burford did have access to Roux's work; see e.g. Burford 1969: 54 n. 2. For references to the architectural data she misses from Roux's monograph, see sub-section 'Quarries' below.

[10] Prignitz 2014.
[11] Cf. DeLaine 1997: 105–106.
[12] See also Pakkanen 2021.
[13] Pegoretti's handbooks were first published in 1843–1844, but I use here the 2nd revised edition of 1863–1864. On the use of Pegoretti's labour rates, see DeLaine 1997: 104–105.
[14] Stanier 1953.

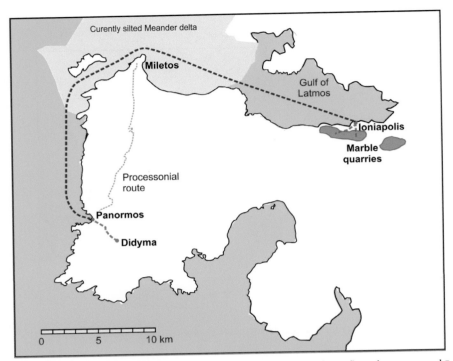

Figure 2. Transport of marble from the quarries to the sanctuary of Apollo at Didyma (based on Borg and Borg 2002a: fig. 3; Slawisch and Wilkinson 2018: fig. 3).

craftsmen to facilitate cross-cultural comparisons. The length of the working day is taken as ten effective hours.[15]

Temple of Apollo at Didyma

The 28 building inscriptions of the Hellenistic temple of Apollo at Didyma provide a detailed picture of the organisation and costs of the building project. Rehm's analyses are based on a detailed study of the accounts and what was known about the temple architecture by the 1940s.[16] In the current study, the inscriptional evidence on the quarrying of material for and construction of the column is compared with the work carried out by Lothar Haselberger, who discovered the Hellenistic work drawing of the shaft profile on the cella wall of the temple and studied the unfinished temple column.[17] Currently, it is possible to form a clear picture of the construction project in the sanctuary of Apollo due to the detailed research on the quarries in the region, the temple, the surrounding landscape, and the inscriptions (**Figure 2**).[18]

Haselberger's measurements of the two bottom drums of the unfinished column allow for a comparison of the actual dimensions with the diameter information inscribed on the drums, the Hellenistic shaft profile drawing, and the finished fluted drums.[19] The data on the column and the inscriptions are summarised in **Figure 3**. This figure is largely based on Haselberger's shaft profile drawing[20] but with new additions. The length of the foot-unit, 296.4±0.4 mm, is known from the design drawings on the cella wall which include a scale drawing of the shaft profile with entasis.[21] The vertical dimension of the shaft is scaled down by the factor of 16 so that one dactyl corresponds to one foot. The two lowest drums have the same inscribed dimension of 7 ft, so 2.072–2.078 m. The measured diameters of the blocks are 2.113 and 2.100 m,[22] so the figure inscribed on the block indicates that finished drums with diameters of 7 ft could be carved out of the two blocks, but they are not indications of the actual diameters of the drums. The inscription on the drum in the middle of the shaft (Drum 10) is very precise and it gives the dimensions down to half a dactyl (6 + 1/4 + 1/8 + 1/16 + 1/32 ft), but the calculated diameter is clearly less than what was required for the shaft at this point because of the

15 Cf. DeLaine 1997: 106. The use of a 10-hour day has the added advantage that person-hours can conveniently be calculated by multiplying the presented figures by 10.
16 Rehm 1958.
17 Haselberger 1980, 1983, 1985b.
18 On the quarries, see Borg and Borg 2002a, 2002b; Attanasio et al. 2006; Toma 2020. On the temple, see Knackfuss 1941; Haselberger 1980, 1983. On the landscape and procession from Miletos to Didyma, see Herda 2006; Slawisch and Wilkinson 2018. On the inscriptions, see Rehm 1958.

19 Haselberger 1983: 115–121. On the columns, see also Knackfuss 1941: 82–95.
20 Haselberger 1983: fig. 5.
21 Haselberger 1980: 193; 1983: 117. Rehm's (1958: 44 n. 2) foot-standard is not quite correct at 0.294 m, so his analyses need to be slightly adjusted. Knackfuss (1941: 62) suggests that the unit is 0.29845 m.
22 Haselberger 1983: 116–117.

convex entasis curve. The most likely interpretation is that the architect and the masons took advantage of the extra layer of quarry stone left all around the drum – the block was most probably initially intended for use higher up in the shaft, but the extra layer of stone of at least 2 cm made it possible to use the drum lower down. On Drum 8, the minimum thickness of the extra stone is 5 cm. It seems, therefore, that the building accounts very likely record the size of the block ordered from the quarry and, therefore, the dimensions used to calculate the block volume in cubic feet to pay for the quarrying and transport of the block. The use of very small foot divisions all the way down to a half-dactyl on the drums themselves (1/2 dactyl = c. 9.3 mm) has a parallel in the precisely recorded dimensions and costs of the building accounts: for example, in *Didyma* II 39.24 the combined surface area of two Ionic capitals is given as [3]77 1/4 square feet and the price of dressing the blocks as 1886 drachmas 1 obol 6 chalkous. Table A1 in the Appendix summarises the costs per column block where the rates in the inscriptions are given per cubic foot. This makes it possible to derive the drachma rates per cubic metre of the delivered blocks from the prices recorded in the inscription. Table A2 in the Appendix summarises the information on the work which was calculated based on the surface area of the blocks rather than the volume.

The measured sizes of the plinths at Didyma are very close to 9 ft × 9 ft × 1.5 ft (measured 2.69 m × 2.69 m × 0.45 m), so I have taken 121.5 cubic feet as the ordered quarry size of a block. In many cases the plinth is made of two separate blocks which both originally had a protective mantle. Based on Hubert Knackfuss's profile drawing of the lower part of the unfinished column and the known bottom diameter of the shaft,[23] it is possible to derive the width of the plinth with its extra layer of quarry stone and estimate the difference between the designed and delivered sizes. The width of the delivered plinth block is 2.754 m, so the thickness of the extra mantle is in this case c. 3 cm. Based on the drums, the extra layer was at least 2 cm, so this figure is used for the dimensions where the actual dimension cannot be measured such as the finished horizontal contact surfaces of the blocks in Tables A1 and A2. The layer was likely thicker than this in most cases, but this estimate gives a minimum estimate for the quarry size of the blocks.

The radius of the spira varies slightly, but Knackfuss gives several examples in his documentation. For example, the finished block with a radius of 1.311 m and the unfinished spira[24] of 1.336 m are both very close to a designed radius of 4.5 ft, so these dimensions are used for calculating the designed and delivered sizes. The

height of the finished block is 0.423 m. In the unfinished standing column, the torus and the lowest convex part of the shaft, the apophyge, are carved as one block.[25] The radius of the torus is 1.222 m and the height of the block 0.346 m. The ordered radius was most likely 4 ft (1.186 m). Combining the torus with the lower part of the shaft is not unique to this column, but the height of these blocks varies, as does that of the drums. The marble beds of the Milesian quarries had difficulties delivering the larger blocks needed for the column drums,[26] and this is also the best explanation for the higher price of the drums compared to the plinths (5.5 and 4 drachmas per cubic foot, respectively). The lower price is used systematically in Table A1 for blocks which have a height of less than 0.5 m.[27] Dimensions of the drums are indicated in **Figure 3**. The reading of the dimension inscription on Drum 9 is uncertain, and I have suggested that it could be 6 1/4 ft (Haselberger's suggestion is 6 1/8 ft). The designed radius of the top drum with an apophyge is known on the basis of the preserved capitals.[28] The size of a finished capital is quite accurately 7 ft × 8.5 ft × 3 ft (measured dimensions 2.056 m × 2.548 m × 0.906 m),[29] so the estimated designed volume of the capital was very likely 178.5 cubic feet or 4.64 m³. These dimensions are confirmed by the building accounts where the size of an Ionic capital delivered from the quarry is recorded.[30] The total ordered volume of quarry stone for the column can be calculated as 63.2 m³ and the minimum actually delivered volume as 69.6 m³, so at least 10% extra material was taken from the quarries to the sanctuary. With column drums it was also possible to take advantage of this extra stone by placing them further down in the shaft than initially planned. Therefore, it was not necessary that the surplus material was just carved away in all cases. The figures indicate that the volume of the ordered blocks was between 84–94% of the delivered quarry material.

The horizontal surfaces of the column blocks had to be finished before lifting and positioning, and the top part of the neck drum and the capital were already completed on the ground (the dimensions used in the volume calculations of the top Drum 1 are indicated in **Figure 3** with light grey). The reduced volume of these blocks is also given in Table A1, and this is used to calculate the costs of lifting and positioning of the blocks given in the table. Due to the more finished state of the blocks, the difference between the designed and actual volume for the erection of the column are quite small. The only exception is the capital which was

---

[23] Knackfuss 1941: pl. 44, Z.337.4. For the diameter as 2.111–2.114 m, see Haselberger 1983: 116–117.

[24] Knackfuss 1941: pl. 44, Z.337.3–4.

[25] Haselberger 1983: pl. 25.

[26] Borg and Borg 2002a: 275.

[27] Rehm (1958: 64) employs the lower cubic foot price only for the plinth.

[28] Approx. 0.930 m; Knackfuss 1941: Z.417, Z.429.

[29] Knackfuss 1941: pl. 52; Rehm 1958: 44.

[30] Rehm (1958: 45) presents a detailed argument about why the recorded size of 175 1/8 1/16 ft³ and the price do not match in *Didyma* II 39.53: the size must be emended to 178 1/8 1/16 ft³.

1. Task	2. Rate	3. Rate Ordered	4. Rate Delivered
Quarry stone (H < 0.5 m)	4 dr./ft³	153.6 dr./m³	131.8 dr./m³
Quarry stone (H ≥ 0.5 m)	5 3/6 dr./ft³	211.2 dr./m³	192.4 dr./m³
Land transport		19.2 dr./(km × m³)	17.4 dr./(km × m³)
Loading to ship	1/6 dr./ft³	6.4 dr./m³	5.8 dr./m³
Sea transport		1.6 dr./(km × m³)	1.4 dr./(km × m³)
Unloading from ship	1/6 + 6/72 dr./ft³	9.6 dr./m³	8.7 dr./m³
Lifting and positioning	1 dr./ft³	38.4 dr./m³	38.0 dr./m³
Fine dressing	2 dr./ft²	22.8 dr./m²	21.6 dr./m²
Fluting	2 dr./ft²	22.8 dr./m²	22.2 dr./m²
Carving Ionic capital	5 dr./ft²	56.9 dr./m²	54.5 dr./m²

Table 1. Temple of Apollo at Didyma. Cost rates as outlined in the inscriptions and based on ordered sizes and actually delivered blocks (likely day wage of a skilled craftsman: 2 Alexandrian/Attic drachmas per day; c. 4.3 g of silver per drachma).

substantially reduced in volume due to the extruding volutes.

The inscriptions at Didyma give very precise prices for the different sections of the transport of stone, from shipping from Ioniapolis to Panormos to hauling of the blocks from the harbour to the sanctuary (see **Figure 2**).[31] The price for the land transport from Panormos to the temple of Apollo is given as 2 drachmas per cubic foot. The length of the distance can be measured as 4.0 km and the height difference between the sea-level and the sanctuary is 74 m, so on average the road slopes gently at 1.1 degrees. Using the calculated volumes of stone, the total price for the quarry stone of the column can be calculated as 4856 drachmas; a total of 63.2 m³ of stone was ordered and purchased, and at least 69.6 m³ of stone was actually delivered. Using these figures, the price of land transport for one cubic metre of quarry stone can be calculated as 19.2 drachmas per kilometre for the volume of ordered stone and as 17.4 drachmas per kilometre for the stone actually delivered (**Table 1**). The topography in the delta of the Meander River has drastically changed since Antiquity because of silting (**Figure 2**), but from the building accounts it is clear that marble was shipped directly from Ioniapolis to Panormos. The modern Lake Bafa Gölü was in Antiquity an open gulf of the Mediterranean (the Gulf of Latmos). The distance of sea transport from Ioniapolis to Panormos can be measured as 41 km, so the rate of 1 drachma 4 obols per cubic foot can be calculated to correspond to a cubic metre rate of 1.6 drachmas per kilometre for the ordered stone and 1.4 drachmas for the delivered blocks. The inscription also gives rates for loading (1 obol per cubic foot) and unloading (1 obol 6 chalkous) of the blocks in the harbours and moving

of the blocks in the harbour at Panormos (1 obol per cubic foot). In addition, Rehm estimates that the cost of transport from the quarry to the harbour at Ioniapolis was 1 drachma per cubic foot (half the rate of transport from the harbour to the sanctuary) and at the sanctuary from the workplace to the temple 1 obol per cubic foot.[32]

Table A2 in the Appendix summarises the data related to the surface area of the column blocks. Fine dressing of the base and horizontal surfaces, fluting of the drums, and carving of the capital were all paid by the size of the treated area rather than volume. For each block, the table lists the surface area as it was ordered and delivered, the rates of carving, and the ratio between the ordered and actually delivered rates. Rehm's suggestion of adopting the price of carving the Ionic capital, 5 drachmas per square foot,[33] also for fine dressing of the vertical surfaces of the plinth, spira, and column shaft is surely exaggerated, as we will also see below in the section comparing the labour rates. The volume of removed stone in the carving of the Ionic capital was significantly more than what was required for other parts of the column, so I have used the rate of 2 drachmas per square foot for the rest of the column. The difference between the rates for the designed and actual total areas of the blocks is quite small at c. 96%. The horizontal surfaces of each block were finalised before erecting the column, as were any vertical sections for which the final carving would have been difficult. Fluting of the column was typically one of the final phases of construction, thus protecting the delicate vertical fillets of the shafts when the heavy entablature blocks were being lifted.

---

[31] Rehm 1958: 63–64.

[32] Rehm 1958: 64.
[33] Rehm 1958: 64.

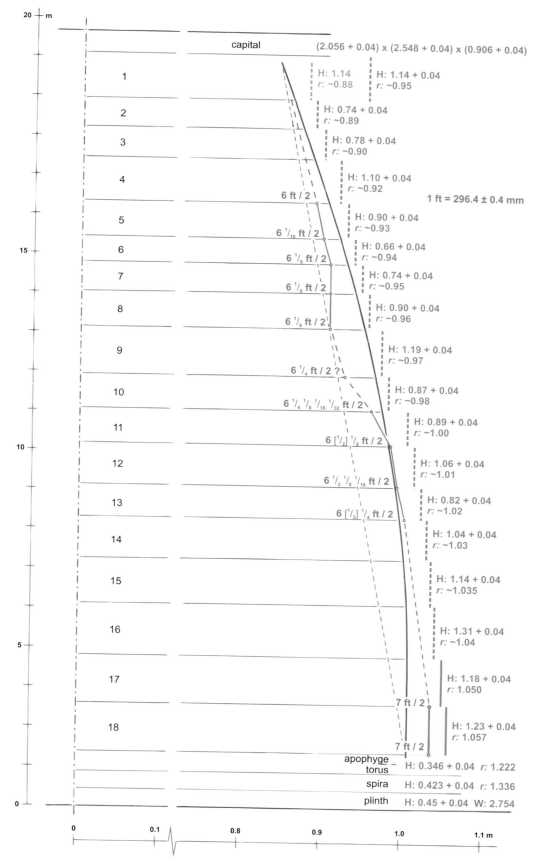

Figure 3. Details of the unfinished column of the temple of Apollo at Didyma. The dimensions inscribed on the drums are indicated with red and the actual dimensions are in blue (revised from Haselberger 1983: fig. 5).

Based on the volumes, surface areas, and rates presented in Tables A1 and A2, the cost of a single column of the temple of Apollo can be summarised as follows:

Quarrying and rough shaping of the blocks for transport	12,952 dr.
Transport (land 8093 dr., sea 5058 dr.)	13,152 dr.
Construction (erecting 2428 dr., dressing 6757 dr.)	9,185 dr.
Total	35,288 dr.

Quarrying and transport are both c. 37% of the total, and the cost for construction makes up the remaining 26% of the c. 35,300 drachmas. The total sum is 9% smaller than Rehm's estimate of 38,800 drachmas. The principal reason is that he adopts the rate paid for the Ionic capital also for the vertical surfaces of the column.

Wages and prices in the Classical and Hellenistic periods

The building accounts give a detailed picture of the construction costs in drachmas in early 2nd-century BC Didyma, and in order to relate these to earlier building projects on the Greek mainland and to later comparative material, a glimpse at the prices and wages in the wider Hellenistic period is necessary. The best time series on commodity prices in the Hellenistic world comes from Babylon where from the late Achaemenid period onwards astronomers meticulously recorded astronomical and meteorological data in Akkadian, as well as the amount of barley and sesame one shekel could buy in the market.[34] The most consistent Hellenistic economic data in the Aegean is from the sanctuary of Apollo on Delos.[35] The administrators kept records of the income and expenditure of the temple and inscribed them on stone, e.g. the prices and quantities of olive oil, pigs, firewood, and barley.[36] Gary Reger correctly emphasises the local conditions and limited scale of the market on Delos,[37] but it is worthwhile contrasting the two data sets from the opposite ends of the Hellenistic world. **Figure 4** presents how many grams of silver were needed to buy 10 kilograms of barley and **Figure 5** the price of 10 litres of sesame seeds in Babylon, the main oil plant, and olive oil on Delos.[38] The effect of instability

at the end of the reign of Alexander, his death in June 323 BC at Babylon, and the following wars of succession are clearly visible in both time series from Babylon. The scale of the y-axes on the two images are different to make room for the high olive oil prices on Delos, but the quick change in the agricultural prices at Babylon in the late 320s BC is evident in both time series. For example, within six months the price of barley had risen to a level four times higher than the previous year, and it takes a quarter of a century of turmoil before the prices return to approximately 4th-century levels at the consolidation of the Seleucid dynasty. The prices in the 3rd and 2nd centuries are marked by some seasonal variation and several clear peaks probably due to bad harvests,[39] but the main characteristic of this period is its high degree of stability. Severe price fluctuations are again visible at the end of the 2nd and beginning of the 1st centuries.

The barley prices on Delos are mostly higher than in Babylon (**Figure 4**), but when expressed in terms of grams of silver, the discrepancies between the two different markets are quite reasonable. Delos is a small island that depended on regionally produced imported grain,[40] and Babylon is located in the highly fertile Euphrates valley with a high volume of production. The spot prices in 250 BC show the range of seasonal variation on Delos, but the principal trend in **Figure 4** is one of constancy over the hundred years of recorded prices (the circles indicate the individual recorded prices and the solid lines the general trend in **Figures 4–5**). The time series on the price of olive oil on Delos is longer and more detailed than that for barley (**Figure 5**). In the early 3rd century there is a sharp fall in the general trend followed by marked stability in the latter half of the records. Reger analyses the early 3rd-century fall on Delos, and he notes that the extreme fluctuations at the end of the 4th century very likely reflect the economic disruption caused by warfare and dependency on imported oil.[41] He argues that the stabilisation of the prices during the 3rd century was probably due to the planting of local and regional olive orchards, but it could also be a reflection of the more stable economic and political climate in the Aegean.[42]

Figure 6 presents the data on day wages in the Aegean. Most of the data is based on Athens,[43] but relevant data

---

[34] Slotsky 1992, 1997; Grainger 1999; van der Spek 2000, 2002; Temin 2002; Pirngruber 2017.

[35] Reger 1993; 1994.

[36] Reger 1994: 127–188.

[37] Reger 1994: 49–83.

[38] The time series for Delos is based on Reger 1994 and for Babylon on data in van der Spek 2002 (the online spreadsheet). For the commodities, including the translation of the Akkadian ideogram *samaššammū* as sesame seeds rather than sesame oil in the context of the *Astronomical Diaries*, see Slotsky 1992: 56–223; 1997: 23–42. For

a summary of recent discussions of the commodities with references, see Pirngruber 2017: 9, n. 13. The general trends for Delos are produced using semiparametric smoothing in statistical package Survo MM; cf. Mustonen 1992: 174–175.

[39] Temin (2002) uses time series analysis methods to demonstrate that the prices are indeed market prices and that they change as would be expected of 'random walks' responding to weather conditions.

[40] Reger 1994: 83–126.

[41] Reger 1994: 155–169.

[42] Cf. Reger 1994: 253–264.

[43] Loomis 1998: 261–323.

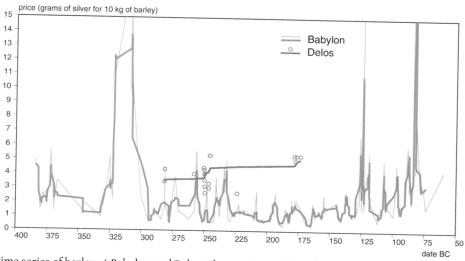

Figure 4. Price time series of barley at Babylon and Delos. The continuous lines for Babylon indicate the spot prices (thin light brown line) and the five-term moving average (thick brown line). The circles give the spot prices for Delos, and the continuous curve gives the general trend (thick red line).

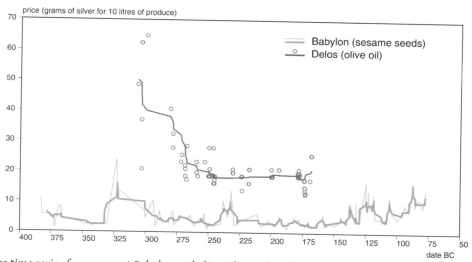

Figure 5. Price time series for sesame at Babylon and olive oil on Delos. The continuous lines for Babylon indicate the spot prices (thin light orange line) and the five-term moving average (thick orange line). The circles give the spot prices for Delos, and the continuous curve gives the general trend (thick green line).

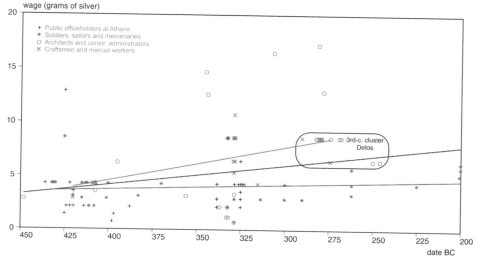

Figure 6. Wages in the Aegean in 450–200 BC. The lines indicate the general linear trend for the whole data set (blue), for craftsmen and manual workers (red), and for soldiers, sailors, and mercenaries (green).

from Delos, Delphi, and Epidauros[44] and on mercenaries has been added.[45] The data covers the period from the mid-5th century to the end of the 2nd century BC. The wage scale (the y-axis) is given in grams of silver because of the different regional currencies.[46] The longest time series on per diem payments is for citizen soldiers, sailors, and mercenaries.[47] In relation to construction, the compensations paid to architects are relatively well known,[48] but the status of an architect suggests that in several cases the compensation should rather be regarded as an acknowledgement of having filled the civic duties of a citizen rather than a living wage.[49] In **Figure 6** data for four different groups are presented:

1. Public officeholders at Athens (plus-sign);
2. Soldiers, sailors, and mercenaries (asterisk);
3. Architects, overseers, and construction project administrators (circle);
4. Craftsmen and manual workers (cross).

The two groups related to building projects received nearly systematically higher daily compensations than officeholders at Athens or the military in the wider Aegean basin, but the deviations in the level of pay the architects received is especially wide. In the 3rd century BC, there is a clear cluster at 1.5–2 Attic drachmas based on the inscriptions from Delos (marked in **Figure 6**). Three different linear trends are fitted to the data using the Linreg-module in Survo MM.[50] Overall, there is a slowly rising trend in the data: clear clustering can be observed in the late 5th century with most of the data coming from Athens, but this pattern breaks up in the Late Classical period (blue line in **Figure 6**). The linear trend of the per diem payments for soldiers and sailors is nearly flat (green line). The sharper slope in the day wages of the craftsmen is largely due to the high payments they received at Eleusis in the late 4th century before stabilising to 1.5–2 Attic drachmas on Delos (red line). Walter Scheidel presents a wider analysis of the long-term wages for unskilled labourers expressed in terms of litres of wheat.[51] His 31 data points are mostly from the eastern Mediterranean and Mesopotamia ranging from 1800 BC to AD 1300. He observes that

the Athenian daily wages, and to a lesser degree, the Delian ones belong to the 'higher income band' and are approximately at the same level as median wheat wages in Europe in AD 1500–1800.[52]

Even though this quick comparison of consumer prices and wages does not give direct evidence for the possible daily payment of a construction worker in early 2nd-century Didyma, the inscriptional evidence and stabilisation of the economy in the 3rd century point towards accepting the recorded levels of payments from Delos as a guideline. Cities in the Greek world minted their own coinage, but the sanctuaries of Apollo both on Delos and at Didyma used Attic (Alexandrian) drachmas in their accounting.[53] In the following section, therefore, I will use 2 Attic drachmas as a day wage for a skilled worker and 1 drachma for a manual labourer, at least at this initial stage of converting the recorded expenses to person-days of labour at Didyma.

Comparison of labour rates

The rates at Didyma, based on the volume calculations, are summarised in **Table 1**. The higher rate gives the price based on the ordered block sizes and the lower one is based on the actual delivered volume of stone. The price of quarry stone is separated into two different categories based on the maximum height of the required blocks.

Quarries

Prignitz's new work on the Epidaurian inscriptions makes possible a fresh look into the quarry, transport, and construction rates in the 4th-century north-eastern Peloponnese.[54] **Table 2** presents a summary of selected quarry, transport, and construction costs for limestone based on the contracts recorded in the building accounts of the temple of Asklepios (IG IV² 102).[55] The temple was built at the beginning of the 4th century BC.[56] Prignitz has reinterpreted several contract sums in the accounts,[57] and the stone quantities presented in the table are recalculated based on Roux's work on the temple.[58] Price rates, stone volumes, and surface areas given by Burford in her monograph should not be trusted:59 [59] for example, she only includes one of the three steps for the volume of the krepis and stylobate, and her cella stone volume

[44] Glotz 1913: 214–215; Lacroix 1914: 307; Larsen 1959: 408–412; Burford 1969: 140, n. 4; 1972: 141; Prignitz 2014: 177.
[45] Griffith 1935: 295–306; Pritchett 1971: 22.
[46] For the different drachma standards, the commonly accepted mass of 4.3 g/dr. is used for the Attic drachma in the conversions and 6.1 g/dr. for the Aiginetan. For a summary of the multiple monetary standards of the Greek world, see Psoma 2015. On the problem of defining the mass of the Athenian drachma, see Pakkanen 2011: 161, n. 28.
[47] Pritchett 1971: 3–29; Loomis 1998: 32–61, 266–269.
[48] Glotz 1913: 214–215; Lacroix 1914: 307; Burford 1969: 140, n. 4; 1972: 141.
[49] Burford 1969: 138–145; 1972: 141–142; Coulton 1977: 23–29.
[50] Mustonen 1992: 168–170.
[51] Scheidel 2010.

[52] Scheidel 2010: 452–454.
[53] Rehm 1958: 40; Reger 1994: 12–13.
[54] Prignitz 2014.
[55] The drachma prices per cubic metre presented in the table are calculated by dividing the contract price given in the inscription by the volume of building stone derived from the reconstruction of the temple of Asklepios.
[56] Prignitz 2014: 248–249 argues for a date of 400–390 BC.
[57] Prignitz 2014: 18–85.
[58] Roux 1961: 83–130.
[59] Burford 1969: 248–250.

Construction task and quantity	Q, T, and C	Q and T	Quarry	Transport	Construction
1. Local limestone for foundations of *peristasis*, 176 m³	4068 dr. 23.1 dr./m³				
2. Local limestone for foundations of cella, 96 m³	1385 dr. 14.4 dr./m³				
3. Corinthian stone for *peristasis* from steps to pediments, 258.7 m³		5700 dr. 22.0 dr./m³			
4. Construction of visible steps and stylobate, 66.9 m³					888 dr. 13.3 dr./m³
5. Construction of colonnade and entablature, 191.8 m³					3068 dr. 16.0 dr./m³
6. Corinthian stone for cella (half), 135.1 m³		6167 dr. 45.6 dr./m³			
7. Corinthian stone for cella (other half), 135.1 m³			4437–4455 dr. 32.8–33.0 dr./ m³	1712–1730 dr. 12.7–12.8 dr./ m³	
8. Construction of the cella, 270.2 m³					3209–3500 dr. 11.9–13.0 dr./ m³
9. Fluting of exterior and interior columns, 574.5 m²					1336 dr. 2.3 dr./m²

Table 2. Temple of Asklepios at Epidauros. Cost rates based on contract prices in the inscriptions and reconstructed stone volume (probable day wage of a skilled craftsman: 1 Aiginetan drachma per day; *c.* 6.1 g of silver per drachma)

is copied directly from Stanier's analysis.[60] Stanier did his work before the publication of Roux's monograph, and for example, he interprets the foundation widths of the cella as the thickness of the wall itself (1.48 and 1.55 m) even though these foundations carried both the cella wall and the interior colonnade; his wall height is too low, but this is not enough to compensate for the exaggerated thickness of the walls. Therefore, he ends up overestimating significantly the total volume of the cella stone, resulting in highly incorrect rates both in his and Burford's work.

Local soft limestone was considered sufficient for the foundations but not for the visible parts of the temple of Asklepios, and it was inexpensive: the whole process of quarrying, transport, cutting to shape, and assembling cost only *c.* 14–23 drachmas per cubic metre (rows 1 and 2 in **Table 2**). The higher rate of *c.* 23 drachmas per cubic metre for the exterior peristyle foundations could possibly be a result of preparing the whole temple area for construction. The usual Greek practice of constructing the exterior colonnade of a temple before the cella[61] is also attested by the order of the account entries for the temple of Asklepios. The ground area of the peristyle foundations is in any case almost twice as large as the cella foundations (120 and 64 m², respectively). The change to Corinthian suppliers instead of local ones was very likely linked to

the quality of the stone and the guaranteed supply from the established quarries.

The rates based on the construction contracts for the visible steps and the stylobate, the exterior order, and the cella reveal that there should not be any great discrepancies in my calculated volumes of the different parts of the temple. The rate for the exterior order, 16.0 drachmas per cubic metre, is slightly higher than for the krepis of the temple, 13.3 drachmas per cubic metre (rows 4 and 5 in **Table 2**). Construction of the columns and the exterior entablature is more difficult than the steps, so a higher rate would have been justifiable. Some final numbers of the cost of the contract for the cella construction are missing,[62] but the space available indicates that the total minimum sum of the missing characters is nine drachmas and the maximum 300 drachmas, so the contract was for 3209–3500 drachmas (row 8 in **Table 2**). The calculated rate is 11.9–13.0 drachmas per cubic metre, so it is in the same range as the krepis rate. In the contracts for the Corinthian quarry stone for the exterior and the cella[63] (rows 3, 6–7 in **Table 2**), the difference between the rates for contracts 3 and 6 is striking: the rate for the first contract is less than half of the latter. It is possible that Lykios from Corinth underestimated the difficulties in transporting the stone over sea and land to Epidauros, so the later contractors demanded a substantially

---

[60] Stanier 1953.
[61] Coulton 1977: 66–67.

[62] *IG* IV² 102.20–21; Prignitz 2014: 22, 46–47.
[63] *IG* IV² 102.3–4, 12–17; Prignitz 2014: 22, 44–46.

higher price. Other explanations could be that some of the stone for the upper parts of the exterior entablature was delivered as part of the cella contract or that the smaller cella wall blocks needed more quarry work to cut to size, though this extra cost was offset by the easier transport of the smaller blocks. The temple is the first monumental building in the sanctuary, so there were quite possibly some initial problems in the temple design and the *chaîne opératoire* of the building project. Therefore, in the following discussion I will combine the data of the four different contracts related to the quarrying and transport of Corinthian stone.

Some of the last figures for the cost of quarrying and transport are missing from the two separate contracts for the second half of the cella stone: however, the total would have been the same as for the first half, 6167 drachmas. Therefore, based on the space for the missing characters,[64] the contract for quarrying was 4437–4455 drachmas and for transport 1712–1730 drachmas. Circa 72% of these two contract prices was, therefore, for quarrying and *c.* 28% for transport (row 7 in **Table 2**). Assuming this ratio applies to the two other contracts (rows 3 and 6 in **Table 2**), the average for the temple quarry stone comes to *c.* 24.6 drachmas per cubic metre[65] and for the combined sea and land transport to *c.* 9.5 drachmas per cubic metre. On the same lines of the inscription as the discussed contracts, the architect of the project, Theodotos, is recorded as having received his conventional annual payment of one Aiginetan drachma a day.[66] The daily wage of a skilled craftsman can, with a relatively high degree of certainty, be taken to be at the same level,[67] so the calculated rates can also be expressed as person-days: 24.6 person-days per cubic metre for quarrying and 9.5 person-days for transport. This opens up the possibility of comparing the inscriptional data with Pegoretti's labour cost rates to gain an understanding of the possible amount of work involved for the Epidaurian contracts.[68]

Corinthian oolitic limestone is a very good material for construction. It is highly homogenous, and the size and shape of extracted blocks were determined by the intended use rather than discontinuities in the matrix, so wastage could also be kept to a minimum. A channel was cut around the stone and the most unpredictable part was breaking the lower surface of the block from the bedrock. Due to lamination of the limestone, the lower surfaces could require significant trimming of the lower face.[69] Keeping in line with the total cost estimate of a single column at Didyma, it is possible to analyse the work involved in quarrying the limestone drums of a single column of the temple of Asklepios. The calculations are based on Roux's proposal that the shaft was constructed of ten drums with an average height of 0.54 m; the lower shaft diameter was *c.* 0.92 m and the upper 0.606 m.[70]

For quarrying limestone, Pegoretti gives rates of 17.5–33.3 h/m^3 for one skilled quarryman assisted by two labourers, 56–224 h/m^3 of skilled labour for roughing-out the shape of the blocks, and 2.4–8.0 h/m^2 for rough dressing of the block surfaces.[71] Assuming a day rate of one Aiginetan drachma for the skilled quarryman and half of that for his assistants, and a ten-hour effective working day, the cost of the first phase of quarrying one cubic metre comes to 1.8–3.3 person-days of skilled and 3.5–6.7 person-days of unskilled labour, or a total of 3.5–6.7 Aiginetan drachmas per cubic metre.[72] With good planning during quarrying,[73] only the lower surfaces of the drums would have required roughing-out. Estimating an average thickness of 0.1 m for this layer, *c.* 20% of the final volume of the drums would have been removed, resulting in a rate of *c.* 1.1–4.5 dr./m^3.[74] Pegoretti's rough dressing of the drums is based on a rate per square metre, but in order to compare the rate with the inscription, it must be converted to a cubic metre rate. In this particular case the rate for the drums comes to 2.1–7.2 dr./m^3, but smaller blocks have a higher surface area per cubic metre, so their rate would be higher. Summing up the three phases, the rate for the drum blocks can be estimated as 6.8–18.3 dr./m^3. Considering the very high total volume of extracted material from the quarries at Corinth[75] and the homogeneity of the material, it is likely that the labour rate at Corinth would have been towards the lower end of the range. Even considering additional

64 *IG* IV^2 102.14–17. For the space for missing characters, see Prignitz 2014: 22.

65 For comparison, the price of Corinthian quarry stone based on mid-4th-century building accounts from Delphi is 16–26 dr./m^3; Roux 1966: 289–290.

66 *IG* IV^2 102.7.

67 Cf. *IG* I^3 475 and 476, the Erechtheion building accounts of 409–407 BC. For detailed analyses of the accounts and wages, see Loomis 1998: 99, 105–108.

68 Pegoretti 1863–1864. These volumes are the 2nd edition revised by A. Cantalupi. On the use of Pegoretti in the context of Roman construction projects, see DeLaine 1997: 104–106.

69 Hayward 2013: 66–68.

70 Roux 1961: 93. For the upper diameter, see Pakkanen 1998: app. D, table D1.

71 Pegoretti 1863: 166–167, 280–281, 338, 466; cf. Russell 2013: 30–31, table 2.1. Russell gives Pegoretti's minimum rate for roughing-out limestone as 56.9 h/m^3, but in Pegoretti 1863: 338 it is 56.0 h/m^3.

72 Hayward (2013: 68) estimates that quarrying a 1.4-m^3 block of Corinthian limestone takes *c.* 25 hours of labour. However, his estimate is based on quarrying marble and Burford's (1969: 247) estimate that Pentelic marble takes five times as long to work as 'poros' limestone. This might well be the case with dressing the stone, but Pegoretti's (1863: 166–167) *quarry* rates are only 1.2–2.3 times higher for marble than for limestone.

73 For the limestone drums in the quarries at Selinous, see e.g. Martin 1965: 148.

74 The average radius of a drum in the temple of Asklepios is r = 0.382 m, so the removed volume can in this case be calculated as $10 \times \pi r^2 \times 0.1\ \text{m} \approx 0.457\ \text{m}^3$. This is 18.5% of the total volume of the shaft of 2.47 m^3.

75 4,000,000–4,500,000 m^3; Hayward 2013: 64.

costs for tools and their maintenance, harbour dues, and also a possible quarry lease paid to the polis,[76] the average price of 24.6 drachmas per cubic metre paid for the stone by the sanctuary at Epidauros would have left a healthy profit margin for the entrepreneur. Assuming that the maximum quarry costs at Corinth could be kept to 12 drachmas per cubic metre, it can be estimated that the contractor was paid at least 2.1 times more than the daily wages for the extraction of the blocks. Returning back to the first contract on quarrying and transport of stone for the exterior of the temple (row 3 in **Table 2**), based on Pegoretti's labour rates it could have been a profitable deal, but there would have been little margin for error.[77] Also, the risks for the quarry contractor at Corinth would also have been substantially lower than for the transport contractor, as we will see below.

A similar comparison can be carried out with the cost of quarry stone at Didyma. Pegoretti's rate for marble quarrying is 40 h/m³ for a skilled quarryman with two assistants, 248.7–350.0 h/m³ for roughing-out, and 9.0–12.5 h/m² for rough dressing.[78] Using the daily wage of two Attic drachmas for skilled and one drachma for unskilled labour, the cost of quarrying comes to 16 dr./m³. The volume of the quarry stone needing to be roughed-out depends on the type of stone. For marble the wastage tends to be greater than for homogenous limestones, so I use 25% in the following calculations.[79] This results in a range of 12.4–17.5 dr./m³. Using the total column block volumes and surface areas at Didyma (**Tables A1–A2**) to estimate the rate for rough dressing the quarry blocks results in a rate of 7.4–10.2 dr./m³. The total range for the work quarrying the column blocks at Didyma based on Pegoretti comes to 35.8–43.7 dr./m³. This means that the lower end of the rate that was actually paid based on the building accounts and delivered stones, 131.8 dr./m³ (**Table 1**), is 3.7 times higher than the lower end of the range based on Pegoretti's figures. This applies to the blocks with a height of less than 0.5 m. The upper end of

the range at Didyma, 192.4 dr./m³, is for the larger blocks, and compared to the upper end of Pegoretti's range, it is 4.4 times larger. The paid rate at Didyma is 3.7–4.4 more than what would be expected on the basis of Pegoretti's labour rates and the daily wage calculations. Based on Pegoretti's data, Corcoran and DeLaine calculated the Roman quarry rate of medium-grained white marble as 26 *denarii* per cubic Roman foot which translates to 32.9 dr./m³ using the Didyma day wages. Consequently, their calculations produce a little lower figure than my minimum estimate based on Pegoretti.[80] Their minimum estimate for the full production costs of Proconnesian marble is based on 15th- and 16th-century AD costs at Luna, and it comes to 50 *denarii*/ft³, or 63.2 dr./m³ in terms of the Didyma prices. This is only 33–48% of the actual quarry stone prices paid at Didyma. These calculations point towards adding at least 50–100% on top of Pegoretti's quarry rates for additional costs such as supervision, tools, their maintenance, higher level of wastage, and moving the large blocks in the quarry.[81] Even with the additional costs, there is enough of a margin for the profit of the contractor. However, these calculations of the quarry costs support that the analysis of the daily wages presented in the previous section can produce a reasonable estimate for the daily wage level of the 2nd-century BC construction project at the sanctuary of Apollo at Didyma.

Land transport

A very significant part of construction project expenses was generated from moving the large limestone and marble blocks into the sanctuaries. The costs of land transport of marble column drums using oxen from the Pentelic quarries to Eleusis are known in detail from a preserved building account.[82] Stanier calculates the price of the transport of an average column drum of *c.* 2.84 m³ as 344 drachmas, but he slightly underestimates the ground distance from the quarries. The distance from the foot of the Pentelic mountain to the sanctuary at Eleusis is *c.* 33 km, so his average rate per cubic metre can be recalculated as *c.* 3.7 drachmas per kilometre. Kevin Clinton argues that in addition to the per diem price of 4 drachmas per yoke, there was an additional cost of 1 drachma per half-day.[83] The smallest recorded payment is 228 drachmas,[84] so accepting Clinton's analysis, the journey to Eleusis

---

76 Burford 1969: 172–175.
77 The minimum cost of quarrying is 6.8 dr./m³ × 258.7 m³ ≈ 1759.2 dr.; the later rates for land transport at Epidauros were certainly much higher: using the Tholos rate of 2.25 Aig. dr./(km×m³), the cost would have been 2.25 dr./(km×m³) × 15 km × 258.7 m³ ≈ 8731 dr., higher than the whole contract price. For the rates of land transport, see the next sub-section. A rough estimate for the minimum price can be estimated on the basis of oxen-days. Assuming that the maximum load per yoke was one tonne and that the return trip from the harbour to the sanctuary could be made in a day, it took a minimum 258.7 m³ × 2.6 tonnes/m³ × 1 oxen-day/tonne = 673 oxen-days. On loads of 500–1000 kg for a single yoke at Epidauros, see Burford 1969: 186–188. In the late 4th century BC, the cost of an oxen-day was *c.* 4 Attic dr. (see nn. 82-83 below for references), so for work carried out earlier in the century, it is unlikely that the price would have been less than 2 Aig. dr. per day. The combined minimum cost of quarrying and land transport comes to 3105 dr., leaving less than half for the operating costs of the quarries and sea transport.
78 Pegoretti 1863: 167, 280–281, 392; cf. Russell 2013: 30–31, table 2.1. For an evaluation of the cost of different marbles in Asia Minor and their use in building in the Roman period, see Barresi 2003: 151–204.
79 Cf. Corcoran and DeLaine 1994: 270.

80 Corcoran and DeLaine 1994, 270. 26 den. / 61 den./person-day × 2 dr./person-day × (0.296 ft/m)³ ≈ 32.9 dr./m³.
81 Cf. Barker and Russell, this volume for a discussion of factoring incidental costs into labour estimates.
82 *IG* II² 1673 (333/2? BC). For discussions of the inscription, see Stanier 1953: 70–71; Burford 1960: 13–15; Clinton 1971: 102–113; Raepsaet 1984; Loomis 1998: 109–110.
83 Clinton 1971: 106–107; cf. Burford 1960:, 13–15; Loomis 1998: 109–110, esp. n. 14.
84 *IG* II² 1673.81.

would have been carried out in two days by 28 yokes,[85] resulting in a minimum rate per cubic metre of 2.3–2.9 Attic drachmas per kilometre.[86]

However, there was no attempt to minimise the transport costs at Eleusis. The number of oxen yokes varied, and the smallest number used was most likely 24 and the highest 38,[87] resulting in loads of only 170–330 kg per yoke. The incentive of the administrators at Eleusis was quite likely to make certain that all yokes and their drivers turning up were given a chance to take part, thus ensuring that a sufficient number of beasts were always present when required. At Epidauros, the transport of 71 Pentelic marble coffers for the Tholos from the harbour to the sanctuary, a distance of 15 km on a cart road rising to 360 metres above sea level (c. 1.4-degree slope), cost 25 drachmas a piece. Burford gives the mass of a single coffer as 1997 kg,[88] so the rate per cubic metre can be calculated as 2.3 Aiginetan drachmas per kilometre, or in terms of the Attic drachma, 3.2 drachmas per kilometre.[89]

Burford estimates the distance as 7 miles,[90] but the more evenly sloped cart road is longer, so the rate per kilometre here is lower than hers. It is possible to compare this rate with DeLaine's land transport cost of 0.52 *kastrensis modii* / (tonne × Roman mile): her rate is 85% of the daily wage of a skilled workman,[91] and expressed in terms of a Roman mile, the rate at Epidauros is 124% of the daily wage of one Aiginetan drachma,[92] so it is higher but still within a comparable range. Because of the lighter mass of the coffers, far fewer oxen yokes would have been required than at Eleusis, but the contractor was not able to deliver the blocks on time. Megakleidas was paid 1775 drachmas for the transport, but he subsequently had to pay a fine of 1080 drachmas because of delay.[93] Using multiple yokes results in loss of efficiency,[94] and taking into consideration the mass of the heavy cart needed, Burford estimates that up to eight yokes would have been needed to pull the heavy blocks.[95] If the Epidaurian farmers were compensated at the same level as the Attic ones, the day-wage of a yoke and the driver would have been 2.8 Aiginetan drachmas, and only the single day of transport from the harbour to the sanctuary would have been covered, not the return trip. This level of compensation would have basically left little chance for Megakleidas to make a profit,[96] so it is likely that he paid less per yoke, tried to use fewer yokes, or even attempted to get away with both means of reducing the costs at the same time. The speed of transport would have depended on the number of yokes and carts available, so in this instance his attempt to get more out of the contract failed and he quite certainly ended up with a significant loss.

The land transport rates at Didyma are approximately five times higher than the average rate of 3.7 drachmas per cubic metre in Attica; however, based on the analysis of the previous section, the daily wages of skilled workmen were probably at the same level at Eleusis and at Didyma. There are some larger blocks at Didyma, but in general the blocks are of similar size, so that is not a sufficient explanation for the difference. At Eleusis, only the working days were covered by the payments and the income was only supplementary for the farmers turning up at the Pentelic mountain. Additional costs of the operation such as loading and unloading the blocks were not included in the price, and even the cost of the drinking troughs for the oxen was covered separately;[97] the heavy carts were also provided by the sanctuary.[98] The transport price at Epidauros is the total price paid to the contractor before the middle of the 4th century BC. The daily wages paid a little later at Eleusis were very high, so Megakleidas probably paid less to the yokes and should have been able to make a decent profit from the contract. It is difficult to find a specific reason why the land transport rates are as high as they are at Didyma by comparison with data from Eleusis and Epidauros, but organisation of transport could have been quite different at Didyma than at these other locations and required a higher level of compensation to cover all related costs.[99]

Carving final surfaces and the cost of a column

Comparison of the rates for column fluting at Epidauros and Didyma with Pegoretti's labour figures is rather straight-forward. Based on the contract price and the estimated surface area of the exterior, in-antis, and interior columns, the rate at Epidauros was 2.3 dr./m² (**Table 2**). Russell's analysis of Pegoretti's labour constants gives the fluting rate for limestones as

---

[85] 28 × 2 days × 4 dr./day + 2 days × 2 dr./day = 228 dr. DeLaine (1997: 108) gives the minimum speed for a heavily laden oxen pair as 1.67 km/h, and with multiple yokes the speed would have been slower; however, the load per yoke at Eleusis was low, so even assuming a minimum speed of 1.5 km/h, it would have been possible to reach the sanctuary in two days of 11 hours (2 × 11 h × 1.5 km/h = 33 km). Bevan (2013: 6) gives a summary of travel speeds and loads for Greek and Roman contexts: his wagon speed is 2–4 km/h and load 200–1000 kg.
[86] The mass of the column drums at Eleusis is 6.5–8.0 tonnes (Burford 1960: 6), so their volume was 2.4–3.0 m³: 228 dr./ (2.4 m³ × 33 km) ≈ 2.87 dr./(m³×km); 228 dr./ (3.0 m³ × 33 km) ≈ 2.33 dr./(m³×km).
[87] Clinton 1971: 103–107; Loomis 1998: 109 n. 14.
[88] Burford 1969: 186.
[89] 1775 dr. / (71 × (1997 kg / 2700 kg/m³) × 15 km) ≈ 2.25 Aig. dr./ (m³×km); 6.1 g / 4.3 g × 2.25 Aig. dr. ≈ 3.2 Attic dr.
[90] Burford 1969: 190.
[91] DeLaine 1997: 210–211. Rate: 0.52 KM / 0.61 KM ≈ 0.852.
[92] 25 dr. / (1.997 tonne × 15 km / 1.481 miles/km) ≈ 1.236.
[93] IG IV² 103, 198–199, 231–232. See also Prignitz 2014: 113–115.
[94] See e.g. DeLaine 1997: 108.
[95] Burford 1969: 186–187.

[96] 4 Attic dr. × 4.3 g / 6.1 g ≈ 2.82 Aig. dr.; 8 × 2.82 Aig. dr. ≈ 22.6 Aig. dr., and the price Megakleidas received was 25 Aig. dr.
[97] IG II² 1673.21.
[98] IG II² 1673.11–43; Burford 1969: 252–253.
[99] For example, if the contractor had to provide and maintain the carts for heavy transport.

7–26 h/m²,[100] so converted using the daily rate of one Aiginetan drachma per person-day, the range comes to 0.7–2.6 dr./m². The compensation actually paid at Epidauros is within this range, so it is possible that the contract price mainly included the daily wages of the stonemasons, the tools, and their maintenance. The rate for fluting marble columns can be calculated as 28.8–40.7 h/m²,[101] so using the estimated skilled wages of 2 Alexandrian (Attic) drachmas a day at Didyma, the range is 5.8–8.1 dr./m².[102] At the temple of Apollo, the most probable rate for fluting, 22.2–22.8 dr./m² (**Table 1**) is 2.7–3.9 times higher than the rate based on the estimated labour, so the compensation must have included substantial additional operational costs and a margin for profit on top of the salaries. The height of the Ionic capital at Didyma is higher than the maximum height given by Pegoretti, but the increase in his figures is based on a linear trend of the height,[103] not the surface area or volume as would be expected. Therefore, calculating a 'Pegorettian' labour estimate for the size of the Didyma capital is uncomplicated.[104] The person-hours can be converted into a rate of 12.5–17.2 dr./m² for the Didyma capital using its finished size in the calculations.[105] The rate for carving the capital is specified in the inscription as 5 dr./ft², so the paid rate of 56.9 dr./m² is 3.3–4.6 times higher than what can be estimated on the basis of Pegoretti's labour costs. This is in line with the analysis of the quarry costs, so 50–100% should be added on top of Pegoretti's marble carving rates for additional costs, such as tools and their maintenance, supervision, and making a profit. It is also possible that the craftsmen contracted to carry out the fluting and capital carving were highly valued specialists and paid at a higher rate than other masons. The recorded expenses for the temple certainly would have allowed such a rate.[106]

Based on the Didyma building accounts, the total cost of quarrying, transporting, erecting, and final carving of a single Ionic marble column of the temple of Apollo would have been *c.* 35,300 drachmas. The total volume of the material was 63.2 m³, so using the day wage of a skilled labourer, the final rate for the project comes to *c.* 280 person-days per cubic metre.[107] For one limestone

column of the temple of Asklepios at Epidauros, the total cost can be estimated as 177 drachmas.[108] The overall rate comes to *c.* 66 person-days per cubic metre, so building at a reasonable scale and employing less expensive materials, the rate for a single column at Epidauros can be calculated as less than a quarter of the of the rate for a column at Didyma. Using marble in monumental buildings made the statement that no costs were spared in these projects.

Cost of stonework for the Parthenon

If used diligently, the labour cost rates based on a comparison of Greek building account inscriptions and 19th-century architectural manuals can provide a way for realistic estimations of costs for monumental construction. The benefit of the inscriptions is that they document actually occurred costs, so studies are not limited to estimating the minimum level of finance for the projects. To give an example of how comparative rates can be used to suggest a cost range for stonework of a specific building, I will present a revaluation of Stanier's estimate for the Parthenon at Athens (447–432 BC).[109] In his calculations, 68% of his total cost comes from the quarrying, erecting, and dressing of the stone. Taking the above analyses as a guideline, the minimum quarry rates are largely based on Pegoretti but take into account operational costs. The maximum rates are based on Didyma but adjusted to the 5th-century Athenian daily wage of one drachma a day (**Table 3**). The rates for the limestone foundations are taken directly from the Epidauros inscriptions.[110] The costs for fine dressing are based on the Didyma inscriptions, and in order to keep comparisons between Stanier's calculations and the new rates as simple as possible, I have not adjusted any of the surface area or volume information nor have I estimated minimum figures for fine dressing of the blocks.

The readjustment of Stanier's rates shows that he has overestimated the cost of stonework for the temple. The range calculated here comes to 610,000–920,000 person-days instead of Stanier's much higher 1,900,000 person-days (**Table 3**). Expressed in Attic drachmas, the more likely range is 100–150 talents instead of 320 talents as estimated by Stanier. This brings down the total price

---

[100] Russell 2013: table 2.1.
[101] Russell 2013: table 2.1.
[102] Burford's (1969: 246) modern comparanda for fluting the Pentelic marble columns in the rebuilding of the Stoa of Attalos in the 1950s result in very high labour rates of 150 and 267 person-hours/m². These rates are 3.7 and 6.6 times higher than Pegoretti's maximum rate, so they are not useful for estimating realistic ancient labour costs.
[103] Pegoretti 1863: 397; cf. Russell 2013: table 2.3.
[104] Minimum 0.90 m / 0.80 m × 1042.67 h ≈ 1173.0 h and maximum 0.90 m / 0.80 m × 1440 h = 1620 h.
[105] 1173.0 h / 10 h/person-day × 2 dr./person-day × (2 × 2.056 m × 2.548 m + 2 × 2.548 m × 0.906 m + 2 × 2.056 m × 0.906 m) ≈ 12.47 dr./m²; 1440 h / 10 h/person-day × 2 dr./person-day × (2 × 2.056 m × 2.548 m + 2 × 2.548 m × 0.906 m + 2 × 2.056 m × 0.906 m) ≈ 17.22 dr./m².
[106] Cf. Barker and Russell, this volume.
[107] 35,288 dr. / 63.22 m³ / 2 dr./person-day ≈ 279.2 person-days/m³.

[108] The volume of the shaft and capital is *c.* 2.70 m³, and the surface area is *c.* 13.9 m². The rates are 24.6 dr./m³ for quarrying, 9.5 dr./m³ for transport, 16.0 dr./m³ for construction, 2.3 dr./m² for fluting, and 0.66 dr./m² for stuccoing. Stuccoing of the peristyle order is not separately listed in the building accounts, but it is quite possible that the task was part of the contract Philargos undertook for 615 dr. (*IG* IV² 102.79–80). If so, the rate for stuccoing the surfaces of the peristyle columns, entablature, and the exterior of the cella wall comes to 615 dr. / 926.6 m² ≈ 0.664 dr./m². Prignitz (2014: 43–75) does not discuss under which contract stuccoing of the exterior order should fall.
[109] Stanier 1953.
[110] Stanier (1953: 70) argues that the drachma rates from Epidauros can be used for the 5th century BC since the difference between the weight of Aiginetan and Attic drachmas matches the rise of prices.

1.	2. Fine Dressing	3. Quarrying	4. Constr.	5. Combined Rate	6. Volume	7. Cost
Walls	–	30.0–65.9 (153.5)	19.0 (16.5)	49.0–84.9 (170.0)	2849	139,601–241,880 (484,188)
Pavement	–	30.0–65.9 (153.5)	19.0 (11.0)	49.0–84.9 (164.5)	1389	68,061–117,926 (228,421)
Foundations	–	(25.6)	(9.3)	14.4–23.1 (34.9)	3251	46,814–75,098 (113,330)
Colonnade	25.37 (35.75)	30.0–65.9 (154.3)	19.0 (68.8)	74.4–110.4 (258.8)	3704	275,466–408,440 (958,521)
+ Fine dressing of walls and pavement, 7065 m² at 10.8 dr./m² (16.35 dr./m²)						76302 (115513)
Total				606244–919646 (1899973) dr. = 101.0–153.3 (316.7) talents		

Table 3. Stonework of the Parthenon on the Athenian Acropolis. Cost rates (2–5): dr./m³; volume (6): m³; cost (7): Attic drachmas. Stanier's figures are given in parentheses in the table (day wage of a skilled craftsman: 1 Attic drachma per day; c. 4.3 g of silver per drachma).

of the Parthenon to 250–310 talents, significantly less than Stanier's 470 talents.[111] Further revaluation of the costs is beyond the scope of this paper, but considering the tendency towards high rates in Stanier's study, it is likely that the lower sum of 250 talents estimated here is closer to the maximum price of the Parthenon, not the minimum.[112] Also, the Athenian practice of directly compensating the craftsmen rather than through a contractor, as is evident in the Erechtheion accounts, would have been an additional factor in reducing the overall costs compared to Epidauros and Didyma.[113]

Conclusions

The comparative analysis of the blocks of the unfinished column of the Hellenistic temple of Apollo at Didyma and the data on costs, rates, and volumes in the building accounts makes it possible to calculate separate labour rates for quarrying, transport, and construction of both the ordered *and* delivered material (**Table 1**). The total cost of a single column can be estimated as c. 35,300 drachmas (or c. 17,600 person-days of skilled labour working effectively ten hours a day). Quarrying and transport comprise c. 37% of the total costs each, and these two categories were more expensive than the actual construction of the column at c. 26% of the total. The new data on the cost of contracts and estimates of the building material

volume of the temple of Asklepios at Epidauros allow the estimation of more reliable cost rates for quarrying of Corinthian limestone, for sea and land transport from Corinth to Epidauros, and for construction at the temple site (**Table 2**). The difference in the scale of the two enterprises is striking: the volume of one column at Didyma is c. 63.2 m³ and at Epidauros only c. 2.7 m³. The total column cost at Epidauros can be estimated as 177 drachmas, and since the day wage of a craftsman was most probably in the range of one Aiginetan drachma, this labour cost is almost exactly one hundredth of the person-days at Didyma. Quarrying made c. 38% of the costs, and even though the distance by sea and land is the same as at Didyma, transport was only 14% of the total, thus leaving 48% for construction. The reduced level of costs for quarrying and transport clearly made Corinthian limestone a viable option for building in the north-eastern Peloponnese and at Delphi. In terms of person-days per cubic metre, the differences between the two projects are equally remarkable: the colossal scale, use of marble throughout, and relatively high transport costs at Didyma result in a rate more than four times as expensive per cubic metre as at Epidauros with imported Corinthian limestone and building at a 'human' scale.

When used carefully, combining data from the buildings themselves, the preserved building accounts, and 19th-century architectural manuals can result in realistic estimations for the total costs of monumental construction.[114] The principle of estimating minimum

---

[111] For a more general evaluation of the cost of major building programmes at Athens compared to income and expenses, see Pakkanen 2013: 72–74.

[112] Stanier (1953) estimates the cost of stone transport as 48 talents; ceiling, roof, and gates as 65 talents; pedimental sculptures and acroteria as 17 talents; cella wall frieze as 12 talents; and metopes as 10 talents.

[113] *IG* I³ 475 and 476; cf. Loomis 1998: 105–108.

[114] On the use of market prices in Attica for estimating the cost of Classical and Hellenistic housing, see Pakkanen 2021. On the documentation and estimation of building volumes for private houses, see also Pakkanen *et al.* 2020: 2–3.

labour costs is in general a sensible approach since in most cases it is very difficult to set the level for reasonable or maximum costs. However, because the Classical and Hellenistic building accounts list the specific payments made to the craftsmen, architects, and contractors, it is possible to derive the actual labour cost rates from the inscriptions and compare them with Pegoretti's 19th-century handbook and later scholarship using his rates. The analysis of the quarry and fine dressing rates from Epidauros and Didyma strongly supports the idea that employing Pegoretti's data also for Greek contexts produces meaningful comparisons: it opens up the possibility of looking into the profits made by the contractors and evaluating the level of skilled daily wages for projects where these data were not recorded in Antiquity. For example, using Pegoretti's labour rates for the work in the quarries provides a minimum baseline for estimating the number of required person-days, including roughing-out the shape of the blocks before transport. Comparing these figures with data from the building inscriptions provides a possibility of estimating the general operational costs of the ancient quarries. The high costs at Didyma can be the combined result of expensive contracts for the transport of marble blocks, entrepreneurs making substantial profits from the work, and the need to pay high enough prices for the times when the work was not progressing. Based on the analyses presented in this paper, the criticism that Pegoretti's figures produce too high labour estimates for ancient monumental building cannot be supported. In the concluding section of this paper, I present a revaluation of the cost of stonework for the Parthenon on the Athenian Acropolis based on a comparison with labour rates from Didyma and Epidauros (**Table 3**). The more realistic estimate of 100–150 Attic talents is only one third to half of Stanier's suggestion.

Acknowledgements

This study started its life as the joint paper 'Econometrics in Greek Architecture: Review and Current Trends' with Ann Brysbaert. It was presented at the Oxford conference in January 2020 honouring Janet DeLaine's defining contribution to the field of labour cost studies. Developing the ideas and discussions during the conference resulted in two separate papers, and both of these are presented in this volume.[115] Special thanks are due to Ann for being able to sound the ideas and for her feedback. I am also grateful to Caroline Waerzeggers for her quick reply to my query regarding the commodity prices in Babylon. This paper picks up on several issues presented in the footnotes of my contribution to the project 'Shipsheds of the Ancient Mediterranean'.[116]

The conference and its publication provided the opportunity of updating and formalising these ideas more thoroughly, so I wish to thank the organisers and Janet for the inspirational occasion.

Bibliography

Attanasio, D., M. Brilli and N. Ogle 2006. *The Isotopic Signature of Classical Marbles*. Rome: L'Erma di Bretschneider.

Barresi, P. 2003. *Province dell'Asia Minore. Costo dei marmi, architettura pubblica e committenza*. Studia Archaeologica 125. Rome: L'Erma di Bretschneider.

Bevan, A. 2013. Travel and interaction in the Greek and Roman World. A review of some computational modelling approaches, in S.E. Dunn and S. Mahony (eds) *The Digital Classicist 2013*: 3–24. Bulletin of the Institute of Classical Studies Supplement 122. London: Institute of Classical Studies.

Blackman, D., B. Rankov, K. Baika, H. Gerding and J. Pakkanen 2013. *Shipsheds of the Ancient Mediterranean*. Cambridge: Cambridge University Press.

Borg, B.E. and G. Borg 2002a. The History of Apollo's Temple at Didyma, as told by marble analyses and historical sources, in L. Lazzarini (ed.) *Interdisciplinary Studies on Ancient Stone. ASMOSIA VI Proceedings of the Sixth International Conference of the Association for the Study of Marble and Other Stones in Antiquity, Venice, June 15–18, 2000*: 271–278. Padova: Bottega d'Erasmo.

Borg, B.E. and G. Borg 2002b. From Small quarries to large temples. The enigmatic source of limestone for the Apollo temple at Didyma, W-Anatolia, in L. Lazzarini (ed.) *Interdisciplinary Studies on Ancient Stone. ASMOSIA VI Proceedings of the Sixth International Conference of the Association for the Study of Marble and Other Stones in Antiquity, Venice, June 15–18, 2000*: 427–436. Padova: Bottega d'Erasmo.

Brysbaert, A. 2013. Set in stone? Socio-economic reflections on human and animal resources in monumental architecture of Late Bronze Age Tiryns in the Argos Plain, Greece. *Arctos* 47: 49–96.

Brysbaert, A. 2015. Set in stone? Technical, socio-economic and symbolic considerations in the construction of the Cyclopean-style walls of the Late Bronze Age citadel at Tiryns, Greece, in C. Bakels and H. Kamermans (eds) *Excerpta Archaeologica Leidensia, Analecta Praehistorica Leidensia* 45: 69–90. Leuven: Peeters.

Brysbaert, A. 2017. Set in stone: an impact assessment of the human and environmental resource requirements of Late Bronze Age Mycenaean monumental architecture. *Antiquity* 91.358, e4: 1–7.

Brysbaert, A. 2022. Labouring and Its Costs During the Aegean Late Bronze Age, in Barker, S.J., C. Courault, J.Á. Domingo and D. Maschek (eds) *From Concept to Monument: Time and Costs of Construction in the Ancient World. Papers in Honour of Janet DeLaine*: 233–265. Oxford: Archaeopress.

---

[115] For her contribution, see Brysbaert Chapter 13 in this volume.
[116] Blackman *et al.* 2013. The project was co-directed by Boris Rankov, David Blackman, and the author of this paper, and it was funded by the Leverhulme Trust in 2003–2007.

Brysbaert, A., V. Klinkenberg, A. Gutiérrez Garcia-M. and I. Vikatou (eds) 2018. *Constructing Monuments, Perceiving Monumentality and the Economics of Building. Theoretical and Methodological Approaches to the Built Environment*. Leiden: Sidestone Press.

Burford, A. 1960. Heavy transport in Classical antiquity. *The Economic History Review* 13: 1–18.

Burford, A. 1969. *The Greek Temple Builders at Epidauros. A Social and Economic Study of Building in the Asklepian Sanctuary, during the Fourth and Early Third Centuries B.C.* Liverpool: Liverpool University Press.

Burford, A. 1972. *Craftsmen in Greek and Roman Society*. London: Thames and Hudson.

Clark, M.G. 1993. The Economy of the Athenian Navy in the Fourth Century B.C., Unpublished D.Phil. thesis. Oxford: Oxford University.

Clinton, K. 1971. Inscriptions from Eleusis. *Archaiologike Ephemeris* 1971: 81–136.

Corcoran, S. and J. DeLaine 1994. The unit measurement of marble in Diocletian's Prices Edict. *Journal of Roman Archaeology* 7: 263–273.

Coulton, J.J. 1977. *Greek Architects at Work. Problems of Structure and Design*. London: Elek Books.

Davies, J.K. 2001. Rebuilding a temple: the economic effects of piety, in D.J. Mattingly and J. Salmon (eds) *Economies beyond Agriculture in the Classical World*: 209–229. Leicester–Nottingham Studies in Ancient Society 9. London: Routledge.

DeLaine, J. 1997. *The Baths of Caracalla. A Study in the Design, Construction, and Economics of Large-Scale Building Projects in Imperial Rome*. Journal of Roman Archaeology Supplement 25. Portsmouth (RI): Journal of Roman Archaeology.

Feyel, C. 2006. *Les Artisans dans les sanctuaires grecs aux époques classique et hellénistique à travers la documentation financière en Grèce*. Bibliothèque des écoles françaises d'Athènes et de Rome 318. Athens: Ecole française d'Athènes.

Glotz, G. 1913. Les salaires à Délos. *Journal des savants* 11: 206–215.

Grainger, J.D. 1999. Prices in Hellenistic Babylonia. *Journal of the Economic and Social History of the Orient* 42: 303–350.

Griffith, G.T. 1935. *The Mercenaries of the Hellenistic World*. Cambridge: Cambridge University Press.

Haselberger, L. 1980. Werkzeichnungen am jüngeren Didymeion. Vorbericht. *Istanbuler Mitteilungen* 30: 191–215.

Haselberger, L. 1983. Bericht über die Arbeit am jüngeren Apollontempel von Didyma. Zwischenbericht. *Istanbuler Mitteilungen* 33: 90–123.

Haselberger, L. 1985a. Befestige Turmgehöfte im Hellenismus auf den Kykladeninseln Naxos, Andros und Kea. Unpublished PhD dissertation, Technische Universität. Munich.

Haselberger, L. 1985b. The Construction plans for the Temple of Apollo at Didyma. *Scientific American* 253: 126–133.

Haussoullier, B. 1926. Inscriptions de Didymes. Comptes de la construction du Didymeion IV. *Revue de philologie, de littérature et d'histoire anciennes* 50: 125–152.

Hayward, C. 2013. Corinthian stone exploitation and the interpretation of inscribed building accounts, in K. Kissas and W-D. Niemeier (eds) *The Corinthia and the Northeast Peloponnese. Topography and History from Prehistoric Times until the End of Antiquity*. Athenaia 4: 63–78. Munich: Hirmer.

Hellmann, M.-C. 1999. *Choix d'inscriptions architecturales grecques*. Lyon: Maison de l'Orient et de la Méditerranée – Jean Pouilloux.

Herda, A. 2006. *Der Apollon-Delphinios-Kult in Milet und die Neujahrsprozession nach Didyma: ein neuer Kommentar der sog. Molpoi-Satzung*. Milesische Forschungen 4. Mainz: Philipp von Zabern.

Knackfuss, H. 1941. *Die Baubeschreibung*. Didyma 1. Berlin: Gebr. Mann.

Lacroix, M. 1914. Les Architectes et entrepreneurs à Délos de 314 à 240. *Revue de philologie, de littérature et d'histoire anciennes* 38: 303–330.

Lancaster 2019. To House and defend: the application of architectural energetics to southeast Archaic Greek Sicily, in L. McCurdy and E.M. Abrams (eds) *Architectural Energetics in Archaeology. Analytical Expansions and Global Explorations*: 95–113. London: Routledge.

Larsen, J.A.O. 1959. Roman Greece, in T. Frank (ed.) *An Economic Survey of Ancient Rome* 4: 259–498. Paterson (NJ): Pageant Books.

Loomis, W.T. 1998. *Wages, Welfare, Costs and Inflation in Classical Athens*. Ann Arbor: University of Michigan Press.

Martin, R. 1965. *Manuel d'architecture grecque*. Paris: A. et J. Picard.

Mustonen, S. 1992. *SURVO. An Integrated Environment for Statistical Computing and Related Areas*. Helsinki: Survo Systems.

Müth, S. and J.-C. Bessac 2018. Economical challenges of building a Geländemauer in the middle of the 4th c. BC: the city wall of Messene as an example. 19th International Congress of Classical Archaeology. Cologne/Bonn, 22–26 May 2018. Viewed 25 March 2020, https://www.aiac2018.de/programme/sessions/session3/panel24/papers/mueth/

Pakkanen, J. 1998. *The Temple of Athena Alea at Tegea. A Reconstruction of the Peristyle Column*. Publications by the Department of Art History at the University of Helsinki 18. Helsinki: Department of Art History at the University of Helsinki.

Pakkanen, J. 2011. Aegean Bronze Age weights, chaînes opératoires, and the detecting of patterns through statistical analyses, in A. Brysbaert (ed.) *Tracing Prehistoric Social Networks through Technology: a Diachronic Perspective on the Aegean*: 143–166. London: Routledge.

Pakkanen, J. 2013. The economics of shipshed complexes: Zea, a case study', in D. Blackman, B. Rankov, K. Baika,

H. Gerding and J. Pakkanen, *Shipsheds of the Ancient Mediterranean:* 55–75. Cambridge: Cambridge University Press.

Pakkanen, J. 2021. Building Big and Greek Classical and Hellenistic Houses? Estimating Total Costs of Private Housing in Attica', in J. Pakkanen & A. Brysbaert, *Building BIG – Constructing Economies: from Design to Long-Term Impact of Large-Scale Building Projects (Panel 3.6)* (Archaeology and Economy in the Ancient World. Proceedings of the 19th International Congress of Classical Archaeology 10): 59–75. Heidelberg: Propylaeum.

Pakkanen, J. and A. Brysbaert (eds) 2021. *Building BIG – Constructing Economies: from Design to Long-Term Impact of Large-Scale Building Projects (Panel 3.6)* (Archaeology and Economy in the Ancient World. Proceedings of the 19th International Congress of Classical Archaeology 10). Heidelberg: Propylaeum.

Pakkanen, J., A. Brysbaert, D. Turner and Y. Boswinkel 2020. Efficient three-dimensional field documentation methods for labour cost studies: case studies from archaeological and heritage contexts. *Digital Applications in Archaeology and Cultural Heritage* 17, e00141: 1–10.

Pegoretti, G. 1863–1864. *Manuale pratico per l'estimazione dei lavori architettonici, stradali, idraulici e di fortificazione per uso degli ingegneri ed architetti.* Biblioteca scelta dell'ingegnere civile 13. 2nd edn rev. by A. Cantalupi, 2 vols. Milan: Galli e Omodei.

Pirngruber, R. 2017. *The Economy of Late Achaemenid and Seleucid Babylonia.* Cambridge: Cambridge University Press.

Pitt, R.K. 2016. Inscribing construction: the financing and administration of public building in Greek sanctuaries, in M.M. Miles (ed.) *A Companion to Greek Architecture:* 195–205. Malden (MA): Wiley Blackwell.

Prignitz, S. 2014. *Bauurkunden und Bauprogramm von Epidauros (400–350): Asklepiostempel, Tholos, Kultbild, Brunnenhaus.* Vestigia 67. Munich: Verlag C.H. Beck.

Pritchett, W.K. 1971. *The Greek State at War* 1. Berkeley: University of California Press.

Psoma, S.E. 2015. Choosing and changing monetary standards in the Greek world during the Archaic and the Classical periods, in E.M. Harris, D.M. Lewis and M. Woolmer (eds) *The Ancient Greek Economy. Markets, Households and City-States:* 91–115. Cambridge: Cambridge University Press.

Raepsaet, G. 1984. Transport de tambours de colonnes du Pentélique a Éleusis au IVe siècle avant notre ère. *L'Antiquité Classique* 53: 101–136.

Reger, G. 1993. The Public purchase of grain on independent Delos. *Classical Antiquity* 12: 300–334.

Reger, G. 1994. *Regionalism and Change in the Economy of Independent Delos, 314–167 B.C.* Berkeley: University of California Press.

Rehm, A. 1958. *Die Inschriften.* Didyma 2. Berlin: Gebr. Mann.

Roux, G. 1961. *L'architecture de l'Argolide aux IVe et IIIe siècles avant J.-C.* Bibliothèque des Ecoles Françaises d'Athènes et de Rome 199. Paris: De Boccard.

Roux, G. 1966. Les comptes du IVᵉ siècle et la reconstruction du temple d'Apollon à Delphes. *Revue archéologique:* 245–296.

Russell, B. 2013. *The Economics of the Roman Stone Trade.* Oxford: Oxford University Press.

Salmon, J. 2001. Temples the measures of men: public building in the Greek economy, in D.J. Mattingly and J. Salmon (eds) *Economies beyond Agriculture in the Classical World:* 195–208. Leicester–Nottingham Studies in Ancient Society 9. London: Routledge.

Scheidel, W. 2010. Real wages in early economies: evidence for living standards from 1800 BCE to 1300 CE. *Journal of the Economic and Social History of the Orient* 53: 425–462.

Scranton, R.L. 1960. Greek architectural inscriptions as documents. *Harvard Library Bulletin* 14: 159–182.

Slawisch, A. and T.C. Wilkinson 2018. Processions, Propaganda, and Pixels: Reconstructing the Sacred Way Between Miletos and Didyma. *American Journal of Archaeology* 122: 101–143.

Slotsky, A.L. 1992. The Bourse of Babylon: An Analysis of the Market Quotations in the Astronomical Diaries of Babylonia. Unpublished PhD dissertation. Yale University.

Slotsky, A.L. 1997. *The Bourse of Babylon. Market Quotations in the Astronomical Diaries of Babylonia.* Bethesda (MD): CDL Press.

Stanier, R.S. 1953. The Cost of the Parthenon. *The Journal of Hellenic Studies* 73: 68–76.

Temin, P. 2002. Price behavior in ancient Babylon. *Explorations in Economic History* 39: 46–60.

Toma, N. 2020. Milet, Türkei. Marmorprovenienz und bauwirtschaftliche Paradoxe (nach Vorarbeiten 2018 und 2019). *e-Forschungsberichte des Deutsches Archäologisches Instituts* 2020.1: 117–123.

van der Spek, R.J. 2000. The Effect of war on the prices of barley and agricultural land in Hellenistic Babylonia, in J. Andreau, P. Briant and R. Descat (eds) *Économie antique. La guerre dans les économies antiques:* 293–313. Saint-Bertrand-de-Comminges: Museé archéologique départemental de Saint-Bertrand-de-Comminges.

van der Spek, R.J. 2002. Commodity prices in Babylon 385–61 BC. Viewed 27 March 2020, <http://www.iisg.nl/hpw/babylon.php> and datafile <http://www.iisg.nl/hpw/babylonia.xls>.

Appendix

1. Block	2. V ord.	3. V del.	4. V hz.	5. rate	6. rate m³	7. pr. ord.	8. rate d.	9. rd/ro	10. TrQIP	11. TrLo	12. TrSea	13. TrUnl	14. TrH	15. TrHD	16. TrD	17. Land	18. Sea	19. Erect.
Plinth	3.164	3.716	3.413	4.0	153.6	486.0	130.8	0.851	121.5	20.2	202.5	30.4	20.2	243.0	20.2	405.0	253.1	121.5
Spira	2.282	2.596	2.372	4.0	153.6	350.6	135.0	0.879	87.6	14.6	146.1	21.9	14.6	175.3	14.6	292.2	182.6	87.6
Torus	1.528	1.811	1.623	4.0	153.6	234.7	129.6	0.844	58.7	9.8	97.8	14.7	9.8	117.4	9.8	195.6	122.2	58.7
Drum18	4.159	4.458	4.317	5.5	211.2	878.4	197.0	0.933	159.7	26.6	266.2	39.9	26.6	319.4	26.6	532.3	332.7	159.7
Drum17	3.990	4.226	4.087	5.5	211.2	842.7	199.4	0.944	153.2	25.5	255.4	38.3	25.5	306.4	25.5	510.7	319.2	153.2
Drum16	4.324	4.587	4.451	5.5	211.2	913.3	199.1	0.943	166.0	27.7	276.7	41.5	27.7	332.1	27.7	553.5	345.9	166.0
Drum15	3.712	3.971	3.837	5.5	211.2	783.9	197.4	0.935	142.5	23.8	237.6	35.6	23.8	285.1	23.8	475.1	296.9	142.5
Drum14	3.333	3.600	3.466	5.5	211.2	704.0	195.6	0.926	128.0	21.3	213.3	32.0	21.3	256.0	21.3	426.6	266.7	128.0
Drum13	2.578	2.811	2.680	5.5	211.2	544.5	193.7	0.917	99.0	16.5	165.0	24.7	16.5	198.0	16.5	330.0	206.2	99.0
Drum12	3.271	3.525	3.397	5.5	211.2	690.9	196.0	0.928	125.6	20.9	209.4	31.4	20.9	251.2	20.9	418.7	261.7	125.6
Drum11	2.695	2.922	2.796	5.5	211.2	569.3	194.8	0.923	103.5	17.3	172.5	25.9	17.3	207.0	17.3	345.0	215.6	103.5
Drum10	2.512	2.746	2.625	5.5	211.2	530.6	193.2	0.915	96.5	16.1	160.8	24.1	16.1	192.9	16.1	321.5	201.0	96.5
Drum09	3.207	3.636	3.518	5.5	211.2	677.5	186.3	0.882	123.2	20.5	205.3	30.8	20.5	246.3	20.5	410.6	256.6	123.2
Drum08	2.330	2.722	2.606	5.5	211.2	492.1	180.8	0.856	89.5	14.9	149.1	22.4	14.9	178.9	14.9	298.2	186.4	89.5
Drum07	1.916	2.212	2.098	5.5	211.2	404.6	182.9	0.866	73.6	12.3	122.6	18.4	12.3	147.1	12.3	245.2	153.3	73.6
Drum06	1.709	1.943	1.832	5.5	211.2	360.9	185.7	0.879	65.6	10.9	109.4	16.4	10.9	131.2	10.9	218.7	136.7	65.6
Drum05	2.282	2.554	2.445	5.5	211.2	482.1	188.7	0.894	87.7	14.6	146.1	21.9	14.6	175.3	14.6	292.2	182.6	87.7
Drum04	2.732	3.031	2.925	5.5	211.2	577.1	190.4	0.901	104.9	17.5	174.9	26.2	17.5	209.9	17.5	349.8	218.6	104.9
Drum03	1.898	2.087	1.985	5.5	211.2	400.8	192.1	0.909	72.9	12.1	121.5	18.2	12.1	145.7	12.1	242.9	151.8	72.9
Drum02	1.760	1.941	1.842	5.5	211.2	371.7	191.5	0.907	67.6	11.3	112.6	16.9	11.3	135.1	11.3	225.2	140.8	67.6
Drum01	3.098	3.346	2.773	5.5	211.2	654.3	195.6	0.926	119.0	19.8	198.3	29.7	19.8	237.9	19.8	396.5	247.8	119.0
Capital	4.747	5.132	2.816	5.5	211.2	1002.6	195.4	0.925	182.3	30.4	303.8	45.6	30.4	364.6	30.4	607.6	379.8	182.3
Total	63.224	69.570	63.904			12952.2		x̄ 0.904			4046.6			4856.0		8093.3	5058.3	2428.0

Table A1. Temple of Apollo at Didyma. Volumes, rates, and costs per block where the rates are defined on the basis of volume in the building accounts.

1. Block: column block. 2. V ord: volume ordered – 3. V del: volume delivered – 4. V hz: Volume after horizontal beds of the blocks have been smoothed (before erection) – 5. rate: rate from inscription (dr./ft³) – 6. rate m³: dr. per m³ (= rate/(0.2964 m)³) – 7. pr. ord: price in dr. as ordered (= V ord. × rate m³) – 8. rate d: rate as delivered (dr./m³) – 9. rd/ro: rate delivered / rate ordered / (= rate d./rate m³) – 10. TrQIP: cost in dr. of land transport from quarry to Ioniapolis – 11. TrLo: Transport, loading to ship at Ioniapolis – 12. TrSea: Transport by sea – 13. TrUnl: Transport, unloading at Panormos – 14. TrH: Transport at the harbour – 15. TrHD: Transport from harbour at Panormos to the sanctuary – 16. TrD: Transport from workplace to place of use at Didyma – 17. Land: total in dr. for land transport (= 10 + 14 + 15 + 16) – 18. Sea: total in dr. for sea transport (= 11 + 12 + 13) – 19. Erect: Lifting and positioning of blocks.

1. Block	2. A ord.	3. A del.	4. rate	5. rate m²	6. pr. ord.	7. rate d.	8. rd/ro
Plinth	21.348	22.605	2	22.77	486.0	21.79	0.948
Spira	14.274	14.766	2	22.77	324.9	22.33	0.972
Torus	11.455	12.039	2	22.77	260.8	22.48	0.964
Drum18	14.779	15.189	2	22.77	336.5	22.34	0.972
Drum17	14.453	14.712	2	22.77	329.0	22.49	0.982
Drum16	15.038	15.356	2	22.77	342.3	22.44	0.979
Drum15	13.803	14.144	2	22.77	314.2	22.39	0.976
Drum14	13.010	13.396	2	22.77	296.2	22.32	0.971
Drum13	11.442	11.792	2	22.77	260.5	22.33	0.971
Drum12	12.773	13.136	2	22.77	290.8	22.34	0.972
Drum11	11.547	11.875	2	22.77	262.9	22.35	0.973
Drum10	11.015	11.391	2	22.77	250.8	22.27	0.968
Drum09	12.316	13.165	2	22.77	280.4	21.74	0.933
Drum08	10.310	11.219	2	22.77	234.7	21.53	0.920
Drum07	9.398	10.088	2	22.77	213.9	21.75	0.934
Drum06	8.941	9.450	2	22.77	203.6	21.98	0.949
Drum05	10.153	10.693	2	22.77	231.1	21.99	0.950
Drum04	11.114	11.677	2	22.77	253.0	22.00	0.950
Drum03	9.179	9.500	2	22.77	209.0	22.26	0.967
Drum02	8.801	9.115	2	22.77	200.4	22.25	0.967
Drum01	12.096	12.475	2	22.77	275.4	22.29	0.969
Capital	15.820	16.504	5	56.91	900.4	54.86	0.958
Total	273.063	284.288			6756.6		$\bar{x}$ 0.961

Table A2. Temple of Apollo at Didyma. Surface areas, rates, and costs per block where the rates are defined on the basis of area in the building accounts.

1. Block: column block. 2. A ord: surface area of the block as ordered – 3. A del: surface area of the delivered block – 4. rate: rate from inscription (dr./ft²) – 5. rate m²: dr. per m² (= rate/(0.2964 m)²) – 6. pr. ord: price in dr. as ordered (= A ord. × rate m²) – 7. rate d: rate as delivered (dr./m²) – 8. rd/ro: rate delivered / rate ordered / (= rate d./rate m²).

15.

On Toolmarks, Sequence of Carving, and Labour Quantification in Roman Stone Carving: The Case of Heroon III at Miletus

Natalia Toma

German Archaeological Institute

natalia.toma@dainst.de

Abstract

This paper aims to explore the method of labour quantification in Roman stone carving by adding a monument-based perspective to determine the sequence of carving and, by doing so, to cross-check the accuracy of estimates. The argument is built upon the results of a broader research project dealing with the dynamics of the building economy in Roman imperial Miletus (DFG TO1102/1-1). In this particular case, the focus is on the marble architecture of the funerary monument known as Heroon III and on the reconstruction of the carving process as revealed by toolmarks. The results indicate a very rational approach to construction by the Roman workforce that obviously aimed more at efficiency than at accuracy of execution. Moreover, it seems that the prevalence of sawing in the preparatory phase of stone carving practiced on the construction site must have been higher than generally acknowledged for ancient practices. In fact, its relevance in Antiquity seems comparable with operations in the Early Modern period. The observations on sawing in Roman Miletus thus legitimise once more the use of Pegoretti's labour figures for ancient carving processes and confirm modern architectural handbooks as indispensable tools for the better understanding of ancient building processes.

Keywords: toolmarks, stoneworking, sawing techniques, labour figures, architectural energetics

Introduction

Roman stone architecture has been traditionally studied in terms of scale, level of ingenuity, or choice of prestigious materials. Yet, the last two decades have seen increasing research interest in the building process and especially its socio-economic dimensions. This development is owed decisively to the breakthrough in the methodology for quantifying the ancient building economy as elaborated by Janet DeLaine in her monograph on the Baths of Caracalla in Rome.[1] DeLaine introduced a civil engineering approach based on 19th-century architectural manuals that exhaustively described the early modern building process and presented labour constants that allow the conversion of material volumes into labour equivalents in order to quantify structures in terms of man-hours. Among numerous sources, Giovanni Pegoretti's handbook *Manuale pratico per l'estimazione dei lavori archittetonici, stradali, idraulici e di fortificazione,* issued in 1843–44 and reprinted in 1863–64, has become the established point of reference for archaeological studies dealing with the quantification of ancient architecture, particularly with regard to massive stone building and especially

to stone carving.[2] Stone carving is a conservative craft, and therefore single operations and tasks of the building process, such as quarrying, transporting, working, carving, and lifting stone, and even the tools described by Pegoretti in the 19th century remained with few exceptions comparable to ancient ones.

The potential of the Pegoretti-based method has been rapidly acknowledged within archaeological research, which has largely embraced it; however this has been done in a rather one-sided way as reflected by the dominating trend of cost estimates.[3] Beyond offering a sense of magnitude, the quantification of ancient building projects also allows us to study major operations of the building process otherwise not described in ancient sources and to weigh them against each other.[4] Nevertheless, the scholarly and historical relevance of using them solely to create estimates remains controversial. This issue was raised in 2012 by

---

[1] DeLaine 1997.

[2] This paper uses Pegoretti's first volume of the second edition, abbreviated as Pegoretti 1863. The content of the chapter referring to stone carving (Articulo VIII. Apparecchio e lavoratura delle pietre da taglio) as well as the tables with the labour figures are identical in both editions, see Pegoretti 1863: 355–467 and Pegoretti 1843: 232–334.

[3] E.g. Barresi 2003; Maschek 2016; Domingo and Domingo 2017.

[4] DeLaine (1997) emphasised that estimates not only give a sense of magnitude but are also a valuable and indispensable tool to understand major operations of the construction process – i.e. the 1:3 ratio between the effective costs for procuring stone material and its transport to the construction site by land routes.

Simon Barker and Ben Russell in a study scrutinising the reliability and the use of Pegoretti's labour figures in quantifying ancient stone carving processes.[5] The crucial point about Pegoretti's handbook is the lack of any instructions on how to use the labour figures he provides. This is not surprising as building processes or related operations and procedures, such as stone carving, do not progress uniformly.[6] On the contrary, the decision on the sequence of work stages or choices of tools differs according to the personal preferences and the skills of the craftsmen and the specific end product.[7]

Therefore, the key for applying Pegoretti's method is identifying the *chaîne opératoire* that acts as an algorithm determining the sequence of work stages (or tasks) that can be afterwards translated into labour equivalents by the given equations. This sequence can be determined in two distinctive ways: a general approach based on commonly accepted assumptions and ideal circumstances, or a reconstruction based on a specific and detailed analysis of the monument itself. The choice of approach is of course directly influenced by the scale and the degree/level of preservation of the monument. Nevertheless, archaeological research has so far favoured the ideal model for reconstructing the carving process.[8]

This paper aims to explore the method of labour quantification in Roman stone carving by adding a monument-based perspective on determining the sequence of carving and, by doing so, cross-checking the accuracy of the estimates. The underlying intention of this paper is to reach a better understanding of ancient construction processes and operations undertaken on the construction site. For the sake of brevity, the focus is exclusively set on the stone carving process. The argument is built upon the results of my research project dealing with the dynamics of the building economy in Roman imperial Miletus, in particular the marble architecture of the so-called Heroon III.[9] The monument was thoroughly architecturally surveyed by B. Weber in the 1990s,[10] while my own fieldwork in 2018 and 2019, though primarily focused on the architectural decoration and the archaeometric study of the construction material, also included a detailed analysis of the stone carving process, with particular regard to toolmarks.[11]

The so-called Heroon III and evidence of sawing in its construction

The so-called Heroon III is a 3rd-century AD monumental funerary complex, most probably commemorating a prominent citizen as suggested by its location within the urban texture of the city and the proximity to the theatre and the Faustina-Baths. The complex occupied the whole width of a north-south oriented *insula* and included a peristyle court, a block of *cubicula* with cult functions at the backside, and a cella-structure for the grave itself (**Figure 1**). Two architectural elements are of specific interest for this investigation: the stylobate slabs of the peristyle and the orthostates of the pedestal-like substructure of the sarcophagus grave.

The colonnade surrounding the unpaved court of the funerary monument stood on a stylobate of mainly longitudinally arranged slabs and consisted of the following elements: pedestals carved from the same block as the pertaining Attic-Ionic base (**Figure 6**), monolithic columns shafts of granite, Corinthian capitals, and a simple entablature of an architrave superimposed with a fluted frieze and a cornice with dentils.

The now-lost monumental sarcophagus exposed in the cella was set on a pedestal-like substructure[12] built of various stone materials and contrasting chromatics (**Figure 2**): on the two-step krepis stood the moulded lower profile of the pedestal whose middle section was faced by four orthostates and topped by a projecting profile. Both profiles were carved in a dark grey marble variety, while the central part – built of blocks of Neogene limestone – was paneled with four thick orthostates of intense white colour. The white marble originated from the Bafa-Lake quarries of Miletus,

---

[5] Barker and Russell 2012; Toma 2022.

[6] Pegoretti's manual addresses primarily 19th-century construction specialists proficient in construction practices and familiar with stone carving. This justifies the abundance of detail and the deliberate consistency in describing each single task or work stage related to a building operation.

[7] This is clearly stated by Pegoretti (1863: 355) whose main concern as a civil engineer was 'pietra da taglio' and not architectural elements that required further carving: 'Compiuti che sia l'apparecchio grossolani delle pietre, alcune volte vengono quest poste in opera senz'altro lavoro, come negli edificj rustici; ma nei lavori architettonici ordinariamente si perfezionano i tagli'.

[8] An idealised *chaîne opératoire* is the only reasonable approach when it comes to understanding a large-scale monument (DeLaine 1997). Though most authors (See Barresi 2003: 163–188, esp. 169 f.; Maschek 2016; Domingo and Domingo 2017) precisely define their methodology and adopt a coherent *chaîne opératoire* complying with the basic rules of construction practice, the lack of a standardised sequence of tasks nonetheless inhibits further comparative studies. For a critical assessment on the varying sequences of tasks, see also Barker and Russell 2012: 87.

[9] This case study summarises preliminary results of the ongoing research project 'Construction dynamics and building materials in Roman Imperial Miletus' (TO1102-1/1) funded by the German Research Foundation (DFG) and established at the German Archaeological Institute (Natural Science Department). I want to thank C. Berns, director of the Miletus excavation, for his support during the field campaigns, and my student assistants, M. Bäßler, J. Schneider, and K. Zielke, for their engagement in the project.

[10] Weber 2004: 101–144.

[11] Toma 2021.

[12] Weber 2004: 118–121, fig. 77 (catalogue), 131 f. (reconstruction).

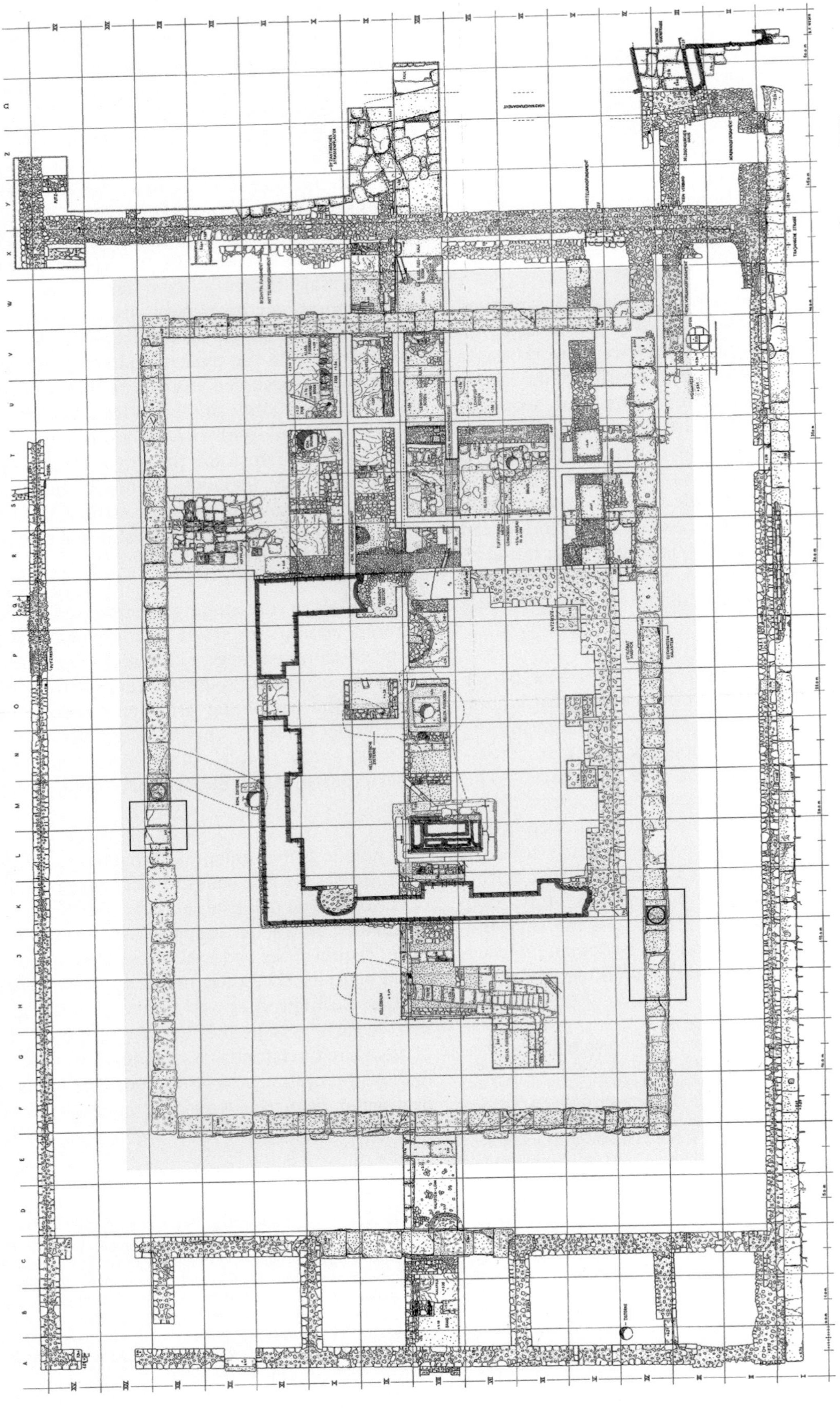

Figure 1. Miletus, Heroon III. Plan of the stone elements of the peristyle court (B. Weber) with labelling by the author.

Figure 2. Miletus, Heroon III. Cella: Pedestal combining moulded profiles of dark grey material with orthostates of white marble (author's photos).

same as the dark grey material.[13] The limestone was most likely quarried on the Milesian peninsula.[14]

The stylobate rested on a limestone *euthynteria*. Excluding the south-west and north-east corners, c. 64 slabs with varying lengths and widths are preserved in situ.[15] The height measured in Roman units (1 Roman ft of 29.6 cm) is approximately 1 Roman ft, while the length of the slabs varies considerably from 2 to 6 Roman ft. The surface treatment of the marble slabs on their front and rear is rather uniform. The front, i.e. the face visible from the peristyle court, shows a smoothed surface worked with a fine tooth chisel, and in most cases, there is a so-called edge-protection-bosse beneath the upper edge (**Figure 3**, above). The rear side of the slab shows alternating bands of curved marks that can be best observed on slabs of the north and east part of the peristyle's stylobate (**Figure 3**, below). This kind of toolmark is typical at quarries where it indicates the use of a quarry pick to cut separating trenches along the sides of the blocks to be detached from the bedrock. The evidence of quarry pick marks on the rear side of the stylobate

slabs indicates that the building material reached the construction site of the Heroon in the state of extraction without undergoing preparatory carving at the quarry.

The upper surfaces of the stylobate's slabs, which were actually the ancient walking level, show no uniform stage of working but rather a wide range of textures: from roughed-out by a point chisel to smoothed with tooth chisels of different formats to evenly polished (**Figure 4**). This last category is of particular interest as polishing is considered a common finish of stone surfaces and therefore the last task in stone carving.[16] Nevertheless, this particular case documents that the polished surface has been deliberately re-worked: first deepened with a point chisel and then subsequently smoothed with a tooth chisel (**Figure 4**). The point chisel is conventionally used at the very beginning of the stone carving process to remove superfluous material; its traces are usually cleared away by the tooth chisel to achieve an even finish, and then the surface is polished using abrasives. This particular example, however, testifies to a reversed sequence of tasks: the toolmarks must be the reason why this slab was previously considered spoliated material.[17] Yet, a close look at the edge of this block reveals a rough margin with a curved outline that diminishes toward the ends (**Figure 4**). This is a typical sawing toolmark, otherwise extensively documented on the rear side of thin panels or profiles for wall revetment or flooring (**Figure 5**).[18] The ancient technique of sawing is well documented, as several depictions of ancient sawing devices and even some of the machines themselves

---

[13] Weber (2004: 105) considers the white marble of local provenance, while the dark grey material is attributed to the quarries of Priene. My own archaeometric investigation on the building material used in Roman imperial times at Miletus, combined with surveys of the local quarries on the shores of Bafa Lake, suggest a local origin for both varieties used for the substructure. The microscopic analysis of the white marble of the orthostates evidences a heteroblastic texture with medium-sized grains and predominantly straight boundaries that is congruent with the microscopic features of the local Milesian deposit. The dark grey marble is a popular choice for architectural decoration in Roman imperial Miletus as evidenced by the stylobate slabs of the Serapeion and the pillars of the *proskenion* of the theatre. In 2019 I could identify several small extraction areas of dark grey marble on the south shore of the Bafa Lake in the proximity of the so-called quarries Miletus-West described by Peschlow-Bindokat 1981. Archaeometric analysis regarding the newly identified ancient sources for dark grey marble is ongoing.
[14] Limestone is found in the immediate vicinity of Miletus, on the Milesian peninsula, and is attested as building material in numerous construction projects in Miletus and Didyma; see Borg and Borg 1998.
[15] For the description of the peristyle's stylobate, see Weber 2004: 102 f.

[16] For polishing as the last task in stone carving, see Koenigs 1981: 144, 146, tab. 51 for Archaic architecture. In Roman imperial times, polished surfaces were a common finish for monolithic shafts. For an early-modern perspective on polishing, see Pegoretti 1863: 359 ('pulimento a lucido dei marmi'), 410 f., who lists it at the end of the stone carving process.
[17] Weber 2004: 103.
[18] Mangartz 2010; Kozelj and Wurch-Kozelj 2012.

Figure 3. Miletus, Heroon III. Colonnade: Stylobate slab – front side with upper edge en bosse(above) and rear side with alternating bands of curved iron point marks (below) (author's photos).

Figure 4. Miletus, Heroon III. Colonnade: Stylobate slab with different toolmarks and surface treatments (author's photo).

are preserved. The saw was usually operated by two workers that pulled a metal blade in sequence on each end and used abrasive sand for the cutting operation. The process of sawing ended a few centimetres above the lower edge of the block to be subdivided. The two parts were split by means of wedges inserted in the sawn channel so that each part bears at its lower edge a thin margin with the curved profile of the saw blade.[19]

The process of subdividing blocks or cutting panels produces, on the surfaces exposed to the metal saw blade, the same effect as the deliberate task of polishing, due to the use of abrasives in both processes. Therefore, traces of sawing can be distinguished from a polished finish only in combination with remains of the splitting margin. This ambivalent interpretation of 'polished' surfaces has several consequences for our understanding of the Roman stone carving process and the procedures undertaken on the construction site.

One example is given by the only base-pedestal still preserved in situ on the eastern side of the colonnade, just next to the stylobate slab that I described above (**Figure 6**). This case is particularly interesting because the pedestal – commonly a free-standing architectural item – was carved from the same block as the stylobate slab; this is not only a distinctive architectural element but also one from another part of the building, the

---

[19] For a detailed description of the sawing process, see Grewe 2009: esp. 439–448. See also Mangartz 2010. For the different forms of cutting edges, see Schwander 1991; Grewe 2009: 445, fig. 15.

Figure 5. Sawing traces. Above: Cornice block with sawing channel (Miletus, Theatre, author's photo); below, left: Rear of a marble slab with splitting margin and traces of rubbing with abrasive material (sand) (author's photo); below, right: Wall veneer profile with sawing notch (incision/Sägekerbe) on the rear (Drawing by B. Weber).

foundations.[20] The original raw block used to carve these two different architectural items measured at least 96 cm in height and was at least 60 cm wide and 83 cm long. This block must have reached the construction site in the quarry state, as suggested by the treatment of the rear side of the stylobate slab where circular paths of the quarry pick can be still identified. It was only on the construction site that raw blocks like this one were further processed, either being roughed-out and dressed for specific architectural elements or subdivided and squared to the required measurements by sawing.

Therefore, sawing must be considered a stoneworking technique with a broader spectrum of applications than already indicated by the common production of veneer panels or the re-working of spoliated material.[21] Sawing should be acknowledged as a common practice on Roman construction sites: saws were used not only to cut stone, mainly as preparatory work in order to subdivide blocks of suitable dimensions from a monolith, but also to adjust blocks and to trim them to the precise required dimensions. The relevance of sawing for the stone carving process in this regard is

---

[20] The fact that this pedestal was carved from the same block as the stylobate slab was most probably the reason why it remained preserved in situ, while all but one of the remaining 38 pedestals are now lost. Its monolithic, bulky format must have increased the difficulty of removing it and prevented any direct reuse.

[21] Schwandner (1991: 216), like Adam (1984), assumes that the saw was used extensively in the production of blocks in the Roman Imperial period. Except for the articles concerned directly with the reconstruction of ancient sawing machines and methods (Grewe 2009; Mangartz 2010), sawing traces are rarely encountered in archaeological literature on ancient building processes (Bessac 1986). In the literature on the marble trade from the imperial period, the opinion that building materials were made to order, prepared, and even prefabricated in the quarries tends to dominate (Toma 2020).

Figure 6. Miletus, Heroon III. Colonnade: Pedestal with Attic-Ionic base carved from the same block as the stylobate slab (author's photo).

comparable to roughing-out and dressing/shaping with a point chisel, except that sawing was less material-consuming and therefore more economical. In fact, adjusting the dimension of an architectural item by using a point chisel to remove the superfluous material produces waste and requires further carving activity to plane and smooth the surface. On the other hand, the use of a saw is not only precise in the execution but the removed material also takes the form of a slab that can be used, for example, for veneer.[22] Furthermore, both surfaces exposed to the rubbing activity of the abrasive material used for the sawing process are even and, except for the splitting margin, also smoothed and polished. Therefore, both surfaces show a nearly-finished state, and both architectural elements can be put in place without undergoing any further substantial carving.

Another aspect resulting from the observation of the sawn surfaces relates to the importance of toolmarks to help reconstruct the sequence of tasks and the complexity and accuracy of the carving process. Polishing is commonly seen as the last task in finishing the carving process of a decorated surface.[23] The fact that the polished surface of the stylobate plate was deliberately roughed-out can be explained by its

function at walking level: a rougher surface would have prevented people from slipping. Nevertheless, this kind of polished surface resulting from the sawing process is not singular within the complex of the so-called Heroon III. It can be observed on the thresholds of the cella, on the front of blocks of the eastern krepis of the pedestal, and most obviously on the two monumental orthostates from the same structure (**Figure 7**).[24] Both orthostates are slab-shaped and measure *c.* 30 cm in depth and 88.8 cm in height, while the length varies according to the state of preservation from 116 cm on the poorly preserved north side to the 286 cm of the complete south orthostate. This slab is slightly tilted from its original position but still inserted in the lower profile of the pedestal. On both narrow sides of the orthostate, two 7 to 13 cm projecting bosses testify to their function as lifting elements. The front of the slab displays on approximately a third of its total surface area a triangular-shaped polished surface, resulting from sawing, that was subsequently re-worked. The lower edge of the slab bears the traces of the typical splitting margin that was removed by the use of a big, rough tooth chisel and then a finer tooth chisel. The rest of the polished surface was partially re-worked, mostly on the borders, with the same two differently toothed chisels. This clearly shows that the intended finish of the front of the visible face was not a polished but a

---

[22] See also Bachmann 2016.
[23] See fn. 16.

[24] Weber 2004: tab. 32. 3; 35. 4 (thresholds).

Figure 7. Miletus, Heroon III. Cella: south orthostate of the pedestal with different toolmarks (author's photo).

fine chiseled surface. The same intentional process to change a polished surface into a chiseled one is also evident on the fragmentary north orthostate. This kind of finish for the orthostates contrasts with the polished treatment of the dark grey moulded profiles framing them (**Figure 2**).

The carving process and its implication for labour quantification

The presented evidence allows us to reconstruct the carving process of the two massive orthostates in the cella of the so-called Heroon III as follows: they were presumably detached from the same block that was divided through sawing.[25] Judging from the traces of the point chisel and the pick on the rear of each slab, the block arrived at the construction site most probably in the quarry state. The sawing of the two slabs occurred after transportation, on the spot. The sawn surfaces were intended as front faces and underwent further carving together with the upper and bottom sides and the narrow sides, while the rear maintained its original treatment.

As the degree of finish of each of the five visible surfaces of the orthostates varies substantially and the finish removed the traces of previous stages of work, the carving sequence can only be partially reconstructed and will be investigated using the case of the fully preserved south orthostate (**Figure 7**). The upper surface shows carefully drafted margins and a planed surface carved with a fine tooth chisel. The same treatment can be assumed for the bottom surface that is not visible. The narrow sides of the orthostate,

though, testify to the use of the iron point to remove excessive material of 0.07 to 0.13 m to reduce the slab to its desired length of 2.68 m. Traces of point chisels are clearly visible only on the bosses, while the rest of the surface was carefully flattened, provided with a drafted margin, and worked with a fine tooth chisel.[26] The bosses were used to manoeuvre the heavy slab, which after being sawn must have been turned 90 degrees to have its future visible face carved and then lifted again in order to be put in place. The fact that the orthostate slab was turned horizontally is evidenced by the toolmarks, which also allow us to reconstruct the position where the stonemason stood and how he moved around the slab while working with the chisel. The re-working of the sawn surface of the south orthostate began at the upper left corner and progressed along its long side as several concentric rows of tooth chisel marks preserved on the upper edge of the slab indicate.[27] The stonemason then turned to the opposite side of the slab and chiseled away the splitting margin but without completely re-working the sawn surface. The orthostate slab was installed in an unfinished state; its visible surface was not uniformly finished.

The carving process as evidenced by the toolmarks differs substantially in terms of complexity and accuracy from the conventional sequence of tasks, commonly applied in archaeological studies. In the tables below I confront two estimates – one based on the toolmarks-based sequence and the other on the

---

[25] Both lengths and depths of the block can be reliably reconstructed to *c.* 286 cm (measured between the two lifting bosses of the south orthostate) and 30 cm, respectively. The height of the slab in its finished state is 88.6 cm - precisely 3 Roman ft.

[26] The narrow side of the north slab has no boss, but there is evidence of its removal by the point chisel. The varying accuracy of carving of the orthostates' narrow sides is most probably due to their different positions. For example, the north slab formed the actual front side of the pedestal, and so its working level is more advanced than that of the south slab positioned at the back of the monument.

[27] In case of the north orthostate, the stonemason stood exactly in the middle of the narrow side and worked from this position as the circular concentric traces of the tooth chisel show.

Surface	Toolmarks-based sequence	Pegoretti's labour figure	Area (m²)/ Volume (m³)	Man-hours (h / MD)	Human factor and qualification
front	sawing	1 *segatura* = 15 h/ m²	2.5 m²	37.55 h / 3 ¾ MD	2 *segatore* / sawyer
	1st planing (tooth chisel)	9a) *cesellatura* = 25h/m²	1.71 m²	42.75 h/ 4 ¼ MD	1 *scalpellino* / stone carver
	2nd planing (tooth chisel)	9a) *cesellatura* = 25h/m²	1.12 m²	28 h / 3 MD	1 *scalpellino* / stone carver
bedding, resting	roughing-out	2a) *scalpelimento* = 200 h/ m³	2 × 0.12 m³	6.86 h / ¾ MD	1 *tagliapietra* / quarry man
	planing	6a) *apparechio rustico* = 9.33 h/m²	2 × 0.858 m²	16.01 /1 ¾ MD	1 *scalpellino* / stone carver
	smoothing	9a) *cesellatura* = 25 h/m²	2 × 0.858 m²	42.75 / 4 ¼ MD	1 *scalpellino* / stone carver
narrow	roughing-out	2a) *scalpelimento* = 200 h/m³	0.018 m³ / 0.035 m³	3.6 h / ½ MD / 7.02 h / ¾ MD	1 *tagliapietra* / quarry man
	planing	6a) *apparechio rustico* = 9.33 h/m²	2 × 0.25 m²	2.33 h / ¼ MD	1 *scalpellino* / stone carver
	smoothing	9a) *cesellatura* = 25 h/m²	2 × 0.27 m²	13.5 h / 1 ½ MD	1 scalpellino / stone carver

Table 1*: Estimate based on the toolmarks-based sequencing of tasks and on Pegoretti's labour figures for white marble.[†]

* The starting point of the carving process is considered a block measuring 2.86 m in length and 0.60 m in width. The height can be estimated to 0.96 m by adding a protection surface of 0.04 m to the lower and upper parts of the block.
[†] Pegoretti 1863: 392–401, tab. V, 4th column (*Tabella quinta. Marmi neri e bianchi / marmi bianchi comuni con frattura concoide di maggior durezza*).

Surface	Typical sequence of tasks	Pegoretti's labour figure	Area (m²)/ Volume(m³)	Man-hours (h)	Qualification
whole volume	roughing-out	2a) *scalpelimento* = 200 h/ m³	0.77 m³	154.4 h	1 *tagliapietra* / quarryman
all six protective surfaces	roughing-out	2a) *scalpelimento* = 200 h/ m³	0.29 m³	58.9 h	1 *tagliapietra* / quarryman
all six at the same degree	planing	6a) *apparechio rustico* = 9.33 h/ m²	7.39 m²	69.06 h	1 *scalpellino* / stone carver
all six at the same degree	smoothing	9a) *cesellatura* = 25 h/m²	7.39 m²	184.75 h	1 *scalpellino* / stone carver
Front	scrapping	27a) *orsatura* = 2.3 h/m²	2.5 m²	5.9 h	1 *politore* / polisher
	polish	30a) *pulimento a lucido* = 10.7 h/m²	2.5 m²	26.75 h	

Table 2*: Estimate based on the conventional reconstruction of the sequence of tasks.

* Estimate based on the assumption that the orthostate slab reached the construction site in the quarry state and that all carving tasks were undertaken with the same degree of accuracy. The starting point of the carving process is considered a block measuring 2.86 m in length, while the width and the height are estimated to approx. 0.38 and 0.96 m, respectively by adding a protection surface of 0.04 m to the lower, upper, front, and rear sides of the block. The task of roughing-out is twice listed: once applied to the whole volume of material as conventionally used by Barresi (2003: 172 f.) and once considering a protective surface of 0.04 m.

conventional succession of tasks in stone carving. The comparative estimates of labour are related to the carving process of the south orthostate of the pedestal structure of the so-called Heroon III (**Figure 7**) and are presented in **Tables 1 and 2**.[28]

The estimated time to carve the south orthostate totals 196.4 h, or approximately 20 man-days,[29] and it involves the activity of four craftsmen with different qualifications.

The estimated time to carve the south orthostate – if the carving progressed uniformly following the conventionally assumed sequence – amounts to about 35 or a maximum of 45 man-days. This difference of 10 days is due to a misinterpretation of Pegoretti's indications regarding roughing-out. Although Pegoretti obviously refers to the volume of removed material, several archaeological studies concerned with estimates apply this labour figure to the whole volume of the raw block.[30]

A comparison between the two techniques (roughing-out and sawing) is difficult, as the initial dimensions of the raw block are not known and the exact volume of the removed material can only be approximated. In modern stone carving, the dimensions of the raw block are only slightly different than those of the final product with an average of a 4-cm high protection surface. If one assumes similar protection surfaces and compares the times given by Pegoretti for sawing the front of the orthostate (0.90 × 2.86 m = 2.54 m²) and those for roughing-out the same surface with an iron chisel (0.90 × 2.86 × 0.04 = 0.10 m³), the latter technique is slightly more efficient, as sawing requires two craftsmen and 3 1/2 man-days and roughing-out more than 2 man-days but only one person. The time required to saw the front of the orthostate is almost twice the time a carver would require to remove the superfluous material (approximately 0.04 m) with an iron chisel, but by sawing one obtains two equally planed and polished surfaces and reduces the time for further carving work. Furthermore, sawing does not require the same

degree of specialisation as carving, as the saw blade can be operated by unqualified workers. Ancient sources are sparing regarding the number and specialisation of craftsmen engaged on a construction site, but modern manuals indicate three different categories of stoneworkers – *segatore* or sawyer, *tagliapietra* or quarryman, and *scalpellino* or stone carver – and the hierarchies on the construction site. Pegoretti's manuals for instance values the work of a sawyer as half of that of a quarryman.[31] This means that, in terms of costs, roughing-out and sawing are interchangeable, as the removal of 0.04 m of superfluous material from a 1 × 1 m surface, i. e. 0.04 m³, takes one quarry man 8 hours and the sawing of a 1 × 1 m surface takes 15 hours and two sawyers.

Conclusion

The evidence of toolmarks at the so-called Heroon III in Miletus indicates a dynamic on the construction site, at least at Miletus, that differs from the typical sequence of carving generally assumed in archaeological studies. The ancient process of carving appears extremely versatile in terms of technical solutions used and at the same time ambivalent with regard to finishing. The evidence from toolmarks also sheds new light on the organisation of the construction site, indicating a diversity of professionals active at the same time.

The toolmarks-based reconstruction of the carving process of the marble orthostates of Heroon III shows a very rational approach by the Roman workforce that obviously aimed more at efficiency than at the accuracy of execution. A visible face could either be polished or chiseled, and both surface treatments could alternate within the same monument.

Moreover, it seems that the prevalence of sawing in the preparatory phase of stone carving practiced on the construction site must have been higher than generally acknowledged for ancient practices. In fact, its relevance in Antiquity seems comparable with operations in the Early Modern period. Pegoretti for instance, lists the activity of sawing at the very beginning of the carving process and notes its ability to be substituted with roughing-out. The observations on sawing in Roman Miletus thus legitimise once more the use of Pegoretti's labour figures for ancient carving processes and confirm modern architectural handbooks as indispensable tools for the better understanding of ancient building processes. Nevertheless, since ancient carving processes do not progress uniformly, the use of 19th-century labour figures should either follow

---

[28] Stage of working per surface: Rear side: quarry state, i.e. no further carving on the construction site. Front surface: sawing, re-working of the splitting margin (flat iron and chisel), and partial chiseling (twice with two different tooth chisels). Narrow sides: removal of superfluous material (except for the bosses) and planing and smoothing the remaining surface and the edges with plain and tooth chisels. Bottom (not visible) and upper surface: planing and smoothing the remaining surface and the edges with plain and tooth chisels; unclear if the block was previously trimmed to the actual dimension and by which technique (sawing or roughing-out).

[29] The conversion of hours to man-days follows the accepted opinion that a working day in the Roman imperial period comprised 10 hours (DeLaine 1997: 104–107; see also Maschek 2016: 398). All the remaining values are rounded up to quarters.

[30] Barresi 2003: 172 f.; Domingo and Domingo 2017: 48–51. Barker and Russell (2012: 87 f.) consider that Pegoretti's labour figure 2a refers to the volume of removed material. My own research based on further modern manuals confirms this; Toma 2022.

[31] Pegoretti 1863: 361: 'Riguardo poi all'assistenta dei manuali si ritiene che ciascuno di questi possa accudire al servizio di quattro o cinque artefici; e la sorvelianza di un capo scalpellino si valuta per cinque tagliapietre e per dieci lustratori o segatori.'

an exact reconstruction of architectural processes, or in case of more generic models, a generally agreed standard chaîne opératoire.

Bibliography

Adam, J.-P. 1984. *La construction romaine. Matériaux et techniques*. Paris: A. and J. Picard.

Bachmann, M. 2016. Präfabrikation und Sägetechnik. Der Einsatz der Steinsäge in der Roten Halle, in Ş. Aktaş, E. Dündar, S. Erkoc and M. Koçak (eds) *Lykiaekhissa. Festschrift für Havva Işkan*: 63–70. Istanbul: Ege Yayınları.

Barker, S.J. and B. Russell 2012. Labour figures for Roman stone-working: Pitfalls and potential, in S. Camporeale, H. Dessales and A. Pizzo (eds) *Archeologia della costruzione III, Les chantiers de construction de l'Italie et des provinces romaines* (Anejos de Archivo Español de Arqueología 64): 83–94. Madrid and Mérida: Consejo Superior de Investigaciones Científicas, Instituto de Arqueología.

Barresi, P. 2003. *Province dell'Asia Minore: costo dei marmi, architettura pubblica e committenza* (Studia Archaeologica 125). Rome: 'L'Erma' di Bretschneider.

Bessac, C. 1986. *L'outillage traditionnel du tailleur de pierre de l'antiquité à nos jours* (Revue archéologique de Narbonnaise, Suppl. 14). Paris: Centre national de la recherche scientifique.

Borg, G. and B. Borg 1998. Die unsichtbaren Steinbrüche. Zur Bausteinprovenienz des Apollon-Heiligtums von Didyma. *Antike Welt* 29(6): 509–518.

DeLaine, J. 1997. *The Baths of Caracalla. A Study in the Design, Construction, and Economics of Large-Scale Building Projects in Imperial Rome* (Journal of Roman Archaeology Supplementary Series 25). Portsmouth, Rhode Island: Journal of Roman Archaeology.

Domingo, J.Á. and J.R. Domingo 2017. El coste del Arco de Caracalla en Theveste (Tébessa, Argelia): verificación empírica de una metodología de cálculo. *Archeologia dell'Architettura* 22: 35–53.

Grewe, K. 2009. Die Reliefdarstellung einer antiken Steinsägemaschine aus Hierapolis in Phrygien und ihre Bedeutung für die Technikgeschichte, in M. Bachmann (ed.) *Bautechnik im antiken und vorantiken Kleinasien* (Byzas 9): 429–454. Istanbul: Ege Yayınları.

Königs, W. 1981. Bauteile aus Myus im Theater von Milet. *IstMitt* 31: 143–147.

Kozelj, T. and M. Wurch-Kozelj 2012. Use of a saw in Roman and Proto-Byzantine period on the Island of Thassos, in A. Gutiérrez García-Moreno, M.P. Lapuente Mercadal and I. Rodà (eds) *Interdisciplinary Studies on Ancient Stone: Proceedings of the IXth Association for the Study of Marbles and other Stones in Antiquity* (Tarragona 2009): 715–722. Tarragona: Institut Català d'Arqueologia Clàssica.

Mangartz, F. 2010. *Die byzantinische Steinsäge von Ephesos. Baubefund, Rekonstruktion, Architekturteile* (Monographien Römisch-Germanisches Zentralmuseum Mainz. Forschungsinstitut für Vor-und Frühgeschichte 86). Mainz: Verlag des Römisch-Germanischen Zentralmuseums.

Maschek, D. 2016. The Marble Stoa at Hierapolis. Materials, Labour Force and Building Costs, in T. Ismaelli and G. Scardozzi (eds) *Ancient Quarries and Building Sites in Asia Minor: Research on Hierapolis in Phrygia and Other Cities in South-Western Anatolia: Archaeology, Archaeometry, Conservation*: 393–402. Bari: Edipuglia.

Pegoretti, G. 1863. *Manuale pratico per l'estimazione dei lavori architettonici, stradali, idraulici e di fortificazione per uso degli ingegneri ed architetti*. Volume primo. Milan: Angelo Monti.

Peschlow-Bindokat, A. 1981. Die Steinbrüche von Milet und Herakleia am Latmos. *JdI* 96: 157–235.

Schwandner, E.-L. 1991. Der Schnitt im Stein. Beobachtungen zum Gebrauch der Steinsäge in der Antike, in A. Hoffmann, E.-L. Schwandner, W. Hoepfner and G. Brands (eds) *Bautechnik der Antike* (Internationales Kolloquium in Berlin 1990): 216–223. Mainz am Rhein: Philipp von Zabern.

Toma, N. 2020. *Marmor – Maße – Monumente. Vorfertigung, Standardisierung und Massenproduktion marmorner Bauteile in der römischen Kaiserzeit*. Wiesbaden: Harrassowitz.

Toma, N. 2021. Geglättet oder gesägt? Werkzeugspuren und die Rekonstruktion antiker Bauprozesse, in V. Apostol, S. Bâlici, L. Nistor and N. Toma (eds) *Arhitectură. Restaurare. Arheologie. In honorem Monica Mărgineanu-Cârstoiu*: 447–459. Bucharest: Editura A.R.A.

Toma, N. 2022. Das Stadion-Osttor in Milet. Unfertigkeit und Effizienzstrategien im kaiserzeitlichen Marmorbau, in F. Rumscheid and N. Toma (eds) *Unfertigkeit in antiker Architektur. Definitionen und Ursachen* (Bonner Jahrbücher, Beiheft 61): 103–133. Darmstadt: Philipp von Zabern

Weber, B. 2004. *Die römischen Heroa von Milet* (Milet I, 10). Berlin: De Gruyter.

16.

Il Peristilio Inferiore della *Domus Augustana* sul Palatino: organizzazione del lavoro e calcolo dei costi di un'impresa imperiale

Francesca Caprioli
Sapienza, Università di Roma
francescacaprioli@mac.com

Alessandro Mortera
Università Ca' Foscari Venezia
alessandro.mortera@unive.it

Patrizio Pensabene
Sapienza, Università di Roma
patrizio.pensabene@uniroma1.it

Javier Á. Domingo
Pontificia Università della Santa Croce
javdomingo78@gmail.com

Abstract

To address the subject of a construction site and its costs, we present the case study of the so-called Lower Peristyle of the *Domus Augustana* on the Palatine Hill. This sector of the Imperial Palace, made up of numerous rooms around a large central courtyard characterised by two superimposed architectural orders, sheds light on many aspects of ancient building practices. The exceptional state of conservation of the structures and the ability to trace different architectural fragments to the two different architectural orders make it possible to investigate certain practices used by the *marmorarii* and to give a reliable evaluation of the marble materials used and their costs. The activity of this highly skilled workforce is attested among other things, by the presence of numerous incised constructions lines on the architectural members.

The theme of the costs of public architecture in Rome takes on a very extraordinary dimension, since the role of the client is played by the emperor, who acts through the public administration. It can therefore be assumed that the raw materials (marble, bricks, timber, etc.) from the *praedia* and the imperial mines and quarries had no direct impact on costs except for transport, production, and installation.

Keywords: Palatine Hill, Lower Peristyle, architectural decoration, building practices, marble veneer

Introduzione

Negli ultimi anni si sta affermando sempre più l'esigenza di capire le modalità di costruzione degli edifici pubblici a Roma, finora affrontate soprattutto dal punto di vista degli organi dell'amministrazione pubblica preposti all'esecuzione e al controllo del lavoro. In questo senso la ricerca è stata già avviata agli inizi del secolo scorso da Otto Hirschfeld che attraverso lo studio della documentazione epigrafica aveva potuto individuare i rami dell'amministrazione che avevano come sfera di competenza l'edilizia pubblica.[1] Di fatto, studi successivi, ma anche recenti, come quello di Anne Daguet-Gagey del 1997 sulle opere pubbliche a Roma tra il 180 e il 305 d.C., hanno continuato sulla stessa direzione,[2] e lavori come quelli di Leon Homo del 1951, con traduzione italiana pubblicata nel 1971 dal titolo "*Roma imperiale e l'urbanesimo nell'antichità*", hanno affrontato soprattutto tematiche sulle superfici occupate dall'edilizia pubblica e privata e sulla legislazione inerente:[3] il nucleo principale delle informazioni non proveniva dunque dall'analisi delle evidenze archeologiche, ma principalmente dalle fonti epigrafiche e storiche, come si riscontra nel lavoro, pur utilissimo, di Gabriella Bodei Giglioni del 1974.[4]

Possiamo dunque rilevare che poco trattato è rimasto il tema di come l'amministrazione pubblica organizzasse i lavori, nel senso di come erano impostati i cantieri, quali fossero i collegi interessati e come avveniva il trasporto delle materie prime in occasione delle varie imprese edilizie; ad esempio nei volumi di Pierre Gros sull'architettura romana vi è solo un brevissimo capitolo dedicato alle associazioni professionali[5] e in

---

[1] Hirschfeld 1905.
[2] Daguet-Gagey 1997.
[3] Homo 1951.
[4] Bodei Giglioni 1974.
[5] Gros 1996: 376–385.

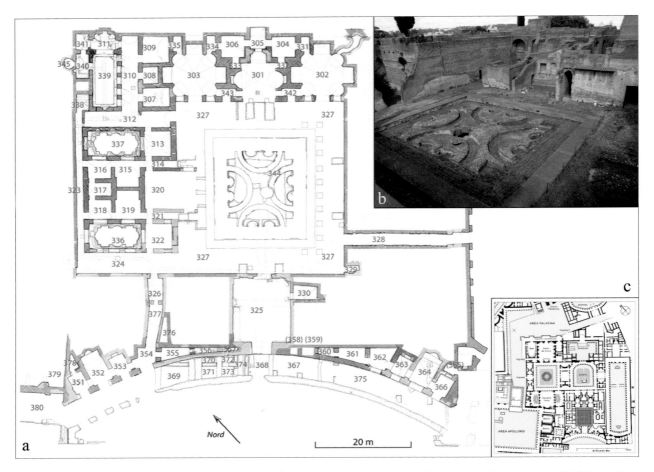

Figura 1. Peristilio Inferiore della *Domus Augustana*: a) pianta con numerazione degli ambienti (da Bitterer 2012); b) l'area del Peristilio dal livello superiore della *Domus Augustana* (foto A. Mortera); c) il Peristilio nel Palazzo imperiale (da Mar 2005).

genere i lavori sui *collegia* nel mondo romano si limitano a ricerche epigrafiche sulle liste collegiali, sui rapporti tra i vari membri, o sulle sedi dei collegi, quando sono note come a Ostia e ad Aquileia.[6] Solo Janet DeLaine nel 1997 ha affrontato dal punto di vista del cantiere lo studio delle Terme di Caracalla e ultimamente nel 2015 Evelyne Bukowiecki e Ulrike Wulf-Rheidt hanno tentato per la *Domus Flavia* una ricostruzione parziale del cantiere, basandosi solo sui laterizi.[7]

Poco affrontato è il tema dei costi in cui incorreva anche l'architettura pubblica.[8] Si può presumere che le materie prime (marmi, laterizi, calce, legname per le impalcature, chiodi e strumenti vari) provenienti dai *praedia* e dai distretti minerari imperiali non incidessero direttamente sulle spese se non per quelle di trasporto, di lavorazione e di messa in opera, ambiti per i quali necessariamente si ricorreva alle associazioni

professionali, qualunque sia stato il numero di schiavi pubblici messi a disposizione dall'amministrazione imperiale.

In questa sede, limiteremo il nostro discorso al calcolo del costo dei marmi per i quali deve considerarsi che, nei casi in cui erano destinati all'edilizia pubblica di Roma, essi provenivano da cave direttamente controllate dall'amministrazione centrale e non gravavano dunque come costo in sé del materiale.[9]

Anche un'opera pubblica destinata a residenza imperiale determinava un investimento finanziario che si distribuiva non solo per l'approvvigionamento delle materie prime, ma anche per i salari della numerosa manodopera specializzata libera e non solo schiavile.[10] Proprio l'attività di questa manodopera altamente specializzata è testimoniata, tra l'altro, dalla presenza

[6] Per Ostia, vedi Chevallier 1986: 152–162; Pavolini 1996: 129–139; per Aquileia, Bollmann 1998: 69, nota 56; Leicht 1946–1947; Panciera 1957: 22–45. Sui *collegia* in generale, vedi Bollmann 1998.
[7] Bukowiecki e Wulf-Rheidt 2015a; DeLaine 1997.
[8] Una utile sintesi sull'utilizzo che si è fatto di tali studi nell'ambito dell'architettura e dell'economia romana è delineata in Maschek 2020: 46–50.

[9] Domingo 2013; Pensabene 2015a; Russell 2013.
[10] Su queste problematiche, vedi Bernard 2017; DeLaine 1997: 103–130, 175–197; Volpe 2017. Per quanto riguarda la realtà delle cave, Domingo 2013: 120–121; Hirt 2010: 155–159, 251–260; Paribeni e Segenni 2017; Pensabene 2015a.

di numerose linee guida di cantiere incise sulle membrature architettoniche.[11]

È ormai un'acquisizione della storia degli studi che per le necessità dei monumenti della capitale, lo sfruttamento delle cave e il trasporto avvenivano attraverso locatari e *rationales* dipendenti della *statio marmorum* di Roma alla quale destinavano i prodotti migliori, mentre ne trattenevano una parte come guadagno. Le spese vere e proprie dovevano dunque riguardare la manodopera impiegata nella lavorazione e messa in opera dei marmi, tenendo conto che su di esse incidevano anche i costi del trasporto per il quale si usufruiva molto probabilmente di imbarcazioni private affittate a tale scopo.[12]

Nel 2002 è stato affrontato da Elisabetta Bianchi e Roberto Meneghini il calcolo della quantità dei marmi impiegati per il Foro di Traiano, sui cui di recente si è intervenuti di nuovo soprattutto a proposito del trasporto delle colonne del tempio del divo Ulpio.[13] Per il Foro difatti si è avvantaggiati dalla conservazione di molte parti delle strutture, in particolare della basilica Ulpia e dei portici che forniscono un dato oggettivo al calcolo delle superficie rivestite di marmo e a quello delle colonne connesse. Con le stesse modalità, nel 2010, è stato intrapreso lo studio volumetrico dei diversi materiali impiegati nel cantiere del Foro di Nerva.[14]

In questa sede presentiamo un calcolo quantitativo dei marmi impiegati per un complesso di committenza imperiale di cui si conserva buona parte delle strutture edilizie: si tratta di quella parte del Palazzo imperiale sul Palatino riservata ai ricevimenti "privati" (*epula*),[15] il cd. Peristilio Inferiore della *Domus Augustana* (**Figura 1**). In questo settore del Palazzo si hanno ancora le murature di decine di ambienti che gravitano attorno ad un ampio spazio centrale scoperto articolato su due ordini architettonici sovrapposti e che in origine erano foderate da lussuosi rivestimenti in marmi bianchi e colorati, dei quali restano pochissimi lacerti *in situ*, i quali sono però attestati dai fori per inserire le grappe che fissavano le lastre di rivestimento alle pareti.[16] In effetti, vedremo come il Peristilio Inferiore è stato spogliato dai suoi marmi ancora in epoca imperiale, anche se avanzata, sostituendoli con intonaci dipinti.[17] Lacerti dei rivestimenti marmorei originari si conservarono, anche se con restauri, solo lungo i percorsi che continuarono ad essere praticati per

Figura 2. Peristilio Inferiore della *Domus Augustana*: a) vano scala 328 (foto M. Maira); b) particolare del rivestimento marmoreo ancora *in situ* (foto A. Mortera).

collegare il Peristilio con il resto del Palazzo.[18] Infatti si riscontrano ancora lastre e impronte sulla malta di allettamento lungo le due scale che dal piano superiore portavano al Peristilio Inferiore (**Figura 2**) e sulle pareti del ninfeo visibile durante la discesa di una di queste scale (**Figura 3**).[19]

---

[11] Vedi *infra*.
[12] Gianfrotta 2008: 87.
[13] Bianchi e Meneghini 2002; Pensabene e Domingo 2017.
[14] Meneghini e Bianchi 2010.
[15] Sojc 2005–2006; Sojc e Winterling 2009.
[16] Molti di questi conservano ancora le zeppe in marmo al loro interno. Sulle possibili articolazioni dei rivestimenti, vedi Bitterer 2012; per la tecnica relativa al fissaggio delle lastre, vedi Bruto e Vannicola 1990: 328, 332–333; Guidobaldi e Angelelli 2005: 34–38.
[17] Vedi *infra*.

[18] Sulle percorrenze all'interno del Palazzo e del Peristilio Inferiore, vedi Mar 2009; Pflug 2014.
[19] Rispettivamente ambienti nn. 328, 338 e 339. Su i rivestimenti di questi vani, vedi Fogagnolo 2009b: 280–281.

Figura 3. Peristilio Inferiore della *Domus Augustana*. Ninfeo 339, parete occidentale: è ben evidente lo strato di allettamento delle lastre di rivestimento con frammenti litici affogati nella malta. In basso, sono visibili alcuni lacerti *in situ* della zoccolatura in lastre di cipollino (foto A. Mortera).

Tuttavia, negli sterri del Peristilio operati nel XIX e XX secolo, sono stati ritrovati migliaia di frammenti di lastre marmoree di rivestimento parietale e pavimentale (accatastati ancora in diversi ambienti) insieme a frammenti architettonici (basi, fusti, capitelli, elementi di trabeazione e di transenne)[20] che testimoniano come non solo le scale e il ninfeo citato ma probabilmente anche le pareti interne delle nicchie degli altri due ninfei e di altri settori del complesso avessero mantenuto parte del rivestimento marmoreo.

Non affronteremo in questa occasione il tema della continuità o discontinuità dei rivestimenti in marmo, ma tenteremo invece un calcolo dei marmi impiegati nella prima fase domizianea del Peristilio Inferiore e nei decenni immediatamente successivi. Si tratterà di un calcolo ipotetico che ci restituisce soprattutto il volume delle superfici occupate dal marmo, ma non quali fossero le qualità impiegate negli specifici settori. Per lo spessore delle lastre ci siamo affidati ai pochi resti ancora *in situ* e al calcolo in percentuale degli spessori dei frammenti di lastre nelle cataste e da noi catalogati.

Questo lavoro vuole soprattutto offrire un esempio di metodo per la ricostruzione dei volumi dei marmi impiegati, che abbiamo classificato per funzioni (lastre di rivestimento, elementi architettonici dei colonnati e delle trabeazioni); solo successivamente si potrà tentare una ricerca su come l'arrivo, il trasporto e il deposito del marmo e la loro messa in opera abbiano inciso sulla storia del cantiere di questa parte della *Domus Augustana*.

P. P.

Il Peristilio Inferiore della *Domus Augustana*

Il caso-studio presentato in questa occasione per analizzare il processo che accompagna un monumento dalla fase di progettazione alla sua realizzazione è il cd. Peristilio Inferiore della *Domus Augustana*,[21] in quanto tra i contesti del Palazzo imperiale sul Palatino studiati da parte della nostra *equipe* di ricerca – e di prossima pubblicazione – risulta essere quello che ha restituito più dati dal punto di vista dell'architettura, della decorazione, del colore del marmo e dei tracciati di cantiere.

I primi scavi nell'area di cui si abbiano notizie, condotti per volere dell'abate Paul Rancoureil, risalgono al 1774–1777. In questa occasione, vennero alla luce gli ambienti del settore nord-occidentale del livello inferiore del Peristilio, dai quale furono recuperati e depredati diversi materiali di pregio, tra cui numerosi marmi e statue.[22] I resoconti di tali operazioni furono pubblicati nel 1785 da Giuseppe Antonio Guattani, il quale riporta come: *"Fra i molti avanzi di colonne, di capitelli, cornicioni, fregi di diverse modinature, superbamente intagliati, in rosso antico, giallo, pavonazzetto, ed altri sceltissimi marmi, vi si trovarono intere due statue di Leda poco meno del vero [...]; la elegantissima statua dell'Apollo Saurottono [...]; una testa di metallo, altri busti, e teste, con frammenti di figure di eccellente scalpello"*.[23] Egli inoltre descrive con grande ammirazione la decorazione di alcuni ambienti: *"Tutto il composto quindi dell'ordine era lavorato in marmo paonazzetto, esclusi i capitelli di giallo, la cornice, ed architrave di rosso, ed il fregio parimente di giallo, in cui erano scolpiti in ottimo stile festoni, e frutti. [...] Non si può accertare cosa stesse ne' fondi de' molti riquadri che vi sono; mentre appena se ne viddero le traccie, e qualche pezzo di marmo paonazzetto, che ne formava la cornice. [...] se quando infiniti pezzi, e frantumi delle cornici si rinvennero qua, e là caduti, ed altri attaccati al loro sito ancora, neppur uno vi*

---

[20] Tali cataste (citate in Voigts 2012: 141, nota 5) furono allestite all'interno degli ambienti coperti (nn. 304, 306, 309, 331, 334–335) negli anni del secondo conflitto mondiale.

[21] Si coglie l'occasione per ringraziare in questa sede la Direzione del Parco Archeologico del Colosseo (dott.ssa A. Russo) e i funzionari responsabili dell'area (dott.ssa P. Quaranta) e dell'Ufficio Catalogo (dott. A. D'Alessio, dott.ssa R. Alteri) per la disponibilità e la collaborazione. In quest'area nel 2018–2019 si è svolto il Seminario *"Decor. Il linguaggio architettonico romano"*, organizzato dalla Cattedra di Archeologia Classica di Sapienza – Università di Roma del Prof. Domenico Palombi in collaborazione con il Parco Archeologico del Colosseo e incentrato sullo studio della decorazione architettonica di questo specifico settore del Palazzo imperiale.

[22] Garcia Barraco 2014: 26–30; Iacopi 1997: 17; Pafumi 2007: 209, 212. Alcuni di questi ambienti vennero reinterrati, mentre altri, tra cui le tre aule centrali (301–303), furono rese frequentabili mediante una scala costruita nel vano 307 e di cui sono ancora leggibili le impronte sulle murature.

[23] Fusco 2012: 356; Guattani 1785: IV-V; Pafumi 2007: 213–217. Alcune di queste sculture raggiunsero presto l'Inghilterra (una di quelle rappresentanti Leda con il cigno, in marmo pentelico, venduta da Gavin Hamilton a Lord Shelburne e dal 1970 al Paul Getty Museum di Malibu), i Musei Vaticani (Apollo Sauroctono), o andarono ad arricchire collezioni private (come nel caso della seconda statua di Leda, da riconoscersi forse con un esemplare a Villa Albani). Tra i rinvenimenti statuari sono ricordati anche un ritratto di Settimio Severo, oggi al British Museum, e un secondo Apollo Sauroctono, oggi a Stoccolma.

Figura 4. L'area del Peristilio Inferiore della *Domus Augustana* durante gli scavi (a), i restauri di Alfonso Bartoli (b) e la fine dei lavori (c). Nell'ultima immagine è visibile la sistemazione di alcuni frammenti architettonici lungo il muro di fondo del braccio nord-occidentale dell'ambulacro, dove molti dei quali si trovano tutt'ora (da *Archeologia in posa* 1994).

fu trovato de' suddetti specchi, o riquadri [...]. È incredibile intanto in quanta copia corniciami, fregi, capitelli (fra' quali due intatti di giallo) ne andarono sopra carrette come vil tavolozza al negozio del marmista Vinelli a Campo Vaccino"; ancora menziona il pavimento dell'ambiente 305, di cui "*[...] restava per anco il suo pavimento intatto buona parte [...] diviso in triangoli, alternativamente variati di giallo bianco, e serpentino*".[24]

È solo nella prima metà degli anni '30 del Novecento però che per l'area della *Domus Augustana* si giunge a un punto di svolta: tra il 1926 e il 1936 Alfonso Bartoli portò infatti a compimento la demolizione di Villa Mills,[25] un edificio in stile neogotico il cui nucleo originario aveva occupato fin dal Cinquecento buona parte del livello superiore della *Domus Augustana*, celandone le strutture superstiti. Nel 1936, egli si dedicò anche allo scavo integrale dell'invaso del Peristilio Inferiore, dal quale emersero numerosi elementi architettonici che furono fin da subito sistemati lungo i quattro bracci dell'ambulacro e che tutt'oggi si trovano nella medesima posizione; contemporaneamente, si procedette alla demolizione di alcune tamponature ritenute di epoca tarda e al restauro delle altre murature (**Figura 4**), lavori che si conclusero entro il 1938.[26]

Nonostante gli scavi e i restauri, il Peristilio Inferiore e la *Domus Augustana* non furono oggetto di studi sistematici fino alla metà degli anni '60, quando venne pubblicato il lavoro monografico di Gisella Wataghin Cantino.[27] Più di recente, l'area della *Domus Augustana* e, nello specifico, quella del Peristilio, sono state oggetto di approfondite indagini e ricerche da parte dell'equipe tedesca coordinata da Natascha Sojc e Ulrike Wulf-Rheidt nell'ambito del *Palatin Projekt*.[28]

Figura 5. Peristilio Inferiore della *Domus Augustana*: a) traccia di uno dei cavi di fondazione dei pilastri del primo ordine (foto A. Mortera); b) cavi di fondazione durante gli scavi Bartoli (da Schmölder-Veit 2012); c) particolare di uno dei cavi svuotati (da Fink e Wech 2012).

Nella sua prima fase domizianea,[29] il Peristilio presentava un primo ordine di semicolonne addossate a pilastri in travertino, com'è stato dedotto dallo scavo delle sottobasi[30] (**Figura 5**) e dal ritrovamento delle

---

[29] Non essendo questa la sede più adatta per un'approfondita disamina dei singoli elementi architettonici, ci limitiamo a sottolineare come la nostra ipotesi di un impianto architettonico e decorativo realizzato in marmo già in epoca domizianea (espressa anche in Coticelli *et al.* 2017: 578–579, 584; Wataghin Cantino 1966: 36) si discosti da quanto sostenuto in precedenza da altri studiosi che hanno proposto a partire dagli stessi frammenti una marmorizzazione dell'elevato solo in epoca adrianea (ciò è vero soprattutto per i capitelli, per cui si veda Freyberger 1990: 78, 86), rimandando ad altra sede per una più opportuna discussione. Cfr. generalmente Voigts 2012 e Wataghin Cantino 1966 per la ricostruzione architettonica del Peristilio.

[30] Wataghin Cantino 1966: 36. "*Una serie di cavi, a ridosso del muretto della vasca, delimitati da muriccioli in opera a sacco a questo ortogonali, è quanto rimane delle fondazioni della struttura esterna del portico. In ognuno di essi, come dimostrano i frammenti rimasti, era collocato un lastrone di travertino; la loro disposizione non è, in senso assoluto, regolare, poiché ne variano le dimensioni e le distanze reciproche: è possibile tuttavia ricavare un interasse costante, che risulta però diverso, nei lati orientali ed occidentali da un lato, settentrionale e meridionale dall'altro*". Vedi anche Fink e Wech 2012: 115–116. I pilastri dovevano presentare forma quadrangolare, con un nucleo di travertino di circa cm 135 × 90, ricostruibile a partire da un frammento di base di rivestimento del pilastro che conserva anche la curvatura per la semicolonna.

---

[24] Guattani 1785: LXXXVI.
[25] Bartoli 1938: 3–5; Garcia Barraco 2014: 37–39; Iacopi 1997: 36, 41. Sulla Villa, Garcia Barraco 2014: 9–40, 77–86, 111–126.
[26] Bartoli 1938: 4; Garcia Barraco 2014: 37–39; Iacopi 1997: 36, 41.
[27] Wataghin Cantino 1966.
[28] Sojc 2012a.

piattabande armate dello stesso materiale, rivestiti di marmo.[31] I fusti delle semicolonne, costituiti da lastre di rivestimento con scanalature e rudenti, posti sulla fronte del pilastro verso la fontana, erano alti m 6,5 con basi composite e capitelli ionici, anch'essi di rivestimento, per un totale della colonna di m 7,14 su cui poggiavano piattabande rivestite da fregi-architrave in lastre e cornici in blocchi in marmo proconnesio, per un'altezza totale di m 8,75 (**Figura 6**). I pilastri erano rivestiti probabilmente sui fianchi e sicuramente sul retro, che presentava con tutta probabilità una lesena al centro, cui è plausibile riferire un frammento in marmo pavonazzetto con scanalature di cm 5,6–6 e listello largo tra cm 2–2,6; i fusti di lesena erano sormontati da capitelli corinzi in marmo lunense larghi anch'essi cm 70. L'ambulacro doveva essere coperto da una volta a botte.[32]

Per quanto riguarda la ricostruzione delle pareti di fondo, la questione risulta di non facile definizione. Secondo il principio di conformità su cui si struttura l'ordine architettonico romano, ai pilastri dovrebbero corrispondere delle lesene, cui potrebbero attribuirsi in via di ipotesi alcuni frammenti di fusti scanalati in giallo antico e capitelli corinzi. In alternativa, in base all'analisi dei numerosi fori da grappa, T. Bitterer vede ricostruita una sequenza paratattica di ortostati nella parte inferiore sormontati da ampie specchiature di marmo colorato incorniciate da piccole lesene al di sopra delle quali corre una trabeazione a lastre.[33] Questo tipo di rivestimento parietale dovrebbe immaginarsi anche per le pareti meridionale e occidentale, mentre si potrebbe pensare ad una variazione dello schema decorativo per quanto riguarda il braccio sul quale si aprono le due sale ottagone (amb. 302 e 303) e l'ambiente centrale (301). Quest'ultimo presenta difatti un'enfatizzazione della sua apertura sulla corte mediante basi composite di circa cm 78 di diametro,[34] plausibilmente sormontate da fusti scanalati in giallo antico dello stesso diametro.[35] Al momento non è stato possibile individuare frammenti di capitello di sicura attribuzione per questi fusti, mentre è ipotizzabile che l'apertura fosse inquadrata da *antae* rivestite da semipilastri con capitelli corinzi, di cui rimangono due esemplari (**Figura 7**).

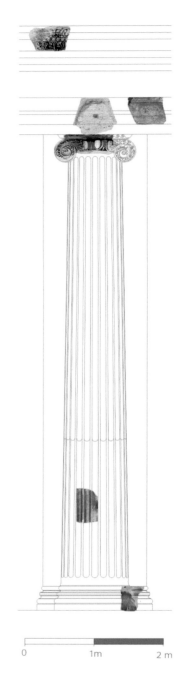

Figura 6. Peristilio Inferiore della *Domus Augustana*. Primo ordine architettonico (disegno E. Pullano; rielaborazione grafica A. Mortera).

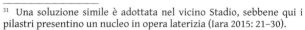

---

[31] Una soluzione simile è adottata nel vicino Stadio, sebbene qui i pilastri presentino un nucleo in opera laterizia (Iara 2015: 21–30).
[32] Voigts 2012: 174; Wataghin Cantino 1966: 37.
[33] Bitterer 2012. Questa ipotesi è tutt'ora ancora al vaglio da parte nostra. Riteniamo che soltanto un accurato rilievo della parete sud-est, dove si conserva il maggior numero di questi fori, potrebbe contribuire a dirimere la questione. L'incertezza legata alla ricostruzione dell'aspetto delle pareti di fondo dell'ambulacro ci ha portato in questa sede ad escludere dal calcolo dei rivestimenti le lesene.
[34] Le basi attualmente visibili sono state ricostruite *in situ* da Alfonso Bartoli in travertino invecchiato, con frammenti originali di marmo inseriti al loro interno. Cfr. Wataghin Cantino 1966: 31–32.
[35] Il diametro è ricostruito a partire da frammenti che alternano listelli di cm 2,5 e scanalature larghe cm 6,7–7. Tali misure ad ogni modo non consentono di ricostruire se non ipoteticamente l'*entasis* dei fusti.

Per il secondo ordine sono ipotizzabili basi composite alte circa cm 30 e dal diametro di cm 56 con fusti scanalati in cipollino[36] e portasanta (ma forse anche giallo antico) alti m 4 e sormontati da capitelli corinzi

---

[36] Negli anni '40 del Novecento Giuseppe Lugli poteva osservare all'interno dell'invaso della fontana centrale numerosi frammenti di fusti di colonne in cipollino (Lugli 1946: 510), permettendo così di ipotizzarne un crollo dall'ordine superiore.

alti cm 60, di cui recentemente è stato possibile l'analisi autoptica di un frammento inserito nella catasta all'interno dell'ambiente 304 e di fattura domizianea, alto cm 66,4 (**Figura 8**).[37] Per il fregio-architrave si può pensare ad un'altezza di cm 72, come dimostra un frammento in buono stato di conservazione nell'area, e a una cornice alta cm 45–50, di cui rimane un esemplare, per un'altezza totale dell'ordine di m 6,27. Tra le colonne trovavano posto balaustre costituite da piedistalli orizzontali in marmo africano, granito grigio del Foro e lunense, che in corrispondenza dei fianchi presentano il negativo delle modanature delle basi tra cui erano posti e che al di sopra ospitavano transenne in marmo bianco (**Figura 9**). Anche per le pareti di fondo dell'ambulacro posto in corrispondenza del secondo ordine si pone il problema dell'esistenza o meno delle lesene a ribattere le colonne, ulteriormente complicata dall'esiguità delle strutture murarie perimetrali conservate.

Sulla corte del Peristilio si affacciano diversi ambienti dei quali sono in corso di elaborazione alcune ipotesi ricostruttive dei loro rivestimenti. Alcuni esempi *in situ*, che corrispondono ai vani scala 328 e 338, o ancora al ninfeo 339,[38] insieme alla presenza di un numero piuttosto ingente di lastre pavimentali e parietali e di *sectilia* rinvenuti nell'area in un'ampia varietà di litotipi tra cui prevalgono quelli colorati (**Figura 10**), restituiscono l'immagine di una corte peristiliare e dei suoi ambienti attigui piuttosto colorata.[39] L'ampio pozzo

---

[37] Nel volume di prossima pubblicazione "Par domus est caelo. *Palazzo dei Flavi sul Palatino: architettura e decorazione architettonica*" si approfondisce l'argomento, riscontrando proprio in questo esemplare una variante più raffinata del secondo dei due *pattern* (con il quale si intende la combinazione di tipo e stile di impatto immediato) dei capitelli corinzi del Palazzo, riconducibile a un'officina meno raffinata e classicheggiante che lavora nel Peristilio Inferiore.

[38] Fogagnolo 2009a; Fogagnolo 2009b: 280–281.

[39] Da questo punto di vista, di grande interesse risultano le tracce superstiti dei rivestimenti pavimentali di alcuni ambienti, tutti collocati nel settore occidentale dell'area del Peristilio, testimoniati perlopiù dalla conservazione di ampi tratti dei rispettivi massetti in cui è possibile osservare le impronte delle lastre o in cui sono inseriti frammenti di lastre, schegge o residui di lavorazione in marmo affogati nella malta di allettamento che consentono di ricostruirne lo schema decorativo (vedi D'Elia e Le Pera Buranelli 1985: 177, fig. 1; Fogagnolo 2009a: 493; Fogagnolo 2009b: 280. Sulla tecnica di messa in opera, Giuliani 2006: 189, 191, fig. 3; Guidobaldi e Angelelli 2005: 34–38). I ninfei 336 e 337 presentano sul fondo delle vasche lunghe lastre rettangolari disposte a giunti sfalsati, alcune delle quali ancora conservate. Nel vano 316 le impronte lasciano presupporre un pavimento articolato in formelle quadrangolari, mentre nell'ambiente 307 il pavimento doveva presentare lastre rettangolari disposte a giusti sfalsati. Assai più articolato doveva invece presentarsi la pavimentazione del vano 318, di cui rimane la preparazione di un *sectile* con quattro grandi quadrati separati da fasce rettangolari, il tutto verosimilmente in contrasto cromatico (Quaranta 2021: 20–22). Le aree di percorrenza, nella fattispecie i corridoi, presentano invece impronte di lastre rettangolari (di dimensioni minori rispetto a quelle dei ninfei) disposte secondo giunti sfalsati (310, 312) o con lastre più grandi e più piccole alternate (323). Assai interessante appare la soluzione adottata in corrispondenza dell'angolo tra i corridoi 310 e 312, dove la tessitura delle lastre ne asseconda l'andamento a 90°. In tutta l'area del Peristilio, le uniche altre lastre conservate e tutt'ora individuabili sono quelle delle vaschette ricavate all'interno dell'ambulacro, in marmo bianco. L'ambulacro doveva verosimilmente essere pavimentato con grandi lastre di marmo bianco.

Figura 7. Peristilio Inferiore della *Domus Augustana*. Frammento di capitello corinzio d'anta (foto A. Mortera).

Figura 8. Peristilio Inferiore della *Domus Augustana*. Capitello corinzio pertinente al secondo ordine architettonico (foto A. Mortera).

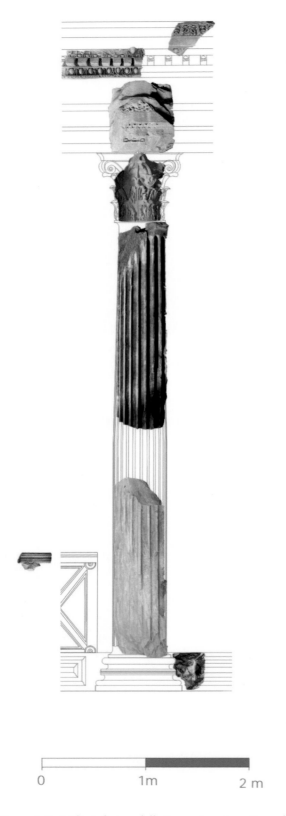

Figura 9. Peristilio Inferiore della *Domus Augustana*. Secondo ordine architettonico (disegno T. Chiaramida; rielaborazione grafica A. Mortera).

di luce costituito dal peristilio stesso rifrangeva la luce sulle specchiature dei marmi impiegati che risultavano combinati per contrasto in uno scintillio di colori,[40] così come descrive Stazio nelle sue *Silvae* come elogio del suo sovrano.[41] Nello stesso passo, l'autore descrive la *regia* dell'augusto Domiziano come l'anello di congiunzione tra la terra e il cielo, così imponente, splendente e colorata da poter far ingelosire gli dei stessi. In questo senso vanno interpretati i dati evinti dall'analisi di un limitato lotto di 3367 frammenti di lastre di rivestimento, in cui prevalgono nettamente marmi pregiati e ampiamente diffusi quali il giallo antico (29%), il pavonazzetto (21,5%) e il serpentino (20%); seguono con un marcato distacco il porfido rosso (5%), il portasanta e il cipollino (entrambi con poco più del 3%), mentre con percentuali più basse trovano attestazione l'africano (2,5%), diverse varietà di granito (del Foro, bianco e nero, minuto) e altri marmi colorati (bigio, bardiglio, verde antico); tra i bianchi, invece, sono presenti il proconnesio (2,3%), il pentelico (1,6%) e il tasio (poco più dell'1%).

Sulla corte centrale (ca. m 21 × 19), affacciano numerosi ambienti disposti lungo i bracci nord-occidentale e nord-orientale dell'ambulacro, mentre sugli altri due si aprono dei passaggi che conducevano alla grande esedra o al piano superiore della *Domus Augustana*.

I vani del settore occidentale risultano aperti con grandi finestre sui cortili interni che successivamente sono stati arricchiti da bacini d'acqua[42] e sono tutti addossati al criptoportico, il quale riceve luce da due finestre poste nei due ambienti destinati a ninfei (amb. 336–337). Questi ultimi presentano vasche rettangolari scandite da nicchie semicircolari e rettangolari. Cinque ulteriori ambienti, di dimensioni più piccole, si dispongono nello spazio tra i due ninfei (amb. 315–319). Una grande sala (amb. 320), la cui parete di fondo è animata da tre nicchie che dovevano essere inquadrate da edicole con colonne sorrette da mensole e frontoni triangolari e curvilinei, affaccia direttamente sulla corte peristiliare.

L'ala settentrionale è composta invece da tre vani, due laterali a pianta ottagonale e uno centrale quadrato, con i due ambienti laterali simmetrici caratterizzati da un'architettura a nicchie e volte a padiglione, secondo uno schema molto simile a quello adottato nella *Domus*

---

[40] Sull'accostamento nei rivestimenti marmorei dei diversi litotipi per contrasto, si vedano le interessanti osservazioni in Grüner 2017.
[41] Stat., *silv.*, IV.2.18–31: "[..]*Tectum augustum, ingens, non centum insigne columnis / sed quantae superos caelumque Atlante remisso / sustentare queant. Stupet hoc vicina Tonantis / regia, teque pari laetantur sede locatum / numina. Nec magnum properes excedere caelum: / tanta patet moles effusaeque impetus aulae / liberior, campi multumque amplexus operti / aetheros, et tantum domino minor; ille penates / implet et ingenti genio iuvat. Aemulus illic / mons Libys Iliacusque nitet, [//] multa Syene / et Chios et glaucae certantia Doridi saxa; / Lunaque portandis tantum suffecta columnis. / Longa supra species: fessis vix culmina prendas / visibus auratique putes laquearia caeli [..]*".
[42] Cfr. Schmölder-Veit 2012: 185–205; Wataghin Cantino 1966: 29, 33–34.

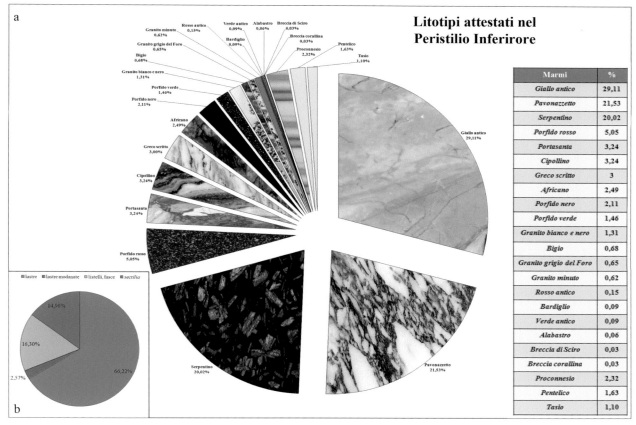

Figura 10. Peristilio Inferiore della *Domus Augustana*. Percentuali dei litotipi dei frammenti di lastre analizzate (a); percentuali delle tipologie di lastre analizzate (b).

Aurea neroniana.[43] L'articolazione spaziale interna di questi vani è contraddistinta da "alcove" decorate da nicchie rettangolari e semicircolari inquadrate da edicole, anch'esse sostenute da colonne su mensole, al cui interno erano probabilmente collocate statue;[44] due stretti corridoi mettono in comunicazione la sala centrale con le due laterali. Da notare è la presenza di numerosi passaggi ed accessi ai vani, che risultavano in tal modo collegati tra loro, al fine di permettere sia l'interazione tra i piccoli gruppi presenti all'interno di questi ambienti, sia di agevolare gli spostamenti dell'imperatore durante lo svolgimento dei *convivia*.[45]

Sul lato meridionale, verso il Circo Massimo, la *Domus* presentava il suo unico prospetto. Su questo lato si apre una sola sala rettangolare (amb. 325),[46] che conduceva a un prospetto curvilineo a esedra. La sala si apre nel settore più orientale del lato meridionale e non si presenta in asse con il peristilio, ma solamente con la vasca centrale configurata a *peltae* contrapposte e con l'ambiente 301 posto sul lato settentrionale. Con tutta probabilità la sala fu aperta nel muro di fondo

del peristilio nel corso di alcuni interventi di restauro realizzati agli inizi del II secolo d.C., quando si decise di monumentalizzare il settore creando un grande prospetto curvilineo sul Circo Massimo che modificò profondamente il progetto originario,[47] il quale prevedeva un andamento rettilineo della facciata. Un frammento della *Forma Urbis* testimonia come l'esedra prevedesse un colonnato sulla fronte prospiciente il Circo Massimo,[48] che dunque modificò profondamente l'aspetto di questa facciata del Palazzo in seguito alla ristrutturazione di inizio II secolo.

Il limite orientale del Peristilio è costituito da una parete continua, che conserva molteplici fori, nel cui angolo sud-orientale si apriva un vano una scala (amb. 328) che consentiva un secondo collegamento con il piano superiore della *Domus Augustana*. Della scala rimangono le impronte e si conservano ancora le ricche *incrustationes* marmoree che ne assecondavano lo sviluppo.

Nell'angolo settentrionale, invece, una serie di piccoli ambienti, tra cui una latrina, gravitano attorno al

---

[43] Sulle aule ottagone del Peristilio, vedi Pflug 2017: 319–323.

[44] Sull'arredo scultoreo del Peristilio Inferiore, vedi Pafumi 2007.

[45] Mar 2009; Pflug 2014.

[46] *Contra* Wataghin Cantino 1966: 15, 27, che non ritiene vi fosse alcuna apertura.

[47] Bukowiecki 2012: 93–94; Bukowiecki e Wulf-Rheidt 2015: 372; Pflug 2012: 72; Sojc 2012b: 25; Wulf-Rheidt 2012: 269–271.

[48] Si tratta del frammento 20b, trasmesso nel Cod. Vat. Lat. 3439, 14r (Carettoni, Colini, Cozza e Gatti 1960: 77–80, tav. XXII). Lugli 1946: 509, che ricorda i cavi di fondazione per il colonnato.

Figura 11. Peristilio Inferiore della *Domus Augustana*. Lacerto di pittura con finte architetture di epoca severiana. In basso a sinistra è indicato il tratto della parete di fondo lungo il braccio nord-occidentale dell'ambulacro dove si trova (A. Mortera).

terzo ninfeo (amb. 339). Questo, visibile da un secondo vano scala di collegamento con il livello superiore del Palazzo (amb. 338), conserva ancora in parte lacerti dei rivestimenti parietali.[49]

Dall'analisi di circa 400 frammenti architettonici e di oltre 3300 lastre di rivestimento, è stato possibile ricostruire la prima importante fase del cantiere flavio che ha inizio con Vespasiano, come ipotizzato dell'analisi di alcune delle murature del settore occidentale, prive di bipedali,[50] e che si protrae nel tempo con una importante fase domizianea che sviluppa il cantiere, con una coda finale, per dare solidità e rifinitura al progetto, fino all'apertura della grande esedra traianea che affaccia sul Circo Massimo. A queste segue una fase di restauro della struttura sicuramente datata all'età severiana, per una serie di frammenti architettonici facilmente inquadrabili nell'epoca di Settimio Severo – tra cui almeno un esemplare di capitello ionico, che copia l'iconografia flavia mantenendone inalterato l'aspetto morfologico –, che dovette forse seguire all' incendio del 192 e al quale si pose rimedio tramite alcuni interventi strutturali;[51] più incerto, invece, è un intervento di restauro posto

attorno alla metà del II secolo e testimoniato da cornici di ordine misto. Ad una fase tardo-severiana sono attribuibili alcune pitture negli ambienti 315 e 327 che sostituiscono il rivestimento marmoreo. La pittura più interessante e meglio conservata occupa un'ampia porzione della parete di fondo del braccio occidentale della corte del Peristilio, nella sua metà settentrionale (**Figura 11**). Qui sono riconoscibili finte architetture, costituite da una sorta di podio articolato in una serie di specchiature di marmo sopra il quale campeggia un fusto tortile di colonna; la scena sembrerebbe contemplare anche due figure umane.[52] Successive modifiche si ebbero poi nel corso del III-IV secolo, quando lungo l'ambulacro vennero create sei piccole vasche.[53]

Il maggior numero dei frammenti può ad ogni modo essere attribuito alla fase originaria e, nello specifico, ad un'officina di epoca domizianea che si contraddistingue per una resa plastica, raffinata e vivace che lavora indifferentemente su marmi bianchi e colorati, membrature architettoniche decorate e lisce, con un alto grado di specializzazione e cartoni di estrema eleganza. Differentemente dal linguaggio palaziale standard riscontrato negli ambienti di rappresentanza

---

[49] Fogagnolo 2009a: 491–492. Sulla latrina, i ninfei e i sistemi idrici, vedi Schölder-Veit 2012.
[50] Vedi *infra*.
[51] A questo intervento potrebbero forse riferirsi due grandi contrafforti eretti contro le due colonne *in antis* dell'ambiente 301 e dei cui elevati in opera laterizia oggi rimangono alcuni filari e il nucelo, fortemente restaurato e caratterizzato dalla presenza di diversi frammenti di basalto e marmo.

[52] Cfr. Bitterer 2012: 242; Pflug 2012: 74; Pflug 2013: 202; Sojc 2012b: 27. Tracce di intonaco privo di pittura sono invece visibili lungo la parete orientale del Peristilio e all'interno delle due sale ottagone. Sulla pittura di epoca severiana, vedi Falzone 2018.
[53] Schmölder-Veit 2012: 210–212. *Contra* Wataghin Cantino 1966: 35, che ritiene queste strutture di epoca flavia.

della *Domus Flavia* da noi studiati,[54] possiamo in sintesi sostenere che il secondo e il terzo livello (quello del cd. *Paedagogium*) dell'architettura arrampicata del Palazzo presentano forse per il loro carattere più privato e i loro ambienti volumetricamente più piccoli un linguaggio distinguibile e miniaturistico fatto per essere apprezzato da vicino, durante gli *epula* privata in una permanenza a lungo termine negli ambienti del Peristilio.

Accenniamo ora solo brevemente in conclusione a due concetti di vitruviana memoria che abbiamo enucleato come strumenti fondamentali del linguaggio del potere e, nello specifico, del linguaggio palaziale. Uno è lo *splendor*, il *nitor*, la capacità di maneggiare la luce attraverso l'uso del materiale e artifizi architettonici, tale da rifrangere la luminosità proveniente dall'esterno e creare un preciso colore nell'atmosfera dei singoli ambienti; l'altro, più noto, è il *decor*, concetto che unisce struttura e decorazione; il *decor*[55] è una precisa scelta formale, strutturale, cromatica, decorativa e di arredo che si rende opportuna attraverso il linguaggio architettonico, distinguibile per ogni edificio ma conforme ad un alfabeto comune, quello imperiale.

Lo *splendor* e il *decor*, insieme, nel meccanismo di consenso della propaganda imperiale attuato attraverso l'architettura, danno luogo nella loro combinazione a un terzo concetto che è quello dello *stupor*, quel sentimento a cui mirano gigantismo, cromatismo e l'esuberanza dell'ornato vegetale che fa leva sull'estetica in senso lato (*aisthanomai*, essere colpiti sensibilmente), che invade di stupore il fruitore e lo proietta immediatamente in una dimensione in cui egli si trova in un livello asimmetrico, obbligato ad ammirare, a rimanere attonito: "in-stupidito". Ed è su questo meccanismo che si instaura tutta la propaganda dei poeti di corte Marziale[56] e Stazio, che incentrano la loro opera sulla lode e la celebrazione del palazzo imperiale e dell'imperatore Domiziano. Il palazzo diventa, quindi, una sorta di tempio del *dominus et deus*,[57] una struttura gigante, splendente, pluridecorato, nel quale l'imperatore si manifesta dentro grandi nicchie semicircolari come una statua, una statua di divinità.

F. C.

I tracciati di cantiere

Come anticipato, nell'ambito del Peristilio Inferiore è stato possibile individuare numerose linee guida, o tracciati di cantiere, qui presenti in una varietà e accuratezza tali da rappresentare per ora, all'interno del Palazzo, un osservatorio preferenziale. Sulla base del supporto materiale su cui essi sono osservabili, è stato possibile individuarne due differenti categorie.

Nel primo caso, si tratta di una serie di linee rosse che contraddistinguono alcune pareti di una decina di ambienti che si trovano nel quadrante occidentale del Peristilio (**Figura 12**).[58] Realizzate con della vernice rosso ocra stesa a mano libera con un pennello dalla punta piuttosto spessa,[59] esse corrono perlopiù orizzontalmente ad altezze comprese tra i m 2 e i m 3,20 circa sull'attuale piano di frequentazione dell'area; il *ductus* appare piuttosto regolare.

Apprestamenti simili sono attestati in pochissimi altri casi. Nell'ambito di Roma sono noti quelli delle cd. *Septem domus Parthorum* e delle cd. Terme di Massenzio sul Palatino, la cui costruzione risalirebbe in entrambi i casi all'epoca severiana;[60] di recente linee tracciate con una vernice rossa sono state osservate su alcune murature di età severiana del *Templum Pacis*.[61] Più complessi, invece, sono i casi delle Terme di Traiano e della Basilica di Massenzio. Nel primo, in corrispondenza di una delle gallerie sostruttive del complesso e della grande esedra sud-occidentale sono state rintracciate numerose iscrizioni dipinte – oltre 250 – il cui scopo era quello di rendere conto dell'avanzamento dei lavori di costruzione.[62] I vari formati di queste iscrizioni hanno portato ad ipotizzare non solo l'esistenza di più squadre che dovevano lavorare insieme, o alternandosi, ma anche un certo grado di alfabetizzazione, quantomeno dei caposquadra.[63] Ulteriori tracce di una verniciatura rossa sono state inoltre notate in corrispondenza di numerosi bipedali e sesquipedali, i quali però sembra fossero utilizzati esclusivamente negli archi di scarico e nelle piattabande del complesso termale.[64] Per

[54] Coticelli, De Martini, Grande e Mancini 2017.

[55] Vitr., I.2.1.

[56] Mart., VIII.36: "*Regia pyramidum, Caesar, miracula ride; / Iam tacet Eoum barbara Memphis opus: / Pars quota Parrhasiae labor est Mareoticus aulae? / Clarius in toto nil videt orbe dies. / Septenos pariter credas adsurgere montes, / Thessalicum brevior Pelion Ossa tulit; / Aethera sic intrat, nitidis ut conditus astris / Inferiore tonet nube serenus apex / Et prius arcano satietur numine Phoebi, / Nascentis Circe quam videt ora patris. / Haec, Auguste, tamen, quae vertice sidera pulsat, / Par domus est caelo, sed minor est domino*".

[57] Suet. *Dom.*, 13.1–2.

[58] Sulla linea, vedi Pflug 2017: 324–325, fig. 6. Gli ambienti in cui essa è almeno parzialmente visibile sono i nn. 313–316, 318–322, 336–337.

[59] In alcuni tratti lo spessore di questa linea è pari a cm 2 circa, mentre in altri raggiunge lo spessore di un laterizio.

[60] Lugli 1957: 573. Sulla datazione dei due complessi, Lugli 1930: 248, 411–412; Carettoni 1972; Mancioli, Ceccherelli e Santangeli Valenzani 1993; Wulf-Rheidt 2012: 271–273; Bukowiecki e Wulf-Rheidt 2015: 333.

[61] Tucci 2017: 268, 277, 281–282. Si veda anche il caso della *domus* al di sotto di S. Maria in *Aracoeli*, dove alcune linee nere marcherebbero gli intradossi delle volte (Tucci 2017: 281, nota 61; sulla *domus*, Tucci 2019).

[62] Volpe 2002; 2008; 2010; Volpe e Rossi 2012; 2014. Verosimilmente, la presenza di date in queste iscrizioni doveva essere funzionale anche al calcolo dei tempi di tiraggio della malta dei tratti murari realizzati, nonché alla rendicontazione del cantiere.

[63] Volpe 2002: 393; Volpe 2008: 243; Volpe 2010: 88.

[64] Carboni 2003: 67; Rossi 2015: 34 e figg. 8–9; Volpe e Rossi 2014: 206–207, dove si ipotizza che la vernice venisse applicata direttamente in fabbrica in modo da indicare fin da subito la destinazione specifica

Figura 12. Peristilio Inferiore della *Domus Augustana*. Linea rossa che corre lungo alcune delle pareti del settore nord-occidentale: a) ambiente 320, pareti settentrionale e occidentale; b) passaggio tra ambiente 320 e corridoio 314; c) ambiente 320, parete occidentale; d) ambiente 315, parete orientale; e) ninfeo 336, parete orientale (foto A. Mortera).

quanto riguarda la Basilica di Massenzio, invece, filari di laterizi rubricati sarebbero stati impiegati per segnalare la quota del sommoscapo delle colonne della navata centrale e il profilo delle modanature della trabeazione.[65]

Al di fuori di Roma, linee ottenute con una vernice rossa sono attestate ad Ostia, nel complesso dei cd. Grandi *Horrea*[66] e in uno degli ambienti del *castellum aquae*,[67] e a Villa Adriana nella cd. Palestra.[68] Qui, nello specifico, piuttosto che semplici linee sono presenti dei veri e propri simboli – come quelli tutt'oggi ancora in uso – per indicare le quote. Anche nelle province non mancano esempi di una simile prassi, come sembrerebbe indicare

il caso di un impianto termale di grandi dimensioni ad *Italica*.[69]

La funzione delle linee rosse del Peristilio non è del tutto chiara, poiché avrebbero potuto assolvere a molteplici scopi. Da una parte, esse non sembrerebbero difatti individuare filari che dovevano svolgere alcuna specifica funzione, se non forse quella di marcapiano o di orizzontamento;[70] anche una loro eventuale connessione con il rivestimento marmoreo – per indicarne magari una variazione nella tessitura o della qualità di marmo da impiegare – sembra potersi escludere: del tutto assenti, infatti, sono in corrispondenza di esse i fori da grappa per il fissaggio delle lastre.[71] Un'altra possibilità è che esse segnalassero l'avanzamento dei lavori di una o più squadre alternate, o ancora che fossero propedeutiche

di questi materiali. Sesquipedali dipinti di rosso caratterizzano la muratura al di sopra del colonnato interno di S. Maria Maggiore (Krautheimer 1971: 39–40, 51; Pensabene 2015b: 259, che ritiene fossero a vista).
[65] Amici 2008: 23 e fig. 20a.
[66] Gismondi 1953: 205; Lugli 1957: 573.
[67] Bukowiecki, Dessales e Dubouloz 2008: 135.
[68] Attoui 2008: 52–66, figg. 6–11, 15–18.

[69] Bukowiecki e Dessales 2008: 200.
[70] In questo settore del Peristilio infatti non sono attestati bipedali, solitamente impiegati a questo scopo (Bukowiecki 2012: 90).
[71] Si veda ad esempio il caso dell'ambiente 320, per il quale un'ipotesi circa lo schema compositivo del rivestimento parietale sulla base della disposizione dei fori da grappa è in Bitterer 2012: 234, fig. 2e.

ad un periodo di fermo prolungato del cantiere. Il fatto che una di queste linee, nel caso specifico dell'ambiente 320 (**Figura 12b**), presenti un tratto obliquo che segna l'ingombro orientale della piattabanda al di sopra del vano di passaggio con il corridoio 314, potrebbe forse consentire di ipotizzare che la funzione di tali segno – o almeno una delle loro funzioni – fosse quella di indicare la quota d'imposta delle ghiere e delle piattabande in bipedali relative alle aperture nelle murature.[72] Sempre per quanto riguarda il vano 320, la linea è ben visibile anche lungo tutta la parete occidentale (**Figura 12c**), in cui si aprono tre nicchie. Lo stato di conservazione di questo elemento piuttosto precario, però, non consente di stabilire se linee simili fossero presenti su altre pareti.[73]

Tale espediente – che al momento sembra attestato solo in questo limitato numero di ambienti del settore occidentale del Peristilio – si rintraccia esclusivamente su murature che fin'ora la storia degli studi ha ricondotto al cantiere vespasiano del complesso, consentendo così di ipotizzarne una contestualità alle strutture e di anticipare l'utilizzo di questa pratica ben prima dell'epoca traianea o della fine del II secolo, come invece sostenuto ormai diversi decenni fa,[74] individuando così una vera e propria consuetudine nell'arte del costruire di epoca imperiale probabilmente con ampia diffusione.[75]

Piuttosto interessante, inoltre, appare la circostanza per cui, dove presenti, queste linee non risultano né precedute né seguite da altri segni simili, a differenza di quanto accade invece nel caso delle terme di Traiano dove le date avevano il chiaro scopo di indicare i progressi delle singole squadre impiegate e l'entità del proprio lavoro. Nel caso del Peristilio, mancano attualmente indizi tali dal poter ipotizzare il numero delle squadre all'opera; anzi, l'assenza di altri tracciati lascerebbe presupporre piuttosto l'avvicendarsi di due sole squadre, o di due cantieri successivi le cui murature realizzate sarebbero state così distinte.[76]

Alla seconda categoria appartengono invece i tracciati individuati su numerosi elementi architettonici conservati nell'area. Questi, come noto, possono essere ricondotti a diversi momenti della "vita" delle membrature architettoniche, relativi alla loro realizzazione o alla messa in opera.[77] Al momento, a quella che è un'analisi preliminare dei frammenti presenti nell'area del Peristilio Inferiore, i tracciati di cantiere riscontrati appaiono perlopiù propedeutici alla realizzazione delle membrature architettoniche e, nella fattispecie, al delineamento delle singole modanature. Questo aspetto dell'architettura e dell'organizzazione del cantiere è allo stato attuale, per il Palazzo e, nello specifico, per il Peristilio, pressoché inedito.[78]

Questo tipo di tracciati di cantiere sono individuabili con una certa facilità a quasi ogni livello dell'alzato architettonico, in particolar modo su basi, fusti e capitelli per un totale di più di 20 elementi.[79]

Nel caso delle basi, sia di colonna che di lesena o di pilastro, tutte composite, si tratta nello specifico di sottili incisioni praticate con uno scalpello a punta fina in corrispondenza dei tori inferiore e superiore e dei tondini sul listello che separa le due *scotiae*. Tali incisioni indicano il punto di maggiore espansione di queste modanature, sulle quali veniva così segnata la circonferenza massima che doveva poi essere progressivamente ridotta.[80] Ciò risulta evidente soprattutto nel caso di un frammento di base di colonna e uno di base di rivestimento di pilastro, entrambi in marmo lunense (**Figura 13a, b**). Simili linee guida sono riscontrabili su almeno altri due frammenti di basi di pilastro (**Figura 13c, d**); nel caso

---

[72] Cfr. Pflug 2017: 325; Tucci 2017: 281. Non è forse improbabile, nell'ambito di un cantiere come quello del Palazzo imperiale, che alcune componenti di maggior impegno delle murature, come le piattabande o gli archi di scarico, potessero essere affidate a squadre specializzate. Ad ogni modo, si deve notare come tutte le piattabande e le gli archi di scarico in questo settore del Peristilio si trovino al di sopra tale linea.

[73] Nel Peristilio, così come nel caso delle terme di Traiano, la conservazione di queste linee molto deve alla natura umida degli ambienti in cui sono state rinvenute. La possibilità che tracce simili caratterizzassero anche altre pareti del complesso è espressa in Bukowiecki 2012: 92.

[74] Vedi nota 66. Sulle murature del Peristilio, vedi Bukowiecki 2012: 88–99; Pflug 2012; Pflug 2017: 325–330.

[75] Così Tucci 2017: 281–282, che ritiene che simili elementi (per i quali utilizza il termine di "bande") dovevano essere utilizzati per dare informazioni a coloro che erano coinvolti nel processo costruttivo.

[76] Pflug 2017: 325.

[77] Di recente, i tracciati di cantiere presenti sugli elementi architettonici hanno suscitato un interesse sempre maggiore da parte di coloro che si occupano di architettura antica, contribuendo alla redazione di una bibliografia di riferimento sempre più corposa. Per un inquadramento generale, vedi Inglese 2000; Inglese e Pizzo 2014; 2016; 2017; Vinci, Ottati e Gorostidi Pi 2020. Già negli anni '80 del Novecento tali apprestamenti furono portati all'attenzione degli studiosi da parte di Lothar Haselberger che si occupò dei tracciati sulle pareti della cella del *Didymaion* (Haselberger 1980; 1983a, b; 1985; 1986) e sul lastricato della piazza del mausoleo di Augusto (Haselberger 1994; 1995; Inglese 2000: 31–36, 37–50). Un ruolo fondamentale ebbero anche i lavori di Patrizio Pensabene (Pensabene 1973: 192–194), Amanda Claridge (Claridge 1982; 1983), Francesco Tomasello (Tomasello 1984; 1986) e di Peter Rockwell (Rockwell 1987–1988; 1989).

[78] Gli unici tracciati pubblicati sono in Inglese e Pizzo 2014: 26, 73. Questo aspetto legato alla realizzazione delle membrature architettoniche è ora in corso di approfondimento da parte di chi scrive anche per altri contesti del Palazzo imperiale, in particolare per quanto riguarda le cd. *Domus Flavia* e *Domus Augustana*.

[79] In questa occasione vengono presentati quelli riscontrati durante lo svolgimento delle attività seminariali di Sapienza – Università di Roma, svolte tra i mesi di maggio e ottobre del 2019.

[80] Inglese e Pizzo 2014: 203, 208; Inglese e Pizzo 2017: 236. Incisioni simili appaiono piuttosto diffuse: si vedano ad esempio i casi del Pantheon, del tempio di Venere Genitrice nel Foro di Cesare, del Foro di Traiano (Inglese e Pizzo 2014: 31, 36, 38–42), delle terme di Nettuno a Ostia (Inglese e Pizzo 2014: 32), o ancora di Villa Adriana (Inglese e Pizzo 2014: 33–35).

Figura 13. Peristilio Inferiore della *Domus Augustana*: a) frammento di base di colonna; b-d) frammenti di base di pilastro; e) base di colonna (foto A. Mortera).

di un'altra base di colonna (**Figura 13e**), sono invece visibili sul piano d'attesa due incisioni longitudinali che ne materializzano l'asse di simmetria.[81]

Per quanto riguarda i fusti di colonna e di lesena, i tracciati riscontrabili sono esclusivamente riconducibili alla realizzazione dei listelli e delle scanalature. La tecnica con cui si ottenevano listelli e scanalature è riscontrabile in diversi casi, tra cui quello di un grande frammento di fusto scanalato di colonna in cipollino con sommoscapo e uno più piccolo in portasanta (**Figura 14a**) ed è nota e documentata da tempo, grazie all'osservazione ravvicinata di alcune delle colonne dell'*Hadrianeum* e di molti altri casi.[82] Affinché ciò fosse possibile venivano praticati sul corpo del fusto ancora liscio una serie di piccoli fori, alle volte inseriti all'interno di piccoli cerchi incisi, che dovevano marcare rispettivamente il centro e la larghezza dei listelli;[83] nello spazio di risulta che veniva a crearsi tra di essi, il marmo veniva scavato ottenendo così le scanalature.

Tra i tracciati di cantiere, questa è forse la tipologia più comunemente attestata, testimoniando così la sistematicità con cui tale pratica era attuata. Questa infatti era applicata non solo nel caso di fusti con listelli piatti, ma anche per quelli i cui listelli presentano dei tondini, come dimostra un frammento di fusto di lesena in pavonazzetto probabilmente riconducibile ad uno degli ambienti interni gravitati attorno alla corte centrale del Peristilio (**Figura 14b**). In questo caso, i fori di trapano sono praticati al centro del tondino sovrapposto; sono invece assenti evidenze di ulteriori segni specifici atti ad individuare la larghezza dei listelli o degli stessi tondini.

Un'altra serie di linee guida funzionali all'individuazione dei listelli e delle scanalature è riscontrabile su di un frammento di fusto di colonna in cipollino, pertinente al secondo ordine architettonico (**Figura 14c**). Sul piano di appoggio sono infatti presenti, oltre ad un piccolo foro che segna il centro geometrico del piano, inserito in una piccola depressione, tre incisioni: due longitudinali, che dovevano indicare uno spigolo di altrettanti listelli – e forse anche segnare il diametro del piano, dividendolo

a metà –; una terza, circolare, doveva invece indicare il diametro del fusto appena al di sopra dell'imoscapo.[84]

I capitelli sono senza alcun dubbio gli elementi architettonici che restituiscono maggiori testimonianze, nonché quelle più elaborate e sistematiche. Essi infatti rappresentano il manufatto architettonico-decorativo la cui realizzazione doveva presentarsi alquanto complessa, necessitando di una serie di operazioni e passaggi precisi e di non facile esecuzione; essi inoltre venivano per buona parte scolpiti sottosopra e solo una volta che la decorazione era in uno stadio avanzato venivano rigirati.[85]

I capitelli ionici delle semicolonne del primo ordine non hanno restituito informazioni circa gli stadi di lavorazione precedenti alla realizzazione degli elementi decorativi. Ciò nonostante, un frammento (**Figura 15**) piuttosto ben conservato appare alquanto interessante: oltre ad una cavità circolare per un perno metallico che attraversa il capitello per tutta la sua altezza,[86] sul retro presenta un *kyma* lesbio continuo che indica come il blocco di marmo lunense in cui esso è intagliato fosse stato verosimilmente in origine destinato all'esecuzione di un altro elemento architettonico.

Diversa è la situazione per i capitelli corinzi di colonna del secondo ordine, di cui sopravvivono almeno cinque esemplari piuttosto ben conservati e svariati frammenti di piccole dimensioni. Nel caso di quelli più integri, in quattro casi è stato possibile osservarne il piano di appoggio parzialmente originario. È su questa superficie che è stato possibile riscontrare il maggior numero di tracciati di cantiere (**Figura 16**): a partire dal centro, evidenziato mediante un piccolo foro, si dipartono molteplici raggi incisi: quattro, sei o otto, a seconda del caso. Ciascuno di questi termina in corrispondenza di altrettanti fori, praticati a cm 3 circa dal margine del piano. Questi, così come i raggi, sono posti in corrispondenza dello spazio di risulta tra le foglie di acanto della prima corona, segnando così il centro delle foglie della seconda;[87] al contrario, non è stato possibile verificare l'esistenza di incisioni simili relative alla disposizione delle foglie della prima corona, come attestato invece in molti casi.[88] Per ciascun capitello, inoltre, quattro raggi

[81] Vedi alcuni esempi da Ostia e Villa Adriana: Inglese e Pizzo 2014: 90, 92–94, 96, 102; Inglese e Pizzo 2017: 235.
[82] In particolare, vedi Claridge 1982; 1983. Simili tracciati sono noti a Roma per quanto riguarda il tempio del divo Vespasiano (Rockwell 1987–1988: 62–68), dei fori di Nerva e di Traiano (Inglese e Pizzo 2014: 57–59), del Pantheon (Claridge 1983: 125, fig. 13), di Villa Adriana (Gutiérrez Deza e Felipe 2009: 130–131; Fileri 2017: 793; Inglese e Pizzo 2014: 49–51) e dell'arco di Costantino (Claridge 1983: 125). Vedi anche Inglese e Pizzo 2014: 203–204, 209–210; Inglese e Pizzo 2017: 236–237. Sulla lavorazione dei fusti, cfr. Pensabene 1992: 81–83; Pensabene 1996: 1116–1122; Pensabene 1998: 293–298.
[83] Tali passaggi, ricostruiti ed ipotizzati a partire dall'osservazione dei contesti indicati nella nota precedente, sono assenti nel passo vitruviano relativo alla teoria sull'articolazione dei fusti scanalati di colonna (Vitr., 3.5.14).
[84] Cfr. alcuni esempi da Villa Adriana (Guitiérrez Deza e Felipe 2009: 132–133), dal tempio di Cordoba (Gutiérrez Deza 1995: 120–124), o dal teatro di *Italica* (Rodríguez Gutiérrez 1997: 222; 2004: 597–598).
[85] Asgari 1988. Cfr. Toma 2014: 89–90; 2015: 816, 818; Wilson Jones 1991: 129–139.
[86] Voigts 2012: 141. Tale cavità presenta un diametro di cm 9,5 circa. Sull'utilizzo di questi perni metallici nel Palazzo, Voigts 2017a, b.
[87] Come riscontrato in un capitello dalle Terme di Agrippa a Roma (Respighi 1930: 116), di diversi esemplari di Villa Adriana (Gutiérrez Deza 2016: 73; Gutiérrez Deza e Felipe 2009: 133–140; Inglese e Pizzo 2014: 69, 205, 211), o del teatro di *Italica* (Rodríguez Gutiérrez 1997: 223–229; Rodríguez Gutiérrez 2004: 598–599).
[88] Così a Villa Adriana (Gutiérrez Deza e Felipe 2009: 136, fig. 11), nel teatro di *Italica* (Rodríguez Gutiérrez 1997: 225 e fig. 9), o a Pergamo nel complesso del *Traianeum* (Rohmann 1998: 35, tav. 13, fig. 4).

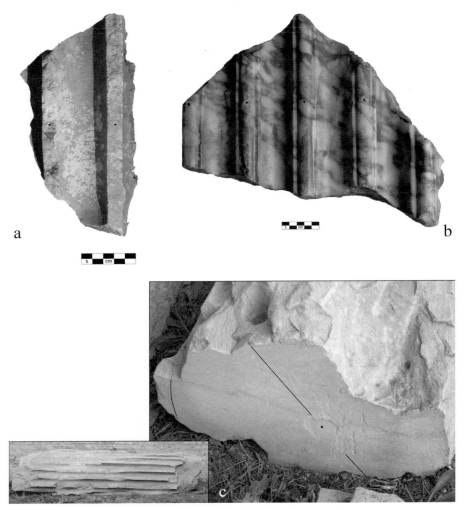

a

b

c

Figura 14. Peristilio Inferiore della *Domus Augustana*: a) frammento di fusto di colonna in portasanta; b) frammento di fusto di lesena con tondini sui listelli in pavonazzetto; c) troncone di fusto di colonna in cipollino con imoscapo (foto A. Mortera).

segnano la posizione dei fiori dell'abaco.[89] Dei tre capitelli più integri, due presentano alcune "anomalie": uno (**Figura 16b**), ha uno dei raggi in corrispondenza di uno dei fiori dell'abaco costituito in realtà da due incisioni appena divergenti; nel secondo caso (**Figura 16d**), invece, sono presenti due raggi doppi, coincidenti con due fiori dell'abaco, e due circonferenze incise. La prima, collega tutti i fori posti lungo il bordo del piano di appoggio del capitello; l'altra, invece, doveva individuare la posizione dei fori da perno per il fissaggio al sottostante fusto, così come spesso si riscontra nell'ambito di fusti di colonna realizzati in rocchi sovrapposti.[90]

Altri tracciati di cantiere sono poi visibili su quattro frammenti relativi agli spigoli dell'abaco di capitelli corinzi di colonna e un frammento di fiore d'abaco. A causa della frammentarietà di questi elementi, i tracciati sono solo parzialmente visibili. In un caso (**Figura 17a**), sono visibili un'incisione che segna la linea di mezzeria dello spigolo, che prosegue anche sullo *scamillus*, e una seconda linea, piuttosto corta, che interseca perpendicolarmente la prima in corrispondenza di un foro. Negli altri due casi sono presenti anche delle incisioni semicircolari che indicano la larghezza dello spigolo dell'abaco o la posizione e la dimensione del fiore dell'abaco (**Figura 17b-c**). Più complesso appare il sistema di incisioni tracciate in corrispondenza del piano di appoggio di un frammento di fiore dell'abaco (**Figura 17d**), in cui sono visibili due circonferenze

[89] Così come sul piano di appoggio di un capitello del tempio di calle Claudio Marcelo di Cordoba (Gutiérrez Deza 2005: 124–126, fig. 6; Gutiérrez Deza 2016: 73–74, fig. 1). Un capitello di piccole dimensioni da Ostia presenta invece due serie di doppie incisioni ad indicare la posizione di due fiori d'abaco praticate sul piano d'attesa (Pensabene 1973: tav. LXXXIX).
[90] Si vedano i casi di Villa Adriana (Fileri 2017: 793, figg. 6–7; Gutiérrez Deza e Felipe 2009: 135–140), Cordoba (Gutiérrez Deza 2005: 124–125,

127–128; Gutiérrez Deza 2016: 75), o di *Italica* (Ahrens 2005: 116, tav. 101; Rodríguez Gutiérrez 1997: 223–228; Rodríguez Gutiérrez 2004: 595–599).

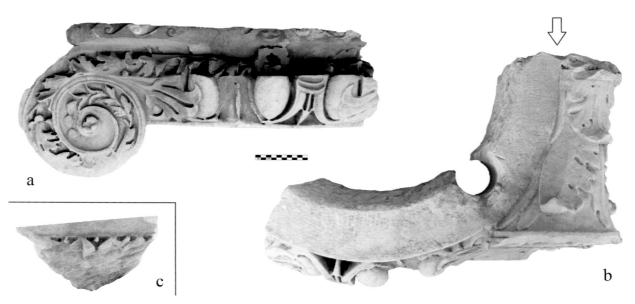

Figura 15. Peristilio Inferiore della *Domus Augustana*. Frammento di capitello ionico di rivestimento di semicolonna del primo ordine: a) fronte; b) piano di appoggio, la freccia indica la posizione del *kyma* lesbio contino; c) particolare del *kyma* lesbio sul retro (foto A. Mortera).

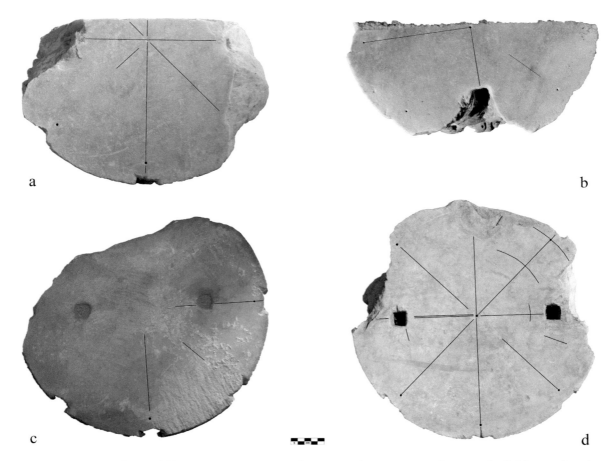

Figura 16. Peristilio Inferiore della *Domus Augustana*. Piani di appoggio di quattro capitelli corinzi (a-d) del secondo ordine sui quali sono leggibili le linee guida propedeutiche al posizionamento e alla realizzazione delle foglie d'acanto e del fiore dell'abaco (foto A. Mortera).

a

b

c

d

Figura 17. Peristilio Inferiore della *Domus Augustana*. Frammenti di spigoli dell'abaco di capitelli corinzi (a-c); frammento di fiore dell'abaco (d) (foto A. Mortera).

tangenti, una retta che passa per il punto di tangenza e infine un segmento obliquo. Così come nel caso del piano di appoggio, anche quello di attesa doveva dunque essere caratterizzato da una raggiera originata da un centro che doveva individuare gli spigoli dell'abaco.[91]

Questa serie di tracciati aveva lo scopo di facilitare il lavoro degli scalpellini impegnati nella realizzazione dei capitelli, materializzando sul blocco di marmo una serie di assi e linee guida funzionali alla distribuzione dei singoli elementi vegetali. Nella fattispecie, i quattro raggi

che indicavano la posizione dei fiori dell'abaco avevano altresì la funzione di dividere il piano di appoggio – e quindi il capitello stesso – in altrettanti quadranti e facce, all'interno di ciascuna delle quali veniva poi indicata la posizione delle foglie di acanto delle due corone.

Alquanto interessante appare il caso di un frammento di fregio-architrave sporgente in proconnesio, contraddistinto da *Rankengottin* e girali con *peopled scrolls*. In corrispondenza del piano di attesa, oltre ad un foro quadrangolare con relativa canaletta di scolo funzionale al fissaggio del blocco di cornice soprastante, è presente una lieve incisione (**Figura 18**): questa, disposta ortogonalmente alla fronte, ne indica il centro; inoltre, si trova in corrispondenza della testa della figura acantiforme che occupa l'asse mediano della fronte. La posizione di tale segno, tutt'altro che casuale, doveva così servire ad indicare l'asse centrale della faccia principale

---

[91] Inglese e Pizzo 2014: 205, 211; Inglese e Pizzo 2017: 237. Vedi il caso di un capitello del Colosseo, uno di Villa Adriana (Inglese e Pizzo 2014: 62, 64) e un altro da *Italica* (Ahrens 2005: 116–117, tavv. 101–102; Rodríguez Gutiérrez 1997: 225; 2004: 595–599). Sulle incisioni sul piano di attesa dei capitelli e il loro legame con il processo di strutturazione del capitello, cfr. Pensabene 1973: 192–194; Toma 2014; Toma 2015; Tomasello 1984; Wilson Jones 1991: 127–139.

Figura 18. Peristilio Inferiore della *Domus Augustana*. Frammento di fregio-architrave sporgente con *Rankengottin* e *peopled scrolls*: in alto a sinistra la fronte; in alto a destra il fianco destro; in basso il piano di attesa (foto A. Mortera).

del blocco e, di conseguenza, il posizionamento della figura antropomorfa.

Da ultimo, si segnala un frammento di piedistallo pertinente ad una transenna, in marmo africano. Esso presenta una delle sue estremità sagomata con le modanature in negativo della base composita cui doveva addossarsi. Su una delle facce sono visibili alcune incisioni che si intersecano ortogonalmente tra loro (**Figura 19**): due, nello specifico, sembrerebbero segnalare l'altezza del listello, mentre le altre tre sono direttamente collegate con la profilatura del toro inferiore.

Seppur ad una rassegna ancora preliminare, il Peristilio Inferiore della *Domus Augustana* sembra quindi restituire un importante numero di testimonianze legate alle pratiche di cantiere, in particolar modo per quanto riguarda le incisioni sulle membrature architettoniche che, normalmente graffite sulle superfici di contatto e

quindi non visibili dopo la messa in opera gli elementi, sorprendono per la facilità e la frequenza con cui queste sono individuabili. Bisogna però considerare che ciò è possibile in quanto, proprio perché queste incisioni erano praticate su quelle che sarebbero divenute superfici di contatto, queste mancavano spesso dello stadio finale di rifinitura. È possibile perciò ipotizzare che questi tracciati sulle membrature fossero ben più diffusi e comparissero su ogni singolo elemento architettonico, piuttosto che supporre che a presentarle fossero dei "prototipi" usati poi come modelli.[92] In tal senso sembrerebbero portare anche i capitelli corinzi e i frammenti di spigoli d'abaco del Peristilio Inferiore qui presentati, ciascuno dei quali mostra una serie più o meno numerosa di incisioni.

L'insieme di queste testimonianze contribuisce a far luce sulle pratiche di cantiere – o di più cantieri – impiegate

---

[92] Rohmann 1998: 35–36; Toma 2015: 816. *Contra*, Siegler 1966: 434; Tomasello 1984: 96.

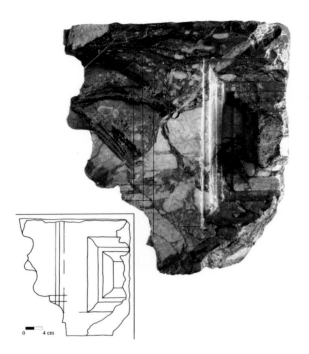

Figura 19. Peristilio Inferiore della *Domus Augustana*.
Frammento di piedistallo per transenna in marmo africano
(foto A. Mortera; disegno T. Chiaramida).

nell'*iter* costruttivo di questo settore del Palazzo imperiale, avviato in epoca vespasianea e ultimato solo decenni più tardi negli ultimi anni del principato domizianeo, con un possibile prolungamento dei lavori fino ai primissimi anni del II secolo d.C.

Tali tracciati, così come la linea rossa sulle murature, testimoniano la particolare premura e attenzione che sottintendeva nello specifico ai cantieri di grandi complessi monumentali pubblici, dove i lavori dovevano essere condotti a ritmi sostenuti impiegando un numero elevato di manodopera più o meno specializzata intenta a portare avanti diverse operazioni allo stesso momento.[93]

La realizzazione delle membrature architettoniche doveva necessariamente essere affidata ad una manodopera specializzata, i *marmorarii*. La sequenza di passaggi per ricavare da un blocco un qualsiasi elemento architettonico, infatti, richiedeva una serie di minuziose operazioni, tanto più durante le fasi della realizzazione delle modanature e delle decorazioni. Affinché i singoli elementi scolpiti rispondessero in egual maniera al progetto, su di essi veniva praticata una serie di linee guida o di piccoli fori atti ad individuare lo schema di base – ritmo, dimensioni – cui i singoli scalpellini avrebbero

poi fatto ricorso durante il loro lavoro.[94] Nell'ambito del Peristilio Inferiore, questo insieme di linee guida appare alquanto omogeneo.[95] Ad ogni modo, a prescindere dal loro numero, il numero sempre maggiore di questo tipo di tracciati di cantiere dimostra quantomeno una certa familiarità con i principi della geometria piana da parte degli addetti ai lavori.[96]

La validità di tale pratica dovette far sì che ben presto essa si affermasse come prassi dell'arte del costruire, divenendo una metodologia comunemente diffusa nell'architettura monumentale pubblica in molteplici aree dell'Impero.[97] Stabilirne una cronologia appare però piuttosto difficile e, verosimilmente, fuorviante. Sicuramente attestata già in epoca augustea,[98] essa godette di una certa fortuna e longevità.[99] In via ipotetica, si può pensare che il processo di standardizzazione che interessò la decorazione architettonica a partire dall'epoca domizianea abbia richiesto, per velocizzare le operazioni di realizzazione delle membrature architettoniche,[100] un'intensificazione dell'uso di queste linee guida. Tale pratica, almeno a Roma, avrebbe trovato grande fortuna nella ricostruzione del centro monumentale della città a seguito del devastante incendio dell'80 d.C.[101] e, nel caso specifico, nella volontà di ultimare il grandioso progetto del Palazzo il più rapidamente possibile. Essa avrebbe poi proseguito per tutto il II e quanto meno il III-IV secolo, come dimostra nel caso del Peristilio il frammento di fregio-architrave con *Rankengottin* e *peopled scrolls*,[102] divenendo una caratteristi precipua dei grandi complessi architettonici di pubblica committenza.

A. M.

[94] Gutiérrez Deza 2016: 73, dove si esprime la possibilità che tali linee potessero essere evidenziate tramite una colorazione, in modo da risultare più evidenti e più facili da seguire.
[95] In alcuni casi, la presenza di tipi di tracciati non sempre uguali tra loro ha dato modo di riconoscere il lavoro di diversi *marmorarii* (cfr. Rodríguez Gutiérrez 1997: 223; Gutiérrez Deza 2005: 134–5).
[96] Inglese e Pizzo 2014: 201–202; Inglese e Pizzo 2017: 234–235.
[97] Si vedano i casi dell'Asia Minore (Inglese 2016; Inglese e Pizzo 2017: 240–242) e della Lusitania (Inglese e Pizzo 2017: 242–243; Pizzo 2016); sono poi inoltre noti singoli casi-studio come quelli di Cordova (Gutiérrez Deza 2005; 2016; Márquez 1996), *Italica* (Rodríguez Gutiérrez 1997: 212–229; 2004: 595–599), *Tarraco* (Vinci e Ottati 2017), Atene (Ottati 2018), Sabratha (Tomasello 1984; Toma 2015: 814–815) e Iasos di Caria (Tomasello 1986), cui abbiamo più volte fatto ricorso.
[98] Il Foro di Augusto difatti dimostra già una certa familiarità con questa pratica (Inglese e Pizzo 2014: 29, 37, 45, 56, 117–118, 152–154, 174–176, 193–194). Tracciati di dettaglio sulle membrature architettoniche compaiono ad ogni modo già in Egitto e in Grecia e Magna Grecia dal VII-VI secolo a.C. (Inglese 2000: 176–185). Per i capitelli, vedi ad esempio il caso dei capitelli dorici di Iasos di Caria (Tomasello 1986).
[99] Inglese e Pizzo 2014: 216–217; Inglese e Pizzo 2017: 239. In Gutiérrez Deza e Felipe 2009: 142–144, si ipotizza una sistematicità di questa pratica a partire dall'epoca adrianea.
[100] Sulla decorazione architettonica di epoca flavia, Pensabene e Caprioli 2009.
[101] Cass. Dio, 64.24.2. Sugli interventi di Domiziano nell'area centrale di Roma, Moormann 2018.
[102] Neu 1972: 178, cat. 39; Toynbee e Ward-Perkins 1950: 23, tav. X, 2. Sulla continuità di questa prassi delle linee guida, Inglese e Pizzo 2014: 216–217; Inglese e Pizzo 2017: 243–244. Vedi anche le linee rintracciate di recente sui frammenti del tempio sul Quirinale (Pensabene 2018: 574–580).

[93] A tal proposito, per quanto riguarda la realizzazione di membrature architettoniche, si vedano le interessanti osservazioni di Jens Rohmann e Johannes Lipps sul numero di scalpellini impiegati per realizzare i capitelli del complesso del *Traianeum* di Pergamo (Rohmann 1998: 22–26, 33) e sulla presenza di molteplici squadre al lavoro contestualmente nell'ambito della Basilica Emilia (Lipps 2011: 173–179).

Il costo del cantiere flavio

Vogliamo affrontare ora la ricostruzione dei costi della decorazione marmorea del Peristilio Inferiore della *Domus Augustana* (**Appendice, Tabella 1a–f**). Abbiamo già visto le caratteristiche architettoniche di questo spazio decorato con marmi provenienti da cave specializzate nella produzione di *marmora* destinati alle esigenze della casa imperiale come il pavonazzetto, il giallo antico, il cipollino, il lunense, il proconnesio, ecc.

Siamo infatti di fronte a un progetto di committenza imperiale che può essere letto come una struttura "pubblica" appartenente allo Stato, perché destinata ad accogliere l'imperatore in carica, mantenendo però allo stesso tempo un certo carattere privato, in quanto parte del nucleo della residenza imperiale non aperto alle pubbliche udienze che doveva essere accessibile solo all'imperatore, al suo circolo di amici, agli invitati e naturalmente al personale di servizio.

L'uso del marmo

Il carattere pubblico della *Domus Augustana* significa che l'amministrazione statale è stata la responsabile dell'organizzazione dei lavori di costruzione. E in tale caso possiamo ritenere:

- che il progetto doveva essere gestito da uno specifico *curator* incaricato del coordinamento del trasporto dei diversi materiali costruttivi, ma non della scelta dei marmi da utilizzare, che spettava al progettista.
- che nell'approvvigionamento dei materiali giocavano un ruolo importante i rapporti personali fra questi *curatori* e i *procuratori* delle cave, le élite locali con interessi in esse e i contatti con gli intermediari, come i *redemptores* e i *negotiatores marmorum* che agivano nelle principali città e presso le cave: possiamo citare ad esempio T. Flavio Onesimo, *redemptor operum Caesar(is)*, attivo nel II sec. d.C. a Roma dove era anche quinquennale del collegio dei *fabri tignuarii* (*CIL* VI, 9034), ma il cui monumento funerario a tempietto è stato trovato a Synnada, nel capoluogo del distretto marmifero a cui appartenevano le cave di pavonazzetto.[103] Questi *redemptores* dovevano giocare un ruolo importante nell'acquisizione dei marmi, dati i loro collegamenti diretti con le cave.

Nell'età domizianea in cui si costruì il Palazzo la distribuzione dei marmi avveniva su due livelli. Il primo organizzato direttamente dall'amministrazione imperiale, che spesso si avvaleva di liberti e schiavi imperiali; il secondo gestito da affittuari delle cave e da *negotiatores* collegati ad essi. Solo a questo secondo livello poteva verificarsi una certa concorrenza fra diverse cave, se alcune qualità di marmi venivano acquistate sul mercato.

Inoltre, nel caso di un'opera di committenza imperiale, è molto probabile che il marmo dalle cave imperiali avesse un costo equivalente a zero (alcuni autori hanno suggerito un costo di circa il 50% del prezzo di mercato[104]). Per cui, riteniamo che le materie prime (marmi, laterizi, calce, legname per le impalcature, chiodi e strumenti vari) provenienti dai *praedia* e dai distretti minerali imperiali non incidessero direttamente sulle spese se non per quelle di trasporto, di lavorazione e di messa in opera, ambiti per i quali necessariamente si ricorreva alle associazioni professionali, qualunque sia stato il numero di schiavi pubblici messi a disposizione dall'amministrazione imperiale.

Ci sono però altri aspetti che dovettero giocare un ruolo importante nella scelta dei marmi. Citiamo ad esempio il colore, che poteva essere usato, come abbiamo visto nella prima parte di questo studio, per definire gli spazi. Nel Peristilio Inferiore si è fatto ricorso alla quadricromia augustea con l'inserimento di nuovi litotipi impiegati dall'età giulio-claudia in poi (porfido, serpentino e granito) e alcune varianti dettate specificatamente dal contesto: una struttura addossata ad un pendio, quasi un pozzo gigantesco che presuppone la provenienza della luce dall'alto. Ciò determina necessariamente l'uso di marmi chiari nella pavimentazione della corte, nel rivestimento della fontana e nei pilastri del portico: elementi tutti questi che sono rivestiti in marmi bianchi.

Anche per il secondo ordine sono stati scelti per le colonne colori chiari come quelli del cipollino, del portasanta (e forse del giallo antico) e sono dunque evitati marmi più scuri come l'africano, se non per creare un contrasto tra la verticalità delle colonne e le transenne chiare.

Il costo dei marmi

Una volta stabilite queste premesse possiamo tentare di ricostruire in maniera approssimativa il costo dei marmi utilizzati nel Peristilio Inferiore, partendo dai dati contenuti nell'Editto di Diocleziano.[105] Bisogna dire che in questa ricostruzione non abbiamo preso in considerazione né i marmi che rivestivano i pavimenti

---

[103] Pensabene 2013: 215.

[104] Barresi 2000: 352.
[105] Sul costo dei marmi vedere Domingo 2012a: 75–91; Lazzarini 2010: 485–490. Per quanto riguarda il costo del travertino, non compreso nell'Editto di Diocleziano, abbiamo immaginato un prezzo di circa 1 HS/p^3, leggermente più economico del travertino rosso delle cave presso Cartagena, in Spagna, con un costo di 1,5–2 HS/p^3, Soler 2012: 212.

dei due livelli del Peristilio, né i marmi che rivestivano il muro di fondo del secondo piano (sul quale non siamo ancora in grado di proporre una ricostruzione attendibile), né ancora i marmi che decoravano la fontana centrale.

Il costo della manodopera

Nella storia degli studi è stato attribuito a un operaio non qualificato della costruzione nel I-II sec. d.C. uno stipendio generico di 2 HS/giorno (valore ottenuto dall'estrapolazione dei dati dell'Editto di Diocleziano in questo periodo storico[106]). Sappiamo però da diverse fonti che i salari percepiti a Roma dovevano essere più elevati.[107] Possiamo ricostruire dunque uno stipendio per le fasi del lavoro che avvenivano direttamente nelle cave (apparato rustico e semilavorazione) di 2,5 HS/giornata, uno stipendio per gli addetti alla messa in opera di 4 HS/giornata e uno stipendio per la manodopera specializzata impiegata nella finitura dei motivi decorativi di 5 HS/giornata.

Il costo dell'apparato rustico

Consisteva nel dare ai blocchi estratti la forma geometrica dell'elemento finale.[108] Questa fase del lavoro era completata direttamente nelle cave, in modo da ridurre al massimo il volume e il peso dei blocchi trasportati, e il suo costo dipendeva dal tipo di materiale usato: pietra calcarea, simile al travertino, 116 ore/m³;[109] marmo a grana fina (lunense, pavonazzetto, giallo antico e portasanta) 157,5 ore/m³;[110] e marmo a grana media (proconnesio, rosso antico, serpentino e cipollino) 210 ore/m³.[111]

Il costo della semilavorazione

Consisteva nel delimitare sul blocco di pietra le linee essenziali dello sviluppo decorativo/formale dell'elemento architettonico finale. Il costo variava in base al tipo di elemento architettonico e al materiale usato. Ad esempio, i capitelli avevano un costo di a(1+0,25/x), dove "a" corrisponde a 4,33 ore di lavoro per il marmo a grana fina o 5,8 ore di lavoro per il marmo a grana media e dove "x" corrisponde al diametro inferiore espresso in metri. Il risultato ottenuto corrisponde a ore lavoro × m² di superficie.[112] I fusti avevano un costo di a(2+0,25/x), dove "a" corrisponde a 4,33 ore di lavoro per il marmo a grana fina o 5,80 ore di lavoro per il marmo a grana media[113] e dove "x"

corrisponde al diametro del fusto espresso in metri. Il risultato ottenuto corrisponde a ore di lavoro per m² di superficie.[114] Le basi avevano un costo equivalente a ⅓ dei loro rispettivi capitelli.[115] E, infine, gli elementi con superfici lineari (modanature, architravi, fregi e cornici) avevano un costo di 4,33 ore/m² se di marmo a grana fina o un costo di 5,8 ore/m² se di marmo a grana media.[116]

Il costo del trasporto

Il costo del trasporto terrestre può calcolarsi con la formula 0,85 denari (I sec. d.C.) / (m³ × miglio).[117] Il trasporto fluviale era 5,5 volte più economico di quello terrestre quando percorso controcorrente e 10,8 volte più economico quando a favore della corrente.[118]

Il trasporto marittimo può essere ricostruito in base ai dati contenuti nell'Editto di Diocleziano.[119] Bisogna segnalare che perfino quando i marmi di titolarità imperiale erano impiegati in costruzioni di commissione imperiale il trasporto era affidato generalmente a privati.[120]

Per il marmo proconnesio bisogna aver presente il costo del trasporto dalla città di Nicomedia a Roma, di 18 denari del IV sec. d.C. × modio castrense = 14 denari del s. I d.C. × m³.[121]

Per il marmo lunense bisogna considerare un primo tragitto terrestre fra le cave e il porto, di circa 20 miglia,[122] e un tragitto marittimo fino a Roma il cui costo, non specificato nell'Editto di Diocleziano, doveva essere simile a quello fra Roma e la Sicilia, di 6 denari del IV sec. d.C. × modio castrense = 4,7 denari del I sec. d.C. × m³.

Per il pavonazzetto bisogna considerare un primo tragitto fluviale fra le cave e Nicomedia, di circa 176 miglia, e un tragitto marittimo fra Nicomedia e Roma.

Per il cipollino possiamo considerare un tragitto marittimo simile a quello da Roma a Tessalonica che, secondo l'Editto di Diocleziano, aveva un costo di 18

---

[106] Barresi 2000: 182, 345; DeLaine 1997: 119–121.
[107] Domingo 2013: 119–143.
[108] Barresi 2003: 171; Pensabene 2007: 390; Pensabene e Bruno 1998: 2.
[109] Pegoretti 1863: 429.
[110] Pegoretti 1863: 402.
[111] Pegoretti 1863: 402.
[112] Pegoretti 1863: 402, 430.
[113] Pegoretti 1863: 423, 430.
[114] Pegoretti 1863: 423, 430.
[115] Barresi 2000: 362; Soler 2012: 216, tab. 5.
[116] Pegoretti 1863: 403 .
[117] Barresi 2003: 175; DeLaine 1997: 210–211; Mar e Pensabene 2010: 527, 531.
[118] Russell 2013: 96.
[119] Giacchero 1974: 310–312. Vedere anche: Arnaud 2007: 321–336.
[120] Gianfrotta 2008: 87.
[121] La conversione si basa nel rapporto: 1 modio castrense = 0,0128 m³, cioè 1 m³ = 78,125 modii (Barresi 2002: 78; Duncan Jones 1976: 53–62). L'estrapolazione dei costi dall'età di Diocleziano al I sec. d.C. si basa sul rapporto: 1 modio castrense = 100 denari in età diocletianea e 1 denario nel I sec. d.C. (DeLaine 1997: 146).
[122] Mar e Pensabene 2010: 531.

denari del IV sec. d.C. × modio castrense[123] = 14 denari del I sec. d.C. × m³.

Per il giallo antico bisogna considerare un tragitto marittimo simile a quello fra la Sicilia e Roma, di 6 denari del IV sec. d.C. × modio castrense[124] = 4,7 denari del I sec. d.C. × m³.

Per il portasanta possiamo supporre un tragitto marittimo simile a quello fra Tessalonica e Roma.

Per il serpentino bisogna considerare un primo tragitto terrestre dalle cave al porto, di circa 5,5 miglia, e un trasporto marittimo fino a Roma simile a quello percorso per il cipollino = 14 denari del I sec. d.C. × m³.

Per il rosso antico possiamo supporre un tragitto marittimo simile a quello del cipollino = 14 denari del I sec. d.C. × m³.

Successivamente i marmi dovevano risalire il Tevere fino al punto di sbarco, che riteniamo fosse la zona del Foro Boario,[125] per un tragitto di circa 20 miglia,[126] e successivamente percorrere via terra un tragitto di circa 0,4 miglia fino al Palatino.

Costo della messa in opera

Quando i monoliti superavano il peso di 1 tonnellata, il costo in ore di lavoro della messa in opera per ogni tonnellata di peso si calcola tramite la formula: 0,20 (imbracatura) + 0,33 × m di distanza (avvicinamento) + 0,2 × m di altezza (elevazione) + 0,1 (posizionamento) + 1 (grappe).[127] Il calcolo in ore di lavoro è fatto per un gruppo di quattro operai.[128]

I blocchi con un peso inferiore a 1 tonnellata avevano un costo, espresso in ore di lavoro, di t + 0,06 t (a-1); dove "t" corrisponde a 0,6 ore per ogni 100 kg di peso e "a" corrisponde all'altezza di elevazione della pietra, espressa in metri. In questo caso, il calcolo in ore di lavoro è basato su una squadra di due operai più un tagliatore di pietra e un manovale.[129]

Costo della finitura

Consisteva nella realizzazione degli ultimi ritocchi ai motivi decorati (basi, fusti, capitelli, fregi, architravi, cornici, ecc.). Per calcolare il costo di questa operazione bisogna distinguere il tipo di elemento architettonico, il materiale usato e le loro dimensioni. Un blocco

squadrato liscio in travertino aveva un costo di 10,67 ore/m² di superficie;[130] le basi un costo equivalente a ¼ dei loro rispettivi capitelli;[131] i fusti scanalati di colonna in marmo a grana media un costo di 13,3 ore/m² di superficie,[132] se in marmo di grana fina un costo di 10 ore/m² di superficie,[133] e se di lesena un costo di circa ¼ dei rispettivi fusti di colonna.[134] Per quanto riguarda i capitelli corinzi, quelli in marmo a grana media con un'altezza 0,50 m hanno un costo di 720 ore[135] (= 432 ore se di lesena[136]). Infine, il costo delle modanature, architravi, fregi e cornici dipende dalle loro dimensioni, dai materiali e dalla complessità dei motivi decorativi.[137]

Considerazioni finali

Il risultato ottenuto permette di arrotondare il costo finale della decorazione marmorea a circa 400.000 HS, mentre il costo del solo materiale, che si è detto non prendiamo in considerazione essendo un'opera di committenza imperiale, ammontava a circa altri 400.000 HS. Il costo stimato in giornate di lavoro sarebbe di circa 75.000, divise nelle diverse fasi di produzione realizzate *in situ* e nelle cave.

Abbiamo potuto osservare l'applicazione di alcune soluzioni tecniche destinate in parte anche a contenere i costi di questa struttura, come il ricorso al piano inferiore di pilastri in travertino rivestiti di marmo e la configurazione delle trabeazioni con un nucleo ancora in travertino rivestito di marmo, ad eccezione delle cornici formate da blocchi marmorei. Queste soluzioni si distinguono da quelle del secondo ordine architettonico, costituito invece da colonne interamente in marmo che sorreggono una trabeazione con blocchi di marmo. In questo caso, però, gli architravi, i fregi e le cornici sono state lavorate unicamente sul lato principale, essendo state lasciate lisce nel lato posteriore.

Il calcolo dei costi di questo settore del palazzo imperiale ci ha offerto l'occasione di studiare con attenzione le tecniche costruttive usate, i marmi impiegati e la volumetria di tutti i componenti di questa struttura, propiziando una migliore comprensione dello sviluppo del cantiere. Un'opera realizzata con la partecipazione di operai altamente qualificati, come mostrano non soltanto il livello artistico degli elementi decorativi, ma anche le tecniche costruttive usate e il preciso sistema di linee guida incise sugli elementi architettonici.

J. Á. D.

---

[123] Arnaud 2007: 336; Giacchero 1974: 301.
[124] Arnaud 2007: 336; Giacchero 1974: 301.
[125] Pensabene e Domingo 2017: 572–582.
[126] Pensabene e Domingo 2017: 582.
[127] Barresi 2000: 363; Mar e Pensabene 2010: 527.
[128] Pegoretti 1864: 217-218.
[129] Barresi 2003: 186; Pegoretti 1864: 217-218.

[130] Domingo 2012b: 410; Domingo 2012c: 158.
[131] Barresi 2000: 362.
[132] Pegoretti 1863: 404.
[133] Pegoretti 1863: 404.
[134] Barresi 2000: 362.
[135] Pegoretti 1863: 408.
[136] Pegoretti 1863: 409.
[137] Pegoretti 1863: 406-407.

Conclusioni

Il complesso del Peristilio Inferiore della *Domus Augustana* doveva rispondere, così come l'intero Palazzo, a esigenze di varia natura: da una parte, infatti, le sue strutture dovevano garantire la realizzazione di un vasto e grandioso complesso esteso a tutto il colle Palatino; dall'altra, a queste architetture era affidata la materializzazione dell'ideologia imperiale promossa da Domiziano.

In questo senso, l'analisi dei dati quantitativi legata ai materiali impiegati per la realizzazione dei due ordini architettonici sovrapposti della corte centrale e dei rivestimenti marmorei delle pareti di fondo dell'ambulacro in corrispondenza del livello inferiore del Peristilio, ha fornito un utile strumento per indagare uno degli aspetti più affascinanti dei cantieri pubblici di epoca imperiale: quello dei costi. Nel caso specifico, l'interesse di un simile approccio è accentuato dalla natura del tutto particolare del contesto preso in esame, il Palazzo imperiale.

All'interno di questo scenario, tutte le operazioni relative al cantiere – confezione delle murature, realizzazione delle membrature e dei rivestimenti marmorei che rispondessero ad un comune linguaggio architettonico palaziale – dovevano sì mirare ad una rapidità di esecuzione del progetto, possibile grazie all'impiego di maestranze specializzate e formate per riprodurre un preciso repertorio decorativo, segno distintivo del *decus* del Palazzo, e verosimilmente meno alla ottimizzazione dei costi. Riteniamo infatti che non fossero tanto questi alla base delle scelte formali, architettoniche e stilistiche adottate in un progetto come quello del Peristilio Inferiore, per il quale la logica del "risparmio" deve essere fugata. A favore di una simile ipotesi deve considerarsi il costo finale presentato in questa sede, così come il fatto che, come abbiamo detto, nel caso della dimora dell'imperatore si può ritenere che il costo delle materie prime provenienti da cave che rientravano nel *patrimonium Caesaris* fosse pressoché nullo. Sebbene frutto di dati parziali e relativi ad una circoscritta parte di tutto il complesso palaziale, la cifra di 400.000 HS ben esemplifica la principale peculiarità della questione dei costi legati ad un'architettura *sui generis* come deve considerarsi quella del Palazzo sul Palatino: questo valore difatti non rappresenta che una minima parte della spesa reale stabilita e affrontata dall'erario per realizzare quella che a tutti gli effetti doveva apparire come un'impresa edilizia sconfinata, la quale, dettata in buona parte da ragioni di propaganda politica, consenso e costituzione di un'ideologia imperiale mirata a sottolineare costantemente la doppia natura del *princeps*, umana e divina, non poteva presentare limiti prestabiliti. Ciò è ancor più degno di nota se si pensa che a una simile spesa, in provincia,

corrisponde la costruzione di un edificio da spettacolo (cfr. in questo volume il contributo di J. Borrego e C. Courault sul teatro di Cordoba).

Il caso del Peristilio Inferiore conferma dunque come in occasione di grandi progetti edilizi di committenza pubblica gran parte delle somme stanziate fossero destinate alla manodopera, spesso specializzata. La presenza di quest'ultima emerge tanto dallo studio della decorazione architettonica, imputabile a un'officina il cui lavoro su marmi bianchi e colorati e su membrature architettoniche decorate e lisce si distingue per una resa plastica e raffinata, quanto da aspetti più tecnici legati alla realizzazione degli elementi marmorei stessi. Molte delle membrature architettoniche conservano difatti delle incisioni su determinate superfici che appartengono perlopiù alla fase di definizione delle modanature o alla disposizione degli elementi decorativi (come nel caso dei capitelli corinzi), risultando omogenee tra loro. Queste inoltre consentono di delineare una pratica comune agli scalpellini e ai *marmorarii* impiegati non solo nell'ambito del cantiere del Peristilio, ma anche in quello di altri importanti cantieri pubblici. Così, per le basi si ricorreva ad incisioni longitudinali per la definizione della circonferenza massima che dovevano assumere tori e tondini; nel caso dei fusti, i listelli e i tondini ad essi sovrapposti erano individuati da piccoli fori e da circonferenze atte ad indicarne la larghezza; per i capitelli invece una doppia serie di raggiere, praticate sui piani di appoggio e di attesa, indicavano la disposizione dei principali elementi morfologici (spigoli dell'abaco, volute, fiore dell'abaco) e decorativi (foglie d'acanto).

Tutto ciò contribuiva a restituire l'idea di un'impresa "faraonica". Nel suo complesso, la costruzione del Palazzo imperiale doveva suscitare stupore, soggezione, senso di inferiorità e costruire intorno alla figura del *dominus* una sorta di alone di "mistero" tale da legittimarne anche la natura divina (*et deus*), delineando così un'architettura "impossibile", in grado di sfidare gravità, altezze e volumetrie terrene. Domiziano costruì così il suo palazzo "infinito" – un labirinto potremmo dire –, che doveva materializzare con la sua sola vista un'operazione non quantizzabile nell'immediato e che anelava ad un'azione divina, come ricordano Stazio e Marziale: un vero e proprio *miraculum*.

F. C., A. M., P. P., J. Á. D.

Bibliografia

Amici, C. 2008. Dal monumento all'edificio: il ruolo delle dinamiche di cantiere, in S. Camporeale, H. Dessales e A. Pizzo (eds) *Arqueología de la costrucción,*

I. Los procesos constructivos en el mundo romano: Italia y provincias occidentales (Mérida, Instituto de Arqueología, 25-26 de Octubre 2007): 13–31. Mérida: Consejo Superior de Investigaciones Científicas.

Archeologia in posa 1994. *Archeologia in posa: cento anni di fotografie del Palatino.* Roma: Edizioni De Luca.

Arnaud, P. 2007. Diocletian's Prices Edict: the prices of seaborne transport and the average duration of maritime travel. *Journal of Roman Archaeology* 20: 321–335.

Asgari, N. 1988. The stages of workmanship of the Corinthian capital in Proconnesus and its export form, in N. Herz e M. Waelkens (eds) *Classical Marble: Geochemistry, Technology, Trade*: 115–125. Dordrecht-Boston: Kluwer Academic Publishers.

Attoui, R. 2008. Segni di cantiere nella "Palestra" di Villa Adriana, Tivoli, in S. Camporeale, H. Dessales e A. Pizzo (eds) *Arqueología de la costrucción, I. Los procesos constructivos en el mundo romano: Italia y provincias occidentale (Mérida, Instituto de Arqueología, 25-26 de Octubre de 2007)*: 49–66. Mérida: Consejo Superior de Investigaciones Científicas.

Barresi, P. 2000. Architettura pubblica e munificenza in Asia Minore. Ricchezza, costruzioni e marmi nelle provincie anatoliche dell'Impero. *Mediterraneo Antico* III, I: 309–368.

Barresi, P. 2002. Il ruolo delle colonne nel costo degli edifici pubblici, in M. De Nuccio e L. Ungaro (eds) *I marmi colorati della Roma imperiale*: 69–81. Venezia: Marsilio.

Barresi, P. 2003. *Provincie dell'Asia Minore. Costo dei marmi, architettura pubblica e committenza.* Roma: L'Erma di Bretschneider.

Bartoli, A. 1938. *Domus Augustana.* Roma: Istituto di Studi Romani.

Bernard, S.G. 2017. Workers in the Roman Imperial Building Industry, in K. Verboven e C. Laes (eds) *Work, Labour, and Professions in the Roman World*: 62–86. Leiden-Boston: Brill.

Bianchi, E. e R. Meneghini 2002. Il cantiere costruttivo del foro di Traiano. *Mitteilungen des Deutschen Archäologischen Instituts, Römische Abteilung* 109: 395–417.

Bitterer, T. 2012. Le incrostazioni marmoree nel Peristilio Inferiore della *Domus Augustana*, in N. Sojc (ed.) *Domus Augustana: Neue Forschungen zum "Versenkten Peristyl" auf dem Palatin*: 229–247. Leiden: Sideston Press.

Bodei Giglioni, G. 1974. *Lavori pubblici e occupazione nell'antichità classica.* Bologna: Pàtron.

Bollmann, B. 1998. *Römische Vereinshäuser. Untersuchungen zu den Scholae der römischen Berufs-, Kult- und Augustalen-Kollegien in Italien.* Mainz: Verlag Philipp von Zabern.

Bruto, M.L. e C. Vannicola 1990. Ricostruzione e tipologia delle *crustae* parietali in età imperiale. *Archeologia Classica* XLII: 325–376.

Bukowiecki, E. 2012. La *Domus Augustana* inferiore: organizzazione del cantiere e principali fasi costruttive, in N. Sojc (ed.) *Domus Augustana: Neue Forschungen zum "Versenkten Peristyl" auf dem Palatin*: 79–105. Leiden: Sideston Press.

Bukowiecki, E. e H. Dessales 2008. Les thermes publics d'Italica: regards compares sur deux chantiers de construction, in S. Camporeale, H. Dessales e A. Pizzo (eds) *Arqueología de la costrucción, I. Los procesos constructivos en el mundo romano: Italia y provincias occidentales (Mérida, Instituto de Arqueología, 25-26 de Octubre 2007)*: 191–207. Mérida: Consejo Superior de Investigaciones Científicas.

Bukowiecki, E., H. Dessales e J. Dubouloz 2008. *Ostie, l'eau dans la ville: châteaux d'eau et réseau d'adduction.* Roma: Ecole Française de Rome.

Bukowiecki, E. e U. Wulf-Rheidt 2015a. Approvvigionamento dei laterizi nei cantieri palatini, in E. Bukowiecki, R. Volpe e U. Wulf-Rheidt (eds) *Il laterizio nei cantieri imperiali. Roma ed il Mediterraneo. Atti del I workshop "Laterizio", Roma 27-28 novembre 2014 (Archeologia dell'Architettura XX)*: 26–30. Firenze: All'Insegna del Giglio.

Bukowiecki, E. e U. Wulf-Rheidt 2015b. I bolli laterizi delle residenze imperiali sul Palatino a Roma. *Mitteilungen des Deutschen Archeologischen Instituts, Römische Abteilung* 121: 311–482.

Carboni, F. 2003. Scavi nell'esedra nord-orientale delle Terme di Traiano. *Bullettino della Commissione Archeologica Comunale di Roma* 104: 65–82.

Carettoni, G., A.M. Colini, L. Cozza e G. Gatti 1960. *La pianta marmorea di Roma antica: Forma Urbis Romae.* Roma.

Carettoni, G. 1972. Terme di Settimio Severo e terme di Massenzio "in Palatio". *Archeologia Classica* XXIV: 96–104.

Chevallier, R. 1986. *Ostie antique: ville et port.* Paris: Les Belles Lettres.

Claridge, A. 1982. Le scanalature delle colonne, in L. Cozza (ed.) *Tempio di Adriano*: 27–30. Roma: De Luca.

Claridge, A. 1983. Roman methods of fluting corinthian columns and pilaster, in K. De Fine Licht (ed.) *Città e architettura nella Roma imperiale. Atti del seminario del 27 ottobre 1981 nel 25° anniversario dell'Accademia di Danimarca (Analecta Romana Instituti Danici 10)*: 119–128. Odense: Odense University Press.

Coticelli, A., S. De Martini, F. Grande e E. Mancini 2017. La declinazione e percezione del linguaggio architettonico nelle varie articolazioni del palazzo flavio sul Palatino, in P. Pensabene, M. Milella e F. Caprioli (eds) Decor. *Decorazione e architettura nel mondo romano, Atti del Convegno, Roma 21-24 maggio 2014 (Thiasos Monografie 9)*: 575–588. Roma: Edizioni Quasar.

Daguet-Gagey, A. 1997. *Les opera publica à Rome (180-305 ap. J.-C.).* Paris: Institut d'Etudes Augustiniennes.

D'Elia, L. e S. Le Pera Buranelli 1985. Rilievo del Peristilio Inferiore della *Domus Flavia*, in *Roma: archeologia nel centro, I. L'area archeologica centrale*: 176–178. Roma: De Luca.

DeLaine, J. 1997. *The Bath of Caracalla. A study in the design, construction, and economics of large-scale building projects in imperial Roma* (Journal of Roman Archaeology, Suppl. 25). Portsmouth (Rhode Island): Journal of Roman Archaeology.

Domingo, J.Á. 2012a. El coste del mármol. Problemas e incertidumbres de una metodología de cálculo. *Marmora* 8: 75–91.

Domingo, J.Á. 2012b. Los costes de la arquitectura romana: el capitolio de Volúbilis (Mauretania Tingitana). *Archeologia Classica* LXIII: 381–418.

Domingo, J.Á. 2012c. El coste de la arquitectura: avances, problemas e incertidumbres de una metodología de cálculo: Volúbilis y Dougga. *Archeologia dell'Architettura* XVII: 144–170.

Domingo, J.Á. 2013. The differences in Roman Construction Costs: the Workers' Salary. *Boreas* 36: 119–143.

Duncan-Jones, R.P. 1976. The size of the modius castrenses. *Zeitschrift für Papyrologie und Epigraphik* 21: 53–62.

Falzone, S. 2018. La pittura parietale: caratteri e contenuti, in A. D'Alessio, C. Panella e R. Rea (eds) *Roma Universalis: i Severi. L'impero e la dinastia venuta dall'Africa* (catalogo della mostra): 116–119. Milano: Electa.

Fileri, P. 2017. I graffiti del marmorario: nuovi tracciati di cantiere e di dettaglio a Villa Adriana, in P. Pensabene, M. Milella e F. Caprioli (eds) Decor. *Decorazione e architettura nel mondo romano, Atti del Convegno, Roma 21-24 maggio 2014* (Thiasos Monografie 9): 789–800. Roma: Edizioni Quasar.

Fink, M e P. Wech 2012. Foundations in *opus caementicium* and their building process in the imperial architecture of the Palatine: typology as a means of dating in a local system, in N. Sojc (ed.) *Domus Augustana: Neue Forschungen zum "Versenkten Peristyl" auf dem Palatin*: 107–137. Leiden: Sideston Press.

Fogagnolo, S. 2009a. Esempi di schemi decorativi dell'*opus sectile* parietale dalla zona inferiore della *Domus Augustana* sul Palatino, in C. Angelelli (ed.) *Atti del XIV Colloquio dell'Associazione Italiana per lo Studio e la Conservazione del Mosaico (Spoleto, 7-9 febbraio 2008)*: 489–500. Tivoli: Scripta Manent.

Fogagnolo, S. 2009b. Rivestimenti marmorei del complesso palaziale di epoca flavia, in F. Coarelli (ed.) *Divus Vespasianus: il bimillenario dei Flavi* (catalogo della mostra): 280–283. Milano: Electa.

Freyberger, K.S. 1990. *Stadtrömische Kapitelle aus der Zeit von Domitian bis Alexander Severus: zur Arbeitsweise und Organisation stadtrömischer Werkstätten der Kaiserzeit*. Mainz am Rhein: von Zabern.

Fusco, R. 2012. G.A. Guattani, l'architettura antica e la *Domus Augustana* al Palatino, in G.M. Di Nocera, M. Micozzi, C. Pavolini e A. Rovelli (eds) *Archeologia e memoria storica. Atti delle Giornate di Studio (Viterbo 25-26 marzo 2009)* (Daidalos 13): 355–369.

García Barraco, M.E. 2014. *Villa Mills sul Palatino e la Domus Augustana*. Roma: Arbor Sapientiae.

Giacchero, M. 1974. *Edictum Diocletiani et Collegarum de pretiis rerum venalium*. Genova: Istituto di Storia Antica e Scienze Ausiliarie.

Gianfrotta, P.A. 2008. Σμειριδες: depositi portuali, marmi di cava e navi. *Orizzonti* IX: 77–89.

Gismondi, I. 1953. Periodo imperiale, in G. Calza, G. Becatti e I. Gismondi (eds) *Scavi di Ostia, 1. Topografia generale*: 195–208. Roma: Libreria dello Stato.

Giuliani, C.F. 2006. *L'edilizia nell'antichità*. Roma: Carocci.

Gros, P. 1996. *L'architecture romaine du début du IIIe siècle av. J.-C. à la fin du Haut-Empire, 1. Les monuments publics*. Paris: Picard.

Grüner, A. 2017. Die Farben des Augustusforum. Der öffentliche Raum als ästhe-tisches System, in M. Flecker, S. Krmnicek, J. Lipps, R. Posamentir e T. Schäfer (eds) *Augustus is tot - Lang lebe der Kaiser. Internationales Kolloquium anlässlich des 2000. Todesjahres des römischen Kaiser vom 20. - 22. November 2014 in Tübingen*: 559–584. Rahden/Westf.: Verlag Marie Leidorf.

Guattani, G.A. 1785. *Monumenti antichi inediti, ovvero notizie sulle antichità e belle arti di Roma*. Roma: stamperia Pagliarini.

Guidobaldi, F. e C. Angelelli 2005. I rivestimenti parietali in marmo (*incrustationes*). La tecnica di fabbricazione e posa in opera come base del progetto di conservazione, in *Wall and Floor Mosaics: Conservation, Maintenance, Presentation, VIIIth Conference of the International Committee for the Conservation of Mosaics (ICCM), Thessaloniki, 29 October - 3 November 2002*: 33–43. Thessaloniki: European Center of Byzantine and Post-Byzantine Monuments.

Gutiérrez Deza, M.I. 2005. Líneas guía para la elaboración de los elementos arquitectónicos en el templo de culto imperial de la provincia *Baetica*. *Romula* 4: 115–136.

Gutiérrez Deza, M.I. 2016. Líneas de planeamiento en el templo romano de Córdoba, in C. Inglese e A. Pizzo (eds) *I tracciati di cantiere: disegni esecutivi per la trasmissione e diffusione delle conoscenze tecniche*: 72–81. Roma: Gangemi.

Gutiérrez Deza, M.I. e A.M. Felipe 2009. Una breve visión de la labor de los marmorarii de Villa Adriana. *Romula* 8: 125–144.

Haselberger, L. 1980. Werkzeichnungen am Jüngeren Didymeion. *Istanbuler Mitteilungen* 30: 191–215.

Haselberger, L. 1983a. Bericht über die Arbeit am Jüngeren Apollontempel von Didyma. *Istanbuler Mitteilungen* 33: 90–123.

Haselberger, L. 1983b. Die Bauzeichnungen des Apollotempels von Didyma. *Architectura: Zeitschrif für Geschichte der Baukunst* 13: 13–26.

Haselberger, L. 1985. Die Werzeichnung des Naiskos im Apollontempel von Didyma, in *Bauplanung und Bautheorie der Antike* (Diskussionen zur archäologischen Bauforschung 4): 111–119. Berlin: Deutsches Archäologisches Institut.

Haselberger, L. 1986. I progetti di costruzione del tempio di Apollo a Didime. *Le Scienze* 210 (febbraio): 96–106.

Haselberger, L. 1994. Ein Giebelriss der Vorhalle des Pantheon die Werkrisse vor dem Augustusmausoleum. *Mitteilungen des Deutschen Archäologischen Instituts, Römische Abteilung* 101: 279–308.

Haselberger, L. 1995. Un progetto architettonico di 2000 anni fa. *Le Scienze* 324 (agosto): 56–61.

Hirschfeld, O. 1905. *Die kaiserlichen Verwaltungsbeamten bis auf Diocletian.* Berlin: Weidmann.

Hirt, A.M. 2010. *Imperial Mines and Quarries in the Roman World. Organizational Aspects 27 BC - AD 235.* Oxford: Oxford University Press.

Homo, L. 1951. *Rome impériale et l'urbanisme dans l'antiquité.* Paris: Albin Michel.

Iacopi, I. 1997. *Gli scavi sul colle Palatino: testimonianze e documenti.* Milano: Electa.

Iara, K. 2015. *Hippodromus Palatii: die Bauornamentik des Gartenhippodroms im Kaiserpalast auf dem Palatin in Rom.* Weisbaden: Dr. Ludwig Reichert Verlag.

Inglese, C. 2000. *Progetti sulla pietra.* Roma: Gangemi.

Inglese, C. 2016. I tracciaci di cantiere nelle province romane dell'Asia Minore, in C. Inglese e A. Pizzo (eds) *I tracciati di cantiere: disegni esecutivi per la trasmissione e diffusione delle conoscenze tecniche*: 29–54. Roma: Gangemi.

Inglese, C. e A. Pizzo 2014. *I tracciati di cantiere di epoca romana. Progetti, esecuzioni e montaggi.* Roma: Gangemi.

Inglese, C. e A. Pizzo (eds) 2016. *I tracciati di cantiere: disegni esecutivi per la trasmissione e diffusione delle conoscenze tecniche.* Roma: Gangemi.

Inglese, C. e A. Pizzo 2017. Lo studio dei tracciati di cantiere nel mondo romano: metodologia e nuove prospettive di ricerca, in L. Roldán, J.M. Macias, A. Pizzo e O. Rodríguez (eds) *Modelos constructivos y urbanísticos de la arquitectura de Hispania. Definición, evolución y difusión del periodo romano a la Antigüedad tardía (MArqHis 2013-2015)* (Documenta 29): 231–244. Tarragona: Institut Català d'Arqueologia Clàssica.

Krautheimer, R. 1971. *Corpus basilicarum christianarum Romae: the early Christian basilicas of Rome (IV-IX cent.), III.* Città del Vaticano: Pontificio Istituto di Archeologia Cristiana.

Lazzarini L. 2010. Considerazioni sul prezzo dei marmi bianchi e colorati in età imperiale, in S. Camporeale, H. Dessales e A. Pizzo (eds) *Arqueología de la Construcción, II. Los procesos constructivos en el mundo romano: Italia y provincias orientales*: 485–490. Madrid-Mérida: Consejo Superior de Investigaciones Científicas.

Leicht, P.S. 1946-1947. I collegi professionali romani nelle iscrizioni aquileiesi. *Atti della Pontificia Accademia Romana di Archeologia. Rendiconti* 22: 253–265.

Lipps, J. 2011. *Die Basilica Aemilia am Forum Romanum. Der kaiserzeitliche Bau und seine Ornamentik.* Weisbaden: Dr. Ludwig Reichert Verlag.

Lugli, G. 1930. *I monumenti antichi di Roma e suburbio.* Roma: Bardi.

Lugli, G. 1946. *Roma antica: il centro monumentale.* Roma: Bardi.

Lugli, G. 1957. *La tecnica edilizia romana con particolare riguardo a Roma e Lazio.* Roma: Bardi.

Mancioli, D., A. Ceccherelli e R. Santangeli Valenzani 1993. Domus Parthorum. *Archeologia Laziale* XI: 53–58.

Mar, R. 2005. *El Palatí: la formació dels palaus imperials a Roma.* Tarragona: Institut Català d'Arqueologia Clàssica.

Mar, R. 2009. La *Domus Flavia*, utilizzo e funzione del palazzo di Domiziano, in F. Coarelli (ed.) Divus Vespasianus: *il bimillenario dei Flavi* (catalogo della mostra): 250–261. Milano: Electa.

Mar, R. e P. Pensabene 2010. Finanziamento dell'edilizia pubblica e calcolo dei costi dei materiali lapidei: il caso del Foro Superiore di Tarraco, in S. Camporeale, H. Dessales e A. Pizzo (eds) *Arqueología de la Construcción, II. Los procesos constructivos en el mundo romano: Italia y provincias occidentales*: 509–537. Madrid-Mérida: Consejo Superior de Investigaciones Científicas.

Márquez, C. 1996. Técnica de talla en la decoración arquitectónica de *Colonia Patricia Corduba*, in M. Khanoussi, P. Ruggeri e C. Vismara (eds) *L'Africa romana: atti dell'XI Convegno di studio, 15-18 dicembre 1994, Cartagine, Tunisia*: 1123–1134. Sassari: Editrice Il Torchietto.

Maschek, D. 2020. Assessing the Economic Impact of Building Projects in the Roman World: the Case of Late Republican Rome, in C. Courault e C. Marquez (eds) *Quantitative Studies and Production Cost of Roman Public Construction*: 45–67. Cordoba: UCOPress.

Meneghini, R. e E. Bianchi 2010. Il cantiere costruttivo del Foro di Nerva, in S. Camporeale, H. Dessales e A. Pizzo (eds) *Arqueología de la Construcción, II. Los procesos constructivos en el mundo romano: Italia y provincias orientales* (Certosa di Pontignano, Siena, 13-15 de Noviembre de 2008): 71–79. Madrid-Mérida 2010: Consejo Superior de Investigaciones Científicas.

Moormann, E.M. 2018. Domitian's remake of Augustan Rome and the *Iseum* Campense, in M.J. Versluys, K. Bülow Clausen e G. Capriotti Vittozzi (eds) *The Iseum Campense from the Roman Empire to the Modern*

Age: temple, monument, lieu de memoire. Proceedings of the international conference held in Rome at the Royal Netherlands Institute in Rome (KNIR), the Accademia di Danimarca, and the Accademia d'Egitto, May 25–27 2016: 161–177. Roma: Edizioni Quasar.

Neu, S. 1972. Römisches Ornament. Stadtrömische Marmorgebälke aus der Zeit von Septimius Severus bis Konstantin. PhD Thesis, Westfälische Wilhelms-Universität Münster. Münster 1972.

Ottati, A. 2018. Considerazioni su sigle e tracciati di cantiere nella Biblioteca di Adriano ad Atene. *Annuario della Scuola Archeologia Italiana di Atene* 96: 251–274.

Paribeni, E. e S. Segenni 2017. Schiavi nelle cave, in C. Parisi Presicce e O. Rossini (eds) *Spartaco: schiavi e padroni a Roma* (catalogo della mostra): 119–123. Roma: De Luca Editori d'Arte.

Pafumi, S. 2007. Per la ricostruzione degli arredi scultorei del Palazzo dei Cesari sul Palatino. *Bulletin Antieke Beschaving. Annual Papers on Classical Archaeology* 82: 207–225.

Panciera, S. 1957. *Vita economica di Aquileia in età romana*. Aquileia: Associazione nazionale per Aquileia.

Pavolini, C. 1996. *La vita quotidiana a Ostia*. Roma-Bari: Laterza.

Pegoretti, G. 1863. *Manuale pratico per l'estimazione dei lavori architettonici, stradali, idraulici e di fortificazione per uso degli ingegneri ed architetti*. Volume Primo (2ª ed.). Milano: Tipografia di Domenico Salvi e C.

Pegoretti, G. 1864. *Manuale pratico per l'estimazione dei lavori architettonici, stradali, idraulici e di fortificazione per uso degli ingegneri ed architetti*. Volume Secondo (2ª ed.). Milano: Tipografia di Domenico Salvi e C.

Pensabene, P. 1973. *Scavi di Ostia, VII: i capitelli*. Roma: Istituto Poligrafico dello Stato.

Pensabene, P. 1992. The method used for dressing the columns of the Colosseum portico, in M. Waelkens, N. Herz e L. Moens (eds) *Ancient Stones: Quarrying, Trade and Provenance. Interdisciplinary Studies on Stones and Stones Technology in Europe and Near East from the Prehistoric to the Early Christian Period*: 81–89. Louvain: Leuven University Press.

Pensabene, P. 1996. Sulla tecnica di lavorazione delle colonne del tempio tetrastilo di Thignica (Aïn Tounga), in M. Khanoussi, P. Ruggeri e C. Vismara (eds) *L'Africa romana: atti dell'XI Convegno di studio, 15-18 dicembre 1994, Cartagine, Tunisia*: 1103–1122. Sassari: Editrice Il Torchietto.

Pensabene, P. 1998. Sulla tecnica di lavorazione delle colonne in marmo proconnesio del portico in *Summa Cavea* del Colosseo, in P. Pensabene (ed.) *Marmi antichi, II. Cave e tecnica di lavorazione, provenienze e distribuzione* (Studi Miscellanei 31): 293–300. Roma: L'Erma di Bretschneider.

Pensabene, P. 2007. Ostiensium Marmorum Decus et Decor. *Studi Architettonici, decorativi e Archeometrici*. Roma: L'Erma di Bretschneider.

Pensabene, P. 2013. *I marmi nella Roma antica*. Roma: Carocci.

Pensabene, P. 2015a. Marmi pubblici e marmi privati. Note in margine ad un recente volume di Ben Russell. *Archeologia Classica* LXVI: 575–593.

Pensabene, P. 2015b. *Roma su Roma: reimpiego architettonico, recupero dell'antico e trasformazioni urbane tra il III e il XIII secolo*. Città del Vaticano: Pontificio Istituto di Archeologia Cristiana.

Pensabene, P. 2018. Appendice VI.6-VI.7. Tracciati di cantiere sugli elementi architettonici del tempio sul Quirinale, in M.G. Picozzi (ed.) *Palazzo Colonna. Giardini. La storia e le antichità*: 574–580. Roma: De Luca Editori d'Arte.

Pensabene, P. e M. Bruno 1998. Aggiornamenti, nuove acquisizioni e riordino dei marmi di cava dal canale di Fiumicino, in P. Pensabene (ed.) *Marmi antichi II. Cave e tecnica di lavorazione, provenienze e distribuzione*: 1–22. Roma: L'Erma di Bretschneider.

Pensabene, P. e F. Caprioli 2009. La decorazione architettonica d'età flavia, in F. Coarelli (ed.) Divus Vespasianus: *il bimillenario dei Flavi* (catalogo della mostra): 110–115. Milano: Electa.

Pensabene, P. e J.Á. Domingo 2017. Il cantiere, l'approvvigionamento dei marmi, il trasporto e i costi dei grandi monoliti in granito del Foro e in Sienite. *Atti della Pontificia Accademia Romana di Archeologia, Rendiconti* Ser. III, LXXXIX: 523–597.

Pflug, J. 2012. Die bauliche Entwicklung des Versenkten Peristyls der Domus Augustana – Erste Ergebnisse der bauforscherischen Untersuchung, in N. Sojc (ed.) *Domus Augustana: Neue Forschungen zum "Versenkten Peristyl" auf dem Palatin*: 47–78. Leiden: Sideston Press.

Pflug, J. 2013. Die Bauliche Entwicklung der *Domus Augustana* im Kontext des südöstlichen Palatin bis in severische Zeit, in N. Sojc, A. Winterling e U. Wulf-Rheidt (eds) *Palast und Stadt im severischen Rom*: 181–211. Stuttgart: Steiner.

Pflug, J. 2014. Der Weg zum Kaiser. Wege durch Kaiserpalast auf dem Palatin in Rom, in D. Kurapkat, P.I. Schneider e U. Wulf-Rheidt (eds) *Die Architektur des Weges: Gestaltete Bewegung im gebauten Raum. Internationales Kolloquium in Berlin vom 08. - 11. Februar 2012 veranstaltet vom Architekturreferat des DAI*: 360–381. Regensburg: Schnell and Steiner.

Pflug, J. 2017. Der Baustellen-Workflow im Ziegelbau. Spuren der Planungs- und Bauprozesse im "Versenkten Peristyl" der *Domus Augustana*, in D. Kurapkat e U. Wulf-Rheidt (eds) *Werkspuren: Materialverarbeitung und handwerkliches Wissen in antiken Bauwesen. Internationales Kolloquium in Berlin vom 13.-16. Mai 2015, veranstaltet vom Architekturreferat des DAI im Henry-Ford-Bau der Freien Universitat Berlin*: 313–332. Regensburg: Schnell and Steiner.

Pizzo, A. 2016. Observacione sobre los trazados de obra de época romana en Lusitania, in C. Inglese e A.

Pizzo 2016 (eds) *I tracciati di cantiere: disegni esecutivi per la trasmissione e diffusione delle conoscenze tecniche*: 55–71. Roma: Gangemi.

Quaranta, P. 2021. Palatino. *Sectilia pavimenta* dalla Domus Augustana: alcune osservazioni preliminari, in C. Angelelli e C. Cecamore (eds) *Atti del XXVI Colloquio dell'Associazione italiana per lo studio e la conservazione del mosaico*: 17–27. Roma: Edizioni Quasar.

Respighi, L. 1930. Identificazione di un capitello del "*Laconicon*" delle Terme di Agrippa conservato nei Musei Vaticani. *Atti della Pontificia Accademia Romana di Archeologia, Rendiconti* VII: 109–117.

Rockwell, P. 1987–1988. Carving instructions on the Temple of Vespasian. *Atti della Pontificia Accademia Romana di Archeologia, Rendiconti* LX: 53–69.

Rockwell, P. 1989. *Lavorare la pietra: manuale per l'archeologo, lo storico dell'arte e il restauratore*. Roma: Carocci.

Rodríguez Gutiérrez, O. 1997. Sobre tecnología romana: algunos datos en torno a la fabricación de elementos aquitectónicos. *Cuadernos de Prehistoria y Arqueología* 24: 209–252.

Rodríguez Gutiérrez, O. 2004. *El teatro romano de Italica. Estudio arqueoarquitectónico*. Madrid: Servicio de Publicaciones de la Universidad Autónoma de Madrid.

Rohmann, J. 1998. *Die Kapitellproduktion der römischen Kaiserzeit in Pergamon*. Berlin: de Gruyter.

Rossi, F.M. 2015. Scelta, lavorazione e messa in opera dei laterizi nell'esedra sud occidentale delle Terme di Traiano, in E. Bukowiecki, R. Volpe e U. Wulf-Rheidt (eds) *Il laterizio nei cantieri imperiali: Roma e il Mediterraneo. Atti del I workshop "Laterizio" (Roma, 27-28 novembre 2014)* (Archeologia dell'Architettura XX): 31–37. Firenze: All'Insegna del Giglio.

Russell, B. 2013. *The Economics of the Roman Stone Trade*. Oxford: Oxford Universiy Press.

Schmölder-Veit, A. 2012. Ninfei e latrine, in N. Sojc (ed.) *Domus Augustana: Neue Forschungen zum "Versenkten Peristyl" auf dem Palatin*: 185–218. Leiden: Sideston Press

Siegler, K.G. 1966. Die einzelnen Grabungsobjekte, *Traianeum*, in E. Boehringer (ed.) *Die Ausgrabungsarbeiten zu Pergamon im Jahre 1965: vorläufiger Bericht mit Hinweisen auf Grabungen und Arbeiten früherer Jahre und des Frühjahrs 1966. Archäologischer Anzeiger*: 415–483 (430–434).

Sojc, N. (ed.) 2012a. *Domus Augustana: Neue Forschungen zum "Versenkten Peristyl" auf dem Palatin*. Leiden: Sideston Press.

Sojc, N. 2012b. Introduction: Research on the Sunken Peristyle of the Domus Augustana, in N. Sojc (ed.) *Domus Augustana: Neue Forschungen zum "Versenkten Peristyl" auf dem Palatin*: 11–46. Leiden: Sideston Press.

Soler B. 2012. Planificación, producción y costo del programa marmóreo del teatro romano de Cartagena, in V. García-Entero (ed.) *El marmor en Hispania: explotación, uso y difusión en época romana*: 193–228. Madrid: Universidad Nacional de Educación a Distancia.

Toma, N. 2014. Von Marmorblock über Halbfabrikat zu korinthischem Kapitell Zur Kapitellproduktion in der Kaiserzeit, in J. Lipps e D. Maschek (eds) *Antike Bauornamentik: Grenzen und Möglichkeiten ihrer Erforschung* (Studien zur antiken Stadt 12): 84–98. Wiesbaden.

Toma, N. 2015. Carving a Corinthian capital. New technical aspects regarding the carving process, in P. Pensabene e E. Gasparini (eds) *Proceedings of the Xth ASMOSIA Conference, Rome, 21st to 26th of May 2012*: 811–821. Roma: L'Erma di Bretschneider.

Tomasello, F. 1984. Un prototipo di capitello corinzio in Sabratha. *Quaderni di Archeologia della Libia* XIII: 87–103.

Tomasello, F. 1986. Un capitello dorico di Iasos: esempio di metodologia progettuale di periodo ellenistico, in *Studi su Iasos di Caria: venticinque anni di scavi della missione archeologica italiana* (Bollettino d'Arte, Suppl. 31–32): 67–82. Roma: Istituto Poligrafico e Zecca dello Stato.

Toynbee, J.M.C. e J.B. Ward-Perkins 1950. Peopled scrolls: a Hellenistic Motif in Imperial Art. *Papers of the British School at Rome* 18: 1–43.

Tucci, P.L. 2017. *The Temple of Peace in Rome*. New York: Cambridge University Press.

Tucci, P.L. 2019. Living on the Capitoline Hill: the *domus* of the Aracoeli and its sculptural and painted decoration. *Papers of the British School at Rome* 87: 71–144.

Vinci, M.S., A. Ottati e D. Gorostidi Pi 2020 (eds). *La cava e il monumento. Materiali, officine, sistemi di costruzione e produzione nei cantieri edilizi di età imperiale*. Roma: Edizioni Quasar.

Voigts, C. 2012. Das zweigeschossige Peristyl der *Domus Augustana*: Untersuchung der Stein-Bauteile und Rekonstruktion der Portiken, in N. Sojc (ed.) Domus Augustana: *Neue Forschungen zum "Versenkten Peristyl" auf dem Palatin*: 139–184. Leiden: Sideston Press.

Voigts, C. 2017a. High-Tech für den römischen Kaiserpalast Hohlbohrer und Gewölbeanker, in D. Kurapkat e U. Wulf-Rheidt (eds) *Werkspuren: Materialverarbeitung und handwerkliches Wissen in antiken Bauwesen. Internationales Kolloquium in Berlin vom 13.-16. Mai 2015, veranstaltet vom Architekturreferat des DAI im Henry-Ford-Bau der Freien Universitat Berlin*: 333–340. Regensburg: Schnell and Steiner.

Voigts, C. 2017b. Trabeazioni di pietra con armature di metallo, in P. Pensabene, M. Milella e F. Caprioli (eds) Decor. *Decorazione e architettura nel mondo romano, Atti del Convegno, Roma 21-24 maggio 2014* (Thiasos Monografie 9): 753–758. Roma: Edizioni Quasar.

Volpe, R. 2002. Un antico giornale di cantiere delle terme di Traiano. *Mitteilungen des Deutschen Archäologischen Instituts, Römische Abteilung* 109: 377–394.

Volpe, R. 2008. Le giornate di lavoro nelle iscrizioni dipinte delle terme di Traiano, in M.L. Caldelli, G. Gregori e S. Orlandi (eds) *Epigrafia 2006. Atti della XVIe Rencontre sue l'épigraphie in onore di Silvio Panciera con altri contributi di colleghi, allievi e collaboratori* (Tituli 9): 453–466. Roma: Edizioni Quasar.

Volpe, R. 2010. Organizzazione e tempi di lavoro nel cantiere delle terme di Traiano sul colle Oppio, in S. Camporeale, H. Dessales e A. Pizzo (eds) *Arqueología de la Construcción, II. Los procesos constructivos en el mundo romano: Italia y provincias orientales (Certosa di Pontignano, Siena, 13-15 de Noviembre de 2008)*: 81–91. Madrid-Mérida: Instituto de Arqueología de Mérida.

Volpe, R. 2017. Liberi e schiavi nei cantieri edilizi, in C. Parisi Presicce e O. Rossini (eds) *Spartaco: schiavi e padroni a Roma* (catalogo della mostra): 95–100. Roma: De Luca Editori d'Arte.

Volpe, R. e F.M. Rossi 2012. Nuovi dati sull'esedra sud-ovest delle Terme di Traiano sul Colle Oppio: percorsi, iscrizioni dipinte e tempi di costruzione, in S. Camporeale, H. Dessales e A. Pizzo (eds) *Arqueología de la Costrucción, III. Los procesos constructivos en el mundo romano: la economía de las obras (Ecole Normale Superieure, Paris, 10-11 de diciembre de 2009)*: 69–81. Madrid-Mérida: Anejos de Archivo Español de Arqueología.

Volpe, R. e F.M. Rossi 2014. Colle Oppio – Terme di Traiano. Lavori di restauro nell'esedra sudoccidentale (2013-2014). *Bullettino della Commissione Archeologica Comunale di Roma* 115: 204–120.

Wataghin Cantino, G. 1966. *La Domus Augustana: personalità e problemi dell'architettura flavia.* Torino: Giappichelli.

Wilson Jones, M. 1991. Designing the Roman Corinthian capital. *Papers of the British School at Rome* 59: 89–150.

Wulf-Rheidt, U. 2012. Die Bedeutung der neuen Erkenntnisse zum Versenkten Peristyl der Domus Augustana für den südöstlichen Teil des Kaiserpalastes, in N. Sojc (ed.) *Neue Forschungen zum "Versenkten Peristyl" auf dem Palatin*: 259–275. Leiden: Sidestone Press.

Ordine	Tipo	Elemento	Materiale	Quantità	Percentuale	Costo (HS/p3)	Altezza (m)	Larghezza / Spessore (m)	Lunghezza (m)	Numero di lesene per muro	Diametro (m)	Lato blocco originale del fusto (m)	Lato (m)	Volume 1 esemplare (m³)	Volume totale (m³)	Volume totale (p3)	Superficie 1 esemplare (m²)	Superficie totale (m²)	Costo totale (denari)	Costo totale (HS)
I - Pilastri	Nucleo		Travertino	32		1	7,50		0,9				1,35	9,21	294,84	11.351,34	40,50	1.296,00	11.351	45.405
I - Pilastri	Semicolonna (fronte)	Base composita	Proconnesio	32		1,6	0,37	0,170					1,06	0,07	2,16	83,25	0,53	16,80	133	533
I - Pilastri	Semicolonna (fronte)	Fusto	Lunense	32		5	6,50	0,050			0,90		6,50	0,29	9,36	360,36	6,50	208,00	1.802	7.207
I - Pilastri	Semicolonna (fronte)	Capitello ionico	Proconnesio	26	80%	5	0,26	0,650					1,10	0,19	4,83	186,09	0,62	16,22	930	3.722
I - Pilastri	Semicolonna (fronte)	Capitello ionico	Proconnesio	6	20%	1,6	0,26	0,650					1,10	0,19	1,12	42,94	0,62	3,74	69	275
I - Pilastri	Trabeazione	Architrave	Lunense	1		5	0,50	0,075	102,0					3,83	3,83	147,26	102,00	102,00	736	2.945
I - Pilastri	Trabeazione	Fregio	Proconnesio	1		1,6	0,50	0,110	102,0					5,61	5,61	215,99	102,00	102,00	346	1.382
I - Pilastri	Trabeazione	Nucleo interno	Travertino	1		1	1,00	0,800	102,0					81,60	81,60	3.141,60	204,00	204,00	3.142	12.566
I - Pilastri	Trabeazione	Cornice	Proconnesio	1		1,6	0,61	0,600	102,0					37,33	37,33	1.437,28	124,44	124,44	2.300	9.199
I - Pilastri	Lesene (retro)	Base composita	Lunense	26		5	0,37	0,170					1,06	0,07	1,73	66,74	0,52	13,47	334	1.335
I - Pilastri	Lesene (retro)	Base	Proconnesio	6		1,6	0,37	0,170					1,06	0,07	0,40	15,40	0,52	3,11	25	99
I - Pilastri	Lesene (retro)	Fusto	Pavonazzetto	16		8	6,50	0,130					0,69	0,58	9,33	359,16	6,18	98,80	2.873	11.493
I - Pilastri	Lesene (retro)	Fusto	Giallo antico	16		8	6,50	0,130					0,69	0,58	9,33	359,16	6,18	98,80	2.873	11.493
I - Pilastri	Lesene (retro)	Capitello	Lunense	32		5	0,75	0,060				0,60	0,70	0,03	1,01	38,81	0,62	19,68	194	776
I - Pilastri	Pilastri (fianchi)	Base	Lunense	26		5	0,37	0,170					1,06	0,07	1,76	67,64	0,53	13,65	338	1.353
I - Pilastri	Pilastri (fianchi)	Base	Proconnesio	6		1,6	0,37	0,170					1,06	0,07	0,41	15,61	0,53	3,15	25	100
I - Pilastri	Pilastri (fianchi)	Fusto	Lunense	64		5	7,62	0,055					1,06	0,44	28,43	1.094,62	8,92	570,59	5.473	21.892
I - Lesene	Lesene muro di fondo	Base	Lunense	32		5	0,37	0,170					1,06	0,07	2,16	83,25	0,53	16,80	416	1.665
I - Lesene	Lesene muro di fondo	Fusto	Pavonazzetto	16		8	6,50	0,130					0,70	0,59	9,46	364,36	6,24	99,84	2.915	11.660
I - Lesene	Lesene muro di fondo	Fusto	Giallo antico	16		8	6,50	0,130					0,70	0,59	9,46	364,36	6,24	99,84	2.915	11.660
I - Lesene	Lesene muro di fondo	Capitello	Lunense	32		5	0,60	0,170					0,70	0,07	2,28	87,96	0,62	19,97	440	1.759
I - Lesene	Trabeazione	Fregio-architrave	Lunense	1		5	1,00	0,170	128,5					21,85	21,85	841,03	257,00	257,00	4.205	16.821
I - Lesene	Trabeazione	Cornice	Rosso Antico	1		8	0,20	0,200	128,5					5,14	5,14	197,89	51,40	51,40	1.583	6.332
II - Colonne	Colonne	Base	Lunense	32		5	0,30				0,56		0,95	0,27	8,66	333,56			1.668	6.671
II - Colonne	Colonne	Fusti	Cipollino	16		4	4,00				0,50	0,60		1,44	23,04	887,04	6,28	100,53	3.548	14.193
II - Colonne	Colonne	Fusti	Portasanta (?)	16		6	4,00				0,50	0,60		1,44	23,04	887,04	6,28	100,53	5.322	21.289
II - Colonne	Colonne	Capitelli corinzi	Lunense	32		5	0,60				0,43		0,80	0,38	12,29	473,09	1,92	61,44	2.365	9.462
I - Colonne	Trabeazione	Fregio-architrave	Lunense	1		5	0,75	0,370	102,0					28,31	28,31	1.089,74	153,00	153,00	5.449	21.795
I - Colonne	Trabeazione	Cornice	Lunense	1		5	0,50	0,400	51,0					10,20	10,20	392,70	51,00	51,00	1.963	7.854
I - Colonne	Trabeazione	Cornice	Proconnesio	1		1,6	0,50	0,400	51,0					10,20	10,20	392,70	51,00	51,00	628	2.513
I - Parete	Parete S-O		Giallo antico	0,4	40%	8	7,40	0,060	34,5	6				15,32	13,04	501,92	255,30	228,77	4.015	16.061
I - Parete	Parete S-O		Pavonazzetto	0,4	40%	8	7,40	0,060	34,5	6				15,32	13,04	501,92	255,30	228,77	4.015	16.061
I - Parete	Parete S-O		Serpentino	0,2	20%	4	7,40	0,060	34,5	6				15,32	14,18	545,83	255,30	242,03	2.183	8.733
I - Parete	Parete S-E		Giallo antico	0,4	40%	8	7,40	0,060	37,5	10				16,65	13,44	517,44	277,50	243,14	4.139	16.558
I - Parete	Parete S-E		Pavonazzetto	0,4	40%	8	7,40	0,060	37,5	10				16,65	13,44	517,56	277,50	243,14	4.139	16.558
I - Parete	Parete S-E		Serpentino	0,2	20%	4	7,40	0,060	37,5	10				16,65	15,05	579,23	277,50	260,32	2.317	9.267
I - Parete	Parete N-E		Giallo antico	0,4	40%	8	7,40	0,060	35,0	10				15,54	9,47	364,75	259,00	177,03	2.918	11.672
I - Parete	Parete N-E		Pavonazzetto	0,4	40%	8	7,40	0,060	35,0	10				15,54	9,47	364,75	259,00	177,03	2.918	11.672
I - Parete	Parete N-E		Serpentino	0,2	20%	4	7,40	0,060	35,0	10				15,54	12,51	481,52	259,00	218,82	1.926	7.704
I - Parete	Parete N-O		Giallo antico	0,4	40%	8	7,40	0,060	40,0	6				17,76	13,88	534,49	296,00	242,87	4.276	17.104
I - Parete	Parete N-O		Pavonazzetto	0,4	40%	8	7,40	0,060	40,0	6				17,76	13,88	534,49	296,00	242,87	4.276	17.104
I - Parete	Parete N-O		Serpentino	0,2	20%	4	7,40	0,060	40,0	6				17,76	15,82	609,13	296,00	269,43	2.432	9.746
I - Parete	Zoccolo / modanatura		Pavonazzetto	1		8	0,37	0,100	101,1					3,79	3,79	145,95	37,91	37,91	1.168	4.670
TOTALE																				428.361

Tabella 1a. Costo della decorazione marmorea del peristilio inferiore della *Domus Augustana*.

APARATO RUSTICO

Caratteristiche	Materiale	Tipo di operaio	Stipendio (HS/giornata)	Tempo (ore/m³)	Volume totale (m³)	Giornate di lavoro totale	Costo totale (HS)
Travertino	Travertino	Marmista	2,5	116,0	376,44	4.366,7	10.917
Marmo grana fina	Lunense	Marmista	2,5	157,5	136,70	2.153,0	5.382
Marmo grana fina	Pavonazzetto	Marmista	2,5	157,5	72,42	1.140,6	2.851
Marmo grana fina	Giallo Antico	Marmista	2,5	157,5	68,63	1.080,9	2.702
Marmo grana fina	Portasanta	Marmista	2,5	157,5	23,04	362,9	907
Marmo grana media	Proconnesio	Marmista	2,5	210,0	57,23	1.201,7	3.004
Marmo grana media	Rosso Antico	Marmista	2,5	210,0	5,14	107,9	270
Marmo grana media	Serpentino	Marmista	2,5	210,0	57,55	1.208,6	3.021
Marmo grana media	Cipollino	Marmista	2,5	210,0	23,04	483,8	1.210
TOTAL					820,18	12.106,1	30.265

Tabella 1b. Costo della decorazione marmorea del peristilio inferiore della *Domus Augustana*.

SEMILAVORAZIONE

Ordine	Tipo	Elemento	Materiale	Tipo di operaio	Stipendio (HS/giornata)	Tempo (ore/m²) Formula generale	Tempo (ore/m²) Formula adattata	Tempo (ore/m²)	Giornate di lavoro 1 esemplare	Giornate di lavoro totale	Costo totale (HS)
I – Pilastri	Semicolonna (fronte)	Base composita	Proconnesio	Marmista	2,5	1/3 capitello	1/3 capitello	2,42	0,13	4,06	10
I – Pilastri	Semicolonna (fronte)	Fusto	Lunense	Marmista	2,5	a(2+0,25/x)	4,33(2+0,25/0,9)	9,86	6,41	205,15	513
I – Pilastri	Semicolonna (fronte)	Capitello ionico	Lunense	Marmista	2,5	a(1+0,25/x)	4,33(1+0,25/1)	5,41	0,34	8,78	22
I – Pilastri	Semicolonna (fronte)	Capitello ionico	Proconnesio	Marmista	2,5	a(1+0,25/x)	5,8(1+0,25/1)	7,25	0,45	2,71	7
I – Pilastri	Trabeazione	Architrave	Lunense	Marmista	2,5		4,33	4,33	44,17	44,17	110
I – Pilastri	Trabeazione	Fregio	Proconnesio	Marmista	2,5		5,8	5,80	59,16	59,16	148
I – Pilastri	Trabeazione	Cornice	Proconnesio	Marmista	2,5		5,8	5,80	72,18	72,18	180
I – Pilastri	Lesene (retro)	Base composita	Lunense	Marmista	2,5	1/3 capitello	1/3 capitello	2,04	0,11	2,75	7
I – Pilastri	Lesene (retro)	Base	Proconnesio	Marmista	2,5	1/3 capitello	1/3 capitello	2,04	0,11	0,64	2
I – Pilastri	Lesene (retro)	Fusto	Pavonazzetto	Marmista	2,5	a(2+0,25/x)	4,33(2+0,25/0,69)	10,23	6,32	101,06	253
I – Pilastri	Lesene (retro)	Fusto	Giallo antico (?)	Marmista	2,5	a(2+0,25/x)	4,33(2+0,25/0,69)	10,23	6,32	101,06	253
I – Pilastri	Lesene (retro)	Capitello	Lunense	Marmista	2,5	a(1+0,25/x)	4,33(1+0,25/0,6)	6,13	0,38	12,07	30
I – Pilastri	Pilastri (fianchi)	Base	Lunense	Marmista	2,5	1/3 capitello	1/3 capitello	2,04	0,11	2,79	7
I – Pilastri	Pilastri (fianchi)	Base	Proconnesio	Marmista	2,5	a(2+0,25/x)	1/3 capitello	2,04	0,11	0,64	2
I – Pilastri	Pilastri (fianchi)	Fusto	Lunense	Marmista	2,5	a(2+0,25/x)	4,33(2+0,25/1,06)	9,68	8,63	552,40	1.381
I – Lesene	Lesene muro di fondo	Base	Lunense	Marmista	2,5	1/3 capitello	1/3 capitello	1,96	0,10	3,29	8
I – Lesene	Lesene muro di fondo	Fusto	Pavonazzetto	Marmista	2,5	a(2+0,25/x)	4,33(2+0,25/0,69)	10,23	6,38	102,12	255
I – Lesene	Lesene muro di fondo	Fusto	Giallo antico	Marmista	2,5	a(2+0,25/x)	4,33(2+0,25/0,69)	10,23	6,38	102,12	255
I – Lesene	Lesene muro di fondo	Capitello	Lunense	Marmista	2,5	a(1+0,25/x)	4,33(1+0,25/0,70)	5,88	0,37	11,73	29
I – Lesene	Trabeazione	Fregio-architrave	Lunense	Marmista	2,5		4,33	4,33	111,28	111,28	278
I – Lesene	Trabeazione	Cornice	Rosso antico	Marmista	2,5		4,33	4,33	22,26	22,26	56
II – Colonne	Colonne	Base	Lunense	Marmista	2,5	1/3 capitello	1/3 capitello	2,28			35
II – Colonne	Colonne	Fusti	Cipollino	Marmista	2,5	a(2+0,25/x)	5,8(+0,25/0,50)	14,50	9,11	145,77	364
II – Colonne	Colonne	Fusti	Portasanta (?)	Marmista	2,5	a(2+0,25/x)	4,33(2+0,25/0,50)	10,83	6,80	108,83	272
II – Colonne	Colonne	Capitelli corinzi	Lunense	Marmista	2,5	a(1+0,25/x)	4,33(1+0,25/0,43)	6,85	1,31	42,07	105
I – Colonne	Trabeazione	Fregio-architrave	Lunense	Marmista	2,5		4,33	4,33	66,25	66,25	166
I – Colonne	Trabeazione	Cornice	Lunense	Marmista	2,5		4,33	4,33	22,08	22,08	55
I – Colonne	Trabeazione	Cornice	Proconnesio	Marmista	2,5		5,8	5,80	29,58	29,58	74
I – Parete	Zoccolo / modanatura	Parete - zoccolo	Pavonazzetto	Marmista	2,5		5,8	5,80	21,99	21,99	55
TOTALE										1.958,99	4.933

Tabella 1c. Costo della decorazione marmorea del peristilio inferiore della *Domus Augustana*.

Materiale	Tipo di Trasporto	TRASPORTO			Volume totale (m³)	Costo totale (denari)	Costo totale (HS)
		Percorso	Distanza (miglia)	Formula (denari/m³)			
Travertino	Terrestre	Cave - Palatino	1	0,85 den/(m³·miglia)	376,44	320	1.280
Lunense	Terrestre	Cave - Mare	20	0,85 den/(m³·miglia)	136,70	2.324	9.295
Lunense	Marittimo	Mare - Porto		4,7 den · m³	136,70	642	2.570
Lunense	Fluviale	Porto - Foro Boario	20	[0,85 den/(m³·miglia)]/5,5	136,70	423	1.690
Lunense	Terrestre	Foro Boario - Palatino	0,4	0,85 den/(m³·miglia)	136,70	46	186
Pavonazzetto	Fluviale	Altintaş - Nicomedia	176	[0,85 den/(m³·miglia)]/10,8	72,42	1.003	4.012
Pavonazzetto	Marittimo	Nicomedia - Porto		14 den · m³	72,52	1.014	4.055
Pavonazzetto	Fluviale	Porto - Foro Boario	20	[0,85 den/(m³·miglia)]/5,5	72,42	224	895
Pavonazzetto	Terrestre	Foro Boario - Palatino	0,4	0,85 den/(m³·miglia)	72,42	25	98
Giallo Antico	Marittimo	Cave - Porto		4,7 den · m³	68,63	323	1.290
Giallo Antico	Fluviale	Porto - Foro Boario	20	[0,85 den/(m³·miglia)]/5,5	68,63	212	848
Giallo Antico	Terrestre	Foro Boario - Palatino	0,4	0,85 den/(m³·miglia)	68,63	23	93
Portasanta	Marittimo	Cave - Porto		14 den · m³	23,04	323	1.290
Portasanta	Fluviale	Porto - Foro Boario	20	[0,85 den/(m³·miglia)]/5,5	23,04	71	285
Portasanta	Terrestre	Foro Boario - Palatino	0,4	0,85 den/(m³·miglia)	23,04	8	31
Proconnesio	Marittimo	Nicomedia - Porto		14 den · m³	57,23	801	3.205
Proconnesio	Fluviale	Porto - Foro Boario	20	[0,85 den/(m³·miglia)]/5,5	57,23	177	708
Proconnesio	Terrestre	Foro Boario - Palatino	0,4	0,85 den/(m³·miglia)	57,23	19	78
Cipollino	Marittimo	Cave - Porto		14 den · m³	23,04	323	1.290
Cipollino	Fluviale	Porto - Foro Boario	20	[0,85 den/(m³·miglia)]/5,5	23,04	71	285
Cipollino	Terrestre	Foro Boario - Palatino	0,4	0,85 den/(m³·miglia)	23,04	8	31
Serpentino	Terrestre	Cave - Mare	5,5	0,85 den/(m³·miglia)	57,55	269	1.076
Serpentino	Marittimo	Mare - Porto		14 den · m³	57,55	806	3.223
Serpentino	Fluviale	Porto - Foro Boario	20	[0,85 den/(m³·miglia)]/5,5	57,55	178	712
Serpentino	Terrestre	Foro Boario - Palatino	0,4	0,85 den/(m³·miglia)	57,55	20	78
Rosso Antico	Marittimo	Mare - Porto		14 den · m³	5,14	72	288
Rosso Antico	Fluviale	Porto - Foro Boario	20	[0,85 den/(m³·miglia)]/5,5	5,14	16	64
Rosso Antico	Terrestre	Foro Boario - Palatino	0,4	0,85 den/(m³·miglia)	5,14	2	7
TOTALE							38.965

Tabella 1d. Costo della decorazione marmorea del peristilio inferiore della *Domus Augustana*.

Ordine	Tipo	Elemento	Materiale	Tipo di operaio	Stipendio (HS/giornata)	Formula (distanza avvicinamento = 20 m) / t=0,6 ore × 100 kg / a = altezza elevazione = ore di lavoro	Peso (Tnn/m³) per ogni tipo de marmo	Peso 1 elemento (tonnelate)	Peso totale (Tonnelate)	Altezza elevazione (m)	Giornate di lavoro totale	Costo totale (HS)
I - Pilastri	Nucleo		Travertino	Operai x 4	4	t + 0,06t(a-1)	2,5	23,03	737,10	3,50	508,6	8.138
I - Pilastri	Semicolonna (fronte)	Base composita	Procomnesio	Operai x 4	4	t + 0,06t(a-1)	2,7	0,18	5,84	0	3,3	53
I - Pilastri	Semicolonna (fronte)	Fusto	Lunense	Operai x 4	4	t + 0,06t(a-1)	2,7	0,79	25,27	3,62	17,5	281
I - Pilastri	Semicolonna (fronte)	Capitello ionico	Lunense	Operai x 4	4	t + 0,06t(a-1)	2,7	0,50	13,05	6,87	10,6	169
I - Pilastri	Semicolonna (fronte)	Capitello ionico	Procomnesio	Operai x 4	4	t + 0,06t(a-1)	2,7	0,50	3,01	6,87	2,4	39
I - Pilastri	Trabeazione	Architrave	Lunense	Operai x 4	4	t + 0,06t(a-1)	2,7	10,33	10,33	7,13	8,5	136
I - Pilastri	Trabeazione	Fregio	Procomnesio	Operai x 4	4	t + 0,06t(a-1)	2,7	15,15	15,15	7,63	12,7	203
I - Pilastri	Trabeazione	Nucleo interno	Travertino	Operai x 4	4	t + 0,06t(a-1)	2,5	204,00	204,00	7,63	171,1	2.737
I - Pilastri	Trabeazione	Cornice	Procomnesio	Operai x 4	4	t + 0,06t(a-1)	2,7	100,80	100,80	8,13	86,4	1.382
I - Pilastri	Lesene (retro)	Base composita	Lunense	Operai x 4	4	t + 0,06t(a-1)	2,7	0,18	4,68	0	2,6	42
I - Pilastri	Lesene (retro)	Base	Procomnesio	Operai x 4	4	t + 0,06t(a-1)	2,7	0,18	1,08	0	0,6	10
I - Pilastri	Lesene (retro)	Fusto	Pavonazzetto	Operai x 4	4	t + 0,06t(a-1)	2,7	1,57	25,19	3,62	17,5	280
I - Pilastri	Lesene (retro)	Fusto	Giallo antico (?)	Operai x 4	4	t + 0,06t(a-1)	2,7	1,57	25,19	3,62	17,5	280
I - Pilastri	Lesene (retro)	Capitello	Lunense	Operai x 4	4	t + 0,06t(a-1)	2,7	0,09	2,72	6,87	2,2	35
I - Pilastri	Pilastri (fianchi)	Base	Lunense	Operai x 4	4	t + 0,06t(a-1)	2,7	0,18	4,74	0	2,7	43
I - Pilastri	Pilastri (fianchi)	Base	Procomnesio	Operai x 4	4	t + 0,06t(a-1)	2,7	0,18	1,09	0	0,6	10
I - Pilastri	Pilastri (fianchi)	Fusto	Lunense	Operai x 4	4	t + 0,06t(a-1)	2,7	1,20	76,77	3,62	53,3	853
I - Lesene	Lesene muro di fondo	Base	Lunense	Operai x 4	4	t + 0,06t(a-1)	2,7	0,18	5,84	0	3,3	53
I - Lesene	Lesene muro di fondo	Fusto	Pavonazzetto	Operai x 4	4	t + 0,06t(a-1)	2,7	1,60	25,55	3,62	17,7	284
I - Lesene	Lesene muro di fondo	Fusto	Giallo antico	Operai x 4	4	t + 0,06t(a-1)	2,7	1,60	25,55	3,62	17,7	284
I - Lesene	Lesene muro di fondo	Capitello	Lunense	Operai x 4	4	t + 0,06t(a-1)	2,7	0,19	6,17	6,87	5,0	80
I - Lesene	Trabeazione	Fregio-architrave	Lunense	Operai x 4	4	t + 0,06t(a-1)	2,7	58,98	58,98	7,13	48,4	774
I - Lesene	Trabeazione	Cornice	Rosso antico	Operai x 4	4	t + 0,06t(a-1)	2,7	13,88	13,88	8,13	11,9	190
II - Colonne	Colonne	Base	Lunense	Operai x 4	4	t + 0,06t(a-1)	2,7	0,73	23,39	8,74	20,6	329
II - Colonne	Colonne	Fusti	Cipollino	Operai x 4	4	t + 0,06t(a-1)	2,7	3,89	62,21	11,04	59,8	957
II - Colonne	Colonne	Fusti	Portasanta (?)	Operai x 4	4	t + 0,06t(a-1)	2,7	3,89	62,21	11,04	59,8	957
II - Colonne	Colonne	Capitelli corinzi	Lunense	Operai x 4	4	t + 0,06t(a-1)	2,7	1,04	33,18	13,01	34,3	548
II - Colonne	Trabeazione	Fregio-architrave	Lunense	Operai x 4	4	t + 0,06t(a-1)	2,7	76,42	76,42	13,61	80,5	1.289
II - Colonne	Trabeazione	Cornice	Lunense	Operai x 4	4	t + 0,06t(a-1)	2,7	27,54	27,54	14,36	29,8	476
II - Colonne	Trabeazione	Cornice	Procomnesio	Operai x 4	4	t + 0,06t(a-1)	2,7	27,54	27,54	14,36	29,8	476
I - Parete	Parete S-O	Lastra	Giallo Antico	Operai x 4	4	t + 0,06t(a-1)	2,7		35,20	4,00	24,9	399
I - Parete	Parete S-O	Lastra	Pavonazzetto	Operai x 4	4	t + 0,06t(a-1)	2,7		35,20	4,00	24,9	399
I - Parete	Parete S-O	Lastra	Serpentino	Operai x 4	4	t + 0,06t(a-1)	2,7		38,28	4,00	27,1	434
I - Parete	Parete S-E	Lastra	Giallo Antico	Operai x 4	4	t + 0,06t(a-1)	2,7		36,29	4,00	25,7	411
I - Parete	Parete S-E	Lastra	Pavonazzetto	Operai x 4	4	t + 0,06t(a-1)	2,7		36,29	4,00	25,7	411
I - Parete	Parete S-E	Lastra	Serpentino	Operai x 4	4	t + 0,06t(a-1)	2,7		40,62	4,00	28,8	460
I - Parete	Parete N-E	Lastra	Giallo Antico	Operai x 4	4	t + 0,06t(a-1)	2,7		25,58	4,00	18,1	290
I - Parete	Parete N-E	Lastra	Pavonazzetto	Operai x 4	4	t + 0,06t(a-1)	2,7		25,58	4,00	18,1	290
I - Parete	Parete N-E	Lastra	Serpentino	Operai x 4	4	t + 0,06t(a-1)	2,7		33,77	4,00	23,9	382
I - Parete	Parete N-O	Lastra	Giallo Antico	Operai x 4	4	t + 0,06t(a-1)	2,7		37,48	4,00	26,5	425
I - Parete	Parete N-O	Lastra	Pavonazzetto	Operai x 4	4	t + 0,06t(a-1)	2,7		37,48	4,00	26,5	425
I - Parete	Parete N-O	Lastra	Serpentino	Operai x 4	4	t + 0,06t(a-1)	2,7		42,72	4,00	30,2	484
I - Parete	Zoccolo / modanatura	Modanatura	Pavonazzetto	Operai x 4	4	t + 0,06t(a-1)	2,7	10,24	10,24	0	5,8	92
TOTALE											1.643,0	26.288

Tabella 1e. Costo della decorazione marmorea del peristilio inferiore della *Domus Augustana*.

| Ordine | Tipo | Elemento | FINITURA | | Stipendio (HS/giornata) | Tempo (ore/m²) | Giornate di lavoro totale | Costo totale (HS) |
			Materiale	Tipo di operaio				
I - Pilastri	Nucleo		Travertino	Marmista	5	10,67	1.382,8	6.914
I - Pilastri	Semicolonna (fronte)	Base composita	Proconnesio	Marmista	5	1/3 capitello	960,0	4.800
I - Pilastri	Semicolonna (fronte)	Fusto	Lunense	Marmista	5	3,0	52,0	260
I - Pilastri	Semicolonna (fronte)	Capitello ionico	Lunense	Marmista	5	90,0	234,0	1.170
I - Pilastri	Semicolonna (fronte)	Capitello ionico	Proconnesio	Marmista	5	120,0	72,0	360
I - Pilastri	Trabeazione	Architrave	Lunense	Marmista	5	83,3	849,2	4.246
I - Pilastri	Trabeazione	Fregio	Proconnesio	Marmista	5	333,3	3.400,0	17.000
I - Pilastri	Trabeazione	Nucleo interno	Travertino	Marmista	5	10,7	217,7	1.088
I - Pilastri	Trabeazione	Cornice	Proconnesio	Marmista	5	407,0	5.064,7	25.323
I - Pilastri	Lesene (retro)	Base composita	Lunense	Marmista	5	1/3 capitello	4.212,0	21.060
I - Pilastri	Lesene (retro)	Base	Proconnesio	Marmista	5	1/3 capitello	972,0	4.860
I - Pilastri	Lesene (retro)	Fusto	Pavonazzetto	Marmista	5	2,5	24,7	123
I - Pilastri	Lesene (retro)	Fusto	Giallo antico (?)	Marmista	5	2,5	24,7	123
I - Pilastri	Lesene (retro)	Capitello	Lunense	Marmista	5	486,0	1.555,2	7.776
I - Pilastri	Pilastri (fianchi)	Base	Lunense	Marmista	5	1/3 capitello	1.920,0	9.600
I - Pilastri	Pilastri (fianchi)	Base	Proconnesio	Marmista	5	1/3 capitello	1.920,0	9.600
I - Pilastri	Pilastri (fianchi)	Fusto	Lunense	Marmista	5	2,5	142,6	713
I - Lesene	Lesene muro di fondo	Base	Lunense	Marmista	5	1/3 capitello	5.184,0	25.920
I - Lesene	Lesene muro di fondo	Fusto	Pavonazzetto	Marmista	5	2,5	25,0	125
I - Lesene	Lesene muro di fondo	Fusto	Giallo antico	Marmista	5	2,5	25,0	125
I - Lesene	Lesene muro di fondo	Capitello	Lunense	Marmista	5	486,0	1.555,2	7.776
I - Lesene	Trabeazione	Fregio-architrave	Lunense	Marmista	5	250,0	6.425,0	32.125
I - Lesene	Trabeazione	Cornice	Rosso antico	Marmista	5	305,3	1.569,0	7.845
II - Colonne	Colonne	Base	Lunense	Marmista	5	1/3 capitello	7.680,0	38.400
II - Colonne	Colonne	Fusti	Cipollino	Marmista	5	13,3	133,7	668
II - Colonne	Colonne	Fusti	Portasanta (?)	Marmista	5	10,0	100,5	503
II - Colonne	Colonne	Capitelli corinzi	Lunense	Marmista	5	720,0	2.304,0	11.520
II - Colonne	Trabeazione	Fregio-architrave	Lunense	Marmista	5	250,0	3.825,0	19.125
II - Colonne	Trabeazione	Cornice	Lunense	Marmista	5	305,3	1.556,8	7.784
II - Colonne	Trabeazione	Cornice	Proconnesio	Marmista	5	407,0	2.075,7	10.378
I - Parete	Parete S-O	Lastra	Giallo antico	Marmista	5	10,8	247,1	1.235
I - Parete	Parete S-O	Lastra	Pavonazzetto	Marmista	5	10,8	247,1	1.235
I - Parete	Parete S-O	Lastra	Serpentino	Marmista	5	10,8	261,4	1.307
I - Parete	Parete S-E	Lastra	Giallo antico	Marmista	5	10,8	262,6	1.313
I - Parete	Parete S-E	Lastra	Pavonazzetto	Marmista	5	10,8	262,6	1.313
I - Parete	Parete S-E	Lastra	Serpentino	Marmista	5	10,8	281,1	1.406
I - Parete	Parete N-E	Lastra	Giallo antico	Marmista	5	10,8	191,2	956
I - Parete	Parete N-E	Lastra	Pavonazzetto	Marmista	5	10,8	191,2	956
I - Parete	Parete N-E	Lastra	Serpentino	Marmista	5	10,8	235,5	1.177
I - Parete	Parete N-O	Lastra	Giallo antico	Marmista	5	10,8	262,3	1.311
I - Parete	Parete N-O	Lastra	Pavonazzetto	Marmista	5	10,8	262,3	1.311
I - Parete	Parete N-O	Lastra	Serpentino	Marmista	5	10,8	291,0	1.455
I - Parete	Zoccolo / modanatura	Modanatura	Pavonazzetto	Marmista	5	83,3	315,6	1.578
TOTALE							58.773,3	293.866

COSTO TOTALE	CON MATERIALE	822.679 HS
COSTO TOTALE	SENZA MATERIALE	394.318 HS
GIORNATE DI LAVORO		74.481

Tabella 1f. Costo della decorazione marmorea del peristilio inferiore della *Domus Augustana*.

Quantifying the Forum of Pompeii: Building Economics, Material, and Labour

Cathalin Recko

Archaeological Institute,
University of Cologne
c.recko@uni-koeln.de

Abstract

The forum of Pompeii houses a number of public buildings of different functions, types, and structures. The quantification of both the material and the labour requirements offers valuable information about the local building traditions and the complex network of material availability, functionality, and efficiency that forms the building 'industry' of Pompeii. Observations obtained by a comparative analysis of differently categorised labour requirements for twelve buildings around the forum help to detect patterns and dynamics within this network. The figures presented, representing 'labour in hours', serve not as a description of time but as an economic value and as the main comparative factor applied to the buildings.

Keywords: architectural energetics, comparative analysis, Temple of Fortuna Augusta, building industry, Roman architecture

Introduction

In the last years, the number of studies concerning the building economy, technical processes, and labour estimation has increased immensely.[1] Since Janet DeLaine's pathbreaking work on the Baths of Caracalla,[2] the methodology of estimating amounts of labour based on pre-industrial engineering handbooks[3] has developed in many directions. On the one hand, our knowledge of building details, materials, or single processes is constantly further refined, and the catalogue of buildings, whose costs are calculated, is growing. On the other hand, there is an urge to address questions that concern overall developments and characteristics of economy, culture, and society. To raise some of these questions on a local scale that goes beyond the analysis of a single building or structure, this paper compares the material and labour requirements of the main public buildings around the forum of Pompeii (**Figure 1**).[4] This method aims at gaining an understanding of how a local building industry works and how single buildings function within it.

Case study: Pompeii's forum

The city of Pompeii, which serves as a case study, is based in Italian Campania in the Sarno river plain. This region is characterised by extensive volcanic activity, which results in a high availability of different building materials:[5] a soft, but durable tuff ('Nocera-tuff'), that was used most versatilely and was later accompanied by a yellow kind; a soft, but cavernous calcareous tufa ('Sarno-limestone'); a hard blue/grey lava; and an extremely porous and lightweight foam lava ('cruma'). These are the bulk materials that were used as building stones for the different wall techniques: *opus incertum*, *opus vittatum*, and *opus caementicium*. All of these stone types except for cruma were further used as larger blocks for doorjambs, thresholds, etc. For decorative purposes that included carving, Nocera-tuff and a white limestone were the most suitable local stones due to their smooth surface. The latter was a hard stone that resembled marble and, thus, was not used as a regular building stone for walls. Beside building stones, brick and timber complete the bulk materials of presumably local origin. However, ceramic building materials became more common as a wall facing only in the 1st century AD. Apart from these local or regional materials, imported marble, especially from Carrara, was used for surface decorations and ornamental objects.

---

[1] This further results in the organisation of conferences such as 'From concept to monument: time and costs of construction in the ancient world' in Oxford, at which I was kindly given the opportunity to speak and from which this paper emerged.
[2] DeLaine 1997.
[3] Most frequently used is Pegoretti 1862/1864. See also Barker and Russell 2012.
[4] The presented figures and results are preliminary and have their origin in Recko 2020.

[5] For a more detailed overview of the characteristics of the local building materials, see Kastenmeier 2010.

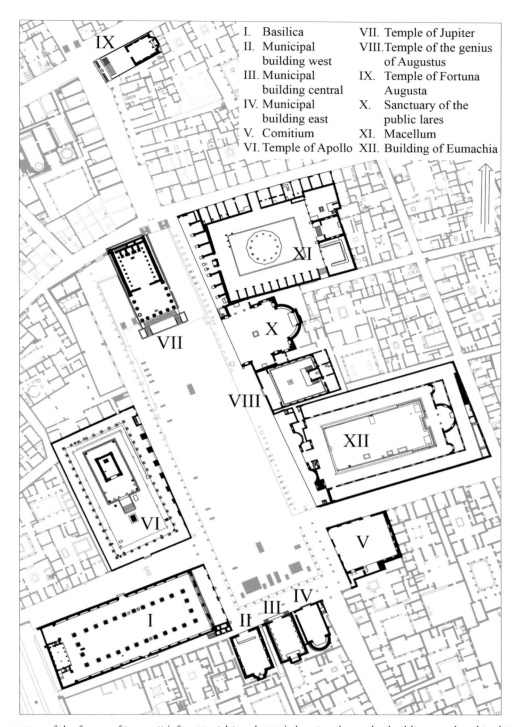

I.   Basilica   VII. Temple of Jupiter
II.   Municipal   VIII. Temple of the genius
      building west   of Augustus
III. Municipal   IX.   Temple of Fortuna
      building central   Augusta
IV.   Municipal   X.   Sanctuary of the
      building east   public lares
V.   Comitium   XI.   Macellum
VI.   Temple of Apollo   XII. Building of Eumachia

Figure 1. Map of the forum of Pompeii (after Morichi *et al.* 2017) showing the twelve buildings analysed in this study.

The use of these materials – regarding both quantity and function – and especially how that affects labour shall be examined by comparing material and labour requirements for a large group of buildings. This group is formed by the public buildings in the area of the forum of Pompeii,[6] which cover administrative, sacred,

and commercial building types. The chronologies of these buildings reach from the 2nd century BC to the period before the destruction of the city in AD 79. Within this timeframe the above listed bulk materials were used in different contexts and their development gives us an impression of the local building traditions.

In total, 12 buildings around the forum have been included in this study, among them there are five administrative buildings, all located on the south end

---

[6] The Temple of Venus, the Forum Baths, and the *horrea* on the west side are excluded from this study because they did not meet the preservation or research standard required for a legitimate quantification.

of the forum. The basilica with its 1.675 m² is by far the largest and grandest administrative building.[7] The rich architectural decorations are made of Nocera-tuff except for the main columns' shafts, which are made of customised petal shaped bricks. The basilica is one of the earlier buildings in the forum and dates presumably to the beginning of the 1st century BC.[8]

Further, there are three municipal buildings with simple rectangular structures and a centralised apse or niche on each south side. No architectural decorations remain, but all buildings once had marble veneer and probably flooring.[9] Their similar composition including the brick structures along the inner walls and the continuous façade shows that all three buildings form some kind of unit. Whereas the western and central municipal buildings date after the earthquake of AD 62, the eastern building is older and underwent structural alterations. In this earlier phase, however, it was probably already connected to the predecessors of the central and western buildings.[10]

The so-called comitium is an open courtyard with one podium facing the inner area and one in a previous phase facing the forum portico.[11] Similar to the municipal buildings, there was no known architectural decorations except possibly for rich marble veneer. Despite the massive brick pillars on the north side and a row of tuff pillars on the west side facing the forum, the prime masonry technique was *opus incertum*.

The sacred buildings form the largest group of building types around the forum. The temple of Apollo[12] and the temple of Jupiter[13] together with the basilica are the earliest buildings, and thus, they are characterised by the heavy use of Nocera-tuff for every kind of architectural decoration. The temple of Jupiter is the main temple facing the north side of the forum. Unlike the temple of Apollo, it has no *temenos* or surrounding structure. With an estimated height of nearly 10 m, the columns of the temple of Jupiter are the largest ones in the forum, as is the podium with its corridors and chambers mostly built of lava *incertum*. Both buildings underwent a number of modifications during the 2nd and 1st centuries BC.

Two further podium temples are the so-called temple of the genius of Augustus[14] and the temple of Fortuna Augusta[15] in the far north. Both were completely covered in marble. In the case of the temple of the genius of Augustus, this holds solely for the very small temple building itself and not for the courtyard and the adjoining rooms. The walls of the courtyard show a decoration system consisting of small stones, brick, and now lost stucco that is very similar to the street facing walls of the building of Eumachia. Whereas the temple of Fortuna Augusta, which must have been finished in the year AD 3, was one of the first buildings with extensive marble decoration, the temple of the genius of Augustus dates to later in the 1st century AD. Extensive marble cladding is also characteristic of the so-called sanctuary of the public lares, which was an open courtyard enclosed only on three sides.[16] The walls were structured by several niches, arches, and an apse consisting of a mixture of brick and rubble with a few patches of *opus (quasi) reticulatum*.

Lastly, there are two very large buildings that run loosely under the function of commercial buildings. The macellum[17] is located on the northeast side of the forum, and it accommodates a *tholos*, a portico on two sides of the open courtyard, and a large number of *tabernae*. Three larger rooms on the east side had ritual and communal functions. The macellum combines many different building techniques and probably numerous building phases and repairs. A precise chronology has not been asserted yet, but a predecessor could go back to the 2nd century BC.

The second commercial area, the building of Eumachia,[18] also consists of the largest portico in the forum and a *taberna*. The two-storey portico that ran on all four sides of the main hall was of marble and is thus not only the largest one in size but also in volume and grandeur. The building is dated to the Augustan age.[19]

Methodology

For this study, the 12 mentioned buildings were reconstructed as simply as possible to maintain the goal of creating minimum figures for the building projects. Due to the lack of detailed knowledge of chronologies and building phases of all the buildings, the quantification was based on each building's last phase. Inevitably, this means that practical issues, such as actual building times in years or numbers of people that worked at the construction site at the same time, had to be disregarded. Instead, the estimated labour requirements are treated as an indicator for economic value and as a comparative factor to track overall phenomena and mechanisms of the building industry.

---

[7] Ohr 1991.
[8] Mogetta 2013: 259–260 refering to Maiuri 1973: 220–223.
[9] Flecker and Kockel 2008: 278–295.
[10] The anticipated final publication of the project on the south part of the forum will hopefully clarify the chronologies and contexts of these buildings. For first observations, see Flecker and Kockel 2008.
[11] Fuchs 1957.
[12] De Caro 1986 and, more recently (though controversial), Cooper and Dobbins 2015.
[13] Gasparini 2014.
[14] Wallat 1997: 107–127.
[15] van Andringa 2012.
[16] Wallat 1997: 129–152.
[17] Wallat 1997: 153–200.
[18] Wallat 1997: 31–105.
[19] Kockel 1986: 457–458.

Not included in the calculations are foundations and all forms of earthworks, as well as temporary facilities such as scaffolding and centering. Due to the complete lack of knowledge, some minor aspects such as the sea transport of iron or iron ore and the production and transport of colour pigments were disregarded as well.

These basic principles and considerations resulted in a methodological framework that for each building allowed an estimate of the amount of labour for producing the building materials, transporting them from the production site to the construction site, and for the actual building processes. A comparative analysis of these figures and thereby determining which buildings differ from others and why they do so, helps to identify the basic mechanisms and characteristics of local building traditions.

After calculating the labour requirements for the 12 buildings, what results is a large amount of data in the form of extremely large numbers, one can neither really understand nor compare with each other. So, the numbers need to be put in different contexts and formats that make them more comparable for all the different types of buildings and sizes. The best way to do so is to look at different ratios, first and foremost the ratio of labour in hours per cubic metre of construction volume. In this case, 'construction volume' means the volume of a building that is filled with a built structure. This is roughly the same as the overall amount of material volume. Using this ratio prevents any bias to building size or structure.

Results

General

The first step is to look for the labour requirements for material production, transport, and construction (**Figure 2**). It is obvious that in this study the material production not only requires the most labour input but is also the most variable factor. This is followed by the labour for processes at the construction site and transport costs. The latter plays a minor role in Pompeii, partly due to the high availability of local stone, ceramic building materials, and pozzolana. However, it should also be noted that the source of the building materials in most cases could only be located to certain areas within the Sarno river plane and not to specific quarries.[20] Further, the course of the Sarno was artificially straightened and highly differs from the meandering river network it once was. Thus, the numbers for transport times are generally to be considered as a very rough estimate.

Table 1 gives an overview of the most basic and relevant figures gained from the labour cost analysis of the forum buildings.[21] It can be seen that there is a rough correlation between the ground area, the construction volume, and the overall labour costs. Only the temples stand out. The four buildings at the bottom of the list – the comitium and the municipal buildings – are the small ones that do not have any (known) architectural decorations. Accordingly, there is a small jump between the overall labour of the comitium and the richly decorated sanctuary of the public lares. From there, the figures rise constantly as the buildings become larger and with more architectural decoration.

The temple of Fortuna Augusta

The building that seems at first glance to be the most interesting one is naturally the one with the highest overall labour in hours per construction volume: the temple of Fortuna Augusta. This might seem surprising, because it is a rather small temple lying outside the actual forum space (**Figure 3, 1 [IX]**). It is a tetrastyle podium temple with a platform between the stairs to hold an altar. The architectural decorations were rather rich and consisted of marble. Next to the eight Corinthian columns of the *pronaos*, the outer walls of the *cella* repeated these columns as pilasters, and the *cella* contained a marble *aedicula*. A fragment of a cornered pilaster shaft shows how these corners were constructed from one piece and not two pieces at a right angle. It is evident therefore that the decorations were of a rather high quality (**Figure 4**). According to an inscription, the temple was dedicated by a *duumvir*, Marcus Tullius, on his own land, and it can be dated to the last decades of the 1st century BC. To understand why this temple was the most time-consuming building and how it differs from the others, the numbers need to be further divided for a more detailed look. Compared to the other buildings under investigation, the ground area of the temple of Fortuna Augusta, 225 m², is rather small (**Figure 1**). There are no surrounding structures or free spaces, and a podium up to a height of 3 m covers the whole area. Therefore, it is no surprise that the ratio of volume to area is rather high with over 3 m³ construction volume per m² ground area (**Table 1**).

As the graph (**Figure 2**) shows, in every building the production of building materials required the most labour input, but the temple of Fortuna Augusta with 183 h per m³ lies far above the forum average. Splitting the labour for material production into more categories further clarifies this phenomenon. The production of the materials for the wall structures – building stones (rubble, reticulate, and small blocks), brick, and mortar

---

20 Kastenmeier 2010.

21 A detailed and transparent demonstration of the applied methodology and formulas for calculations cannot be provided in this paper but are derived from Recko 2020.

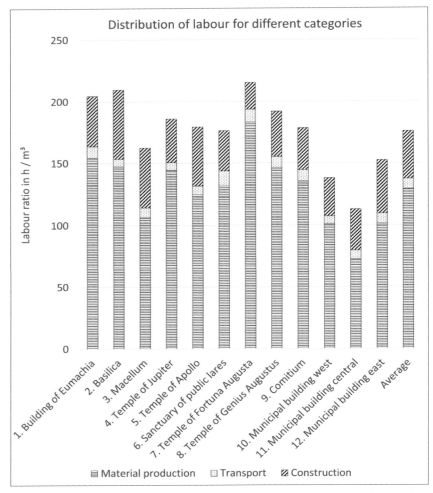

Figure 2. Graph showing labour ratios of different categories across all the buildings under study.

Figure 3. Temple of Fortuna Augusta in Pompeii (picture: C. Recko). Su concessione del Ministero della Cultura - Parco Archeologico di Pompei.

	Dimensions			Overall labour and main categories					Categories of material production				Categories of processes at the construction site			
	Ground area in m²	Construction volume in m³	Ratio of volume in m³ per area in m²	Overall labour in h	Overall labour in h/m³	Material production labour in h/m³	Transport labour in h/m³	Construction labour in h/m³	Walls labour in h/m³	Simple blocks labour in h/m³	Decorative blocks labour in h/m³	Surface decorations labour in h/m³	Walls labour in h/m³	Transport on site labour in h/m³	Surface decorations labour in h/m³	Blocks labour in h/m³
1. Building of Eumachia	**2804**	**3542**	1.3	**724,737**	**205**	154	9	41	41	359	**1190**	255	12	3	141	64
2. Basilica	1670	2502	1.5	524,809	**210**	147	6	**56**	**101**	559	**337**	34	12	6	**245**	24
3. Macellum	2031	2594	1.3	421,244	162	107	7	48	43	231	1244	116	11	2	176	51
4. Temple of Jupiter	540	2233	4.1	415,303	186	144	6	35	99	470	**317**	39	9	2	**459**	38
5. Temple of Apollo	1855	2215	1.2	397,325	179	125	7	48	31	255	**390**	33	8	3	**222**	36
6. Sanctuary of the public lares	529	1340	2.5	236,193	176	131	12	32	31	441	1038	338	8	1	105	**116**
7. Temple of Fortuna Augusta	**225**	**754**	**3.3**	**162,337**	**215**	**183**	**11**	**22**	**28**	**770**	**1028**	**781**	**8**	**3**	**81**	**102**
8. Temple of Genius Augustus	460	694	1.5	133,185	192	146	9	37	38	378	1104	328	10	1	142	62
9. Comitium	402	446	1.1	79,534	178	135	9	34	44	194	-	458	10	1	115	23
10. Municipal building west	189	503	2.7	69,350	138	101	6	31	36	304	-	492	9	1	134	40
11. Municipal building central	166	489	2.9	55,253	113	72	7	34	34	15	-	321	9	1	162	40
12. Municipal building east	161	345	2.1	52,610	152	101	8	43	41	331	-	360	11	1	164	33
Average	919	1471	2.0	272,657	169	129	8	38	47	359	831	296	10	2	179	52

Table 1. Overview of the main results of the labour quantification. The numbers, to which the text specifically refers, are **bold**.

Fig. 4: Remains of the architectural decorations and a pilaster shaft of the Temple of Fortuna Augusta (picture: C. Recko).
Su concessione del Ministero della Cultura - Parco Archeologico di Pompei.

– actually lies far below the average with 28 h / m³; however, in every other category – simple stone blocks, decorative stone blocks, and surface decorations (walls and floors) – the temple lies above the average. Even further, labour for simple stone blocks and decorations again show the overall highest ratio for all buildings. Both categories show an average time per m³ that is more than double the forum average, which needs to be explained by looking at the material itself. 'Simple stone blocks' are in this study defined as mostly simply squared blocks, and they function for example as steps, lintels, or gutters.[22] Usually, these types of stones were made of Nocera-tuff, because it is easy to carve, suitable for all carving, and is local. However, the simple blocks from the temple of Fortuna Augusta are mostly made of white limestone. Limestone is a material, which has a significantly higher specific weight than soft tuff, and it is a lot harder to carve. This results in higher labour figures for quarrying, processing, and transporting. On the other hand, it has a smooth texture and its white colour resembles marble. At the temple of Fortuna Augusta, the limestone blocks were comparably large, forming the whole platform for the altar, the stairs, and the substructure of the podium. This concentration of one type of hard stone with the complete absence

of simple tuff blocks is something that we do not see in other buildings and that is why the ratio of labour requirements per m³ of simple blocks is so high.

Alternatively, the decorative stone blocks – columns, entablatures, and profiled blocks – are usually made of either Nocera-tuff or marble and in a few cases of white limestone.

The basilica, the temple of Apollo, and the temple of Jupiter are three buildings whose architectural decorations consist solely of Nocera-tuff in large volume. As carving limestone and marble requires roughly double the time of carving Nocera-tuff, the overall forum average is low, because it includes buildings with exclusively tuff decorations. Therefore, the margin between the forum average and the buildings with marble architectural decorations, such as the temple of Fortuna Augusta, is neither unusual nor a specific characteristic of individual buildings.

The surface decorations of the temple are mostly gone, but it is assumed that the temple was almost completely covered with marble. This would have included the fluted pilasters (most likely with bases and capitals) that structured the outer walls of the *cella* and which would have been more time-consuming to produce than plain veneer. As neither the walls nor the floors

---

[22] So simple carvings like a concave block also count as simple blocks as long as the carving is not ornamental or of a decorative nature.

– both have limited expansion – give any reason to reconstruct a combination of marble covering with more modest floors or plastered walls,[23] the marble surface decorations are both of a time-consuming material and a time-consuming quality. These two factors cause the highest ratio of labour per volume to be for the surface decorations.

So far, all the characteristics concern the immediately visible parts of the temple, but the underlying would have been the main construction necessary for a building. Still, it is obvious that their share in the labour requirements of this temple is marginal. The tasks for producing wall stones include quarrying, squaring, and rough shaping. This last step is less labour intensive than the numerous steps of stone carving, e.g. removing material, shaping, creating dowel holes, different kinds of surface treatments, etc. Further, except for lava, the stones used for constructing walls are all soft and thus easier to shape. Brick, on the other hand, as an artificial material requires several different raw materials and tasks for its production, including the collection of fuel for the kiln.

The labour for the production of material for the walls of the temple of Fortuna Augusta (28 h per m3) is not only below the forum average but also on the lowest of all the buildings studied (**Table 1**). That is because the percentage of rubble in this building is quite high, and rubble – especially of the local soft stones, calcareous tufa (so-called Sarno-limestone) and scoria (so-called cruma) – is easy and fast to produce and to transport. Large amounts of rubble went into the podium, and the walls are mostly made of *opus incertum* with few quoins of *opus testaceum* (brick) or of *opus vittatum* (small rectangular stone blocks). In fact, quoining of the inner corners of the *cella* was completely left out, and the corners were irregularly formed with rubble stones. This is a phenomenon that does appear in other Pompeiian buildings, but it is certainly not the standard. Unfortunately, the walls are currently in a bad state of preservation, but next to the missing quoins there are some other hints in the material remains that suggest that the walls never were particularly neat. The quoins' edges, for example, are quite rough and less regularly set than in other buildings. Where they were prepared for veneer and on the east side, where the apse was probably added at a later stage, the surfaces were so irregular and battered that the original structure is hard to make out. Further, the north and south walls of the *cella* each contain two niches and the back walls of these niches are remarkably thin (about 8 to 12 cm roughly estimated), which is visible through a small hole in one of these back walls. In other buildings containing niches, e.g. the macellum, the building of Eumachia, or the comitium,

the surrounding walls reach a thickness that makes sure to hold the depth of the niches as well as a regular-sized back wall. It is clear that the focus for construction and labour investment at the temple of Fortuna Augusta, on the other hand, was not directed to basic elements such as the walls but rather to the more prominent and immediately visible parts of the building.

When turning to the processes on the construction site, we see a similar phenomenon (**Table 1**). The labour for the walls is equally low, because for example, laying the large amount of *opus caementicium* for the podium is comparatively fast. In addition, the decorations (which means surface decorations like veneer and not architectural decorations like columns) had a total volume of 59 m3 which is the lowest volume among all the forum buildings and took only 81 h per m3 to construct. This volume is even lower than buildings with an equally small ground area such as the municipal buildings or the comitium. The reason for this is partly the distinct structural requirements of building a podium temple compared to a regular building. For instance, the temple podium adds significant construction volume but presents only a limited amount of surface for decoration because the podium lacks inner walls and the parts containing stairs need neither wall veneer nor a floor. In case of the temple of Fortuna Augusta, the whole east side of the podium and *cella* did not need any decorative finish, because it was not visible from the outside due to the alignment with the walls of the adjacent building (**Figure 1**).

In contrast to the low labour ratios for walls and decorations, what stands out through both an overall high ratio and a high difference to the forum average are the blocks that needed to be set in place. As we have already seen, only hard stones were used for both simple and decorative blocks. Since the process of lifting and setting in place is directly related to the weight of the blocks,[24] the heavy hard stones needed more time to be set than lighter soft stones. The same relationship between the object's weight and the necessary labour input applies to the horizontal transport at the construction site. This would have been necessary as the large amounts of building material probably reached the construction site successively and needed to be stored in an intermediate location to guarantee a smooth construction progress.

In summary, the temple of Fortuna Augusta can be characterised as a building where the heavy use of hard prestigious stones like limestone and marble required labour requirements in both material production and construction that were well above the average. In contrast, the walls were of a rougher nature and were executed with less care. Their share in the labour requirements, both for the material production and

---

[23] Of course, this is a debatable issue about the reconstruction, especially concerning the heights that are not preserved today.

[24] Pegoretti 1864: 13–15.

the processes at the construction site, is accordingly marginal.

The structural specifics of a free-standing podium temple further intensify the high ratios of labour per m³. First, a temple has a rather simple format, where the whole outside and the inside are equally important. This means that the overall volumes of some of the materials can be lower than in other building types, but at the same time the fewer possibilities to vary between different types of materials and treatments result in high labour ratios. In larger buildings, there are always side rooms or back walls that are not immediately visible, and thus, they often have more modest furnishings. If we look back at the simple blocks, the low variation of blocks necessary for a temple structure can still result in high labour ratios. And of course, certain aspects of decorative stones such as the columns and entablature must be a part of a classic temple building. So, very simply put, in larger buildings with more structural variety one can get more output from the same amount of labour input.

Observations on other buildings and outliers

After discussing the characteristics of the temple of Fortuna Augusta that make this building the most labour intensive structure in the forum of Pompeii, some observations can be made on other buildings to clarify how the different characteristics of the buildings (structural and material) affect the labour required for their construction.

Looking at the overall labour requirements, the building of Eumachia was the most labour intensive with over 724,000 h (**Table 1**). If 50 people worked at the same time for 10 h a day all year long, this translates to a period of 1449 days or about 4 years.[25] Of course, this building is on top of the list partly because it is the one with the largest ground area as well as the highest construction volume. But even when looking at the ratio of overall labour per m³, it ranges only a bit lower than the temple of Fortuna Augusta. In general, ornamental and decorative carving on hard materials like limestone and especially marble, is the component that determines the labour comparison the most. Accordingly, the 1190 h per m³ for producing decorative blocks for the building of Eumachia reflect the inclusion of a two-story marble portico running on four sides around the large courtyard and a limestone *chalcidicum* in front of the building. Further, the difference between processing hard stones and soft stones is clearly visible when comparing all the figures for labour per m³ for decorative blocks. The three buildings that solely use Nocera-tuff – the basilica, the temple of Apollo, and the temple of Jupiter – show a labour ratio that is only half

of the forum average. Alternatively, applying the surface decorations on the construction site is noticeably more time-consuming for the same three buildings. This is because in addition to covering plain walls and floors, all the decorative elements made from Nocera-tuff, such as the columns and entablatures, needed a stucco coating, whereas marble elements remained plain.

What brings the basilica to the second highest overall labour ratios (210 h per m³) despite its use of soft Nocera-tuff, is partly the heavy use of compact lava as the only component of the high and massive *opus incertum* walls. Quarrying this hard stone is significantly more time-consuming than all the other local stones, and it makes the basilica and the temple of Jupiter, which also uses it frequently for the *cella* walls and the podium, stand out with their figures for the production of wall materials.

Usually, compact lava was not used as a rubble stone due to its hardness but as blocks for locations under high stress, e.g. thresholds. As stylobate stones it was used at the sanctuary of the public lares. As there were not many simple blocks in this building in general, the ratio of 116 h per m³ for setting blocks in place is accordingly high.

Conclusions: the local building industry

The above observations provide a picture of the local building industry of Pompeii. From early on, a range of building materials were available in the wider area around the city. These materials were used in strong accordance to their technical properties. Thus, there were soft and easily workable stones that as rubble could be flexibly used for foundations, walls, and cores (Nocera-tuff, yellow tuff, Sarno-limestone, and cruma). Lava as a hard stone was used for thresholds or other locations under high pressure. Further, the smooth and easy to cut tuff was suitable for ornamentation and a range of other functions. Increasingly during the first century AD, there was also brick, which was especially useful for corners, niches, and arches.

The comparative analysis of quantified labour requirements put these characteristics in a mathematical setting and enabled the identification of outliers. The temple of Fortuna Augusta, for example, turned out to be the most labour-intensive buildings in the forum, which can be explained by a strong emphasis on high quality materials especially on the visible outside of the temple. The underlying wall structures on the other hand seem less considered.

Before the temple of Fortuna Augusta preluded the marble preference at the forum, the use of compact lava in *opus incertum* walls and cores had visible impact on the labour figures. For the higher-than-average walls of the basilica and the massive podium of the temple of Jupiter, the builders might have felt more secure

---

[25] This by no means refers to an actual building period. It is only to help the reader to better relate to the high numbers of labour in hours.

using a particularly hard and stress-resistant material even though that meant a noticeable increase in labour requirements. In this case, the increase was in a category of labour tasks (producing stone materials for walls) that usually has only a small share in the overall amount of labour. In contrast to prestige, functionality might be the main motivation in this context. However, that does not mean that architectural decorations played a minor role in these earlier buildings in general. Instead, all three buildings had extensive decoration schemes,[26] but they were made of soft tuff. In turn, though, the labour requirements for applying surface decorations at the construction site was very high, because the tuff décor always received stucco.

With this selection of materials and a long tradition at hand, producing materials for wall structures and constructing them might have been a process that was more or less set. Also, although the walls count for the main part of the construction volume – on average 73 % – their share in the overall labour was only 24 % on average. This is potentially one of the reasons that the wall techniques in Pompeii did not develop as dynamically as they did for example in Rome or Ostia. Opus *reticulatum* never became a standard in Pompeii, and even *opus testaceum* was mostly chosen where the structural advantage of bricks was useful. Instead, what really had a significant impact was when marble replaced Nocera-tuff as the prime material for decorative stones. This clearly cannot be explained with functionality.

It is also interesting to note that the temple of Fortuna Augusta with its complete exterior of hard stone was built relatively early and the buildings on the east side of the forum, all of which at least partly used marble, followed.

Unfortunately, the development of the local building industry of Pompeii was cut short at a relatively early stage in AD 79. We do not know in which direction the use of *opus testaceum* over *opus incertum* may have developed, and if at a certain point, marble would have replaced Nocera-tuff altogether. However, by quantifying the materials and the labour to produce, transport, and build with them, this paper has shown how the builders approached different materials and how different characteristics – of materials as well as of building types – affected the labour requirements. In this way, we gain a better economic understanding of the complex local systems of builders, buildings, and topography.

---

[26] A comparison to smaller buildings with more modest tuff decorations is not possible at the forum of Pompeii in its latest phase.

Bibliography

Barker, S.J. and B. Russell 2012. Labour figures for Roman stone-working. Pitfalls and potential, in S. Camporeale, H. Dessales and A. Pizzo (eds) *Arqueología de la Construcción III. Los procesos constructivos en el mundo romano: la economía de las obras.* (Anejos de Archivo Español de Arqueologa 64): 83–94. Madrid: Consejo Superior de Investigaciones Científicas - Instituto de Arqueología de Mérida.

Bologna, F. 2019. Water and stone. The economics of wall-painting in Pompeii (A.D. 62–79). *Journal of Roman archaeology* 32: 97–128.

Cooper, J.G. and J.J. Dobbins 2015. New Developments and New Dates within the Sanctuary of Apollo at Pompeii. *The Journal of Fasti Online* 340: 1–7.

De Caro, S. 1986. *Saggi nell'area del tempio di Apollo a Pompei. Scavi stratigrafici di A. Maiuri nel 1931–32 e 1942-43.* Napoli: Istituto universitario orientale (Annali / Dipartimento di studi del mondo classico e del Mediterraneo antico. Sezione di archeologia e storia antica. Quaderno 3).

DeLaine, J. 1997. *The baths of Caracalla. A study in the design, construction and economics of large-scale building projects in imperial Rome* (Journal of Roman Archaeology Supplementary series 25). Portsmouth, RI: JRA.

Flecker, M. and V. Kockel 2008. Forschungen im Südteil des Forums von Pompeji. Ein Vorbericht über die Arbeitskampagnen 2007 und 2008. *Mitteilungen des Deutschen Archäologischen Instituts. Römische Abteilung* 114: 271–303.

Fuchs, G. 1957. Fragmenta saeptorum. *Mitteilungen des Deutschen Archäologischen Instituts. Römische Abteilung* 64: 154–197.

Gasparini, V. 2014. Il culto di Giove a Pompei. *Vesuviana* 6: 9–94.

Kastenmeier, P. 2010. The source of stone building materials from the Pompeii archaeological area and its surroundings. *Periodico di Mineralogia* 79 (special issue): 39–58.

Kockel, V. 1986. Archäologische Funde und Forschungen in den Vesuvstädten 2. *Archäologischer Anzeiger* 1986: 443–569.

Maiuri, A. 1973. *Alla ricerca di Pompei preromana. Saggi stratigrafici.* Napoli: Società editrice napoletana.

Mogetta, M. 2013. *The Origins of Concrete in Rome and Pompeii.* PhD dissertation. University of Michigan.

Morichi, R., R. Paone and F. Sampaolo 2017. *Pompei - nuova cartografia informatizzata georiferita* (Quaderni di Nova Bibliotheca Pompeiana. Series maior 2). Roma: Arbor Sapientiae Editore.

Ohr, K. 1991. *Die Basilika in Pompeji* (Denkmäler antiker Architektur 17). Berlin: de Gruyter.

Pegoretti, G. 1862/1864. *Manuale pratico per l'estimazione de lavori architettonici, stradali, idraulici e di fortificazione per uso degli ingegneri ed architetti*

(Biblioteca scelta dell'ingegnere civile 14). Milano: Domenico Salvi e C.

Recko, C. 2020. Bauökonomische Untersuchung zum Forum von Pompeji. Quantifizierung und vergleichende Analyse von Baumaterial, Bauprozessen und Arbeitszeit. Unpublished PhD dissertation. University of Cologne.

van Andringa, W. 2012. Pompéi. M. Tullius et le temple de Fortune Auguste. Campagnes de fouilles et d'études 2011. *Chronique des activités archéologiques de l'École française de Rome* 355: 359–366.

Wallat, K. 1997. *Die Ostseite des Forums von Pompeji.* Frankfurt am Main i.e.: Lang.

18.

Pompeian Wall Painting in Figures: Labour and Materials

Francesca Bologna

Università di Verona, Dipartimento di Culture e Civiltà
francescabologna@live.com

Abstract

The quantitative analysis of the materials and labour force involved in the realisation of specific building projects has now become more common in the study of architecture in Antiquity. This approach allows us to assess the costs incurred by the patrons funding such projects, as well as the logistics of these endeavours. Past studies often focused on public buildings rather than private houses, and their painted decoration was usually neglected. Yet wall paintings played a crucial role in everyday life in Antiquity, for they adorned not only public buildings and elite houses but also more modest dwellings.

Assessing labour figures and production costs for Roman wall painting allows us to fully appreciate this craft as an economically embedded practice. In this paper I will use ancient and post-antique sources, as well as experimental archaeology, to reconstruct the actions, materials, people, and ultimately, the costs involved in the decoration of an 'average' Pompeian house. I will then investigate how painters could meet their clients' demands by adjusting to their different needs and finances, thus using quantitative analysis to shed light on ancient craftspeople's working practices. Lastly, I will comment on the use of different pigments and their prices.

Keywords: wall painting, plaster, pigments, costs, labour figures

Even since Janet DeLaine's revolutionary work on the Baths of Caracalla,[1] the scholarly world has become aware of the importance of investigating the economic aspects of the ancient construction industry, examining in turn materials and their supply, transport, labour, and workforce organisation. This has led to the development of a new field of study, keen on assessing monumental building not in terms of design and aesthetics but rather treating construction techniques and building materials as important aspects of economic performance, as well as of societal organisation.

Past and current research has mostly focused – understandably – on public buildings, for they are often better preserved and documented, thus offering better case studies. At the same time, they were the results of substantial private and/or imperial investments, bound to have significant economic repercussions, often not only locally but also on a regional or even empire-wide scale. Yet projects of such scale were necessarily outliers, if highly impactful ones; the norm was to have smaller, sub-elite private commissions, which without being necessarily as far-reaching, would still sustain the local market. In this paper I will not focus on monumental projects but rather on smaller-scale, domestic ones within the city of Pompeii. Moreover, I will not concentrate on the time and labour involved in the construction of domestic buildings but rather on those necessary to decorate them, specifically to realise their wall decoration.

Wall painting is intrinsically linked with architecture, and it plays a significant role in ancient building projects, both public and private. Wall paintings adorned not only public buildings and elite houses but also more modest dwellings and commercial properties (from shops and bars to brothels), thus forming an integral part of everyday life in the Roman world. Recent studies investigating the logistics and economic importance of the construction industry in Antiquity have usually focused on the sculpted architectural material of ancient buildings, aided by the figures that can be extrapolated from post-antique building manuals.[2] This analysis of labour rarely has been applied to the study of painted decoration, despite the interesting insights it could offer into wall painting as an economically embedded craft.

Painting is arguably the most 'democratic' form of art consumption in Antiquity, for colours made their appearance on most visible surfaces, from public architecture to sculpture, from houses to retail units, adorning the dwellings of elite, sub-elite, and lower classes alike. This of course resulted in very different levels of commission, as interestingly noted by de Vos in her investigation of lower-class houses in Pompeii.

---

[1] DeLaine 1997.

[2] See for example Barresi 2004; 2015; Maschek 2016; and papers in Camporeale, Dessales and Pizzo 2008; 2010. See Maschek's contribution in this volume for and in-depth discussion with bibliography.

1 cm thickness × 1 m²	Rendering (rabboccatura/ gobetage)	Floating (arricciatura/crépi)	Setting (intonacatura fina/enduit)	TOT. (drying time not included)	workforce
Pegoretti 1864	0.25	1.25	1.25	0.58	1 mason + labourer
Rea 1902	0.13	0.27	0.27	0.19	1 plasterer + labourer + boy
Hurst 1905	0.24	0.4	0.48	0.33	1 plasterer + labourer + boy
Rondelet 1862	-	-	-	0.42	1 mason + labourer
Claudel and Laroque 1870	0.1	0.24	0.25	0.2	1 mason + boy
Morisot 1820		0.33	0.45	0.36	1 mason + boy
AVERAGE	0.18	0.50	0.54	0.35	2 men

Table 1. Labour figures for plastering expressed in hours, listed by author and activity.

De Vos assigned different wall decorations to a specific workshop, dubbed 'bottega di via di Castricio', thanks to the identification of recurring motifs, which in turn highlighted a peculiar decorative strategy based on the reworking and simplification of the most common and fashionable decorative elements of the time.[3] According to de Vos, this showed a desire, on the painters' part, to conform to current trends while at the same time allowing for their clients' limited financial resources. Mythological panels were thus replaced with simpler subjects, such as still-life paintings, the architectural views were dilated, the *bordures ajourées* were substituted with garlands, the chromatic range was rather limited, and the figurative repertoire was quite simple. Whether one agrees in assigning all decorations which show these elements to the same workshop or not, de Vos's study has the undeniable value of showing how different levels of demand existed and could be met by Roman painters. Still, among high-quality forms of domestic decoration in Pompeii, panel pictures appear to have been the most widespread, as a considerable number of them appear in houses which did not belong to the municipal elite, in contrast with what can be observed, for example, for *opus vermiculatum* mosaics or sculptures.[4]

Labour figures

Painting is intrinsically connected with plastering. Not only must a wall be plastered before it can be painted but it also must be plastered in a very specific way, applying consecutive coats, which differ in terms of both thickness and composition.

19th- and 20th-century building manuals offer accurate estimates for plastering times, even differentiating between various qualities of plasters, which can be easily linked with what we know about Roman plastering techniques from ancient sources and archaeological evidence. To calculate the time necessary to spread what Vitruvius refers to as *trullisatio*, estimates for rendering can be used. Floating times can be employed for the application of the intermediate layer(s) of plaster and sand (often referred to as *arriccio* in current scholarship), while figures for setting can be used for the *intonachino*, the last fine layer of plaster on which colours are applied. After collecting all data connected with plastering times from the main pre-industrial building manuals, I calculated an average that was used for my calculations. The collected results are summarised in **Table 1**. All estimates refer to 1 cm of plaster per 1 m², times are expressed in hours, and whenever possible the times were calculated and converted based on a constant workforce comprised of 2 men.

Estimating painting times can be difficult, especially since ancient sources do not offer any clues on the topic, while practices described in post-antique sources are not easily comparable with Roman wall painting. Despite these issues, experimental archaeology can offer some insights, and in order to obtain an estimate for painting times, I turned to two experimental frescoes realised in France in 1996 and 2014.

In 1996 a group of archaeologists and restorers from the *Centre d'étude des peinture murales romaines* (CEPMR) realised an experimental fresco at Saint-Savin, trying to emulate the Roman style and technique.[5] The team,

---

[3] De Vos 1981: 125–126.
[4] Flohr 2019: 113.

[5] Barbet and Coutelas 2002.

composed of eight people, plastered and painted a surface of 9.85 m² in four days. On the third day of the experiment, each group comprised of two people painted 1 m² in half a day. The people involved were not professional painters, thus the director of the project suggested that an experienced painter could achieve the same results in half the time, for a painting output of *c.* 0.22 m² per hour. This estimate was confirmed in 2014 when, as part of the exhibition *L'empire de la couleur* held at the Musée Saint Raymond in Toulouse, another experimental fresco was produced.[6] This time it was realised by two experienced painters and restorers, who plastered and painted a surface of 9.38 m² in 12 days, which translates into an average painting output of 0.19 m² per hour. If we calculate the average between the two, we obtain a painting time of 0.21 m² per hour, a figure I will be using in the following calculations.

Painting an 'average' Pompeian house: labour

We now have all the figures necessary to calculate how much time was needed to paint a Roman house, but is there such a thing as an 'average' Roman house? The city of Pompeii offers a rather substantial dataset, which was compiled into a comprehensive database by Miko Flohr.[7] The collected evidence provides an average area for a Pompeian house of 393.5 m² and an average of 17.3 rooms. Therefore, in this hypothetical average house, an average room would measure 22.8 m² with a wall length of *c.* 4.8 m. If we then assume a wall height of *c.* 3 m, the surface of each wall within the room would be of *c.* 14.3 m², for a total wall surface per room of *c.* 43 m².[8] By multiplying this figure for the average number of rooms within a house (17.3), we can estimate a total surface of 742 m² to be painted. This is, of course, an approximation and it is important to highlight that it does not account for the possible existence of upper floors, which are mostly lost to us. Still, it offers a reliable starting point.

After calculating labour figures and the total area to be painted, the last variable to consider is the number of people at work. When modelling the labour force connected with the construction of public buildings, the maximum manpower necessary to complete the project in the minimum amount of time is generally used, yet with private commissions we can hardly expect patrons to consistently employ the highest possible number of craftspeople necessary to complete the job. Private, sub-elite domestic commissions pose a rather different case study, for we have an almost

endless list of possibilities influenced by the different financial situations of the patrons, while we must also consider the practicalities linked with carrying out work in buildings currently in use. Assumptions made for craftspeople at work on a new monument cannot always be applied to those working on the decoration of an inhabited domestic building; for example, the owner of the house might prefer the hired workforce to proceed by completing just one or two rooms at a time, to avoid turning the whole house into an inaccessible working site.[9] Therefore, when assessing decoration works carried out within domestic buildings, it is perhaps more sensible to explore a range of possibilities. I will first reconstruct the times and actions necessary to complete the painted decoration of an average house using the minimum man-power necessary to carry out the work. A productive unit or team is usually considered as comprised of four to six people,[10] thus I use this figure to reconstruct the work sequence. I will then repeat my calculations with a higher manpower figure.

In total, 3,530 work hours are necessary to paint 742 m² (the wall surface of an average Pompeian house) at 0.21m²/h. If we assume one team composed of six painters at work in the house, moving from room to room, then the time necessary to complete the whole project appears incredibly long: 589 work hours, which translates into *c.* 59 work days assuming a work day of 10 hours. Thus, about 2 months would be necessary in order to repaint the house, without considering – as already noted – the possible presence of upper floors or the time necessary to plaster the walls before painting them. Even if this possibility cannot be discarded out of hand, it stills seems more likely that Roman house owners would have hired larger teams.

If we repeat the calculations assuming an average of 1.5 painters per room,[11] then we reach the rather high total of 26 painters, who could paint a whole house in 14 work days; however, this would have made it extremely difficult for the whole household to live in the building while the work progressed. Smaller groups of 20 or 15 painters could complete the same amount of work in 18 and 24 work days respectively. If we assume the average daily wage for a skilled worker in 1st-century AD Italy to be 6 HS,[12] then we reach a

[6] Mulliez 2014. See also Musée Saint Raymond and GK Vision, *Tectoria Romana: à la recherché de la fresque antique*, viewed 24 February 2020 <http://www.tectoria-romana.com/>.
[7] Flohr 2018.
[8] Wall surface was multiplied by 3 rather than 4 to account for wall width and other openings, such as windows.
[9] In the Casa dei Pittori al Lavoro (IX.12.9) in Pompeii, for example, two different rooms (12) and (4) were being painted at the same time, while room (3) had been temporarily turned into a deposit, thus making most of the ground floor unusable (Varone and Béarat 1997: 200–202).
[10] For wall painting see, among others, Ling 1991: 215–216; for mosaicists, see Wootton 2015: 279–280 with bibliography; for pottery workshops, see Hasaki 2011: 18 and 26–27.
[11] A fair assumption with an average area of 22.8 m² per room.
[12] See Maschek 2016: 400 with bibliography.

total of more than 2,000 HS to pay for the wages of these painters.

Still, all of these estimates focus on painting without considering plastering times. The most extensive review of Pompeian plaster remains to-date the one carried out by Augusti in 1950, whose 54 samples were collected from a wide range of buildings.[13] He concluded that it was quite common in Pompeii to have only two layers of plaster applied to the wall: one rough coat (trullisatio) 4 cm thick and the intonachino 0.8 cm thick. This translates into 1.4 h/m² to apply the rough coat and 0.9 h/m² for the intonachino, for a total of 2.3 h/m² without including drying times. Applied to the 'average' Pompeian house, this amounts to 1710 work hours: 29 days for a team of 6 workers, 7 days for 26 workers, 9 days for 20 workers, and 11 days for 15 workers. 119 work hours would have also been necessary to mix and sieve the plaster (22.7 m³).[14] At 6 HS/day, this translates into 1100 HS, while if we assume a lower wage for this slightly less specialised task (4 HS/day) the total would be 730 HS. This roughly corresponds to an extra 50% to add to painting times and costs, to which we should also add the price of materials.[15] When considering plastering, however, we are faced with a great variety within the site of Pompeii, ranging from just one layer of thin plaster to four or five different ones of varying thicknesses, so it is quite hard to generalise. Consequently, the calculations I just presented can only offer a general sense of the time necessary to decorate an average Pompeian house. They are a starting point to assess the financial and personal burden sustained by Pompeian patrons, yet the city offers such a wide variety of case studies that for more precise estimates it is advisable to proceed on a case-by-case basis. In other words, there was no standard commission, Pompeian or otherwise, and we must always keep in mind that Roman building projects came in all shapes and sizes.

Cutting corners

At this stage, it is interesting to reflect on how painters might try to meet the different needs of their clients, influenced by their financial resources or other practicalities. Recently, different studies have focused on assessing how reuse and recycling could impact the final cost of a building project, highlighting how this could result in a lower investment on the patron's part.[16] Since painters were hired not only by the members of the elite but also by commissioners belonging to very different levels of society, it is

worthwhile to at least address different measures which they might have employed in order to cut costs.

The first, obvious way to reduce production times is evident by looking at archaeological evidence and comparing it with what is described by ancient authors. Even a cursory review of surviving wall paintings clearly shows that the number of layers of plaster applied to the walls hardly ever met the requirements dictated by Vitruvius and Pliny.[17] In order to meet the very high standards set by Vitrivius – 7 coats of plaster – more than 6 hours would have been necessary to plaster 1 m².

Trullisatio (rendering) 5 cm → 1.8 h

3 coats lime + sand (floating) 1 cm → 1 h × 3= 3 h

3 coats lime + marble dust (setting) 0.5 cm → 0.5 h × 3= 1.5 h

It should be noted, however, that this does not include drying times, which are of paramount importance when painting a fresco. Two experimental frescoes realised in Cologne in 1995 and in Saint-Savin in 1996 allow us to reach a rough estimate for drying times.[18] In both cases the rough coat was left to dry for about 24 hours before applying the next one, while for the following layers a drying time of about 5 hours was enough, roughly the equivalent of half a day of work. Even prior to the application of the painted decoration, it was necessary to allow for the finishing coat to at least start drying before applying the colour. Of course these necessary pauses could be absorbed by proceeding with the plastering and/or painting of the rest of the room or another room altogether, but still these breaks should be considered.

Plastering times could, however, be reduced if, as was usually the case, fewer coats were applied to the walls. For example, 2 hours per m² would be necessary when applying three layers of plaster, which was indeed more common in the city of Pompeii, where there are no surviving examples of painted walls with seven plaster coats.[19]

Trullisatio 2.5 cm → 0.9 h

Arriccio 0.6 cm → 0.6 h

Intonachino 0.35 cm → 0.4 h

Yet another way to reduce costs for plastering is connected with the choice of materials, and indeed in Pompeii we find no traces of the marble dust whose use is recommended by both Vitruvius and Pliny.

---

[13] In her more recent study of Pompeian plaster, Freccero (2018) does not focus on plaster thickness.
[14] Pegoretti 1864: 234 (Analisi 283).
[15] See infra.
[16] See, among others, Barker 2018.

[17] Vitr. 7, 3, 5–6; Plin. HN, 36, 55.
[18] Häfner 1997; Barbet and Coutelas 2002.
[19] Figures for plaster thickness used in the calculations come from Augusti 1950: 334–335.

Figure 1. Third-Style decoration underneath later Fourth-Style wall paintings, note the hacking of the previous decoration. From the so-called Thermae of Baia, Sosandra sector, SW corner of the peristyle.

Figure 2. Fragment of Romano-British painted plaster with traces of repaint (BM 1856,0701.778).
© The Trustees of the British Museum.

Plastering times could also be reduced by simply repainting on top of pre-existing decorations. In this case, rather than removing the whole *tectorio* and applying it anew, craftspeople would simply proceed by hacking the existing painted plaster to ensure a better adherence, then applying only one thin layer of plaster on which to paint (see **Figures 1–2**). This in turn leads to another decorative strategy, one that is often observed in Pompeian houses, where earlier decorations were preserved or, occasionally, even retouched following damages caused by the earthquake which hit the city in AD 62.[20] The decision

to maintain existing painted decorations appears to have often, but not always, been the result of economic reasoning. Pompeians show a tendency to maintain older Third-Style decorations in rooms gravitating around the atrium, probably as a result of a twofold trend: on one hand the desire to somehow preserve and display the household's illustrious past, especially in a traditional area such as that of the atrium, on the other hand the newfound eminence of the peristyle and the rooms opening on it, which would prompt owners to focus their Fourth-Style redecorations in this area. However, those large households which were thoroughly and lavishly refurbished by their wealthy new owners usually retain only a few Third-Style decorations, often in secondary or downgraded parts of the house, such as *alae* turned into storage rooms. Usually only small or medium-sized houses show an almost complete Third-Style decoration.[21] This shows that, even if there are social and cultural aspects which cannot be forgotten when assessing wall paintings, costs would necessarily have been an important variable considered by patrons. It makes perfect sense, in economic terms, for them to focus their redecorating efforts on the main rooms of their house, leaving old decoration in secondary ones.

[20] 73 buildings in Pompeii retain one or more rooms decorated in the Third Style. On the strategies adopted by Campanian homeowners in dealing with pre-existing wall decorations, see Ehrhardt 2012.

[21] A notable exception is the Casa del Gruppo dei Vasi di Vetro (VI.13.2), whose owner deliberately decided to preserve the original wall paintings, possibly as a way of distancing himself from 'wealthy newcomers'.

Yet another aspect of wall painting production that has important economic repercussions is the use of the so-called *picturae ligneis formis inclusae*, figurative scenes painted on plaster encased in wooden trays, similar to what was done with *emblemata* in mosaic production. These 'prefabricated' panels are quite rare, indicating that the practice never became common in the Vesuvian area.[22] Indeed applying a pre-painted panel to a wall required less work and was less time consuming than painting it on site, but this reasoning does not consider the whole picture. These panels would have to be realised in a studio, likely by a highly specialised painter. The fact that they were usually identified in important buildings and within prominent reception rooms speaks to their exclusivity; we can therefore assume that their quality was expected to be higher than average. Superior quality would necessarily result in an increased value, thus even if their use would save a certain amount of work hours on site, it would not necessarily lower costs, quite the opposite. It should be noted, however, that in some cases parts of old wall decorations could be excised and re-employed within the same house.[23] In these cases alone we can indeed assume that this practice would result in a lower expense, especially since the process often resulted in the fracture of the wall fragments, especially when they were not treated with the necessary care or skill.

Pigments

Lastly, production costs are always strongly influenced by materials. In the case of wall painting, pigment prices played an important role in decoration costs, and the archaeological evidence proves that painters – and their patrons – were aware of a number of solutions which could allow similar end results with significantly different costs. First and foremost, similar colours could be obtained using differently priced pigments: the expensive cinnabar could be substituted with red ochre and red lead, green earths were generally used in place of malachite, and chalk was largely employed instead of the higher quality aragonite. These substitutions might be applied to the whole building, or the cheapest pigments could be used in secondary rooms, while the more expensive ones were more sparsely employed in important reception rooms.

The latter solution was the one employed, among other examples, in the Domus Aurea in Rome. Pigment analysis carried out on some fragments of painted plaster from Nero's palace currently held at the British Museum shows that the choice of pigments was influenced by room function.[24] The wall paintings in the British Museum collection come from two different rooms within the Esquiline wing of the palace, the long service corridor 92 and room 119, the so-called Room of Achilles at Skyros, close to the famous Octagonal Suite. The fragments are dominated by blue, green, and red hues on a white ground (**Figures 3–4**). Egyptian blue was used in both rooms, even though in the corridor the shade is lighter and the pigment is less thickly applied. When we turn to green, however, we can observe how two distinct pigments were used: green earth in corridor 92 and a coarser, brighter, copper-based pigment with frit-like appearance in room 119 (Egyptian green or possibly malachite). Yet the most telling distinction can be perceived when turning to the colour red. All painted fragments from room 119 show a widespread use of cinnabar (HgS, the Roman *minium*), which was generously and thickly applied, mixed with varying quantities of red ochre and red lead. On the other hand, paintings from corridor 92 show no traces of the expensive pigment; here, red is obtained exclusively from red ochre and red lead, and it is more thinly applied. To this we should add that traces of gilding were only detected in fragments from the so-called Hall of Achilles. In this case, the two different functions of the rooms – reception and passage – very clearly resulted in distinct decorating strategies and choices of pigments.

Unfortunately, we have no way of quantifying the exact impact of these choices on total costs, for ancient sources are rather inconsistent when it comes to pigment prices; however, it is still possible to reach some general conclusions. According to Pliny, the regulated price for cinnabar from *Baetica* was 70 HS per *libra*,[25] and the price for generic cinnabar was 50 HS per *libra*,[26] while high quality red lead could cost half as much, 24 HS per *libra*.[27] It is hard to gauge how much could be paid for red ochre, but *sinopis* of the best quality was apparently valued at 48 HS per *libra* – almost as much as cinnabar – while low quality kinds could cost as little as 2 HS.[28] As for greens, malachite (*chrysocolla*) could cost 24, 20, or 12 HS per *libra* depending on quality,[29] while the price given by Pliny for green earths is 1 HS per *libra*.[30] Whether we

[22] Four examples in Herculaneum and six in Pompeii according to Donner (Helbig 1868), five in Herculaneum and 34 in Pompeii according to Maiuri (Maiuri 1938, 1940), to which we can now add the three *picturae ligneis formis inclusae* in the Casa del Centenario (IX.8.6). Even if we were to accept all the panels identified by Maiuri, some of which are dubious, these amount to about 4% of the 901 panel pictures in Pompeii (figure from Hodske 2007).
[23] Five examples in the Villa dei Misteri and one in the Casa dei Quattro Stili (I.8.17) according to Maiuri (1940). See also Carrive 2017.

[24] Payne and Booms 2014.
[25] Plin. *HN*, 33.40.
[26] Plin. *HN*, 33.39.
[27] Plin. *HN*, 35.20 (*usta*, 6 denarii/*libra*).
[28] Plin. *HN*, 34.18.
[29] Plin. *HN*, 33.27 (7, 5, 3 denarii/*libra*).
[30] 'There are also two colours of very inferior quality, which have

Figure 3. Fragment of wall decoration from the Domus Aurea, corridor 92 (BM 1908,0417.8).
© The Trustees of the British Museum.

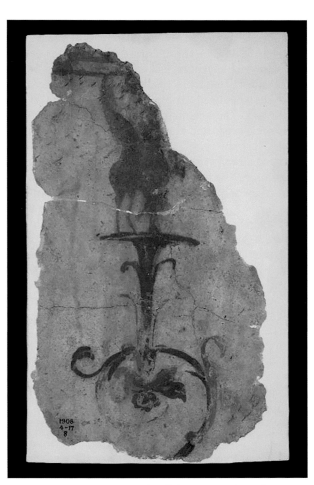

Figure 4. Fragment of wall decoration from the
Domus Aurea, room 119 (BM 1908,0417.5).
© The Trustees of the British Museum.

take these figures to be exact or not, they still suggest that substituting cinnabar for red ochre and red lead or using green earths rather than more expensive pigments could result in a considerable saving.

Egyptian blue offers a different case, for it was detected in the fragments pertaining to both corridor 92 and room 119. Unlike more expensive pigments such as cinnabar or malachite, Egyptian blue appears to have been consistently used in the realisation of wall paintings throughout the Roman Empire; it was repeatedly detected at various sites in Italy, Gaul, and Britain. Yet, according to Pliny, the price for one *libra* of high quality *vestorianus* was 44 HS,[31] comparable with what was paid for the rarely employed cinnabar and the other 'florid' colours.[32] Other blues referenced in Pliny's work are still considerably expensive,[33] an occurrence which casts some doubts on his reliability when compared with archaeological evidence.

The only other document we can use to infer pigment prices is Diocletian's Edict, which, however, was promulgated more than two centuries later. Still, it is possible, to some extent, to compare prices in the Edict with those recorded in the *Historia Naturalis* by using the wheat ratio as a conversion factor.

been recently discovered. One of these is the green known as *appianum*, a fair imitation of *chrysocolla*; just as though we had not had to mention sufficient of these counterfeits already. This colour, too, is prepared from a green chalk, the usual price of it being one sesterce per pound.' Plin. *HN*, 35.29.

[31] Plin. *HN*, 33.57.
[32] On this, see also Ceci and Becker 2020.
[33] *Lomentum* 40 HS, *caeruleum* 32 HS, *armenium* 24 HS (Plin. *HN*, 33.57 and 35.28).

For wheat prices in 1st- to 2nd-century AD Italy, I followed Rathbone in estimating an average price of 4 *sesterces* per *modius* of wheat.[34] If we compare this price with the 100 *denarii* per *modius castrensis* in Diocletian's Edict, it follows that one 1st-century AD *denarius* = 66.67 AD 301 *denarii*.[35] I used this figure to convert pigment prices recorded in the *Edictum de pretiis* into 1st-century AD prices (see **Table 2**). When we compare the two sets of prices, both similarities and discrepancies become apparent: the Edict's price for yellow ochre falls within the range presented by Pliny, and the price for cinnabar is considerable, even though not as expensive as in the *Historia Naturalis*. The main difference is offered by Egyptian blue, for the maximum cost for one *libra* of high quality pigment is considerably lower than the price for *vestorianus* recorded by Pliny (9 instead of 44 HS). Of course such a discrepancy might be connected with the difference in dates between these two sources, as well as with the fact that the Edict might have been mainly aimed at the eastern provinces of the empire. Yet, the lower price for Egyptian blue recorded in Diocletian's Edict appears to be more in line with its generally widespread use in Roman times.

If anything, this brief review proves that, with the evidence currently available, it is extremely difficult to assess pigment prices with a desirable degree of certainty, thus limiting our ability to fully appreciate all the productive and economic aspects connected with the making of Roman wall paintings.

Painting an 'average' Pompeian house: materials

If we now return to our 'average' Pompeian house, we can apply the prices collected in **Table 2** to reach a rough estimate of the cost of the pigments used to paint it. I first created a hypothetical painted wall,

inspired by those that can be observed throughout Pompeii in terms of both decorative motifs and colour, measuring *c.* 14.3 m² (**Figure 5**). I then used colour cluster analysis to calculate the quantity of pigments needed to paint it, by converting decorated surfaces into grams of pigments used. To do so, I applied Delamare's estimate of about 100 grams of pigment per square metre painted, a figure that was confirmed during the realisation of the Saint-Savin experimental fresco.[36] Colour cluster analysis was used to identify and quantify the representative colours of the different sections of the wall, which were listed by the software used for the task in the form of percentages.[37] The actual painted surface was obtained by simply multiplying the percentages for the total area of the wall that was being examined. In order to account for the presence of overlapping layers of colour, background colours were considered as covering the whole surface of the corresponding wall zone, while upper zone and interpanels were considered as painted directly on the last layer of plaster.

The reconstructed wall and resulting estimate do not include the figure panel in the centre of the wall. In order to calculate the quantity of pigments needed to paint the mythological scene, five figure panels were selected and the results of their colour cluster analyses were used to obtain an average of the colours employed. The selected samples are all intact and well preserved, and they represent scenes with two or more characters.[38] These figures were then added to those already calculated for the rest of the painted decoration. The total amount of pigments necessary to paint the analysed wall is c. 1170 grams (see **Table 3**).[39]

We can now proceed and multiply the amounts of different pigments by the prices recorded in ancient sources. Pliny's figures were favoured, using an average price where different ones were presented for varying qualities of the same type of pigment. There are only two exceptions: black and blue. The *Historia Naturalis* does not include prices for black pigments, instead I

[34] Rathbone 2009: 307–309. In suggesting 4 HS per *modius* as the iconic price for wheat, Rathbone turns to a number of different sources, such as Tacitus' *Annales*, where the author relates that during a shortage in AD 19 Tiberius set a maximum price and compensated merchants with 2 *nummi* (HS) per *modius* (Tac. *Ann.*, 2.87), possibly implying a subsidised price of 4 HS/*modius*. To this he adds an epigraph from the Forum Sempronii dated around AD 100–150, where it is recorded that a benefactor provided wheat at 1 *denarius* (4 HS) per *modius* (CIL XI, 6117), while in AD 93/4 the Roman governor of Antioch ordered for surplus stocks of wheat to be sold at a maximum price of 1 *denarius* per *modius* (AE 1925, 126b). The same price also appears in rabbinic texts, even though it might refer to the *modius castrensis* (Sperber 1974/1991: 102). The price of 1 *denarius* per *modius* can also be inferred from soldiers' pay before AD 84: if we assume that they received 5 *modii* of wheat per month, then the deduction of 240 *denarii* for rations amounts once again to our iconic price. Moreover, Seneca (*Ep. Mor.*, 80.7) calculates an allowance for a slave of 5 *modii* of wheat and 5 *denarii* per month, if we assume an half-and-half package, then the price for wheat appears to be once again 4 HS/*modius*. Lastly, Rathbone remarks on how almost all *alimenta* in Italy around AD 100 appear to be multiples of 4 HS.
[35] In calculating the wheat ratio between AD 79 and AD 301 *denarii* the difference in units of measure for grain was also considered: 1 *modius castrensis* = 1.5 standard *modii*. Once again I followed Rathbone (2009: 301).

[36] Delamare 1983: 74; Barbet and Coutelas 2002: 39.
[37] Image Color Summarizer v.0.76 © Martin Krzywinski. The number of colour clusters is inputted by the user.
[38] 'Alexander and Roxane' and 'Bacchus and Ariadne' from the Casa del Bracciale d'Oro (VI.17.42) at Pompeii (Pompei, Soprintendenza Archeologica, inv. 41657-41658); 'Sacrifice of Iphigenia' from the Casa del Poeta Tragico (VI.8.3) at Pompeii (Napoli, Museo Archeologico Nazionale, inv. 9112); 'Perseus freeing Andromeda' from the Casa dei (VI.9.6) at Pompeii (Napoli, Museo Archeologico Nazionale, inv. 8998); 'Io and Argos' from the Casa di Meleagro (VI.9.2) at Pompeii (Napoli, Museo Archeologico Nazionale, inv. 9556). See also Bologna 2019: 106–109 for a similar approach in the analysis of the Casa dei Pittori al Lavoro.
[39] Pale green was broken down into its components assuming a 1:2 ratio between green and white. Brown/dark orange was calculated as obtained by mixing 2 parts red, 1 part white, 1 part green. For pink a 1:2 ratio between red and white was assumed, for dark red a 1:1 ratio between red and black.

Pigment	Pliny	Diocletian's Edict conversion 1st c. AD	Diocletian's Edict
White (best quality) Aragonite?	c. 33 HS (paraetorium)		
White earth	1 HS (melinum)		
Cerussite/white lead	cerussa		
Yellow ochre (best quality)	8 HS (Attic sil)		
Yellow ochre	4 HS (marmorosum)		
Yellow ochre	3 HS? (pressum, Scyricum)	6 HS	100 denarii
Yellow ochre (low quality)	2 HS (from Achaia)		
Yellow ochre (low quality)	1.5 HS (lucidum, Gaul)		
Hematite/red ochre (best quality)	48 HS (sinopis)		
Hematite/red ochre (low quality)	2 HS (African, cicerculum)		
Cinnabar (best quality)	≤70 HS (from Baetica) 50 HS	30 HS	500 denarii
Cinnabar (lower quality)		18 HS	300 denarii
Red lead (best quality)	24 HS (usta/purpurea)		
Red lead (low quality)	1.25 HS (artificial sandaraca from burnt ceruse)		
Sandyx	0.6 HS (half rubrica half sandaraca, mineral origin, not from madder lake)	2.4 HS	40 denarii (organic or mineral?)
Egyptian blue (best quality)	44 HS (vestorianus)	9 HS	150 denarii
Egyptian blue (lower quality)		4.8 HS	80 denarii
Pale blue	40 HS (lomentum)		
Azurite	32 HS (caeruleum)		
Azurite	24 HS (armenium, in the past 300 HS)		
Blue (low quality)	1.25 HS (lomentum tritum)		
Malachite (different qualities)	28 – 20 – 12 HS (chrysocolla)		
Green earths (low quality)	1 HS (appianum)		
Purple (organic, from murex)	4 to 120 HS (purpurissum)		
Indigo	68–80 HS (indicum)		
Carbon black		0.72 HS	12 denarii (ink)

Table 2. Pigment prices expressed in HS per libra, from Pliny's *Historia Naturalis* and Diocletian's Edict. Prices in the Edict were converted to 1st-century AD prices based on wheat price.

	Activity	Man-hours
Extraction and manufacturing	Quarrying	1,328,670
	Roughing-out	1,915,200
Transport	Loading wagons	31,920
	Transport by wagons (quarry-river, 1.5 km)	64,638
	Unloading wagons	15,960
	Loading ship	31,920
	Transport by ship (river, 20 km)	53,850
	Unloading ship	63,840
	Loading wagons	31,920
	Transport by wagons (river-construction site, 0.3 km)	13,167
	Unloading wagons	15,960
	TOTAL	**3,567,045**

Table 1. The effort required by the different activities connected to the stone supply for the façade of the amphitheatre of Verona.

been necessary for the roughing-out of the stone blocks, an activity which took place in the quarries.[15]

Subsequently, the stone blocks had to be transported from the quarries to the construction site. First, they had to be loaded onto wagons to be transferred from the extraction basin to the embarkation point on the river Adige, to cover a distance of about 1.5 km. Assuming the use of wagons drawn by a pair of oxen and capable of carrying one tonne of stone,[16] we can calculate that about 112,500 man-hours would have been necessary to transport the material from the quarries to the river (including the loading and unloading activities, which involved three men minimum).[17] Once the wagon was unloaded, the blocks were loaded onto a ship, which would have sailed from Valpolicella to Verona, covering a distance of about 20 km. Assuming the use of boats with a capacity of 20 tonnes,[18] the transport of all the stone blocks employed in the amphitheatre would have required about

1,800 trips[19] of 30 hours each (round trip), for a total of about 54,000 man-hours of work.[20] Considering also the loading and unloading operations, the river transport would have required about 150,000 man-hours of work in total.[21] Lastly, once unloaded from the ships, the stones had to be loaded again onto a wagon to reach the construction site, to cover a distance of 300 m, an activity that would have required 61,000 man-hours of work.[22] All things considered, a minimum of 3,500,000 man-hours of work were needed to get the stone necessary to build the façade of the amphitheatre of Verona (**Table 1**).

[15] According to Pegoretti, the roughing-out requires 144 h/m³ (Pegoretti 1843: 298, tab. 9, 2a). This equates to 13,300 m³ × 144 h = 1,915,200 man-hours.

[16] Considering the loading limit for an ox-cart (presumably with a single yoke) can vary between 400 and 640 kg (for bibliographical references, see DeLaine 1997: 108), I have assumed that the loading limit for a wagon pulled by two oxen would be around 1000 kg = 1 tonne.

[17] Assuming that each wagon could transport 1 tonne of stone, we can calculate that to transport 13,300 m³ of stone (= 35,910 t, given that the calcare della Valpolicella weighs 2.7 t/m³) 35,910 trips were necessary. Assuming a maximum speed of 1.67 km/h (DeLaine 1997: 98 and 108), we can calculate that each trip required 1.8 hours, and so 35,910 trips required 64,638 man-hours. The loading activities (Pegoretti 1843: 176) required 0.8 h/m³, for a total of 10,640 hours of work of 3 men (=31,920 man-hours), and the unloading activities 0.4 h/m³, for a total of 5,320 hours of work of 3 men (=15,960 man-hours).

[18] This capacity is suggested by the data provided by the cargo of some shipwrecks found in the rivers of northern Italy (Previato and Zara 2014).

[19] 35,910 tonnes / 20 tonnes per boat = 1,795 trips.

[20] Assuming a speed of 1.65 km/h for the outward trip, downstream, and a speed of 1.1 km/h for the return trip, upstream, we can calculate that the outward trip required about 12 hours (20 km/1.65 km/h = 12.12 h), and the return trip 18 hours (20 km/1.1 km/h = 18.18 h), for a total of about 30 hours for the round trip. As a result: 1,795 trips × 30 hours = 53,850 hours. The rate of travel was calculated based on information provided by *Philostratus* about the time needed to go up the river Tiber from Ostia to Rome (Philostr., *Vit. Apoll.*, VII, 16 and Le Gall 2005: 287), according to which to cover a distance of about 28 km upstream 3 days were necessary. This means that the boats sailed at a speed of about 1.1 km/h. This rate was used for the return trip from Verona to Valpolicella (upstream), while for the outward trip I assumed a speed of 1.65 km/h, which I calculated proportionally based on the ratio between the values proposed by Pegoretti for transport by river, that were considerably higher (Pegoretti 1843: 16).

[21] The loading activities (Pegoretti 1843: 176) required 0.8 h/m³, for a total of 10,640 hours of work of 3 men (=31,920 man-hours), and the unloading activities 1.6 h/m³, for a total of 21,280 hours of work of 3 men (=63,840 man-hours).

[22] For the number of trips and man-hours required for loading and unloading, see footnote 17. Considering a speed of 1.67 km/h, each trip required about 22 minutes. As a consequence, 35,910 trips required 790,020 minutes (=13,167 hours). hours of work of 3 men (=15,960 man-hours).

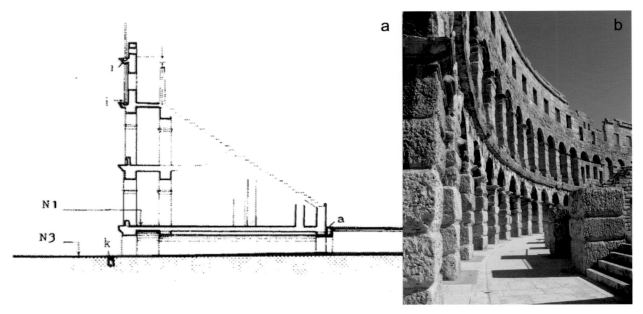

Figure 6. The façade of the amphitheatre of Pola: a) section (from Tosi 2003); b) photo by the author.

The amphitheatre of Pola

The second building examined is the amphitheatre of Pola.[23] As in Verona, the building was situated outside the city walls, in the proximity of a road which connected Pola to Tergeste, the Via Flavia. The construction of the amphitheatre dates to the 1st century AD: most scholars agree that the building was built within the Augustan period and then enlarged during the reign of Claudius.

The building measured 132.45 x 105.10 m and could contain about 22,000 spectators. It was partly built on substructures and partly on the slope of a hill. The cavea was made of 40 steps divided into two maeniana. The façade was composed of two orders of 72 arches overlapped by an attic of 64 rectangular windows. It was enriched by four towers (one for each quadrant), each of which contained a wooden staircase and was provided with two tanks on the top, maybe used for sparsiones (**Figure 6**). With regard to the building materials and techniques employed in the amphitheatre, the substructures and the radial walls were constructed in opus caementicium with a wall facing in opus vittatum, while the external ring (façade and towers) was built in opus quadratum. The stone blocks of the façade were large and heavy monoliths with bossed faces, similar to those of Verona.

Different types of limestone were employed in the building. In the inner parts, where stone elements of relatively small dimensions or slabs were needed, a limestone from the immediate vicinity of Pola (the Rakalj quarry) and another stone possibly from the Solina Bay (near Rovinj) were used. For the façade, which was made of large and massive blocks, a different type of limestone was used from the 'Cava Romana' or Vinkuran quarry, situated 4 km south to Pola (**Figure 7**).[24] This extraction site was selected by the builders of the amphitheatre because of the quality of the natural rock, which permitted the extraction of blocks without limitations in height.

Let us now focus on the effort required for the construction of the façade. Considering the dimensions of its different parts, we can calculate that about 15,800 m³ of limestone were necessary to complete the construction, including the towers.[25] To quarry such a quantity of stone, assuming the values provided by Pegoretti, we can calculate that about 1,580,000 man-hours of work by three men were needed[26] and an additional 2,275,000 hours were necessary to rough-out the blocks.[27]

The heavy blocks extracted in the quarry then had to be transferred to the construction site. It is likely that this was done by sea, taking advantage of the small

[23] On the amphitheatre of Pola: Mirabella Roberti 1939; Mlakar 1976; Golvin 1988: 159 and 171–173; Tosi 2003: 521–523; Maggi 2007: 45–47.

[24] The provenience of the stones employed in the façade was established by archaeometrical analysis carried out on samples taken from the external ring, which were compared with samples taken in the Vinkuran quarry. On the origin of the stones of the amphitheatre of Pola: Crnkovic 1991.
[25] The precise number is 15,812 m³. The calculation was based on the published dimensions of the amphitheatre and on those derived from plans and sections of the building.
[26] To extract 15,800 m³ of stone 526,140 hours were needed. Considering the effort of 3 men: 526,140 h × 3 men = 1,578,420 man-hours. See fn. 14 for the rate.
[27] This equates to 15,800 m³ × 144 h = 2,275,200 man-hours. See fn. 15 for the rate.

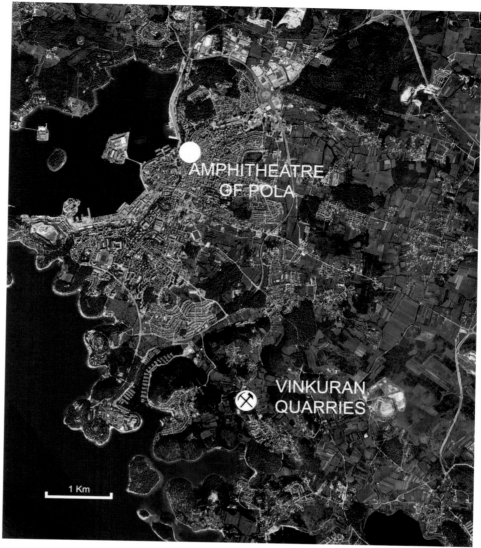

Figure 7. The position of the Vinkuran quarries with respect to the amphitheatre of Pola (Google Earth with additions by author).

distance between the quarry and the shore (1 km) and between the construction site and the coast (200 m), as well as the distance to be covered by ship (about 13 km). The first step of this route was the transport of the blocks from the quarry of Vinkuran to the seaside. The blocks were probably carried on ox-wagons, which had to cover a distance of about 1 km. Considering the time required both by the trip and by the loading and unloading activities, we can calculate that about 108,000 man-hours were needed to complete this operation.[28] The blocks then had to be taken by the ship

to the construction site, covering a distance of about 13 km by sea, and then unloaded. Assuming also in this case the use of ships with a capacity of 20 tonnes, we can hypothesise that 2,133 trips by sea would have been needed, requiring about three hours each (round trip), for a total of about 7,400 hours.[29] Considering also the loading and unloading operations, the transport of the stone by sea required roughly 121,000 man-hours of work.[30] Finally, another 67,000 hours would have been necessary to transport the stone from the seaside

---

[28] Assuming that each wagon could transport 1 ton of stone, we can calculate that to transport 15,800 m³ of stone (= 42,660 t, given that the limestone of the Vinkuran quarry weighs 2.7 t/m³) 42,660 trips were necessary. Considering a speed of 1.67 km/h, a round trip required 72 minutes. As a consequence, 42,660 trips required 51,192 hours (42,660 × 72 minutes = 3,071,520 minutes = 51,192 hours). The loading activities (Pegoretti 1843: 176) required 0.8 h/m³, for a total of 12,640 hours of work of 3 men (=37,920 man-hours), and the unloading activities 0.4 h/m³, for a total of 6,320,000 hours of work of 3 men (=18,960 man-hours).

[29] The distance to be covered was about 13 km. Assuming a speed of 7.4 km/h (= 4 knots; this value was selectedbased on information provided by DeLaine 1997: 108 and Russell 2013: 110–111), we can calculate that a round trip required 3.5 hours (13 km/7.4 km/h = 1.75 h). This equates to 2,133 trips × 3.5 hours = 7,465 hours.

[30] The loading activities (Pegoretti 1843: 176) required 0.8 h/m³, for a total of 12,640 hours of work, and the unloading activities 1.6 h/m³, for a total of 25,280 hours of work for 3 men (=75,840 man-hours).

	Activity	Man-hours
Extraction and manufacturing	Quarrying	1,579,998
	Roughing-out	2,275,200
Transport	Loading wagons	37,920
	Transport by wagons (quarry-sea, 1 km)	51,192
	Unloading wagons	18,960
	Loading ship	37,920
	Transport by ship (sea, 13 km)	7,465
	Unloading ship	75,840
	Loading wagons	37,920
	Transport by wagons (sea-construction site, 0.2 km)	9,954
	Unloading wagons	18,960
	TOTAL	**4,151,329**

Table 2. The effort required by the different activities connected to the stone supply for the façade of the amphitheatre of Pola.

to the construction site.[31] As a result, to get the stone necessary to build the façade of the amphitheatre of Pola a minimum of about 4,150,000 man-hours of work would have been needed (**Table 2**).

The amphitheatre of Padova

The third case study examined is the amphitheatre of Padova.[32] Also in this case, the building was situated outside the city wall, very close to the river *Meduacus*, which passed through the city in ancient times. It was built in the first half of the 1st century AD, measured 134.26 x 97.3 m, and could contain about 17,000 spectators. Therefore, it was smaller than the amphitheatres of Verona and Pola, but at the same time shared features, such as construction on substructures: the *cavea* in fact was supported by a series of galleries, partially walkable. The internal walls of the building were built in *opus caementicium*, with a revetment in *opus vittatum*, while the façade was built in *opus quadratum*. Two different stone materials were employed to construct it: a limestone quarried on the Berici Hills was used in the wall facing of the internal walls, while the Euganean trachyte was used in the external ring and for the load-bearing structures. The

latter is a magmatic stone, which was quarried in the Euganean Hills, an extraction district situated about 15 km west of Padova which in the Roman period was largely exploited for stone employed in the city and in many other urban centres of Northern Italy (**Figure 8**).[33] As regards the façade of the amphitheatre, it is characterised by a lower degree of preservation than those of the amphitheatres of Verona and Pola, but the information provided by the excavations of the last century and the examination of the stone blocks uncovered permitted a hypothetical reconstruction of the original layout of the external ring.[34] According to the majority of scholars, it is believed that it was composed of two orders of 80 arches overlapped by an attic, for a total height of about 16 metres (**Figure 9**).

Let us now focus on the effort required to build the façade. Considering its layout, we can calculate that about 7,200 m³ of trachyte were necessary to build it.[35] Assuming the values provided by Pegoretti, we can calculate that to quarry such a quantity of trachyte about 1,500,000 man-hours of work would have been needed,[36] while another roughly 1,530,000 hours would have been necessary for shaping and

---

[31] The distance to be covered was about 200 m. Considering the use of ox-wagons with a capacity of 1 tonne, 42,660 trips were necessary. Assuming a speed of 1.67 km/h, we can calculate that each round trip required 14 minutes, meaning that 42,660 trips required 597,240 minutes = 9,954 hours. Another 37,920 and 18,960 man-hours respectively were needed for the loading and unloading operations (see fn. 28).

[32] On the amphitheatre of Padova: Brunelli Bonetti 1916; *Anfiteatro Padova* 1981; Golvin 1988: 120; Tosi 2003: 514–516; Maggi 2007: 43–44; Bressan 2018a, 2018b.

[33] On the use and trade of Euganean trachyte, see Zara 2018 and Germinario *et al.* 2018. Euganean trachyte was largely exported and used in many cities of northern and central Italy to pave the urban streets.

[34] Fardin *et al.* 1996.

[35] The precise number is 7,208 m³. Also in this case, the calculation was based on the published dimensions of the amphitheatre and on those extractable from plans and sections of the building.

[36] According to Pegoretti (Pegoretti 1843: 78, analisi 5), quarrying 1 m³ of a siliceous stone requires 70 h/m³. Therefore, to extract 7,208 m³ of stone 504,560 hours were needed. Considering the effort of 3 men: 504,560 h × 3 men = 1,513,680 man-hours.

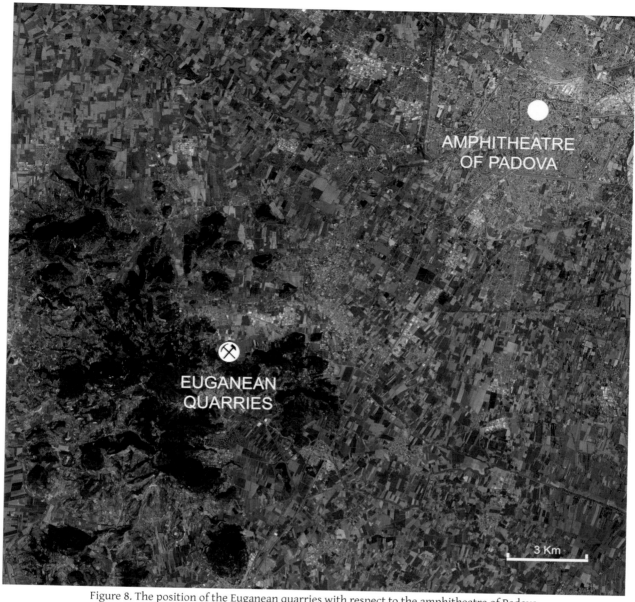

Figure 8. The position of the Euganean quarries with respect to the amphitheatre of Padova (Google Earth with additions by author).

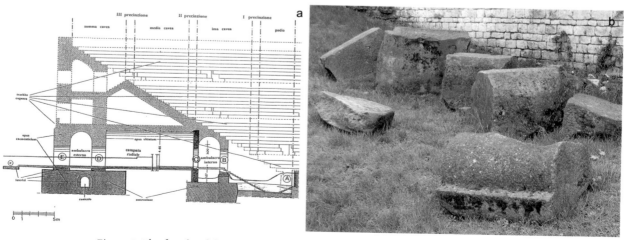

Figure 9. The façade of the amphitheatre of Padova: a) section (from Fardin *et al.* 1996); b) photo by the author.

	Activity	Man-hours
Extraction and manufacturing	Quarrying	1,513,680
	Roughing-out	1,537,682
Transport	Loading ship	17,299
	Transport by ship (sea, 13 km)	28,860
	Unloading ship	34,598
	Loading wagons	17,299
	Transport by wagons (sea-construction site, 0.2 km)	8,981
	Unloading wagons	8,649
	TOTAL	**3,167,048**

Table 3. The effort required by the different activities connected to the stone supply for the façade of the amphitheatre of Padova.

roughing-out activities.[37] Once extracted and shaped, the stone blocks had then to be transported to Padova. The transport was facilitated also in this case by the presence of waterways which passed in the vicinity of the quarries and permitted easy access to the urban centres of the region. In particular, the connection between the Euganean Hills and Padova was guaranteed by the river Bacchiglione, which flows to the north of the hills and then through the city. It is precisely this river which was used to transfer the stone blocks extracted in the Euganean Hills to the construction site of the amphitheatre of Padova. Although the quarries were situated about 4 km from the river, thanks to the presence of several canals, the stone blocks could have been directly loaded onto boats. The distance to be covered by sailing was 20 km. As a consequence, considering the quantity of stone to be transferred and assuming the use of boats with a capacity of 20 tonnes, we can calculate that about 960 trips (round trip) would have been necessary,[38] for a total effort of about 80,600 man-hours of work, considering also the loading and unloading operations.[39] Once in Padova, the stone blocks were probably unloaded at the fluvial harbour of the city, which was situated just 400 m south of the amphitheatre. It is likely that to transport the stones from the harbour to the construction site ox-wagons were used. Assuming the use of wagons with a capacity

of 1 tonne and considering the distance to be covered (400 m), we can calculate that this activity required approximately 35,000 man-hours of work.[40] As a result, to get the stone necessary to build the façade of the amphitheatre a minimum of about 3,200,000 man-hours would have been needed (**Table 3**).

The dynamics of stone supply in the construction process of the amphitheatres of Regio X: a comparison

The quantitative analysis of the dynamics of stone supply can be accomplished in relation to buildings similar in respect to both architectural features and distance/connectivity to the quarries but different in terms of type of stone employed. By comparing the data, we notice that the figures obtained are different in regard to the total number of man-hours required in the supply process, but have some similarities in the ratio between the effort required by the different activities connected with the stone supply (**Figure 10**). In fact, the time needed for the first two stages (extraction and roughing-out of the blocks) for all cases is significantly greater than the time needed for the transport of the stone blocks from the quarries to the construction sites. Moreover, we notice that the first two steps of the production process are the most costly, in the case of the amphitheatres of Verona and Pola the most expensive activity is the roughing-out (respectively 54% and 55% of the total effort) followed by the quarrying (37% and

[37] According to Pegoretti, the roughing-out requires 213.33 h/m³ (Pegoretti 1843: 291, tab. 8, 2a). As a consequence: 7,208 m³ × 213.33 h = 1,537,682 man-hours.

[38] Assuming that 7,208 m³ = 19,245 tonnes (given that the Euganean trachyte weighs 2.67 t/m³), by using boats with a capacity of 20 tonnes, 962 trips were necessary (19,245/20 = 962).

[39] The distance to be covered was about 20 km. 962 trips × 30 hours = 28,860 hours; see fn. 20 for the rates. The loading activities (Pegoretti 1843: 176) required 0.8 h/m³, for a total of 5,766 hours of work of 3 men (=17,299 man-hours), and the unloading activities 1.6 h/m³, for a total of 11,533 hours of work for 3 men (=34,598 man-hours).

[40] To transport 7,208 m³ of stone, 19,245 trips were necessary. Assuming a speed of 1.67 km/h, each round trip required 28 minutes. As a consequence, 19,245 trips required 538,860 minutes, that is 8,981 hours. The loading activities (Pegoretti 1843: 176) required 0.8 h/m³, for a total of 5,766.4 hours of work of 3 men (=17,299 man-hours), and the unloading activities 0.4 h/m³, for a total of 2,883.2 hours of work for 3 men (=8,649.6 man-hours).

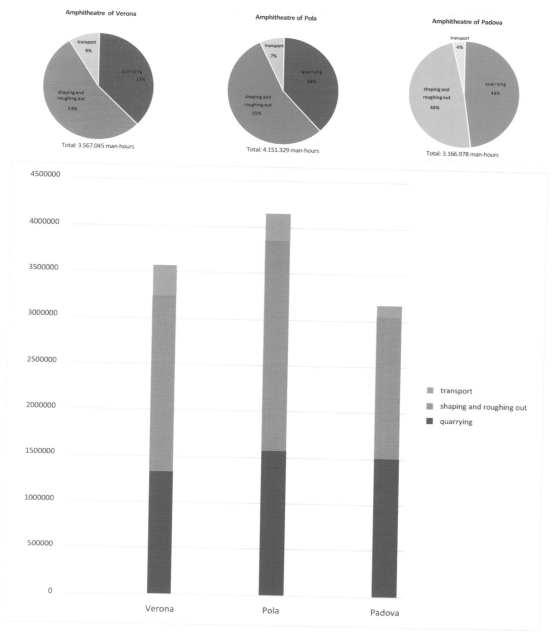

Figure 10. Graphs showing the total effort required by supplying stone for the façades of the amphitheatres of Verona, Pola, and Padova.

38%), while in the case of the amphitheatre of Padova the effort required by these two activities is identical (48% for the quarrying and 48% for the roughing-out).

In contrast, the transport figures look very similar: in the three cases examined the effort required to transfer the stone from the quarries to the building site was very low and would have had a low impact on the economics of the construction process (4–9% of the total effort). The lowest travel rate is that of the amphitheatre of Padova, even though the waterway used (river) and the distance (20 km) to transfer the stone to the construction site are identical to that of the

amphitheatre of Verona. This difference is attributable to the fact that, in the case of Padova, the supplying of trachyte required only two modes of transport (boat and then wagon), while in the case of Verona, three different modes of transport were needed (wagon – ship – wagon) to transfer the Valpolicella limestone with an additional trans-shipment necessary to bring the stone blocks from the quarries to the construction site. Despite these differences, the transport rate in all cases looks very low in respect to the effort required by the quarrying and manufacturing activities. More generally, this shows the convenience of the use of waterways in the stone trade and the important

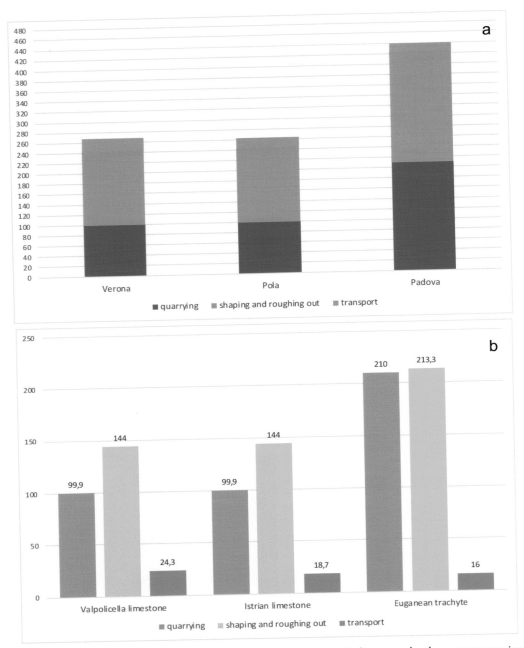

Figure 11a–b. Graphs showing the different effort required to get 1 m³ of stone in the three cases examined.

role played by the accessibility of the quarries to the economics of ancient construction processes.[41]

However, in comparing the figures obtained we should not forget that the quantity of stone required for the construction of the three buildings was different due to their size. Therefore, to have a realistic picture of the economic impact of the stone supply, we should compare the effort required to obtain the same quantity of stone, for example 1 m³ (**Figure 11a**). By doing so, the differences become more visible.

In general, we notice that while the labour required to obtain 1 m³ of Valpolicella limestone for the amphitheatre of Verona looks very similar to that required to get 1 m³ of Vinkuran limestone for the amphitheatre of Pola, the labour necessary to obtain the same quantity of trachyte was far greater. This is due to the different effort required by the first two activities of the production process (quarrying and roughing-out the stone blocks). Moreover (**Figure 11b**), we can observe that quarrying 1 m³ of trachyte required twice

---

[41] On these topics and more in general about the economics of the stone trade in ancient times: Russell 2013 and Russell 2018.

the effort as the extraction of 1 m³ both of limestone of Valpolicella and of limestone of Vinkuran, while roughing-out 1 m³ of trachyte was one and a half times more challenging than roughing-out 1 m³ of limestone.

These differences clearly are due to the different features of the types of stone employed in the three buildings. The limestone of Valpolicella and the limestone of the Vinkuran quarry in fact, employed respectively in the amphitheatre of Verona and Pola, are very similar: they are both compact limestones with an identical specific weight (2.7 kg/m³). In contrast, the trachyte of the Euganean Hills employed in the amphitheatre of Padova, is a magmatic rock which is very difficult both to quarry and work.

This points to the fact that with equal accessibility of the quarries (similar distance from the construction site and similar connectivity by means of waterways), limestones were generally cheaper than magmatic stones. Clearly the choice of the type of stone to be employed in a building was crucial for the overall budget of a construction project. This choice was obviously influenced by the type of resources available to the builders in the territory and the financial resources of the commissioner. In the case of the amphitheatre of Padova, for example, to construct the façade another kind of stone could have been used, that is the limestone of the Berici Hills. This limestone was easier to quarry and work and was available to the builders, as proven by the fact that they employed it in the internal walls of the building. However, the disposable funds of this project provided the possibility to select and use the Euganean trachyte, which was more expensive but also more appropriate for the load-bearing structures which composed the façade of the amphitheatre.

The cost of the amphitheatres

To conclude, by comparing the data provided by the quantitative analysis some considerations on the dynamics of stone supply in *Regio X* at the beginning of the imperial period and, more generally, on the dynamics of stone supply in ancient times can be drawn.

The analysis carried out shows that similar construction projects in different cities of the same region followed similar patterns in the dynamics of stone supply. In all the cases examined, the ancient builders chose stones of good quality that were easily accessible from the cities where the amphitheatres were built. All the selected quarries in fact were situated at a distance not exceeding 15 km from the construction site and were well connected to the city by means of waterways (river/sea). We do not have information about the ownership of the quarries from which the stone was taken, but it is likely that they were property of the cities where the

construction process took place or of wealthy citizens of those cities.[42] Such connections would have impacted the choice of these materials for construction.

Despite these similarities, by quantifying the price per cubic metre required to supply the stones for the three amphitheatres, we obtain different values and can draw up a sort of price list. The 'price' of the first two stones is really similar: the cost of one cubic metre of Valpolicella limestone in fact can be quantified at about 268 man-hours of work, with the cost of the Vinkuran limestone at 263 man-hours per cubic metre. The cost of the trachyte instead looks far higher and almost double compared to the first two: in fact, it can be quantified at 439 man-hours per cubic metre. This shows that the trachyte was more expensive due to the fact that it was harder to quarry and work than limestone. As a consequence, the construction of a building made of trachyte in Padova was more expensive than building an analogous building in Verona or Pola using the limestone quarried in the vicinity of those cities, even though the distance and connectivity between the quarries and the construction sites were similar. Therefore, on the basis of the figures obtained we cannot exclude that this difference in cost influenced the construction projects and also the size of the amphitheatres built in these cities. Maybe the amphitheatres of Verona and Pola were larger than the one of Padova because of the different cost required for the supply of the building stone?

To really conclude... some final remarks about methodology

To really conclude my paper, I would like to point out some final remarks about the quantification methodology derived from my personal experience in this field of study.

In my opinion, the quantitative approach successfully introduced by Janet DeLaine in the 1990s has been a great innovation in the study of ancient architecture, firstly because its application obliges scholars to deeply reflect on the different stages of the chaîne opératoire of the construction process. Secondly, it can really help to analyse the economics of ancient buildings.

In applying this approach and in order to limit the number of errors, it is undoubtedly very important to have a deep knowledge of the context in which a building is situated in terms of geography, connectivity, natural resources, etc., as well as of the building itself in terms of dimensions, layout, and construction characteristics. However, the reconstruction of the building process in terms of energetics is a path full of pitfalls due to the large number of variables and because

---

42 Buonopane 1987: 207–208.

it is not always easy to understand and select the right formulas and values provided by building manuals like that of Pegoretti. Therefore, the final figures obtained could be incorrect. In addition, different scholars frequently apply the same formulas in different ways, and so their results look incomparable. So, how to solve these issues?

As regards the final figures, the application of the quantitative method is still valuable, because even if it provides figures which may not be correct in absolute terms, it can provide an order of magnitude of the economics of an ancient building, and this is already a great achievement. However, to make it even more valuable, the results obtained by different scholars on different buildings should be comparable. This is possible only if in the future all scholars discuss their approach and strive to standardise their formulas. By applying the same formulas in the same way, it would be possible to make comparisons between different buildings and different construction processes, and to shed light on the economics of the construction industry in a specific context or in a specific chronological framework, as I tried to do within my research on the amphitheatres of *Regio X*.

Bibliography

Anfiteatro Padova 1981 = *L'anfiteatro di Padova. Miscellanea di Studi* (Supplemento di Archeologia Veneta). Padova: Società archeologica veneta.

Arich, D. and F. Spaliviero (eds) 2002. *L'Arena di Verona. Duemila anni di storia e di spettacolo.* Verona: Accademia di Belle arti G.B. Cignaroli.

Basso, P. 1999. *Architettura e memoria dell'antico. Teatri, anfiteatri e circhi della Venetia romana.* Roma: «L'Erma» di Bretschneider.

Basso, P. 2013. Le tecniche edilizie: qualche considerazione, in P. Basso and G. Cavalieri Manasse (eds) *Storia dell'architettura del Veneto. L'età romana e tardoantica*: 160–165. Venezia: Marsilio.

Bolla, M. 2012. *L'Arena di Verona.* Sommacampagna: Cierre.

Bonetto, J. and C. Previato 2018. The construction process of the Republican city walls of Aquileia (northeastern Italy). A case study of the quantitative analysis on ancient buildings, in A. Brysbaert, V. Klinkenberg, A. Gutiérrez Garcia-M. and I. Vikatou (eds) *Construction monuments, perceiving monumentality and the economics of building*: 309–330. Leiden: Sidestone Press.

Bressan, M. 2018a. L'anfiteatro romano di Padova. Un secolo e (quasi) mezzo di ricerca archeologica e prospettive future, in R. Deiana (ed.) *La Cappella degli Scrovegni nell'anfiteatro romano di Padova: nuove ricerche e questioni irrisolte*: 59–89. Padova: Padova University Press.

Bressan, M. 2018b. L'anfiteatro romano di Padova. Uno studio degli ambienti sotterranei, in F. Veronese (ed.) *Livio, Padova e l'universo veneto* (Venetia 6): 149–169. Roma: «L'Erma» di Bretschneider.

Brugnoli, P. (ed.) 1999. *Marmi e lapicidi di Sant'Ambrogio in Valpolicella dall'età romana all'età napoleonica.* Sant'Ambrogio in Valpolicella: Centro di documentazione per la storia della Valpolicella.

Brunelli Bonetti, F. 1916. Studi intorno all'anfiteatro romano di Padova. *Atti e Memorie dell'Accademia Patavina di Scienze, Lettere e Arti* XXXII: 352–362.

Buonopane, A. 1987. Estrazione, lavorazione e commercio dei materiali lapidei, in E. Buchi (ed.) *Il Veneto nell'età romana*, 1: 187–224. Verona: Banca Popolare di Verona.

Crnkovic, B. 1991. The origin of the dimension stone of the Arena in Pula. *Rudarsko-geološkonaftni zbornik* 3: 63–67.

Courault, C. 2015. La fondation de Cordoue à partir d'une étude quantitative de la muraille républicaine. Un premier essai. *Romula* 14: 29–51.

DeLaine, J. 1997. *The baths of Caracalla. A study in the design, construction, and economics of largescale building projects in imperial Rome* (Journal of Roman Archaeology. Supplementary series 25). Portsmouth, Rhode Island: JRA.

DeLaine, J. 2015. The Pantheon Builders: Estimating Manpower for Construction, in T.A. Marder and M. Wilson Jones (eds) *The Pantheon. From Antiquity to the Present*: 160–192. New York: Cambridge University Press.

DeLaine, J. 2017. Quantifying Manpower and the Cost of Construction in Roman Building Projects: Research Perspectives. *Archeologia dell'Architettura* 22: 13–19.

DeLaine, J. 2018. Economic choice in Roman construction: case studies from Ostia, in A. Brysbaert, V. Klinkenberg, A. Gutiérrez Garcia-M. and I. Vikatou (eds) *Construction monuments, perceiving monumentality and the economics of building*: 243–269. Leiden: Sidestone Press.

Fardin, A., E. Rossato and S. Tiepolo 1996. L'anfiteatro di Padova: la conoscenza della forma architettonica e nuova ipotesi della configurazione originaria. *Bollettino del Museo Civico di Padova* LXXXV: 21–47.

Germinario *et al.* 2018 = Germinario, L., A. Zara, L. Maritan, J. Bonetto, J.M. Hanchar, R. Sassi, S. Siegesmund and C. Mazzoli 2018. Tracking trachyte on the Roman routes: provenance study of Roman infrastructure and insights into ancient trades in northern Italy. *Geoarchaeology* 33: 417–429.

Golvin, J.C. 1988. *L'amphitéâtre romain. Essai sur le théorisation de sa forme et de ses fonctions.* Paris: Diffusion de Boccard.

Lazzarini, L. and M. Van Molle 2015. Local and imported lithotypes in Roman times in the Southern part of the X Regio Augustea Venetia et Histria, in E.

Gasparini and P. Pensabene (eds) ASMOSIA X: 699–711. Roma: «L'Erma» di Bretschneider.

Le Gall, J. 2005. *Il Tevere fiume di Roma nell'antichità*. Roma: Quasar.

Maggi, S. 2007. *Anfiteatri e città nella Cisalpina romana (dall'antichità al contemporaneo)*. Pavia: Pavia University Press.

Mar, R. and P. Pensabene 2010. Finanziamenti dell'edilizia pubblica e calcolo dei costi dei materiali lapidei: il caso del Foro Superiore di Tarraco, in S. Camporeale, A. Pizzo and H. Dessales (eds) *Arqueología de la construcción II. Los procesos constructivos en el mundo romano: Italia y provincias orientales* (Anejos de Archivo Español de Arquelogía 57): 509–537. Madrid-Mérida: Consejo Superior de Investigaciones Científicas.

Maschek, D. 2016. The marble stoa at Hierapolis. Materials, labour force and building costs, in T. Ismaelli and G. Scardozzi (eds) *Ancient quarries and building sites in Asia Minor. Research on Hierapolis in Phrygia and other cities in south-western Anatolia: archaeology, archaeometry, conservation*: 393–402. Bari: Edipuglia.

Mirabella Roberti, M. 1939. *L'Arena di Pola*. Pola: Stab. Tip. F. Rocco.

Mlakar, S. 1976. *Das Amphitheater in Pula*. Pula: Archäologisches Museum Istriens.

Pakkanen, J. 2013. The Economics of Shipshed Complexes: Zea, a Case Study, in D. Blackman, B. Rankov, K. Baika, H. Gerding and J. Pakkanen (eds) *Shipsheds of the Ancient Mediterranean*: 55–75. Cambridge: Cambridge University Press.

Pegoretti, G. 1843. *Manuale pratico per l'estimazione dei lavori architettonici, stradali, idraulici e di fortificazione per uso degli ingegneri ed architetti*. Milano: Monti.

Pensabene, P. 1983. Osservazioni sulla diffusione dei marmi e sul loro prezzo nella Roma imperiale. *Dialoghi di Archeologia* III/1: 55–63.

Previato, C. 2015. Tra monti, fiumi e mare: l'estrazione e il commercio della pietra nella Regio X - Venetia et Histria, in F. Cambi, G. De Venuto and R. Goffredo (eds) *I pascoli, i campi, il mare. Paesaggi d'altura e di pianura in Italia dall'Età del Bronzo al Medioevo* (Storia e Archeologia Globale 2): 31–49. Bari: Edipuglia.

Previato, C. 2018. Aurisina limestone in the Roman Age: from Karst quarries to the cities of the Adriatic basin, in D. Matetić Poljak and K. Marasović (eds) *ASMOSIA XI - Interdisciplinary Studies of Ancient Stone*, Proceedings of the Eleventh International Conference of ASMOSIA (Split, 18–22 May 2015): 933–939. Split: University of Split.

Previato, C. and A. Zara 2014. Il trasporto della pietra di Vicenza in età romana. Il relitto del fiume Bacchiglione. *Marmora* 10: 59–78.

Previato, C. and A. Zara 2018. A Database and GIS project about quarrying, circulation and use of stone during the Roman age in Regio X - Venetia et Histria. The case study of Euganean trachyte, in D. Matetić Poljak and K. Marasović (eds) *ASMOSIA XI - Interdisciplinary Studies of Ancient Stone*, Proceedings of the Eleventh International Conference of ASMOSIA (Split, 18–22 May 2015): 597–609. Split: University of Split.

Russell, B. 2013. *The economics of the Roman stone trade*. Oxford: Oxford University Press.

Russell, B. 2018. Stone Use and the Economy. Demand, Distribution, and the State, in A. Wilson and A. Bowman (eds) *Trade, commerce and the State in the Roman world*: 236–263. Oxford/New York: Oxford University Press.

Spettacolo in Aquileia e nella Cisalpina Romana 1994 = *Spettacolo in Aquileia e nella Cisalpina Romana* (Antichità Altoadriatiche 41). Udine: Arti grafiche friulane.

Tosi, G. 1994. Gli edifici per spettacolo di Verona, in *Spettacolo in Aquileia e nella Cisalpina Romana*: 241–251.

Tosi, G. 2003. *Gli edifici per spettacoli nell'Italia romana*. Roma: Quasar.

Trivisonno, F. 2015/2016. Le cave di calcare dei Colli Berici. Archeologia e valorizzazione, Tesi di laurea magistrale. Padova: Università degli Studi di Padova.

Zara, A. 2018. *La trachite euganea. Archeologia e storia di una risorsa lapidea del Veneto antico* (Antenor Quaderni 44). Roma: Quasar.

Templi romani giganteschi in Asia Minore:
Problemi di costi e di finanziamento

Paolo Barresi

Faculty of Classical, Linguistic and Formation Studies, Università Kore, Enna

paolo.barresi@unikore.it

Abstract

The Roman marble temples at Cyzicus, merchant city near the marble quarries of Proconnesus, and Tarsus in *Cilicia*, both of which were probably connected to the imperial cult (*neokoria*), have recently been the subject of excavation and research. It is therefore now possible to undertake a more detailed study on the quantity of marble used for their construction. The large dipteral temple at Cyzicus, built between the Hadrianic and Severan periods, was one of the greatest temples in the Roman world, but there are only scanty remains still on site. The large temple peristyle, with columns of 70 Roman feet and a substructure in local stone and *opus caementicium*, used a large amount of marble from the the nearby by Proconnesus quarries. The so-called *Donuk Taş*, a a pseudo-dipteral temple at Tarsus (21 x 10 columns), had roughly the same dimensions and chronology, but it was built with a different architectural techniqu and less marble (also from Proconessus). The management of their construction and the quantities of marble used are on par with (and even exceed in many aspects) the large temples of Rome. With a method based on 19th-century building manuals, it is possible to evaluate the amount of work needed for quarrying, transport, and construction for the large marble blocks used in these two, very similar, temples which were were constructed in two different cities in Asia Minor.

Keywords: Temple, marble, Cyzicus, Hadrian, cost

Introduzione

Il grande tempio di Cizico e il "*Donuk Taş*" di Tarso possono essere considerati i templi più grandi del mondo romano: ambedue furono costruiti tra età adrianea ed età antonina in Asia Minore, e in ambedue il marmo di Proconneso fu usato in grandi quantità. I due templi, che in genere si assegnano al culto imperiale, oggi sono in gran parte distrutti, e le rovine furono saccheggiate a più riprese; recenti campagne di scavo si sono svolte però negli ultimi anni, consentendo di verificare vari dettagli della loro costruzione. Vorremmo partire dall'analisi e dal confronto tra le architetture dei due templi, per verificare come fossero affrontate nell'Asia Minore di età romana i grandi progetti edilizi che coinvolgevano grandi quantità di marmo.

Il tempio di Cizico: questioni preliminari

Inizieremo col tempio di Cizico, meglio noto; sulle indicazioni delle fonti antiche e dei viaggiatori di età moderna, rimandiamo al contributo di Andrea Barattolo[1] dove sono ampiamente discusse. Ci soffermiamo brevemente però sulla datazione della prima neokoria di Cizico, collegata alla costruzione del tempio. Cizico ebbe il titolo di *neokoros*[2] non dopo

il 139 d.C., quando per la prima volta vi si tennero le feste *koinà Asias*, e la prima attestazione di un *archiereus tēs Asias naou en Kyzikō* può datarsi alla fine dell'età adrianea o nella prima età antonina:[3] il grande tempio è certamente collegato a tale momento. Le più antiche monete con legenda *Kyzi(kēnōn) neōkorōn* documentano però l'assegnazione della neokoria alla città solo alla fine del regno di Antonino Pio (*coin type 1*):[4] in esse appare il nome dell'arconte Claudius Hestiaios,[5] che si legge anche in monete cizicene, sempre con legenda *Kyzi(kēnōn) neōkorōn*, battute sotto Marco Aurelio e Lucio Vero (*coin type 2*).[6] Tali monete potrebbero però

---

146) in onore di Antonia Tryphaena (Burrell 2004: 86). Appena pochi anni prima, nel 25 d.C., Tiberio aveva punito Cizico togliendole i privilegi accordati da Agrippa, a causa di un'ignota trasgressione nel campo del culto imperiale (Tac. *Ann.* IV, 36: *incuria caerimoniarum divi Augusti*) o, secondo Cassio Dione (LVII, 24, 6), per non avere iniziato a costruire un *heroon* ad Augusto.

[3] Cagnat 1927, IV: n. 155; Cagnat 1927, IV: nn. 160, 162; Hasluck 1910: 187–188; Buechner 1888: 67; Barattolo 1995: 67–69. È vero che l'istituzione di feste *Adrianeia Olympia*, nel 135 d.C., non doveva necessariamente coincidere con l'assegnazione della neokoria, ma i *koinà Asias*, che appaiono a partire dal 139, come afferma Luigi Moretti (1954: 283 nt. 3, 286 nt. 1), sono da considerare elemento costitutivo della neokoria (Burrell 2004: 92).

[4] Burrell 2004: 89.

[5] *Epì Hestiaiou archontos / ar(chontos) Hestiaiou / epi archontos Kl(audiou) Hestiaiou* (Münsterberg 1985: 66).

[6] *Epì Kl(audiou) Hestiaiou neōkorou Kyzikēnōn* (Burrell 2004: 91), dove però si ricorda non la neokoria in quanto tale, ma un Claudius Hestiaios *neōkoros* di Cizico. Simile titolo (*neōkoros* "della splendida metropoli dei Ciziceni") è attribuito ad Antonius Claudius Alphenus Apollinaris, di Thyatira, nell'età di Caracalla, al tempo della seconda neokoria di Cizico (Petzl 2007, V.2: n. 935, ll. 15–17).

---

[1] Barattolo 1995.

[2] La più antica menzione del titolo di *neokoros* imperiale in Asia, riferito ad una città, è in un'iscrizione di Cizico (Cagnat 1927, IV: n.

essere dell'inizio, piuttosto che della fine del regno di Antonino Pio, ipotizzando che gli *Hestiaioi* citati nei *coin types 1* e *2* fossero due personaggi diversi,[7] anche se legati da parentela. Allora sarebbe possibile datare il *coin type 1* all'inizio dell'età antonina, intorno al 139 d.C., dunque al momento dell'istituzione dei *koinà Asias*, che coinciderebbero con l'assegnazione della prima neokoria, e probabilmente con l'inaugurazione del tempio, la cui costruzione potrebbe essersi protratta per l'intera età di Adriano, quando le fonti parlano di un intervento economico imperiale per l'edificio.[8] Antonino Pio, da governatore della provincia Asia in età adrianea, era rimasto in buoni rapporti con la città, dove la sua statua da proconsole avrebbe ricevuto la corona che prima era stata posta sull'immagine di un dio, *omen* della futura carica imperiale[9]. Il *coin type 2*, di media età antonina, si riferirebbe pertanto ad una parziale ricostruzione, successiva ad un terremoto avvenuto intorno al 160 circa,[10] giustificando così una seconda emissione per la stessa neokoria, alcuni decenni dopo la prima.

Una seconda neokoria, attestata da diversi coni monetali con legenda *Kyzikē(nōn) dis neōkorōn*, fu assegnata a Cizico sotto Caracalla. Il *coin type 4* mostra l'imperatore mentre consegna il modellino di un tempio periptero a una dea, che ne tiene in mano un altro, con un altare tra i due:[11] immagine che si potrebbe anche interpretare come un contributo finanziario dell'imperatore alla costruzione. Nei *coin types 5-6* si fronteggiano poi due facciate templari, una a 9 colonne e una ottastila; nel *coin type 7* è raffigurato un tempio periptero con facciata a 9 colonne assieme ad un edificio circolare, con ingresso inquadrato da due torce su cui si avvolgono serpenti, identificato con un edificio pertinente al tempio dedicato alla dea Kore, che a Cizico era oggetto di un celebre culto misterico.[12]

Il nome dell'*archiereus* Aelius Onesiphoros appare sui *coin types 4, 5* e *6* ma non nel *coin type 7*, unico anche nel mostrare, oltre al periptero, l'edificio circolare, la cui presenza può essere interpretata variamente,[13] non esclusa l'attribuzione del nuovo culto imperiale allo stesso edificio.[14] La menzione della seconda neokoria sparisce poi dalle monete di Cizico, per tornare brevemente sotto Alessandro Severo una prima volta (*coin type 10*), e sotto Valeriano e Gallieno una seconda volta, quando i *coin types 15* e *13* ripetono con qualche variante i *coin types 6* e *7* di Caracalla: le cause di questa alternanza non sono chiare, ma è possibile che si debba al fatto che la città non avesse mai realmente portato a termine uno o ambedue i templi di culto imperiale provinciale.[15]

Non è del tutto chiarito a quale divinità fosse dedicato il tempio.[16] In base all'iscrizione *Theiou Adrianou* tramandata da Malala, generalmente è l'imperatore Adriano ad essere considerato il titolare del culto.[17] Simon Price[18] ha proposto, soprattutto in base all'istituzione di *Adrianeia Olympia*, che il tempio fosse dedicato a Zeus Olimpio identificato con Adriano, certo dopo il 131 d.C., quando viene attribuito ad Adriano l'epiteto *Olympios*. Il tempio era anche connesso con le feste *Olympia*, come attesta Elio Aristide,[19] ma ciò non implica né che l'imperatore fosse la divinità principale, né che lo fosse Zeus Olimpio. Non escludiamo, dunque, che un grande tempio extraurbano, già esistente in età tardo ellenistica, sia stato ricostruito con fondi pubblici a partire dall'età adrianea, per essere utilizzato come tempio di culto imperiale provinciale, come ritenne già Hasluck, ma anche lo stesso Ciriaco d'Ancona, il viaggiatore del Rinascimento al quale si devono molte informazioni sullo stato del tempio, prima dei saccheggi degli ultimi tre secoli.[20] In questo

---

[7] *Klaudios Hestiaios II, hipparchēs, neōkoros* nella moneta di Cizico, è citato anche in altre monete tra la fine del regno di Antonino Pio e l'inizio di quello di Marco Aurelio e Lucio Vero (*RPC*: volume IV, 2, nn. 677, 680, 2993, 11693).

[8] Schol. Luc. Icaromen. 24, 107 ed. Rabe; Adriano visitò Cizico nel 123 d.C.: Ioh. Malalas XI, 279 ed. Dindorf.

[9] *Hist.Aug.* Pius 3; Marquardt 1836: 87. Le monete ciziche di Antonino Pio e magistrato Hestiaios, con facciata ottastila, sono datate "c. 138–142 (?)" (*RPC*: volume IV,2, nn. 670, 2321, 2322 e 11185).

[10] Cass. Dio LXX 4, 1–2. Questo sisma rientra nella serie di terremoti che coinvolse varie città della provincia Asia, datata da Elio Aristide (*Or.* XLIX Keil, 38) quando era proconsole d'Asia L. Antonius Albus. Il periodo del suo proconsolato è però ancora dibattuto: per G.W. Bowersock (1968), più convincente, si data tra 160 e 161 d.C., mentre altri (Alföldy 1977: 213; Thomas 2007: 39), preferiscono un periodo tra 147 e 149 d.C. Dopo tale seconda ricostruzione, sotto Marco Aurelio e Lucio Vero, Elio Aristide avrebbe pronunziato la sua orazione di inaugurazione (Aristid. *Or.* XXVII ed. Keil) in cui magnificava il tempio di Cizico (DeLaine 2002).

[11] Burrell 2004: 94. Secondo Marquardt (1836: 88), tuttavia, una moneta di Settimio Severo con legenda *dis neōkoros* (Mionnet 1830: 338, n. 368) e Vittoria alata sul rovescio, starebbe a documentare l'attribuzione della seconda neokoria a Cizico già sotto Settimio Severo, in onore della vittoria su Pescennio Nigro, nel 193 d.C.

[12] Sul culto di Kore *Sōteira* a Cizico, App., *Mith.* 70, Plut. *Luc.*, 10. Cfr. Hasluck 1910: 210–213; Martin 2003.

[13] L'edificio circolare potrebbe aver ospitato il culto di Adriano, o il nuovo culto imperiale (con l'enneastilo a simboleggiare il nuovo edificio severiano o il tempio adrianeo), ovvero i due edifici potrebbero essere semplicemente segni di orgoglio civico; viene esclusa una seconda neokoria per il culto di Kore (Burrell 2004: 95).

[14] Durante gli scavi degli anni '90 nel tempio adrianeo sono state trovate testimonianze che potrebbero essere attribuite ad un culto imperiale di età severiana (Yaylali and Özkaya 1993: 542–43; vedi però Burrell 2004: 95).

[15] Burrell 2004: 97–98.

[16] Barattolo (1995: 67) ritiene che il nome della divinità non fosse ricordato in quanto era a tutti noto.

[17] Si tratta comunque sempre di fonti tarde, come Sozom., *Hist. Eccl.* III, 23, 59 ("i Ciziceni dichiararono Adriano tredicesimo dio": ma onori divini non implicano che gli fosse dedicato un tempio) o *Anth. Pal.* IX, 656 ("tempio di Adriano"; ma si potrebbe sempre pensare che si intendesse "fatto da Adriano", non "dedicato ad Adriano").

[18] Price 1984: 153–154.

[19] Barattolo 1995: 65; Burrell 2004: 93.

[20] Hasluck 1910: 187, nt. 7. Ciriaco, o forse il suo biografo Scalamonti, nel 1431 aveva identificato il grande tempio con il "*delubrum*" citato da Plin. *HN* XXXVI, 22, con fili d'oro tra i blocchi, dedicato al culto di Giove (Bodnar and Mitchell 1996: 61; Meyer 2014: 36), mentre nella sua lettera del 1444 lo definiva "*nobilissimum illud Proserpinae templum*" (Bodnar and Foss 2003: 72). La traduzione latina di un'iscrizione cizicena che sarebbe stata vista da Ciriaco (Reinach 1890: 529; Bodnar and Mitchell 1976: 62, nt. 33), definiva l'edificio "*illud Proserpinae*

caso, il tempio periptero enneastilo raffigurato sulle monete di Cizico sotto Caracalla (*coin type 7*)[21] sarebbe da identificare con il tempio severiano di culto imperiale, che avrebbe giustificato il secondo titolo di *neokoros*, mentre il tempio della prima neokoria sarebbe la ricostruzione di un antico *Persephoneion*, rappresentato sulle monete di Cizico o come periptero ottastilo (a fianco di un nuovo ottastilo, della seconda neokoria), o come edificio circolare in opera quadrata con statue sulla sommità, raffigurato a fianco del nuovo tempio, che appariva dotato di nove colonne come a distinguerlo dal tempio ottastilo "di Adriano". Si comprenderebbe così anche il dato delle fonti, sull'intervento di Adriano a completamento di un tempio, già iniziato a costruire. È vero che i resti archeologici non sembrano mostrare prove evidenti di un lungo periodo costruttivo: le sostruzioni voltate in opera cementizia, fanno pensare ad una costruzione *ex novo* terminata in pochi decenni, salvo le ricostruzioni dovute a danni sismici.[22] Il problema della mancanza di una fase ellenistica o primo imperiale potrebbe essere superato, però, pensando ad un totale rifacimento, o interpretando come resti di una fase più antica solo i muri di sostruzione in blocchi squadrati connessi da grappe, ossia quelli al di sotto dei muri della cella (mentre gli altri muri hanno un nucleo in opera cementizia).[23] I blocchi uniti da grappe consentirebbero di ipotizzare una fase precedente, che avrebbe coinvolto soltanto la cella, mentre i colonnati, le cui fondazioni utilizzano opera cementizia con cortine in blocchi squadrati senza grappe o pietrame, sarebbero stati completati solo in età imperiale. Si è poi spesso osservato che i templi di altre divinità poterono essere usati come templi di culto imperiale per ottenere una neokoria.[24]

Ricostruiamo così la sequenza dei fatti: un grande tempio extraurbano di Cizico, dedicato alla dea principale della città, Kore *Sōteira*, non finito e

fortemente danneggiato dal terremoto del 120 d.C., fu iniziato a ricostruire con i fondi stanziati allo scopo da Adriano, dopo la sua visita alla città nel 123. Intorno al 139 fu concessa a Cizico la prima neokoria, anche grazie all'avanzato (se non totale) completamento del tempio, divenuto sede di culto imperiale: l'iscrizione *Theiou Adrianou* vista da Malala (XI, 279 ed. Dindorf), infatti, sembra posteriore alla morte di Adriano, ed essendo al genitivo, non era una dedica.[25] Dopo un terremoto intorno al 160 d.C., i danni furono rapidamente riparati e il tempio nuovamente aperto al culto (*coin type 2*) con l'orazione di Elio Aristide (*Or.* XXVII ed. Keil). Nel *coin type 3*, la facciata colonnata con clipeo al centro del frontone è associata all'effigie di Commodo, assieme alla legenda *Kyzi(kēnōn) neōkorōn*, come nel *coin type 1*: potrebbe segnalare un'ulteriore fase di completamento. Una seconda neokoria fu concessa sotto Caracalla, per la costruzione di un secondo tempio di culto imperiale provinciale: potrebbe trattarsi di un nuovo edificio, o del rifacimento dello stesso grande tempio, finanziato con contributo dell'imperatore.

Il tempio di Cizico: ricostruzione ipotetica

In base a questi dati e ai pochi elementi architettonici allora noti,[26] A. Barattolo ha sostenuto l'ipotesi di un tempio diptero con 8 x 17 colonne, una cella a tre navate con semicolonne addossate a pilastri ed architravi, mentre le arcate sostenute da colonne con fusto a tralci di vite, attestate dai disegni di Bartolomeo Fonzio, avrebbero trovato posto in un propileo esterno. Un'altra ricostruzione, con 15 colonne sui lati lunghi, basata sui dati di Ciriaco e su osservazioni in loco, si deve ad una tesi di dottorato scritta nel 1981 da Antony Smith: se il podio con scalinata centrale è da respingere, sembrano ben congegnate le volte di sostruzione,[27] con gli interassi che recepivano il ritmo delle feritoie, i corridoi laterali piegati ad angolo retto sui lati Est ed Ovest, anch'essi dotati di feritoie.[28]

Da parte nostra, riteniamo che il tempio colossale di Cizico possa ricostruirsi come un diptero (8 x 16 colonne), con una cella dotata di pronao profondo, aperto verso Nord con una porta monumentale, forse comunicante con una scala interna alle ante (**Figura 1**). La pianta diptera si collega agli analoghi esempi

---

templum", menzionando un altare (*ara*), e terminava con il testo dell'epigrafe di Aristenetos, che appare in greco nel disegno della porta monumentale (*cod. Bodleianus* 133 v.). Secondo Andrea Barattolo (1995: 76, nt. 155), all'origine di queste ricostruzioni di Ciriaco vi sarebbe una confusione accidentale tra le sue schede epigrafiche; secondo Reinach (1890: 530) la pseudo-iscrizione dell'altare va considerata una combinazione tra l'epigrafe di Aristenetos e un decreto di epoca imperiale copiato da Ciriaco stesso presso il grande tempio (Reinach 1890: 537–538, n. 2), che menzionava alcuni sacerdoti di Kore *Sōteira*, divinità principale di Cizico (*App.*, *Mith.* 74–75).
[21] Burrell 2004: 94.
[22] In tal caso, l'accostamento con l'*Olympieion* di Atene, suggerito dallo scoliasta di Luciano, potrebbe essersi limitato all'aspetto finanziario, ossia al completamento (parziale) con fondi pubblici (Burrell 2004: 87). La notizia sul mancato completamento del tempio è però confermata dal ritrovamento di frammenti di colonne non finite (Koçhan 2014: 284), ma ciò non avrebbe pregiudicato la possibilità di dedicarlo o utilizzarlo, come documentano altri esempi di templi colossali nel mondo greco e romano (Papini 2019: 115–118).
[23] La pianta e le osservazioni di Andrea Barattolo (1995: 81–82, fig. 1) evidenziano la differenza tra le cortine, ma per la parte centrale delle sostruzioni, solo dei saggi in profondità potrebbero verificare se i muri avevano nuclei in opera cementizia.
[24] Martin 2003: 145.

[25] La proposta di Reinach (1890: 517) di correggere l'iscrizione vista da Malala in *Theiō Adrianō*, al dativo, accettata da Barattolo (1995: 64, nt. 58), non è sorretta da prove. Piuttosto, il genitivo di Adriano divinizzato si spiegherebbe come patronimico di Antonino Pio, che doveva essere poi citato al nominativo – come finanziatore – o al dativo, come dedicatario.
[26] Frammenti di fusti e capitelli di grandi dimensioni, e un frammento di grande fusto con tralci di vite da scavi del 1948, al museo di Erdek, alto intorno a 34 p.r., più un fusto di pilastro con semicolonna in proconnesio decorato con tralci di vite al museo archeologico di Istanbul, alto 16 p.r. (Barattolo 1995: 86–88).
[27] Thomas (2007: 39–40, fig. 25) pubblica i disegni dell'inedita tesi di dottorato del 1980 di Antony Smith.
[28] Koçhan and Meral 2015: 63.

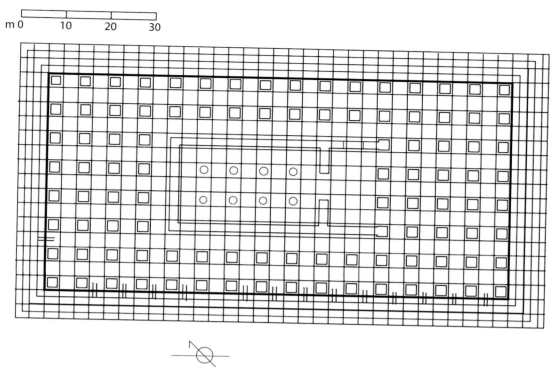

Figura 1. Cizico, tempio colossale. Planimetria ricostruita (disegno Autore).

adrianei di Atene (*Olympieion*), Roma (Venere e Roma), forse anche Efeso (tempio del *Koressos*) e Smirne (tempio del *Değirmentepe*).[29] Il pronao si potrebbe identificare con la "testa del tempio" di Bonsignore Bonsignori,[30] termine che potrebbe adattarsi al lato di fondo di un edificio. Sia davanti che dietro la cella avremmo così 4 file di colonne, più due colonne *in antis* del pronao, che potrebbero giustificare la menzione di 5 file di colonne da parte di Ciriaco. L'interno della cella sarebbe poi diviso in tre navate da colonne a fusto decorato da tralci di vite, con arcate, secondo i disegni di Bartolomeo Fonzio:[31] esse dovevano trovarsi all'interno della cella, disposte in senso Est-Ovest e in due file, in quanto le sei grandi colonne corinzie visibili sullo sfondo non possono che essere quelle rimaste in piedi su uno dei lati lunghi, proprio perché Ciriaco ammette che quelle nel pronao e nell'opistodomo non erano più conservate.[32] Per lo stesso motivo, si può identificare la grande porta con iscrizione ipoteticamente attribuita all'architetto Aristenetos,[33] aperta nella parete in blocchi isodomi

disposta davanti ad altre tre colonne sullo sfondo, con quella che si apriva a Nord (*tramontana*) descritta nel 1498 da Bonsignore Bonsignori,[34] non con un'eventuale porta sul lato breve della cella.[35]

Le informazioni delle fonti scritte e numismatiche vanno ora confrontate con le osservazioni sul monumento e con i dati di scavo. Il basamento, lungo circa m 120, largo circa 50, era costituito da sette gallerie voltate longitudinali e otto spessi muri in opera cementizia[36] che costituivano le fondazioni di cella e colonnati (**Figura 2**). La galleria centrale era più larga delle altre, con una scala e un piccolo ambiente circolare, coperto da cupola, al centro; le tre gallerie sotto la cella sono meglio conservate, mentre nei settori Est e Ovest esse risultano molto danneggiate.[37] Inoltre, la parte Est delle fondazioni della cella, rilevata da Guillaume nel 1864,

[29] Barattolo 1978 (Roma e Atene); Schorndorfer 1999: 151 (Efeso); Kılıç and Gülbay 2010 (Smirne). L'ipotesi di pianta pseudodiptera (Schulz and Winter 1990) va scartata, in quanto urta contro le difficoltà poste da colonnati laterali estremamente ampi, incompatibili coi dati di Ciriaco sulla distanza tra cella e colonne.
[30] Borsook 1973: 191–192.
[31] Cod. Bodleianus ff. 132 v. e 133 r. Ashmole 1956. Cfr. Ciccuto 1996.
[32] Meyer 2014: 42–45; Thomas 2007: fig. 25b (ricostruzione di A. Smith).
[33] Cod. Bodleianus f. 133 v.; Cagnat 1927, IV: n. 140. Consideriamo non originale l'iscrizione di Aristenetos: secondo Donderer (1996: 287–288) lo stile magniloquente, insolito nelle consuete epigrafi di architetti di età romana, la rende sospetta. Anche P. Fane-Saunders

(2016: 242) ritiene che l'iscrizione sia stata creata per rendere più illustre il tempio, prendendo spunto da altre epigrafi sul sito, e da una frase di Plinio il Vecchio – certamente nota a Ciriaco – che ricordava come il tempio di Artemide ad Efeso fosse stato finanziato dall'intera Asia (factum a tota Asia... tota Asia extruente: Plin. HN XXXVI, 21 e XVI, 79).
[34] Borsook 1973: 165, 191–192, doc. 13; Schulz 1995; Rebaudo 2016.
[35] Anche la sua attribuzione ad un eventuale *temenos* (Schulz 1995: 119) si deve dunque respingere.
[36] Barattolo 1995: fig. 1.
[37] Guillaume and Perrot 1864; Guillaume *et al.* (1872, II: pl. III), è l'unico a proporre un rilievo completo di questo settore centrale, descritto anche da Barattolo (1995: 81–82, fig. 18). Il vano coperto a cupola, ricavato nel muro Nord della galleria centrale, ospitava una sorgente che raccoglieva acqua dalla falda freatica su cui è costruito il tempio (Meyer 2014: 57–58).

Figura 2. Cizico, tempio colossale. Tratto centrale dei resti della crepidine sul lato Sud (foto M. Spanu).

presentava due corpi a "L" (non considerati nella pianta di Barattolo), che formavano un corridoio sotterraneo trasversale davanti alle tre gallerie, consentendo di ipotizzare in quest'area una serie di sostruzioni voltate perpendicolari. I tratti di galleria longitudinale definiti "5a" e "3a" nella pianta di Barattolo[38] dovevano comunicare con questa galleria trasversale mediante aperture a livello inferiore; nel pronao potrebbero esserci state gallerie trasversali parallele, tra pilastri su cui si sarebbero impostate le basi delle colonne, collegati da passaggi voltati.

Non tutto è chiarito però su tali sostruzioni: un recente studio sui viaggiatori in età moderna a Cizico ha portato all'attenzione alcune descrizioni seicentesche del "palazzo di Priamo", come era chiamato allora il sito del tempio, che sembrano contraddire le tradizionali ricostruzioni.[39] Guillaume nel 1864 poté rilevare almeno i tre corridoi centrali, meglio costruiti, e in seguito produsse una pianta con le tre gallerie poste sull'angolo Ovest di un'area quadrata formata da quattro corridoi in senso Nord-Ovest – Sud-Est, tagliati ad angolo retto da altre due gallerie.[40] Sulla base di tale planimetria si è pensato che le tre gallerie parallele costituissero un altro edificio, diverso dal tempio.[41] Come si è visto, però,

le indagini di Barattolo, confermate dagli scavi turchi degli ultimi anni, hanno localizzato quattro gallerie parallele ai lati di tre centrali, per un totale di sette; la mancanza delle gallerie perpendicolari è solo apparente, e deriva dallo stato precario di conservazione delle volte: secondo D. Sestini, nel XVIII secolo, l'edificio si poteva paragonare ad un mercato coperto turco (*bedesten*).[42] Lo stato attuale dei resti impedisce una verifica; occorrerà attendere che gli scavi arrivino al centro dell'edificio. Il problema delle sostruzioni è posto poi anche dagli scavi sul lato Ovest del tempio, attualmente in corso.[43]

Tali scavi archeologici si sono svolti in due serie di campagne annuali, una dal 1989 al 1997,[44] l'altra dal 2006 ad oggi, liberando finora i lati Sud, Est ed Ovest del tempio.[45] Con lo scavo dell'angolo Sud-Ovest,

[38] Barattolo 1995: fig. 1.

[39] Meyer 2014.

[40] Guillaume *et al.* 1872, II, pl. III ; Guillaume 1864.

[41] Secondo Meyer (2014: 53), le tre gallerie rilevate da Guillaume si riferirebbero ad una basilica, e non sarebbero da identificare con le tre gallerie più ampie, al centro del sistema di sette gallerie (da considerare inventato) identificato da Barattolo, che costituiva il basamento del tempio. Diremo solo che ci sembra inverosimile che

Barattolo e altri possano essersi equivocati a tal punto; Guillaume ha certamente sbagliato nel non inserire le tre gallerie al centro delle altre, come ha sbagliato nel rendere quadrata, e non allungata, l'area del tempio. L'azimut del tempio, 300° N, coincide con quello delle tre gallerie di Guillaume (Koçhan and Meral 2015).

[42] Sestini 1785: 52 A.

[43] Koçhan *et al.* 2016; Koçhan *et al.* 2017. Nel 2017 e 2018 non risultano campagne di scavo, mentre nel 2019 si è arrivati all'angolo NO (Koçhan and Meral 2020: 30).

[44] Yaylali 1990; Yaylali, Koçhan and Başaran 1991; Yaylali and Özkaya 1992; Yaylali and Özkaya 1993; Yaylali and Özkaya 1994; Yaylali and Özkaya 1995; Yaylali and Özkaya 1996; Yaylali and Özkaya 1997. Nel 1997 sono emerse lastre di pavimentazione a Sud del tempio (Yaylali and Özkaya 1998: 372, res. 6). Negli anni precedenti vi erano stati solo alcuni saggi (Ertüzün 1964; Barattolo 1995: 64).

[45] Koçhan and Meral 2007; Koçhan and Meral 2008; Koçhan and Meral 2009; Koçhan *et al.* 2010; Koçhan and Meral 2011; Koçhan and Meral 2012; Koçhan and Meral 2013; Koçhan 2014 (in inglese); Koçhan and Meral 2014; Koçhan *et al.* 2015; Koçhan *et al.* 2016; Koçhan *et al.* 2017; Meral 2018; Koçhan and Meral 2020.

la lunghezza totale della crepidine è stata fissata a m 116,23, mentre per lo stilobate la misura è meno precisa, attorno a m 107. Dopo lo scavo dell'angolo Nord-Ovest,[46] nel 2019, la larghezza della crepidine è stata stimata a m 62,4. Si è confermata l'esistenza di prese d'aria orizzontali tra la crepidine e i corridoi laterali seminterrati delle sostruzioni, disposte con un ritmo variabile tra m 6,30 - 6,60 - 6,78 (media m 6,56 = 20 piedi dorici).[47] L'interasse sui lati lunghi doveva dunque essere compreso all'interno di queste misure, e sembra adeguata la misura di 22 piedi riportata da Ciriaco (= m 6,51, se piedi romani), registrata sull'architrave raffigurato nel disegno di Bartolomeo Fonzio.[48]

Apriamo qui una parentesi: riteniamo che l'unità di misura scelta dagli architetti del tempio fosse il piede dorico (m 0,328), nonostante il fatto che nel II secolo d.C. sia più logico preferire il piede romano, soprattutto perché in tal modo si ottiene un interasse di 20 piedi, multiplo di 10, più facile da usare nella progettazione modulare. Dobbiamo anche ricordare che a Cizico la tradizione nel campo architettonico probabilmente non ha mai avuto battute di arresto, sostenuta dal continuo approvvigionamento di marmo dalle cave di Proconneso, e non è difficile pensare che il piede dorico, unità di misura usata fino a tutta l'età ellenistica, sia stato mantenuto in uso fino al periodo imperiale. Era comunque sempre possibile un'equivalenza con il piede romano, necessaria per dialogare con fornitori e committenti, sulla base del rapporto 9:10 tra le due unità.[49] La griglia di modulo 10 piedi (da m 0,328) si adatta anche alle larghezze delle gallerie e dei muri intermedi: nei colonnati laterali, sommando la larghezza di un muro e di una galleria (12 ½ + 7 ½ p.) si ottengono 20 p., ossia un interasse. Nei tre interassi mediani della fronte, la maggiore larghezza della galleria centrale, 10 p., è compensata da larghezze di 11 p. e 8 p. nelle altre due, ma la somma delle sette larghezze è comunque 70 p.; si hanno così in tutto 7 interassi regolari da 20 p. (140 p. = m 45,92). Il piede usato nella descrizione di Ciriaco e nei disegni di Fonzio potrebbe essere il piede romano, o un piede ad esso vicino, sia che fosse ancora in uso in Italia centrale nel XV secolo, sia che fosse un piede utilizzato nell'area egea durante quel periodo.

Una novità è emersa dallo scavo sull'angolo Sud-Ovest, tra 2013 e 2016, che ha portato alla luce un'area vuota di strutture davanti alle imboccature delle gallerie 1 e 2,

anche in punti in cui avrebbero dovuto trovarsi le fondazioni delle colonne.[50] Gli scavatori hanno allora abbandonato l'ipotesi iniziale, con le colonne della peristasi collocate logicamente negli spazi intermedi tra le prese d'aria,[51] proponendo una nuova soluzione, in cui le colonne venivano a trovarsi direttamente sopra tali prese d'aria.[52] Tuttavia, anche così non si risolve del tutto il problema, in quanto gli intervalli tra le feritoie variano fino a 30 cm rispetto alla misura dell'interasse, e comunque mancano sempre le fondazioni per le colonne nella parte Sud del pronao. Occorre allora pensare a una diversa soluzione, ipotizzando che le colonne fossero impostate su fondazioni in blocchi di calcare, in seguito asportate dopo il crollo della zona dell'opistodomo, per farne calce, come gran parte dei marmi del tempio. Potrebbe essere rimasta qualche traccia di tali fondazioni alla quota del piano di calpestio delle gallerie, sotto le volte, che risultano ancora ingombre per più di metà altezza, non essendo state ancora toccate dallo scavo.

Elementi architettonici in marmo del grande tempio a Cizico

Nei resoconti di scavo, dal 1990 ad oggi, è stata data notizia del rinvenimento di una serie di elementi architettonici in marmo proconnesio che consentono di precisare la struttura del tempio. Tegole piane con coppi angolari, in marmo, di grandi dimensioni, dimostrano come il tempio avesse almeno in parte una copertura.[53] Sono stati trovati diversi frammenti di blocchi di sima orizzontale ed obliqua su gola, alta cm 80, decorata da *anthemion* di palmette con foglie a nastro alternatamente aperte e chiuse; le grondaie a teste di leone sembrano appartenere a fasi stilistiche distribuite tra prima metà e fine del II secolo d.C.[54] I frammenti di sima obliqua pubblicati mostrano palmette disposte in verticale, su un piano di appoggio costituito da un *kyma* ionico, che seguiva l'inclinazione del frontone, per cui tra esse e il piano si formava un angolo di 70°; ne risulta che il frontone aveva angoli laterali di 90° - 70° = 20°, e di conseguenza l'angolo centrale di 140°, con proporzioni simili ai frontoni del tempio di "Serapide" sul Quirinale a Roma[55] e di Giove Eliopolitano a Baalbek.

I frammenti della cornice del tempio pubblicati finora (**Figura 3**), mostrano un *kyma* di foglie posto tra la sima

[46] Koçhan and Meral 2020: 30 nt. 2.
[47] Yaylali and Özkaya 1992: 228, çiz. 2; Koçhan and Meral 2011: 259, çiz. 3.
[48] Il disegno di Fonzio (Cod. Bodleianus f. 135 v., Barattolo 1995: 105) mostrava un architrave intero; l'interasse è stato calcolato sulla base delle prese d'aria in Yaylali and Özkaya 1996: 410. Gli scavi recenti hanno restituito frammenti di architrave con lacunare decorato a treccia (Koçhan and Meral 2011: 261, res. 8), a meandro, o con motivi vegetali, non abbastanza conservati per definirne la lunghezza.
[49] Una simile equivalenza tra piede dorico e piede attico, vicino a quello romano, è notata da Mark Wilson Jones (2000 b: 86, nt. 50).

[50] Koçhan and Meral 2013: res. 2; Koçhan and Meral 2015: çiz. 3; Koçhan et al. 2017: çiz. 2. Cfr. Barattolo 1995: fig. 1.
[51] Koçhan 2014: fig. 40; Koçhan and Meral 2011: çiz. 1.
[52] Koçhan et al. 2015: çiz. 1.
[53] Lunghezza m 1,04, larghezza m 0,85 (Yaylali 1990: 174, res. 8; Koçhan and Meral 2007: 14, res. 4).
[54] Yaylali 1990: 176, res. 5 e 15 (N. Koçhan); Yaylali and Özkaya 1996: 413, res. 10; Koçhan and Meral 2008: 165, res. 1; Koçhan and Meral 2010: 190, res. 9 (*cyma reversa*); Koçhan and Meral 2011: 261, res. 7; Koçhan and Meral 2013: 377, res. 5. Dimensioni: altezza m 0,80, larghezza m 2,08 - m 2,40, spessore m 1,15 - 1,46.
[55] Trunk 2014.

Figura 3. Cizico, tempio colossale. Frammento di cornice della peristasi con resto di mensola ornata da foglia di acanto (foto M. Spanu).

compatibili con tale fregio, che una volta editi costituiranno un documento eccezionale delle officine scultoree microasiatiche di età imperiale, in particolare della media età antonina.[59] Un colossale lastrone frammentario, trovato nel 2008, sembra pertinente a un soffitto, e presenta un campo quadrato decorato da un tondo a rilievo, in cui si conserva una figura femminile nuda di spalle, nell'iconografia delle Cariti:[60] si potrebbe attribuire all'interno della cella, assieme ad altre lastre più piccole di soffitto con decorazione a conchiglia centrale e motivi curvilinei.[61] Sono anche emersi frammenti di altri cassettoni monolitici (inediti), che potrebbero aver coperto gli intercolumni della peristasi.

Solo pochi frammenti delle colonne sono scampati alla distruzione del tempio in età moderna. Un capitello frammentario[62] trovato durante gli scavi degli anni '90, pertinente alla peristasi, presenta una peculiare decorazione delle zone d'ombra, con orlo ovoidale sottolineato da un bordo rialzato, come in una nota serie di capitelli attici di età adrianea, e nei grandi capitelli del *Kizil Avlı* a Pergamo.[63] Nel 2013 è stato trovato un capitello corinzio della peristasi quasi integro (alto in tutto m 2,5 = 8 ½ p.r. = 7 ½ p. dorici), caratterizzato da foglie di acanto asiatico databili ad età medio - tardo antonina, con abaco ornato da *kyma* ionico in alto e *kyma* lesbio trilobato in basso,[64] alti ognuno m 0,185, per un totale di m 0,37 (**Figura 4**). I frammenti di base sono stati trovati più raramente, ma dagli scavi del

e la corona, decorata a can corrente (altezza circa cm 30), mentre la mensola (alta circa cm 50, lunga m 0,85), con due volute e palmetta che riempie lo spazio tra voluta posteriore più grande e piano di appoggio, era rivestita in basso da una foglia di acanto e coronata da *kyma* ionico, esteso anche agli spazi intermedi sul retro; questi sono decorati a loro volta da *anthemion* di tralci intermittenti obliqui a nastro con fogliette e volute, da cui nascono palmette aperte alternatamente diritte e rovesce, e infine un *kyma* ionico con fila di perline (alto cm 30 circa) separa la sopracornice dai dentelli (altezza circa cm 50).[56] Non è noto come fossero decorati i cassettoni tra le mensole, forse con rosette a sei petali, almeno in qualche caso.[57] In totale, cornice e sima erano alte circa m 2,30–2,40.

Prima degli scavi recenti, era noto solo un frammento del fregio figurato della peristasi, purtroppo oggi perduto, alto m 1,52: raffigurava cavalieri in costume orientale.[58] A partire dal 1990 sono emersi nuovi frammenti di rilievo con figure umane, di dimensioni

[56] Yaylali, Koçhan and Başaran 1991: 206, res. 5; Yaylali and Özkaya 1992: 226, res. 12; Yaylali and Özkaya 1994: 328, fig. 7; Yaylali and Özkaya 1995: 314, res. 7; Yaylali and Özkaya 1997: 372, res. 7; Koçhan and Meral 2009: 54, res. 10; Koçhan *et al.* 2010: 190, res. 6. Confronti interessanti si trovano nella decorazione del teatro della vicina Parion, datata alla seconda metà del II secolo, recentemente scavato: una cornice con corona decorata a can corrente, sopra un *kyma* di foglie di acanto (Başaran and Yıldızlı 2018: 54 fig. 2), un *anthemion* a tralci intermittenti e foglie seghettate, con *kyma* lesbio confrontabile con quello dell'abaco del capitello di Cizico (Başaran and Yıldızlı 2018: 60, fig. 10b). Cfr. anche Başaran and Yıldızlı 2016. Parion era una colonia romana di età augustea che ottenne benefici da Adriano (Magie 1950, II: 1473–1474).
[57] Yaylali and Özkaya 1992: 227, res. 13.
[58] Sono stati ravvisati confronti stilistici con il "monumento partico" di Efeso (Laubscher 1967: 215; Barattolo 1995: 104–105), ma i cavalieri raffigurati non sembrano Parti, in quanto indossano il *torques*: se si tratta di Galati, potrebbe trattarsi di un riferimento all'invasione del 278 a.C. dei Galli Trocmi, da cui Cizico si salvò grazie a Filetero di Pergamo, come testimoniato da un'iscrizione (Hasluck 1910: 174–175; Smith and De Rustafjaell 1902: 193–201, n. 3).

[59] Yaylali 1990: 174, res. 6 (alt. m 1,55); Yaylali, Koçhan and Başaran 1991: res. 9; Yaylali and Özkaya 1994: res. 11–14. Si distinguono una testa elmata, calcificata dal fuoco delle fornaci (Yaylali and Özkaya 1996: 415, res. 13); una testa di satiro, con iridi incise (Koçhan and Meral 2008: 164, res. 3; Koçhan *et al.* 2010: 190, res. 8). Altre sculture sono datate al periodo di Marco Aurelio e Lucio Vero su base stilistica (Koçhan and Meral 2011: 261, res. 9; Koçhan and Meral 2012, 338, res. 8–10; Koçhan and Meral 2014a: 193, res. 6–9; Koçhan *et al.* 2015: 437, res. 7, Koçhan *et al.* 2016: 225, res. 3; Koçhan *et al.* 2017: 250, res. 3). Il tema del fregio potrebbe essere stato sui racconti mitologici e storici collegati a Cizico, a partire dagli Argonauti (connessi con il fondatore eponimo Kyzikos), fino al momento della costruzione del tempio, con l'intervento divino (Kore) che salvava la città nei momenti critici. Le corazze anatomiche di alcuni guerrieri (Koçhan and Meral 2013: 377, res. 4) trovano confronti con quelle raffigurate nel sarcofago con amazzonomachia a Kütahya da Aizanoi, di età medio antonina (Koch 2011: 113, fig. 2), in marmo docimeno, che documentano così la circolazione di schemi iconografici simili tra maestranze di età imperiale che lavoravano marmi diversi in Asia Minore.
[60] Koçhan and Meral 2009: 52; Koçhan and Meral 2014b: 234, res. 16–17. Lunghezza massima m 2,55, lato ricostruito del quadrato m 3,66: si pensa ad una collocazione sopra le colonne della peristasi. A Cizico esisteva un portico (*pastas*) dedicato alle Cariti, dove era stata dedicata una parte (*stylis*) della più antica trireme, inventata da Atena (*Anth. Pal.* VI, 342).
[61] Koçhan and Meral 2009: 53, res. 4–5; Koçhan 2014: 285, fig. 36.
[62] Nel disegno f. 136 v. di Fonzio il capitello corinzio era alto 9 p. (Schulz and Winter 1990: 69, fig. 6; Barattolo 1995: tav. 38). Sono emersi in seguito altri frammenti di capitelli corinzi (Schorndorfer 1999: 148; Barattolo 1995: 90–91), alcuni dei quali databili tra II e III secolo (Yaylali and Özkaya 1994: 109, res. 5–6; Koçhan and Meral 2008: 165, res. 4).
[63] Yaylali and Özkaya 1996: 413, res. 11. Su questo capitello sono stati osservati anche resti di doratura (Koçhan and Meral 2020: 32, res. 10), che appariva anche in frammenti scultorei del fregio (Koçhan 2014: 285).
[64] Schulz and Winter 1990: 70.

Figura 4. Cizico, tempio colossale. Capitello corinzio della
peristasi quasi integro, rinvenuto nel 2013
(foto P. Pensabene).

m 2,1 circa;[70] rispetto ad esso, però, il diametro inferiore del fusto, misurato all'*apophyge*, doveva essere piuttosto più stretto. Nel *Didymaion* di Mileto, tempio colossale con misure simili a quelle di Cizico, la differenza tra diametro inferiore del fusto (all'*apophyge*) e diametro del toro di base era nell'ordine di 16 cm;[71] sottraendo tale misura dal diametro superiore della base di Cizico, si ottiene quella del diametro inferiore del fusto, o modulo (M): m 2,1 – 0,16 = m 1,94 = 6 ½ p.r. = 6 p. dorici circa. Se il fusto era di 8 M, come di solito nelle colonne romane di età imperiale, sarebbe stato alto 6 p. x 8 = 48 p.d. (53 1/3 p.r.); sommando l'altezza del capitello (m 2,5 = 7 ½ p.d.) e della base (m 1,64 = 5 p.d.), la colonna risulterebbe alta 48 + 7 ½ + 5 = 60 ½ p.d. = m 19,68, circa 10 volte il diametro inferiore del fusto (H = 10 d x 6 p. dorici = 60 p.d.); avremmo anche un rapporto normale tra altezza totale della colonna e altezza del fusto, ossia H/h = 6/5 = 60 p.d. / 48 p.d. = 8 M x 6 p.d. In piedi romani, l'altezza totale corrisponderebbe a 67 p.r. circa, comunque non lontana dai 70 piedi di Ciriaco. Tuttavia, l'intercolumnio risulta così non più di 14 piedi (= m 4,14 = 12 ½ p. dorici), come afferma Ciriaco, ma 22 - 6 ½ = 15 ½ p.r. È possibile però che l'intercolumnio di Ciriaco si riferisse allo spazio tra i plinti, ognuno di lato m 2,53 = 8 ½ p. = 7 ½ p. dorici: in tal caso sarebbe possibile conciliare tutti i dati (spazio tra plinti: 20 – 7 ½ = 12 ½ p. dorici = 14 p.r.). Il fusto marmoreo non era monolitico, come afferma Cassio Dione: secondo Bonsignore Bonsignori, che visitò il tempio nel 1498, era formato da dieci rocchi.[72] Negli *excerpta* di Xifilino, tratti da Cassio Dione, le dimensioni del tempio potrebbero essere state "gonfiate" (75 p. = 50 cubiti romani invece di 67 p. = 44 cubiti romani di altezza della colonna, e 4 *orgyiai* invece di 3 ½ circa per la circonferenza del diametro), per arrivare a misure tonde, più eclatanti.

Tra i disegni di Fonzio sono raffigurate tre serie di semicolonne corinzie decorate da tralci di vite, addossate a pilastri (ff. 132 v. – 133 r. con arcate; f. 134 r. più slanciate, inquadrano un *gorgoneion* a rilievo dalla parete; ff. 134 v. – 135 r. – 135 v. – 136 r. sostengono trabeazioni a parete con capitelli a doppia corona di foglie, fregio figurato piuttosto alto).[73] Un frammento di fusto di semicolonna addossata a pilastro, con decorazione vitinea, nell'antiquarium di Erdek, è probabilmente da assegnare all'ordine interno della cella;[74] se ne conosce il diametro inferiore, di m 1,258, da cui si può ricavare l'altezza totale, m 12,58 (10 D) = 42 ½ piedi. Le sue dimensioni si adattano a quelle delle colonne vitinee sotto arcate del disegno di Fonzio (f. 132v. – 133 r.), che abbiamo proposto di collocare entro la cella: il concio superiore dell'archivolto, di 13 piedi

2009 sono emersi un plinto frammentario (alto m 1, largo m 2,53), con l'inizio del toro inferiore, e una base, ambedue sbozzati;[65] grazie a un disegno di Guillaume del 1864 si conosce anche una base frammentaria[66] alta m 0,64, dunque la base composita era alta in tutto m 1,64 = 5 p. dorici = 5 ½ p.r. Rimangono solo frammenti dei fusti, alcuni con scanalature eseguite, altri con la sola sbozzatura,[67] mentre sono noti diversi frammenti di sommi scapi, con la parte superiore delle scanalature decorata da vasi a due anse; da uno di essi si ricava anche il diametro di m 1,9, misurato al tondino superiore.[68]

È possibile dunque ricostruire l'altezza della colonna, in base alle regole di M. Wilson Jones,[69] ricordando che per Ciriaco era 70 piedi, mentre per Cassio Dione 75 piedi (50 cubiti), e la circonferenza del fusto 4 *orgyiai* (dato destinato a impressionare: equivale all'apertura di braccia di quattro uomini). Anche se non si è conservato alcun frammento di imo scapo, è possibile ricavarne il diametro grazie a quello del toro superiore della base, di

[65] Koçhan 2014: 290, figs 42–43.
[66] Guillaume and Perrot 1864; Schulz and Winter 1990: 59, fig. 2.
[67] Fusto non lisciato (Koçhan 2014: fig. 35); scanalature solo delineate (Koçhan and Meral 2011: 261, res. 6).
[68] Koçhan and Meral 2009: res. 3; Koçhan and Meral 2020: 31, çiz. 2, res. 3.
[69] Wilson Jones 2000a.
[70] Koçhan 2014: 291.
[71] Knackfuss 1941: taf. 44.
[72] Borsook 1973: 191; Schulz 1995: 118.
[73] Barattolo 1995: tavv. 32–39.
[74] Barattolo 1995: 88, tavv. 28–30. Proviene probabilmente dagli scavi di Ertüzün (1964).

di corda (f. 136 r.), consente di ricostruire in linea di massima l'ordine, con un arco di 18 piedi circa di luce in totale, e colonne di circa 35–40 piedi di altezza. Una semicolonna addossata a pilastro al Museo di Istanbul, reimpiegata in un edificio bizantino di Costantinopoli, è formata da una semicolonna decorata da tralci di vite, addossata a un pilastro ornato su due lati da pannelli con tralci di acanto: presenta una base attica senza plinto, sormontata da una doppia corona di foglie di acanto, su cui si imposta il fusto decorato, attribuite ad un eventuale secondo ordine all'interno della cella.[75]

È certamente inusuale trovare arcate su colonne entro un tempio: i rari confronti si trovano piuttosto in basiliche e porticati,[76] ma esiste a Cizico stessa un confronto molto calzante. Si tratta di un blocco con inizio di doppio archivolto, da collocare sopra il capitello e da integrare con il concio centrale; l'iscrizione ΚΑΙϹΑΡΕΙΑΝ ΠΑΝΚΡΑΤΙΝ e la corona con palma nell'area libera tra i due inizi di archivolto lo pone in un contesto di ginnasio;[77] la larghezza di m 1,45 = 5 p.r. è vicina a quella del blocco centrale nel disegno di Fonzio. Si può allora proporre la ricostruzione dell'alzato del tempio: la colonna alta m 19,68, più l'architrave alto circa come il fregio, di m 1,52 (m 3,04 in tutto), più m 2,40 di cornice: in tutto m 25,12 (76 ½ p.d. = 85 p.r.). Le colonne all'interno potevano essere alte p.d. 38 ¾ (m 12,71).

Pochi templi romani si avvicinano alle dimensioni del tempio di Cizico, tra cui il tempio grande di Baalbek,[78] di I sec. d.C., il c.d. tempio di Serapide a Roma,[79] di età severiana, ed il tempio colossale di Tarso (cfr. qui sotto). Il tempio adrianeo di Venere e Roma[80] aveva dimensioni inferiori: a quanto si può ipotizzare dai pochi frammenti rimasti, la colonna era alta 60 p.r. con un diametro inferiore di 6 p.r., e il capitello, se è da identificare con un esemplare solo sbozzato nelle cave di Proconneso,[81] avendo una diagonale d'abaco lunga m 3,6, doveva essere alto circa m 2,1.

La ricostruzione planimetrica qui adottata si basa sulle misure derivate dagli scavi più recenti, sovrapposte alla pianta delle sostruzioni,[82] e dall'adozione di un interasse di m 6,56 circa = 20 piedi dorici, con 8 x 16 colonne. Ne risulta una crepidine di m 116,23 = 355

p.d. (17 interassi e ¾) per 62,3 = 190 p.d. (9 ½ interassi), mentre lo stilobate sarebbe lungo attorno a m 102 (15 ½ interassi = 310 p.d. = m 101,68 = 344 p.r. circa) e largo m 49,2 (7 ½ interassi = 150 p.d. = m 49,2 = 166 p.r.), misure vicine a quelle di Ciriaco (p.r. 360 = m 106,56 e p.r. 165 = m 48,84).[83] Il marmo usato è tutto proconnesio, e Cizico era il centro di smistamento di tale marmo.

Ricostruzione dei costi del tempio di Cizico

Premettiamo che non si sono considerate le tegole in marmo, non essendo certo fino a che punto il tempio fosse coperto, né la decorazione interna della cella, per le incertezze che ancora esistono riguardo alla sua ricostruzione, che si auspica saranno risolte nella prosecuzione degli scavi. Inoltre, per le parti dell'edificio in pietra calcarea e cementizio, si è calcolato solo il costo di manifattura e messa in opera, ma non il costo del materiale, che non è noto.

Il volume del marmo necessario (**Tabella 1**) è stato calcolato in tutto 16063 m³, così diviso: 98 fusti (probabilmente in otto o dieci rocchi), ognuno da 47 m³, ed altrettanti capitelli e basi, rispettivamente 6,4 e 8,13 m³ ciascuno; blocchi di architrave e fregio, nessuno dei quali si conserva integro, 14,7 m³ ciascuno, per 168 esemplari rispettivamente; blocchi di cornice e sima, 15,74 m³ per ogni interasse, cui si deve aggiungere il volume dei rivestimenti della peristasi e i blocchi della cella, per un volume stimato[84] di 4400 m³. Ad un costo di 15 ½ denari per m³, derivato dall'Editto di Diocleziano,[85] si raggiungono così 16063 m³ x 15,5 = 248976,5 denari circa, per il solo marmo proconnesio in cava.

Il trasporto sul cantiere era certo relativamente economico, dato che l'isola di Proconneso da cui proveniva il marmo si trovava di fronte a Cizico,[86] ma va considerato il costo del breve viaggio via mare, comprese le operazioni di carico e scarico, che valutiamo a 8 ½ denari per metro cubo,[87] dunque 136535,5 denari circa.

---

[75] Barattolo 1995: tav. 29. Andrea Barattolo (1995: 87–88, tav. 31.4) ritiene che sopra le fondazioni centrali all'interno della cella vi fossero due ordini sovrapposti; assegna poi un fregio figurato, di cui sono noti frammenti al museo di Istanbul, alti almeno m 0,68, all'ordine inferiore della cella. Cfr. Schulz 1995: 119–120.

[76] Thomas 2007: 40.

[77] Chaniotis et al. 2012: 933. Il blocco è stato trovato in ricerche di superficie ad Ovest del teatro della città, piuttosto distante dal tempio (Yaylali and Özkaya 1995: 318, res. 17).

[78] Wilson Jones 2000a: 221–224.

[79] Töbelmann 1923: 81–82.

[80] Barattolo 1978: 400.

[81] Wilson Jones 1991: 134 n. 54.

[82] Barattolo 1995: fig. 1

[83] La lunghezza dello stilobate risulta maggiore in Ciriaco di circa 3,5 m (mezzo interasse): probabilmente ciò si deve al fatto che sui lati brevi la crepidine era più lunga (aveva gradini più brevi e in maggior numero) rispetto a quella sui lati lunghi, e Ciriaco potrebbe non averne tenuto conto.

[84] Crepidine: lastre rettangolari da m 3,28 x 1,64 x 0,5 = 2,69 m³. Numero = (19 x 4 =76) + (19 x 5 = 95) + (31 x 4 x 2 = 248) = 419 x 2,69 = 1127 m³; pavimento peristasi: lastre quadrate da m 3,28 x 3,28 x 0,5 = 5,38 mc. Numero = 15 x 31 – (area muri cella) = 465 – 35 = 430 x 5,38 = 2313 m³; muri cella: lastre di rivestimento 1,64 x 0,82 x 0,15 = 0,2 m³. Numero = (15 x 60 x 2 = 1800) + (7 x 60 = 420) + (3 x 60 = 180) = 2400 x 2 = 4800 x 0,2 mc = 960 m³. Ai fini del calcolo si è ipotizzato che i componenti fossero tutti uguali tra loro.

[85] Ritengo che vadano accolti in linea di massima i costi dei marmi documentati nell'Editto, che per me sono basati sul piede cubico (Barresi 2003: 168–170).

[86] Monna and Pensabene 1977: 169–170.

[87] Ho discusso altrove le questioni relative (Barresi 2003: 175–178).

ELEMENTI	DIMENSIONI mc/mq x n.	TOT. mc	MATERIALE (den)	TRASPORTO (den)	I LAV. (den)	II LAV. (den)	POSA (den)	TOT. (den)
Fusti	47 / 94 x 98	4606	71393	39151	36157	8340	22572	177613
Capitelli	6,4 /20 x 98	627	9718,5	5329,5	6583,5	1773	3073	26477,5
Basi	8,13 /27 x 98	797	12353,5	6774,5	8368,5	2394	3905	33795,5
b. architrave	14,7 /52 x 168	2470	38285	20995	25935	7906	12104	105225
b. fregio	14,7 /52 x 168	2470	38285	20995	25935	7906	12104	105225
cornice e sima (x 1 interasse)	15,74 / 68 x 44	693	10741,5	5890,5	7276,5	2707	16980	43595,5
Altre lastre e blocchi	4400 / 29442		68200	37400	34540	26645	21562	188347
Totali	16063 mc		248976,5	136535,5	144795,5	57671	92300	680278,5

Tabella 1. Cizico, opere in marmo.

La prima lavorazione sul posto può essere valutata in ore di lavoro:[88] 157 ore al metro cubo di marmo per fusti e blocchi, e 210 ore al metro cubo di marmo per gli elementi con decorazione. Valutando il salario giornaliero di una giornata media di 10 ore di lavoro a 0,5 denarii, si ottengono così quote di 36157 denari (fusti) e 34540 denari (blocchi della crepidine e della cella), mentre capitelli, basi e trabeazione sono valutati in tutto 74098,5 denari: in tutto 143178,5 denari.

La decorazione architettonica era poi sottoposta ad una lavorazione successiva alla messa in opera, che si valuta complessivamente 18,1 ore al metro quadro di superficie:[89] 8340 denari per i fusti, 15812 complessivi per fregi e architravi, 6869 denari circa per basi, capitelli e cornici, e 26645 denari per blocchi e lastre di pavimentazione e rivestimento. Alcuni frammenti di decorazione marmorea, come si è visto, non hanno avuto l'ultima finitura; non includiamo dunque il costo della scultura architettonica, perché non è possibile sapere quanta parte della decorazione sia stata rifinita. Del resto, anche in un altro tempio colossale, con tempi di costruzione che si sono prolungati dal medio ellenismo all'età imperiale, come il Didymaion di Mileto, si è osservato che parte della decorazione è rimasta parzialmente incompiuta, specie se in punti poco visibili.[90]

Per valutare la messa in opera, per ogni tonnellata di marmo, si presuppongono due operai, un tagliapietre, 4 manovali, con una distanza di avvicinamento in media di 100 m e un'altezza media di 10 m;[91] poiché il peso totale del marmo impiegato risulta circa t 43343, il numero di ore di lavoro per la messa in opera ha

un costo totale di 92300 denari. Il costo totale delle parti marmoree dovrebbe dunque aggirarsi sui 680278 denari.

Va aggiunto il costo delle opere per scavo e costruzione di sostruzioni e fondazioni.[92]

Le dimensioni considerate sono circa m 120 in lunghezza, m 60 in larghezza e m 8 in altezza. Si calcola (Tabella 2) un volume complessivo di terra scavata di circa 57600 m³, per un calcolo del lavoro necessario in 13133 giornate di lavoro / uomo. Si aggiunge la costruzione dei muri, circa metà dei quali in calcare e metà in opera cementizia, spessi in media m 2,72, e delle volte a botte; risulta più costosa la costruzione di muri in blocchi squadrati di calcare, in tutto 229532 giornate,[93] mentre per i muri in opera cementizia[94] 94606 giornate, e per le sette volte a botte parallele 64262.[95] Il totale è dunque 441499 giornate di lavoro, che al salario ipotizzato di mezzo denaro a giornata, si valutano 220749,5 denari circa, dallo scavo alla costruzione. Il costo totale del tempio è quindi dell'ordine di 900000 denari.

Il grande tempio di Tarso

Il Donuk Taş[96] a Tarso è un colossale basamento rettangolare di m 123 x 42,90, alto m 11,56, costituito da opera cementizia colata tra blocchi squadrati di calcare, di cui oggi restano solo le impronte, essendo

---

[88] Pegoretti 1863, I: 392.
[89] Pegoretti 1863, I: 407–409.
[90] Barresi 2015: figs 2–3.
[91] Pegoretti 1863, II: 216.
[92] Abbiamo utilizzato il calcolo di Janet DeLaine (1997) per le terme di Caracalla.
[93] Pegoretti 1863, I: 16, 279, 355; II: 137.
[94] Pegoretti 1863, II: 83, 140; DeLaine 1997: App. 5.
[95] Pegoretti 1863, II: 78.
[96] "Pietra ghiacciata" (Donuk) o "pietra sottosopra" (Dönük): Held 2008: 164. Sarebbe il tempio della I neokoria di Tarso (Draeger 1993: 128), per alcuni dedicato a Ercole fondatore della città, identificato con Commodo (Baydur 2001: 229), spiegando podio e scalinata frontale con l'influenza dei grandi templi siriaci.

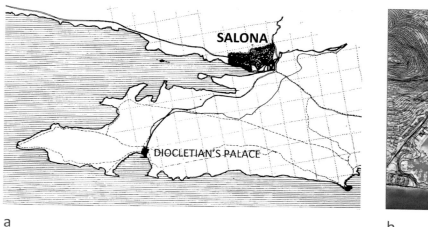

a

b

Figure 1. a) Salona, the *ager* of Salona, and Diocletian's Palace (drawing: J. Marasović); b) original coastline of the Split bay shown on an orthophoto (drawing: J. Marasović, updated by K. Marasović).

to the *fabrica*.[6] Belamarić believes that another factory, the *gynaeceum Iovensis Dalmatiae – Aspalatho* (imperial weaving factory producing woollen clothing), also listed in *Notitia Dignitatum Occidentalis XI*, could have existed in Diocletian's time and been situated somewhere in the vicinity of the Palace or even within the Palace in the zone north of the *decumanus*.[7]

State ownership of the land has also recently been mentioned again as one of the factors that may have influenced the choice of this particular location for the Palace. Two hypotheses have been suggested: Basić, basing his argument on Roman agrimensorial practices, suggests that since the land divisions (*centuriae*) lacked a regular shape due to the coastline, they fell under the *ius subsecivorum* and were, as such, declared state property (**Figure 1a**). This legal status facilitated the process of land acquisition for the construction of the Palace.[8] Alternatively, Cambi suggests that the land was part of the imperial estate of Probus on the basis of an inscription fragment dedicated to the emperor Probus (*CIL* III, 8707) and a fragment of a frieze depicting weapons, both of which were found near the west wall of Diocletian's Palace. He connects them both to a triumphal monument dedicated to the emperor located on the estate. According to Roman law, since Probus had no direct descendants, after his death the land reverted to state property, which Diocletian could legitimately use to construct his Palace.[9]

No matter what the specific reasoning behind the Palace's location was, its position in the vicinity of the provincial capital impacted a number of factors related

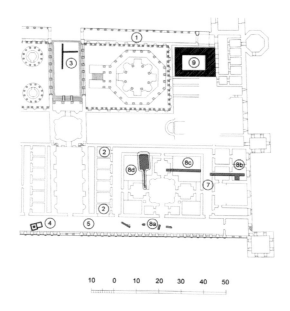

Figure 2. Vestiges of an earlier complex discovered under the Palace (drawing: S. Perojević, J. Marasović and K. Marasović).

to its construction, from the engagement of labour to the use of local workshops and the availability of stockpiled building material.[10] The Split peninsula was inhabited in the pre-Diocletianic period as indicated by numerous archaeological finds related to earlier settlements, including necropoleis with gravestones. Moreover, the Peutinger map marks two toponyms on the peninsula: *ad Dianam* (temple) situated on the Cape of Marjan hill and Spalatum situated within the area of the bay where the Palace was later constructed. The vestiges of a settlement, perhaps a *vicus*, were found on the peninsula

---

[6] Cambi 2005: 137–139.
[7] Belamarić 2003; 2004. An important part of Belamarić's hypothesis, namely, his calculation of the capacity of the aqueduct of Diocletian's Palace, proved to be incorrect; Marasović and Margeta 2018.
[8] Basić 2012a.
[9] Cambi 2016b.

[10] It can be assumed that such storage depots existed in Salona, although there is currently no archaeological evidence to support this.

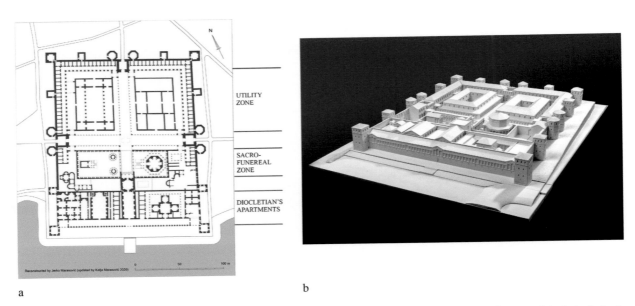

a   b

Figure 3. a) Ground plan of Diocletian's Palace (drawing: J. Marasović, updated by K. Marasović); b) 3D model of Diocletian's Palace (drawing: J. Marasović, updated by K. Marasović).

in the areas east and west of the Palace.[11] The remains of an earlier building complex were also discovered under the Palace (**Figure 2**). Although the layout, function, and development of this earlier structure remain to be determined, several finds including architectural elements – a stone seat from an auditorium, an architrave, and several cornice blocks – provide some clues. The shape of the stone seat and the cornice blocks indicate that they belonged to a building of semi-circular, circular, or elliptical shape.[12] Moreover, stylistic analysis of the motifs on the cornice blocks suggest a date for the complex in the second half of the 2nd century AD.[13]

The preexisting complex must have influenced the overall construction cost of the Palace, as it had to be demolished and may have provided material for reuse. According to Marasović *et al.*, the limestone blocks of this complex were reused for the construction of Diocletian's Palace, while blocks with architectural decoration were discarded in the sewage canal where some of them were found during archaeological campaigns carried out in 1995–1996.[14] It is also possible that its marble bases, column shafts, and capitals were reused in the Palace. All told, this would have likely reduced both the cost and the duration of the Palace's construction.

The site of the Palace's construction also had a bearing on the overall construction cost. The position of the Palace

immediately on the coast, within the Gulf of Salona (Kaštela Bay), provided excellent access to maritime transport, which meant that all of the construction material (limestone blocks extracted from the nearby quarries, Plata, Stražišće, Rasohe on the island of Brač, and probably from the quarries of Seget and Sutilija situated in the vicinity of city of Trogir, as well as imported elements of architectural decoration, etc.) could be transported directly to the construction site using the more economical option of sea transportation (**Figure 1b**).[15]

The architectural design of the Mausoleum and its specific location within the Palace were also important for the cost of construction. The Mausoleum is situated in the so-called sacral (or sacro-funereal) zone, one of the three distinct main zones of the Palace (along with the utility zone situated north of the *decumanus* and the zone of Diocletian's apartments, which occupied the southern part of the Palace). The sacral zone is situated between the *decumanus* and the apartments (**Figure 3a and b**). It consists of two *temenos* areas of different size, positioned symmetrically on the east and west sides of a rectangular courtyard (traditionally identified as the peristyle of Diocletian's Palace). The larger *temenos* in the west contains three buildings: two smaller circular buildings and a building in the form of a prostyle temple. The *temenos* in the east contains the Mausoleum

---

[11] See Bašić 2012a for a review of the different theories suggested.
[12] Marasović *et al.* 2000: 178–180; Perojević *et al.* 2009: 51–66.
[13] See Marasović and Marasović 1965 for pers. comm. from Kähler, proposing a date in the 1st or 2nd century. See Marasović 2005: 364 for pers. comm. from Cambi, proposing a date to the 2nd century. Matetić Poljak 2014a: 193 dates the blocks to the Hadrianic-Antonine period.
[14] Marasović *et al.* 2000: 178–179; Perojević *et al.* 2009: 57.

[15] For identification of the local quarries providing the limestone blocks, see Miliša and Marinković 2018. For a summary of the archaeological investigation carried out in front of the southern façade of Diocletian's Palace and the various discoveries relating to the ancient waterfront, see Delonga 2007; Delonga and Alajbeg 2007. See also Marasović 2019, who presents a reconstruction of the waterfront during the Diocletianic period.

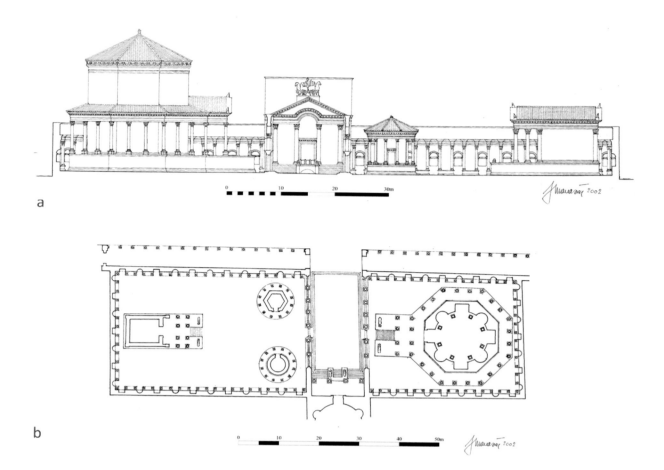

a

b

Figure 4. Reconstruction of the sacro-funereal zone: a) view of the sacro-funereal zone (drawing: J. Marasović); b) ground plan of the sacro-funereal zone (drawing: J. Marasović).

of Diocletian. Both *temenoi* were enclosed by a high wall on three sides. The fourth side is delimited by a peristyle colonnade. The access to the *temenos* area is gained through the fifth intercolumniation (counting from the *decumanus*) (**Figures 4a,** and **b**). The location of the Mausoleum therefore meant that only three sides of the octagon were visible from the peristyle, which allowed blocks used on the other sides to be left unfinished, thus reducing the overall cost of the Mausoleum project (see below).

The precise start date for the construction of Diocletian's Palace is unknown. It is widely accepted that the project must have begun shortly after the Tetrarchy had been established in AD 293 (in which the planned abdication of the senior Augusti represents a key element). If started at this date, the period of construction might have been approximately 12 years (until Diocletian's abdication in AD 305 at the insistence of Galerius).[16] In comparison, a period of 7 to 8 years has been estimated for the construction of the Baths of Diocletian in Rome. Since the Baths were almost three times larger in surface area than the Palace (*c.* 120,000 m^2 compared to nearly 39,600 m^2), 12 years seems overly long for its construction.[17] However, if we assume that the precise year (or date) of Diocletian's abdication was not fully determined when the Tetrarchy was established, the construction of the Palace could have started later, lasting less than 12 years. It is possible that upon Diocletian's decision to abdicate, the construction was accelerated in order to complete the work and make all of the arrangements necessary to receive the emperor. As is discussed below, there is abundant evidence for the use of unfinished architectural decoration in the Palace, including a number of elements belonging to the Mausoleum. We can perhaps speculate that the inclusion of unfinished material was a consequence of the construction timeframe being accelerated as a result of Diocletian's decision to abdicate.

[16] Lactantius, De Mortibus Persecutorum 19.

[17] Marasović and Margeta 2018: 215. The Palace has a width of 180 m and a length of 220 m. The central quadrangle of the *Baths of Diocletian* measures approximately 37,700 m^2; Lombardi and Santucci 2015: 78.

Figure 5. Mausoleum – Split Cathedral, an aerial view
(photo: T. Bartulović).

History of the Mausoleum

The Mausoleum was converted into a cathedral dedicated to the Assumption of the Blessed Virgin Mary in the early Middle Ages (**Figure 5**).[18] The position of the Mausoleum inside the Palace has given rise to debate about its original function and if it was indeed Diocletian's Mausoleum. While historical sources record that Diocletian died in the Palace, they do not specify the location of his tomb.[19] The first historical source to mention the octagonal building (the cathedral) as Diocletian's burial site is Constantine Porphyrogenitus.[20] The text, belonging to the 11th-century and dubiously attributed to Adam of Paris, references it as *Templum Iovi*. Two centuries later, Thomas the Archdeacon likewise refers to the building as *Templum Iovis*.[21] The 15th-century texts of Cyriacus of Ancona and Marko Marulić and the 16th-century texts

of Giambattista Giustinian, Antonio Proculiano, and Pietro Niccolini refer to the building as the Temple of Jupiter. The first monographs on the Palace by Robert Adam and Vicko Andrić (the first conservator in Split in the 19th century) also refer to the Mausoleum as the Temple of Jupiter.[22]

At the beginning of the 20th century, Niemann identified the building as Diocletian's Mausoleum.[23] Hébrard and Zeiller posited that in addition to functioning as a mausoleum, it also served as a kind of pseudo-temple of Jupiter since Diocletian regarded himself as the son of Jupiter.[24] This interpretation was also accepted by Bulić and Karaman.[25] In general, modern scholarship identifies the octagonal building as Diocletian's Mausoleum based on an identification attributed to Porphyrogenitus, the form of the building, which corresponds to Roman (Tetrarchic) imperial mausolea in Late Antiquity,[26] the figural motifs of the architectural decoration,[27] and fragments of red porphyry, which have been identified as Diocletian's sarcophagus. These fragments were found in the vicinity of the building[28] but their identification is still debated.[29] Alternatively, some scholars have suggested that the building was both the Temple of Jupiter and Diocletian's Mausoleum or the Divii Diocletiani,[30] with Hesberg proposing that the tomb was located in the crypt beneath the cella of the *templum*.[31]

Description of the Mausoleum and its dimensions

The importance of the Mausoleum building is also emphasised by its dimensions (it is the highest building in the Palace) and by its position in the *temenos* area of the Palace. The *temenos* wall was articulated by an alternation of semicircular and rectangular niches, in front of which were pedestals carrying columns and an

---

[18] Basić 2016; 2017. See Marasović 2011, for an overview of various problems related to the date for the conversion of the Mausoleum into a cathedral. Basić believes that the Christianisation of the Mausoleum occurred in several stages over the course of the early Middle Ages (from the 6th to 9th centuries).
[19] Lactantius (*De Mortibus Persecutorum* 42, 3) and Saint Jerome (*Hyeronimi Chronicon*, ed. 1913: 230.) both record Diocletian's death in the Palace. Ammianus Marcellinus (Rerum *gestarum libri qui supersunt* XVI, 8, 3-7) in AD 356 mentions the theft of a purple garment from Diocletian's tomb. Sidonius Apollinaris (Carmen XXIII) in AD 495 also records Diocletian's burial site as being in Dalmation Salona (...*ille cuius bustum Dalmaticae vident Salonae...*).
[20] Constantine Porphyrogenitus, *De Administrando Imperio*, ch. 29.
[21] T. Arhiđakon (Thomas the Archdeacon), ed. 2003: ch. IV, 16, 18. An overview of historical sources is given by McNally 1996: 30; Marasović 1998; Basić 2016; 2017.

[22] On the the original function of the building, see the overviews by Marasović 1995; McNally 1996: 30; Marasović *et al.* 2006; Basić 2016; 2017.
[23] Niemann 1910: 62–79.
[24] Hébrard and Zeiller (1912: 78) argued that the 'real' Temple of Jupiter in the Palace would have been a prostyle temple located in the western *temenos*.
[25] Bulić and Karaman 1927: 75.
[26] For domed, circular, or octagonal Tetrarchic mausoleum types, see Johnson 2009. The closest comparison is the so-called Mausoleum of Maximian at San Vittore, Milan.
[27] McNally 1996: 32; Marasović *et al.* 2006.
[28] The fragments are kept in the Archaeological Museum in Split. On the sarcophagus, see Marin 2006; Bujević 2019.
[29] Some opponents to the identification of the building as Diocletian's Mausoleum cite the location inside the Palace, cf. Duval 1997; 2003: 298–299. Alternatively, Čurčić 1993 believes that the building is a *heroon* erected in honour of the founder of the new palace-city. Vasić 1997 argues that the octagon was a temple dedicated to the cult of Jupiter, the Jovian dynasty, and other gods. Babić (2018 and 2019) connects the relief of Diocletian's wife Prisca with the goddess Isis and therefore suggests that the octagonal building was a temple dedicated to the goddess Isis Panthea.
[30] On Diocletian's possible deification, see Eutropius: IX, 28; Cambi 2010: 185; 2016a: 120–121.
[31] Hesberg 1978: 967.

Figure 6. Section through the Mausoleum (drawing: G. Niemann).

entablature. The relationship between the architectural order of the *temenos* walls and the Mausoleum is rather unusual. According to Marasović's reconstruction (**Figure 4a**), on the north and south sides the distance between the walls and the Mausoleum is 1.5 m, while on the east side it is only 0.5 m.

The Mausoleum has an octagonal ground plan in front of which projects a rectangular *pronaos*. The high podium carries the cella surrounded by a portico (**Figure 6**). The building was constructed on a platform made of two layers of roughly rectangular stones set on a rubble layer of smaller stones.[32] This platform extends over the entire area of the eastern *temenos*. The foundations of the Mausoleum and the *prostasis* (porch) rest on a lower platform layer. This consists of three rows of roughly

worked blocks with a lower row 0.50 m high and two upper rows 0.40 m high. The upper layer of the platform extended over the area between the Mausoleum and the *temenos* wall. The area between the top layer of the platform and the final row of foundation blocks was filled with soil.

Crypt

A circular, domed crypt (12.75 m in diam.), articulated with eight pylons enclosing seven wedge-shaped niches, was built in the podium of the structure (**Figure 7a**). The entrance to the crypt was below soil level. The narrow access passage, which turns at a 90-degree angle, leads into the crypt. The lower layer of stones of the platform also forms the floor of the crypt. A well with a water source is also set within the crypt floor. The upper layer (representing the top of the platform)

---

[32] McNally *et al*. 1976: 49.

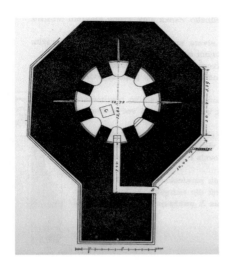

a

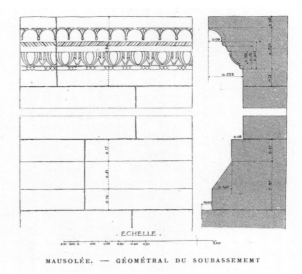

b

. ECHELLE .

MAUSOLÉE. — GÉOMÉTRAL DU SOUBASSEMEMT

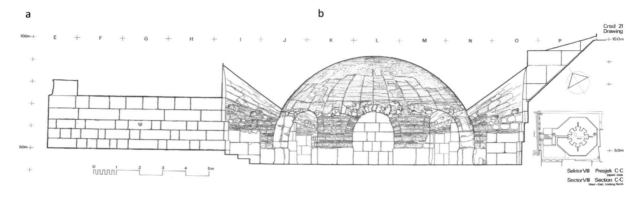

c

Figure 7. Crypt: a) ground plan (drawing: G. Niemann); b) podium base and cornice moulding (drawing: E. Hébrard and J. Zeiller); c) section through the crypt (drawing: A. Čipin).

forms the floor of the passage leading to the crypt. The height difference between these two levels of the floor was solved by adding two steps (**Figure 7c**). The crypt is not decorated. The niche pylons were constructed of a single row of limestone blocks, above which are rows of rough stones and bricks. The dome is made of rough tuff stones. The inner side of the perimeter wall of the crypt is constructed of rectangular limestone blocks. The lack of decoration and the fact that there is no evidence that the crypt was accessible in the Diocletianic period suggest that it served as a sort of 'crawl space' supporting the cella (funeral chamber).[33]

The exterior wall of the podium is constructed of prismatic limestone blocks at each corner of the octagon (two sides enclosing the angle of 135 degrees). Between them, along each side of the octagon, vertical

rectangular orthostates are placed (usually eight orthostate blocks per side).

The exterior of the podium has a simple base moulding (with an oblique plane and fillet) on which the protrusions used to lift the blocks into place are still preserved. The podium's cornice is composed of a superposition of bead and reel, egg and dart, fillet, astragal with cable motif, cavetto with shear-shaped leaves, and a fillet (**Figure 7b**).[34] The crypt was made from a total of 2645 m³ of stone.[35]

[33] Marasović *et al.* 2006: 501.

[34] The decorative architectural elements from the Mausoleum have been studied in detail by McNally 1996 and Matetić Poljak 2009b.
[35] For measurements, see Niemann 1910: 64–65; Johnson 2009: 61 and fig. 38. The measurements are as follows, internal diameter: 8.66 m; height, from the floor of the crypt to the floor of the cella: 5.73 m; the roof formed by a dome: 7.99 m in diameter and 2.41 m in height; thickness of the dome at the top: 0.32 m; depth of the niches: 2 m; dimensions of the open door on the south side: 1.82 m tall × 1.02 m wide; dimensions of the corridor connecting the door with the internal hall: width: 1.02 m, length divided into two sectors of 6 m

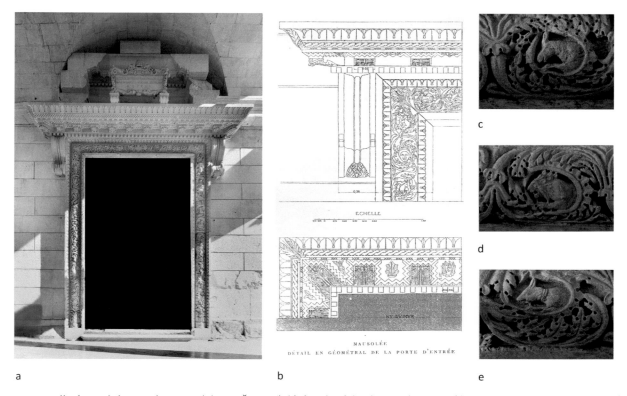

Figure 8. Cella door: a) door and cornice (photo: Ž. Bačić); b) details of the door and cornice (drawing: E. Hébrard and J. Zeiller); c-e) animal protomes in the inhabited scroll (photo: D. Matetić Poljak).

Cella

The cella's monumental doorway is surrounded by a finely carved limestone frame with inhabited acanthus scroll decoration, above which is a richly decorated Corinthian cornice set on two S-shaped consoles, all of which served to emphasise the cella's entrance (**Figure 8a**). The inhabited acanthus scroll motif has been documented only within the sacro-funereal zone of the Palace. The scroll decoration features protomes of different animals and a single mask (**Figures 8c, d** and **e**).[36] The two large S-shaped consoles are not original

but replicas belonging to the 19th century.[37] The copies are each decorated with a finely indented acanthus leaf on the lower volute. The Corinthian cornice is richly decorated by a superposition of various elements and decorative motifs: dentils, consoles, fillet, bead and reel, guilloche, fillet, shear-shaped leaf, and dart. Cornice modillions are of S-shaped type, they feature a leaf bundle on the front side and an acanthus spinosus leaf applied to the bottom side. The soffit coffers are decorated either with a vegetal or floral motif. The modillions and soffit coffers are framed by a zig-zag motif (**Figure 8b**).

The interior of the cella is circular (13.30 m in diameter), articulated with eight alternating semicircular and rectangular niches. The entrance to the cella is positioned within the western rectangular niche. The cella walls are constructed with blocks held together with iron clamps and laid using the *isodomum* technique.[38] The cross-section of the wall, now visible as a result of a door and a window cut into the wall of the eastern rectangular niche during the 16th century, shows that it was composed of at least three rows of

---

and 7.5 m; height of the external upper moulding of the podium: 0.54 m; projection of this moulding: 0.25 m; length of this moulding: 84 m; height of the lower moulding at the base of the crypt: 0.54 m; projection of this moulding: 0.25 m; dimensions of the podium blocks: height: 2.07/2.10 m and thickness: 1.00 m. The calculation of the stone volume for the crypt was based on the formula 4 × L (side) × apo (apothem or distance from the centre of the octagon to the centre of one side), which equals: 4 × 10.67 m × 12.59 = 537 m², with the volume being 537 m² × 5.73 m (height) = 3077 m³, from which value the internal space of the niches as well as the internal corridor and the dome must be subtracted. The niches measure: depth 2 m, width 1.74 m, height 2.40 m, with a total volume of 8.35 m³ × 8 niches, which equals 67 m³. The internal corridor measures: height 1.82 m, width 1.02 m, length 13.5 m, giving a volume of 25 m³. For the volume of the dome it is necessary to start with the diameter of the interior of the crypt, which equals 8.66 m. Using the following formula: $4/3\pi r^3$, we get: $4/3 × 3.1416 × 4.33^3 = 4/3 × 255$, which gives a total volume of 340 m³.
[36] Matetić Poljak 2014b.

[37] Part of the original cornice is now stored in the Archeological Museum in Split.
[38] Nikšić 1995.

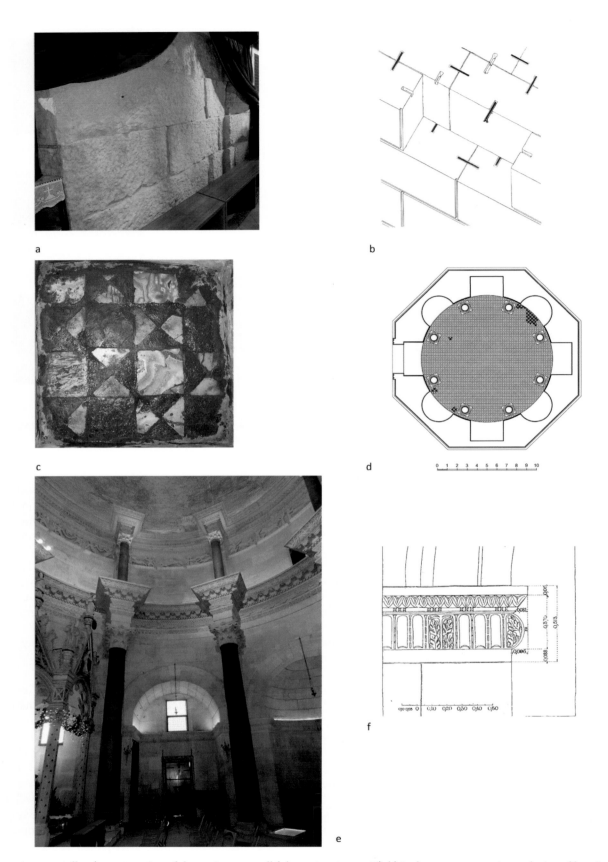

Figure 9. Cella: a) construction of the perimeter wall (photo: K. Marasović); b) *isodomum* construction technique (drawing: G. Nikšić); c) *opus sectile* pavement (photo: Z. Sunko); d) reconstruction of the original Mausoleum pavement (drawing: K. Marasović, V. Marinković); e) two architectural orders of the cella (photo: K. Marasović); f) impost (drawing: E. Hébrard and J. Zeiller).

stone blocks (Figures 9 and b). Overall, the cella required a total of 1474 m³ of stone for its construction.[39]

Various archaeological excavations have uncovered an *opus sectile* pavement of a rather simple geometric pattern composed of squares arranged in chromatic contrast. It is composed of whole squares measuring 13 by 13 cm (Guidobaldi's Q motif) or squares of the same dimensions but composed of four small triangles (Guidobaldi's Qt motif)[40] (**Figure 9c**). On the basis of visual identification, the stones have been identified as *alabastro, bigio antico, pavonazzetto, Rosso Cario (Iassense),* an unidentified bluish marble, and a black limestone of unknown origin that was also used for mosaic floors elsewhere in the Palace.[41] The *opus sectile* pavement covered the entire circular area of the cella, while more roughly made limestone slabs were discovered at the same level as the *opus sectile* floor in the niches. According to Marasović and Marinković, the floor of the niches was raised in the form of a limestone platform, similar to the one preserved in the western rectangular niche in which the entrance to the Mausoleum is placed (**Figure 9d**).[42] Due to the difficulties reconstructing the proportions of each type of marble used in the floor, it has been excluded from the cost calculations generated for the Mausoleum.

Architectural decoration of the cella

The architectural decoration of the cella is composed of several elements, including convex imposts within the wall, archivolts in the niches, two superimposed architectural orders, and a separate frieze (**Figure 9e**). The convex imposts run under the niche's calottes uninterruptedly around the entire cella wall. It is decorated with both plain hollow tongues and hollow tongues containing indented acanthus leaves, while its crown, representing a raking fillet, is decorated with a bead and reel motif and a zig-zag composed of leaves (**Figure 9f**). The archivolts in the niches have two fasciae and a crown representing a raking fillet.

The lower architectural order is Corinthian and the upper is Composite. Both orders have the entablature *en ressaut.* Excessive restoration of the cella during the 19th century resulted in all capitals of both orders, several pilasters of the lower order, and most of the entablature blocks being replaced by copies. The originals are currently located outside the Palace near the northern perimeter wall or in the Archaeological Museum in Split.

The eight columns of the lower order have limestone Ionic-Attic bases with plinths.[43] The column shafts are monolithic, and their slightly different heights suggest that they are *spolia.* Six of the columns are probably in Aswan red granite, to which we have attributed an average cost of 100 *denarii*/ft³, with the remaining two carved from Traodense granite. The columns are arranged so that the two shafts in Troadense granite accentuate the rectangular niche located directly opposite the entrance (**Figure 13; Table 1, no. 26–27**).[44] The limestone capitals are of normal Corinthian type. Their decoration corresponds to other Corinthian limestone capitals elsewhere in the Palace such as the capitals of the Mausoleum's portico and the capitals of the peristyle and prothyron. The decoration of the capitals places them stylistically in the Diocletianic period (**Figure 10b**).[45]

The entablature is composed of three blocks: an Ionic architrave with two fasciae and a crown moulding ornamented with an egg and dart motif; a convex frieze with an overlapping laurel leaf motif, and a

---

[39]   The cella has an internal diameter of 13.30 m, an external length from corner to corner of 20.30 m, a height from floor to roof of 21.70 m, several open niches on the walls, 3.50 m wide, and one in front of the door measuring 4.70 m, 5.44 m tall, and 2.58 m deep (see Niemann 1910: 74; Johnson 2009: 60, 64). The jambs of the cella entrance are 5.65 m tall, 0.57 m wide, 1.17 m thick, with a lintel 0.57 m tall and 4.14 m long. The cornice above the entrance has a height of 0.64 m, a thickness of 0.80 m, and a length of 6.20 m. The S-shaped consoles supporting the cornice have a height of 1.10 m, a width of 0.37 m, and a projection from the wall of 0.42 m. The width of the cella walls varies, since it is a circle inside an octagon. On average the walls are *c.* 2.74 m at the sides and 3.30 m at the corners of the octagon. The stone blocks used for the wall's construction measure: 0.54 × 0.58, 0.54 × 0.73, and 0.54 × 1.24. They are joined with a band of *caementicium.* The volume calculations are based on: the area of the octagon (in plan) multiplied by the height of the cella. These dimensions were applied with the following formula: 4 × L (side) × apo (apothem or distance from the centre of the octagon to the centre of a side) = 4 × 7.69 m × 9.13 m = 281 m² × 13.95 m (height of the cella without the dome) = 3920 m³. To this we need to add the area and volume of the interior of the cella (which is cylindrical in shape) and subtract this value from the volume of the octagon. Here we used a cylinder volume formula: πr²·h (height) = 3.1416 × 6.675² × 13.95 m = 1.953 m³. Next, the area of the semi-circular niches was multiplied by their height to obtain their volume. This total volume was then multiplied by four to give the total volume of semi-circular niches, which was subtracted from the total volume of the octagon. This was calculated as follows: width 3.50 m, height 5.44 m, depth 2.58 m, using the area of the circle = πr² = 3.1416 × 2.58² = 21m²/2 = 10.5 m² semicircle × 5.44 m height = 57.12 m³ × 4 niches = 228.5 m³. Finally, the area of the rectangular niches was multiplied by their height to get the volume of these elements. As with the semi-circular niches, this total was then multiplied by four and the total subtracted from the volume of the octagon. This was calculated as follows: width 4.70 m, height 5.44 m, depth 2.58 m = 66 m³ × 4 niches = 264 m³. All together, this gives a total of 1474 m³ for the cella.

[40]   Guidobaldi 2003: 18, fig. 3.

[41]   Marasović *et al.* 2015; Marasović and Marinković 2018: 841.

[42]   Marasović and Marinković 2018: 841.

[43]   The dimensions of this architectural order are as follows: plinth under the bases: height from 0.13 to 0.16 m and length from 1.18 to 1.128 m; bases: height from 0.40 to 0.45 m; monolithic shafts: height from 5.84 to 6.10 m, with an average value of 5.97 m, lower diameter from 0.74 to 0.79 m, with an average value of 0.76 m; limestone Corinthian capitals: height from 0.87 to 1.04 m, abacus length from 1.11 to 1.18 m.

[44]   Marasović *et al.* 2015: 1005.

[45]   The style of the acanthus leaf, which consists of a broad flat midrib, two or three pairs of lobes, and a bent top leaflet with deeply carved folios and eyelets in the shape of a curved teardrop with rectangular bases, is typical for this type of capital; Scrinari 1957: 48; Matetić Poljak 2009a: 203.

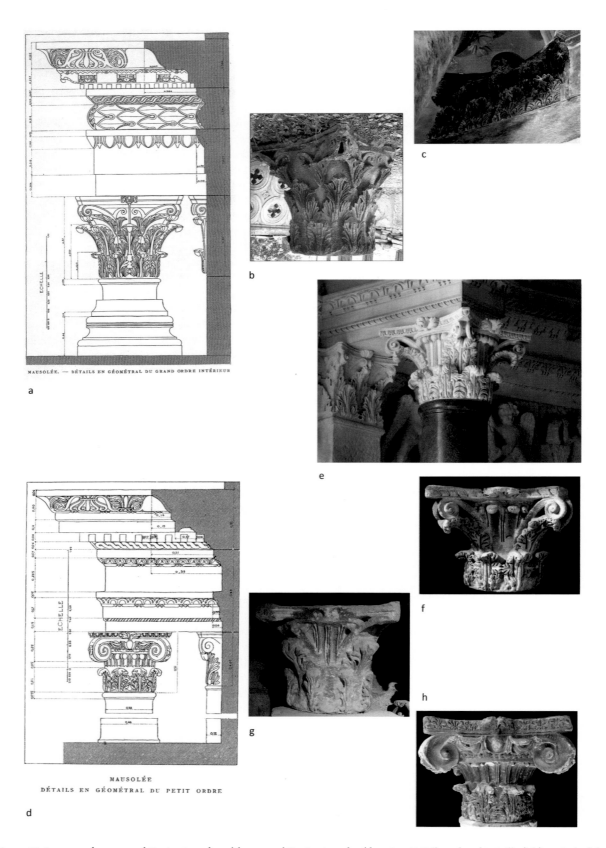

Figure 10. Lower and upper architectonic order: a) lower architectonic order (drawing: E. Hébrard and J. Zeiller); b) capital of the lower architectonic order (photo: D. Matetić Poljak); c) pilaster capital of the lower architectonic order (photo: D. Matetić Poljak); d) upper architectonic order (drawing: E. Hébrard and J. Zeiller); e) pilaster capital of the upper architectonic order (photo: D. Matetić Poljak); f) Corinthicising capital (photo: D. Matetić Poljak); g) Corinthicising capital with acanthus spinosus leaves (photo: D. Matetić Poljak); h) Composite capital (photo: : D. Matetić Poljak).

guilloche carved on an oblique part of the crown; and a Corinthian-type cornice.[46] The latter consists of dentils, S-type modillions decorated with a leaf bundle on the front and an acanthus leaf on the bottom, and soffit coffers decorated with either a floral or vegetal motif, bordered by a zigzag motif, which extends to the crown of the modillions, and a *cyma recta* with anthemion composed of alternating acanthusized and closed flame palmettes (**Figure 10a**).

Behind each of the column capitals a pilaster capital projects from the wall. Unlike the upper order, the pilaster capitals do not have shafts and bases.[47] The pilaster capitals are carved in limestone and belong to the Corinthian type with two rows of leaves, two volutes, and two or more helices. The leaves of the pilaster capitals are of two different types: two feature the acanthus spinosus leaf that is typical of 'Diocletianic stylisation', while six examples feature fine indented leaves (**Figure 10c**).

The upper Composite order has eight columns deployed without bases (**Figure 10d**).[48] The column shafts, which differ slightly in height and are therefore probably *spolia,* are of two types of marble. The four columns of the main axis are red porphyry, while the remaining four are granito del foro (**Figure 13; Table 1, no. 31–38**). On the lower part of one of the red porphyry shafts, part of an apophyge was cut in order to adjust its height to the required dimension. All of the capitals are of grey, probably Proconnesian marble, which has

been used here as the basis for calculating their cost. Of the eight capitals, three are Composite and five are of Corinthicising type (**Figures 10f** and **h**). All capitals have fine indented acanthus leaves, with the exception of one belonging to the Corinthicising type, on which acanthus spinosus leaves are applied (**Figure 10g**).

Even though the capitals have been dated to the Diocletianic period, as Scrinari has pointed out, they might also be *spolia*.[49] The style of the indented leaves of the capitals in the Mausoleum differs from the type of fine indented leaves applied to other limestone elements in the Mausoleum. To a certain degree, they are similar to the stylisation of the leaves on a capital from Antalya dated to the second half of the 2nd century, two capitals from Tyre now dated to the second half of the 2nd century,[50] and capitals of the third order of the scaenae frons of the theatre in Hierapolis in Phrygia that are dated to the beginning of the 3rd century.[51] The anthemion on one Composite-type capital differs from the motifs discovered elsewhere in the Palace. Moreover, the presence of one capital with acanthus spinosus leaves in the upper order suggests that this capital had to be substituted for a capital that had been damaged during transport or construction.

The entablature, carved in local limestone, is composed of an architrave-frieze and Ionic cornice. The architrave has two fasciae divided by a cable motif, and a bead and reel divides the upper fascia from the top crown moulding, which is decorated with a stirrup framed leaf and dart motif. The frieze is plain and articulated with bead and reel decoration under the crown, which is decorated with shear-shaped leaves. The Ionic cornice consists of the following superimposed decorative elements: a motif of guilloche, dentils, plain corona, raking fillet, and *cyma recta* with anthemion of the same type as that of the lower order. Directly behind the columns of the upper order are eight pilasters shafts in Brač limestone and Corinthian capitals in local limestone that were decorated with acanthus spinosus leaves but some with the sides only semi-finished (**Figure 10e**).[52]

A frieze composed of 24 panels runs beneath the entablature of the upper architectural order. The panels have three iconographic themes: two erotes carrying garlands below a mask, erotes in hunting scenes, or scenes of erotes in a chariot race (**Figure 11e**). In addition, three panels show two erotes carrying a laurel wreath inside which busts appear. Two of the busts have been identified as Diocletian (**Figure 11c**) and his wife

---

[46] The dimensions of this entablature are as follows: architrave: 0.77 m in height, 0.67 m in thickness; frieze: height from 0.50 to 0.52 m, 0.95 m in thickness; cornice: height from 0.50 to 0.56 m, 1.38 m in thickness, length of a whole block: 1.40 m; imposts: 1.50 m in length and 1.00 m in width.

[47] These elements are similar in height to the columns, e.g. around 0.96 m (Matetić Poljak 2009a: 225), with an abacus length of 1.10 m.

[48] The dimensions of this architectural order are as follows. For the monolithic shafts: height from 3.11 to 3.15 m, with an average value of 3.13 m; smaller diameter: from 0.45 to 0.47 m, with an average value of 0.46 m. For the capitals: height from 0.47 to 0.52 m, with an average value of 0.50 m, abacus length: from 0.61 to 0.72 m, with an average value of 0.66 m. For the architrave/frieze blocks: height from 0.34 to 0.67, 0.45 m in thickness, and 2.40 m in length; cornice: 0.52 m, 1.30 m in thickness, with a block length of 1.52 m. The dimensions of each of the capitals are as follows, for the pseudo-Corinthian capitals with *finemente dentellate* leaves: one is 50.5 cm in height, 39 cm in diameter, with an abacus length of 66 cm, another is 47 cm in height, 39 cm in diameter, with an abacus length of 65 cm; another is 48 cm in height, 38.5 cm in diameter, with an abacus length of 64 cm; another is 52 cm in height, 37 cm in diameter, with an abacus length of 67 cm; see Matetić Poljak 2009a: 223, fig. 67, 68, 69, 70, respectively. Regarding the three Composite capitals with *finemente dentellate* leaves, two of them are of superior quality and are currently exhibited in the lapidarium (Matetić Poljak 2009a: 224, figs 72–73). These capitals, for which we do not know if they correspond to *spolia* or were made *ex novo* for the Palace, could have served, in both cases, as a model for the entire series and could have been manufactured in situ using blocks of imported marble. They have the following dimensions: one of them is 50 cm in height, 38.5 cm in diameter, with an abacus length of 61 cm (Matetić Poljak 2009a: 224, fig. 71); another is 47 cm in height, 38.5 cm in diameter, with an abacus length of 56 cm (Matetić Poljak 2009a: 224, fig. 72); another is 53 cm in height, 39 cm in diameter, with an abacus length of 56 cm (Matetić Poljak 2009a: 224, fig. 73).

[49] Matetić Poljak 2009a: 224; Scrinari 1957: 90; Matetić Poljak 2009a: 224.

[50] Stube 1987: tab. d and e; Rohman 1995: 120; Kawhagi-Janho 2014: capital II-1, fig. 13-20, and capital II-2, fig 21.

[51] Pensabene 2007b: 342, fig. 19.

[52] Matetić Poljak 2009a: 208.

Figure 11. Frieze and dome: a) laurel wreath with the bust of Prisca (photo: D. Matetić Poljak); b) laurel wreath with the head of Hermes Psychopompus (photo: D. Matetić Poljak); c) laurel wreath with the bust of Diocletian (photo: D. Matetić Poljak); d) plate with unfinished figures (photo: D. Matetić Poljak); e) part of the frieze (photo: D. Matetić Poljak); f) dome (photo: K. Marasović).

Prisca (**Figure 11a**), while the third has a head with a wing-like form on the top and has been identified as Hermes Psychopompus (**Figure 11b**).[53] The majority of the frieze panels are only summarily executed with some left unfinished (**Figure 11d**). One panel opposite the entrance is missing. It was destroyed in the 16th century when its was replaced by a window. It has been suggested that the panel featured a motif symbolising Diocletian's divinisation, probably an eagle.[54]

Dome

The dome is 3.5 m tall[55] and is constructed of two layers of bricks with a total thickness of 68 cm. The intrados of the dome is composed of twelve brick arches. In the lower part of the dome the bricks are laid horizontally, the middle zone consists of smaller brick arches arranged in fan-shaped rows, and the upper zone has horizontal rows of bricks which continue up to the very top of the dome. The extrados of the dome is in the form of bricks laid in rows (**Figure 11f**).[56] During the conservation and restoration works undertaken in 2012/2013, iron nails were discovered in situ. These acted as reinforcing elements that enabled the mortar bedding of the dome's original mosaic decoration to adhere more securely to the brick surface of the dome. Glass and stone *tesserae* belonging to the original mosaic decoration were found under the medieval pavement. The dome's mosaic decoration was probably destroyed at some point during the Middle Ages.[57] When viewed from ground-level, the strong projection of the entablature of both the lower and upper architectural orders acts like two frames emphasising the dome, leading the viewer's eye upwards to what would originally have been the dome's mosaic decoration. The dome has not been taken into consideration for the cost estimation of the Mausoleum due to the difficulty of analysing the techniques and materials used with the necessary precision.

Portico

The exterior of the Mausoleum consisted of a 3.5-m wide podium with a colonnaded portico of the Corinthian order.[58] It consisted of 24 columns, 19 of which are still in situ, separated by an intercolumniation of 2.6 m.[59] The column shafts are set on limestone pedestal-bases (of Ionic-Attic type with plinth) carved from the same block (**Figure 12a**). Those located at the octagonal corners of the podium are prismatic in form. The columns of the south-west corner and two on the eastern side of the Mausoleum were destroyed during the construction of the Baroque choir (**Figure 13; Table 1, no. 11, 12, 18**). The column shafts are most likely *spolia,* due to their different dimensions,[60] and are of different types of marble. The quarry origins of these have been inconsistently identified by scholars (**Figure 13; Table 1**).[61]

Only three sides of the octagonal portico were visible through the peristyle colonnade – the north-western, western, and south-western sides. On the visible sides of the portico the architect arranged columns symmetrically with respect to the main axis of the Mausoleum, while on the non-visible sides the approach was less systematic.[62] Two fluted column shafts of Proconnesian marble were positioned on the north-east and south-east corners of the portico. A fragment of a fluted Proconnesian column shaft was reused in the medieval house which was erected nearby on the south *temenos* wall. It can likely be connected with one of the missing shafts from the eastern side of the portico since, with the exception of the three fluted column shafts of the portico, no columns in the Palace are fluted. One would expect to find the fluted shafts in the porch, and their rather peculiar position confirms their origin as *spolia*. Some shafts of the portico may have belonged to the aforementioned complex that preceded the construction of the Palace. For three shafts belonging to the portico and executed

---

[53] The identification of the male bust as the emperor Diocletian is widely accepted. However, opinion is still divided as to the identification of the female bust. While most scholars identify the bust as Prisca, others favour a divinity: Čurčić (1993) has suggested the goddess Tyche; Babić (2004) suggested Isis or Tyche, although more recently he considers it to be a representation of Aurelia Prisca as Isis (cf. Babić 2018; 2019). The third head depicted in the wreath is generally identified as Hermes Psychopompus, although the identification as a Gorogona or personification of the wind has also been proposed, see Babić 2018: 221; McNally 1996: 59 and Cambi 2016a: fig. 26, respectively.
[54] Kähler (1974: 817) proposed that this was a depiction of Sol. Rendić Miočević (1992) has suggested a depiction of an eagle of apotheosis and Babić (2018) suggested that the missing panel could have represented figures associated with the cult of Isis and Serapis.
[55] Johnson 2009: 67.
[56] Doljanin *et al.* 2013.
[57] Doljanin *et al.* 2013. The *tesserae* are exhibited in the Treasury of the Split Cathedral.
[58] Johnson 2009: 60. The dimensions of this architectural order are as follows: height of the square pedestals under the columns, from 0.84 to 1.03 m; width of the square pedestals from 0.79 to 0.94 m; number of square pedestals, 20 (14 + 6); height of the polygonal pedestals, from 0.86 to 1.02 m; width of the polygonal pedestals from 0.79 to 0.94; number of polygonal pedestals, 8; height of the monolithic shafts from 4.56 to 4.84, with an average value of 4.70 m; lower diameter, from 0.52 to 0.62 m, with an average value of 0.57; Corinthian limestone capitals (24 + 4 *prostasis*), abacus length of 1.28 m, height from 0.68 to 0.79 m, with an average value of 0.73 m (Matetić Poljak 2009a: 205). One of the capitals from one of the southern corners is not in situ but was found nearby in 1972. This capital is 0.75 m in height and less than 0.53 m in diameter (Mirnik 1989: 17; Matetić Poljak 2009a: 205–206, fig. 2, no. 4 in the diagram). Another capital is 0.74 m in height, 0.46 m in diameter, with an abacus length of 1.28 m (Matetić Poljak 2009a: 206, no. 1 in the diagram).
[59] Johnson 2009: 61.
[60] For the suggestion that both the diversity of material and varying sizes of the column shafts indicate that they were *spolia*, see Johnson 2009: 68. In fact, the difference in height of the column shafts was corrected through the dimensions of the plinths supporting the columns; Johnson 2009: 61.
[61] Ward Perkins 1970: Appendix and fig. 1; Marasović *et al.* 2015: 1007, fig. 4.
[62] Marasović *et al.* 2015: 1005.

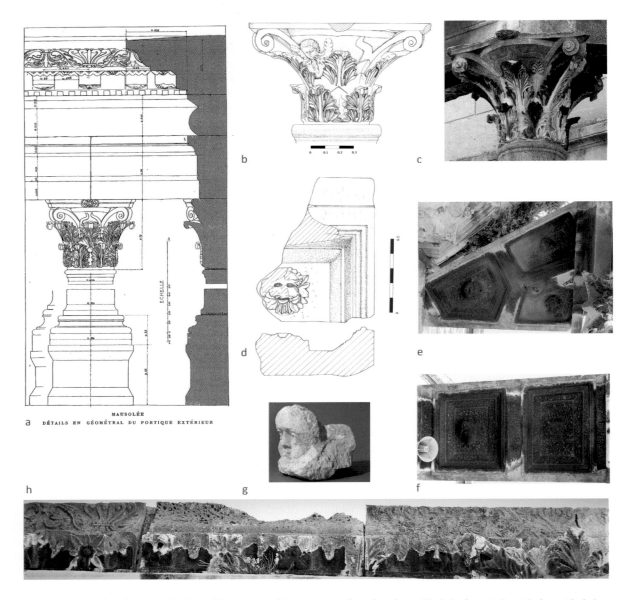

Figure 12. Portico: a) architectural order of the portico (drawing: E. Hébrard and J. Zeiller); b-c) capitals with five-sided abacus (drawing and photo: D. Matetić Poljak); d) fragment of the rectangular coffered slab (drawing: D. Matetić Poljak); e) pentagonal coffered slab (photo: D. Matetić Poljak); f) rectangular coffered slab (photo: D. Matetić Poljak); g) antefix-imbrex (photo: Z. Sunko); h) different stages of completion of cornice blocks (photo: D. Matetić Poljak).

in an unidentified stone, we attributed a hypothetical cost of 75 *denarii*/ft³ for our cost calculations.

The capitals are limestone and of free Corinthian type with the calices omitted. The capitals on the octagonal corners have pentagonal abacuses. Frequently the capital diameters do not match the upper diameter of the shafts, with the capital diameter sometimes being significantly larger than the astragal of the column shaft (**Figures 12b** and **c**). The entablature of the colonnade consists of three parts: an Ionic architrave, a frieze, and a cornice. Currently, 16 of the architrave blocks remain in situ. Their outer and

inner faces consist of two fasciae and a crown moulding consisting of cavetto and fillet, separated by a half-round moulding. The architrave integrated into the Mausoleum wall belongs to the same type. The convex frieze is plain with simple crown moulding representing a raking fillet.

The cornice is Corinthian with eight blocks still in situ and additional fragments located in the *temenos* area outside of the Palace's north wall and in the substructures of Diocletian's Palace. Furthermore, several blocks are now stored in the Archaeological Museum in Split. The cornice is similar to the lower order of the cella with a

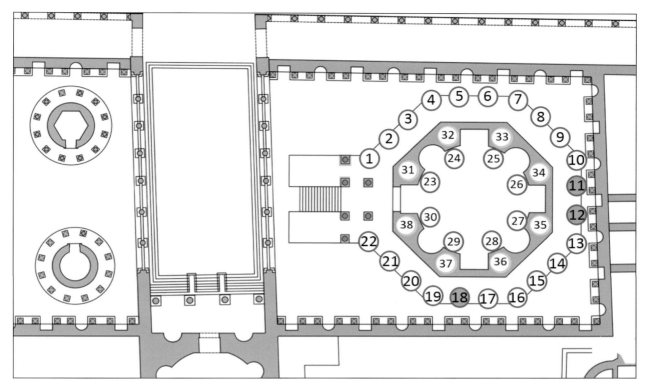

Figure 13. Distribution and types of stone used in the column shafts of Diocletian's Mausoleum. Columns highlighted in red belong to the internal colonnade of the lower order; those in yellow belong to the internal colonnade of the upper order; and those in blue are the columns of the exterior colonnade, of which the solid blue circles indicate shafts whose original position is uncertain (see Table 1).

superimposed scheme of dentils, consoles, soffit coffers, corona, *cyma recta* decorated with an anthemion of alternating acanthusising and closed flame palmettes, and a plain fillet. The consoles are of two types: one of a parallelepiped shape and ones of an S-shape form, similar to a two-volute type. The underside of the cornice blocks have different motifs: human heads, human and animal masks, acanthus leaves of Diocletianic style, and floral or vegetal motifs.63 [63] The soffit coffers have either a floral or vegetal motif. The consoles and soffit coffers are framed by a zig-zag motif.

It should be noted that some of the cornice blocks are unfinished, either with a plain or half-carved anthemion motif within the *cyma recta* or with unfinished motifs on the undersides of consoles and in the soffit coffers. Several of the unfinished blocks are positioned in situ on the south and south-east sides of the portico (**Figure 12h**). It is not possible to determine the original location within the portico for several of the unfinished blocks now located in the above-mentioned locations. However, we can probably assume that they were positioned on the sides of the portico which were not visible.

The portico was covered with flat stone coffered slabs and a roof. The coffered slabs rest on architraves above columns and extend across the portico incorporated into the Mausoleum wall.[64] Five slabs are still in situ, while a large number can now be found in the *temenos* area. There are two types of slabs: ones with two coffers that were used along the sides of the portico, which were rectangular or slightly trapezoidal in form, depending on whether they were positioned in the middle of the portico or towards the side corners; and those used at the corners of the portico which were pentagonal with three coffers (**Figures 12d, e,** and **f**). The coffers are decorated with different motifs including masks, human and animal heads, and floral and vegetal motifs.[65] According to Hébrard and Zeiller's partial reconstruction of the portico, there were 64 coffered slabs in total (56 rectangular and 8 pentagonal).[66] Although the portico was covered by a roof, only one decorative element has been identified - an antefix-imbrex with a human head. It is possible that it was originally located on one of the eaves of the portico roof (**Figure 12g**).[67]

---

[63] Verzár Bass (2004: 213) has identified the heads as representations of Jupiter and Heracles. For a discussion of the decorative motifs found on the consoles, see Matetić Poljak 2009b: 268–271.

[64] This element has a height of 0.75 m, a projection of 0.83 m, and a total length of 54.36 m.
[65] For attempts to identify human heads, see Mirnik 1977: 53; 1989: 18; McNally 1996: 45; Babić 2004: 722-727.
[66] Hébrard and Zeiller 1912: 78.
[67] Marinković 2014: 295–301; 2017.

Column number (Figure 13)	Height	Diameter	Material: Marasović *et. al.* 2015: 1003–1019	Material: Ward-Perkins 1970: 38–44	Material: Pensabene, personal notes	Observations
1	4.84	0.62	Granito del Foro	Granito del Foro	Granito del Foro	
2	4.76	0.55	Red granite	Red granite	Aswan granite	
3	4.82	0.52	Red granite	Red granite	Aswan granite	
4	4.80	0.56	Red granite	Red granite	Aswan granite	
5	4.69	0.58	Breccia Corallina	Breccia Corallina	Breccia Corallina	
6	4.76	0.59	Breccia Corallina	-----	Breccia Corallina	
7	4.74	0.58	Breccia Corallina	Breccia Corallina	Breccia Corallina	
8	4.69	0.59	Proconnesian	Proconnesian	Bigio Antico	
9	4.69	0.58	Proconnesian	Proconnesian	Proconnesian	
10	4.68	0.60	Proconnesian	Proconnesian	White marble	Fluted column shaft.
11	-----	-----	Proconnesian	-----	-----	There is a fragment in Proconnesian to be attributed to columns 11 or 12. Fluted column shaft.
12	-----	-----	Proconnesian	-----	-----	
13	4.75	0.60	Proconnesian	Proconnesian	White marble	Fluted column shaft.
14	4.73	0.58	Proconnesian	Proconnesian	Bigio Antico	
15	4.63	0.59	Troadense granite	Troadense granite	Troadense granite	
16	4.74	-----	Troadense granite	Troadense granite	Troadense granite	
17	4.78	0.58	Troadense granite	Troadense granite	Troadense granite	
18	4.71	0.59	Breccia Corallina	Breccia Corallina	Breccia Corallina	
19	-----	0.58	Breccia Corallina	-----	-----	A fragment in Breccia Corallina found in the *temenos* area, perhaps to be attributed to this column.
20	4.56	0.53	Red granite	Red granite	Aswan granite	
21	4.80	0.54	Red granite	Red granite	Aswan granite	
22	4.74	0.62	Granito del Foro	Granito del Foro	Granito del Foro	
23	6.10	-----	Red granite	Red granite	Aswan granite	
24	5.89	0.76	Red granite	Red granite	Aswan granite	
25	5.92	0.78	Red granite	Red granite	Aswan granite	
26	>6.00	0.79	Troadense granite	Red granite	Granito del Foro	
27	>6.00	0.79	Troadense granite	Red granite	Granito del Foro	
28	6.10	0.74	Red granite	Red granite	Aswan granite	
29	6.00	0.78	Red granite	Red granite	Aswan granite	
30	5.84	0.74	Red granite	Red granite	Aswan granite	
31	3.14	-----	Red granite	Porphyry	-----	The lower part of the stem has been cut.
32	3.11	0.47	Red granite	Granito del Foro	-----	
33	3.11	0.46	Red granite	Granito del Foro	-----	
34	3.14	0.45	Red granite	Porphyry	-----	
35	3.14	0.45	Red granite	Porphyry	-----	
36	3.11	0.47	Granito del Foro	Granito del Foro	-----	
37	3.11	0.47	Granito del Foro	-----	-----	
38	3.15	0.45	Red granite	Porphyry	-----	

Table 1. Measurements of the shafts and materials used.

a

b

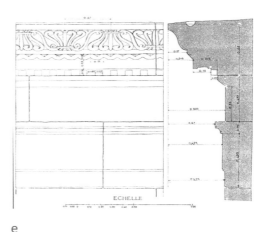

c

d

e

Figure 14. Roof: a) *tegulae* imprints on the roof (photo: T. Bartulović); b) detail of the entablature crowning the Mausoleum (photo: Mediterranean Centre for Built Heritage Split); c) holes on the upper side of the cornice (photo: G. Nikšić); d) Romanesque acroterium (photo: T. Bartulović); e) entablature crowning the Mausoleum (drawing: E. Hébrard and J. Zeiller).

Mausoleum roof

The entablature crowning the Mausoleum is composed of three blocks:[68] an architrave with two fasciae and crown moulding with cavetto and fillet, a flat undecorated frieze with crown moulding in the form of a raking fillet, and an Ionic cornice with dentils, corona, raking fillet decorated with zig-zag motif on its oblique part, and *cyma recta* with an anthemion composed of closed flame palmettes (**Figures 14b** and **e**). The Mausoleum is roofed with an eight-sided structure that has a Romanesque acroterium in the centre (**Figure 14d**). The current roof structure does not rest directly upon the cornice but is separated from it by a further section of wall *c.* 80 cm high. However, a series of evenly spaced holes were found on the upper side of the cornice blocks (**Figure 14c**), leading scholars to suggest that the current roof is not

original but rather a later one concurrent with the Romanesque acroterium.[69] If this is the case, the holes in the upper side of the cornice blocks may have been used to fix the antefixes of an earlier, originally Diocletianic roof.[70] However, those who consider the current roof to be the original Diocletianic version have argued that these holes were used to fix marble or metal plates that covered the wall.[71] During conservation and restoration work on the roof carried out in 1996, a total of 534 *tegulae* were found, two of which have the inscription PANSIANA and two other *tegulae* are inscribed with Q CLODI(I) AMBROSIAN(I) (**Figure 14a**).[72]

---

[68] This element has a height of 0.80 m (Marasović *et al.* 2006: 504) and a length of 62.42 m.

[69] Kečkemet 1993: 108. Nikšić (1997: 119) provides a synthesis on this hypothesis.

[70] Andrić reports finding an antefix decorated with a human head with horns. For this, see Kečkemet 1993: 108 and for details of the antefix, see Nikšić 1997: 119 and Marinković 2017.

[71] Marasović *et al.* 2006.

[72] Nikšić 1997: 116.

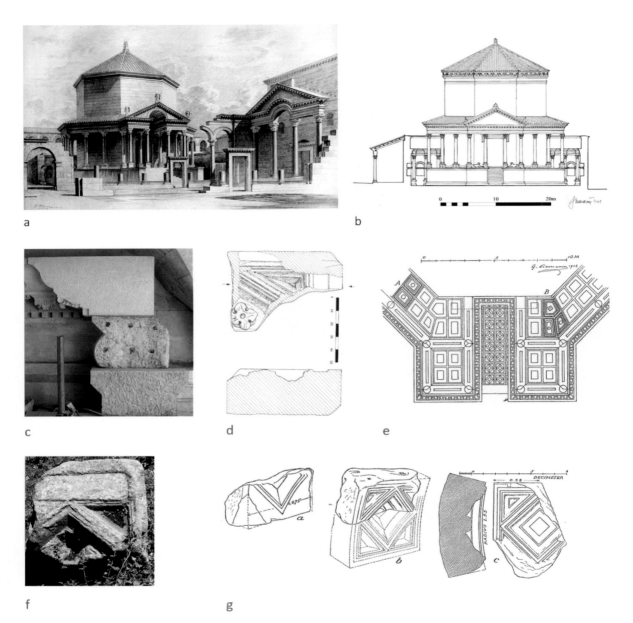

Figure 15. Porch: a) reconstruction of the porch by G. Niemann; b) reconstruction of the porch by J. Marasović;
c) entablature under the barrel vault (photo: D. Matetić Poljak); d) fragment of the coffered slab of the porch
(photo: D. Matetić Poljak); e) reconstruction of the coffered ceiling of the porch (drawing: G. Niemann);
f) fragment of the coffered barrel vault (photo: D. Matetić Poljak); g) coffers of the barrel vault (drawing: G. Niemann).

Porch

Unfortunately, the construction of a medieval belfry caused the destruction of the original architectural order of the Mausoleum's porch. The porch originally had four columns of unknown marble. Kähler has suggested that the fragment of column shaft in red porphyry found in the *temenos* area at the beginning of the 20th century belonged to the porch.[73] However, this is by no means certain. The architectural order on the lateral sides of the porch was probably the same type as the one on the portico. The central part of the porch was covered with a barrel vault, while two lateral sides were covered with coffered rectangular slabs (**Figure 15e**). Five blocks from the barrel vault still survive and show that they were curved blocks with coffers decorated with a central square set at a 45-degree angle within a square (**Figure 15f** and **g**).[74] Several of the coffered slabs were only partially visible, because they were partly hidden by the projection of the cornice. These block show that the decoration was left unfinished in the invisible parts. It is possible that the slabs of the lateral sides also had coffers with a similar decorative scheme (**Figure 15d**).

---

[73] Kähler 1974: 810.

[74] Matetić Poljak 2009b: 790–792.

A small part of the entablature which carried the barrel vault is preserved above the cella entrance, although the elements have partly been replaced by copies (**Figure 15c**). The entablature consists of three blocks: an Ionic architrave with two fasciae separated by a half-round moulding and crown with raking fillet, a plain convex frieze with the crown of the same type as the one of the architraves below, and a cornice composed of a superposition of dentils, S-type consoles, plain corona, *cyma recta,* and fillet. To date, three reconstructions of the porch have been proposed, each based on a different reading of the original function of the arch situated above the cella door. Niemann suggested that it was a relieving arch for the door and therefore reconstructs the arch of the porch with a barrel vault and a so-called Syrian pediment covered by a roof (**Figure 15a**). Alternatively, Hébrard and Zeiller have argued that the arch acted as a window allowing light through to the cella and therefore suggest the arch should be reconstructed a as barrel vault and triangular pediment covered by a terrace to allow the window to function.[75] Finally, Marasović has suggested that the arch acted as a relieving arch and consisted of a barrel vault and triangular pediment (**Figure 15b**). Unfortunately, no elements belonging to the pediment have been found, and therefore it impossible to reconstruct this part of the building with any certainty. As a result, this part of the Mausoleum has not been taken into account in our cost calculations.

The sacro-funereal zone of the Palace employed the widest array of decorative architectural motifs. As far as can be currently established, the complex, inhabited scroll motifs applied to the limestone frame surrounding the Mausoleum entrance were only used in this zone of the Palace. All told, the different figurative motifs used on the frieze under the dome as well as the cornice consoles and coffered slabs of the portico show a high degree of iconographic harmony, irrespective of whether they are interpreted as sepulchral or religious. Nonetheless, the elements are surprisingly executed in a rather summary manner. Such treatment might be explained by the desire to economise on the execution of less visible elements that were either positioned high up on the Mausoleum or located in non-visible locations due to the *temenos* wall. In general, the decorative carving of the architectural blocks is relatively restrained in terms of the number of different motifs employed (e.g. anthemion, egg and darts, leaf and darts, shear-shaped leaves, bead and reel, zig-zag motif, guilloche, cable), however, a good degree of visual variety was obtained through the combination of these different motifs on the Mausoleum's entablatures. Moreover, the combination of pedestal-bases, bases, and capitals in limestone with different spoliated marble column shafts made it possible to obtain the

required column heights, as the height of the various limestone elements could be adjusted as necessary.

The cost of the Mausoleum

The estimated cost of this monument has been carried out by directly applying the prices and wages contained in the Price Edict of Diocletian. Here, the Edict can be applied in its correct time period and geographical setting to study the Mausoleum which remains, despite some later modifications, in an excellent state of conservation. Nevertheless, the monument still presents several issues which have a bearing on both the cost calculation process and the results obtained. For example, since the Mausoleum was part of an imperial palace intended for an emperor who had renounced his public office, it might be seen as 'private' rather than 'public/state' architecture. The potential 'dual' interpretation of the monument as both public and private makes it difficult to identify the financial resources used for its construction. For instance, what were the costs and supply chains for the materials used, most of which came from 'imperial' quarries? What were the purchase methods and the costs of the *spolia* used in many areas of the monument? Did the *spolia* come from public monuments? The answers to these questions depend in part on how we interpret the 'status' of the Mausoleum as either an imperial public commission or a 'private' commission, even if initiated by an emperor. We must therefore try to reconstruct the economic cost of the Mausoleum with these problems in mind, analysing the whole construction process on a step-by-step basis, starting with the identification of the workforce and the different types of materials used (**Appendix Tables a–f**).

Labour costs

The Price Edict of Diocletian informs us of the sums paid to construction workers, which changed according to the activities carried out and their degree of specialisation. On the basis of wages listed in the Edict, we can attribute a theoretical cost to the workforce employed for each phase of the Mausoleum's construction: for the roughing-out of stone elements, we have assumed a specialised workforce with a daily wage of 60 *denarii*; likewise we have assumed that the pre-preparation of stone elements was undertaken by skilled marble workers also receiving a daily wage of 60 *denarii*. For construction processes (e.g. the installation of stone architectural elements, brickwork, etc.), we have assumed the slightly lower daily wage of 50 *denarii*, and finally, for finishing the decorative elements we have assumed the use of skilled marble workers with a daily wage of 60 *denarii*. In determining the cost of labour we have also considered several other factors such as

---

[75] Hébrard and Zeiller 1912: 72.

the origin of the workforce, their status (free, slave, or military), and possible membership in a particularly prestigious workshop. As has already been pointed out, since the building was most likely constructed on imperial land, we have assumed it was probably a public construction, although this assumption is not certain.

A detailed analysis of the decorative motifs of the Mausoleum's stone elements suggests not only a degree of specialisation amongst the stoneworkers but also the possible presence of foreign artisans. The type of *finemente dentellato* acanthus found on some of the (possibly Proconnesian marble) capitals of the upper internal order of the cella and on six of the pilasters of the lower order carved in local stone suggests the participation of Anatolian sculptors.[76] While it is possible that the capitals were imported from the quarries in a finished state, as was often the case at Proconnesus during this period, it is also possible that they were completed in situ by an Anatolian workshop.[77] The use of spinosus acanthus leaves on the pilasters carved in local stone, in a form that is very similar to those seen on capitals from Izmir that probably came from Diocletian's Palace in Nicomedia,[78] also points to the potential employment of an eastern workshop in the service of the emperor.[79]

As for the status of the workers, it is possible to imagine the participation, in some phases of the work, of the soldiers who made up the emperor's guardhouse, for whom part of the palace was reserved. Even if this was the case, we cannot determine if a military workforce was used consistently across all areas of the building or only for public areas. We also know that some of the marble and granite used in the Mausoleum came from quarries where the presence of slave labour and workers condemned *ad metalla* can be documented in the Diocletian age. For example, in the Mons Porphyrites quarries, Aurelius Aristides (*Or.* XXXVI, 67) refers to the presence of condemned Christians in AD 308.[80] Later, in AD 357, another group of condemned Christians, including some bishops, is record at the quarries (Athanasius, *Historia Arianorum* 72). Condemned Christians were also attested at the quarries of Proconnesus in AD 307[81] and again later, in AD 373 (Theodoret, *Hist. Eccl.* 4.22.26).[82] In Diocletian's time, Christians known as *I Quattro Coronati* were condemned to work in a quarry, the location of which has been identified by some as Pannonia, near Sirmium (modern Sremska Mitrovica), or more probably at a quarry in Aswan, Egypt.[83]

Construction materials

The Mausoleum used a variety of different types of stone, such as limestone from the nearby island of Brač, which was located off the coast almost directly opposite the Palace. Brač limestone was mainly used for structural work in the walls of the Mausoleum, but it was also employed for some decorative architectural elements. Various types of marble and granite were used for the Mausoleum's column shafts, including Proconnesian marble, breccia corallina, porphyry, red granite, Troadense granite, granito del foro, and Aswan granite. The dome of the crypt was constructed using local tufa (travertine), probably extracted from quarries located *c.* 7.5 km from the Žrnovnica river, or at quarries in the vicinity of the Krka or Cetina rivers, located *c.* 147 km and 21.5 km (?) from the Palace, respectively.

Using the Price Edict of Diocletian, we can estimate the cost of the main types of marble and granite used in the Mausoleum, which we have reconstructed at the following rates: granito del foro at 100 *den.*/ft³, Aswan granite at 100 *den.*/ft³, Troadense granite at 75-100 *den.*/ft³, red porphyry at 250 *den.*/ft³, Proconnesian marble at 40 *den.*/ft³, and breccia corallina at 75-100 *den.*/ft³. However, the Edict provides no information on the cost of limestone from Brač. We have therefore assumed that the cost of this limestone was similar to local stones, such as limestone from Zerhun (North Africa), which cost 1.5 HS/ft³ at the beginning of the 3rd century AD,[84] the equivalent of about 3 HS/ft³ (= 0.75 *den.*/ft³) in the Diocletianic period.

Since the marble and granite used came from imperial-owned quarries, which was perhaps also the case for the Brač quarries,[85] the cost of stone when used for an imperial construction project may well have been zero.[86] On the other hand, the column shafts and some of the capitals appear to have been *spolia*. As noted above, the column shafts are all of different materials and dimensions, and a number of the capitals pre-date the construction of the Mausoleum. It is also likely that many of blocks in local stone used in the Mausoleum's

---

[76] Matetić Poljak 2009a: 200 and 222.
[77] Matetić Poljak 2009a: 230.
[78] Matetić Poljak 2009a: 200.
[79] Mirnik 1989: 13. Similarities with examples from the eastern empire can also be observed in other decorative elements of the Palace. These include the semi-column capitals used at the intersections of streets, which are similar to the capital from the column commemorating Diocletian in Alexandria, and a capital in the sanctuary of Diocletian in Luxor; see Babić 2009: 187. Moreover, the capitals of the *decumanus* are similar to some examples from Thessalonica and the Villa in Piazza Armerina in Sicily, all of which were produced in the quarries of Proconnesus; see Matetić Poljak 2009a: 212.
[80] Millar 1984: 140.
[81] Millar 1984: 141; Gustafson 1994: 429.

[82] Gustafson 1994: 429.
[83] On this issue, see Pensabene 2013: 249–251; Maskarinec 2017.
[84] Domingo and Domingo 2017: 43
[85] Miliša and Marinković 2018: 967.
[86] On this point, see Caprioli *et al.* in this volume. Some authors, however, adopt a value equivalent to about 50% of the market cost; see, for example, Barresi 2000: 352.

structure had originally been used for earlier structures which preceded the Palace, although this is not certain.

The use of *spolia* was a very common practice in the time of Diocletian, as can be seen from the use of earlier materials in the Baths of Diocletian in Rome. For the Baths' construction, numerous cornices, architraves, and capitals from the Flavian and Severan ages were reused alongside elements produced *ex novo*.[87] Equally, the honorary columns erected by the same emperor in the Forum Romanum in Rome were also likely *spolia*.[88] Given the frequent use of *spolia* in this period, it is likely that a specific organisation existed for the recovery of large architectural elements destined for reuse in new constructions. For example, in the Vespasianic period, an inscription from Rome records the *curator* of a *collegium* of *subrutores*, who were perhaps artisans specialising in the recovery of materials destined for reuse (*CIL* VI, 940). Later, towards the end of the 4th century AD, John Chrysostom mentions that he had recourse to hire specialised workers to dismantle pagan sanctuaries of Phoenicia (Theod. *HE* V, 30).[89]

Unfortunately, we do not have the necessary historical data to reconstruct the economic value of *spolia*. It is probable that their cost would have depended on several factors, such as if the material came from public or private monuments, whether it was taken directly from a monument or from a public or private marble warehouse, etc. Some clues point to the *spolia* reused in the Mausoleum coming from public monuments, such as the large dimensions of the column shafts (those used for the lower order of the cella, for example, are about 6 m tall) and the materials of the column shafts themselves, which originated in quarries intended exclusively for imperial commissions (e.g. Mons Porphyrites or Mons Claudianus). Given this, we believe it is likely that these materials were purchased from a (probably state-owned) warehouse, perhaps located in the nearby city of Salona—where at least five to seven red granite column shafts have been identified. However, we do not know whether they had been imported into the city at an earlier point or if they were imported as *spolia* after originally being used in another region of the empire. If the latter, they may well have been transported first to the island of Brač before being transported for use at the Palace. A space intended for the sorting of much of the marble used in the Palace has been identified there.[90] A workshop specialising in stonework, perhaps in connection with the *collegium lapidariorum* of Salona,[91] has also been identified at this site. Given the probable public origin of the *spolia* and the fact that it was therefore already in state ownership,

the cost would probably have been zero given its further use for an imperial/public monument.

Given the uncertainties noted above about the price paid for the *ex novo* materials and for the *spolia*, we have assumed a dual approach; one with all the materials *ex novo* and one with the probability that a part of the materials, the shafts, and some capitals were *spolia* with a cost equal to zero in our cost estimations for the Mausoleum. On this basis, it is therefore possible to determine a range from the maximum price to the minimum price, which should include the real cost of the Mausoleum.

Roughing-out

The first phase of stone processing, after extraction, consisted of working the quarried blocks into the basic geometric forms of the intended finished architectural elements.[92] This phase was completed in the quarries in order to minimise the volume and weight of the blocks prior to their transportation to the site of construction.[93] The cost of this work depends on the type of material used. The following rates have been assumed in this stage of production: for fine-grained marble blocks (e.g. Carrara, pavonazzetto, Pentelic, breccia corallina, and fior di pesco) a rate of 157.5 hours/m³ was applied;[94] for medium-grained marble (e.g. Proconnesian and cipollino) a rate of 210 hours/m³ was applied;[95] for granite (e.g. granito del foro, Aswan, porphyry, and Troadense) a rate of 256 hours/m³ was applied;[96] and for the limestone quarried on Brač a rate of 116 hours/m³ was applied.[97] In case of *spolia*, this operation would only have been necessary if some of the reused elements required further work to adapt them to their new use. Here we have estimated, as a hypothesis, that about 1/3 of the total *spolia* in the Mausoleum needed additional work.

Rough-shaping

This phase consisted of adding further definition to form the basic decorative/formal details of the final architectural element, creating a surface which could be easily smoothed and detailed with the flat chisel. The following rates have been assumed for this operation: for the capitals, applying the formula a(1+0.25/x), where

---

[87] Pensabene 2015: 79.
[88] Pensabene 2015: 79.
[89] Marsili 2016: 149.
[90] Miliša and Marinković 2018: 965.
[91] Miliša and Marinković 2018: 974–976.

[92] Pensabene and Bruno 1998: 2; Barresi 2003: 171; Pensabene 2007a: 390.
[93] Examples from the 2nd century found at Carrara include various signatures which appear to contain the term *politura*: [De Monte Gamiano / ex casura et politura / Iuli Celsi loco V; De M(onte) G(amiano) loc(o) X caesur(a) Hippa(rchi) poli(tura) Aurelio(rum); De Monte Ga(miano) loco XXXV / cae(sura) pol(itura) Aur(eliorum)]. This is believed to refer to a workshop in the quarries, which was responsible for the roughing-out of blocks (cf. Segenni 2015: 448).
[94] Pegoretti 1863: 402.
[95] Pegoretti 1863: 402.
[96] Pegoretti 1863: 422.
[97] Pegoretti 1863: 429.

'a' is equivalent to 4.33 hours of work for fine-grained marble, 5.8 hours of work for medium-grained marble,[98] or 5.6 hours for limestone, and where 'x' is equivalent to the diameter expressed in metres. The result obtained corresponds to working hours/m² of surface.[99] For the monolithic shafts in granito del foro, Aswan and Troadense, we applied the formula a(2+0.50/x), where 'a' is equivalent to 12 hours of work and 'x' to the shaft diameter expressed in metres.[100] The results obtained are expressed as hours of work/m² of surface.[101] For the monolithic marble shafts, the formula a(2+0.25/x) was applied, where 'a' is equivalent to 4.33 hours of work for fine-grained marble (breccia corallina), 5.8 hours of work for medium-grained marble (Proconnesian),[102] and where 'x' is equivalent to the diameter of the shaft in metres. The results obtained are expressed as hours of work/m² of surface.[103] The rate to produce the bases is assumed to have been about 1/3 of their respective capitals,[104] while the working rate for the linear decorative elements (e.g. architraves, friezes, and cornices) is taken as 4.33 hours/m² for fine-grained marble, 5.8 hours/m² for medium-grained marble,[105] or 5.6 hours/m² for limestone.[106]

Transport

To estimate the cost of transport, it is necessary to consider the total volume of material being transported, the total distance travelled, and the type of vehicle used. The cost of land transport can be calculated using the formula 0.85 2nd-century AD denarii / (m³ × miles),[107] which becomes, when adjusted for inflation to the beginning of the 4th century AD, 85 denarii / (m³ × miles).[108] River transport is taken as 5.5 times cheaper than land transport when travelling against the current or 10.8 times cheaper when travelling upstream.[109] Here, maritime transport has been reconstructed based on the data contained in the Price Edict of Diocletian.[110] It is very probably, as Gianfrotta pointed out, that even when marble from imperial quarries was used for imperial commissions, transport was generally entrusted to private individuals.[111]

The stone from Brač was transported a distance of about 23.5 km (or 16 miles assuming 1 mile = 5000 feet = 1.48 km) by sea. As the Edict of Diocletian does not offer data on the cost of maritime transport for such a short distance as this, we can reconstruct its cost, albeit in an approximate way, considering a value similar to that attributed to river transport when travelling upstream. This is because we can suppose that the stone blocks would be transported using small boats, similar to those used in river transport. The transport of the granito del foro must have taken place in several stages: firstly, 120 km (= 82 miles) by land through the desert from the Mons Claudianus quarries to the Nile, using a route with watering stations set up at regular intervals to provide for the draft animals;[112] a distance of 651.6 km (= 440 miles) down the River Nile to the Port of Alexandria, most likely on special flat-bottomed barges; and lastly, from the Port of Alexandria to Dalmatia via the sea. The total cost for this journey is calculated at 18 denarii × modius castrensis in the 4th century AD,[113] which equals 1406 4th-century denarii/m³.[114] The transport of the Aswan granite from the Syene quarries, very close to the River Nile, and then onwards downstream to the Port of Alexandria (a distance of 1050 km = 706 miles) and then via sea from the Port of Alexandria to Dalmatia is assumed to have a cost equivalent to that assumed for granito del foro. The transport of the porphyry, whose quarries were also very close to those of Mons Claudianus is likewise assumed to have had a similar cost to that of granito del foro.

Proconnesian marble extracted from the quarries located in the north part of Marmara Island[115] was most likely transported at first to the city of Nicomedia,[116] and then between Nicomedia and Salona. The cost is estimated as 14 denarii × modius castrensis in the 4th century AD,[117] which equals 1094 4th-century denarii/m³.[118] Troadense granite, extracted from the quarries near Alexandria Troas, was also probably transported first to the city of Nicomedia[119] and then from Nicomedia

---

[98] Barresi (2004: 265) believes this marble falls within Pegoretti's 'medium-grained' category.

[99] Pegoretti 1863: 402, 430.

[100] Pegoretti 1863: 423.

[101] Pegoretti 1863: 423.

[102] Pegoretti 1863: 403.

[103] Pegoretti 1863: 423.

[104] Barresi 2000: 362; Soler 2012: 216, tab. 5.

[105] Pegoretti 1863: 403.

[106] Pegoretti 1863: 403. Mar and Pensabene (2010: 527) attribute the variable of 10.5 hours/m² to this work on limestone.

[107] DeLaine 1997: 210–211; Barresi 2003: 175; Mar and Pensabene 2010: 527, 531.

[108] The evolution of the price is based on the price of modius castrensis of wheat, e.g. 1 denarius in the 2nd century AD equals 100 denarii at the beginning of the 4th century AD. Therefore, 0.85 denarii in the 2nd century AD corresponds to 85 denarii in the time of Diocletian.

[109] Russell 2013: 96.

[110] Giacchero 1974: 310–312. For the parameters that should be considered when calculating the cost of shipping, see Arnaud 2007: 321–336.

[111] Gianfrotta 2008: 87.

[112] Maxfield 2001: 157–165; Pensabene 2013: 239.

[113] Giacchero 1974: 311; Arnaud 2007: 336.

[114] The conversion is based on the following equivalence: 1 modius castrensis = 0.0128 m³, with 1 m³ = 78.125 modii (cf. Duncan Jones 1976: 53–62; Barresi 2002: 78). Therefore, 4th-c. denarii × 1 modius castrensis = 18 denarii × 0.0128 m³ = 1406.25 4th-c. denarii × 1 m³.

[115] Pensabene 2013: 315.

[116] Ward-Perkins 1980: 329; Pensabene 2013: 315.

[117] Giacchero 1974: 311; Arnaud 2007: 336.

[118] The conversion is based on the following equivalence: 1 modius castrensis = 0.0128 m³, i.e. 1 m³ = 78.125 modii (Duncan Jones 1976: 53–62; Barresi 2002: 78) [14 denarii in the 4th century AD × 1 modius castrensis = 14 denarii in the 4th century AD × 0.0128 m³ = 1093.75 denarii in the 4th century AD × 1 m³].

[119] Pensabene 2013: 315. The Punta Scifo shipwreck in Crotone sank while transporting Proconnesian and pavonazzetto marble, most likely coming from the port of Nicomedia; Pensabene 2010: 81.

to Salona, the cost of which has been assumed to be similar to that of the cost for transporting Proconnesian marble. The transport of the breccia corallina from the quarries located on the west coast of Turkey, in the Karaburun Peninsula or in the area of Vezirken in the province of Bilecik, *Bithynia*,[120] was likewise estimated at a cost similar to that of Proconnesian marble.

Laying

For stone elements that exceed a weight of 1 tonne, the cost in hours of work for the installation for each tonne of weight was calculated using the following formula: 0.20 (for slinging) + 0.33 × m distance (of approach) + 0.2 × m height (for raising) + 0.1 (for positioning + 1 (setting clamps).[121] The calculation, expressed in hours of work, envisages a group of four workers.[122] Since all the column shafts are monolithic, we have assumed an approach distance of about 20 m. For blocks weighing less than 1 tonne, the cost, expressed in hours of work, was calculated using the following formula: t + 0.06 t (a-1); where 't' corresponds to 0.6 hours for every 100 kg of weight and 'a' corresponds to the elevation height of the stone, expressed in metres. We have assumed this operation would have been carried out by four workers, including two workers plus a stone cutter and a labourer.[123] In applying these formulae the following weights of different types of stone have been used:[124] 2.5 tonnes/m³ for Brač limestone,[125] 2.8 tonnes/m³ for granito del foro, porphyry, Aswan, and Troadense granite, 2.7 tonnes/m³ for Proconnesian marble, and 2.5 tonnes/m³ for breccia corallina.

Finishing

This phase consisted of adding careful definition to the planned form of the decorative motifs of the capitals, bases, shafts, friezes, architraves, mouldings, etc. This work is assumed to have been carried out by four highly skilled workers. The following actions and rates have been adopted: for finishing Corinthian limestone capitals with a height of 0.44 m, a total of 384 hours was assumed,[126] with 230 hours for pilasters;[127] for capitals with a height of 0.73 m a total of 864 hours was

assumed,[128] with 518.40 hours for pilasters;[129] and for capitals with a height of 0.96 m a total 1,152 hours was assumed,[130] with a total 691.20 hours for pilasters.[131] For the Corinthian capitals in medium-grained marble (e.g. Proconnesian) with a height of 0.50 m, a total of 720 hours was assumed,[132] with 432 hours for pilasters.[133] For composite capitals in medium-grained marble (e.g. Proconnesian) with a height of 0.50 m, a total of 720 hours was assumed,[134] with 432 hours for pilasters.[135] For the bases, we have assumed a total of about 1/3 that of their respective capitals.[136] To smooth the granite column shafts (e.g. granito del foro, Aswan, and Troadense granite), the rate of 13.50 hours/m² for 4 workers was adopted.[137] For fluted shafts in coarse-grained marble (e.g. porphyry), the rate of 21.9 hours/m² of surface was used,[138] while the lower rate of 13.3 hours/m² of surface was use for fluted shafts in medium-grained marble (e.g. Proconnesian).[139] For fluted shafts in fine-grained marble (e.g. breccia corallina), a rate of 10 hours/m² of surface has been applied.[140] For the pilaster shafts, we have assumed a rate of *c.* 1/4 of that adopted for column shafts.[141] For smooth squared limestone blocks a rate of 10.67 hours/m² of surface is assumed,[142] with the simple decoration of limestone architraves and friezes calculated at a rate of 80.80 hours/m² and 177.60 hours/m², respectively.[143] For the more complex friezes with figurative decorations a much higher rate of 426.67 hours/m² has been assumed.[144] Likewise, for the cornices a rate of 296 hours/m² was assumed.[145] For the mouldings a rate of 115.20 hours/m² was used.[146] For the roof of the portico with coffered decorations, a rate of 177.60 hours/m² was used,[147] and for polishing the surface of the marble floor slabs, a rate of 10.80 hours/m² has been assumed.[148]

Conclusions

Estimating the cost of Diocletian's Mausoleum presents a number of problems, not least how to understand the monument. Should we view the Mausoleum as an example of public or 'private' architecture? These two

[120] Pensabene 2013: 393.
[121] Barresi 2000: 363; Mar and Pensabene 2010: 527.
[122] Pegoretti 1864: 217-218.
[123] Pegoretti 1864: 217-218; Barresi 2003: 186.
[124] Pegoretti 1863: 266-267.
[125] Brač limestone must have been similar in weight to the local stone used for the Arch of Caracalla in Thebeste and Zerhoun stone, which was used for many buildings in Volubilis, both of which weigh *c.* 2.5 tonnes/m³ (cf. Luquet 1964: 356). The local biocalcarenite stone from El Mèdol in Tarragona (2.75 tonnes/m³, cf. Mar and Pensabene 2010: 527) and the local stone of Segóbriga in *Hispania* (2.4 tonnes/m³, cf. Pensabene *et al.* 2012: 169) are also similar to Brač limestone.
[126] Pegoretti 1863: 436.
[127] Pegoretti 1863: 436.

[128] Pegoretti 1863: 436.
[129] Pegoretti 1863: 436.
[130] Pegoretti 1863: 436.
[131] Pegoretti 1863: 436.
[132] Pegoretti 1863: 408.
[133] Pegoretti 1863: 409.
[134] Pegoretti 1863: 408.
[135] Pegoretti 1863: 409.
[136] Barresi 2000: 362.
[137] Pegoretti 1863: 434.
[138] Pegoretti 1863: 404.
[139] Pegoretti 1863: 404.
[140] Pegoretti 1863: 404.
[141] Barresi 2000: 362.
[142] Domingo 2012a: 410; 2012b: 158.
[143] Pegoretti 1863: 434.
[144] Pegoretti 1863: 434.
[145] Pegoretti 1863: 434.
[146] Pegoretti 1863: 434.
[147] Pegoretti 1863: 434.
[148] Pegoretti 1863: 434.

	If *ex novo*		With *spolia* with a cost equal to zero	
	Cost (*denarii*)	Days	Cost (*denarii*)	Days
Material	496,966	---	139,229	---
Rough-out	3,466,667	57,778	3,324,728	55,412
Pre-preparation	120,714	2,012	52,358	873
Transport	541,052	---	50,075	---
Laying	180,798	904	180,798	904
Finishing	6,260,341	26,085	5,933,617	24,723
TOTAL	11,066,539	86,778	9,680,804	81,912
TOTAL without material	10,569,572		9,541,757	

Table 2. Total cost of the Mausoleum if it was built *ex novo* or with *spolia* with a cost equal to zero.

interpretations, as noted above, require us to change the way we reconstruct the cost of the materials used, most of which either came from imperial quarries or were *spolia*, most likely dismantled from public monuments or taken from state-owned warehouses. We have argued here that because the building was most likely constructed on imperial land, it is probable that the Mausoleum was a public project, although we cannot be completely certain of this fact. In attempting to account for these difficulties, we have presented two reconstructions for the cost of the Mausoleum adopting two points of view. Firstly, a scenario assuming all the material were created *ex novo* and another in which the use of *spolia* is taken into account. Here the cost of the *spolia* was assumed to be zero as it was probably property of the Roman state.

The result obtained, in which the marble floor of the cella, the dome, and the tympanum of the propylon were excluded, suggests only a small difference in cost between these two hypotheses (**Table 2**). In total, a cost of about 11 million *denarii* has been estimated if all the materials are assumed to be *ex novo*, or 10.5 million if we exclude the cost for the material. If the materials were *spolia*, the cost is estimated at about 9.6 million *denarii*, or the slightly lower sum of 9.5 million *denarii*, if we take into account the possibility that *spolia* has a cost equal to zero. The latter figure is most plausible if, as we said, we assume that the Mausoleum was a public project.

This small difference between the maximum and minimum cost estimates stands in stark contrast to the considerable difference in costs estimated for other late-antique monuments which employed large amounts of *spolia*. For example, the use of *spolia* in the 4th-century AD walls of the cities of Cordoba and Geneva, both of which used large quantities of recycled materials, have been estimated to have generated an economic saving of *c*. 90% and 80% in their construction, respectively.[149] Likewise, cost estimates for the Arch of Constantine in Rome, built almost entirely with *spolia*, suggest a savings of about 78% compared to the use of newly produced materials, with a further 65% reduction in time needed to construct the Arch.[150] The huge difference in the estimated costs is due to the massive use of *spolia* in these constructions. However, this is not the case for Diocletian's Mausoleum, where the reused materials were only employed for some parts of the building, such as the column shafts and a number of the capitals. Here we should also remember that we do not know whether some of the Brač limestone blocks used in the Mausoleum actually came from pre-existing architectural structures demolished for the Palace / Mausoleum's construction.

The total sum estimated for the construction of the Mausoleum seems reasonable for the building's size and form. We do not know the 'real' cost of other structures datable to this period with which to make a direct comparison. However, we can compare the figure for the Mausoleum with the reconstructed cost for the internal colonnade of St. Peter's Basilica in Rome (100 columns), built during the reign of the emperor Constantine and most of the material for which came from *spolia*, estimated at *c*. 1 million *denarii*,[151] or with the reconstructed cost of the Arch of Constantine in Rome, again built almost entirely with *spolia*, estimated at *c*. 1 million *denarii* (or 4.5 million if it had been built with *ex novo* material).[152]

---

[149] Courault 2020: 395–450; Courault and Ruiz Arrebola 2020: 489–517.
[150] Domingo *et al.* 2020: 167.
[151] Pensabene and Domingo 2016: 2347–2372.
[152] Domingo *et al.* 2020: 159–169.

Alternatively, adjusting the cost estimate for the Mausoleum using the price for a *modius castrensis* of wheat as a basis,[153] we can extrapolate the maximum price obtained for the Mausoleum of 11 million Diocletianic *denarii* to *c.* 450,000 HS in the 1st century AD, a total in keeping with a number of buildings in Italy for which we have epigraphic costs: 352,000 HS paid for the thermal baths of Corfinium in the first half of the 2nd century AD, 300,000 HS for a temple and several statues for the forum of Sinuessa, and two million HS for the Baths of Neptune in Ostia Antica, built in AD 139.[154] Epigraphic costs from North Africa also provide comparable values such as the 600,000 HS paid for the temple of Genius in Lambaesis, between the end of the 2nd century AD and the beginning of the third century AD, or the 200,000 HS paid for the temple of Magna Mater in Leptis Magna in AD 72.[155] We can also compare the estimated expenditure for the Mausoleum with several known example of imperial euergetism such as the emperor Hadrian's donation of 98 columns for the *Aleipterion* in Smyrna, perhaps a representative hall, estimated at a total cost of 1.5 million *denarii*.[156] The total amount when converted to Diocletianic *denarii*, of course, would have been considerably higher.

The estimated costs for Diocletian's Mausoleum presented here are part of a much larger project which aims to calculate the total economic investment made in the late Roman Palace in Split. Of course, this sum would be enormously important in understanding the overall scale of economic resources required for the construction of one of the most important imperial residences of the time. At the same time, the calculation of the number of days of work needed to complete each single phase of the construction process, which was likely completed in a maximum period of 12 years, will also allow us to establish the minimum number of workers needed, further contextualising the economics of the Palace's construction.

Bibliography

Arnaud, P. 2007. Diocletian's Prices Edict: the prices of seaborne transport and the average duration of maritime travel. *Journal of Roman Archaeology* 20: 321–335.

Babić, I. 2004. Egipatski utjecaji u Dioklecijanovoj palači. *Vjesnik za arheologiju i historiju Dalmatinsku* 96: 719–739.

Babić, I. 2009. The tower of Split Cathedral as a stone monument collection, in N. Cambi, J. Belamarić and T. Marasović (eds) *Diocletian, Tetrarchy and Diocletian's Palace on the 1700th Anniversary of Existence* (Split 2005): 181–196. Split: Književni krug.

Babić, I. 2018. Aurelia Prisca as Isis. *Vjesnik za arheologiju i historiju Dalmatinsku* 111: 215–244.

Babić, I. 2019. Hramovi u Dioklecijanovoj palači i štovanje egipatskih božanstava. *Prilozi povijesti umjetnosti u Dalmaciji* 44: 387–407.

Barresi, P. 2000. Architettura pubblica e munificenza in Asia Minore. Ricchezza, costruzioni e marmi nelle provincie anatoliche dell'Impero. *Mediterraneo Antico* III, I: 309–368.

Barresi, P. 2002. Il ruolo delle colonne nel costo degli edifici pubblici, in M. De Nuccio and L. Ungaro (eds) *I marmi colorati della Roma imperiale*: 69–81. Venezia: Marsilio.

Barresi, P. 2003. *Provincie dell'Asia Minore. Costo dei marmi, architettura pubblica e committenza*. Roma: L'Erma di Bretschneider.

Barresi, P. 2004. Anfiteatro Flavio di Pozzuoli, portico *in summa cavea*: una stima dei costi, in E. De Sena and H. Dessales (ed.) *Archaeological Methods and Approaches: Ancient Industry and Commerce in Italy*: 262–267. Oxford: BAR – Int. Series 1262.

Basić, I. 2012a. Spalatum – ager Salonitanus? Prilog tumačenju pravnoposjedovnoga položaja priobalja Splitskoga poluotoka u preddioklecijanskome razdoblju. *Povijesni prilozi* 31, No 42: 9–42.

Basić, I. 2012b. Najstariji urbonimi kasnoantičkog i ranosrednjovjekovnog Splita: Aspalathos, Spalatum i Jeronimov *palatium villae* u svjetlu povijesnih izvora/The oldest Late Antique and early Medievel Split Urbonyms: Aspalathos, Spalatum and Jerome's *palatium villae* in the Light od Historic Sources, in M. Jurković and A. Milošević (eds) *Munuscula in honorem Željko Rapanić. Zbornik povodom osamdesetog rođendana / Festschrift on the occasion of his 80th birthday*: 115–155. Zagreb–Motovun–Split: International Research Center for Late Antiquity and Middle Ages.

Basić, I. 2016. Nova razmatranja o kristijanizaciji Dioklecijanovog mauzoleja. *Starohrvatska prosvjeta* III, 43: 165–196.

Basić, I. 2017. Pagan tomb to Christian church: The case of Diocletian's mausoleum in Split, in E.M. Schoolman (ed.) *Pagans and Christians in the Late Roman Empire. New evidences, new approaches (4th – 8th century)*: 241–271. Sághy, Budapest: Central European University, Department of Medieval Studies; Univesity of Pécs: CEU Press.

Belamarić, J. 2003. The date of foundation and original function of Diocletian's Palace at Split. *Hortus Artium Medievalium* 9: 173–85.

Belamarić, J. 2004. Gynaeceum Iovense Dalmatiae - Aspalatho, in A. Demandt, A. Goltz and H. Schlange-Schöningen (eds) *Diokletian und die Tetrarchie. Aspekte einer Zeitenwende*: 141–62. Berlin: Walter de Gruyter.

---

[153] DeLaine 1997: 119–121, who suggested 1 *denarius* in the 1st century AD was worth 100 *denarii* in the Diocletianic period.
[154] Duncan Jones 1974: 157.
[155] Duncan Jones 1974: 90.
[156] Barresi 2003: 155–156; IvSmyrna 697. The total of 98 columns is assumed as 72 columns of Phrygian marble, 20 of giallo antico marble, and 6 of porphyry.

Bulić, F. 1908. Materiale e provenienza della pietra, delle colonne, nonché delle sfingi del Palazzo di Diocleziano a Spalato e delle colonne ecc. delle basiliche cristiane a Salona. *Bulletino di Archeologia e Storia Dalmata* 31: 86–127.

Bulić, F. 1916. L'Imperatore Diocleziano. Nome, patria e luogo della sua nascita; anno, luogo e genere della sua morte. *Bulletino di Archeologia e Storia Dalmata* 39: 1–90.

Buljević, Z. 2019. Dioklecijanov porfirni sarkofag? *Prilozi povijesti umjetnosti u Dalmaciji* 44, No 1: 429–441.

Bulić, F. and Lj. Karaman 1927. *Palača cara Dioklecijana u Splitu.* Zagreb: Izdanje Matice hrvatske.

Cambi, N. 2005. Antička baština Samostana sv. Frane u Splitu. *Adrias* 12: 135–159.

Cambi, N. 2010. Dioklecijan u Splitu. *Radovi Zavoda za hrvatsku povijest* 42: 169–194.

Cambi, N. 2016a, *Diocletian. Vir prudens, moratus callide et subtilis ili inventor scelerum et machinator omnium malorum. Historical controversis and current dilemmas.* Split: Književni krug - Filozofski fakultet Sveučilišta u Splitu.

Cambi, N. 2016b. Dva natpisa otkrivena u neposrednoj blizini Dioklecijanove palace. *Miscellanea Hadriatica et Mediterranea* 3. 1: 139–156.

Cambi, N. 2019. Salona i Spalatum dvije funkcionalno povezane luke / Salona and Spalatum, two ports, mutually connected by their function, in N. Cambi and A. Duplančić (eds) *Pomorski Split do početka XX. stoljeća, Zbornik radova s međunarodnog znanstvenog skupa održanog u Splitu 26. i 27. rujna 2016. godine*: 55–74. Split: Književni krug Split.

Constantius Porphyrogenitus (ed. 1840). *De Tematibus et De Administrando Imperio, accedit synecdemus cum bandurii et wesselingii commentariis, recognovit Immanuel Bekkerus.* Bonnae: Impensis Ed. Weberi.

Courault, C. 2020. Démanteler Nyon pour édifier le rempart tardo-antique de Genève. Une première approche sur l'économie du phénomène spolia à partir de la trame découverte Rue de la Taconnerie / Rue Hôtel de ville, in C. Courault and C. Márquez (eds) *Quantitative studies and production cost of roman public construction*: 395–450. Córdoba: Editorial Universidad de Córdoba.

Courault, C. and J.R. Ruiz Arrebola 2020. Del desmantelamiento del Teatro a la edificación de las torres Tardoantiguas (ss. IV-V d.C.) en Córdoba. Un estudio petrográfico y económico como reflexión al fenómeno spolia, in C. Courault and C. Márquez (eds) *Quantitative studies and production cost of roman public construction*: 489–517. Córdoba: Editorial Universidad de Córdoba.

Čurčić, S. 1993. Late Antique Palace: The Meaning of Urban Context. *Ars Orinetalis* 23: 67–90.

DeLaine, J. 1997. *The Bath of Caracalla. A study in the design, construction, and economics of large-scale building projects in imperial Roma* (Journal of Roman Archaeology Suppl. 25). Portsmouth (Rhode Island): Journal of Roman Archaeology.

Delonga, V. 2007. Split-Riva (južno pročelje Dioklecijanove palače). *Hrvatski arheološki godišnjak* 4: 513–517.

Delonga, V. and Z. Alajbeg 2007. *Arheološka istraživanja na splitskoj Rivi 2006.-2007*, katalog izložbe. Split: Muzej hrvatskih arheoloških spomenika.

Doljanin, A., P. Ajduković and I. Gjerga Bratić 2013. The dome of the Diocletian's mausoleum, in P. Battinelli and J. Striber (eds) *Conservation and restoration works, Serbia - Italia, Italian-Serbian Bilateral Workshop on Science for Cultural Heritage, November 12, 2013, Museum of Yougoslav History Belgrade*: 71–90. Belgrado: Associazione Italiani e Serbi Scenziati e Studiosi.

Domingo, J.Á. 2012a. Los costes de la arquitectura romana: el capitolio de Volúbilis (Mauretania Tingitana). *Archeologia Classica* LXIII: 381–418.

Domingo, J.Á. 2012b. El coste de la arquitectura: avances, problemas e incertidumbres de una metodología de cálculo: Volúbilis y Dougga. *Archeologia dell'Architettura* XVII: 144–170.

Domingo, J.Á. and J.R. Domingo 2017. El coste del Arco de Caracalla en Theveste (Tébessa, Argelia): verificación empírica de una metodología de cálculo. *Archeologia dell'Architettura* XXII: 35–53.

Domingo, J.Á., C. Courault and P. Pensabene 2020. El Arco de Constantino: la gestión y el coste económico del reaprovechamiento de materiales antiguos en la Roma del s. IV d.C., in P. Mateos and C.J. Morán (eds) Exemplum et Spolia. *La reutilización arquitectónica en la transformación del paisaje urbano de las ciudades históricas, Mérida 2019* (Mytra 7): 159–169. Mérida: Instituto de Arqueología de Mérida.

Duncan-Jones, R.P. 1974. *The Economy of the Roman Empire. Quantitative Studies.* Cambridge: Cambridge University Press.

Duncan-Jones, R.P. 1976. The size of the modius castrenses. *Zeitschrift für Papyrologie und Epigraphik* 21: 53–62.

Duval, N. 1997. Les résidences impériales : leur rapport avec les problèmes de légitimité, les partages de l'Empire et la chronologie des combinaisons dynastiques, in F. Paschout and J. Sizdat (eds) *Usurpationene in der Spätantike: Akten des Kolloquiums 'Staatssreich und Staatlichkeit', 6-10 März 1996* (Solothurn/Bern): 127–153. Stuttgard: Franz Steiner Verlag.

Duval, N. 2003. Hommage à Ejnar et Ingrid Dyggve, La théorie du Palais du Bas Empire et les fouilles du Thessalonique. *Antiquité Tardive* 11: 273–300.

Eusebius Werke, Siebten Band ed. 1913. *Die Chronik des Hieronymus / Hieronymi Chronicon*, Erster Teil, Text, R. Helm (ed.). Leipzig: J. C. Hinrichs'sche Buchhandlung.

Giacchero, M. 1974. *Edictum Diocletiani et Collegarum de pretiis rerum venalium.* Genova: Istituto di Storia Antica e Scienze Ausiliarie.

Gianfrotta, P.A. 2008. Σμειριδες: depositi portuali, marmi di cava e navi. *Orizzonti* IX: 77–89.

Guidobaldi, F. 2003. Sectilia pavimenta e incrustationes: i rivestimenti policromi pavimentali e parietali in marmo o materiali litici e litoidi dell'antichità romana, in A. Giusti (a cura di) *Eternità e nobiltà di materia. Itinerario artistico tra le pietre policrome*: 15–75. Firenze: Edizioni Polistampa.

Gustafson, M. 1994. Condemnation to the Mines in the Later Roman Empire. *Harvard Theological Review* 87,4: 421–433.

Hébrard, E. and J. Zeiller 1912. *Le palais de Dioclétien*. Paris: Ch. Messin Éditeur.

Hesberg von, H. 1994. *I sepolcri romani e loro architettura* (Monumenta, Biblioteca di archeologia 22). Milano: Longanesi.

Kähler, H. 1965. Split i Piazza Armerina rezidencije dvaju careva tetrarha. *URBS* 4: 97–109.

Kähler, H. 1974. Domkirche, in E. Akurgal and U.B. Alkım (eds) *Mansel'e Armağan: Mélanges Mansel*, vol. II: 809–820. Ankara: Türk Tarih Kurumu Yayınları.

Kahwagi-Janho, H. 2014. Chapiteaux corinthiens d'époque romaine à Tyr. *Syria* [Online] 91, viewed on 10. September 2020. URL: http://journals.openedition.org/syria/2250

Johnson, M.J. 2009. *The Roman Imperial Mausoleum in Late Antiquity*. Cambridge: Cambridge University Press.

Lucii Caecilii Firmiani Lactantii ed. 2005. *De mortibus persaecutorum*, Proslov, predgovor, bilješke i kazalo: N. Cambi; prijevod N. Cambi i Branislav Lučin, Split: Književni krug.

Lombardi, L. and E. Santucci 2015. Gli impianti techici delle Terme di Diocleziano, in R. Friggeri and M. Magnani Cianetti (eds) *Le Terme di Diocleziano. La Certosa di Santa Maria degli Angeli*: 77–103. Firenze: Mondadori Electa.

Luquet, A. 1964. Volubilis: Restauration du Capitole. *BAM* V: 351–356.

Mar, R. and P. Pensabene 2010. Finanziamento dell'edilizia pubblica e calcolo dei costi dei materiali lapidei: il caso del Foro Superiore di Tarraco, in S. Camporeale, H. Dessales and A. Pizzo (eds) *Arqueología de la Construcción, II. Los procesos constructivos en el mundo romano: Italia y provincias occidentales*: 509–537. Madrid-Mérida: Consejo Superior de Investigaciones Científicas.

Marasović J., S. Buble, K. Marasović and S. Perojević 2000. Prostorni razvoj jugoistočnog dijela Dioklecijanove palače. *Prostor* 8, No 2 (20): 175- 238.

Marasović, J., K. Marasović and S. Perojević 2006. Le Mausolée de Dioclétien à Split: construction et restitution, in J.-Ch. Moretti and D. Tardy (eds) *L'architecture funéraire monumentale: la Gaule dans l'Empire romain. Actes du colloque* (Lattes 2001): 497–506. Paris: Éditions du CTHS.

Marasović, J. and M. Marasović 1965. Pregled radova Urbanističkog biroa na istraživanju i zaštiti Dioklecijanove palače od 1955. do 1965. godine. *URBS* 4: 23–54.

Marasović, J. and T. Marasović 1970. *Diocletian's Palace*. Zagreb: Zora.

Marasović, K. 2019. Luka Dioklecijanove palače/The Port of the Diocletian's Palace, in N. Cambi and A. Duplančić (eds) *Pomorski Split do početka XX. stoljeća: zbornik radova s međunarodnog znanstvenog skupa održanog u Splitu 26. i 27. rujna 2016*: 77–96. Split: Književni krug.

Marasović, K. and J. Margeta 2018. L'approvvigionamento dell'acqua di Palazzo di Diocleziano, in *Cura aquarum. Adduzione e distribuzione dell'acqua nell'Antichità* (Antichità Altoadriatiche LXXXVIII): 215–232.

Marasović, K. and V. Marinković 2018. Marble revetements of the Diocletian's Palace, in D. Matetić Poljak and K. Marasović (eds) *ASMOSIA XI* (Split 2015): 839–853. Split: University of Split, Arts Academy in Split; University of Split, Faculty of Civil Engineering, Architecture and Geodesy.

Marasović, K., D. Matetić Poljak and Đ. Gobić Bravar 2015. Colored marbles of Diocletian's Palace in Split, in P. Pensabene and E. Gasparini (eds) *ASMOSIA X* (Roma 2012): 1003–1019. Roma: L'Erma di Bretschanider.

Marasović, T. 1995. O hramovima Dioklecijanove palace. *Petriciolijev zbornik 1, Prilozi povijesti umjetnosti u Dalmaciji* 35: 89–103.

Marasović, T. 2005. O preddioklecijanovskoj arhitekturi na prostoru splitske Palače, in M. Sanader (ed.) *Illyrica antiqua: ob honorem Duje Rendić Miočević; radovi s međunarodnog skupa o problemima antičke arheologije, Zagreb 6.-8.XI.2003*: 361–366. Zagreb: Odsjek za Arheologiju, Filozofski Fakultet.

Marasović, T. 2011. *Dalmatia Praeromanica: ranosrednjovjekovno graditeljstvo u Dalmacji. Svezak 3. Koprus arhitekture Srednja Dalmacija*. Split-Zagreb: Književni krug Split, Muzej Hrvatskih arheoloških spomenika Split, Arhitektonski fakultet Sveučilišta u Zagrebu.

Marin, E. 2006. La tomba di Diocleziano. *Rendiconti. Atti della Pontificia accademia romana di archeologia* LXXVIII/2005–2006: 499–526.

Marinković, V. 2014. Several new portraits in Diocletian's Palace. *Vjesnik za arheologiju i historiju dalmatinsku* 107: 291–308.

Marinković, V. 2017. Nove potvrde o izvornoj dekoraciji krova Dioklecijanova Mauzoleja. *Kulturna baština* 42–43: 229–236.

Marsili, G. 2016. Il riuso razionale: cantieri di smontaggio e depositi di manufatti marmorei nella documentazione archeologica ed epigrafica di età tardoantica, in M.C. Parello and M.S. Rizzo (a cura di) *Paesaggi urbani tardoantichi. Casi a confronto. Atti delle Giornate Gregoriane*: 149–156. Bari: Edipuglia.

Maskarinec, M. 2017. Hagiography as History and the enigma of the Quattro Coronati. *RACr* 93: 345–409.

Matetić Poljak, D. 2009a. Les chapiteaux du Palais de Dioclétien, in N. Cambi, J. Belamarić and T. Marasović (eds) *Diocletian, Tetrarchy and Diocletian's Palace on the 1700th Anniversary of Existence* (Split 2005): 197–234. Split: Književni krug.

Matetić Poljak, D. 2009b. Le décor architectural du Palais de Dioclétien à Split, Unpublished PhD dissertation. Aix-Marseille Université.

Matetić Poljak, D. 2014a. Les blocs à décor architectural antérieurs au palais de Dioclétien à Split, in I. Koncani Uhač (ed.) *Akti XII. Međunarodnog kolokvija o rimskoj provincijalnoj umjetnosti. Datiranje kamenih spomenika i kriteriji za određivanje kronologije, Pula 23-28.V. 2011*: 189–193. Pula: Arheološki muzej Istre.

Matetić Poljak, D. 2014b. Le motif du rinceau peuplé dans le palais de Dioclétien à Split, in S. Bourdin, J. Dubouloz and E. Rosso (eds) *Peupler et habiter l'Italie et le monde romain. Études d'histoire et d'archéologie offertes à Xavier Lafon*: 149–156. Aix-en-Provence: Presses universitaires de Provence.

Maxfield, V.A. 2001. Stone quarrying in the eastern desert with particular reference to mons claudianus and mons porphyrites, in D.J. Mattingly and J. Salmon (eds) *Economies beyond agriculture in the classical world*: 143–170. London-New York: Routledge.

McNally, Sh. 1996. *The Architectural ornament in Diocletian's Palace at Split* (Bar International Series 639). Oxford.

McNally Sh., J. Marasović and T. Marasović 1976. Diocletian's Palace, Report on Joint Excavation, Part two. Split: Univeristy of Minnesota, Urbanistički zavod Dalmacije.

Miliša, M. and V. Marinković 2018. Marmore Lavdata Brattia, in D. Matetić Poljak and K. Marasović (eds) *ASMOSIA XI* (Split 2015): 974–976. Split: University of Split, Arts Academy in Split; University of Split, Faculty of Civil Engineering, Architecture and Geodesy.

Millar, F. 1984. Condemnation to hard labour in the Roman Empire, from the Julio-Claudians to Constantine. *PBSR* LII: 124–147.

Mirnik, I. 1977. On some architectural fragments from Dioclteian's palace at Split. *Archeologia Iugoslavica* XVII: 45–56.

Mirnik, I. 1989. Roman Architectural Fragments, in S. McNally and I. Dvoržak (eds) *Diocletian's Palace. American - Yugoslav joint excavations*: 5–40. Minneapolis: Kendall/Hunt Publishing Company.

Niemann, G. 1910. *Der Palast Diokletians in Spalato*. Wien: Alfred Hölder.

Nikšić, G. 1995. Prilog o arhitekturi Dioklecijanovog mauzoleja i rekonstrukciji splitske katedrale, *Prilozi povijesti umjetnosti u Dalmaciji* 35, 1: 105–122.

Pegoretti, G. 1863. *Manuale pratico per l'estimazione dei lavori architettonici, stradali, idraulici e di fortificazione per uso degli ingegneri ed architetti*. Volume Primo (2ª ed.). Milano: Tipografia di Domenico Salvi e C.

Pegoretti, G. 1864. *Manuale pratico per l'estimazione dei lavori architettonici, stradali, idraulici e di fortificazione per uso degli ingegneri ed architetti*. Volume Secondo (2ª ed.). Milano: Tipografia di Domenico Salvi e C.

Pensabene, P. 2007a. Ostiensium Marmorum Decus et Decor. *Studi Architettonici, decorativi e Archeometrici*. Roma: L'Erma di Bretschneider.

Penabene, P. 2007b. Gli elementi marmorei della scena, in D. de Bernardi Ferrero, G. Ciotta, and P. Pensabene (eds) *Il teatro di Hierapolis di Frigia*: 229-388. Roma-Genova: Università degli studi di Roma 'La sapienza', Facoltà di lettere e filosofia, Dipartimento di scienze dell'antichità; Università degli studi di Genova, Facoltà di architettura, Dipartimento POLIS.

Pensabene, P. 2010. Cave di marmo bianco e pavonazzetto in Frigia. Sulla produzione e sui dati epigrafici. *Marmora* 6: 71–134.

Pensabene, P. 2013. *I marmi nella Roma antica*. Roma: Carocci.

Pensabene, P. 2015. *Roma su Roma: reimpiego architettonico, recupero dell'antico e trasformazioni urbane tra il III e il XIII secolo*. Città del Vaticano: Pontificio Istituto di Archeologia Cristiana.

Pensabene, P. and M. Bruno 1998. Aggiornamenti, nuove acquisizioni e riordino dei marmi di cava dal canale di Fiumicino, in P. Pensabene (ed.) *Marmi antichi II. Cave e tecnica di lavorazione, provenienze e distribuzione*: 1–22. Roma: L'Erma di Bretschneider.

Pensabene, P., R. Mar and R. Cebrián 2012. Funding of public buildings and calculation of the costs of the stone materials. The case of the Forum of Segóbriga (Cuenca, Spain), in A. Gutiérrez, P. Lapuente and I. Rodà (eds) *Interdisciplinary Studies on Ancient Stone. Proceedings of the IX International Conference ASMOSIA, Tarragona 2009*: 161–175. Tarragona: Institut Català d'Arqueologia Clàssica.

Pensabene, P. and J.Á. Domingo 2016. Un tentativo di calcolo dei costi delle colonne della basilica costantiniana di San Pietro a Roma, in O. Brandt and V. Fiocchi Nicolai (ed.) *Acta XVI Congressvs Internationalis Archaeologiae Christianae* (Roma 2013): 2347–2372. Città del Vaticano.

Perojević, S., K. Marasović and J. Marasović 2009. Istraživanja Dioklecijanove palače od 1985. do 2005. godine, in N. Cambi, J. Belamarić and T. Marasović (eds) *Diocletian, Tetrarchy and Diocletian's Palace on the 1700th Anniversary of Existence* (Split 2005): 51–94. Split: Književni krug.

Rendić Miočević, D. 1992. O uništenom središnjem motivu friza Dioklecijanova mauzoleja u Splitu, *Prijateljev zbornik I, Prilozi povijesti umjetnosti u Dalmaciji* 32: 99–114.

Russell, B. 2013. *The economics of the Roman Stone Trade*. Oxford: Oxford University Press.

Scrinari, V. 1957. Studi particolari nell'ambito del corpus dei capitelli -Capitelli di Spalato, in *Atti del V Convegno Nazionale di Storia dell'Architettura* (Perugia, 23 settembre 1948): 87–94. Firenze: R. Noccioli.

Segenni, S. 2015. Proprietà, amministrazione e organizzazione del lavoro nelle cave lunensi in età romana, in E. Paribeni and S. Segenni (a cura di) *Notae Lapicidinarum dalle cave di Carrara*: 441–450. Pisa: Pisa University Press.

Sidoine Appolinaire, *Poèmes*, Tome I, Texte établie et traduit par André Loyen. Les Belles Lettres, Paris 1960.

Soler B. 2012. Planificación, producción y costo del programa marmóreo del teatro romano de Cartagena, in V. García-Entero (ed.) *El marmor en Hispania: explotación, uso y difusión en época romana*: 193–228. Madrid: Universidad Nacional de Educación a Distancia.

Stube, Ch. 1983. Die Kapitelle von Quasr Ibn Wardan. Antiochia und Konstantinopel im 6. Jahrhundert. *Jahrbuch für Antike und Christentum* 26: 56–106.

Toma Arhiđakon (ed.) 2003. *Historia Salonitana povijest salonitanskih i splitskih prosvećenika. Predgovor, latinski tekst, kritički aparat i prijevod na hrvatski jezik Olga Perić; povijesni komentar Mirjana Matijević Sokol; studija Toma Arhiđakon i njegovo djelo Radoslav Katičić*. Split: Književni krug.

Vasić, Č. 1997. Simbolics of the sacral complex at Romuliana, in M. Lazić (ed.) *Uzdarje Dragoslavu Srejoviću. Povodom šezdesetpet godina života od prijatelja, saradnika i učenika*: 463–470. Beograd: Univerzitet u Beogradu, Filozofski fakultet.

Verzár Bass, M. 2009. Riflessioni sulle mensole figurate del Palazzo di Diocleziano a Spalato, con particolare attenzione alla figura di Acheloos, in N. Cambi, J. Belamarić and T. Marasović (eds) *Diocletian, Tetrarchy and Diocletian's Palace on the 1700th Anniversary of Existence* (Split 2005): 163–181. Split: Književni krug.

Ward-Perkins, J.B. 1970. Dalmatia and the marble trade. *Disputationes Salonitanae*: 38–44.

Ward-Perkins, J.B. 1980. Nicomedia and the Marble Trade. *PBSR* 48: 23–69.

Appendix

MATERIAL

Order	Type	Material	Qty	Spolia	Cost (den./ft³)	Height	Width / Projection	Length	Ø	Side	Surface, one element (m²)	Total volume (m³)	Total volume (ft³)	Cost (denarii)
Crypt	Walls	Stone of Brač			0.75							2,645.00	101,832.50	76,374
Crypt	External moulding	Stone of Brač			0.75	0.42	0.40	84.00			35.28	14.11	543.31	407
Crypt	External plinth	Stone of Brač			0.75	0.56	0.38	84.00			47.04	18.11	697.25	523
Cella	Walls	Stone of Brač			0.75							1,474.00	56,749.00	42,562
Cella	External middle moulding	Stone of Brač			0.75	0.75	0.83	54.36			40.77	33.84	1,302.81	977
Cella	External upper moulding	Stone of Brač			0.75	0.80	0.29	62.42			49.94	14.48	557.54	418
Cella	Internal upper frieze	Stone of Brač			0.75	0.92	0.15	61.50			56.58	8.49	326.75	245
Portico	Column plinth + base	Stone of Brač	28		0.75	0.95	0.87				3.31	20.13	775.14	581
Portico	Shafts - monolithic	Granito del Foro	2	Yes	100	4.70			0.57	0.67	8.42	4.22	162.46	16,246
Portico	Shafts - monolithic	Aswan granite	5	Yes	100	4.70			0.57	0.67	8.42	10.55	406.14	40,614
Portico	Shafts - monolithic	Breccia Corallina	5	Yes	75	4.70			0.57	0.67	8.42	10.55	406.14	30,461
Portico	Shafts - monolithic	Proconnesian	6	Yes	40	4.70			0.57	0.67	8.42	12.66	487.37	19,495
Portico	Shafts - monolithic	Troadense	3	Yes	75	4.70			0.57	0.67	8.42	6.33	243.69	18,276
Portico	Shafts - monolithic	Indeterminate	3	Yes	75	4.70			0.57	0.67	8.42	6.33	243.69	18,276
Portico	Capitals - Corinthian	Stone of Brač	28		0.75	0.73		1.28			3.74	33.49	1,289.32	967
Portico	Architrave	Stone of Brač			0.75	0.37	0.47	61.50			22.75	10.60	408.25	306
Portico	Frieze	Stone of Brač			0.75	0.23	0.31	61.50			14.14	4.38	168.22	127
Portico	Cornice	Stone of Brač			0.75	0.27	0.71	61.50			16.60	11.79	453.90	340
Portico	Roof	Stone of Brač			0.75	0.50	3.50	61.60			215.60	107.80	4,150.30	3,113
Prothyron	Plinth of the columns	Stone of Brač	4		0.75	0.95	0.87				3.31	2.88	110.73	83
Prothyron	Shafts	Porphyry / Aswan	4	Yes	100	4.70			0.57	0.67	8.42	8.44	324.91	32,491
Prothyron	Capitals	Stone of Brač	4		0.75	0.73		1.28			3.74	4.78	184.19	138
Prothyron	Architrave	Stone of Brač			0.75	0.37	0.47	26.00			9.62	4.52	174.07	130
Prothyron	Frieze	Stone of Brač			0.75	0.23	0.31	26.00			5.98	1.85	71.37	53
Prothyron	Cornice	Stone of Brač			0.75	0.27	0.71	26.00			7.02	4.98	191.89	145
Cella – 1 – Columns	Base - Attic	Stone of Brač	8		0.75	0.45				1.22		5.36	206.29	155
Cella – 1 – Columns	Shafts	Red granite	6	Yes	100	5.97			0.76	0.86	14.25	26.49	1,019.96	101,996
Cella – 1 – Columns	Shafts	Troadense	2	Yes	75	5.97			0.76	0.86	14.25	8.83	339.99	25,499
Cella – 1 – Columns	Capitals - Corinthian	Stone of Brač	8		0.75	0.96				1.10	4.22	9.29	357.77	268
Cella – 1 – Columns	Architrave	Stone of Brač			0.75	0.80	0.47	90.00			72.00	33.84	1,302.84	977
Cella – 1 – Columns	Frieze	Stone of Brač			0.75	0.51	0.31	90.00			45.90	14.23	547.82	411

Appendix Table a. Cost of Diocletian's Mausoleum by construction phases - Material.

MATERIAL

Order	Type	Material	Qty	Spolia	Cost (den./ft³)	Height	Width / Projection	Length	Ø	Side	Surface, one element (m²)	Total volume (m³)	Total volume (ft³)	Cost (denarii)
Cella – I –Columns	Cornice	Stone of Brač			0.75	0.53	0.71	90.00			47.70	33.87	1,303.88	978
Cella – I –Semicol.	Capitals - Corinthian	Stone of Brač	8	Yes	0.75	0.96				1.10	4.22	4.65	178.89	134
Cella – I –Semicol.	Architrave	Stone of Brač			0.75	0.80	0.47	90.00			72.00	33.84	1,302.84	977
Cella – I –Semicol.	Frieze	Stone of Brač			0.75	0.51	0.31	90.00			45.90	14.23	547.82	411
Cella – I –Semicol.	Cornice	Stone of Brač			0.75	0.53	0.71	90.00			47.70	33.87	1,303.88	978
Cella – II –Columns	Shafts	Porphyry	4	Yes	250	3.13			0.46	0.56	4.52	3.93	151.16	37,790
Cella – II –Columns	Shafts	Granito del Foro	4	Yes	100	3.13			0.46	0.56	4.52	3.93	151.16	15,116
Cella – II –Columns	Capitals - Corinthian	Procomnesian	4	Yes	40	0.50				0.66	1.32	0.87	33.54	1,342
Cella – II –Columns	Capitals - Composite	Procomnesian	4		40	0.50				0.66	1.32	0.87	33.54	1,342
Cella – II –Columns	Architrave	Stone of Brač			0.75	0.34	0.45	90.00			30.60	13.77	530.15	398
Cella – II –Columns	Frieze	Stone of Brač			0.75	0.34	0.45	90.00			30.60	13.77	530.15	398
Cella – II –Columns	Cornice	Stone of Brač			0.75	0.52	1.30	90.00			46.80	60.84	2,342.34	1,757
Cella – II –Semicol.	Shafts	Stone of Brač	8		0.75	3.13			0.46	0.56	4.52	3.93	151.16	113
Cella – II –Semicol.	Capitals	Stone of Brač	8		0.75	0.50				0.66	1.32	0.87	33.54	25
Cella – II –Semicol.	Architrave	Stone of Brač			0.75	0.34	0.45	90.00			30.60	13.77	530.15	398
Cella – II –Semicol.	Frieze	Stone of Brač			0.75	0.34	0.45	90.00			30.60	13.77	530.15	398
Cella – II –Semicol.	Cornice	Stone of Brač			0.75	0.34	1.30	90.00			46.80	60.84	2,342.34	1,757
TOTAL														**496,966**

Appendix Table a cont. Cost of Diocletian's Mausoleum by construction phases - Material.

ROUGH-OUT

Material	Formula: hours/m³	Type of labour	Salary / day (denarii)	Spolia	Volume total (m³)	Days	Cost (denarii)
Stone of Brač	116.00	Specialised	60		4,775.33	55,394	3,323,630
Stone of Brač	116.00	Specialised	60	Yes	4.65	54	3,234
Proconnesian	210.00	Specialised	60		0.87	18	1,098
Proconnesian	210.00	Specialised	60	Yes	13.53	284	17,048
Granito del Foro	256.00	Specialised	60	Yes	8.15	208	12,512
Aswan granite	256.00	Specialised	60	Yes	45.48	1,164	69,859
Troadense	256.00	Specialised	60	Yes	15.16	388	23,286
Porphyry	256.00	Specialised	60	Yes	3.93	100	6,031
Breccia Corallina	157.50	Specialised	60	Yes	10.55	166	9,969
TOTAL						57,778	3,466,667

Appendix Table b. Cost of Diocletian's Mausoleum by construction phases - Rough-out.

Order	Type	Material	Quantity	Spolia	Type of labour	Salary / day (denarii)	Formula: hours/m² or General formula	Days	Cost (denarii)
Crypt	External moulding	Stone of Brač			Marble worker	60	5.6	20	1,185
Crypt	External plinth	Stone of Brač			Marble worker	60	5.6	26	1,581
Cella	External middle moulding	Stone of Brač			Marble worker	60	5.6	23	1,370
Cella	External upper moulding	Stone of Brač			Marble worker	60	5.6	28	1,678
Cella	Internal upper frieze	Stone of Brač			Marble worker	60	5.6	32	1,901
Portico	Column plinth + base	Stone of Brač	24		Marble worker	60	5.6	44	2,666
Portico	Column base	Stone of Brač	24		Marble worker	60	1/3 capital	26	1,549
Portico	Shafts - monolithic	Granito del Foro	2	Yes	Marble worker	60	a(2-0.5/x)	58	3,487
Portico	Shafts - monolithic	Aswan granite	5	Yes	Marble worker	60	a(2-0.5/x)	145	8,718
Portico	Shafts - monolithic	Breccia Corallina	5	Yes	Marble worker	60	a(2+0.25/x)	44	2,666
Portico	Shafts - monolithic	Proconnesian	6	Yes	Marble worker	60	a(2+0.25/x)	71	4,285
Portico	Shafts - monolithic	Troadense	3	Yes	Marble worker	60	a(2-0.5/x)	87	5,231
Portico	Shafts - monolithic	Indeterminate	3	Yes	Marble worker	60	a(2-0.5/x)	87	5,231
Portico	Capitals - Corinthian	Stone of Brač	24		Marble worker	60	a(1+0.25/x)	77	4,646
Portico	Architrave	Stone of Brač			Marble worker	60	5.6	13	765
Portico	Frieze	Stone of Brač			Marble worker	60	5.6	8	475
Portico	Cornice	Stone of Brač			Marble worker	60	5.6	9	558
Portico	Roof	Stone of Brač			Marble worker	60	5.6	121	7,244
Prothyron	Plinth of the columns	Stone of Brač	4		Marble worker	60	5.6	7	444
Prothyron	Base	Stone of Brač	4		Marble worker	60	1/3 capital	4	258
Prothyron	Shafts	Porphyry / Aswan	4	Yes	Marble worker	60	a(2-0.5/x)	116	6,974
Prothyron	Capitals - Corinthian	Stone of Brač	4		Marble worker	60	a(1+0.25/x)	13	774
Prothyron	Architrave	Stone of Brač			Marble worker	60	5.6	5	323
Prothyron	Frieze	Stone of Brač			Marble worker	60	5.6	3	201
Prothyron	Cornice	Stone of Brač			Marble worker	60	5.6	4	236
Cella - I -Columns	Base - Attic	Stone of Brač	8		Marble worker	60	1/3 capital	9	539
Cella - I -Columns	Shafts	Red granite	6	Yes	Marble worker	60	a(2-0.5/x)	273	16,367
Cella - I -Columns	Shafts	Troadense	2	Yes	Marble worker	60	a(2-0.5/x)	91	5,456
Cella - I -Columns	Capitals - Corinthian	Stone of Brač	8		Marble worker	60	a(1+0.25/x)	27	1,617
Cella - I -Columns	Architrave	Stone of Brač			Marble worker	60	5.6	40	2,419
Cella - I -Columns	Frieze	Stone of Brač			Marble worker	60	5.6	26	1,542
Cella - I -Columns	Cornice	Stone of Brač			Marble worker	60	5.6	27	1,603
Cella - I -Semicol.	Capitals - Corinthian	Stone of Brač	8	Yes	Marble worker	60	a(1+0.25/x)	27	1,617

Appendix Table c. Cost of Diocletian's Mausoleum by construction phases - Pre-preparation.

					PRE-PREPARATION				
Order	Type	Material	Quantity	Spolia	Type of labour	Salary / day (denarii)	Formula: hours/m² or General formula	Days	Cost (denarii)
Cella – I –Semicol.	Architrave	Stone of Brač			Marble worker	60	5.6	40	2,419
Cella – I –Semicol.	Frieze	Stone of Brač			Marble worker	60	5.6	26	1,542
Cella – I –Semicol.	Cornice	Stone of Brač			Marble worker	60	5.6	27	1,603
Cella – II –Columns	Shafts	Porphyry	4	Yes	Marble worker	60	$a(2+0.5/x)$	67	4,021
Cella – II –Columns	Shafts	Granito del Foro	4	Yes	Marble worker	60	$a(2+0.5/x)$	67	4,021
Cella – II –Columns	Capitals - Corinthian	Proconnesian	4	Yes	Marble worker	60	$a(1-0.25/x)$	5	284
Cella – II –Columns	Capitals - Composite	Proconnesian	4		Marble worker	60	$a(1-0.25/x)$	5	284
Cella – II –Columns	Architrave	Stone of Brač			Marble worker	60	5.6	17	1,028
Cella – II –Columns	Frieze	Stone of Brač			Marble worker	60	5.6	17	1,028
Cella – II –Columns	Cornice	Stone of Brač			Marble worker	60	5.6	26	1,572
Cella – II –Semicol.	Shafts	Stone of Brač	8		Marble worker	60	$a(2-0.25/x)$	51	3,092
Cella – II –Semicol.	Capitals	Stone of Brač	8		Marble worker	60	$a(1+0.25/x)$	10	587
Cella – II –Semicol.	Architrave	Stone of Brač			Marble worker	60	5.6	17	1,028
Cella – II –Semicol.	Frieze	Stone of Brač			Marble worker	60	5.6	17	1,028
Cella – II –Semicol.	Cornice	Stone of Brač			Marble worker	60	5.6	26	1,572
TOTAL								2,012	120,714

Appendix Table c cont. Cost of Diocletian's Mausoleum by construction phases - Pre-preparation.

		TRANSPORT					
Material	The transport route	Type of transport	Distance (miles)	Spolia	Formula (denarii × m³)	Volume total (m³)	Cost (denarii)
Stone of Brač		Maritime	1		[85 den. /(m³· mile)]/10.8	4,775.33	37,584
Stone of Brač		Maritime		Yes		4.65	0
Proconnesian	Nicomedia – Salona	Maritime			1,093.75	0.87	953
Proconnesian	Nicomedia – Salona	Maritime		Yes	1,093.75	13.53	14,799
Granito del Foro	Quarries – Nile	Land	82	Yes	85 den. /(m³· mile)	8.15	56,777
Granito del Foro	Nile – Alexandria	River	440	Yes	[85 den. /(m³· mile)]/10.8	8.15	28,209
Granito del Foro	Alexandria – Spalato	Maritime		Yes	1,406.25	8.15	11,455
Aswan granite	Nile – Alexandria	River	706	Yes	[85 den. /(m³· mile)]/10.8	45.48	252,714
Aswan granite	Alexandria – Spalato	Maritime		Yes	1,406.25	45.48	63,958
Troadense	Nicomedia – Salona	Maritime		Yes	1,093.75	15.16	16,582
Porphyry	Quarries – Nile	Land	82	Yes	85 den. /(m³· mile)	3.93	27,366
Porphyry	Nile – Alexandria	River	440	Yes	[85 den. /(m³· mile)]/10.8	3.93	13,597
Porphyry	Alexandria – Spalato	Maritime		Yes	1,406.25	3.93	5,521
Breccia Corallina	Nicomedia – Salona	Maritime		Yes	1,093.75	10.55	11,538
TOTAL							541,052

Appendix Table d. Cost of Diocletian's Mausoleum by construction phases - Transport.

Order	Type	Material	Quantity	Spolia	Weight Tn/m³	Salary /day (denarii)	Volume, one element (m³)	Elevation height	Formula	Days	Cost (denarii)
LAYING											
Crypt	Walls	Stone of Brač			2.5	50	2,645.00	1.00	t+0.06(a-1)	421	84,111
Crypt	External moulding	Stone of Brač			2.5	50	14.11	1.65	t+0.06(a-1)	2	462
Crypt	External plinth	Stone of Brač			2.5	50	18.11	0.30	t+0.06(a-1)	3	562
Cella	Walls	Stone of Brač			2.5	50	1,474.00	6.52	t+0.06(a-1)	235	46,984
Cella	External middle moulding	Stone of Brač			2.5	50	33.84	5.40	t+0.06(a-1)	6	1,164
Cella	External upper moulding	Stone of Brač			2.5	50	14.48	10.31	t+0.06(a-1)	3	647
Cella	Internal upper frieze	Stone of Brač			2.5	50	8.49	13.83	t+0.06(a-1)	3	526
Portico	Column plinth + base	Stone of Brač	24		2.5	50	0.72	1.95	7.9 + 0,2 × alt	20	3,979
Portico	Shafts - monolithic	Granito del Foro	2	Yes	2.8	50	2.11	3.72	7.9 + 0.2 × alt	2	346
Portico	Shafts - monolithic	Aswan granite	5	Yes	2.8	50	2.11	3.72	7.9 + 0.2 × alt	4	864
Portico	Shafts - monolithic	Breccia Corallina	5	Yes	2.5	50	2.11	3.72	7.9 + 0.2 × alt	4	864
Portico	Shafts - monolithic	Proconnesian	6	Yes	2.7	50	2.11	3.72	7.9 + 0.2 × alt	5	1,037
Portico	Shafts - monolithic	Troadense	3	Yes	2.8	50	2.11	3.72	7.9 + 0.2 × alt	3	519
Portico	Shafts - monolithic	Indeterminate	3	Yes	2.8	50	2.11	3.72	7.9 + 0.2 × alt	3	519
Portico	Capitals - Corinthian	Stone of Brač	24		2.5	50	1.20	4.98	7.9 + 0.2 × alt	21	4,270
Portico	Architrave	Stone of Brač			2.5	50	10.60	5.40	t+0.06(a-1)	2	425
Portico	Frieze	Stone of Brač			2.5	50	4.38	5.77	t+0.06(a-1)	1	235
Portico	Cornice	Stone of Brač			2.5	50	11.79	6.00	t+0.06(a-1)	2	475
Portico	Roof	Stone of Brač			2.5	50	107.80	5.15	t+0.06(a-1)	18	3,511
Prothyron	Plinth of the columns	Stone of Brač	4		2.5	50	0.72	1.95	7.9 + 0.2 × alt	3	663
Prothyron	Shafts	Porphyry / Aswan	4	Yes	2.8	50	2.11	3.72	7.9 + 0.2 × alt	3	691
Prothyron	Capitals - Corinthian	Stone of Brač	4		2.5	50	1.20	4.98	7.9 + 0.2 × alt	4	712
Prothyron	Architrave	Stone of Brač			2.5	50	4.52	5.40	t+0.06(a-1)	1	232
Prothyron	Frieze	Stone of Brač			2.5	50	1.85	5.77	t+0.06(a-1)	1	154
Prothyron	Cornice	Stone of Brač			2.5	50	4.98	6.00	t+0.06(a-1)	1	258
Cella - I -Columns	Base - attic	Stone of Brač	8		2.5	50	0.67	1.95	7.9 + 0.2 × alt	7	1,326
Cella - I -Columns	Shafts	Red granite	6	Yes	2.8	50	4.42	5.50	7.9 + 0.2 × alt	5	1,080
Cella - I -Columns	Shafts	Troadense	2	Yes	2.8	50	4.42	5.50	7.9 + 0.2 × alt	2	360
Cella - I -Columns	Capitals - Corinthian	Stone of Brač	8		2.5	50	1.16	8.20	7.9 + 0.2 × alt	8	1,526
Cella - I -Columns	Architrave	Stone of Brač			2.5	50	33.84	9.18	t+0.06(a-1)	6	1,240
Cella - I -Columns	Frieze	Stone of Brač			2.5	50	14.23	10.02	t+0.06(a-1)	3	633
Cella - I -Columns	Cornice	Stone of Brač			2.5	50	33.87	10.50	t+0.06(a-1)	6	1,267
Cella - I -Semicol.	Capitals - Corinthian	Stone of Brač	8	Yes	2.5	50	0.58	8.20	7.9 + 0.2 × alt	8	1,526
Cella - I -Semicol.	Architrave	Stone of Brač			2.5	50	33.84	9.18	t+0.06(a-1)	6	1,240
Cella - I -Semicol.	Frieze	Stone of Brač			2.5	50	14.23	10.02	t+0.06(a-1)	3	633

Appendix Table e. Cost of Diocletian's Mausoleum by construction phases - Laying.

LAYING

Order	Type	Material	Quantity	Spolia	Weight Tn/m³	Type of labour	Salary / day (denarii)	Volume, one element (m³)	Elevation height	Formula	Days	Cost (denarii)
Cella – I –Semicol.	Cornice	Stone of Brač			2.5	Construction worker × 4	50	33.87	10.50	t+0.06(a-1)	6	1,267
Cella – II –Columns	Shafts	Porphyry	4	Yes	2.8	Construction worker × 4	50	0.98	12.55	7.9 + 0.2 × alt	4	833
Cella – II –Columns	Shafts	Granito del Foro	4	Yes	2.8	Construction worker × 4	50	0.98	12.55	7.9 + 0.2 × alt	4	833
Cella – II –Columns	Capitals - Corinthian	Proconnesian	4	Yes	2.7	Construction worker × 4	50	0.22	14.18	7.9 + 0.2 × alt	4	860
Cella – II –Columns	Capitals - Composite	Proconnesian	4		2.7	Construction worker × 4	50	0.22	14.18	7.9 + 0.2 × alt	4	860
Cella – II –Columns	Architrave	Stone of Brač			2.5	Construction worker × 4	50	13.77	14.67	t+0.06(a-1)	4	711
Cella – II –Columns	Frieze	Stone of Brač			2.5	Construction worker × 4	50	13.77	14.96	t+0.06(a-1)	4	717
Cella – II –Columns	Cornice	Stone of Brač			2.5	Construction worker × 4	50	60.84	15.42	t+0.06(a-1)	11	2,223
Cella – II –Semicol.	Shafts	Stone of Brač	8		2.5	Construction worker × 4	50	0.49	12.55	7.9 + 0.2 × alt	8	1,666
Cella – II –Semicol.	Capitals	Stone of Brač	8		2.5	Construction worker × 4	50	0.11	14.18	t+0.06(a-1)	11	2,136
Cella – II –Semicol.	Architrave	Stone of Brač			2.5	Construction worker × 4	50	13.77	14.67	t+0.06(a-1)	4	711
Cella – II –Semicol.	Frieze	Stone of Brač			2.5	Construction worker × 4	50	13.77	14.96	t+0.06(a-1)	4	717
Cella – II –Semicol.	Cornice	Stone of Brač			2.5	Construction worker × 4	50	60.84	15.42	t+0.06(a-1)	11	2,223
TOTAL											904	180,798

Appendix Table e cont. Cost of Diocletian's Mausoleum by construction phases – Laying.

FINISHING

Order	Type	Material	Quantity	Spolia	Type of labour	Salary / day (denarii)	Formula: time (hours/m²)	Days	Cost (denarii)
Crypt	External moulding	Stone of Brač			Marble worker × 4	60	115.20	406	97,542
Crypt	External plinth	Stone of Brač			Marble worker × 4	60	115.20	542	130,056
Cella	External middle moulding	Stone of Brač			Marble worker × 4	60	115.20	470	112,721
Cella	External upper moulding	Stone of Brač			Marble worker × 4	60	115.20	575	138,063
Cella	Internal upper frieze	Stone of Brač			Marble worker × 4	60	426.67	2,414	579,384
Portico	Column plinth + base	Stone of Brač	24		Marble worker × 4	60	10.67	85	20,318
Portico	Column base	Stone of Brač	24		Marble worker × 4	60	1/3 capital	691	165,888
Portico	Shafts - monolithic	Granito del Foro	2	Yes	Marble worker × 4	60	13.50	23	5,454
Portico	Shafts - monolithic	Aswan granite	5	Yes	Marble worker × 4	60	13.50	57	13,634
Portico	Shafts - monolithic	Breccia Corallina	5	Yes	Marble worker × 4	60	10.00	42	10,100
Portico	Shafts - monolithic	Proconnesian	6	Yes	Marble worker × 4	60	13.30	67	16,119
Portico	Shafts - monolithic	Troadense	3	Yes	Marble worker × 4	60	13.50	34	8,181

Appendix Table f. Cost of Diocletian's Mausoleum by construction phases - Finishing.

				FINISHING					
Order	Type	Material	Quantity	Spolia	Type of labour	Salary / day (denarii)	Formula: time (hours/m²)	Days	Cost (denarii)
Portico	Shafts - monolithic	Indeterminate	3	Yes	Marble worker × 4	60	13.50	34	8,181
Portico	Capitals - Corinthian	Stone of Brač	24		Marble worker × 4	60		2,074	497,664
Portico	Architrave	Stone of Brač			Marble worker × 4	60	80.80	184	44,126
Portico	Frieze	Stone of Brač			Marble worker × 4	60	177.60	251	60,292
Portico	Cornice	Stone of Brač			Marble worker × 4	60	296.00	491	117,962
Portico	Roof	Stone of Brač			Marble worker × 4	60	177.60	3,829	918,973
Prothyron	Plinth of the columns	Stone of Brač	4		Marble worker × 4	60	10.67	14	3,386
Prothyron	Base	Stone of Brač	4		Marble worker × 4	60	1/3 capital	115	27,648
Prothyron	Shafts	Porphyry / Aswan	4	Yes	Marble worker × 4	60	13.50	45	10,908
Prothyron	Capitals - Corinthian	Stone of Brač	4		Marble worker × 4	60		346	82,944
Prothyron	Architrave	Stone of Brač			Marble worker × 4	60	80.80	78	18,655
Prothyron	Frieze	Stone of Brač			Marble worker × 4	60	177.60	106	25,489
Prothyron	Cornice	Stone of Brač			Marble worker × 4	60	296.00	208	49,870
Cella – I –Columns	Base - Attic	Stone of Brač	8		Marble worker × 4	60	1/3 capital	307	73,728
Cella – I –Columns	Shafts	Red granite	6	Yes	Marble worker × 4	60	13.50	115	27,710
Cella – I –Columns	Shafts	Troadense	2	Yes	Marble worker × 4	60	13.50	38	9,237
Cella – I –Columns	Capitals - Corinthian	Stone of Brač	8		Marble worker × 4	60		922	221,184
Cella – I –Columns	Architrave	Stone of Brač			Marble worker × 4	60	80.80	582	139,622
Cella – I –Columns	Frieze	Stone of Brač			Marble worker × 4	60	177.60	815	195,644
Cella – I –Columns	Cornice	Stone of Brač			Marble worker × 4	60	296.00	1,412	338,861
Cella – I –Semicol.	Capitals - Corinthian	Stone of Brač	8	Yes	Marble worker × 4	60		553	132,710
Cella – I –Semicol.	Architrave	Stone of Brač			Marble worker × 4	60	80.80	582	139,622
Cella – I –Semicol.	Frieze	Stone of Brač			Marble worker × 4	60	177.60	815	195,644
Cella – I –Semicol.	Cornice	Stone of Brač			Marble worker × 4	60	296.00	1,412	338,861
Cella – II –Columns	Shafts	Porphyry	4	Yes	Marble worker × 4	60	21.90	40	9,510
Cella – II –Columns	Shafts	Granito del Foro	4	Yes	Marble worker × 4	60	13.50	24	5,862
Cella – II –Columns	Capitals - Corinthian	Procconnesian	4		Marble worker × 4	60		288	69,120
Cella – II –Columns	Capitals - Composite	Procconnesian	4		Marble worker × 4	60		288	69,120
Cella – II –Columns	Architrave	Stone of Brač			Marble worker × 4	60	80.80	247	59,340
Cella – II –Columns	Frieze	Stone of Brač			Marble worker × 4	60	177.60	543	130,429
Cella – II –Columns	Cornice	Stone of Brač			Marble worker × 4	60	296.00	1,385	332,467
Cella – II –Semicol.	Shafts	Stone of Brač	8		Marble worker × 4	60	1/4 shaft	12	2,931
Cella – II –Semicol.	Capitals	Stone of Brač	8		Marble worker × 4	60		346	82,944
Cella – II –Semicol.	Architrave	Stone of Brač			Marble worker × 4	60	80.80	247	59,340
Cella – II –Semicol.	Frieze	Stone of Brač			Marble worker × 4	60	177.60	543	130,429
Cella – II –Semicol.	Cornice	Stone of Brač			Marble worker × 4	60	296.00	1,385	332,467
TOTAL								26,085	6,260,341

Appendix Table f cont. Cost of Diocletian's Mausoleum by construction phases - Finishing.